# Lecture Notes of the Institute for Computer Sciences, Social Informatics and Telecommunications Engineering 255

More information about this series at http://www.springer.com/series/8197

Raheem Beyah · Bing Chang
Yingjiu Li · Sencun Zhu (Eds.)

# Security and Privacy in Communication Networks

14th International Conference, SecureComm 2018
Singapore, Singapore, August 8–10, 2018
Proceedings, Part II

Springer

*Editors*
Raheem Beyah
Klaus Advanced Computing Building
Georgia Institute of Technology
Atlanta, GA, USA

Bing Chang
Singapore Management University
Singapore, Singapore

Yingjiu Li
School of Information Systems
Singapore Management University
Singapore, Singapore

Sencun Zhu
Pennsylvania State University
University Park, PA, USA

ISSN 1867-8211         ISSN 1867-822X  (electronic)
Lecture Notes of the Institute for Computer Sciences, Social Informatics
and Telecommunications Engineering
ISBN 978-3-030-01703-3         ISBN 978-3-030-01704-0  (eBook)
https://doi.org/10.1007/978-3-030-01704-0

Library of Congress Control Number: 2018940136

This Springer imprint is published by the registered company Springer Nature Switzerland AG
The registered company address is: Gewerbestrasse 11, 6330 Cham, Switzerland

# Preface

We are delighted to introduce the proceedings of the 14th European Alliance for Innovation (EAI) International Conference on Security and Privacy in Communication Networks (SecureComm 2018), held in Singapore, in August 2018. SecureComm seeks high-quality research contributions in the form of well-developed papers. Topics of interest encompass research advances in all areas of secure communications and networking.

The technical program of SecureComm 2018 consisted of 33 full papers and 18 short papers in the main conference sessions. The conference sessions were: Session 1, IoT Security; Session 2, User and Data Privacy; Session 3, Mobile Security I; Session 4, Wireless Security; Session 5, Software Security; Session 6, Cloud Security I; Session 7, Mobile Security II; Session 8, Social Network and Enterprise Security; Session 9, Network Security I; Session 10, Applied Cryptography; Session 11, Network Security II; Session 12, Cloud Security II; and Session 13, Web Security.

Aside from the high-quality technical paper presentations, the technical program also featured two keynote speeches and one technical workshop. The two keynote speeches were given by Prof. Robert Deng from Singapore Management University, Singapore, and Prof. Zhiqiang Lin from Ohio State University, USA. The workshop organized was the 6th International Workshop on Applications and Techniques in Cyber Security (ATCS 2018). The ATCS workshop focused on all aspects of techniques and applications in cybersecurity research. The purpose of ATCS 2018 was to provide a forum for the presentation and discussion of innovative ideas, cutting-edge research results, and novel techniques, methods, and applications on all aspects of cyber security and machine learning.

Coordination with the Steering Committee co-chairs, Imrich Chlamtac and Guofei Gu, was essential for the success of the conference. We sincerely appreciate their constant support and guidance. It was also a great pleasure to work with such an excellent Organizing Committee team for their hard work in organizing and supporting the conference. In particular, we thank the Technical Program Committee, led by our co-chairs, Dr. Raheem Beyah and Dr. Sencun Zhu, who completed the peer-review process of technical papers and compiled a high-quality technical program. We are also grateful to the conference coordinator, Dominika Belisova, for her support and all the authors who submitted their papers to the SecureComm 2018 conference and workshops.

We strongly believe that the SecureComm conference provides a good forum for all researchers, developers, and practitioners to exchange ideas in all areas of secure communications and networking. We also expect that future SecureComm conferences will be successful and stimulating, as indicated by the contributions presented in this volume.

September 2018

Raheem Beyah
Bing Chang
Yingjiu Li
Sencun Zhu

# Organization

## Steering Committee Co-chairs

Imrich Chlamtac — University of Trento, Italy
Guofei Gu — Texas A&M University, USA

## Steering Committee Members

Krishna Moorthy Sivalingam — IIT Madras, India
Peng Liu — Pennsylvania State University, USA

## Organizing Committee

### General Chair

Yingjiu Li — Singapore Management University, Singapore

### Technical Program Committee Co-chairs

Raheem Beyah — Georgia Tech, USA
Sencun Zhu — Pennsylvania State University, USA

### Publications Chair

Bing Chang — Singapore Management University, Singapore

### Publicity and Social Media Co-chairs

Yangguang Tian — Singapore Management University, Singapore
Zhao Wang — Peking University, China
Sankardas Roy — Bowling Green State University, USA

### Web Chair

Ximing Liu — Singapore Management University, Singapore

### Panels Chair

Min Suk Kang — National University of Singapore, Singapore

### Local Chair

Li Tieyan — Shield Lab (Singapore), Huawei Technologies Co., Ltd., Singapore

**Conference Manager**

Dominika Belisova                 EAI - European Alliance for Innovation

# Technical Program Committee

| | |
|---|---|
| Elisa Bertino | Purdue University, USA |
| Alvaro Cardenas | The University of Texas at Dallas, USA |
| Kai Chen | Institute of Information Engineering, Chinese Academy of Sciences, China |
| Yu Chen | State University of New York – Binghamton, USA |
| Sherman S. M. Chow | The Chinese University of Hong Kong, SAR China |
| Jun Dai | California State University, Sacramento, USA |
| Mohan Dhawan | IBM Research, India |
| Birhanu Eshete | University of Illinois at Chicago, USA |
| Debin Gao | Singapore Management University, Singapore |
| Le Guan | Pennsylvania State University, USA |
| Yong Guan | Iowa State University, USA |
| Yongzhong He | Beijing Jiaotong University, China |
| Lin Huang | Qihoo 360 Technology Co. Ltd., China |
| Heqing Huang | IBM Research, USA |
| Shouling Ji | Zhejiang University, China |
| Yier Jin | University of Florida, USA |
| Issa Khalil | Qatar Computing Research Institute (QCRI), Qatar |
| Lee Lerner | Georgia Institute of Technology, USA |
| Ming Li | University of Arizona, USA |
| Qinghua Li | University of Arkansas, USA |
| Qi Li | Tsinghua University, China |
| Xiaojing Liao | College of William and Mary, USA |
| Yue-Hsun Lin | JD.com, USA |
| Zhiqiang Lin | The Ohio State University, USA |
| Yao Liu | University of South Florida, USA |
| Anyi Liu | Oakland University, USA |
| Giovanni Livraga | Università degli Studi di Milano, Italy |
| Javier Lopez | University of Malaga, Spain |
| Rongxing Lu | University of New Brunswick, Canada |
| Liran Ma | Texas Christian University, USA |
| Aziz Mohaisen | University of Central Florida, USA |
| Goutam Paul | Indian Statistical Institute, India |
| Rui Qiao | LinkedIn, USA |
| Sankardas Roy | Bowling Green State University, USA |
| Pierangela Samarati | Università degli Studi di Milano, Italy |
| Seungwon Shin | KAIST, South Korea |
| Kapil Singh | IBM Research, USA |
| Anna Squicciarini | Pennsylvania State University, USA |
| Martin Strohmeier | University of Oxford, UK |

Xiao Shu     George Mason University, USA

Scienci Zhao     Florida International University, US

Zhiguo Wang     Shandong University, China

Cong Wang     The University of Hong Kong SAR China

Wei Wang     Purdue Ross and Intosh, China

Elaine Watkins     Johns Hopkins University, USA

Edgar Wright     SBA Research, Berlin

Dingbao Wu     Pennsylvania State University, USA

Hongbin Xiao     Rome State University, USA

Kaijia Xiang     University of South Florida, USA

Qin Xiong     ... University, USA

Shuhuan Pan     University of Texas at San Antonio, USA

Ya Zang     Jiangnan University, USA

Deming Zhao     Virginia Tech, USA

Kui Zeng     George Mason University, USA

Chu Zhang     Tsinghua University, China

Robert Zhang     Wayne State University, USA

Yuqing Zhong     University of Chinese Academy of Sciences, China

Jiafya Zhang     Wright State University, USA

Wenbiang Zhang     Iowa State University, USA

Yongtai Zhao     The Chinese University of Hong Kong SAR China

...hui Zhao     Fudan University, China

Guo Zou     University of Central Florida, USA

# Contents – Part II

**Applied Cryptography**

**Web Security**

# ATCS Workshop

A TCS Workshop

# Contents – Part I

## Mobile Security

## Wireless Security

## Software Security

## Cloud Security

# Social Network and Enterprise Security

# A Mobile Botnet That Meets Up at Twitter

Yulong Dong, Jun Dai[✉], and Xiaoyan Sun

California State University, Sacramento, 6000 J Street, Sacramento, CA 95819, USA
{dong,jun.dai,xiaoyan.sun}@csus.edu

**Abstract.** Nowadays online social networking is becoming one of the options for botnet command and control (C&C) communication, and QR codes have been widely used in the area of software automation. In this paper, we orchestrate QR codes, Twitter, Tor network, and domain generation algorithm to build a new generation of botnet with high recovery capability and stealthiness. Unlike the traditional centralized botnet, our design achieves dynamic C&C communication channels with no single point of failure. In our design, no cryptographic key is hard-coded on bots. Instead, we exploit domain generation algorithm to produce dynamic symmetric keys and QR codes as medium to transport dynamic asymmetric keys. By using this approach, botnet C&C communication payload can be ensured in terms of randomization and confidentiality. We implement our design via Twitter and real-world Tor network. According to the experiment results, our design is capable to do C&C communication with low data and minimal CPU usage. The goal of our work is to draw defenders' attention for the cyber abuse of online social networking and Tor network; especially, the searching feature in online social networks provides a covert meet-up channel, and needs to be investigated as soon as possible. Finally, we discuss several potential countermeasures to defeat our botnet design.

**Keywords:** Mobile botnet · Online social networking · QR code

## 1 Introduction

With the fast development of mobile industry and technology, the number of mobile users has dramatically increased. As the most popular open-source mobile platform in the world, over 2 billion monthly Android devices were found active by May, 2017 [1]. To turn the huge number of mobile devices into an army to perform attacks like Distributed Denial of Service (DDoS), SMS interception, and spamming, attackers started to build mobile botnets [2,3].

Two common command and control (C&C) topologies are found in traditional PC-based botnets: centralized and Peer-to-Peer (P2P)-based structures. In centralized botnets, the C&C communication latency is short and the botmaster can monitor the number of available bots using single or limited amount

© ICST Institute for Computer Sciences, Social Informatics and Telecommunications Engineering 2018
R. Beyah et al. (Eds.): SecureComm 2018, LNICST 255, pp. 3–21, 2018.
https://doi.org/10.1007/978-3-030-01704-0_1

of C&C servers [4]. However, centralized botnets suffer from single point of failure, i.e. the botnet can be easily disabled by the defenders via shutting down the C&C channels. Moreover, the botmaster is directly exposed to defenders when the C&C channel is monitored.

On the other hand, P2P-based botnets have no single point of failure and achieve better stealthiness for the botmaster. However, P2P-based botnets suffer from the looseness of network structure, lack message transmission guarantee, and tend to have longer latency for message delivery [4–6]. Also, P2P-based botnets require higher network overhead to keep the botnets robust [7,8].

Compared with traditional PC-based botnets, mobile botnets are inherently restricted by the features of mobile platforms: low CPU capacity, small network bandwidth, limited battery and expensive data usage. Given the above comparative study about botnet topology, a centralized botnet design is more desirable for the mobile environment. However, the drawbacks of centralized design need to be addressed for robustness and stealthiness, especially the single point of failure problem.

Our paper is an effort to solve these issues by exploiting the automation feature in QR codes and the Twitter search engine to build dynamic C&C channels with high recovery abilities. The following paragraphs introduce the techniques that are essential for our solution, as well as rationales to exploit them.

*Quick Response (QR) code*: QR codes have been widely used in mobile software automation in the past few years. Compared with traditional masquerading techniques, QR codes are more stealthy since it has been widely used in daily life for other purposes and cannot be distinguished by human beings. Researchers [9–11] report that QR codes have been used in several attacking methods such as phishing and social engineering attacks. However, the automatic detection and removal of malicious QR codes for security is still a fairly new topic in the area.

*Online Social Networking (OSN)*: As one of the most popular public networking services, OSN draws attention from researchers [12–14] to use it for building C&C channels. Compared with other botnet C&C communication mediums, OSN has several advantages, such as the simplicity in implementation, the portability over multi-platform environments, and the stealthiness. Nowadays, some OSN platforms like Twitter and Sina Blog (a popular Chinese OSN platform) provide searching interface to allow users to find interested posts by keywords. We find that the search feature provides a possibility to build dynamic C&C channels instead of static (i.e. hard-coded) ones. The dynamic C&C channels can help avoid single point of failure, and thus deliver better robustness and high recovery capabilities.

*Domain Generation Algorithm (DGA)*: DGA from Conficker [15] in 2008 is a solution to avoid single point of failure in the centralized topology. In general, DGA takes one or multiple seeds as inputs to produce random domain names. Based on the actual implementation, DGA may hugely increase the difficulty of predicting the next generated domain name, and make it computationally impossible to stop the attack through banning all possible DGA outputs [16]. In our botnet design, we vary DGA to produce random strings instead of domain names. The DGA generation results play as countersigns (left by the botmaster) to help bots find the meetup place at Twitter.

*Tor network*: Internet was born as a public network, while the second generation onion router (Tor) [17] provisions an ideal technique to achieve anonymity. Tor was invented with ready-to-use client proxy and web browser. It is natural to think of Tor network to keep botmaster's C&C communication anonymous. Today, Tor has been integrated with the mobile platform, such as Orbot [18] for Android. With the appearance of Orbot, the implementation complexity of Tor-based network applications on Android is dramatically decreased, and the botmaster can easily use mobile Android devices to issue commands to botnet with fair stealthiness.

By creatively orchestrating QR codes, OSN, DGA and Tor network, our botnet design successfully enables the following features to overcome the natural limitation in traditional centralized and P2P-based botnets.

- Constructing a new OSN-based mobile botnet with no single point of failure.
- Building dynamic C&C channels with high recovery capability based on the Twitter search engine and QR codes.
- Using dynamic asymmetric key pairs and DGA with random seeds to keep the confidentiality of C&C communication traffic.
- Using Tor network to hide the identity of botmaster.
- Simple implementation and huge potential threats to all OSNs that include searching features.

Our design is generic for both mobile and PC platforms, while our proof of concept and corresponding analysis is conducted on Android platform. **To the best of our knowledge, we are the first to use QR codes as C&C communication medium in OSN-based botnet**.

The rest of the paper is constructed as follows: in Sect. 2, we introduce the related work. In Sect. 3, we elaborate our botnet design. In Sect. 4, we present the proof of concept, including a walkthrough to demonstrate our botnet workflow. In Sect. 5, we evaluate our work. In Sect. 6, we discuss potential countermeasures to our botnet design. In Sect. 7, we conclude this paper. More design rationales and implementation details are presented in [19], and the prototype code can be provided upon request for research purposes.

## 2   Related Work

Researchers have proposed a variety of approaches to build botnets on both PC and mobile platforms, either in traditional centralized or P2P-based topologies. We introduce related botnet research and designs in Sect. 2.1, and summarize our literature review in Table 1. The related QR code research is introduced in Sect. 2.2.

**Table 1.** List of related botnet research & Designs

| Research | Year | Platform | Botnet topology | C&C channel | Masquerade technique |
|---|---|---|---|---|---|
| Hua et al. [20] | 2011 | Mobile | P2P | SMS | N/A |
| Zeng et al. [21] | 2012 | Mobile | P2P | SMS | Plain encrypted text |
| Faghani et al. [22] | 2012 | Mobile | Centralized | SMS/OSNs | N/A |
| Nagaraja et al. [23] | 2011 | PC | Centralized | OSNs | Steganography (JPEG) |
| Cui et al. [12] | 2011 | PC | Centralized | OSNs | Steganography (JPG) |
| Singh et al. [13] | 2013 | PC | Centralized | OSNs | N/A |
| Yin et al. [14] | 2014 | PC | Centralized | OSNs | Plain encrypted Text |
| Compagno et al. [24] | 2015 | PC | Centralized | OSNs | Unicode stenography |
| Koobface [25–27] | 2010 | PC | Centralized | OSNs/web server | Plain encrypted text |
| Elirks [28] | 2012 | PC | Centralized | OSNs | Plain encrypted text |

## 2.1  Botnet Research and Design

Since Short Message Service (SMS) is a common technology in mobile environments, several researches have addressed SMS as C&C channel in botnet design. In 2011, Hua et al. [20] built a botnet with SMS and flooding algorithm. Hua's design successfully spreads one command to 90% of 20,000 bots in 20 min with each bot sending less than 4 messages. However, Hua's design suffers from the natural limitation of flooding algorithm, i.e. if defenders shut down a bot that is very close to the first one, the botmaster loses the rest of bots in the flood.

In 2012, Zeng et al. [21] proposed a SMS and P2P-based botnet design. Their research concludes that the ubiquitousness of SMS, the simplicity of accommodating offline bots, and the capability of hiding C&C commands make SMS suitable for C&C communications in mobile environment. However the malicious text messages in their botnet design is directly exposed to phone owners, and the monetary cost of SMS may attract the owners' attention even without anti-malware alerts.

On the other hand, Faghani et al. [22] designed Socellbot which compares SMS and OSNs as communication medium in mobile environment. Based on their experiment results, OSNs excel in lower network traffic load and faster propagation speed, and hence are more suitable for mobile environment than SMS.

Nagaraja et al. [23] introduced a botnet design by combining steganography and OSNs. In Nagarajia's research, all the C&C communication commands are hidden in JPEG images. The botmaster and bots use two hard-coded OSN accounts as C&C channels. In Nagaraja's design, the C&C traffic is stealthy, but the botnet suffers from single point of failure. If the hard-coded OSN accounts are detected and banned by defenders, the botmaster loses control of the whole botnet.

Similar to Nagaraja's idea, Cui et al. [12] designed an OSN-based botnet called Andbot. Andbot combines URL-flux (a variation of IP-flux), steganography, and Microsoft blog to decrease the threat of single point of failure and increase the stealthiness of C&C communication. In their design, the blog works as a C&C channel. Bots use a hard-coded DGA algorithm to assemble an URL to find the blog built by the botmaster. After the blog is connected, bots download steganographic images to receive the botmaster's commands.

Following up with Cui's research, Yin et al. [14] reported a newer generation of botnet design combining Sina blog and Nickname Generation Algorithm (a variation of DGA) to build dynamic C&C channels. In Yin's design, the botnet has no single point of failure and high resistance to destruction. However, there is still a bottleneck that the network load capacity of each C&C channel is limited. In a large group of bots, botmaster needs to build multiple C&C channels in order to allow all the bots to retrieve the commands. Also, the identity of botmaster is directly exposed to the blog website without any protection.

Singh et al. [13] applied Twitter as the C&C communication platform for a centralized botnet. In their design, they take advantage of the OAuth mechanism provided by Twitter to ensure the origin of C&C commands. The botmaster posts C&C commands through its Twitter account. The drawback of this design is that it suffers from single point of failure. On the other hand, a list of commands are hard-coded on each bot which may be prone to the detection of any anti-virus systems.

In addition to image stenography, Compagno et al. [24] found and proved Unicode encoding can be used as a masquerading technique. In their research, the botmaster takes advantage of Unicode and hides the C&C communication using invisible Unicode characters. Compagno's botnet design is able to survive from the traditional botnet detection and defense strategies, but may be captured by character filtering and statistical analysis on the OSN posts.

Beside the above botnet designs from research, OSNs are already practically observed in real-world malware. For example, in 2010 Koobface was detected and investigated by researchers [25–27]. As a network worm, OSNs are used by Koobface to download different pieces of malicious content, and do C&C communication through several hard-coded OSN accounts and web servers. The specific OSN accounts can be banned, which causes Koobface suffer from single point of failure.

Researchers [28] also captured and investigated wild botnets with their C&C communication methods. An OSN-based botnet called Eliriks was detected based on their observation. In Eliriks, the botmaster posts the information of the C&C web server on a microblogging service called Plurk. For the C&C server's information, the botmaster uses a modified Tiny Encryption Algorithm (TEA) and modified Base-64 encoding to further masquerade the C&C server's sensitive information. The defenders were able to successfully extract the Plurk accounts used by Elriks by the time that the corresponding paper was published. In other words, Eliriks did not survive from the threat of single point of failure.

## 2.2   QR Code Research

In 2010, Kieseberg et al. [10] did a security research on QR codes. Based on their research, the automation feature in QR codes is vulnerable to SQL injection, command injection, fraud, phishing, and social engineering attacks. Krombholz et al. [9] lists several experimental examples to prove that the threats from Kieseberg can actually be implemented in real-world environment.

On the other hand, Kharraz et al. [11] investigated 94,770 QR codes from 14.7 million unique web pages in 2014. In their report, they found 145 real-world malicious QR codes were used in phishing and malware distribution.

Although there is already proof of the existence of malicious QR codes, the research about QR code security is still falling behind. Yao et al. [29] did a security investigation on 31 commercial QR code scanners. Based on their evaluation, only two of them include security warnings after users scan a QR code. This is due to lack of research on the detection of suspicious QR codes.

Our botnet design has four fundamental advantages in contrast with the above related work. First, compared with other OSN-based botnets, our botnet design leverages the OSN searching feature to further randomize the locations that the C&C account appears. Theoretically, the botmaster could use any account in OSNs to publish the C&C commands. Second, beyond other masquerading techniques, we use QR codes to disguise the botnet C&C posts to ensure their stealthiness. Third, instead of hard-coded keys, we use dynamic symmetric and asymmetric keys to ensure the confidentiality of botnet C&C communication. Fourth, Tor network is successfully integrated in our botnet design to hide the identity of botmaster.

## 3    Methodology

We exploit the Twitter search engine, DGA, and QR codes to ensure the botnet robustness and stealthiness. Specifically, we leverage Tor, RSA [30], and Advanced Encryption Standard (AES) [31] cryptographic algorithm respectively to achieve anonymity, integrity, and confidentiality for the botnet C&C communication.

No matter how the botnet topologies evolve, pushing, pulling, and listening are the common options for bots to do C&C communications. In this section, we first give a overview of our botnet design. After that, four major parts of our botnet design are introduced in the following subsections: initialization, command pulling, information collection, and command pushing.

In this paper, the terminologies are denoted as follows: the DGA is denoted as $DGA()$, the DGA seeds as $Seed_1$, $Seed_2$, ... to $Seed_n$, the generated results from DGA as $S_1$, $S_2$, ... to $S_n$, the RSA key pair as $Key_{pub}$ and $Key_{priv}$, and a special token as $Token$. The DGA algorithm is hard-coded on bots, with the DGA seeds derived from timestamps, for synchronization with the botmaster. The special token is a random string concatenated (with a delimiter) with its digital signature signed by the botmaster, i.e. encrypted by $Key_{priv}$. The token is hard-coded on all bots for authentication purpose. No RSA key pairs are hard-coded.

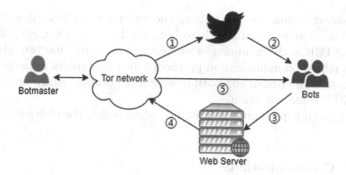

**Fig. 1.** Botnet design overview

## 3.1 Botnet Design Overview

As shown in Fig. 1, our botnet design involves five major parts: botmaster, Tor network, Twitter, bots, and a movable web server built by botmaster. The botmaster's duty is to set up the web server, prepare and publish Twitter posts, and send commands to bots. Twitter's role is to hold a Twitter post as a temporary C&C channel that allows bots to pull a QR code image from the botmaster. The Twitter post contains two major sections: a keyword generated from DGA and a QR code image. The web server is set up by the botmaster to collect information from each bot, such as IP address and device ID. The IP of the web server is propagated to bots as part of the QR code, and thus could be dynamic. The combination of the web server and Twitter posts works as C&C channels which allow bots to do command pulling and information uploading. In addition, every bot sets up a TCP server on its own device. Through information uploading, bots encrypt and upload their identify-sensitive information to the web server. When the botmaster wants to send commands to bots, it downloads and decrypts the bot uploaded data from the web server, and then sends commands to bots via Tor network.

In our botnet design, only the DGA algorithm and a special token are hard-coded on both botmaster and bot sides. The current date (i.e. timestamp) is used as a key factor to produce exactly the same DGA seeds on both botmaster and bot sides. Based on the actual implementation, DGA can take any format of seeds that is generated by the current date. All botnet C&C communication is encrypted by AES or RSA, and no key is hard-coded on bots. The symmetric keys used by AES are generated from DGA, and the public key used by RSA is spread as part of the QR code from botmaster's Twitter post. The special token is used to verify the identity of botmaster and validate the data source after decryption.

The communication between the botmaster and outside networks is via Tor. As Fig. 1 illustrates, there are five steps in our botnet design. Step ① serves as the initialization process for the botmaster to prepare and publish the Twitter post. Step ② is used by bots to download data from the botmaster's Twitter post. Then, bots upload their IP and device information to the web server in Step ③.

The botmaster downloads bot data from the web server in Step ④, and uses the downloaded data to send commands to bots via Tor network in Step ⑤. In our design, using TCP as the communication protocol in Step ⑤ has two advantages. First, it is a reliable communication protocol which guarantees message delivery. Second, it makes the design compatible with Tor network, which only supports TCP or HTTP communication.

A walkthrough is presented in Sect. 4 to demonstrate the above botnet workflow.

## 3.2   C&C Communication

**Initialization.** The botmaster needs to perform a few initialization procedures before the C&C communication starts. First, the botmaster sets up a web server. Second, the botmaster generates two random strings $S_1$ and $S_2$ from $DGA(Seed_1)$ and $DGA(Seed_2)$. After $S_1$ and $S_2$ are generated, the botmaster collects the web server's address information, as well as a pre-generated RSA key pair $Key_{pub}$ and $Key_{priv}$. Third, botmaster combines the current web server address, the hard-coded token $Token$, and $Key_{pub}$ as a command, and then encrypts the combined command with $S_2$. Fourth, the botmaster encodes the combined command into a QR code image. Finally, the botmaster uses a random Twitter account to publish a post, which contains $S_1$ and the QR code image.

**Command Pulling.** Bots regularly conducts command pulling, and succeed whenever the botmaster's Twitter post is available. First, similar to the botmaster, bots generate two strings $S_3$ and $S_4$ from $DGA(Seed_3)$, and $DGA(Seed_4)$. In our design, in order to ensure the synchronization between the bots and botmaster, $S_3$ must be equal to $S_1$ and $S_4$ must be equal to $S_2$. This is ensured by applying the same algorithms to timestamps for getting equivalent seeds at both bot and botmaster sides, and then using the same seeds for DGA algorithms. Bots use $S_3$ as the **keyword to query the Twitter search engine** to find the post from the botmaster. Bots download the QR code image based on the query response. After the QR code image is downloaded, bots first decode the QR code to retrieve raw data and use $S_4$ to do decryption. The botmaster's public key $Key_{pub}$ and the special $Token$ are contained in the decrypted data, and the bots can use $Key_{pub}$ to verify whether $Token$ is generated by the real botmaster using the paired $Key_{priv}$.

**Information Collection.** The web server is important to maintain the robustness of the botnet, as all bots are instructed to upload their real IP and device ID to the web server after IP spoofing. IP spoofing helps disguise the bot identities during C&C communications, in case they are tracked down. In order to keep their uploaded data safe, all data from bots are encrypted by $Key_{pub}$, and remains ciphered in database storage at the web server. This way, the botmaster can monitor and get the information of available bots in the botnet via the web server safely.

**Command Pushing.** The botmaster can send commands to bots at any time. For command pushing, all available bots have their current IP addresses stored on the web server. When command pushing is needed, the botmaster first generated $S_5$ from $DGA(Seed_5)$. Then, the botmaster combines the command for bots and $Token$ as one string, and encrypts the combined string with $S_5$. The botmaster queries the web server to collect each bot's IP address and decrypt the result using $Key_{priv}$. After that, the botmaster extracts the IP addresses of bots and broadcasts the encrypted command via TCP-based Tor network. After TCP packages are received, bots generate $S_6$ from $DGA(Seed_6)$. Similar to Step ① and ②, $Seed_6$ is set (via synchronized timestamps) equal to $Seed_5$ to ensure the bots can decrypt the TCP payload. After checking the existence of $Token$ for validity of the command origin as botmaster or not, bots perform tasks included in the command.

Throughout the above communications, **only the DGA algorithm and the special token are hard-coded** on both botmaster and bot sides. The rationale for hard-coding the special token will be elaborated in Sect. 3.3. The various seeds for DGA are synchronized between the botmaster and bots by applying the same computing algorithms towards the date/timestamp information. To avoid single point of failure, our **Twitter post account and the web server are dynamic**. Each time the botmaster publishes a new Twitter post, the QR code contains the information to redirect bots to the new address of the web server. If the Twitter post is banned by defenders, the botmaster can publish another post from a different and unpredictable account. If the web server is banned, the botmaster sets it up in a new address and generates a new QR code image which contains the new server address. Thus, no matter how defenders destroy the C&C channels, the botmaster always has a way to reconstruct the botnet.

### 3.3  Cryptography and Botnet Robustness

As we mentioned eariller, all the C&C communication in our botnet design is encrypted either by AES or RSA. Step ①, ② and ⑤ are protected by AES. Step ③ and ④ are protected by RSA. It's fully understood that RSA requires more resources than AES for computing. However, AES will require hard coding of symmetric keys for Step ③ and ④, while RSA can avoid this. Taking an extreme example, when a bot falls into a honeynet, defenders may easily track down the web server address once the bot is detected. If defenders further manage to get all the encrypted data from the web server and decipher them with cryptanalysis, other bots in the same botnet may get their IP addresses and device IDs directly exposed to defenders. Using the RSA as the encryption algorithm can dramatically decrease the risk of such situation.

In addition to strengthening the data encryption in communication and storage, using the RSA algorithm helps the bots authenticate the connections and commands from the botmaster. For example, if the defense side succeeds in reverse engineering the bot samples and obtaining the hard-coded token with botnet workflow information, the botmaster identity may be faked to hijack the ownership of the botnet. This can be defeated by using the asymmetric encryption, i.e. the RSA algorithm. Specifically, the special $Token$ includes the digital signature generated by using the $Key_{priv}$, which is only owned by the real botmaster. Hence, only the real botmaster could initiate the authentic C&C communication, as nobody else could provide the corresponding $Key_{pub}$ to verify the signatures associated within $Token$. It's possible that the reverse engineer defenders use an intercepted $Key_{pub}$ to fake as a botmaster to issue a bogus web server address to bots. But again, thanks to RSA algorithm used in Step ③ to encrypt all upload data, the faked botmaster will not be able to decipher the bot connection information for further actions. Defenders could not track down the bot addresses as well, as Step ③ enforces bots to upload data based on IP spoofing. Deciphering the uploaded data on the web server is the only chance to push commands to bots, and only the authentic botmaster can achieve that.

# 4    Proof of Concept

To further illustrate our botnet design, in this section we present a quick walk-through with essential implementation details of our botnet prototype. To demonstrate our botnet design in Sect. 3, we use and run 10 Genymotion emulators on our workstation, one Google Nexus 6 phone, the Tor network, one randomly generated Twitter account, one apache server, and one MySQL database in an orchestrated way. In our demonstration, each emulator acts as one infected bot and the Nexus phone acts as the botmaster.

In order to emulate an attack, we build a victim website to let bots to perform DDoS attack after Step ⑤. As Fig. 2 shows, after each bot processes all the steps for command pulling, information collection, and command pushing, the botmaster pushes a command to bots to coordinate them to conduct a DDoS attack against a victim web server. The TCP payload in Step ⑤ contains an encrypted command which includes the information of $Token$, the length of the attack, the frequency of the attack, and the IP address of the victim website. We present some command construction details in Sect. 4.2. In our demonstration, the botmaster's web server for information collection and the victim website are both running based on apache. The emulators in Fig. 2 are performing a DDoS attack to the victim website. A full video demonstration is available at [33].

## 4.1    Botnet Workflow

**Initialization.** In our botnet implementation, we configure the botmaster to process the initialization on daily base. All the botmaster's communications with the public network (i.e. the communications with Twitter and Internet) are through Tor network. In our experiments, the botmaster generates new QR codes and DGA strings every single day. Depending on the botmaster's choice, it can also be hourly or monthly to update the QR codes and Twitter them accordingly. No matter how often the Twitter posts are published, the current timestamp is used as a key factor for DGA synchronization across the bots and

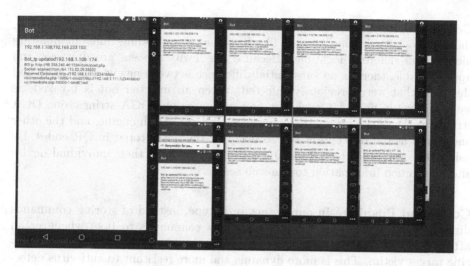

**Fig. 2.** Demonstration of botnet DDoS attack

botmaster. Whenever needed, the botmaster can choose to renew the address of the web server and let the bots know the change through a new QR code Twitter post. The botmaster also has the option to choose whether to use a standard or a modified QR code encoding and decoding library. After the QR code and DGA strings are ready, as Fig. 3 illustrates, the botmaster could post them with any (unpredictable) Twitter account. In our experiments, the Twitter post stays public until the next one is published by botmaster. The Twitter accounts used to post the QR code can vary everyday.

**Fig. 3.** Publishing a Twitter post

**Command Pulling and Information Collection.** In our botnet prototype, there is no initialization process like Koobface downloading different malware pieces from different locations. Because our Twitter posts are dynamic and unpredictable, there is no substantial difference between newly added bots and the bots that were previously infected. When an infected bot is invoked, as we discussed in Sect. 3.2, each bot first generates two DGA strings: one DGA strings works as the keyword to query the Twitter search engine, and the other one works as the decryption key to decipher the data stored in QR codes. By using the decrypted data from QR codes, bots submit their individual device and connection information to the web server.

**Command Pushing.** In our botnet prototype, instead of storing commands directly in QR codes, the botmaster pushes commands to bots whenever an attack (such as DDoS attack in our demonstration) is desired against some specific target victim. This is more dynamic and more resistant to anti-virus detection. Instead of a straightforward DDoS attack to the web server, our bots launch the reflection DDoS attack to take down the MySQL server at the backend of the victim web site. As the DDoS attack is conducted, the available connections for the MySQL server are exhausted quickly and normal users ultimately receive the MySQL connection error while loading the web page.

## 4.2   Command Structure

Our botnet implementation uses two type of command structures, and the summary of the command structures is given in Table 2. Command structure No. 1 is used in Step ① and ②, and command structure No. 2 is used in Step ⑤ . In command structure No. 1, commands use "]][[" as delimiters to differentiate different sections. Specifically, $Key_{pub}$, the current IP address or the URL of the web server, and $Token$ are the sections for command structure No. 1.

**Table 2.** C&C command structure

| No. | Detailed command structure |
|-----|----------------------------|
| 1 | $Key_{pub}$ + "]][[" + Address of the web server + "]][[" + $Token$ |
| 2 | $IP_{victim}$ + "-" + Attack Length + "-" + Attack Frequency + "-" + $Token$ |

Compared with command structure No. 1, command structure No. 2 uses "-" as delimiters. Command structure No. 2 is used when the botmaster wants to issue commands to bots via the Tor network in Step ⑤. In command structure No. 2, the IP of victim site, the length of the attack, the frequency of the attack, and the hard-coded $Token$ are included. $Token$ is used to authenticate the source of the command. The attack frequency and attack length are specified with milliseconds as units.

## 4.3   Implementation Subtleties

Besides the fundamental design and implementation details of our botnet prototype, some specific subtleties can play to gain improved stealthiness and performance. Based on our observation, these tricks or their variants are applicable to the majority of the OSNs.

Welcome to example.com !
Here is our special code for today:
mrf[Vbdp[pNyZna`

**Fig. 4.** Twitter post example

**OSN Post Masquerading.** Ideally, the Twitter post from the botmaster is accessible to all the public. Hence, it is necessary for the botmaster to disguise the post. A typical Twitter post in our botnet design includes a section of misleading information, a keyword, and a QR code image. As Fig. 4 shows, the random string started with *mrf* is the searching keyword. The other characters are misleading information to masquerade the post. Using this approach, the botmaster is able to fake the malicious Twitter post as a real-world commercial post which looks normal.

**QR Code Fetching.** After the botmaster's post is set up, bots can locate the URL of the QR code image from the Twitter search engine. Specifically, based on the REST API provided by Twitter, bots send GET requests by using $S_3$ as the query keyword. In our design, the bots retrieve real-world time together with time zone information from the mobile device. By using the real-world time from the device, the botmaster and bots are able to keep synchronized and ensure $S_3$ from bots is quivalent to $S_1$ from the botmaster.

**Fig. 5.** Twitter search response example

In the response data from the Twitter search engine, the actual URL of the QR code image can be extracted. Based on our experimental results, the images from Twitter posts are stored under the domain of https://pbs.twimg.com/media/, as shown in Fig. 5. In addition, a special unique ID is assigned by Twitter for each image, and the image format is specified in terms of suffix at the very end. By combing the domain name, the unique image ID, and its suffix, bots could identify the URL of the QR code image and download it without any authentication.

**Data Usage Deduction.** Data usage deduction is desired to minimize mobile device's resource consumption by both defenders and adversaries. Hence, we can leverage whatever facilitates supported by the OSNs. For example, Twitter provides Mobile Twitter Search [32] to adapt mobile data usage for bandwidth limitations. By taking advantage of Mobile Twitter Search, the data usage in Step ② can be minimized. Specifically, Twitter provides a service to shrink the size of an uploaded image. After the image URL is extracted, bots can add : *small* to the end as shown in Fig. 5, which can shrink a 770*770 QR code to 680*680 without hurt to the image quality.

## 5 Evaluation

In this section, we evaluate our botnet prototype from below perspectives: C&C data usage, CPU and memory usage, and the complexity of the DGA computation results.

**C&C Data Usage.** In our botnet design, bots use REST API to communicate with Mobile Twitter Search. Figure 6 shows our monitoring results with

*Wireshark.* 24 packages are found used for searching for the Twitter post and 45 packages for downloading the QR code image. In total, 2,595 bytes are used by bots in communication with Mobile Twitter Search, and 4,240 bytes are used to download the image.

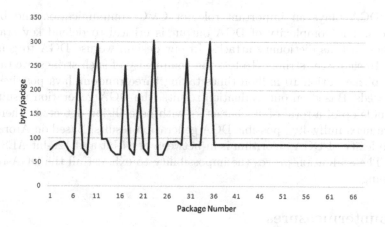

**Fig. 6.** Bot network traffic monitoring result

After bots complete the command pulling process from Twitter, bots upload information to the web server. In our implementation, bots send their IP addresses and device IDs to the web server. In this step, since the payload is encrypted by RSA, the size of package is larger than the original plain text. Based on Wireshark, each bot uploads a 731-byte HTTP packet to the web server. The last is the C&C communication between botmaster and bots in step ⑤. In our implementation, bots receive the TCP package from botmaster with a total length of 90 characters.

To conclude, bots use around 7-KB data to communicate with Twitter, around 700-byte data to upload their individual information to the web server, and around 400 bytes to receive the TCP package from the botmaster.

**Bot CPU and Memory Usage.** CPU usage has significant impact on battery life and user experience of a mobile device. Since a TCP server is created and dedicated to listen on each bot, it is necessary to estimate the CPU usage of the TCP server while bots are awaiting commands. Based on our experiment results, the TCP server thread consumes almost no CPU cycles and around 25 megabytes of memory after it is set up. The memory usage is caused by a simple Android application UI that helps track the actions of each bot, and thus we consider it as acceptable.

We also evaluated the CPU and memory usage for RSA encryption that takes place on bot side. It was found that this entire process only takes around 0.7 seconds, consuming up to 6.83% of CPU cycles and about 0.3 megabytes. In contrast, the RSA decryption that occurs on botmaster side takes around 0.7 seconds as well, occupying up to 12.08% of CPU cycles and about 0.2 megabytes. Overall, the cipher and decipher operations are not burdens for both bot and botmaster sides.

**DGA.** DGA plays an important role for C&C communication and botnet robustness. The complexity of DGA output is critical to defend key cracking techniques such as dictionary attacks. In our design, we use DGA to generate random 16-character strings. To test the complexity of such strings, we ran our DGA implementation 10 million times taking three random Java positive integers as seeds. Based on our evaluation results, the DGA generation results are found made up of a total of 49 characters with no collision detected. Therefore, there are maximally $49^{16}$ possible DGA generation results. Based on Arora [34], the complexity of DGA algorithm is in-between of 64-bit and 128-bit AES algorithms. The evaluation proves the impossibility to exhaust all the DGA results for banning.

## 6   Countermeasures

Different countermeasures may be taken to defend our botnet. In this section, we discuss the countermeasures based on the perspectives of botnet detection and defense. Although the various approaches introduced below could be used against our botnet design, it is still a big challenge for defenders to fully kill a botnet like this.

### 6.1   Botnet Detection

As one of the most popular approaches in the field of malware detection and analysis, honeynet can be used to trap bot infections and collect information for botnet detection in real-world. If bots fall into any honeynet, the compromised devices can be detected by using behavior detection models. For instance, Gu et al. [35] proposed BotMiner to use clustering analysis of network traffic to detect suspicious behavior in a honeynet. Since the C&C protocol for our botnet is HTTP-based, monitoring the header and content of the HTTP packets may statistically reveal the botnet network traffic to defenders.

In addition to honeynet, local botnet abnormal behavior detection approaches may be leveraged to detect our botnet. The Android application store can leverage malware detection software to detect the bot-infected application before it passes their security test. For example, the tool from [36] can be used to detect and visualize traffic flowing to unexpected websites, based on monitoring application activities and building an app-specific attack-neutral activity graph.

Android users can also install and run anti-virus applications on individual devices to help detect the unexpected URL visits (such as Twitter visits in our botnet design). In addition to URL visits, monitoring the mobile application's

CPU usage and network usage can also help detect bot infections, given the fact that a bot will be commanded to launch attacks (like DDoS), which will consume CPU and network resources intensively in a burst. However, till today most customers are still reluctant to run extra software on their devices, due to the limited computing power and battery capacity of the mobile devices.

## 6.2   Botnet Defense

The most straightforward while efficient defense strategy specifically for our botnet design is to exhaust all the possible DGA-generated keywords and black-list them in Twitter search engine. The main issue of this method is the scale of DGA results. The aforementioned evaluation result of our implementation shows that the scale of the DGA results can be too large for defenders to completely ban them. A bigger challenge is that such a black-list requires, as the prerequisite, the success of reverse engineering the corresponding bot samples, as the prediction of DGA outputs needs to know the seeds fed to the DGA algorithm. Any variance in the DGA setting will cause the difference of DGA-generated keywords. Hence, it's almost an unfeasible task to black-list the query keywords in Twitter search engine.

To mitigate the threat of our botnet, we recommend all the OSN platforms to consider to leverage filter bubble [37] to prevent abnormal searching behavior. Filter bubble, as a technology that can be used by modern OSN design to consider peer relationships, could make the OSN post from the botmaster not searchable by others, i.e. bots, as they are not linked to botmaster in OSN. Based on our botnet design, this may prevent the bots to meet up in Twitter.

## 7   Conclusion

In this paper, we proposed a new OSN-based botnet design with strong robustness. In our botnet design, the botmaster orchestrates QR codes, Twitter search, and a movable web server to build dynamic C&C channels, which effectively avoid single point of failure for botnet's high recovery capability. Cryptography (DGA, AES, and RSA) is used to ensure the confidentiality of the C&C communications. Last but not least, our design takes advantage of the Tor network to achieve the botmaster's anonymity, i.e. to ensure that the botmaster is never directly exposed to the public network. To the best of our knowledge, this paper is the first to exploit QR codes as C&C communication medium in OSN-based mobile botnet.

# References

1. Google announces over 2 billion monthly active devices on android. https://www.theverge.com/2017/5/17/15654454/android-reaches-2-billion-monthly-active-users
2. Eslahi, M., Rostami, M.R., Hashim, H., Tahir, N.M., Naseri, M.V.: A data collection approach for mobile botnet analysis and detection. In: The IEEE Symposium on Wireless Technology and Applications (ISWTA), pp. 199–204. IEEE, Kota Kinabalu (2014)
3. Felt, A.P., Finifter, M., Chin, E., Hanna, S., Wagner D.: A survey of mobile malware in the wild. In: The 1st ACM Workshop on Security and Privacy in Smartphones and Mobile Devices, pp. 3–14. ACM, Chicago (2011)
4. Cooke, E., Jahanian, F., McPherson, D.: The zombie roundup: understanding, detecting, and disrupting botnets. In: The Steps to Reducing Unwanted Traffic on the Internet on Steps to Reducing Unwanted Traffic on the Internet Workshop, p. 6. USENIX, Cambridge (2005)
5. Bailey, M., Cooke, E., Jahanian, F., Xu, Y., Karir, M.,: A survey of botnet technology and defenses. In: The Conference for Homeland Security on Cybersecurity Applications & Technology (CATCH09), pp. 299–304. IEEE, Washington (2009)
6. Eslahi, M., Salleh, R., Anuar, N.B.: MoBots: a new generation of botnets on mobile devices and networks. In: IEEE Symposium on Computer Applications and Industrial Electronics (ISCAIE), pp. 262–266. IEEE, Kota Kinabalu (2012)
7. Malatras, A., Freyssinet, E., Beslay, L.: Mobile botnets taxonomy and challenges. In: European Intelligence and Security Informatics Conference, pp. 149–152. IEEE, Manchester (2015)
8. Dagon, D., Gu, G., Lee, C.P., Lee, W.: A taxonomy of botnet structures. In: 23rd Annual Computer Security Applications Conference, pp. 325–339. IEEE, Miami Beach (2007)
9. Krombholz, K., Frühwirt, P., Kieseberg, P., Kapsalis, I., Huber, M., Weippl, E.: QR code security: a survey of attacks and challenges for usable security. In: Tryfonas, T., Askoxylakis, I. (eds.) HAS 2014. LNCS, vol. 8533, pp. 79–90. Springer, Cham (2014). https://doi.org/10.1007/978-3-319-07620-1_8
10. Kieseberg, P., et al.: QR code security. In: 8th International Conference on Advances in Mobile Computing and Multimedia, pp. 430–435. ACM, Paris (2010)
11. Kharraz, A., Kirda, E., Robertson, W., Balzarotti, D., Francillon, A.: Optical delusions: a study of malicious QR codes in the wild. In: the IEEE/IFIP International Conference on Dependable Systems and Networks (DSN), pp. 192–203. IEEE, Atlanta (2014)
12. Cui, X., Fang, B., Yin, L., Liu, X., Zang, T.: Andbot: towards advanced mobile botnets. In: the 4th USENIX Conference on Large-scale Exploits and Emergent Threats, p. 11. USENIX, Boston (2011)
13. Singh, A., Toderici, A.H., Ross, K., Stamp, M.: Social networking for botnet command and control. Int. J. Comput. Netw. Inf. Secur. 5, 11–17 (2013)
14. Yin, T., Zhang, Y., Li, S.: DR-SNBot: a social network-based botnet with strong destroy-resistance. In: 9th IEEE International Conference on Networking. Architecture, and Storage, pp. 191–199. IEEE, Tianjin (2014)
15. Shin, S., Gu, G.: Conficker and beyond: a large-scale empirical study. In: the 26th Annual Computer Security Applications Conference, pp. 151–160. ACM, Austin (2010)
16. Conficker's estimated economic cost? $9.1 billion. http://www.zdnet.com/article/confickers-estimated-economic-cost-9-1-billion/

17. Dingledine, R., Mathewson, N., Syverson, P.: Tor: the second- generation onion router. In: the 13th Conference on USENIX Security Symposium, p. 21. USENIX, San Diego (2004)
18. Orbot. https://www.torproject.org/docs/android.html.en
19. Dong, Y.: An Android botnet that meets up at Twitter. http://csus-dspace.calstate.edu/handle/10211.3/198844
20. Hua, J., Sakurai, K.: A SMS-based mobile botnet using flooding algorithm. In: Ardagna, C.A., Zhou, J. (eds.) WISTP 2011. LNCS, vol. 6633, pp. 264–279. Springer, Heidelberg (2011). https://doi.org/10.1007/978-3-642-21040-2_19
21. Zeng, Y., Shin, K.G., Hu, X.: Design of SMS commanded-and- controlled and P2P-structured mobile botnets. In: The 5th ACM Conference on Security and Privacy in Wireless and Mobile Networks, pp. 137–148. ACM, Tucson (2012)
22. Faghani, M. R., Nguyen, U. T.: Socellbot: A new botnet design to infect smartphones via online social networking. In: 25th IEEE Canadian Conference on Electrical and Computer Engineering, pp. 1–5. IEEE, Montreal (2012)
23. Nagaraja, S., Houmansadr, A., Piyawongwisal, P., Singh, V., Agarwal, P., Borisov, N.: Stegobot: a covert social network botnet. In: Filler, T., Pevný, T., Craver, S., Ker, A. (eds.) IH 2011. LNCS, vol. 6958, pp. 299–313. Springer, Heidelberg (2011). https://doi.org/10.1007/978-3-642-24178-9_21
24. Compagno, A., Conti, M., Lain, D., Lovisotto, G., Mancini, L.V.: Boten ELISA: A novel approach for botnet C&C in online social networks. In: IEEE Conference on Communications and Network Security, pp. 74–82. IEEE, Florence (2015)
25. Koobface: inside a crimeware network. https://www.nartv.org/2010/11/12/koobface-inside-a-crimeware-network/
26. Thomas, K., Nicol, D.M.: The Koobface botnet and the rise of social malware. In: The 5th International Conference on Malicious and Unwanted Software, pp. 63–70. IEEE, Nancy (2010)
27. Web 2.0 Botnet Evolution Koobface Revisited. https://www.trendmicro.de/cloud-content/us/pdfs/security-intelligence/white-papers/wp_web-2-0-botnet-evolution-koobface.pdf
28. Chasing Advanced Persistent Threats (APT). https://www.secureworks.com/research/chasing_apt
29. Yao, H., Shin, D.: Towards preventing QR code based attacks on android phone using security warnings. In: The 8th ACM SIGSAC Symposium on Information, Computer and Communications Security, pp. 341–346. ACM, Hangzhou (2013)
30. Rivest, R.L., Shamir, A., Adleman, L.: A method for obtaining digital signatures and public-key cryptosystems. Commun. ACM **21**, 1–5 (2012)
31. Daemen, J., Rijmen, V.: The Design of Rijndael: AES - The Advanced Encryption Standard. Springer, New York (2013). https://doi.org/10.1007/978-3-662-04722-4
32. Mobile twitter search. https://mobile.twitter.com/search
33. Botnet prototype demonstration. https://youtu.be/LkfYa4OgvYI
34. How secure is AES against brute force attacks. https://www.eetimes.com/document.asp?docid=1279619
35. Gu, G., Perdisci, R., Zhang, J., Lee, W.: BotMiner: clustering analysis of network traffic for protocol and structure-independent botnet detection. In: The 17th USENIX Security Symposium, pp. 1–5. USENIX, San Jose (2008)
36. Gopalan, S., Kulkarni, A., Shah, A., Dai, J., Ouyang, J., Muyan-Ozcelik, P., Sun, X.: Dont be surprised: i see your mobile app stealing your data. In: ICNC 2018-Mobile Computing & Vehicle Communications Symposium, to appear. ICNC, Hawaii (2018)
37. Filter bubble. https://www.techopedia.com/definition/28556/filter-bubble

# Detecting Suspicious Members
# in an Online Emotional Support Service

Yu Li[1(✉)], Dae Wook Kim[2], Junjie Zhang[1], and Derek Doran[1]

[1] Wright State University, 3640 Colonel Glenn Hwy, Fairborn, OH 45435, USA
{li.137,junjie.zhang,derek.doran}@wright.edu
[2] Eastern Kentucky University, 521 Lancaster Ave, Richmond, KY 40475, USA
daewook.kim@eku.edu

**Abstract.** Online emotional support systems provide free support to individuals who experience stress, anxiety, and depression by bridging individuals (i.e., users) with a crowd of voluntary paraprofessionals. While most users tend to legitimately seek mental support, others may engage maliciously by attacking volunteers with trolling, flaming, bullying, spamming, and phishing behaviors. Besides attacking the mental health of trained paraprofessionals, these suspicious activities also introduce threats against the long-term viability of the platform by discouraging new volunteers and encouraging current volunteers to leave. Towards curtailing suspicious users, we propose a novel system, namely *TeaFilter*, that effectively detects suspicious behaviors by integrating a collection of light-weight behavioral features together. We have performed extensive experiments based on real user data from 7 Cups, a leading online emotional support system in the world. Experimental results have demonstrated that our system can accomplish a high detection rate of 77.8% at a low false positive rate of 1%.

## 1 Introduction

There is great need for online platforms that offer emotional supports through live, anonymous chat to individuals who experience stress, anxiety, and depression. Such platforms have been explored theoretically [1,21] and implemented practically, where examples include 7 Cups, BlahTherapy, and CrisisChat. 7 Cups is a canonical example of an online emotional support service that offers crowdsourced emotional support. It bridges individuals who are in need of emotional support (named as members in 7 Cups) with trained paraprofessionals (named as listeners) through confidential and anonymous communication channels. Listeners are volunteers who are trained in Active Listening [27]. 7 Cups has shown a remarkable growth in the context of number of registered active listeners and members since its inception, demonstrating the great need of online emotional support services.

Along with the increasing popularity of social networks including aforementioned emotional support services, a growing number of suspicious activities such

© ICST Institute for Computer Sciences, Social Informatics and Telecommunications Engineering 2018
R. Beyah et al. (Eds.): SecureComm 2018, LNICST 255, pp. 22–42, 2018.
https://doi.org/10.1007/978-3-030-01704-0_2

as unpleasant conversations, offensive communications, and even online harassment emerge. In fact, a survey [12] showed that 73% of adult Internet users have observed online harassment and 40% have personally experienced it. These activities have been observed to result in negative psychological effects such as depression, low self-esteem and even suicidal tendencies. While both members and listeners doubtlessly suffer from online harassment, listeners could have especially harmful repercussions. In addition to suffering from potential psychological attacks, listeners harassed by nefarious members may become demotivated to participate in online emotional support platforms, leading to fatal effects on the viability of online emotional support services that rely on a crowd of supportive listeners to function.

Understanding suspicious activities and detecting suspicious members are therefore essential to secure online emotional support platforms and to protect their voluntary force of listeners. Our work begins with answering an important question - What are the different types of online suspicious activities and how significant they are in this online emotional support service? The answer to this question offers an empirical basis to understand the nature of suspicious activities in online emotional support services. However, suspicious activities are labelled with natural languages rather than predefined types, making it challenging to categorize suspicious activities. In order to address this challenge, we have leveraged the topic modeling method to extract topics from language-based labels.

Our work also focuses on designing an effective detection system, which faces multiple challenges. First, the suspicious activities do not have to rely on elements (e.g., URLs and binaries) that are essential to traditional spamming and phishing attacks. Therefore, it becomes challenging to detect such attacks based on network information (e.g., domain names, IP addresses, and HTTP redirection chains) and malicious logic (e.g, through static and dynamic binary analysis). Second, members and listeners have total freedom to adopt any language for conversation. As a consequence, it faces great obstacles to analyze multilingual conversations such as parsing dialogs, mining text, and modeling topics. Third, information of social structures (e.g., friendship, followed, and following relationship), which is pervasively available for typical online social networks such as facebook and twitter, is usually absent in online emotional support platforms. This is because social structure on an emotional support service is bipartite: users interact with listeners, but members do not communicate with other members and listeners do not communicate with other listeners. Only temporal information about member to professional connections is available as a detection feature.

To effectively and automatically detect suspicious members in online emotional support systems by overcoming the aforementioned challenges, we have designed the novel system *TeaFilter*. *TeaFilter* employs a collection of lightweight behavioral features to characterize a member. These features aim to characterize a user from three aspects including (i) how she starts conservations, (ii) how she chats during a conservation, and (iii) the public reputation of this member inside the community. *TeaFilter* integrates these features using a statistical classifier to discriminate between suspicious and benign members. To the best of our knowledge, this work represents the first effort to systematically detect suspicious members in an online emotional support system. We have evaluated our system using data collected from 7 Cups, a leading website (also an app) that provides free support to people experiencing emotional distress by connecting them with trained listeners via anonymous and confidential communications. Our experimental results have demonstrated that *TeaFilter* can achieve a high detection rate of 77.8% with a low false positive rate of 1%.

The rest of this paper is organized as follows. Section 2 introduces the related work. Section 3 briefly discusses the background of 7 Cups and how data was collected and labeled. We present the system design in Sect. 5 and evaluation results in Sect. 6. The discussion is provided in Sect. 7 and Sect. 8 concludes.

## 2   Related Work

An October 2014 Pew research survey offers the evidence that online harassment is a major phenomenon that impacts Internet and social media users [12]. Academic studies have also demonstrated the negative factors associated with online harassment that attack U.S. teenagers, and unearthed the fact that bullying is intrinsic to users rather than to a particular platform [4]. Our study lies in the intersection of online harassment on online social systems, understanding the nature of online suspicious activities, and designing automated detection systems. Previous studies on online harassment focus on the effects of the practice on individual victims, which is an extremely worthy endeavor [18]. Our study takes the unique perspective of exploring the effect of harassment on the overall health and viability of the online social system itself. We do so by evaluating how listeners may be bullied and discouraged from participating in the service by members. Moreover, our exploration is data rather than survey driven.

Given the increasing popularity of online social networks (OSNs), detecting suspicious users in OSNs becomes of great importance. Many detection methods have been proposed [7–9,13,19,20,24,29]. Considering the prevalence of spamming in OSNs, these methods almost exclusively focus on detecting accounts that send spams, where a spam message is usually initialized by an attacker, flows through one or a series of suspicious accounts, and finally reaches a victim account. Despite the fact that these methods differ in their specific design, they generally take advantage of partial or all of three sources for detection including (i) the content of the spam message, (ii) the network infrastructure that hosts the malicious information (e.g., exploits), and (iii) the social structure among suspicious accounts and victim accounts. For example, Gao et al. [16] designed a method to reveal campaigns of suspicious accounts by clustering those accounts that send messages with similar content. Lee et al. [22] devised a method to track HTTP redirection chains initiated from URLs embedded in an OSN message, group messages that lead to webpages hosted in the same server, and use the server reputation to identify suspicious accounts. Yang et al. [30] extracted a graph from the following relationship of twitter accounts and then propagate maliciousness score using the derived graph; Wu et al. [29] proposed a social spammer and spam message co-detection method based on the posting relations between users and messages, and utilized the user-message relations, user-user relations, and message-message relations to improve the performance of both social spammer detection and spam message detection.

Compared to existing methods on detecting spamming OSN accounts, designing a system to perform effective detection of suspicious users in online emotional support systems faces great challenges. First, elements that are important for spamming attacks such as URLs and binaries do not have to be present to enable successful offensive communications and harassment attacks. Second, both the member and the listener have total freedom to adopt any language for conversation. Third, online emotional support systems only maintain user-professional relationship and social structures (e.g., friendship, followed, and following relationship), which are typical for existing online social networks, will be unavailable. Therefore, we need to design a new system to address these new challenges. This system needs to be capable of detecting suspicious users without relying on the communication content, malicious network infrastructure, or the social structures.

**Table 1.** Summary of the dataset. "Affected Listeners" refer to listeners that were exposed to at least one suspicious activity.

| Users | Count | Percentage |
|---|---|---|
| Num. of members | 452,605 | - |
| Num. of listeners | 169,372 | - |
| Conversations | 3.2 M | - |
| Suspicious members | 19,281 | 4.26% |
| Active suspicious members | 15,305 | 3.38% |
| Affected listeners | 37,262 | 22% |

# 3  Background and Dataset

7 Cups[1] is a website (also an application) that provides free support to people experiencing anxiety, stress & depression by connecting them with trained listeners. 7 Cups was launched in July 2013 and has developed into a popular online therapy & counseling platform with reportedly 600,000 registered users that can generate 90,000 conversations per week by 2015 [6]. 7 Cups has two types of users [5, 11]:

---

[1] https://www.7cups.com.

– **Listeners** are individuals trained with active listening skills. A listener must be at least 16 years old. Each listener is required to complete an hour-long video and text-based training course before she is given a practice conversation with a computer robot that impersonates an individual suffering from depression. A qualified listener will then have the opportunity to proceed with a variety of other training videos. A listener gradually accumulates credits from conversations in which she was involved; the level of a listener will be promoted after a certain amount of credits are obtained. Listeners are the core to the viability of the platform.

– **Members** are individuals who are seeking for stress relief by engaging themselves in active discussion with listeners through the 7 Cups website. Any network user can register as a member. Members obtain "growth points" for conducting activities such as exchanging messages with listeners and posting on the forum. Obtaining sufficient "growth points" will result in the upgrade of "member level" of a member, a metric that implies the progress towards improved mental health.

A member-listener conversation starts with a request from a member to an online listener. A member can search for a listener by offering certain criteria; the 7 Cups platform can also randomly assign an active listener to this member. Once established, the conversation between a member and a listener will last until it is terminated by either end.

Two types of actions, including block and ban, are taken against misbehaving members. A block means the member who has been blocked can no longer have one-one conversation with the listener who blocked her. A ban on the other hand is a more severe restriction which is imposed by the administrators of the website, which stops the banned member from using the service. Usually, a listener offers comments in natural language when blocking a member who shows undesirable behaviors. It is worth noting that comments are offered in natural language. The administrators of 7 Cups will be notified by listeners' actions towards members' misbehaviors and they can take further to ban a misbehaving member permanently according to the 7 Cups community comment policy [25]. It is worth noting that the detection of suspicious members is purely based on manual efforts at current stage. In our current dataset, if a member is blocked by a listener or banned by an administrator, we will label this member as a suspicious member.

We have collected data from 7 Cups. In the dataset, identities of all members and listeners have been properly anonymized and content of conversations has been removed to protect user privacy. The dataset identifies conversations of 452,605 members from December 2013 to August 2015. Among all these members, 19,281 are involved in suspicious activities, representing 4.26% of 452,605 members in total. A large percentage of 22% of listeners have been exposed to at least one suspicious activity, indicating the gravity of online threats against the platform viability. The dataset contains various types of raw data such as the registration date, the login information, the starting time, duration, the member level of each member, and comments from listeners and the administrator.

We analyze all members for types of suspicious activities. In contrast, for detection, we focus on detecting suspicious members that experience persistent activities. Detecting suspicious members with persistent activities is of particular importance for two reasons. First, they are more likely to be trusted by listeners as committed members who seek for serious assistance compared to transient members, thereby being much easier to attack listeners. Second, suspicious members with persistent activities usually accumulate an extensive amount of conversation records with mixed behaviors, which usually require significant time and efforts for manual analysis and efforts, thereby making an automated method highly demanded. In the current implementation of our method, we consider a member with persistent activities if this member (i) has registered for at least 6 weeks and (ii) has initiated more than 3 conversations. We have totally identified 15,305 active suspicious members. Detailed information of the dataset is summarized in Table 1.

## 4   The Analysis of Suspicious Activities

The first step is to build an empirical basis to facilitate the understanding of the suspicious activities in emotional support services. Towards this end, we take advantage of the comment offered by a listener or an administrator when she reports, blocks, or bans a member with inappropriate behaviors. Unfortunately, all comments are in natural languages and their syntactic representations may vary despite they have similar semantic meanings. Table 2 shows a few comments for blocking suspicious activities with different syntax.

**Table 2.** Example comments for suspicious activities

| |
| --- |
| Sexual behavior toward me |
| Just here to flirt |
| Saying sexual things |
| Seemed racially insensitive |
| Threatening me |
| Very vulgar and abusive language |
| Asking personal questions about listeners |
| Member requesting too much personal information |
| Asking for age, address etc |

We use an unsupervised topic modeling method to generalize individual comments with significant syntactical diversity into high-level topics. Specifically, we use LDAVIS [28], a topic modeling tool that extracts the latent topics of a corpus of documents using Latent Dirichlet Allocation [2]. LDAVIS is particularly effective in addressing the challenge introduced by common words in documents

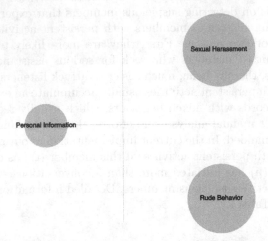

**Fig. 1.** LDAVIS identifies three topics including "sexual harassment", "rude behavior", and "soliciting personal information"

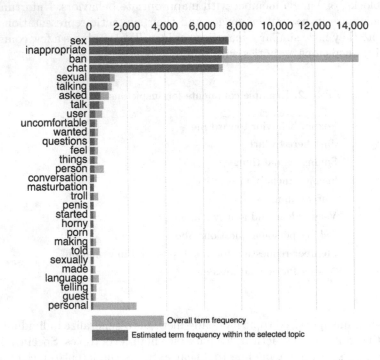

**Fig. 2.** The most relevant terms for the "sexual harassment" topic

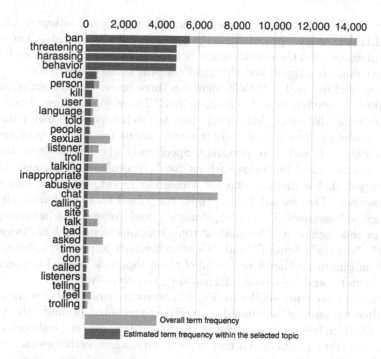

**Fig. 3.** The most relevant terms for the "rude behavior" topic

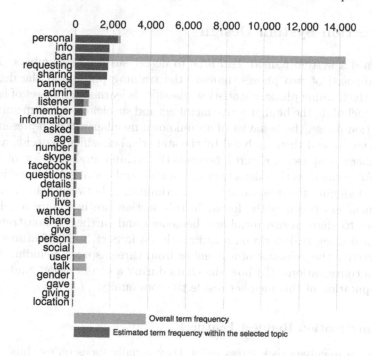

**Fig. 4.** The most relevant terms for the "soliciting personal information" topic

and hence making the meaning or semantics of a topic more interpretable. The input of LDAVIS is a corpus of documents, where each document is a comment in our application, and the output contains groups of documents (i.e., each group is corresponding to a topic) and the most relevant terms for each topic.

As presented in Fig. 1, LDAVIS identifies three broad topics from comments that explain a member report, block, or ban. These topics show significantly large inter-topic distances, indicating they are well separated based on their semantic meaning. The top-30 most relevant terms for these topics are presented in Figs. 2, 3, and 4, respectively. Specifically, the largest topic (i.e., for Fig. 2) is characterized by terms such as "sex", "porn", "naked", and "nude", which suggest that a main reason for a member report, block, or ban is sexual harassment. The second largest topic (i.e., for Fig. 3) is characterized by terms such as "aggressive", "rude", "angry", and "offensive", indicating this topic is for rude behavior. The smallest topic contains terms such as "personal", "number", "details", "email", and "location", which imply the solicitation of personal information. Therefore, we label three topics as "sexual harassment", "rude behavior", and "personal information", respectively.

Our findings are quite similar to [15], where researchers found that the majority of online harassment accounted to receiving unwanted pornography (sexual harassment) from harassers, followed by threats and insults (i.e., rude behaviors). However, our results indicated a new type of harassment activities on soliciting users' information.

## 5    Detection System Design

We designed a system named *TeaFilter* to detect suspicious members. *TeaFilter* is composed of two phases, namely the training phase and the detection phase. In the training phase, a statistical classifier is learned from a set of labelled members including the benign active members and suspicious active members. In the detection phase, the behavior of an unknown member will be represented by a feature vector and then analyzed by the statistical classifier to decide whether this member is suspicious. Figure 5 presents the architectural overview of *TeaFilter*. *TeaFilter* can directly take advantage of all popular statistical classifiers and therefore designing features capable of discriminating between benign and suspicious members becomes the focus. In this section, we introduce a collection of features to characterize members' behaviors and further demonstrate their effectiveness using real-world data as introduced in Sect. 3. The features intend to characterize the behavior of a member from three aspects including (i) how she starts conversations, (ii) how she chats during a conservation, and (iii) the public reputation of this member inside the community.

### 5.1    Conversation-Request Features

Since benign members seek stress relief, they usually focus on establishing and maintaining a few but meaningful connections with listeners that are more likely

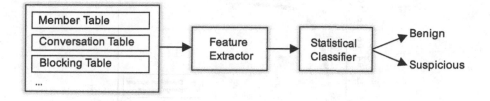

**Fig. 5.** The architectural overview of the system

to result in free expression of anxiety, active interactions, and finally tangible relief. In contrast, suspicious members tend to solicit a large number of listeners for unpleasant conversations. In addition, some listeners may realize the actual intentions of suspicious members and consequently refuse to respond or even terminate the ongoing conversations. In response, suspicious members usually quickly switch to new listeners after they fail to get prompt feedback from current listeners. In other words, while benign members aim to establish high-quality conversations with listeners, suspicious members tend to focus more on accomplishing a large number of conversations for harassment. Therefore, suspicious members are likely to trigger more conversations compared to benign members. We therefore define the following feature.

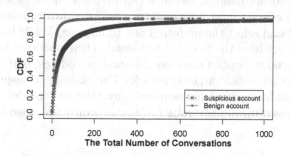

**Fig. 6.** Feature 1: the total number of conversations

- *Feature 1: The Total Number of Conversations.* The feature characterizes total number of conversations in which a member is involved.

- *Feature 2: The Average Number of Conversations Per Day.* For each member, we count the average number of conversations that are successfully established per day. We only count those days in which the member establishes at least one successful conversation.

Both features quantify the conversations for a member. Figures 6 and 7 present the distribution of values for these two features for benign and suspicious members, respectively. The comparisons indicate that suspicious members

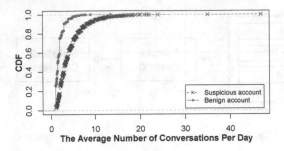

**Fig. 7.** Feature 2: the average number of conversations per day.

indeed involve more conversations than benign ones. Specifically, as indicated in the distribution of Fig. 6, more than 60% suspicious members have total conversations higher than 50 while larger than 96% benign members have their feature values lower than 50. Figure 7 shows that nearly 90% of benign members participate in less than 4 conversations per day. Comparatively, more than 50% of suspicious members have more than 4 conversations per day.

As discussed in Sect. 3, a member has two ways to identify a listener for conversation establishment. On the one hand, a member can ask the 7 Cups platform to assign a listener based on the profile of the member and those of listeners. On the other hand, a member can first search for candidate listeners based on certain criteria (e.g., age, country, and keywords contained in the profile of a listener) and select the preferred one to interact. While both benign and suspicious members have the freedom to identify their preferred listeners, suspicious members tend to depend more on searched candidates, partially due to the higher possibility to launch targeted attacks. For example, a suspicious member who plans to conduct sexual harassment may infer the gender of a potential target listener based on the portraits (or avatar icons) uploaded by listeners.

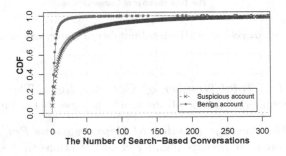

**Fig. 8.** Feature 3: the number of search-based conversations

– *Feature 3: The Number of Search-Based Conversations.* For each member, we calculate the total number of conversations to listeners who are discovered through the search function.

Figure 8 presents the distribution of feature values, where suspicious members tend to generate more search-based conversations compared to benign members. Specifically, more than 65% of suspicious members have more than 20 search-based conversations while about 10% of benign accounts have more than 20 search-based conversations.

## 5.2 Chatting Behaviour

Once a conversation is established, a member can interact with a listener until the conversation is explicitly cancelled. We next propose features that can capture differences between benign and suspicious members during such conversations.

A suspicious member is inclined to be more active in sending messages to either attract listeners' attention or disturb their normal consulting activities. Therefore, we use the number of messages sent by a member to quantify her level of activity in sending messages.

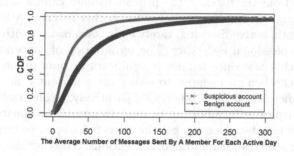

**Fig. 9.** Feature 4: the average number of messages sent by a member for each active day

– *Feature 4: The Average Number of Messages Sent By A Member For Each Active Day.* For a member, we count the total number of messages she has sent and divide it using the total number of days in which this member sends out at least one message.

Figure 9 presents the distribution of this feature for both benign and suspicious members. Specifically, nearly 80% of benign members have less than 40 messages per each active day. In contrast, suspicious members are more active, where approximately 80% of them send more than 40 messages per each active day.

Different from typical online chatting systems, the state of a conversation of 7 Cups will be maintained even if the member or listener in this conversation

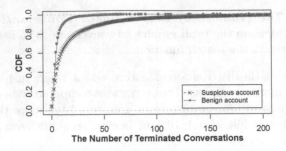

**Fig. 10.** Feature 5: the number of terminated conversation

logs out; the state will also be maintained when the network connection is disrupted. In this case, both the member and listener can re-engage themselves in the previously-established conversation to continue discussion, tremendously fostering long-term, trustworthy, and high-quality interaction between the listener and member. However, a conversation will be discontinued if either side explicitly terminates it. Usually, a conversation between a listener and a benign member is terminated for a few reasons. For example, the member has obtained sufficient mental support from the listener; the present listener cannot satisfy the needs of the member and the member switches to another listener. A listener, who is trained to maintain active listening, rarely ends conversation with an individual who seeks for professional assistance. The termination of conversation happens infrequently in this case since it takes a significant amount of interactions (and thus time) for the benign member to either get sufficient relief or assess the professional proficiency of the listener. Comparatively, a conversation between a listener and a suspicious member can be more frequently terminated. For example, a suspicious member does not get the expected responses from the listener after she sends messages with unfriendly intentions; a listener simply terminates the conversation after she realizes the harassment attempts from a suspicious member. To summarize, we expect a suspicious member tends to experience more terminated conversations compared to a benign member. Therefore, we define the following feature.

– **Feature 5: The Number of Terminated Conversations.** This feature summarizes the total number of conversations experienced by a member that are terminated either by listeners or by this member.

Figure 10 presents the distribution of this feature for both benign and suspicious members. Specifically, more than 90% of benign members have less than 20 terminated conversations. In contrast, approximately 40% of suspicious members have more than 20 terminated conversations.

A benign member usually initiates a conversation request. If the request is accepted by the listener, the conversation will be established. The dialog usually starts with greetings from the member and the subsequent response from the listener. Comparatively, a suspicious member may start a collection of conversations with no message exchanged, where such conversations are denoted as blank conversations in this paper. A suspicious member may trigger blank conversations for two reasons. First, blank conversations can possibly lead to denial of service (DoS) attacks by wasting listeners' time, energy, and enthusiasm to help benign members who actually need emotional support. This type of possible DoS attacks is stealthy since it is challenging for the listener to assess the intention of this member without getting any messages; the listener may falsely classify a suspicious member as one who is slow in typing. Second, a suspicious member may start many conversations simultaneously with a collection of listeners and begin to greet each of them sequentially. When the suspicious member gets response from a listener, she may stop greeting the following ones, introducing blank conversations. In contrast to suspicious members, benign members are much less motivated to generate blank conversations. We therefore define the following feature to quantify such observation.

– *Feature 6: The Number of Blank Conversations.*

Figure 11 presents the distribution of this feature for both benign and suspicious members. Approximately 80% benign members had less than 20 blank conversations. Comparatively, over 60% suspicious members initiated more than 20 blank conversations; about 10% of suspicious members generated a large number of (i.e., more than 100) blank conversations.

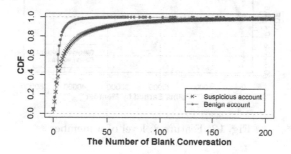

**Fig. 11.** Feature 6: the number of blank conversations

## 5.3   Reputation Features

Members are provided with the capabilities to block listeners in case the listeners behave inappropriately. Since listeners are extensively trained, the chance for them to start inappropriate conversation is extremely low. Unfortunately, this method might be misused by suspicious members. Specifically, when the suspicious member finds that her suspicious intention is identified by the listeners and she is subject to be reported, she can block the listener proactively to either disrupt the listener from reporting her or confuse the administrator to avoid being banned.

Comparatively, benign members treat listeners as their private mental therapists and are therefore extremely less likely to misuse this function. The following feature is accordingly designed.

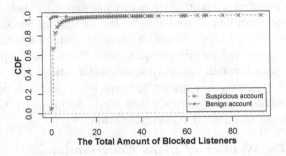

**Fig. 12.** Feature 7: the total amount of blocked listeners

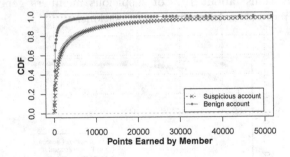

**Fig. 13.** Feature 8: level of a member

- *Feature 7: Total Number of Blocked Listeners.* For each member, we count the total number of listeners she has blocked.

Figure 12 presents the distribution of this feature for both benign members and suspicious members. Specifically, 98% of benign members never blocked any listener. Comparatively, almost 70% of suspicious members blocked at least 1 listener.

- *Feature 8: Level of A Member.*

It is a common feature in many online social networks that a user can earn more "points" by participating various activities such as logining and establishing conversations. Such feature usually reflects the loyalty of users to the online social network. The 7 Cups platform uses the "level" to characterize a member for this purpose. A member with high level implies her high degree of loyalty and frequent usage of the platform. While a certain amount of benign members tend to seek emotional support regularly, most suspicious members tend to be frequent users who are highly active in logining and establishing conversations. Therefore, we expect that suspicious members are inclined to have higher levels compared to benign members. We therefore use the level of a member as a feature. Figure 13 presents the distribution for this feature: while approximately 90% of benign users have growth points less than 2000, 50% of suspicious accounts accumulate more than 2000 growth points.

# 6 Evaluation

We have performed extensive evaluation of *TeaFilter* using real-world data collected from the 7 Cups platform. We have used records of 15,305 suspicious members and those of 15,305 benign members to conduct the experiments, which serve as a balanced dataset for training statistical classifiers. Our evaluation focuses on *TeaFilter*'s overall detection performance and the correlation among different features.

## 6.1 Detection Accuracy

We evaluate the detection performance of *TeaFilter* when three different statistical classifiers including Random Forest [3], Support Vector Machine [10], and Gradient-Boosted Tree [17] are employed. We used 10-fold cross-validation, where we randomly partition the data set into 10 folds and then employ 9 folds for training and the remaining 1 fold for detection. The area under the ROC curve (AUC) [14] values are summarized in Table 3 when these three statistical classifiers are used in *TeaFilter*, respectively. The high AUC values indicate the overall high detection accuracy of the proposed system; they also imply that the high detection performance of *TeaFilter* is rooted in the proposed features. Figure 14 further visualizes the receiver operating characteristic (ROC) when Random Forest is adopted as the statistical classifier for *TeaFilter*, which illustrates the trade-off between the detection rate and the false positive rate. Specifically, given a false positive rate of 1%, it can accomplish a high detection rate of 77.8%.

**Table 3.** AUCs for three classifiers

| Classifier | AUC |
| --- | --- |
| Random forest | 0.9851 |
| SVM | 0.9673 |
| Gradient-boosted tree | 0.9766 |

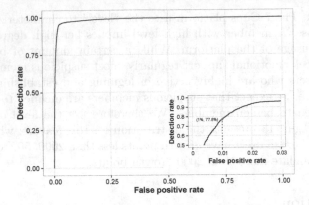

**Fig. 14.** ROC curve on 8 features

We also investigate the relative importance of the proposed features in the context of Random Forest classifier, which has accomplished the best detection accuracy according to our experiments. We employed the variable importance of each feature to the Random Forest classification model using permutation test [26]. It is interesting to note that the reputation features designed are the most important ones for TeaFilter to make a classification decision. Feature 7, corresponding to the number of listeners a member blocked, is many times more important than any other feature in discriminating suspicious and unsuspicious users. This lends support to our hypothesis that suspicious users obtain a sense of when a punitive action will be taken against them, blocking the connection prematurely. It also suggests another kind of attack, where members may troll listeners by starting a conversation, launching an attack quickly, and then terminate the conversation. Moreover, benign users with good intentions may find no need to ever block a listener as conversations persist on 7 cups. The importance of feature 8, the level of a member, reinforces our intuition that longstanding members who make positive contributions to the community (hence increasing their point total and account level) are very low risk for transforming into a suspicious member in the future (Table 4).

## 6.2   Feature Correlation

The purpose of correlation analysis is to determine if many pairs of features used in TeaFilter are linearly correlated, which can hinder classification accuracy as correlated features that essentially encode the same information to a classifier. We use Pearson's $r$ [23], also known as the Pearson correlation coefficient, to measure the strength of correlation. Pearsons $r$ correlation coefficient is defined as: $r = \{\sum(f_1 - \bar{f}_1)(f_2 - \bar{f}_2)\}/\{\sqrt{\sum(f_1 - \bar{f}_1)^2}\sqrt{\sum(f_2 - \bar{f}_2)^2}\}$, where $\bar{f}_1$ and $\bar{f}_2$ denote the means of the $f_1$ and $f_2$, respectively. The Pearson's $r$ takes on values between -1 and 1. The absolute value (i.e, $|r|$) represents the degree of the correlation, ranging from being perfectly negative correlated $(-1)$ and perfectly

**Table 4.** Feature importance rank of *TeaFilter* by Random Forest

| Rank | Variable importance |
|---|---|
| Feature 7 | 815.4 |
| Feature 8 | 131.8 |
| Feature 2 | 80.6 |
| Feature 1 | 49.4 |
| Feature 6 | 46.9 |
| Feature 4 | 43.1 |
| Feature 5 | 36.6 |
| Feature 3 | 33.5 |

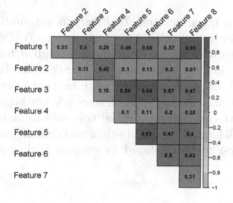

**Fig. 15.** Upper triangular matrix of pearson correlation coefficient

positively correlated (1). Note that $|r| = 0$ indicates no correlation either negatively or positively. If the Pearson's $r$ between two features is close to 1 (or $-1$), then the pair of these features are highly correlated. Figure 15 represents that most of our features are not highly linearly-correlated each other. For example, there is only one pair of features, Feature 5 (*The Number of Terminated Conversations*) and Feature 6 (*The Number of Blank Conversations*), experiences a relatively high coefficient value of 0.93.

## 7   Discussion

Suspicious members may attempt to evade the detection after they know the design of *TeaFilter*. Specifically, they may alter their behaviors to make themselves indistinguishable from benign members. However, successfully evading *TeaFilter* will fundamentally diminish the effectiveness and efficiency for these attacks, thereby significantly raising the bar for suspicious members. For example, suspicious members can increase the average interval between two consecutive conservations and meanwhile reduce the number of conservations. They can start a new conversation after terminate the previous one to bypass the feature that describes the number of blank conversations. All these attempts will decrease the efficiency of malicious activities (i.e., reducing the number of listeners to be harassed). Finally, it is worth noting that the labeling of suspicious activities is based on the interpretation of individual listeners. Therefore, a member blocked by one listener might not be considered unacceptable by another listener. As an example, a listener, who is not comfortable talking about porn addiction, may block the member but the member may be genuinely looking for help. A potential solution is to train a customized detection engine for each listener, which falls into our future work.

## 8   Conclusion

This paper presents a novel system, *TeaFilter*, to automatically detect suspicious members in an online emotional support system. *TeaFilter* leverages three categories of light-weight features to accomplish high detection performance. Although the design and the evaluation of *TeaFilter* are based on real-world data collected from 7 Cups, one leading platform that offers online emotional support, the features and the detection framework are generally applicable to popular social networks including potential new online emotional support platforms. Particularly, all features are lightweight and context-independent, thereby showing great promise to be deployed in systems that support multiple languages.

## References

1. Binik, Y.M., Cantor, J., Ochs, E., Meana, M.: From the couch to the keyboard: psychotherapy in cyberspace. Cult. Internet, 71–100 (1997)
2. Blei, D.M., Ng, A.Y., Jordan, M.I.: Latent Dirichlet allocation. J. Mach. Learn. Res. **3**(Jan), 993–1022 (2003)
3. Breiman, L.: Random forests. Mach. Learn. **45**(1), 5–32 (2001)
4. Calvete, E., Orue, I., Estévez, A., Villardón, L., Padilla, P.: Cyberbullying in adolescents: modalities and aggressors profile. Comput. Hum. Behav. **26**(5), 1128–1135 (2010)
5. Calzarossa, M.C., Massari, L., Doran, D., Yelne, S., Trivedi, N., Moriarty, G.: Measuring the users and conversations of a vibrant online emotional support system. In: 2016 IEEE Symposium on Computers and Communication (2016)
6. Carpenter, D.: Free app provides emotional support for students. http://www.iowastatedaily.com/news/student_life/article_21540770-b496-11e4-9dcd-df0295772d43.html (2015)
7. Chen, Y.R., Chen, H.H.: Opinion spammer detection in web forum. In: Proceedings of the 38th International ACM SIGIR Conference on Research and Development in Information Retrieval. ACM (2015)
8. Chu, Z., Gianvecchio, S., Wang, H., Jajodia, S.: Detecting automation of twitter accounts: are you a human, bot, or cyborg? IEEE Trans. Dependable Secur. Comput. **9**(6), 811–824 (2012)

9. Chu, Z., Gianvecchio, S., Koehl, A., Wang, H., Jajodia, S.: Blog or block: detecting blog bots through behavioral biometrics. Comput. Netw. **57**(3), 634–646 (2013)
10. Cristianini, N., Shawe-Taylor, J.: An Introduction to Support Vector Machines and Other Kernel-based Learning Methods. Cambridge University Press, Cambridge (2000)
11. Doran, D., Yelne, S., Massari, L., Calzarossa, M.C., Jackson, L., Moriarty, G.: Stay awhile and listen: user interactions in a crowdsourced platform offering emotional support. In: Proceedings of the 2015 IEEE/ACM International Conference on Advances in Social Networks Analysis and Mining (2015)
12. Duggan, M.: Online harassment. Pew Research Center (2014)
13. Fakhraei, S., Foulds, J., Shashanka, M., Getoor, L.: Collective spammer detection in evolving multi-relational social networks. In: Proceedings of the 21th ACM SIGKDD (2015)
14. Fawcett, T.: An introduction to ROC analysis. Pattern Recognit. Lett. **27**(8), 861–874 (2006)
15. Finn, J.: A survey of online harassment at a university campus. J. Interpers. Violence **19**(4), 468–483 (2004)
16. Gao, H., Hu, J., Wilson, C., Li, Z., Chen, Y., Zhao, B.Y.: Detecting and characterizing social spam campaigns. In: Proceedings of the 10th ACM SIGCOMM Conference on Internet Measurement. ACM (2010)
17. Han, J., Kamber, M., Pei, J.: Data Mining: Concepts and Techniques. Morgan kaufmann, Los Altos (2006)
18. Hinduja, S., Patchin, J.W.: Bullying, cyberbullying, and suicide. Arch. Suicide Res. **14**(3), 206–221 (2010)
19. Hu, X., Tang, J., Liu, H.: Leveraging knowledge across media for spammer detection in microblogging. In: Proceedings of the 37th International ACM SIGIR Conference on Research & Development in Information Retrieval (2014)
20. Hu, X., Tang, J., Liu, H.: Online social spammer detection. In: Proceedings of the 28th AAAI Conference, pp. 59–65. AAAI (2014)
21. Huang, M.P., Alessi, N.E.: The internet and the future of psychiatry. Am. J. Psychiatry **153**(7), 861–869 (1996)
22. Lee, S., Kim, J.: WarningBird: detecting suspicious URLs in twitter stream. In: NDSS, vol. 12, pp. 1–13 (2012)
23. Lee Rodgers, J., Nicewander, W.A.: Thirteen ways to look at the correlation coefficient. Am. Stat. **42**(1), 59–66 (1988)
24. Miller, Z., Dickinson, B., Deitrick, W., Hu, W., Wang, A.H.: Twitter spammer detection using data stream clustering. Inf. Sci. **260**, 64–73 (2014)
25. Moriarty, G.: 7 cups member agreement. https://www.7cups.com/inc/memberTOS.html
26. RColorBrewer, S., Liaw, M.A.: Package randomForest (2012)
27. Rogers, C.R., Farson, R.E.: Active listening. Industrial Relations Center of the University of Chicago (1957)
28. Sievert, C., Shirley, K.E.: LDavis: a method for visualizing and interpreting topics. In: Proceedings of the Workshop on Interactive Language Learning, Visualization, and Interfaces, pp. 63–70 (2014)

29. Wu, F., Shu, J., Huang, Y., Yuan, Z.: Social spammer and spam message co-detection in microblogging with social context regularization. In: Proceedings of the 24th ACM International on Conference on Information and Knowledge Management, pp. 1601–1610. ACM (2015)
30. Yang, C., Harkreader, R.C., Gu, G.: Die free or live hard? Empirical evaluation and new design for fighting evolving twitter spammers. In: Sommer, R., Balzarotti, D., Maier, G. (eds.) RAID 2011. LNCS, vol. 6961, pp. 318–337. Springer, Heidelberg (2011). https://doi.org/10.1007/978-3-642-23644-0_17

# Towards a Reliable and Accountable Cyber Supply Chain in Energy Delivery System Using Blockchain

Xueping Liang[1,2,3], Sachin Shetty[1], Deepak Tosh[4], Yafei Ji[2(✉)], and Danyi Li[2]

[1] Virginia Modeling Analysis and Simulation Center, Old Dominion University,
Norfolk, VA 23529, USA
[2] Institute of Information Engineering, Chinese Academy of Sciences,
Beijing 100093, China
jiyafei@iie.ac.cn
[3] School of Cyber Security, University of Chinese Academy of Sciences,
Beijing 100190, China
[4] Department of Computer Science, Norfolk State University,
Norfolk, VA 23504, USA

**Abstract.** The cyber supply chain arises as the emerging business model of today's IT infrastructure in enterprise-level energy delivery system, which relies on different software or hardware vendors. Due to the heterogeneous services provided and various roles involved for each system entity to maintain the IT infrastructure, the attack surface expands dramatically, thus putting enterprise systems at high risks of data breaches or compromises. This paper firstly presents an overview of the typical cyber supply chain system, including system entities and processes, and then two attack scenarios are illustrated. Following the analysis of cyber supply chain security requirements and countermeasures, we integrate the power of blockchain technology that has a trustless and decentralized architecture, to the cyber supply chain to achieve reliability and accountability. A basic framework for blockchain assured energy delivery system is introduced as a case study to provide guidelines for future blockchain adoption in achieving provenance of cyber supply chain systems in any industries.

**Keywords:** Cyber supply chain · Distributed ledger · Reliability
Accountability · Energy delivery system

## 1 Introduction

Cyber supply chain [7] is the entire set of key actors that are involved in the cyber infrastructure, including system end-users, policy-makers, acquisition specialists, system integrators, network providers, and software/hardware suppliers. Various sectors maintain cyber supply chains, such as finance, healthcare and energy systems.

R. Beyah et al. (Eds.): SecureComm 2018, LNICST 255, pp. 43–62, 2018.
https://doi.org/10.1007/978-3-030-01704-0_3

Typically industrial systems have several critical components that are associated with personal identification information, payment and system configuration parameters or business sensitive data. As a result, cyber supply chains face threats and risks of data breaches from both insiders and outsiders. Insiders could be compromised and turned into a leakage point of data and intelligence. Outsiders are attempting to plant malware using command and control techniques. Risks exist in every phase of the supply chain life cycles of vendor products and services (software, firmware and hardware), including the procurement, deployment, operation and maintenance. To mitigate cyber security risks and achieve the reliability and accountability of system operation and maintenance, the design and implementation of secure controls for cyber supply chain systems are needed. The control of access to the critical system components by system entities should be addressed.

The Energy Delivery System (EDS), as a critical infrastructure for national security, are faced with severe cyber supply chain security risks than ever before [17]. The notion of smart grid system, highlighting the combination of the physical components with cyber services and products, implicates the critical role of cyber entities that supply the power system and related services such as software development, hardware manufacturing, product reselling and system integration. Developing techniques and tools to provide assured cyber supply chain provenance are top priority for addressing cyber supply chain risks such as, counterfeits, unauthorized production, tampering, theft, insertion of malicious software and hardware, as well as poor manufacturing and development practices [37]. There is a lack of tools or technologies that can protect the entire cyber supply chain and ensure that all software and firmware verified for their trustworthiness before they are integrated into system operational technology (OT) in critical systems such as energy delivery systems. Assured data provenance techniques to certify the software component at all stages of a cyber supply chain should be developed so that the end-users can easily verify whether the purchased electronic component's software or firmware is tampered with or not.

There exist solutions that leverage enhanced security testing, side-channel fingerprinting, reverse engineering, and several formal methods. The aforementioned solutions are mostly deployed at the chip level to detect presence of counterfeit electronic components. However, these methods cannot be scaled to protect the whole cyber supply chain. These discrete solutions create inconsistencies when ensuring the genuineness of purchased electronic components and insufficient to assess chain of custody or products. In order to scale the process of protecting the cyber supply chain, a top-down system-level methodology should be developed beforehand to guide the formalization of the whole supply chain protection. In this paper we adopt a decentralized and trustless architecture, blockchain, to address these challenges. Blockchain technology, originated from Bitcoin [30] where data are stored in a public, distributed and immutable ledger and maintained by a decentralized network of computing nodes, provides the robustness against failure and attacks, functions for data provenance [26] and access control [18]. In this way, we use blockchain to track and record supply chain data, which ensures confidentiality, integrity and availability. The contribution of this paper includes: (1) We present a system overview of the cyber supply chain as a new business and operation model and point out the security concerns. (2) We propose a blockchain integration framework for cyber supply chain security with a set of functions including identity management, product verification, access control, contract execution, and monitoring. (3) We propose a blockchain-based cyber supply chain architecture and implement a prototype of a blockchain-assured cyber supply chain provenance for energy delivery system.

The rest of the paper is organized as follows. An overview of the typical cyber supply chain, including system entities, processes, and two attack scenarios, are introduced in Sect. 2. Section 3 introduces blockchain capabilities, analyses cyber supply chain security requirements, and proposes to integrate blockchain technology to the cyber supply chain for reliability and accountability purposes. A basic framework for blockchain assured energy delivery system is introduced in Sect. 4 as a case study to provide guidelines for future blockchain adoption in real cyber supply chain systems. Section 5 summarizes related work and concludes the work.

## 2   Cyber Supply Chain Demystification

The globalization of cyber supply chain has resulted in electronic components, software and firmware developed by mostly offshore enterprises and has resulted in tremendous savings for the EDS sector. However, the dependency on third-party services has resulted in increase in threats across several stages in the cyber supply chain. Specifically, there is a need for tools or technologies that can adequately address risks involved in processes, sourcing, third party vendor management (every actor that has physical or virtual access to software code and/or systems), acquisition of compromised software/hardware purchases from suppliers, embedded malware in hardware, counterfeited hardware and third party data storage or data aggregators [17]. In this section we start from the system entities that play important roles in cyber supply chain, and then dive into each system process and analyze the possible attacks.

### 2.1   System Entities

Cyber supply chain systems mainly have three critical roles that constitute the cyber supply chain backbones. While there are other roles such as registrars, certifiers and standards organizations, this paper focuses on these roles shown in Fig. 1 that interact frequently with each other and influence the cyber supply chain dynamics.

**Vendor.** According to the definition of NERC (North American Electric Reliability Corporation) [34], vendors include developers or manufacturers of information systems, system components, or information system services, product

**Fig. 1.** The cyber supply chain system entities

resellers and system integrators. They provide hardware/software, hosted services and physical network infrastructure/equipment/facilities, enabling both system operators and end-users to participate and interact within the cyber supply chain. System operators purchase physical devices or IT services from vendors. End-user feedback is also retrieved by vendors for customer retention and profit growth. Moreover, security measurements and risk mitigation techniques are crucial to maintain the prestige of trusted vendor reputation.

**System Operator.** System operators are responsible for receiving, transmitting and distributing physical components and software code from vendors. They are motivated to balance the need for system fidelity and assurance, as well as end-user satisfaction to gain maximized revenue, control cost and complete tasks on time [7]. In some cases, system integration requires collaboration between system operators and vendors for a stable implementation in the production environment. System operators play a vital role for providing system functions to end-users and is directly communicating with end-users for system maintenance and periodic update. During system setup, various hardware and software services are purchased from vendors, which is illustrated in detail as the procurement phase in Sect. 2.2, introducing attack vectors and thus a weak point. During system maintenance, interference from vendors for product updates and remote access is also carried out to ensure system security levels up-to-date, introducing another system weak point as well.

**System End-User.** System end-users rely on the system for resources consumption or services. For example in energy delivery systems, end-users can purchase electricity, oil and gas. This role is generally seen as the customers that set expectations and specifications, as well as accept all incoming deliverables, inherently defining the cyber supply chain of a specific system. User experience usually provides cyber supply chain visions and system goals so that the cyber supply chain could be improved towards that vision. Also end-users have the limitation of budgets so both the system operators and the vendors are in need of cost controlling and service upgrades to ensure all deliverables are satisfying in the perspective of end-users. In this sense, system end-users are at the core position of the cyber supply chain and drive the cycling in positive directions. In some way, system operators could be recognized as the system end-users in the vendor's point of view. From the security standpoint, protecting system operations and ensuring end-users satisfaction is the ultimate expectation for vendors.

**Other Roles.** Registrars provide actors of the cyber supply chain a unique identity, ensuring the authenticity of each participant and the supply chain capability to identify each actor. Standards organizations are neutral parties that deliver technical standards or suggestions for industrial practices. There are certifiers which professionally perform checks against each participant and issue certificates to those qualified, serving as a checkpoint and is reliable. In most cases, certifiers related to the cyber supply chain would visit the vendors for on-site inspection and then make conclusion of whether certain standards and specifications are met by those products before they enter the cyber supply chain [4]. A certificate will be issued to the vendor when it is verified, as a proof of quality and reliability for future procurement phase.

## 2.2 System Process

**Procurement Phase.** Procurement phase should identify and document cyber security risks during designing and developing processes. The security objective is to prevent vulnerabilities or attacks resulting from the procuring and utilizing vendor devices or software, as well as the transitions from previous vendor(s) to another. Meanwhile, the business contract during procurement phase should be negotiated and provisioned with plans to address future risk settlement [34]. In an energy delivery system, in order to provide energy to end-users, for example power supply, the system should deploy physical network to generate, transmit and distribute electricity. This requires not only hardware components such as switchers, sensors and actuators that physically monitor and control the system, but also computer systems for data analysis and storage, as well as the communication systems connecting the physical components and the cyber services. Meanwhile, to identify end-users for billing and payment, the identity based services are necessary. These services actually provide security checkpoints during procurement. Hardware manufacturers are required to meet international or industrial standards to compete and gain profit. Vendors with certificated products are more capable of providing resilient functions and have higher scores to be procured. For example, software vendors should adopt industry-driven safe code development and have the software assurance awareness to ensure software resilience and authenticity. Besides procuring and installing vendor software and equipment, there are cases when the system changes from one vendor to another either because of the end of the contract or a better choice, there are operations such as uninstalling, to make the transition. During the transition, sensitive data access could happen and privileged roles are assigned. All of the above requires that risk mitigation measures and options be in place.

**Operation Phase.** System operations are regular practices to maintain the system functionality and performance, including security check, periodic assessment, logging and monitoring. There are software updates from vendors either for performance improvement or security-related enhancement. The integrity and authenticity of software patches should also be verified and validated to ensure the trustworthiness of software pieces. Some vendor updates require operations from vendor side which allows the vendor to have temporary remote access to the system. This creates the privileged accounts for the convenience of system operations. Some systems would get a complete solution from vendors which will be responsible for the system component maintenance and updates. It is required that risk assessment plan and mitigation measures be reviewed every 15 calender months to remain up-to-date [34] and better address new risks and vulnerabilities. Logging and monitoring are typical measures to detect malicious behaviors in an early stage before potential attacks, which is significantly effective against APT (Advanced Persistent Threat) [38].

## 2.3   Attack Scenarios

Cyber threats and vulnerabilities are difficult to predict and they evolve faster than the current system ability to deploy countermeasures. Typical cyber attacks apply in cyber supply chain systems and this section analyzes two of them specifically which are the most representative.

**Attack via Manufacturer Source Code or Product.** Considering three types of products the manufacturer provides, there are three levels of attack surfaces existing in the manufacturer side, namely software level, firmware level and hardware level. A software or hardware manufacturer could be compromised by attackers planting malwares that modifies source code which will then be distributed to potential enterprises in need of the software. From the attacker's perspective, it is possible to make the product faulty before it is put into use and becomes operative [44]. This attack will render the security measures taken after the products become operational not sufficient or even useless. It is reported that the energy sector faced with this type of attacks since 2011 [20], leading to power outages affecting hundreds of thousands of people. To plant malwares into manufacturer source code, attackers mainly adopt three methods, including phishing emails, trojanized software and watering hole websites. Most phishing emails are targeted at software developers by way of social engineering. Template injection, reported by Cisco [33], is a typical method to plant malicious code via emails. In this case, a word document is attached in an email and that document contains a script or macro that executes malicious code. This is hard to detect because the email and the attachment itself contain no malicious code until it is opened as a doc file and the macro function is enabled. Trojanized software is usually posted on the manufacturer's website as a genuine software by attackers and made available for downloads. Watering hole attacks aims to harvest online credentials, by compromising websites that are likely to be frequently visited by those personnel involved in the system operation [10]. Firmware provides a software-driven interface between physical outputs and the high-level software, and includes boot loader code that initializes and loads the operating system.

Firmware information could be retrieved by reverse engineering and binary code inspection, which can then be modified and reloaded. The firmware modification attack on PLC (Programmable Logic Controllers) existing in industrial control systems is analyzed in [6]. Malicious modification or counterfeiting of PLC firmware enables an attacker to take full control of a certain industrial control device and in turn place any physical system components that are under the control of that device at high risks of compromise. Hardware could also be counterfeited due to the complexity of the chips and micro-units it consists of. This process happens along the life cycle of a hardware from the original materials to the destination.

**Attack via Vendor Remote Access.** A software vendor's credential for remote access to the system that is being used by the enterprise, for which the vendor provides services, could be faced with theft, resulting in the infiltration of the enterprise network from the vendor network which was once a trusted source [35]. Not only network credentials but also multi-factor token data [45] could be stolen, leading to significant supply chain data breach.

## 3   Blockchain Integration for Cyber Supply Chain Security

### 3.1   Blockchain Overview

Blockchain is a new technology which uses a distributed public ledger to record transactions and facilitate trusted delivery of transactions across a distributed network without involvement of centralized authority or intermediaries. Blockchains have the following advantage over centralized databases: (1) Ability to directly share databases across diverse boundaries of trust in situations where it is difficult to identify a trusted centralized arbitrator to enforce constraints of proof of authorization and validity. Blockchain transactions leverage self-contained proofs of validity and authorization based on a verification process enforced by multiple validating nodes and a consensus mechanism that ensures synchronization. (2) Ability to provide robustness in an economical fashion without the need for expensive infrastructure for replication and disaster recovery. Blockchains provide built-in technical mechanisms to handle tasks which would otherwise require complex institutional processes. Nodes in a blockchain automatically self-configure, connect and sync with each other in a peer-to-peer fashion. The feature of built-in redundancy avoids the need for closely monitoring and provides the ability to tolerate multiple communication link failures. External users are allowed to broadcast transactions to any node, and it is ensured that disconnected nodes will be caught up on missed transactions. The detailed capabilities that enable blockchain as a compelling technology to serve as solutions to some critical security issues are discussed in the following.

**Tamper Resistance.** Each mined block in the blockchain contains a list of transactions which are then hashed as a Merkle root. This attribute can be used to handle sensitive information and maintain the integrity of data. The hash of the previous block is involved in the generation of the current block hash, making the block capable to prevent and detect any form of tampering. Manipulation of block data is impossible without being detected. This immutability of blockchain benefits the protection of cyber supply chains by way of providing the reliability of data provenance and implicit linkability between lists of transactions on a time basis.

**Authenticity Verification.** Based on the timestamping function and the chain based architecture, mathematical certainty over the provenance and tracking of every component could be assured in the system. Any record anchored on the blockchain cannot be modified and thus the recorded event sequencing is preserved. The validation of the data integrity is provable by traversing the blockchain state which is maintained by distributed nodes. Any attempt to modify or counterfeit the product would be recorded and detected eventually by tracing back the transaction lists.

**Accountability.** Combined with cryptography algorithms and timestamping function, it is difficult for attackers to modify a past event. Blockchains assume the presence of adversaries in the network and nullify the adversarial strategies by harnessing the computational capabilities of the honest nodes, making the information exchanged resilient to manipulation and destruction [27]. The reconciliation process between entities is sped up due to absence of trusted central authority or intermediary. Tampering of blockchains are extremely challenging due to use of a cryptographic data structure and no reliance of secrets. The blockchain networks are fault tolerant which allows nodes to eliminate compromised nodes.

**Smart Contract.** Contract Negotiation and execution constitute the blockchain processing logic, making the network capable of executing various types of transactions instead of the basic function of payment transfer. Different interactions between system entities can be abstracted and simulated on the blockchain network. For example, to monitor and detect potential threats with established specifications, the automated code execution could be conducted in a distributed but trusted manner. Detecting rules can be established so that a rule based intrusion detection mechanism [19] could be utilized for malicious detection and providing timely alerts.

A set of rules can be defined to govern the system operation and control remote access from vendors, as well as user interactions and data exchanges [39]. These rules can also be stored on the blockchain to prevent from being altered without the awareness and verification of all the nodes.

**Robustness and Reliability.** Computation and data operation process can be deployed among multiple untrusted parties, but the computation and data operation results are trusted. This can effectively reduce the risks of single point of failures and the DDoS attack [13]. The completely decentralized architecture in blockchain network helps to provide robustness for data assurance, fully aligning with the requirements of cyber supply chains where participants are equally distributed and participating, without the built-in trust. All the data records, including identity registration for system entities and products, as well as system operations from both insiders and outsiders, are published either in original format or in hashed strings, which extremely enhances the transparency of every elements in the cyber supply chain.

### 3.2 Blockchain Integration Concerns

**Data Scalability.** Data volume in cyber supply chain could be a heavy load for the processing unit in terms of both time frame and concurrent records. To deal with multiple data streams and operation records, it is required that the blockchain should manage frequent data records and handle large data sets during a limited time span. However, blockchain based architecture requires a specific time cost for both block mining and consensus scheme.

**Data Interoeprability.** Data sets from various vendor domains are formatted differently during record creation, exchange and storage. It is even more complex to process, understand and manage data that is transmitted across boundaries of several subsystems. The data interoperability poses a challenging task for blockchain integration, especially for the design logic of blockchain program such as smart contract in Ethereum [46].

**Data Access.** The public nature of blockchain architecture is a huge challenge for dealing with sensitive data especially when it comes to the market and customer domain. Security measures are required to make sure that only authorized access is allowed, and user privacy is not at risk. Some blockchain implementations, such as Hyperledger, support channel scheme [12] which provides an isolated communication method but this still adds to the risks of data leakage during channel participation.

### 3.3 Blockchain Integration Framework

Based on both the two typical attack scenarios and the blockchain integration concerns discussed above, a resilient cyber supply chain should be able to address the following requirements. First of all, to secure the cyber supply chain from the very beginning, the procurement phase should address the process or the coordination of various security risks. During vendor selection, the vendor's experience and tracking records related to security vulnerabilities and subsequent fixes of its products, as well as vendor overall security reputation should be taken into serious consideration. ISO certificates and documented product secure development adds to the vendor trustworthiness. The vendors should be identified for

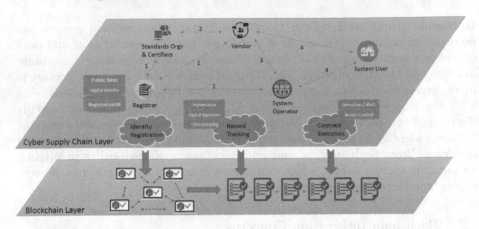

**Fig. 2.** Blockchain-based cyber supply chain system architecture

each critical IT component and software embedded in the products and systems at a fine-grained level. Lower-tier suppliers should be traced back while both open source and commercial programs should be tested thoroughly [22]. The vendor security events could cause severe results to enterprise systems using their products. Therefore, once there are security events reported, the enterprise system should be notified in a timely manner to reduce the security risks and minimize losses. There is a need for a communication channel between security departments of both parties so the enterprise using the vendor services could have timely updates on vendor security reports. Moreover, the vendors are usually granted a remote access temporarily to the enterprise system for deployment and maintenance. So during procurement, the access from vendors in the future should be restricted ahead. Unnecessary permissions should also be removed to avoid future modification and operation. Therefore, further protection against unauthorized access should be in place. Countermeasures include techniques to block malicious emails, as well as attachments such as word documents, sent by potential attackers, and to identify malicious outbound connections. Vendors should be able to identify malicious binary code and build protection into commercial products. Each product should come with a digital signature from manufacturers which is updated on a regular basis. Periodic monitoring and risk assessment should also be in place to counter with potential threats in the future.

Current blockchain based industry solutions for addressing supply chain threats either use the Ethereum platform based on Proof-of-Work consensus, which requires investment of computational resources and can process fewer than 20 transactions per second and transaction validation time takes several minutes [3], or the Hyperledger fabric platform [9] which cannot guarantee privacy in case of a data breach among the validating nodes. To certify that both software components and equipment from vendors at all stages of a cyber supply chain are trusted so that the end-users can easily verify that the purchased electronic components' software or firmware is not tampered with, a blockchain-based cyber supply chain system is proposed, as is shown in Fig. 2. The goals of reliability and accountability are achieved while all concerns mentioned above are addressed. The proposed framework focuses on the following: (1) Identity for each participator in the cyber supply chain is digitally established so as to generate a unique identifier for each vendor and ensure that the others cannot pretend to be the so-called vendor without the private key and other essential information provided. (2) Tamper-proof records are tracked and anchored to the blockchain network so that the records are permanently stored and cannot be modified. (3) Smart contract execution for maliciousness detection and timely alert, as well as vendor access control, are enforced in a decentralized architecture. Considering interactions between different roles of the participants in cyber supply chain, the detailed description of the functions provided by the framework are as follows.

**Identity Establishment.** On entering the cyber supply chain, the very first step for each participant is to create a digital identity with well-protected keys generated by participants themselves. For both participants and cyber assets, a validated identity increases the reliability and trust [25]. In Fig. 2, the registrar is responsible for managing all identity registrations from standards organizations and certifiers, as well as vendors and system operators. Considering different roles in the cyber supply chain, different identity management strategy can be adopted [48]. Verified identities for standards organizations and certifiers ensure the authenticity and trustworthiness of the reports they deliver, regarding to the vendor products as well we vendor qualifications for certain device production. Verified identities for vendors ensure the authenticity of product origins and reduce the possibility of counterfeited products transmitted by phishing emails or websites. Verified identities for system operators allows vendors to communicate confidently that the system operators are exactly from the system, preventing man-in-the-middle attacks [32]. The whole process of identity establishment and maintenance is observed by blockchain nodes which are responsible for anchoring event records as transactions to be validated. For privacy concerns, system users are not necessarily enrolled with the registrar.

**Product Authenticity and Verification.** To verify software integrity, hash algorithms are used to detect changes of code and program execution logic [11]. Digital signature is also an effective methods of detecting tampering [16] using asymmetric encryption algorithms. Watermarks [43] can implicitly render the critical software modules. With blockchain, these methods can be enhanced with improved security and robustness. Blockchain nodes can reach agreements on the verification result and provide timestamping to every corresponding record, regardless of the techniques adopted. By utilizing a decentralized architecture, the code verification process is captured as an event omitted and then permanently anchored to the blockchain network. Moreover, malicious code could be inserted during system integration. There will be interactions between vendors and system operators who will examine the integration process with necessary techniques. For hardware and firmware verification, the process is similar but differs regarding to the specific verification methods. For some cases where the manufacturer source codes are not accessible by system operators, it is essential that the vendor selling the products has the necessary certificate or digital signatures generated by standards organizations or certificate authorities, as well as documented product testing by the manufacturer itself. Similar design principles apply to the cases where there are software updates from manufacturers or vendors to ensure the product authenticity.

**Access Control Management.** For access requests from vendors to systems, the request is examined by first validating both the vendor identity and the access token or credential owned by the vendor, ensuring that the vendor is authenticated and authorized to access system components with appropriate permission to perform product configuration or updates. For vendor maintenance after the product is procured, a temporary remote access is granted. During this period, the operations performed by the vendors should also be captured and recorded on the blockchain. After finishing the maintenance, remote access should be revoked immediately in case of potential threats in the future.

**Contract Negotiation and Execution.** During procurement, there are business contracts to be signed by vendors, which are related to product specifications, prices and customer support issues. Blockchain nodes support smart contract execution, which are pre-defined rules and scripts running against the network. Two major functions can be realized by deploying smart contracts. First, to manage identity registration and authentication, each participant utilizes a blockchain client to communicate with other participants. Second, to implement separation of duty and control access of specific accounts, the related identity is posed under the supervision of a specially-assigned system operator which are represented by a set of blockchain nodes. Each set of nodes are responsible for managing system state changes of the distributed ledger.

**Logging, Monitoring and Auditing.** Detailed product information on parts and materials should be recorded to ensure quality, integrity and backstop warranties [21]. More specifically, the parts, lower level suppliers and production process should be visible along the entire cyber supply chain. Anti-counterfeiting tools adopted should also be recorded. From the logging records, the capability to distinguish between design flaws and deliberate defects is achieved. The following information should also be collected and analyzed, namely control logs, endpoint device logs, firewall logs, anti-virus logs, personnel information and in-scope equipment, aside from traditional network streams and server logs [21]. With all data records available for validation on the blockchain by continuously logging and monitoring, data auditing and decision making can be launched based on the trusted data sets. The data records are stored in a time-based order and are accountable with a trusted data origin. Depending on the application scenarios of how the cyber supply chain is formed, either a synchronized or asynchronized logging is performed. Data auditing is critical for detecting anomaly based on the command records from the control system and the vendors. Based on the auditing results, effective decisions can be made to prevent and mitigate APT attacks or DDoS attacks from the very beginning.

## 4 Case Study: Assured Cyber Supply Chain Provenance for Energy Delivery System

Cyber supply chain provenance tracks products from raw material and program source code to supply chain partners, to manufacturing, to distribution, and to end-consumer use (and beyond, if needed) [5]. To illustrate how we integrate blockchain into cyber supply chain and provide both reliability and accountability, we dive into a case study where we implement a prototype of a blockchain-assured cyber supply chain provenance for energy delivery systems. Besides the identity registration module, there are two other modules, namely the off-chain module and on-chain module. The off-chain module is implemented using Javascript, acting as an interface between the cyber supply chain operators and the blockchain nodes, and is responsible for supply chain formation in the cyber space. System state changes and operations are captured as events by Event Capturer and are verified by Event Verifier. The on-chain module is a set of contracts designed to automatically execute pre-defined logic for system operations and access control.

### 4.1   System Details

**Identity Registration.** System components need to register first before entering the supply chain. Identity information is provided to the registrar in JSON format. An example identity for a software vendor is represented as follows.

```
{
"Identifier":"17692",
"Type":"manufacturer",
"Timestamp":"1475679929",
"PublicKey":"",
"Certificate":"",
"Product":"software001",
"AffiliatedCom":"",
"IPAddress":"",
"Remarks":""
}
```

**Event Capturer.** This is an off-chain module to capture events for logging and is responsible for communicating with the smart contract for updating states that are maintained by blockchain nodes. The event of a software procurement is captured in the following JSON format.

```
{
"EventID":"1279652",
"Type":"Procurement",
"Timestamp":"1475679940",
"Subject":"17692",
```

"Object":"software001",
"Operation":"",
"Data":"",
"Remarks":""
}

After the event is captured, a list of events will be handled to be anchored to the blockchain network [2]. For publishing data records to blockchain network, the Chainpoint standard [1] is adopted. Chainpoint is an open standard for creating a timestamp proof of any data, file, or series of events, which proposes a scalable protocol for publishing data records on the blockchain and generating blockchain receipts. By anchoring an unlimited amount of data to multiple blockchains and verifying the integrity and existence of data without relying on a trusted third-party, Chainpoint standard is widely used in blockchain applications. According to Chainpoint 2.0, data records are hashed so that each Merkle tree can host a large number of records. The target hash of the specific record and the path to the Merkle root constitute the Merkle proof of the provenance data, which is a JSON-LD document that contains the information to cryptographically verify that a piece of data is anchored to a blockchain. It proves the data existed at the time it was anchored. The Merkle root for each Merkle tree is related to one transaction in the blockchain network. The event handling process is shown in the Algorithm 1.

---

**Algorithm 1.** Cyber Supply Chain Event Handling

---
1: **procedure** EVENTHANDLING( )
2:      $S \leftarrow$ a set of *events*
3:      *len* $\leftarrow$ *number of events in S*
4:      $i \leftarrow 0$
5:      $mRoot \leftarrow hash(S(i))$
6:      **while** $i < len$ **do**
7:          **if** $i \% 2 == 0$ **then**
8:              $mRoot \leftarrow hash(hash(S(i)) + mRoot)$
9:          **else**
10:              $mRoot \leftarrow hash(mRoot + hash(S(i)))$
11:          **end if**
12:          $i \leftarrow i + 1$
13:      **end while**
14:      **if** $anchor(mRoot)$ **then return** true
              **return** false
15:      **end if**
16: **end procedure**

---

**Event Verifier.** This is an off-chain module to verify events logged on blockchains, responsible for communicating with the smart contract for retrieving states, which is conducted on request by system operators, end-users or auditors. The event verification result can be represented as follows.

```
{
"EventID":"7294652",
"Result":"True",
"Timestamp":"1475679980",
"BlockNum":"7692",
"Confirmations":"6139",
"Entity":"17692",
"Data":"",
"Result":"True",
"Remarks":""
}
```

The event records constitute the product provenance along the supply chain, which can be validated by reconstructing the Merkle tree from the provenance data. Each provenance record is stored along with other records in the blockchain network as a transaction, which is accessible by querying the ledger state. Since the transaction attribute height represents the block index, the exact block information can be identified as well. Both information are used to verify the record for authenticity.

**Rule Checker.** This is an on-chain module to actually execute smart contract and is responsible for communicating with each smart contract participant for automatic verification and validation of actions and remote access. Our previous work proposed to use the channel scheme to isolate communications between various parties [28]. Based on top of the above work, this paper adopts the channel scheme by isolating different cyber supply chains for each system, maximizing the efficiency of transaction confirmation and validation. In our system, there are three types of rules, resulting in three channel types. One is the procurement evaluation for competing vendors, where there are prerequisites to be a qualified software vendor, making the procurement process transparent and standardized. The second type is the access control management, where each access is granted based on an authenticated token issued during the procurement or system operation process. The third one is the cyber supply chain management where product provenance validation is requested by system users or auditors under some circumstances. Our system is based on a set of scripts that defines various rules. The following script presents the access control policy for vendor remote access. The other two types of rules can be defined similarly.

```
rule VendorAccessToSystemComponents {
    description: "Allow authorized vendor full access"
    participant(p): "org.acme.sample.SampleVendor"
    operation: ALL
    resource(r): "org.acme.sample.SampleComponent"
    condition: (r.vendor.getToken() === p.getToken())
    action: ALLOW
}
```

The identity registration process ensures that each entity is communicating with the authenticated parties. Event capturer addresses data scalability by tree-based method and data interoperability by following a JSON format. Event verifier ensures data integrity while rule checker controls data access to authorized entities. To sum up, the proposed framework meets the security requirements and removes the concerns mentioned in Sect. 3.3.

## 4.2   Security Analysis and Performance

Four types of threats [44] are pointed out for supply chain of industrial devices, namely sabotage, tampering, counterfeiting and theft. Sabotage refers to built-in malicious logic, backdoors and intentional vulnerabilities, which can be mitigated via code checking during the software development or circuit testing during hardware manufacturing. Tampering happens to firmware, software, operating system, internal logic and sensitive data, while counterfeiting exists in hardware, especially chips and circuits. Theft refers to the loss of intellectual property, by the compromise of confidentiality and integrity. These four threats are consistent with the proposed two attack scenarios we summarized. Manufacturer source code attack could lead to sabotage, tampering, counterfeiting and theft while vendor remote access attack could lead to tampering and theft. The proposed framework emphasizes the important role of identity registrar, certificate and standards organizations before the procurement for early detection of sabotage, tampering and counterfeiting. By access control management, the unauthorized remote access can be prevented and the theft is mitigated in this sense. The proposed blockchain-based cyber supply chain framework in energy delivery system not only addresses the four threats above, but also other concerns raised during blockchain integration. First, data sets are handled in a tree-based structure, minimizing the time cost for data processing occured during cyber supply chain formation. Second, by adopting JSON format during data collection and communication, the interoperability of data sets from various subsystems are achieved with flexibility. Third, the access control scheme not only addresses system entity permissions, but also applies to the blockchain network where different roles are assigned to blockchain nodes.

For performance evaluation, we present the system performance in terms of the response time needed for the process of different numbers of events with increasing payloads, which is practical in the case of energy delivery systems where dynamic number of nodes are interacting with the system components, as shown in Fig. 3. Payload length represents the data size collected by the Event Capture and can be adjusted according to different subsystem requirements.

In Fig. 3, the X-axis represents the number of events recorded on the blockchain from 1, 20, 40, 60, 80, 100 to 200, whereas the Y-axis represents the average response time. There are six lines in different colors representing increasing payload sizes from 8 Bytes to 256 Bytes. It can be observed that the system is capable of handling concurrent events without sacrificing significant time cost under 100 events. In the peer-to-peer environment, the communication cost for message broadcast increases dramatically when there are large number of nodes and messages. This figure also shows that for large number of nodes and increasing data size, the response efficiency drops above 100. For a specific number of events, varying payload size brings trivial cost to the average response time, making the system stable and scalable. Compared to the evaluation results in [23], the proposed system architecture has better performances with events number under 100. This makes our system a practical solution where in cyber supply chains for energy delivery systems, there are not as many events as in the

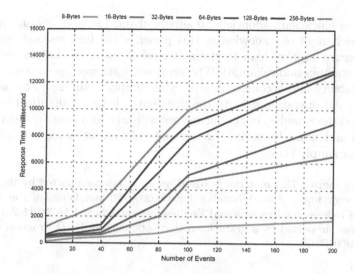

**Fig. 3.** Experiment results for blockchain-assured cyber supply chain in EDS

cloud computing environment and most system components are fixed regarding to the vendor selection during system establishment and system operations during system running. For other cyber supply chain systems such as in medical and financial sectors, the proposed system should be adjusted and improved accordingly.

## 5   Related Work and Conclusion

Our previous work developed cryptographic methods to ensure privacy for blockchain applications even when some participants are compromised [26]. [31] points out the blockchain usage in the future Procurement 4.0, as a potential solution to substantiate Industry 4.0. Information sharing is [42] emphasized that to improve flexibility of supply chain and enable monitoring of risks as well as to establish preventive actions [36,40]. Design principles for application of Bitcoin data structure in supply chain management is explored in [14]. The application of semantic blockchains in supply chain is proposed to solve the issue of supply chain data integration with flexibility [8]. The POMS (Product Ownership Management System) for supply chain is proposed using blockchain to generate proof of possessions for products and prevent counterfeits [41]. To improve the interoperability of data to be recorded on a blockchain, ontology-driven blockchain is designed for supply chain provenance, providing a real-time tracking system [24]. Blockchain adoption in the shipment information tracking along the supply chain is implemented in [47], providing a validated physical distribution visibility. To sum up, blockchain applications in supply chain provide traceability, visibility and transparency, while removing single point of trust and thus single point of failure [15].

There are blockchain adoptions in supply chains for food [39] and medicine [29]. To the best of our knowledge, this paper is the first research work proposed to secure supply chain in the cyber space using blockchain technology with accountability and reliability. The proposed framework is capable of assuring the reliability and accountability of cyber supply chain assets by anchoring transaction and operation data to the distributed ledger maintained by decentralized blockchain nodes. In the future, we will take into consideration of both adversarial and non-adversarial threats and vulnerabilities for a resilient and robust cyber supply chain.

**Acknowledgment.** This material is based on upon work supported by the Department of Energy under Award Number DE-OE0000780 and Office of the Assistant Secretary of Defense for Research and Engineering agreement FA8750-15-2-0120. The work was also supported by a grant from the National Key R&D Program of China (2016YFB0800500).

**Disclaimer**

# References

1. Chainpoint: A scalable protocol for anchoring data in the blockchain and generating blockchain receipts. http://www.chainpoint.org/
2. Tierion API. https://tierion.com/app/api
3. Ethereum reaches 50 (2017). http://www.trustnodes.com/2017/05/17/ethereum-reaches-50-bitcoins-transaction-volumes
4. Abeyratne, S.A., Monfared, R.P.: Blockchain ready manufacturing supply chain using distributed ledger (2016)
5. Awaysheh, A., Klassen, R.D.: The impact of supply chain structure on the use of supplier socially responsible practices. Int. J. Oper. Prod. Manag. **30**(12), 1246–1268 (2010)
6. Basnight, Z., Butts, J., Lopez, J., Dube, T.: Firmware modification attacks on programmable logic controllers. Int. J. Crit. Infrastruct. Prot. **6**(2), 76–84 (2013)
7. Boyson, S., Corsi, T.: Building a cyber supply chain assurance reference model (2009)
8. Brewster, C.: Semantic blockchains in the supply chain
9. Cachin, C.: Architecture of the hyperledger blockchain fabric. In: Workshop on Distributed Cryptocurrencies and Consensus Ledgers (2016)

10. Cert-UK: Cyber-security risks in the supply chain (2015). https://www.ncsc. gov.uk/content/files/protected_files/guidance_files/Cyber-security-risks-in-the-supply-chain.pdf

11. Chen, Y., Venkatesan, R., Cary, M., Pang, R., Sinha, S., Jakubowski, M.H.: Oblivious hashing: a stealthy software integrity verification primitive. In: Petitcolas, F.A.P. (ed.) IH 2002. LNCS, vol. 2578, pp. 400–414. Springer, Heidelberg (2003). https://doi.org/10.1007/3-540-36415-3_26

12. Dhillon, V., Metcalf, D., Hooper, M.: The hyperledger project. Blockchain Enabled Applications, pp. 139–149. Apress, Berkeley, CA (2017). https://doi.org/10.1007/978-1-4842-3081-7_10

13. Douligeris, C., Mitrokotsa, A.: Ddos attacks and defense mechanisms: classification and state-of-the-art. Comput. Netw. **44**(5), 643–666 (2004)

14. English, S.M., Nezhadian, E.: Application of bitcoin data-structures & design principles to supply chain management. arXiv preprint arXiv:1703.04206 (2017)

15. Gallay, O., Korpela, K., Tapio, N., Nurminen, J.K.: A peer-to-peer platform for decentralized logistics. Epublication (2017)

16. Graunke, G., Rozas, C.: Method and apparatus for integrity verification, authentication, and secure linkage of software modules. US Patent 6,105,137, 15 August 2000. https://www.google.com/patents/US6105137

17. Group ESCSW, et al.: Roadmap to achieve energy delivery systems cybersecurity. Energetics Inc. (2011). https://energy.gov/oe/downloads/roadmap-achieve-energy-delivery-systems-cybersecurity-2011

18. Hardjono, T., Pentland, A.S.: Verifiable anonymous identities and access control in permissioned blockchains

19. Ilgun, K., Kemmerer, R.A., Porras, P.A.: State transition analysis: a rule-based intrusion detection approach. IEEE Trans. Softw. Eng. **21**(3), 181–199 (1995)

20. Threat Intelligence: Dragonfly: cyber attacks on the energy sector (2017). https://www.symantec.com/blogs/threat-intelligence/dragonfly-energy-sector-cyber-attacks

21. Jon, B.: Integrating cybersecurity into supply chain risk management (2016). https://www.rsaconference.com/writable/presentations/file_upload/integrating_cybersecurity_into_supply_chain_risk_management.pdf

22. Jon, O.: Vmware and the need for cyber supply chain security assurance (2015). https://www.vmware.com/content/dam/digitalmarketing/vmware/en/pdf/vmware-esg-cyber-supply-chain-security-assurance-white-paper.pdf

23. Kaku, E.: Using blockchain to support provenance in the internet of things. Ph.D. thesis (2017)

24. Kim, H.M., Laskowski, M.: Towards an ontology-driven blockchain design for supply chain provenance (2016)

25. Kshetri, N.: 1 blockchain's roles in meeting key supply chain management objectives. Int. J. Inf. Manag. **39**, 80–89 (2018)

26. Liang, X., Shetty, S., Tosh, D., Kamhoua, C., Kwiat, K., Njilla, L.: ProvChain: a blockchain-based data provenance architecture in cloud environment with enhanced privacy and availability. In: Proceedings of the 17th IEEE/ACM International Symposium on Cluster, Cloud and Grid Computing, pp. 468–477. IEEE Press (2017)

27. Liang, X., Zhao, J., Shetty, S., Li, D.: Towards data assurance and resilience in IoT using blockchain

28. Liang, X., Zhao, J., Shetty, S., Liu, J., Li, D.: Integrating blockchain for data sharing and collaboration in mobile healthcare applications

29. Mackey, T.K., Nayyar, G.: A review of existing and emerging digital technologies to combat the global trade in fake medicines. Expert Opin. Drug Saf. **16**(5), 587–602 (2017)
30. Nakamoto, S.: Bitcoin: a peer-to-peer electronic cash system (2008)
31. Nicoletti, B.: The future: procurement 4.0. Agile Procurement, pp. 189–230. Springer, Cham (2018). https://doi.org/10.1007/978-3-319-61085-6_8
32. Ornaghi, A., Valleri, M.: Man in the middle attacks. In: Blackhat Conference Europe (2003)
33. Sean, B., Earl, C., Erick, G., Christopher, M., Marshall, J.: Attack on critical infrastructure leverages template injection (2017). http://blog.talosintelligence.com/2017/07/template-injection.html
34. Seller, C., Murphy, J.: Cyber supply chain risk management (2017)
35. Shackleford, D.: Combatting cyber risks in the supply chain. SANS.org (2015)
36. Skipper, J.B., Hanna, J.B.: Minimizing supply chain disruption risk through enhanced flexibility. Int. J. Phys. Distrib. Logistics Manage. **39**(5), 404–427 (2009)
37. National Institute of Standards and Technology: Cyber supply chain risk management (2017). https://csrc.nist.gov/projects/supply-chain-risk-management/
38. Tankard, C.: Advanced persistent threats and how to monitor and deter them. Netw. Secur. **2011**(8), 16–19 (2011)
39. Tian, F.: A supply chain traceability system for food safety based on HACCP, blockchain & Internet of Things. In: 2017 International Conference on Service Systems and Service Management (ICSSSM), pp. 1–6. IEEE (2017)
40. Tomlin, B.: On the value of mitigation and contingency strategies for managing supply chain disruption risks. Manage. Sci. **52**(5), 639–657 (2006)
41. Toyoda, K., Mathiopoulos, P.T., Sasase, I., Ohtsuki, T.: A novel blockchain-based product ownership management system (POMS) for anti-counterfeits in the post supply chain. IEEE Access (2017)
42. Urciuoli, L.: Cyber-resilience: a strategic approach for supply chain management. Technol. Innov. Manage. Rev. **5**(4), 13 (2015)
43. Voyatzis, G., Pitas, I.: The use of watermarks in the protection of digital multimedia products. Proc. IEEE **87**(7), 1197–1207 (1999)
44. Waalewijn, D.: Cyber security in the supply chain of industrial embedded devices (2014)
45. William, J.: RSA confirms its tokens used in Lockheed hack (2011)
46. Wood, G.: Ethereum: a secure decentralised generalised transaction ledger. Ethereum Proj. Yellow Pap. **151** (2014)
47. Wu, H., Li, Z., King, B., Ben Miled, Z., Wassick, J., Tazelaar, J.: A distributed ledger for supply chain physical distribution visibility. Information **8**(4), 137 (2017)
48. Xu, L., Chen, L., Gao, Z., Lu, Y., Shi, W.: CoC: secure supply chain management system based on public ledger. In: 2017 26th International Conference on Computer Communication and Networks (ICCCN), pp. 1–6. IEEE (2017)

# Social Bot Detection Using Tweets Similarity

Yahan Wang[1], Chunhua Wu[1(✉)], Kangfeng Zheng[1], and Xiujuan Wang[2]

[1] Beijing University of Posts and Telecommunications, Beijing, China
wuchunhua@bupt.edu.cn
[2] Beijing University of Technology, Beijing, China

**Abstract.** Social bots are intelligent programs that have the ability to receive instructions and mimic real users' behaviors on social networks, which threaten social network users' information security. Current researches focus on modeling classifiers from features of user profile and behaviors that could not effectively detect burgeoning social bots. This paper proposed to detect social bots on Twitter based on tweets similarity which including content similarity, tweet length similarity, punctuation usage similarity and stop words similarity. In addition, the LSA (Latent semantic analysis) model is adopted to calculate similarity degree of content. The results show that tweets similarity has significant effect on social bot detection and the proposed method can reach 98.09% precision rate on new data set, which outperforms Madhuri Dewangan's method.

**Keywords:** Social bot · LSA · Tweets similarity · Machine learning

## 1 Introduction

In recent years, with the rapid development of the Internet, social network has become an indispensable part for most people. Social network is convenient and interesting and it enables people to connect with friends and families to share life moments anywhere at any time. People also like to browse news and express their own opinions on the social network.

There is no doubt that the emergence of social network provides a lot of convenience for our life. However, with the rapid development of artificial intelligence, many bots appear on social network. Accounts controlled by programs are called Social bots which are employed to receive instructions and mimic real users' behaviors on social networks such as Twitter and Facebook. It is reported that [6] "Facebook thinks 83 million of its users are fake" and that "Up to 29.9%of Barack Obama's 17.82 million [Twitter] followers and 21.9% of Mitt Romney's 814000 followers may be fake". What's more, one study has estimated that over half of the accounts on Twitter are not human [17].

Project supported by National Key R&D Program of China (2017YFB0802703), National Natural Science Foundation of China (61602052).

© ICST Institute for Computer Sciences, Social Informatics and Telecommunications Engineering 2018
R. Beyah et al. (Eds.): SecureComm 2018, LNICST 255, pp. 63–78, 2018.
https://doi.org/10.1007/978-3-030-01704-0_4

These social bots can be used to swing voters in political activities, launch political attacks, and manipulate public opinions. And some social bots are used for marketing, such as advertising, leading fashion trends and so on. These behaviors have certain negative impact on the authenticity of social network contents. And more importantly, social bots bring a variety of security risks [11]. One of risks is that social bots can establish contacts with network users to obtain users' personal information, such as birthday, e-mail, phone number, address, etc. After obtaining the information, social bots controllers can use the user's personal information to build the trust relationship with the target of social engineering attack, which has become an emerging threat for social networks.

Therefore, the social bot detection is a very meaningful work that can help to purify social network environment, protect users' personal information security, and help users against social engineering attacks, thereby maintaining a healthy and safe environment for legitimate users on social network.

Currently, there have had many studies on social bot detection, but most studies are concerned with behaviors of accounts, while the studies about content are limited. A new method of social bot detection should be put forward.

The main contributions of this paper are as follows:

- It analyzes tweets from accounts and proposes a detection method using tweets similarity.
- It defines tweets similarity in a more detailed way. Tweets similarity is divided into four parts: content similarity, tweet length similarity, punctuation usage similarity and stop words similarity.
- It compares three computing methods of content similarity and analyzes difference among these methods. After thorough analysis, this paper applies the Latent Semantic Analysis (LSA) model to measure the similarity of content.
- It evaluates the proposed features and proves that the features proposed in this paper have contribution to a better classification result.

This paper is organized as follows: Sect. 2 reviews prior studies, introducing relevant research methods and achievements. Section 3 analyses behaviors of social bots and proposes common features in detection. Specially, it redefines tweets similarity and uses a new algorithm to compute. In Sect. 4, this paper first describes new data set and experimental design. Then, it presents the empirical results. Section 5 summarizes and concludes the research and points out the future work direction.

## 2   Related Works

Many of the prior studies focus on spammer users on social network. Although spammers and social bots may share common features, there are still differences in detection methods. There are two main existing methods for social bot detection: one is based on the honeypot, the other is based on machine learning.

The number of researches on social bot detection based on honeypot is less. The most famous one is Kyumin Lee's a seven-month experiment [12]. Kyumin

Lee put 60 honeypots on Twitter, which were Twitter accounts and posted meaningless contents. So, normal users would not follow these accounts, only social bots followed these honeypots in order to get more influence. Finally Kyumin Lee tracked down 36,000 candidate content polluters.

Social bot detection based on machine learning algorithms is more common. The extracted features are mainly divided into the following two categories: one is user metadata and the other is text-based features. Onur Varol and Emilio Ferrara [21]extracted 1150 features of Twitter accounts for training, and established a scoring system [4], the higher score means that the account has greater possibility of being a social bot. John P. Dickerson [6] used a number of sentiment-related factors as the key to the bots identification, including tweet sentiment flip-flops, tweet sentiment variance and monthly tweet sentiment variance. Nikan Chavoshi [2]developed a method to identify abnormal user accounts on Twitter, which were very unlikely to be manually operated. His detection approach considered cross-correlating user activities and required no labeled data. Zi Chu [3] proposed a classification system that included four parts: an entropy-based component, a machine-learning-based component, an account properties component, and a decision maker. What's more, DARPA held a 4-week competition in February/March 2015, when multiple teams supported by the DARPA Social Media in Strategic Communications program competed to identify a set of previously identified influence bots, which served as ground truth on a specific topic within Twitter. Aram Galstyan's paper [19] introduced the DARPA Challenge and the methods used by the top three teams. The major features of detection include user profile features, tweet syntax features, network features and so on.

Current researches on social bot detection focus on user profile, behaviors of account and network features. However, according to the research [10], social bots have become more and more intelligent in recent years. They can search real users' information on the network to set up fake profiles and social relations. In addition, they can even imitate human schedules and generate the same tweets peak time. This trend makes it difficult for traditional methods to detect social bots, hence it is necessary to find a new way to detect social bots. Different from previous researches, the paper focuses on devising novel features based on tweets similarity.

# 3 Proposed Approach

## 3.1 Analysis of Social Bot Behavior

As the account controlled by program, social bot is designed to resemble human as close as possible. However, confined by the available technology, there are still some differences in behaviors between social bots and human being. Therefore, we can find out some behavior patterns through analysis.

In order to find out the difference between social bots and normal users, this paper analyzes some real accounts and selects some social bots from the list [18], which offered well-known intelligent social bots. Accordingly, some normal users' accounts are captured in top world trends to be compared with social bots. We manually inspected their timelines to find the difference.

Social bots can be roughly divided into two types based on observation. One group of social bots is relatively simple. They are widely involved in top world trends to draw as much attention as possible. However, they are blindly involved in hot topics. Their contents are not very relevant to topics.

While the other kind of social bots focuses on publishing relevant contents in particular fields. When they gain some attention in one area, they can use their influence to affect the opinions of their followers and even carry out social engineering attacks. According to the research [17], an effective social engineering strategy is first posting a lot of picture tweets (to gain attention and a large follower base), and then posting more new tweets which use phishing site address to phish users. Due to the authenticity of their previous sharing, followers will click without suspicion. Therefore social engineering attacks occur.

Beyond that, the differences between the social bot and spammer are also worth our attention. The method of detecting spammer is not entirely suitable for detecting social bot. Social bots work in a more intelligent way than spam accounts do. They can capture hot topics initiatively. Compared with the general spammers, social bots have more specific themes.

Normal users pay more attention to using social media to communicate or share life with families and friends. Therefore, there are more interactions among normal users, which is reflected in the following aspects: more "Likes", using "@" to reply, a reasonable ratio of followers/ followed. What's more, human life is very rich and people are normally interested in many things. Therefore, the normal accounts publish more diverse tweets than social bots do.

## 3.2   Existing Features Description

At present, the features used for social bot detection center on user profile and behaviors of account. Commonly used features are as follows:

**Average number of hashtags:** On Twitter, people use "#" as a hashtag. People can browse tweets about interesting topic by clicking the hashtag. In general, social bots use more hashtags than normal users do in order to get more influence.

**Average number of mentions:** When people want to remind other people to notice the tweet or reply someone, they can use "@".

**Average number of links:** Some social bots post more links to circulate some information. If other users click these links, they may be linked to advertising website or phishing and malware websites.

**Retweet counts:** Ratio of user forwarding other users' tweets to total tweets. On social network, users often forward tweets that are interesting or meaningful. For some social bots, forwarding others' tweet can't achieve their purpose, so majority of the tweets that they post are original tweets. However, some social bots can search related tweets by control programs, in this case, the retweet counts may be high than normal users.

**Number of favorites:** This is the number of "likes" for other users' tweets. On Twitter, if you want to express your like or agreement to a tweet, you can click likes. In general, this happens when users browse timelines. Social bots don't act like this, so they have fewer favorites than human users do.

**Ratio of followers to number followed:** Social bots usually follow a large number of users in order to expand their influence. But because they don't have friends in reality, so they don't have many followers.

**Tweet source:** Social network normal users can post tweets by kinds of official platforms, such as "http://twitter.com/download/android(iphone)", and so on. On the other hand, social bots controlled by program often post tweets by unofficial platform, for example, a personal home page "https://github.com/xxx".

**The average difference between two consecutive tweets:** Due to the limitations of social bot program scripts, tweets publication time may have a certain pattern, while posting time for normal users is more flexible.

The social bot detection using these features can have a good performance. However, with the development of artificial intelligence technology, emerging social bots can effectively avoid these features. Therefore, we need to find new features for detection. At present, only a few papers use tweets similarity as a feature. And the similarity calculation method is limited to word frequency based methods. According to our observation and analysis of social bots' behaviors, this paper redefines tweets similarity, expands the concept of tweets similarity. What's more, the new method of similarity calculation is used to optimize the performance.

### 3.3 Tweets Similarity Features

According to the behavior analysis of social bots in Sects. 3.1 and 3.2, we find that most social bots' tweets have some similarities due to creators' purposes and current technology limitations. In general, social bots' tweets have a comparatively fixed theme in order to achieve their purposes, for example, swinging voters or promoting products. And because of that, these tweets often use similar synonyms or sentences. In contrast, normal users usually have richer expressions than social bots, because they are not controlled by program. Therefore, we take tweets similarity into consideration.

Tweets similarity can be divided into the following sections:

**The similarity of content:** The similarity of content mainly refers to the semantic similarity of the original tweets. In this paper, we select the LSA model (it will be introduced later) as the calculation algorithm of similarity.

**The similarity of tweet length:** In the analysis of social bot behavior, it can be found that the length of tweet post (the number of words) is more fixed than the normal account. Therefore, we choose the variance of the number of words in the original tweets to measure the similarity of tweet length.

**The similarity of punctuation usage:** Everyone has its own punctuation usage custom, so the similarity of punctuation usage is also chosen as a feature.

We measure the similarity of punctuation usage by calculating the variance of the frequency of punctuation usage in each tweet post from an account.

**The similarity of stop words:** stop words usually refers to the most common words in a language. These are some of the most common, short function words, such as "the", "is", "at", "which", and "on". Stop words generally do not have a specific meaning, but can still reflect a user's writing style. We count the frequency of common stop words in each tweet and then calculate the frequency variance to measure the similarity of stop words.

These features reflect the tweet similarity from various angles. It can help us to distinguish the difference between social bot and normal user.

### 3.4   Selection of Content Similarity Calculation Algorithm

For the similarity calculation of tweet length, punctuation and stop words, we choose the variance to measure according to the actual situation of the problem. After calculation, each account has a variance value as the final feature vector. Lower variance value means more similarity.

For the content similarity calculation, there are two mainstream ideas at present. The starting points of different methods are different. One is based on statistic the frequency of the word which only takes the occurrence of the same words in different texts into consideration. This method is easy to understand but ignores the latent semantic in different words. The other method is based on semantic analysis which can consider the semantic relations among different words.

Three algorithms are introduced for the selection of content similarity calculation:

*A. Unigram Matching-based Similarity Algorithm:*
Unigram matching-based similarity algorithm is a simple and easy to understand statistical algorithm. It is calculated using Eqs. (1) and (2)[15]:

$$Sim(S_i, S_j) = \frac{2 \times |S_i \bigcap S_j|}{|S_i| + |S_j|} \tag{1}$$

$$Sim_k = \frac{\sum_{i=1}^{m} \sum_{j=i+1}^{m} Sim(S_i, S_j)}{\frac{1}{2}m(m-1)} \tag{2}$$

$Sim(S_i, S_j)$ is used to calculate the similarity between different tweets from the same account. $|S_i|$ is defined as the number of words in tweet-i. $|S_i \bigcap S_j|$ means the number of same words between two tweets. Therefore, $Sim_k$ equals to the average value of pairwise tweet similarity within user-k. The number of tweet for each user-k is represented by m.

*B. SimHash Algorithm:*
SimHash is a technique for quickly estimating how similar two sets are. It is created by Moses Charikar [1]. This algorithm is used by the Google Crawler to find near duplicate pages. A hash function usually hashes different values to

totally different hash values. First, we need to initialize a f-dimensional vector V to zero and break the tweet up into features. Each feature is hashed using normal 32-bit hash algorithm. For each hash, if $bit_i$ of hash is set then add 1 to V[i], if $bit_i$ of hash is not set then take 1 from V[i]. SimHash $bit_i$ is 1 if $V[i] > 0$ and 0 otherwise. Finally, the SimHash of two tweets can be calculated by Hamming distance to measure the similarity.

## C. Latent semantic analysis (LSA):

LSA is a technique in natural language processing, in particular distributional semantics, of analyzing relationships between a set of documents and the terms they contain by producing a set of concepts related to the documents and terms. In the context of information retrieval, it is sometimes called Latent Semantic Indexing (LSI). LSA assumes that words that are close in meaning will occur in similar pieces of text (the distributional hypothesis). A matrix containing word counts per paragraph (rows represent unique words and columns represent each paragraph) is constructed from a large piece of text and a mathematical technique called singular value decomposition (SVD) is used to reduce the number of rows while preserving the similarity structure among columns [8].

In linear algebra, the singular-value decomposition (SVD) is a factorization of a real or complex matrix. For a matrix A of m by n, it can be decomposed into the following three matrices:

$$A_{m \times n} = U_{m \times m} \sum_{m \times n} V_{n \times n}^T \tag{3}$$

Sometimes to reduce the dimension of the matrix to k, the decomposition of SVD can be approximated as

$$A_{m \times n} \approx U_{m \times k} \sum_{k \times k} V_{k \times n}^T \tag{4}$$

In the context of its application to tweets content similarity, it can be explained: Input m tweets, the tweet has n words. $A_{ij}$ is the eigenvalue of the j-th word of the i-th tweet. And k is the number of subjects we assume, generally less than the number of tweets. $U_{il}$ is the relevance of the i-th tweet and the l-th topic. $V_{jm}$ is the relevance of the j-th word and the m-th semantic. $\sum_{lm}$ is the relevance of the l-th topic and m-th semantic.

The text subject matrix obtained by LSA can be used for text similarity calculation. The calculation method generally uses the cosine similarity. Words are compared by taking the cosine of the angle between the two vectors (or the dot product between the normalizations of the two vectors) formed by any two rows. Values close to 1 represent very similar words while values close to 0 represent very dissimilar words [7].

LSA has many applications in natural language processing. It can be used to find similar documents and relations between terms (synonymy and polysemy). It also can translate a given query of terms into the low-dimensional space, and find matching documents (information retrieval). What's more, LSA can expand the feature space of machine learning or text mining systems [9].

### 3.5 Framework of Proposed Method

Figure 1 illustrates the proposed social bot detection system architecture. The Twitter data are collected from the internet by using Twitter API, which is called Tweepy. The raw data include users' profiles and users' tweets. The Twitter user meta-data are extracted from user profile. In tweets procession, tweets are employed to find out the content features. After acquiring feature vectors, we use labeled data to train well-known classifiers. The optimal classifier model is chosen to answer the question: Is social bot? Unlabeled data need to be extracted from feature vectors and input to classifier model. Then we can get the final predicted result.

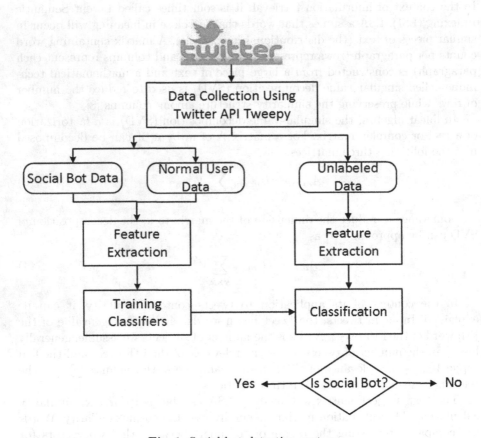

**Fig. 1.** Social bot detection system

The experimentation and results are showed in Sect. 4.

## 4    Experiments and Results

This paper conducts three experiments. Firstly, to decide what kind of algorithm is most effective in calculating content similarity, this paper uses three similarity algorithms. In this experiment, we also want to validate the hypothesis that which social bots have higher content similarity. In the second experiment, Pearson correlation coefficient is chosen as the evaluation index of features. We intend to prove that tweets similarity has great significance for social bot detection by using correlation coefficient of each feature. Finally, we train classifiers using feature vectors to detect social bots. For comparison, we selected the feature set which is proposed in Madhuri Dewangan's paper [5]. We use the same classifiers and parameters to prove that our feature set is valid.

### 4.1  Collecting Corpus

In recent researches on social bots detection, there is no benchmark corpus on social network. The data set obtained by the honeypot system [12] has a certain authority, but the existing social bots become more intelligent. The old data set can't reflect the current trend of the social bots. Many researchers used Twitter data crawled by themselves [5] and manually marked labels to build the data set.

According to the statistics [20], the number of monthly Twitter active users exceeds 230 million and over 100 million daily active users generate about 500 million tweets daily. Accordingly, there are also a large number of active social bots on the Twitter platform. Therefore, Twitter is a typical representative of social network platforms.

The social bots data set in our study comes from Botwiki [13]. Botwiki is an open online website that provides information of various types of bots, including the rapidly growing social bots. From Botwiki we get information about Twitter bot and the list of social bots accounts on Twitter that are maintained by the relevant person. We use the web crawler technology to get these social bots account ID. Unlike other data sets in social bots detection studies, the authenticity of our social bots accounts obtained from Botwiki can be guaranteed, and these accounts can also avoid the possibility of misinterpretation of Twitter accounts by manually labeled. The normal user ID data set is from a study [21] in 2017 by monitoring a Twitter stream.

Our study uses Twitter official API interface Tweepy [16] to crawl user data, including user's published tweets and user meta-data. The raw data set is preprocessed through following steps: (1) only the accounts which post tweets in English are retained due to the generality of English at present. (2) In order to calculate the tweets similarity, we filter out the accounts which the number of original tweets less than 10.

As shown in Table 1, we have 2010 accounts' data in total, including 1119 social bots' data and 891 normal users' data.

### 4.2  Similarity Algorithms Comparison

In this part, three similarity algorithms (Unigram matching-based similarity algorithm, SimHash algorithm and LSA algorithm) are selected in Sect. 3.4 to compare which algorithm is more suitable for calculating the content similarity.

**Table 1.** Data set composition

| Data | Number of accounts |
|------|--------------------|
| Normal user | 891 |
| Social bot | 1119 |
| Total | 2010 |

In order to ensure the validity of the comparison, we do the same pretreatment on the crawled tweets before calculating the text similarity, including cleaning URL, mentioned accounts and hash-tags, and forwarding tweets.

Firstly, we use python NLTK (Natural Language Toolkit) to process the tweets data which we crawl by the API called Tweepy. Because forwarded tweets cannot reflect the tweet style of a user, we remove these retweeted tweets and leave only the original tweets. In those tweets, we leave texts after word segmentation, deleting stop word and other processes.

We use the same processed data in these three different tweet similarity algorithms. The calculated similarity of each account's tweets is used to train classifiers as the only feature. Three machine learning algorithms are chosen as classifiers to verify performance. The performance statistics reported here is based on 10-fold cross validation over the data set.

As shown in Fig. 2, LSA model-based similarity algorithm has better performance than other algorithms in the three classical classifiers we selected. Therefore, we use LSA model to analysis tweets similarity.

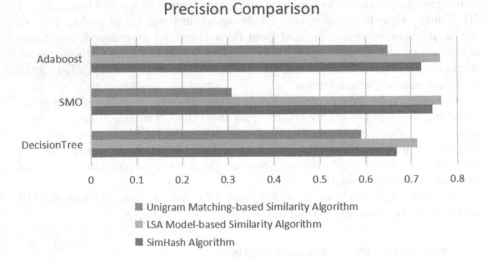

**Fig. 2.** Content similarity algorithms comparison

First, we train the LSA model, then we randomly selected 10 tweets in each user original tweets as the index contents, and the other tweets for similarity comparison. We select the average as the feature of tweets similarity.

After we calculate the tweets similarity, we randomly select 500 social bots' and 500 normal users' tweets similarity to verify the hypothesis. The test result suggests that our assumption is rational.

The tweets similarity of social bots and normal users is clearly presented in Fig. 3. The result shows that the content similarity of most social bots is higher than normal users'. However, there are also a few normal users have high similarity. Tracing the reason, we find some normal users are accustomed to using other APP to share photos or videos, so this type of tweets will have a fixed beginning sentence, to a certain extent, increases the content similarity.

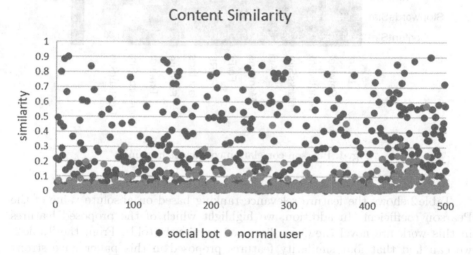

**Fig. 3.** Content similarity test performance using LSA model

## 4.3   Feature Ranking

In order to prove the tweets similarity features proposed in this paper are helpful for social bot detection we use the Pearson correlation coefficient for correlation analysis of features and labels.

Pearson coefficient measures the linear correlation between two variables X and Y, which is the covariance of the two variables divided by the product of their standard deviations.

In calculation, the normal user's label is 1, and the social bot's user label is 0. From Fig. 4, we can find the linear relationship between feature and label. The greater the absolute value of the Pearson coefficient, the stronger the correlation. Relevance ranking is as follows in Table 2.

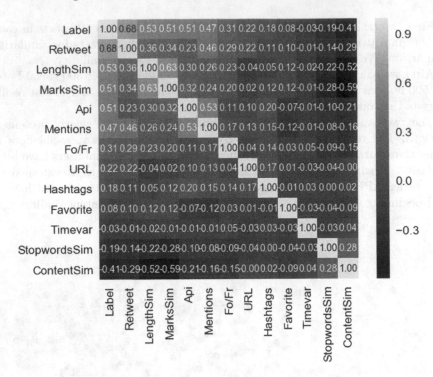

**Fig. 4.** Pearson correlation coefficient heat map

Table 2 shows the feature relevance ranking based on absolute value of the Pearson coefficient. In addition, we highlight which of the proposed features in this work are novel (new) or discussed previously (old). From the Table 2, we can find that four similarity features proposed in this paper have strong correlation with the label. Further analysis of the results shows that higher content similarity means that the account is more likely to be a social bot. The other three similarities are measured by variances. Therefore, lower value means more similarity. What's more, according to the relevance results, we can find that the normal users' tweet length and punctuation are more diverse than those in social bots' tweets, but have a more fixed stop word usage.

Pearson correlation coefficient verifies the previous assumptions in this paper and proves that four similarities of tweets have strong significance for social bot detection.

## 4.4   Classifiers Training and Performance Analysis

In order to show the importance of tweets similarity feature in the detection of social bots and whether there is a positive effect on the improvement of the detection accuracy, we choose Madhuri Dewanga's paper on social bots detection as baseline and repeat it on our dataset.

**Table 2.** Feature relevance ranking

| Rank | Feature | Pearson correlation coefficient | Old/New |
|---|---|---|---|
| 1 | Ratio of retweet to total tweets | 0.68 | Old |
| 2 | The similarity of tweet length | 0.53 | New |
| 3 | The similarity of punctuation usage | 0.51 | New |
| 4 | Tweet source(Api) | 0.51 | Old |
| 5 | Average number of mentions | 0.47 | Old |
| 6 | The similarity of content | −0.41 | New |
| 7 | Ratio of followers to number followed | 0.31 | Old |
| 8 | Average number of links | 0.22 | Old |
| 9 | The similarity of stop words | −0.19 | New |
| 10 | Average number of hashtags | 0.18 | Old |
| 11 | Number of favorites | 0.08 | Old |
| 12 | The average difference between two consecutive tweets | −0.03 | Old |

We use three different supervised learning algorithms by scikit-learn in python: Random Forest, GradientBoostingClassifier and AdaboostClassifier. All performance statistics reported here are based on 10-fold cross validation over the data set.

Experiment 1 runs with features which we need to compare with in Madhuri Dewangan's paper. In Experiment 2 uses all features which we propose in this paper, including tweets similarity.

Precision is a popular measurement on social bot detection performance currently. Precision is important as it helps to avoid a real user being deleted from the site [14]. But if an algorithm only considers precision, it will have many false-negatives especially for imbalanced data. As it will only predict the most acute examples of bots, leaving many bots undetected. Therefore, we chose precision, recall and F1 as indicators of our social bot detection model. The indicators can be defined as follows:

$$Precision = \frac{True\ positive}{True\ positive + False\ positive} \tag{5}$$

$$Recall = \frac{True\ positive}{True\ positive + False\ negative} \qquad (6)$$

$$F1 = \frac{2 \times Precision \times Recall}{Precision + Recall} \qquad (7)$$

The results are shown in the following Tables 3, 4 and 5.

**Table 3.** Precision performance

|  | Random forest | GradientBoostingClassifier | AdaboostClassifier |
|---|---|---|---|
| Compared paper | 0.964414 | 0.968311 | 0.963993 |
| Method in this paper | 0.978421 | 0.980915 | 0.977031 |

**Table 4.** Recall performance

|  | Random forest | GradientBoostingClassifier | AdaboostClassifier |
|---|---|---|---|
| Compared paper | 0.963679 | 0.968179 | 0.963204 |
| Method in this paper | 0.977627 | 0.980109 | 0.976137 |

**Table 5.** F1 performance

|  | Random forest | GradientBoostingClassifier | AdaboostClassifier |
|---|---|---|---|
| Compared paper | 0.966144 | 0.967699 | 0.963213 |
| Method in this paper | 0.978115 | 0.981098 | 0.976103 |

From the results comparison, we can easily find that the tweets similarity features are meaningful for social bots detection. It can improve the performance of social bots detection using a variety of machine learning algorithms.

As for the choice of machine learning algorithms, besides the classic Random Forest algorithm, we also choose two kinds of boosting algorithms. A special point of boosting algorithm is that it combines some weak classifiers with undetermined methods to get a better performance model.

GradientBoostingClassifier is an iterative decision tree algorithm, this algorithm consists of multiple decision trees, the conclusions of all trees add up to make the final answer. It was considered as an algorithm which has a strong ability of generalization.

AdaboostClassifier can be used in conjunction with many other types of learning algorithms to improve their performance. The weighted average of the weak classifiers output represents the final output of the boosted classifier. AdaBoost is adaptive in the sense that subsequent weak learners are tweaked in favor of those instances misclassified by previous classifiers.

Among these three classifiers, GradientBoostingClassifier has the best performance in total. The method proposed in the paper can reach 98.09% precision,

98.01% recall and 98.11% F1. Compared with those in Madhuri Dewangan's paper, all the evaluation indexes in this paper have been improved. All the results prove that the proposed method is effective.

## 5  Conclusion

In this paper, the tweets similarity (including content similarity, length similarity, punctuation usage similarity and stop wards similarity) is proposed for social bot detection. The LSA algorithm is used to find the potential semantic model of tweet content. This paper provides a new angle on social bots detection. Experimental results show that the proposed method outperforms traditional method in terms of precision/recall/F1 with the new data set. There is no doubt that the detection of social bots on social network is very important. What's more, to certain extent, these researches can reduce the threats posed by social engineering attacks to social network users.

Although the detection of social bots has reached a certain effect, prior researches do not utilize differences of social bots. With the development of artificial intelligence, social bots will become more and more intelligent and the areas involved will be more comprehensive. Admittedly, many social bots are meaningful. They can facilitate people's life in many ways, such as broadcasting weather forecasts and providing real-time traffic information. Therefore, how to recognize bot attributes in social bots detection, that is, how to identify malicious social bots will become the future research direction. In addition, because the current researches about social bots detection are mainly focusing on the Twitter platform, applying the existing research results to other social network platforms is also a need for further research.

## References

1. Charikar, M.S.: Similarity estimation techniques from rounding algorithms. In: Proceedings of ACM Symposium on Theory of Computing, STOC, pp. 380–388 (2002)
2. Chavoshi, N., Hamooni, H., Mueen, A.: Identifying correlated bots in Twitter. In: International Conference on Social Informatics, pp. 14–21 (2016)
3. Chu, Z., Gianvecchio, S., Wang, H., Jajodia, S.: Who is tweeting on Twitter: human, bot, or cyborg? In: Computer Security Applications Conference, pp. 21–30 (2010)
4. Clayton A. Davis, Onur Varol, E.F.: Bot or not? http://truthy.indiana.edu/botornot/
5. Dewangan, M., Kaushal, R.: SocialBot: Behavioral Analysis and Detection. Springer, Singapore (2016). https://doi.org/10.1007/978-981-10-2738-3_39
6. Dickerson, J.P., Kagan, V., Subrahmanian, V.S.: Using sentiment to detect bots on Twitter: are humans more opinionated than bots? In: IEEE/ACM International Conference on Advances in Social Networks Analysis and Mining, pp. 620–627 (2014)

7. Dumais, S.T.: Latent semantic analysis. Ann. Rev. Inf. Sci. Technol. **38**(1), 188–230 (2015)
8. Evangelopoulos, N.E.: Latent semantic analysis. Wiley Interdisc. Rev. Cogn. Sci. **4**(6), 683–692 (2013)
9. Glvez, R.H., Gravano, A.: Assessing the usefulness of online message board mining in automatic stock prediction systems. J. Comput. Sci. **19**, 43–56 (2017)
10. Golder, S.A., Macy, M.W.: Diurnal and seasonal mood vary with work, sleep, and daylength across diverse cultures. Science **333**(6051), 1878–1881 (2011)
11. Hill, K.: The invasion of the Twitter bots (2012). http://www.forbes.com/sites/kashmirhill/2012/08/09/the-invasion-of-the-Twitter-bots/
12. Lee, K., Eoff, B.D., Caverlee, J.: Seven months with the devils: a long-term study of content polluters on Twitter. In: International Conference on Weblogs and Social Media, Barcelona, July 2011
13. McNally, L.: Botwiki. https://botwiki.org/resources/Twitterbots/
14. Morstatter, F., Wu, L., Nazer, T.H., Carley, K.M., Liu, H.: A new approach to bot detection: striking the balance between precision and recall. In: IEEE/ACM International Conference on Advances in Social Networks Analysis and Mining, pp. 533–540 (2016)
15. Perdana, R.S., Muliawati, T.H., Alexandro, R.: Bot spammer detection in Twitter using tweet similarity and time interval entropy. J. Inorgan. Biochem. **105**(4), 518–524 (2015)
16. Roesslein, J.: Tweepy. www.tweepy.org (2009)
17. Shafahi, M., Kempers, L., Afsarmanesh, H.: Phishing through social bots on Twitter. In: IEEE International Conference on Big Data, pp. 3703–3712 (2017)
18. Sharma, R.: 15 awesome Twitter bots you should follow (2016). https://beebom.com/best-twitter-bots/
19. Subrahmanian, V.S.: The darpa Twitter bot challenge. Computer **49**(6), 38–46 (2016)
20. U.S. Securities, E.C.: Amendment no. 1 to form s-1 (2014). http://www.sec.gov/Archives/edgar/data/1418091/000119312513400028/
21. Varol, O., Ferrara, E., Davis, C.A., Menczer, F., Flammini, A.: Online human-bot interactions: detection, estimation, and characterization. In: The 11th International AAAI Conference on Web and Social Media (2017)

# Network Security

# A Multi-protocol Authentication Shibboleth Framework and Implementation for Identity Federation

Mengyi Li[1], Chi-Hung Chi[2(✉)], Chen Ding[3], Raymond Wong[4], and Zhong She[5]

[1] Tsinghua University, Beijing, China
[2] Data61, CSIRO, Canberra, Australia
chihungchi@gmail.com
[3] Ryerson University, Toronto, Canada
[4] University of New South Wales, Kensington, Australia
[5] IntelShare Initiative, Melbourne, Australia

**Abstract.** One of the challenges for Single Sign-On (SSO) is the multiprotocol federation in identity management. Even though projects such as Shibboleth provide good identity management framework, they usually support single protocol such as Security Assertion Markup Language (SAML). With the movement of increasing service collaboration in the cloud, identity federation needs to be extended to cover multiple identity protocol standards. In this paper, we propose an online distributed multi-protocol identity management framework Sh-IDaaS (Shibboleth-based Identity-as-a-Service) which could discover multiple user identity services in the Shibboleth environment. The framework enables federation of various identity services by binding different identity providers to a special discovery service, even if they support different identity protocols. Based on the Shibboleth framework, we describe the detailed design and implementation of our pluggable Sh-IDaaS architecture. Analysis of interoperability and performance of our Sh-IDaaS framework prototype is also provided to justify its feasibility and practicability.

**Keywords:** Authentication · Identity · Single Sign-On · Identity-as-a-Service

## 1 Introduction

With the movement of increasing collaboration among difference cloud service providers, identity access management has become a big issue. Users not only want to aggregate multiple independent component services together to form composite services, but they also want to subscribe to more than one composite service from their partners for business process orchestration. As a result, the overhead for service providers to manage the associated user identities has become a burden; and for users, paying extra efforts to handle identity related issues is also troublesome.

The idea of single sign-on (SSO) has been proposed to solve this problem. In addition, with the increasing demand for establishing a federated environment to achieve SSO among different service providers, SSO platforms such as OpenSSO [1]

© ICST Institute for Computer Sciences, Social Informatics and Telecommunications Engineering 2018
R. Beyah et al. (Eds.): SecureComm 2018, LNICST 255, pp. 81–101, 2018.
https://doi.org/10.1007/978-3-030-01704-0_5

and Shibboleth [2], and identity management related protocols such as Security Assertion Markup Language (SAML) [3], Liberty Alliance [4], Information Cards [5], and OpenID [6], emerge almost simultaneously. However, despite the effort of SSO across multiple systems, one complication is that different service providers might have different security requirements and use different standards and protocols [7].

To address this issue, it would be beneficial if a distributed, online, third party identity management service can be provided. Such a service is known as Identity-as a-Service (IDaaS). By supporting different major identity management standards and protocols, IDaaS can help manage identity related issues of software services by binding itself to them, in a similar fashion as in service composition. This not only offloads the burden of identity management from the service providers, but it also provides a robust, cost-effective way of handling identity management for them.

When involving multiple service providers in an identity federation, identity discovery becomes an essential issue. The challenge here is, for enterprise federation in which each enterprise holds its own identity management service separately, how to discover an identity provider for users. Among SSO platforms currently available, Shibboleth [8] is one of the most popular open sources for local identity and access management [9]. However, Shibboleth by itself is still not a complete IDaaS solution because it only supports SAML protocol [3]. When resources are offered by independent service providers with different access requirements using different identity protocols, it does not function anymore.

In this paper, we propose a distributed, online, Shibboleth-based, multi-protocol authentication framework Sh-IDaaS (Shibboleth-based IDaaS) to address this problem. Even though the concept of cross-protocol federation has been around for some time, there is still no multi-protocol identity federation framework available. To achieve the extensibility, we design our Sh-IDaaS as a pluggable framework so that any identity provider can be plugged in through some sort of transformation according to its related identity management standard. Being able to federate third party services with different identity protocols is extremely attractive to users because "single sign on" for the usage of multi-protocol services becomes possible.

The outline for the rest of this paper is as follows. Section 2 gives background knowledge on two main identity protocols, SAML and OpenID, together with an introduction to Shibboleth-based identity federation. It also discusses the mechanisms of the multi-protocol authentication framework for identity federation, and analyzes the reasons of choosing Shibboleth as our base reference. Section 3 reviews related work on identity federation, in particular those related to Shibboleth environment. Section 4 describes how to integrate multi-protocol identity providers together using the concept of a convertor bridge and shows the overall architectural design of the Sh-IDaaS framework. Section 5 explains in detail the actual implementation of the pluggable Sh-IDaaS prototype system. The main focus is on the SAML convertor and the architecture of the Sh-OpenID (Shibboleth-based OpenID) provider. Section 6 illustrates the interoperability and extensibility of Sh-IDaaS with two representative use cases. Section 7 presents the results of the performance tests on the handling and conversion between the two identity protocols, SAML and OpenID. And finally Sect. 8 concludes the paper.

# 2  Background of Shibboleth-Based Identity Federation

## 2.1  SAML, OpenID, and Shibboleth

Security Assertion Markup Language, or SAML [10, 11], is an XML-based open standard for exchanging authentication and authorization data between Identity Providers (IdP) and Service Providers (SP). SAML Core refers to the general syntax and semantics of SAML assertions as well as the protocol used to request and transmit these assertions from one system entity to another. By defining XML-based assertions, protocols, bindings and profiles, SAML provides important support to Web SSO.

Among all the identity related standards, the most distinguished one on handling identity discovery is the open source OpenID framework [12, 13]. Different from SAML, OpenID focuses on user-centric digital identity [14]. Due to its decentralization nature, it is easy for users to sign up and access web accounts, replacing the common login process that uses the pair of login name and password. It allows a user to login once by a unique OpenID identifier (usually an "http" or "https" URL or XRI) and gain access to the resources of OpenID Relying Parties (RP). With the user centric feature, OpenID solves the troublesome pre-configuration problem which SAML demands. No central authority must approve or register RPs to OpenID Providers (OP). An end user can freely choose which OP to use.

Based on the SAML protocol, Shibboleth Federation Software [15] was developed to provide web SSO functionality, addressing many issues including accessing online resources both inside and outside an organization, requiring multiple username-password pairs for multiple software services, facilitating rapid, effective and secure integration of disparate third-party services, and so on. For example, one of the valuable benefits of Shibboleth is described as "Build and Manage Locally, Access Globally", which means that based on Shibboleth identity and access management system for applications, an organization can use it for federation of third-party collaborators. Shibboleth has already become one of the most widely adopted federated access management software in research and education communities. In this paper, our work extends the Shibboleth federation system as a multi-protocol Sh-IDaaS framework.

## 2.2  Discovery Service

One limitation of the SAML protocol is its restriction on binding between SPs and multiple IdPs. Because of the passive nature of SP, how to distinguish federated deployment (also known as IdP discovery service) comes up as a fundamental problem: is there an effective and efficient solution for the SP to recognize where to send the user agent? Although numerous solutions have been put forward, most of them lead to an increased interference due to per-site prompts, or other extra work for SPs. For instance, one straightforward approach is to ask users of each SP, but this requires each user to understand how to make unambiguous selection for the SP. Obviously, these solutions put extra burden on both users and SPs. In this paper, we focus on the WAYF (Where Are You From) service provided by Shibboleth; the idea is that discovery should be regarded as a service for large federation of IdPs. In this case, Discovery Service (DS) should act as a proxy for the SP, relaying a request to the selected IdP.

Discovery Service (DS) [16] can be used during the web-based SSO when an SP needs to establish an association with a particular IdP. In theory, DS is attractive since every SP can share a single point of discovery, and the user experience can seamlessly cross over all services. Figure 1 demonstrates how the DS integrates with SPs and IdPs and how the messages are exchanged between them; it illustrates the fundamental ideas behind Sh-IDaaS (it is assumed that the user uses a standard HTTP user agent [17]). Below we list the details of the workflow, which consists of 8 steps:

1–2. When a user visits an SP for resources, the SP will first redirect the user agent to DS, which is configured in advance with a set of parameters that make up the request.

3. From the user agent's point of view, with the HTTP Redirect request to DS, it will be provided an HTML webpage with a list of all available IdPs for the user to choose from.

4. The DS sends the user agent another HTTP Redirect request to a particular IdP selected by the user in Step 3 with an HTTP Request for the login page.

5. The DS interacts with the user via the user agent to associate one or more suitable IdPs with the validity check on user's username-password pair.

6. By confirming the validity of username and password provided, the DS then sends an HTTP Redirect request again to the user agent to forward the user back to the resource initially requested in Step 1. At the same time, the user agent receives a handle that can be forwarded to the SP together with the redirect request.

7–8. The SP forwards an attribute request directly to the IdP by sending the handle it just received from Step 6. At the IdP side, the handle received from the SP gets checked. If valid, the requested user attributes are transmitted to the resource according to the principal's authority provided by the SP.

Although there are many redirections that interact with the DS, most of them are actually transparent to the user; they happen between the SP and the IdP automatically. The user only experiences an additional process of IdP selection as shown in Step 3.

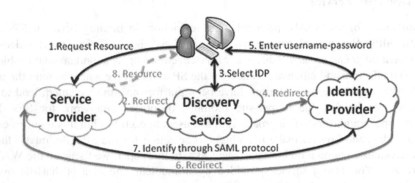

**Fig. 1.** Workflow between SP and IdP with DS

## 2.3 Analysis and Selection of Shibboleth

Even though the Shibboleth System extends the capability of Web-based applications by implementing identity management for secure access among multiple organizations, it only supports the SAML protocol. In real life, different protocols are likely to be used by different organizations. Therefore, it is very important to consider the situation when the identity federation contains multiple identity management related protocols. A more prominent related issue is whether it is possible to compose software services in the Shibboleth environment in which the identity management of these services could be handled by protocols other than SAML as well.

From the previous discussion, we argue that most of the identity related protocols (e.g., SAML and OpenID) have provided reasonable approaches for web SSO [18]. Even though these protocols use dissimilar methods on exchanging authentication and authorization data, they all rely on a third-party online service to identify the principal. Usually when a user requests resources from the SP, the corresponding IdP will pass an assertion to the SP via the DS (as shown in Fig. 1). On the basis of this assertion, the SP could make an access control decision. Based on this concept, we therefore put forward an online, extensible, identity management related, third-party service that supports multi-protocol authentication.

Through a comprehensive survey, we choose the open-source Shibboleth System (including IdP and DS) to be the basic authentication framework for our multi-protocol IDaaS because it meets our prototype requirements: Shibboleth is based on the SAML protocol, and it also handles account management with the DS. Some of the major questions that we need to ask include: What if IdPs based on different identity related protocols are interested to join in? How could the SPs connect to different IdPs sharing the same context to achieve the overall SSO? Since the combination between the SAML protocol and other identity related protocols will be the key topic of investigation in this paper, we will take OpenID, which is totally different from the SAML protocol as an example to illustrate our approach. If the framework can support the OpenID protocol, it will minimize the dependency on central servers or previous configurations, making entities more autonomous and capable of making trust decisions.

# 3 Related Work

In recent years, with the importance of federation issues being recognized by software services, there already exists some identity federation concepts [19–25]. Nenadic et al. [20] put forward an architecture aimed at providing multi-level user authentication service for Shibboleth. It points out that Shibboleth does not specify all the necessary components for authentication and authorization services. Therefore, by integrating FAME and PERMIS components into Shibboleth respectively, the whole architecture could provide a more complete solution for the IdP's local authentication system and the SP's access control engine. However, it leaves the task of integrating other authentication IdPs to the Shibboleth System. Hiroyuki and Takeshi [21] proposed a federation of hierarchical IdPs in the Shibboleth environment to solve the problem of complex structures of IdPs. They focused on the connection between organizations and sub-organizations through authentication delegation. However, the prototype they implemented only relies on the SAML protocol because they only used Shibboleth without considering other authentication components that may extend to different protocols. Almenárez et al. [22] mentioned the importance of federation for identity management and analyzed several federation frameworks such as the Liberty Alliance Identity Federation Framework, Shibboleth, OpenID and WS-Federation. Medsen [23] and Hatakeyama et al. [24, 25] also proposed the idea of federation proxy as the bridge for cross domain identity federation. However, it is still in the idea stage and no implementation has been done. Furthermore, information exchange among providers in these proposals is limited. There is some work on the design and implementation of web forward proxy with Shibboleth Authentication [26], but the solution does not address the multi-protocol issue.

There are "Identity 2.0" solutions such as OAuth [27] or Higgins [28] that have already integrated OpenID [29]. However, they inherit some security risks that OpenID has, including Phishing, replay attacks, and web application logic flaws. Kim et al. [19] proposed a common interoperable authentication framework regardless of the authentication methods and ID management technologies (e.g., SAML, Cardspace, and OpenID). However, it only presents the concept without defining the detailed contents such as authentication protocols, message formats, policies and operations to manage the ID lifecycle and other implementation details.

In this paper, we not only propose a well-defined authentication framework for cross-protocol identity federation, but also present the overall architecture design and implementation details, as well as the interoperability of the framework and the evaluation on its performance.

## 4    Proposed Solution

As mentioned in Sect. 2.3, we choose Shibboleth as the back-end authentication module so that IdPs that support other identity related protocols do not need to care about the information of principals' identities. In Sect. 3, we pointed out that the Shibboleth framework does not provide identity sources or authentication systems to keep the user information. Therefore, in order to use databases, Lightweight Directory Access Protocols (LDAP), or Kerberos connection, we need to use the Shib Proxy and the Data Connector which are integrated inside the Shibboleth project so that user's profile information can be shared in the databases or LDAP. However, there is one more intractable problem we need to solve, that is how to share the login context among multiple IdPs which adopt different identity protocols. For example, when a user logins in an IdP, through what mechanisms can other IdPs save that login session automatically, thus keeping the user in its own trust federation?

### 4.1    Convertor as Bridge Between Shibboleth IdP and Other IdPs

To address the issue mentioned above, we propose a universal framework that could integrate any identity protocols into the Shibboleth environment by plugging in a middleware – an identity convertor. Using this convertor as bridge between the Shibboleth IdP with other IdPs, IdPs supporting different identity protocols could share the same login context to achieve SSO when an end user sends a request for resources in the service provider. Such a middleware layer not only helps achieve the interoperability of the whole framework, but it also allows any new identity service could be added in without affecting existing services. Figure 2 illustrates the design of the middleware built to support multi-protocol IdPs in the Shibboleth environment.

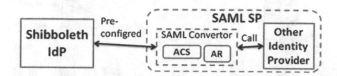

**Fig. 2.** Middleware design between Shibboleth IdP and other IdPs

In our design, we encapsulate a SAML convertor [30] (including ACS – Assertion Consumer Service and AR – Attribute Requestor components) that implements the basic authentication and authorization mechanism as the general SAML SP. Then we plug it into a regular IdP that may support any identity related protocol by taking the steps as we mentioned in Sect. 2.2. Note that in Fig. 2, the original IdP (the right part in Fig. 2) is now bridged to Sh-IdP. Therefore, from the perspective of a back-end Shibboleth IdP, Sh-IdP can be treated as a common SP using the SAML protocol when handling authentication and authorization. It can handle the original IdP authentication operation as well as the extended the SAML protocol to handle the final authentication process. With this architectural support, a generic structure that contains all the identity related information can be implemented using the middleware layer between Sh-IdP and other IdPs, providing the function of mapping service's identity related information from one format to the other.

## 4.2 Overall Architecture Design of Multi-protocol Framework

Figure 3 illustrates the overall architecture design of our multi-protocol authentication framework in the Shibboleth environment.

DS is located at the center of the framework, which is responsible for the "WAYF" service mentioned in Sect. 2.2. By presenting a front page containing a list of all the SPs, the DS allows an end user to choose which IdP for identification. Note that SPs are in fact bound to the DS directly. Any IdP that would like to join the identity federation could be transformed into a Sh-IdP by plugging a SAML convertor, and then delegating the original authentication request to the pre-configured Shibboleth IdP as shown in Fig. 2. The configuration between the Sh-IdP and the DS is the same as the deployment between the SAML SP and the DS. As long as it is configured correctly, Sh-IdP will be part of the multi-protocol framework to achieve SSO seamlessly.

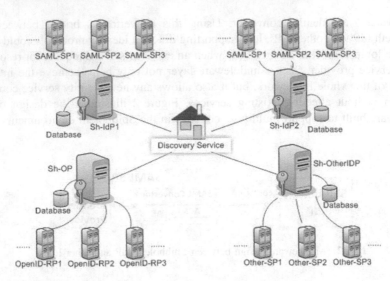

**Fig. 3.** Overall architecture design of our multi-protocol framework

# 5    Implementation of Pluggable Sh-IDaaS

## 5.1    Configuration of Shibboleth Environment

Shibboleth is a complex environment with multiple components and containers. The main components involved in our implementation of Shibboleth IdPs are: Apache 2.2 (version httpd-2.2.15) with mod_auth_mysql, mod_proxy_ajp, mod_ssl, Tomcat 6.0 (version apache-tomcat-6.0.26) and Shibboleth IdP (version shibbolethidp-2.0). We set SSO endpoint on port 443 by using X.509 certificate and then set Attribute Authority endpoint on port 8443 by using a self-signed certificate. In order to enable Tomcat to act as a back-end application server for the Shibboleth IdP and receiving authentication requests coming from Apache, we load mod_proxy_ajp built in Apache by adding a few requisite lines in httpd.conf.

Installation of Shibboleth IdP 2.0 is a standard procedure, just executing the install. sh file and configuring the path and hostname. However, to secure the traffic on the SSO login page and the communication between the SAML IdP and SP, X.509 certificates are required to be installed. This is to make sure that the users can verify that they are submitting their credentials to a server they trust. During the installation, we first create the key pair and the CSR (Certificate Signing Request) named idp.key and idp.crt by OpenSSL, and then load them into the metadata file folder of Shibboleth IdP. At the same time, we ensure the attribute query handler to be SSL-protected so that authentication of attribute requests is secured. These directives instruct the Apache server to request a client certificate during the SSL (Secure Socket Layer) exchange. The actual certificate processing is performed by Shibboleth, but Apache is still required to secure a connection to retrieve and feed the certificate to the IdP. This is the main reason to define a new SSL virtual host in ssl.conf on port 8443, then fill in the values of [SSLCertificateFile] and [SSLCertificateKey File] with idp.crt and idp.key which we generate in the IdP metadata file to refer to the proper key and certificate for the federation.

Since Shibboleth 2.0 does not authenticate principals, a relational database with a JDBC connector directory is recommended. Here, we choose MySQL as the database. To support MySQL, an authentication mechanism used to protect a < Location > block in Apache Basic authentication, mod_auth_mysql that is built in Apache is assumed to be in action accordingly.

## 5.2    Setup of a Traditional OpenID Provider

To implement a pluggable Sh-IDaaS by adding multi-protocol IdPs into the Shibboleth environment, we take OpenID Provider as an example in our prototype. The OpenID Provider (OP) is programmed in PHP and deployed on Apache Web Server. We implement the OpenID module based on some existing libraries and software packages that feature OpenID capabilities developed and maintained in openid.net [31] with version openid-php-2.2.2. Several main files and file folders we deploy are as follows:

- Folder OpenID mainly contains files that deal with OpenID server protocol and logic.
- Folder Yadis provides core PHP Yadis implementation, offering service discovery using the XRDS document format defined by OASIS.
- Folder Render contains resources and defines main pages for OP.
- File commer.php provides functions of doing or cancelling authentication between an OpenID server and a consumer.
- File session.php defines functions for session cookie actions.
- File action.php defines OpenID server action handlers. When converted into ShOP, the main file that needs to be modified for original OP is action.php. Since the functions defined in the action.php are encapsulated well, the modification of the authentication related function codes is minimal.

## 5.3    Implementation of SAML Convertor

The module we choose for the SAML convertor as a bridge between the Shibboleth IdP and OP is SimpleSAMLphp [32]. Since not all the modules provided by SimpleSAMLphp are needed, we extract the main modules that implement the SAML protocol as a simple SAML SP and is installed in our server as a SAML convertor. To make sure that it works well with the OP and functions as a new SAML SP, we put all the related folders into the same directory. To convert the original OP into a Shibboleth managed system, certain codes need to be modified. These include codes that communicate with the SAML convertor – the SAML SSO toolkit installed on the OP machine. All authentication issues would be delegated from OP to the SAML convertor. This delegation process has three steps. As the first step during the conversion, we need to request the SAML convertor library in the original OP. Next, in order to prepare the OP's SSO entry point, we invoke an SSO identification request, and then parse and analyze the SAML convertor's identification result. Finally, we redirect the user to his/her personal dashboard (the restricted target information) based on the information returned by the SAML convertor.

For the implementation, the main step is to convert the OP into Sh-OP is to change the original local authentication method by delegating the SimpleSAML_Auth_Simple object defined in the SAML convertor to pass the authentication operation to Shibboleth IdP, and then process authorization through the SAML protocol. Taking extensibility into consideration, we add a Sh-login function in the same file with the original login action function (both located in the action.php file of the original OP) instead of modifying the codes in the login action directly. We create a new object "$as = new SimpleSAML_Auth_Simple ('defaultsp')", and then call the method $as->requireAuth() to establish the association between Sh-OP and Shibboleth IdP.

However, according to the SAML protocol, in order to allow the SAML convertor to collaborate with remote Shibboleth IdP servers, we need to specify the remote Shibboleth IdP's metadata in the SAML convertor's shib20-idp-remote.php file, including the attributes of entityid, metadata-set, certFingerprint, certData, SingleSignOnService, scopes, ArtifactResolutionService, and so on. All these information are located in the Shibboleth metadata folder we generated earlier.

To add a Sh-OP to the pre-defined Sh-IdP, the description of the middleware SAML convertor also needs to be added to the Shibboleth configuration files. This can be done by first creating the SAML SP metadata that contains the information required by the Sh-IdP for the converted Sh-OP, and then adding the formatted information of the SAML convertor in the relying-party.xml file that is located in the metadata folder of the Shibboleth IdP. This is a key step to enable the collaboration between the Sh-OP and the Sh-IdP via the SAML convertor. Note that the content of these files might be different according to the actual deployment of the SAML convertor middleware. Till now, we have implemented the conversion from an original OP into a special Sh-OP. The architecture and message flow details of the middleware framework will be given in the next section.

## 5.4  Architecture and Implementation of Our Middleware Framework

Figure 4 shows the middleware implementation we bring forward in the previous section. In our middleware framework model, we use Shibboleth 2.0 programmed in Java (as we described in Sect. 5.1) as the back-end IdP to perform the final authentication (the left part in Fig. 4). By encapsulating the SAML convertor into the regular OP and adding a Sh-SSO button in the front-page of the original OP, we transform it to a Sh-OP as we discussed in Sect. 5.3 (the right part in Fig. 4).

Through the SAML convertor, a user taking a web browser as the user agent might be able to share the login context by keeping a PHPSession cookie generated by ShOP and a JSession cookie generated by Shibboleth IdP even if they are using different programming languages and in a cross-domain environment. The main message flow Sh-OpenIDProvider handles for the cross-protocol authentication is depicted in Fig. 5.

Based on the high level architecture in Fig. 4, we integrate the converted Sh-OpenIDProvider and Shibboleth IdP with the middleware part built in the framework. We call it Sh-IDaaS (shown in Fig. 5). The main message flow is as follows:

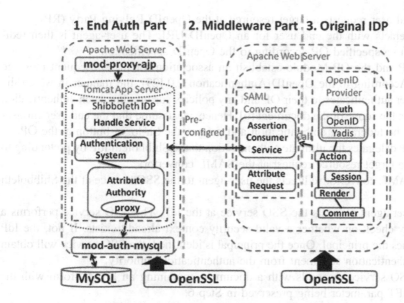

**Fig. 4.** Architecture of a Sh-OpenID provider

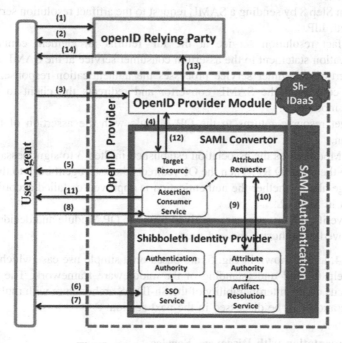

**Fig. 5.** Message flow inside Sh-IDaaS

1. The end user requests a target resource at the OpenID Relying Party (RP).
2. RP interacts with the end user for an OpenID URI. The user-agent is then redirected to a specified OP according to the OpenID specification.
3. The RP and the OP Module establish an association for the subsequent message flow. According to the OpenID Authentication 2.0 [29], the manner in which the end user authenticates to their OP and any policies surrounding such authentication is not in the scope of the document [6]. Hence, we assume that the end user chooses to use the federation authentication and presses the Sh-login button at the OP.
4. The OP delegates the ultimate authentication to the Shibboleth IdP by pretending to create a target resource request at the SAML convertor.
5. The SAML convertor redirects the user-agent to the SSO service at the Shibboleth IdP.
6. The user-agent requests the SSO service at the IdP. The SSO service performs a security check on whether a valid security context already exists. If not, the IdP identifies the principal. Once the principal is identified, the SSO service will obtain the authentication statement from the authentication authority.
7. The SSO service responds with a document containing an HTML form with the TARGET parameter being preserved in Step 6.
8. The user-agent issues a POST request to the assertion consumer service at the SAML convertor.
9. The assertion consumer service validates the request and dereferences the artifact created in Step 8 by sending a SAML request to the artifact resolution service at the Shibboleth IdP.
10. The artifact resolution service at the IdP returns an element containing the authentication statement to the assertion consumer service at the SAML convertor.
11. The assertion consumer service processes the authentication response, creates a security context at the SAML convertor and redirects the client to the target resource module.
12. The target resource returns to the OP Module with the assertion of the profile validation.
13. The OP Module uses the association established in Step 3 to sign messages which is sent to the OpenID RP. Then the OP redirects the user-agent back to the RP with a message about whether the authentication is approved or failed according to the assertion in Step 12.
14. The RP verifies those messages received from the OP Module and decides whether it is allowed to authorize the end user.

Step 1–14, as are shown in Fig. 5, are based on a simple use case which is mainly created to help the full understanding of the middleware framework. The major use cases that focus on the interoperability of the Sh-IDaaS architecture with multi-protocol identity federation will be discussed in the next section.

## 5.5   Implementation with Discovery Service

In Figs. 4 and 5, the Sh-OpenIDProvider and Shibboleth 2.0 IdP are physically separable if we configure the metadata in both SAML convertor and Shibboleth 2.0 IdP as the regular SAML SP and IdP do. Therefore, in our prototype implementation that combines SAML and OpenID protocol in the Shibboleth environment with the DS (as is shown in Fig. 3), we consider ShOP or Sh-OtherIDP as a traditional SAML SP. This implies that it can be configured with any Shibboleth IdP it trusts in the framework for its final authentication. Furthermore, we deploy a DS model as the center service and configure all the IdPs and SPs according to what are shown Fig. 3.

The DS we deploy is the version discoveryservice-1.0 from the Shibboleth project website. In order to perform the workflow of the Sh-IDaaS prototype, we deploy 11 Service Provider websites based on Drupal open source packages [33]. For each SP that supports local authentication originally, we add an SSO button in the front page, transform them into either OpenID supported or SAML supported SPs, and deploy them with a certain Sh-IdP or Sh-OpenID Provider and DS by configuring the metadata information respectively. Detailed workflow for the Sh-IDaaS prototype will be illustrated in the next section.

# 6 Interoperability of Sh-IDaaS Prototype

Interoperability means the ability to exchange and use information, usually in a large heterogeneous network. It is of extreme importance in a federation environment, where the sites in the community might use different federating software. Our pluggable Sh-IDaaS is designed for this purpose, offering multi-protocol support by ensuring that it will interoperate well with any software services.

To explain the interoperability of Sh-IDaaS with multi-protocol identity federation in details, two main use cases will be described in this section. Figures 6 and 7 portray the process how an end user using a web browser as a user agent handles Web-SSO through multiple protocols respectively. Here, we take Sh-OpenIDProvider and unconverted Shibboleth IdP as an instance.

## 6.1 Use Case When the SAML SP Is Visited First, then the OpenID Relying Party

Figure 6 shows the workflow when an end user first requests protected resources in SAML-SP with his/her username-password pair, then visits an OpenID RP with his/her OpenID identifier. Sh-IdP stands for Shibboleth IdP and Sh-OP stands for ShOpenIDProvider. The SP interacting directly with the Sh-OP is a common OpenID Relying Party (RP). The other SPs are common SAML SPs. As is shown in the figure, Step 1–6 explicate the process when an end user requests a SAML-SP for the first time. The interactions among the web browser, the SAML-SP, the selected Shibboleth IdP, and the DS are the same as Step 1–7 in Sect. 2.2. During the accessing process, Shibboleth IdP chosen by the user to implement the identity authentication would first gather a set of attributes about the principal using the attribute resolver by collecting the user data from the backend sources (in our implementation, we deploy MySQL by calling mod_auth_mysql in Apache2). Each attribute is attached with encoders for security purpose. The principal's information is thus packaged into a form ready for the response to be sent to the SAML-SP in Step 5 using the encoders attached earlier,

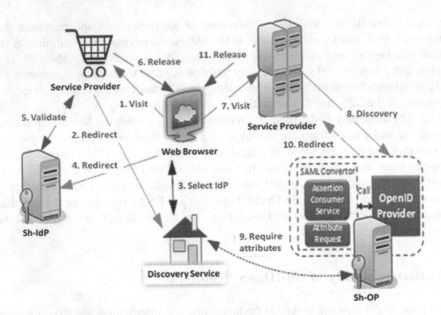

**Fig. 6.** Workflow of Sh-IDaaS (Use Case 1)

typically in a SAML assertion (called an artifact too). This artifact will be signed with the Sh-IdP's key and encrypted with the SAML-SP's key for security and privacy purposes. Then it is placed into a response that will be passed through the web browser back to an ACS endpoint in SAML-SP. On the other hand, in the web browser, a set of session cookies that contain the name-value pairs will be created by the DS, including an important session cookie containing a set of the principal's attributes released by the IdP. They may be encrypted for information privacy and data security purposes.

Subsequent accesses to the protected resource (Step 7–11) are granted directly until the timeout of the Shibboleth session. Afterwards, it will require a fresh handle to be issued by the DS. Without closing the web browser, the user visits the OpenID RP, filling in his/her special OpenID identifier offered by the Sh-OP (a formatted URL) portrayed in Step 7. Through the OpenID discovery process (Step 8), the web browser will establish an association to the Sh-OP. Although the original authentication phase is replaced by the SSO authentication in the Sh-OP, this is transparent to the RP. In fact, the interaction between the RP and the Sh-OP is totally the same as what the OpenID specification describes. The only difference is on how the Sh-OP validates the principal and the attributes the Sh-OP obtains from the principal. Sh-OP no longer acquires principal's attributes from an identity source or an authentication system by asking the end user directly. Instead, by preconfiguration with the DS, the SAML-convertor inside the Sh-OP would get the principal's information by resolving the HTTP response from the DS. SAMLconvertor transforms the information, and passes it to the Sh-OP. However, all these redirections between the SAML convertor and the DS are transparent to the end user. What he/she experiences is that he/she accesses the protected resources of the OpenID RP seamlessly with his/her attributes and authority issued by the Sh-IdP when he/she logs in earlier in Step 1–6.

## 6.2 Use Case When OpenID Relying Party Is Visited First, Then SAML SP

Figure 7 shows the interoperability of the Sh-IDaaS when an end user first visits an ordinary SP supporting identity protocol other than SAML. The workflow in this figure uses OpenID as the example. The case starts with an end user entering the OpenID RP with an OpenID identifier (Step 1). Once the RP has successfully performed discovery and created an association with the discovered Sh-OP endpoint URL, it can send an authentication request (an indirect request) to the Sh-OP to obtain an assertion. At the same time, the RP redirects the web browser to the Sh-OP for authentication (Step 2). The SAML convertor is called, performing as an ordinary SAML SP with the DS (Step 3–6). During this process, the end user should choose a Shibboleth IdP and identify himself/herself. The Shibboleth IdP then creates an artifact containing the principal's information for response to the SAML convertor and the DS keeps a set of session cookies shown in Step 1–6 in Fig. 6. According to the principal's attributes parsed from the SAML-convertor, the Sh-OP will decide whether the end user is authorized to perform the OpenID authentication. The Sh-OP redirects the web browser back to the RP with either an assertion that authentication is approved or a message that authentication fails by examining the "relay state" information returned (Step 7–8).

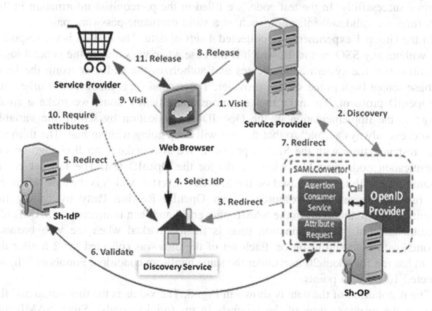

**Fig. 7.** Workflow of Sh-IDaaS (Use Case 2)

Without closing the browser, the end user accesses the SAML-SP (Step 9). At this time, the access occurs in the context of a set of session cookies stored within the web browser. Therefore the browser is finally redirected to the protected resource without login again as the normal SAML SSO process does in Step 9–11. All the complicated redirections are still transparent to end users.

# 7  Evaluation of Sh-IDaaS Prototype

In this section, we present the results of the performance tests on our Sh-IDaaS prototype. Since Sh-IDaaS contains many redirections as well as reading and writing operations which are all time consuming, we evaluate the performance of Sh-IDaaS mainly by analyzing the response time recorded in the logs.

There are two groups of experiments, one to test the basic SSO response time without using the discovery service (i.e. Group 1), and the other when using the Sh-IDaaS framework with the discovery service (i.e. Group 2). We implemented a set of test programs to simulate the accessing operations, allowing the web browser to request the resources from the SP continuously for several hours. The tests were carried out by tracking the redirections of the web browser. In order to avoid the interference between the cookies and the local cache in the web browser, we started a new process every time a new user logs on. The response time is defined as the elapsed time from the start time, which is the time when the web browser posts a resource request to an SP, to the termination time, which is the time when the web browser obtains the response resource successfully. In the test code, we filled in the prerequisite information in the login form for valid authentication such as a valid username-password pair.

In the Group 1 experiment, we collected 4 sets of data. The first set is the response time without any SSO protocols, which is the case when we simulate the general login operations that the system authenticates and authorizes the end user using the local database source built in the service provider. The second set is the response time with the OpenID protocol. To make the test more conveniently done, we make a small change to the implementation of the OpenID authentication by setting the variable "logsuccess" always as "ok" so that the test will keep going without halt. The third set is the response time with the SAML protocol. We also make a small change on the authentication code, just like what we do for the OpenID test. The last set is the response time with OpenID based on the SAML convertor, which is the case when the web browser requests for resources in an OpenID Relying Party by calling the authentication module built in the SAML convertor, and then redirects to a SAML IdP for authentication. The termination time is finally marked when the web browser responds with the valid resource. Each set of the data was collected for 2 h after the system has run for about 20 min under the same hardware condition. For about 2 h, we collected 10000 data points.

The distribution of the data is shown in Fig. 8. The x-axis is the timestamp and the y-axis is the response time of the requests in ms (mini-seconds). Since SAML and OpenID have been applied in a lot of communities with satisfying performance, we take the first 3 sets of data in Group 1 as the reference benchmark. Table 1 shows the

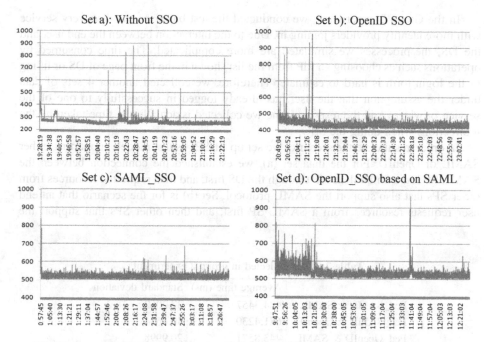

**Fig. 8.** Data collected from group 1 experiment on evaluation of Sh-IDaaS prototype

average response time and the standard deviation for each set respectively, which illustrates the dispersion degree of the response time under different conditions.

From Fig. 8 and Table 1, we can see that applications using OpenID or SAML services do have non-negligible overhead cost when compared to the one without using them. Furthermore, applications using SAML perform more stable than the others. Even though the average time of OpenID_SSO plus SAML_SSO is about 950 ms, when composing them together into the Sh-OpenID framework to perform the authentication process, its average time is 529 ms, which is just 9 ms more than the one for SAML_SSO alone. Therefore, the implemented prototype that plugs a SAML convertor into the OpenID authentication process has a relatively satisfactory performance.

**Table 1.** Data collected from group 1 experiment

|                                      | Average time (ms) | Standard deviation |
| ------------------------------------ | ----------------- | ------------------ |
| With SSO                             | 263.5781          | 26.2352            |
| OpenID_SSO                           | 434.4885          | 25.6883            |
| SAML_SSO                             | 520.5102          | 11.5978            |
| OpenID based on SAML convertor       | 529.7865          | 22.1367            |

In the Group 2 experiment, we conducted the test based on the discovery service with more identity providers joining in. Due to the interaction between the end user and the DS, the processes we simulated are more complicated. The time consumed by operations such as choosing an IdP from the list shown in the front page of DS or filling in the login form is hard to estimate. Therefore, we collected another 4 sets of data under the assumption that the user has already logged in successfully to one of the service provider. And the response time we collected is actually the time taken by the redirections when doing the SSO.

In order to simulate the scenario, we set up 11 SPs as test models supporting either SAML or OpenID. For the data set (a), we established the connection between the SAML SP and a Shibboleth IdP through the DS first, and then requested resources from other SPs that also support the SAML protocol. Set (b) is for the scenario that an end user requests resources from a SAML SP first, and then other SPs that support the

**Table 2.** Data collected in group 2 experiment

|  | Average time (ms) | Standard deviation |
|---|---|---|
| Fed_SAML & SAML | 484.3457 | 37.2062 |
| Fed_SAML & OpenID | 681.4230 | 40.4654 |
| Fed_OpenID & SAML | 443.8571 | 20.9998 |
| Fed_OpenID & OpenID | 653.5704 | 17.5313 |

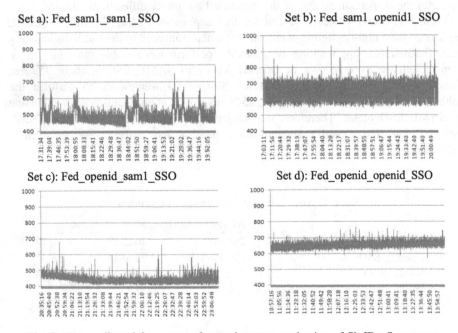

**Fig. 9.** Data collected from group 2 experiment on evaluation of Sh-IDaaS prototype

OpenID protocol. Set (c) is for the scenario that a user logs into an OpenID RP first, and then other SPs that support the SAML protocol. Set (d) is for the scenario that an end user successfully logs in through the OpenID protocol, and then he/she visits other SPs that also support the OpenID protocol. In our experiment, we choose data set (a) as the reference benchmark. The distribution of the data is shown in Fig. 9. The x-axis is the timestamp and the y-axis is the response time for the requests in ms.

Table 2 shows the average response time and the standard deviation calculated for each set respectively. From Fig. 9 and Table 2, we can see that in the Sh-IDaaS framework, a SSO service does have the time overhead. Since the redirections between the OpenID RP and the Shibboleth IdP through the DS operate more frequently, with the SSO OpenID RP, it almost takes 200 ms more than that for the SSO SAML SP. However, compared to the average time cost for Set (a), other sets of data are all less than 1 s, which should be acceptable by the end user. The standard deviation shown in Table 2 shows better result when compared to data of Set (a). Therefore, the pluggable Sh-IDaaS prototype we design and implement has a relatively satisfying performance.

## 8 Conclusion

In this paper, we propose a new Sh-IDaaS framework to address the challenge of controlling access to resources offered by multiple third-party providers supporting different identity protocols. The Sh-IDaaS prototype we design and implement achieves the combination not only between SAML IdPs but also with OpenID Providers. By supporting the OpenID protocol in the Shibboleth framework, the Sh-IDaaS solves the pre-configuration problem which SAML has. We implemented the framework by adding a convertor to delegate the authentication requests to SAML SSO in the Shibboleth framework together with the Discovery Service and the Identity Provider. Furthermore, a more generic proposal for identity federation by designing a pluggable multi-protocol authentication framework in the Shibboleth environment is also given. From the experiment results, we can see that the performance of the Sh-IDaaS prototype is satisfactory, which demonstrates both the feasibility and practicability of our proposal.

## References

1. OpenSSO. https://opensso.dev.java.net/
2. The Shibboleth Project 2007. http://shibboleth.net/
3. OASIS Security Assertion Markup Language (SAML) V2.0, April 2005. http://www.oasis-open.org/
4. The Liberty Alliance Project. http://www.projectliberty.org/
5. Nanda, A.: Identity selector interoperability profile V1.0. Microsoft Corporation (2007)
6. OpenID Specifications, OpenID Foundation (2007). http://openid.net/developers/specs/
7. Blaze, M., Kannan, S., Lee, I., Sokolsky, O., Keromytis, A., Lee, W.: Dynamic trust management. IEEE Comput. **42**(2), 44–52 (2009)

8. Cantor, S. (ed.): Shibboleth Architecture. Protocols and Profiles, 10 September (2005). https://wiki.shibboleth.net/confluence/download/attachments/2162702/internet2-mace-shibboleth-archprotocols-200509.pdf

9. Grimm, C., Groeper, R.: Trust issues in Shibboleth-enabled federated grid authentication and authorization infrastructures supporting multiple grid middleware. In: Proceedings of the 3rd IEEE International Conference on e-Science and Grid Computing, pp. 569–576 (2007)

10. Ragouzis, N., et al.: Security Assertion Markup Language (SAML) V2.0 Technical Overview. OASIS Committee Draft, Document ID sstc-saml-tech-overview-2.0-cd-02, March (2008). http://www.oasis-open.org/committees/download.php/27819/sstc-saml-tech-overview-2.0-cd-02.pdf

11. Lewis, K.D., Lewis, J.E.: Web single sign-on authentication using SAML. Int. J. Comput. Sci., 2 (2009)

12. Reed, D., Chasen, L., Tan, W.: OpenID identity discovery with XRI and XRDS. In: Proceedings of the 7th Symposium on Identity and Trust on the Internet, pp. 19–25 (2008)

13. Recordon, D., Reed, D.: OpenID 2.0: a platform for user centric identity management. In: Proceedings of the 2nd ACM Workshop on Digital Identity Management, pp. 11–16 (2006)

14. Rieger, S.: User-centric identity management in heterogeneous federations. In: Proceedings of the 4th International Conference on Internet and Web Applications and Services, pp. 527–532 (2009)

15. Barton, T., et al.: Identity federation and attribute-based authorization through the globus toolkit, Shibboleth, GridShib, and MyProxy. In: Proceedings of the 5th Annual PKI R&D Workshop (2006)

16. Widdowson, R., Cantor, S. (ed.): Identity Provider Discovery Service Protocol and Profile. 27 March (2008). http://www.oasis-open.org/committees/download.php/28049/ sstc-saml-idpdiscovery-cs-01.pdf

17. RFC 2109: HTTP State Management Mechanism, http://www.ietf.org/rfc/rfc2109.txt

18. Hodges, J.: Technical Comparison: OpenID and SAML, Draft 6. 17 January (2008). http://identitymeme.org/doc/draft-hodges-saml-openid-compare-06.html

19. Kim, S.H., Jin, S.H., Lim, H.J.: A concept of interoperable authentication framework for dynamic relationship in identity management. In: Proceedings of the 12th International Conference on Advanced Communication Technology, pp. 1635–1639 (2010)

20. Nenadic, A., Zhan, N., Chin, J., Goble, C.: FAME: adding multilevel authentication to shibboleth. In: Proceedings of IEEE Conference on e-Science and Grid Computing, p. 157 (2006)

21. Hiroyuki, S., Takeshi, N.: Federated authentication in a hierarchy of IdPs by using shibboleth. In: Proceedings of the 11th IEEE/IPSJ International Symposium on Applications and the Internet, pp. 327–332 (2011)

22. Almenárez, F., Arias, P., Marín, A., Díaz, D.: Towards dynamic trust establishment for identity federation. In: Proceedings of the Euro American Conference on Telematics and Information Systems: New Opportunities to increase Digital Citizenship, Article No. 25 (2009)

23. Madsen, P.: Proxy Assurance Between OpenID & SAML (2009). http://kantarainitiative.org/confluence/download/attachments/3408008/ntt-madsen-rsa/concordia.pdf

24. Hatakeyama, M., Shima, S.: Privilege federation between different user profiles for service federation. In: Proceedings of the 4th ACM Workshop on Digital Identity Management, pp. 41–50 (2008)

25. Hatakeyama, M.: Federation proxy for cross domain identity federation. In: Proceedings of the 5th ACM Workshop on Digital Identity Management, pp. 53–62 (2009)

26. Takaaki, K., Hiroaki, S., Noritoshi, D., Ken, M.: Design and implementation of web forward proxy with shibboleth authentication. In: Proceedings of the 11th IEEE/IPSJ International Symposium on Applications and the Internet, pp. 321–326 (2011)
27. OAuth. http://oauth.net/
28. Higgins. http://wiki.eclipse.org/Higgins_2.0/
29. OpenID Authentication 2.0 Final, 5 December (2007). http://openid.net/specs/openid-authentication2_0.html
30. SWITCH AAI ArpViewer, http://www.switch.ch/aai/support/tools/arpviewer.html
31. OpenID.Net, http://openid.net/developers/libraries/
32. SimpleSAMLphp. http://SimpleSAMLphp.org/
33. Drupal. http://drupal.org/

# SDN-Assisted Network-Based Mitigation of Slow DDoS Attacks

Thomas Lukaseder[✉], Lisa Maile, Benjamin Erb, and Frank Kargl

Institute of Distributed Systems, Ulm University,
Albert-Einstein-Allee 11, 89081 Ulm, Germany
{thomas.lukaseder,lisa.maile,benjamin.erb,frank.kargl}@uni-ulm.de
http://uni-ulm.de/in/vs

**Abstract.** Slow-running attacks against network applications are often not easy to detect, as the attackers behave according to the specification. The servers of many network applications are not prepared for such attacks, either due to missing countermeasures or because their default configurations ignores such attacks. The pressure to secure network services against such attacks is shifting more and more from the service operators to the network operators of the servers under attack. Recent technologies such as software-defined networking offer the flexibility and extensibility to analyze and influence network flows without the assistance of the target operator.

Based on our previous work on a network-based mitigation, we have extended a framework to detect and mitigate slow-running DDoS attacks within the network infrastructure, but without requiring access to servers under attack. We developed and evaluated several identification schemes to identify attackers in the network solely based on network traffic information. We showed that by measuring the packet rate and the uniformity of the packet distances, a reliable identificator can be built, given a training period of the deployment network.

**Keywords:** DDoS mitigation · Slow-running DDoS attacks
Slow HTTP · Network-based mitigation · Software-defined networking

## 1 Introduction

On the Internet, Distributed Denial of Service (DDoS) attacks represent common attack mechanisms that aim for the availability of their target. For this purpose, DDoS attackers drain relevant resources of the victims (e.g., network bandwidth or computing power of a host), eventually rendering their services unavailable for the users. A key to these attacks is the imbalance between resources invested by the attackers and resourced drained at the targets at the expense of the victim. Some DDoS mechanisms exploit properties of network protocols (e.g., SYN flooding during TCP connection establishment or amplification attacks with DNS replies), while others rely on excessive traffic generated by a large number

© ICST Institute for Computer Sciences, Social Informatics and Telecommunications Engineering 2018
R. Beyah et al. (Eds.): SecureComm 2018, LNICST 255, pp. 102–121, 2018.
https://doi.org/10.1007/978-3-030-01704-0_6

of attacking entities (e.g., by leveraging botnets). Most often, a combination of both is used.

Slow-running DDoS attacks represent a specific attack mechanism that takes advantage of the properties of many connection-oriented, request/response-based client/server protocols, especially HTTP. Instead of simply flooding the victim, a malicious client of a slow-running DDoS attack spawns connections to the target server and tries to keep these connections established as long as possible. At the same time, the client tries to minimize its own network bandwidth for those connections. Therefore, the attacker delays the completion of its initial request by purposefully fragmenting and trickling a valid request with extended periods of no transmissions. Such slow connections then tie up finite resources at the victim's server (e.g., threads for request handling) and eventually hinder the service availability for legitimate users.

So far, countermeasures against slow-running DDoS attacks have been primarily considered for the actual servers under attack, as we highlight in Sect. 2. We argue that this host-based approach is not sufficient in several scenarios and opt for a network-based approach instead. In particular, a host-based approach requires appropriate adaptations to the individual server setups and configurations by all of their operators. In a network-based approach, the network of the target actively provides detection and mitigation capabilities, independent of the actual victim server. The main contribution of our work is presented in Sect. 3, when we adapt our network-based, SDN-assisted DDoS mitigation framework to mitigate slow-running DDoS attacks. Our framework enables us to protect arbitrary servers in our network against such attacks, without any changes to the servers. In Sect. 4, we evaluate the capabilities of our framework using real-world network traffic. Next, we give an outlook and point to practical implications when applying network-based mitigation schemes against slow-running DDoS attacks and summarize our findings in Sect. 5.

## 2  Background

Unlike many other DDoS attack variants, slow-running attacks do not rely on excessive network traffic to bring down a target host. Instead, a number of tentatively valid connections with very low bandwidth are used to drain server resources over time. For the detection and mitigation of such connections, suspicious connection properties must be identified. Because it is very difficult to distinguish attackers from regular slow clients, the detection of slow DDoS attacks is often challenging.

### 2.1  Slow DDoS Attacks

Slow DDoS attacks target application-level protocols that rely on a connection-oriented transport protocol (e.g., TCP) and use client/server-based architectures. As most of these protocols employ a request/response-based message exchange pattern, we do only consider this pattern.

Under the premise that a server handles an incoming connection by providing a dedicated resource (e.g., a request handler thread or process), it is the aim of a slow DDoS attack to deplete the pool of available connection resources. Note that these resources still remain idle most of the time, as the mechanism is attacking their availability, not their utilization.

**General Mechanism.** Given a generic connection-oriented, request/response-based application protocol, a client first establishes a connection, then sends (1) a request with its headers, optionally followed by (2) a request payload. After fully receiving the request, the server handles the request and replies with a response, consisting of (3) response headers and potentially (4) a response payload.

In either four of these steps, an attacker can deliberately slow down communication. While sending the request, the attacker can use very low transmission bandwidths and introduce artificial delays between sending chunks of data on the application level. When receiving a response, the attacker can delay and reduce the speed of the read operations, effectively announcing small receiving buffers and hence forcing the server to also use low bandwidths.

Apart from this agnostic approach, attackers can also exploit explicit properties of the application-level protocol to delay transmissions, prevent timeouts, or render a detection difficult due to valid behavior in line with the protocol specifications.

**Slow DDoS Attacks Against HTTP.** Although slow-running DDoS attacks work against other protocols such as IMAP, SMTP, or FTP, the HTTP protocol is the most prominent victim of this attacking scheme yet.

*Slow Header HTTP Attack.* This attack is also known as slowloris [1] and is the predominant slow HTTP attack. It was successfully used in 2009 against Iranian government servers [14]. In the slow header HTTP attack, a malicious client starts with a regular HTTP request line. After that, the client waits a certain period of time before it sends an additional custom request header (e.g., "X-abcd: 1234"). The client then waits another period and repeats the previous step with another random custom header. According to the specification of HTTP [3], clients are allowed to add such custom headers. This mechanism does not only slow down the initial request, in fact, it does not terminate the request at all. Unless the server applies countermeasures such as maximum request duration time, an ongoing slow request can bind server resources for an arbitrary period.

*Slow Body HTTP Attack.* This variant is also known as the slow POST attack, as it relies on the HTTP POST method. This method allows the client to submit a request entity such as form data or file to be uploaded. While regular behavior is used for the request header, the attacker either slows down the transmission of the request entity, or provides a Content-Length which is deliberately larger than the actual entity. In turn, this requires the server to wait for additional data. Alternatively, an attacker can use the chunked transfer encoding mode in order to send arbitrarily slow chunks of a request entity.

*Slow Read HTTP Attack.* In this variant, the attacker requests a large resource using a regular HTTP request [10]. Once the server starts to send the HTTP response entity, the attacker consumes the incoming stream at an extremely slow rate, which forces the HTTP server to slow down the transmission due to the small receive buffer resp. full window [11]. This attack requires much more resources from the attackers as the packets from the server need to be acknowledged and is therefore less common than the aforementioned attacks.

## 2.2   Countermeasures Against Slow DDoS Attacks

There are commercial vendors claiming that their tools are able to mitigate slow-running attacks. Unfortunately, these vendors do not publish their mechanisms, nor are their tools freely available for open, comparative analyses. However, there are scientific publications in the area of our research that we elaborate on in the following.

While it is rather easy to detect slow-running connections, it is very difficult to determine whether these connections are from valid clients with bad network connections, or from malicious clients that execute an attack. Countermeasures conducted directly by the server under attack have been receiving the majority of attention in the literature (e.g., [4,9,12]). As server applications terminate connections on the application layer, host-based mechanisms can take advantage of protocol-specific properties and metrics to estimate malicious behavior. E.g., a webserver can specify limits for the minimum data rate required for a client when sending an HTTP request. It can also use more aggressive timeout values for the initial HTTP request lines, subsequent header lines or chunks of HTTP messages. A drawback of host-based mechanisms is the fact that attack victims and attack deflectors are the same instances.

We opt for a network-based approach which provides protection for threatened services on a network level. So far, only Hong et al. [5] have suggested a network-based defense method against Slow HTTP DDoS attacks by using SDNs. Their method introduces an SDN-based defense application that is triggered by a webserver, but then handles potentially malicious HTTP traffic instead of the webserver. The approach relies on assistance by the webserver under attack, as the webserver actively initiates the attack check routine and forwards message fragments to the defense application and requires access to the application level payload.

Unlike the method of Hong et al., our approach does not require any active assistance of the threatened servers. Instead, we only probe the servers in a way which is transparent to the servers and does not require any modifications to the services.

## 2.3    Network-Based Mitigation

Mitigation of DDoS attacks can be achieved at different locations in the network. On the one hand, the target host itself can deploy mitigation mechanisms. As previously mentioned, there are host-based mitigation mechanisms against slow attacks. However, these mechanisms require the administrator of the target service to become active. Many service operators do not have the resources or knowledge to mitigate attacks on their end. Therefore, mitigating of DDoS attacks is often handled by network operators and offered as a service in form of DDoS Protection Services that become increasingly popular [6].

A differentiation amid network-based mitigation mechanisms can be made whether the mechanism is transparent for the target host and acts autonomously or whether the target has to actively request the mitigation from the mitigation service providers and has to cooperate for the mitigation to be effective. The aforementioned mechanism by Hong et al. is a network-based mitigation mechanism based on SDN against slow HTTP attacks that identifies attackers based on timeouts. The proposed mechanism relies on the cooperation of the target host [5].

Fayaz et al. [2] propose Bohatai as a "Flexible and elastic DDoS defense" tool for SDN, NFV, network-based mitigation system. However, they do not consider slow attacks.

In prior work, we proposed a network-based mitigation system utilizing SDN. The system is transparent to the target system and acts autonomously. However, it is only capable of identifying attackers in flooding attacks [7]. The attack detection and mitigation mechanism is attack agnostic and can therefore also be used for slow attacks.

## 3    Framework

In the following, we describe the attacker model underlying our system. Based on that, we describe the architecture of the system on a conceptual level followed by a description of the schemes to identify attackers and the description of our implementation.

### 3.1    Attacker Model

The attackers in these scenarios have access to a large number of distributed network resources (e.g. a bot net). Attackers making use of DDoS attacks are differing greatly in resources and technical knowledge. We differentiate between two types of attackers. On the one hand, the simple attacker. The simple attacker uses tools that are readily available for their attacks and several of those exist for slow attacks. We also make use of these very tools and the options they provide to emulate the behavior of this attack type. The second attacker model features a more sophisticated attacker that knows how the attacks work, understands how these attacks are usually mitigated, and built their own or made adjustments to the attacking tool to circumvent detection.

## 3.2   Architecture

The architecture of the mitigation system is based on our previous work. In [7], we have introduced our framework and the underlying concepts. We have also implemented the framework, including identification schemes for flooding attacks. In an evaluation, we have shown the system's capabilities to mitigate TLS, HTTP, and SYN flooding attacks measuring detection times, times until the last attacker was blocked, and the overall downtime of the server. The system has proven to be capable of detecting and mitigating these attacks at 10 Gbps throughput on commodity hardware with few falsely identified clients. The concept is shown in Fig. 1.

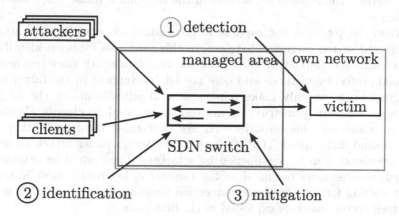

**Fig. 1.** Sketch of the framework architecture, as described in full detail in [7]. The contribution of this work focuses primarily on phase 2, the identification of attackers.

We have divided the functionality of our framework in three phases. The detection phase (1) responsible for detecting an attack, the identification phase (2) identifying the attackers, and the mitigation phase (3) where the attackers are excluded from the network. The system is a network-based mitigation system capable of detecting arbitrary DDoS attacks and mitigating flooding attacks.

In the *detection phase* (1), the system observes the network to find attackers. For that, the status of servers that are under protection of the system is monitored. If a server cannot be reached, the system assumes an attack and starts to analyze the traffic data in the identification phase.

The *identification phase* (2) for the target system is activated to identify the attackers. For this, the SDN controller instructs the SDN-enabled switches upstream of the target to mirror the target's incoming traffic and to forward it to a network monitor. The monitor then identifies possible attackers by applying the different identification schemes and relays this information to the SDN controller. For flooding attacks, we use a scoring-based identification scheme. Clients are given a score dependent on the assumed load a packet of that type would inflict on the target system. For example, an *IP* packet would give one point, a *TLS client hello* 20.

Lastly, in the *mitigation phase* (3), the SDN controller instructs the switches to block further connection attempts by the attackers and terminates the attacker's open connections to the target by injecting spoofed RST messages to the target system. This way, the target system recovers faster as it does not wait for the connections to actually time out. The process is repeated until the target system is reachable again and the observation phase cannot identify any additional attackers.

We have chosen an SDN-based architecture as it offers enough flexibility and extensibility to allow for an extensible system. Using SDN especially helps when setting up the identification phase and in the mitigation phase when blocking the attackers.

However, as yet, it is not capable of responding to potential slow attacks once detected at the targets. Therefore, in this work, we focus on identifying slow attackers and mitigating these attacks. Our framework does not require host-based protection methods and does not rely on support by the target host.

For this work, we only make minor, internal adjustments to the original framework. We focus primarily on the techniques used to classify clients as benign or malicious. One important change concerning the framework is the option to send RST-flagged TCP packets to the server under attack to deliberately terminate connections opened by attackers. Thus, when an attacker is identified, the resources occupied at the target can be freed almost instantly without waiting for the very long connection timeout of the server that is the very attack vector that gets exploited in the first place.

### 3.3 Identification Schemes

Identification of slow attackers is hindered by several factors. The attacking clients behave according to specification, the data rate of the attack is low, and—in case of a highly distributed attack—each client only opens a small amount of connections. This leads to intrusion detection systems not being able to successfully distinguish attacks from regular server traffic [13]. Currently, many servers such as Apache can be configured to mitigate the effect of slow HTTP attacks by reducing the maximum time a server waits to receive a full request. However, these changes also block legitimate requests from clients with slow Internet connections and an attack still has a noticeable impact on the server's performance [9]. Moreover, this mitigation technique requires the administrator to become active and is therefore not a viable option for our use case.

Attacks conducted by the most common tools, however, also show common characteristics in terms of network traffic patterns. Based on this traffic (and extending on preliminary deliberations [8]), we identified six attacker identification schemes that we took into account for our evaluation:

*Long Connections (LC).* A very basic method measures the duration $d$ of connections and deems very long connections suspicious. This method, however, needs to wait for the connection to last longer than a certain threshold in the area of minutes and, thus, the identification of attackers can take longer than with other methods. This could also lead to many false positives when the time out is set too short. This is the closest to the already established mitigation method of changing the aforementioned server settings.

*Low Packet Rate (LPR).* One of the core characteristics of slow attackers is a low packet rate $p$ as the attackers try to send as little packets as possible while still keeping the connection open. This scheme alone might also lead to slow regular clients to be blocked. The packet rate is defined as the amount of packets divided by the elapsed time since the first packet of the connection.

*Packet Distance Uniformity (PDU).* Even time intervals between packets are a feature that can be observed with scripted attacks. The assumption is that non-scripted real clients would send with varying packet rates due to the user behavior, network utilization, and available processing resources. Especially clients with bad connections that could be mistaken for attackers by the LPR metric experience differing packet distances. To reduce load, we only consider the packet distance for three consecutive packets in a row. The packet distance between two subsequent packets is defined as the difference between their receiving time stamps. The PDU is defined as the absolute value of the difference between the packet distances of three consecutive packets abbreviated as $\Delta$.

*Combination of LPR and PDU (LPR-PDU).* LPR can reliably detect slow clients while PDU can reliably detect constant clients while both mechanisms cannot assess the other trait. Therefore, a combination of both schemes could lead to better results. Both traits are present in attackers but should not be common in benign clients. The combination of the two metrics evaluates whether a client shows two characteristics typically attributed to an attacker. As a combination scheme, this scheme requires two thresholds $p$ and $\Delta$.

*Low Mean Packet Rate (MPR).* The mean packet rate $\bar{p}$ of an attack connection should be high compared to benign clients and could therefore also be used as an indicator for an attack.

*Low Packet Rate Variance (PRV).* The mean packet rate of an attack connection should be more consistent compared to benign clients because of the periodically generated traffic for keep alive. Therefore, we also analyze whether the packet rate variance $\sigma^2$ can be used as an indicator for attackers.

During our preliminary tests, we have noticed that these schemes (except for LC) behave differently whether the TCP handshake is taken into account. Therefore, we evaluate these with and without measuring the handshake packets.

The chosen schemes require very little calculation effort, work solely on the network layer with therefore comparatively minor privacy implications, and have very low storage requirements (at max, two values per client need to be stored). In addition to the aforementioned schemes, we also identify two schemes we choose not to evaluate further as they do not fulfill our requirements of a light-weight network-based scheme:

*Incomplete Application-Layer Messages.* This scheme operates on the same conceptual level as the approach of Hong et al. [5] for detecting Slow HTTP attacks. Benign clients typically do not send incomplete headers on application layer. However, incomplete headers are an inherent feature of slow attacks. Therefore, this method helps to identify attackers reliably. However, it relies heavily on the application layer protocol, a specific detector per protocol and attack type is necessary. For slow HTTP header attacks, for instance, the identification of incomplete packets needs to check GET requests for only one end-of-line character at the end or compare the Content-length definition with the actual body length of messages. This identification method is quite resource intensive as deep packet inspection is necessary and requires access to the application layer of the connections. In contrast to the other schemes, encrypted communication (e.g. TLS) cannot be analyzed.

*Scoring-Based Mechanism.* A scoring-based system based on our prior work used to mitigate flooding attacks would rate every connection depending on the load caused at the target. For example, a scoring system would rate Slow POST attacks by giving a high score to packets belonging to a POST request. To prevent non-distributed DoS attacks, the number of connections per single clients can be considered. Thereby, any additional connection will increase the score which is assigned to a client. If other methods fail to identify attackers correctly, this mechanism can at least provide the support for a small subgroup of slow HTTP attacks (non-distributed attacks). Preliminary tests have shown that this scheme is very unreliable for slow attacks and is therefore excluded from the evaluation.

## 3.4 Implementation

The network monitor for the observation phase is based on Bro 2.5-372[1], which provides an easy to extend event-based system. Bro already offers some of the metrics necessary for the analysis such as the packet rate as built-in functions. Other metrics such as the packet rate without the TCP handshake have to be calculated without a built-in function of Bro. This can lead to more processing effort for these schemes as the built-in functions have been potentially optimized over the years while the newly added features might be less efficient.

Bro provides an API to the Ryu SDN controller[2] called broccoli. As Ryu also satisfies our other requirements of extensibility, sufficient support of the Open-Flow protocol and our switches, we choose Ryu in version 4.6 for our prototype.

Attackers for the first attack scenario are simulated with the tools slowloris 0.1.4[3] for slow header attacks and slowhttptest 1.6[4] for slow body attacks.

---

[1] https://bro.org.
[2] https://osrg.github.io/ryu/.
[3] https://github.com/gkbrk/slowloris.
[4] https://github.com/shekyan/slowhttptest.

For the second attack scenario, we modify the original slowloris tool and create a variant with a less predictable behavior, called slowloris-ng[5].

# 4 Evaluation

The following chapter presents the evaluation results of the schemes introduced as part of the mitigation framework. We describe the setup and workloads based on real-life traffic scenarios. We then present the results and discuss their implications.

## 4.1 Setup

Each scheme can be configured with specific parameters, for example, for the long connection scheme a threshold defines after how many seconds a connection is considered suspicious. For other schemes, such as low packet rate, the optimal rate needs to be determined. The optimal values are extracted in Sect. 4.3 by testing the behavior of the framework with a one-day traffic pcap, as described in Sect. 4.2. The number of suspicious packets per client (number of strikes) necessary to deem a client an attacker is another parameter under investigation. Its purpose is to reduce false positives when a benign client sends only one packet or a very small amount of packets that incidentally fall below the threshold. However, this should have an impact on the detection time.

## 4.2 Evaluation Workloads

We use three different evaluation workloads with benign traffic to test the mitigation system in terms of precision and accuracy (Table 1). All test traces have been captured as actual live traffic from real deployments and merged with labeled attack traffic from the three attack tools under investigation.

**Table 1.** Overview over the data sets used.

|       | Start date  | Duration | #hosts | Size (header only) |
|-------|-------------|----------|--------|--------------------|
| SUEE1 | 2017-11-02  | 24 h     | 1634   | 164 MB             |
| SUEE8 | 2017-11-05  | 8 d      | 8286   | 1871 MB            |
| ICSI  | 2004-10-04  | 20 min   | 461    | 677 MB             |

For one, two recordings from the student union for electrical engineering at Ulm University[6] have been used, one containing 24 hours (2nd to 3th November 2017 with 1,634 clients, SUEE1) and another containing eight days (5th to 13th

---

[5] https://github.com/vs-uulm/slowloris-ng.
[6] https://fs-et.de.

November 2017 with 8,286 clients, SUEE8) of traffic data respectively. The web server of the student union offers information about the union on its main site, provides public real-time transport information for bus stops in the city which is used primarily on mobile devices via mobile networks, as well as several external and internal services.

Additionally, we use a recording of an internal enterprise network of the Lawrence Berkeley National Laboratory/International Computer Science Institute (LBNL/ICSI) (from the 4th October 2004 between 10:03 pm and 10:23 pm with 461 clients, in the following called ICSI)[7].

All three pcap files contain only header data since the data sets were anonymized and do not contain application layer payload due to privacy concerns. There have been no attacks reported during the times of recording of the benign data sets. The data sets serve the following purpose in our analysis: SUEE1 is used as training data set to determine the best thresholds for each detection scheme. SUEE8 then is used to determine whether the trained mitigation system is capable to mitigate attacks adequately. The ICSI set is used as an indicator whether the parameters could hold universal value or if training for a specific network is necessary.

For the first attack scenario, the attacking tools are adapted to allow IP spoofing to simulate distributed attacks and are left in standard configuration apart from that. The parameters for slowhttptest are 30 s intervals, 8192 bytes for the Content-length header, 10 bytes POST-body length per packet and one socket per client. Slowloris is also configured to use only one socket per client. The default configuration is left in place in all other settings, resulting in a packet interval of 15 s.

For the second scenario, slowloris-ng includes several changes compared to the original slowloris. The additional features implement randomized behavior, which is configured to send in intervals of 15 s with a randomization interval of 5 s and sending the header lines as bursts of single messages per character. This tool shows how applicable the presented schemes are for highly improved attackers compared to easily accessible attacking scripts. For each of these tools, 49 to 50 clients are started simultaneously with different IP addresses to attack the web server. These attacks are run in parallel with the benign pcaps presented before. Due to the vast differences between the attacks, we choose to determine the best thresholds for each of the three attacks separately and evaluate these thresholds against all attacks.

We have combined the SUEE data sets with the attack recordings. We have published the data sets with a more detailed description on github[8]. The MAC and IP addresses are anonymized, i.e. new addresses are set. Benign clients IP addresses in the anonymized data sets are moved to the 192.168.0.0/16 block, while attacking clients are in the 128.10.0.0/16 block.

---

[7] https://www.icir.org/enterprise-tracing/download.html.
[8] https://github.com/vs-uulm/2017-SUEE-data-set.

## 4.3  Results

The evaluation thresholds are determined by testing the mitigation system with the SUEE1 data set with induced attacks of each type. The number of strikes for a detection is set to one. The thresholds are found using the bisection method starting with two extreme values that would result in detection of all clients—benign and attackers—and detection of no clients respectively. The balanced accuracy is used as quality metric. We have decided to use balanced accuracy over accuracy, as it takes the unbalance of the data sets into account (only 49 to 50 attackers versus up to 8,286 benign clients). Otherwise, a completely worthless classifier that classifies everything as benign would result in an accuracy of up to 0.994, while the balanced accuracy would be 0.5, similar to a coin toss, resulting in a much more accurate indicator. Compared to precision/recall and receiver operating characteristic (ROC), balanced accuracy has the advantage of resulting in one clear value, that can be taken as a good estimation of the quality of a scheme. Balanced accuracy (BACC) is defined as $BACC = (\frac{TP}{TP+FN} + \frac{TN}{TN+FP}) \cdot 0.5$ with the true positive values TP, false positive FP, true negative TN, and false negative FN.

**Table 2.** Overview of the ideal thresholds for each scheme and attack for data set SUEE1.

| Scheme | TCP handshake | slowloris | slowhttptest | slowloris-ng |
|---|---|---|---|---|
| LC | N/A | $d = 2.1e{-}5$s | $d = 2.1e{-}5$s | $d = 0.0999727$s |
| LPR | Yes | $p = 0.091756$ Hz | $p = 0.01739$ Hz | $p = 0.783869$ Hz |
|  | No | $p = 0.079935$ Hz | $p = 0.03806$ Hz | $p = 0.77687$ Hz |
| PDU | Yes | $\Delta = 5.9e{-}5$s | $\Delta = 2.5e{-}5$s | $\Delta = 2.5e{-}5$s |
|  | No | $\Delta = 1.4e{-}5$s | $\Delta = 0.000631$s | $\Delta = 1e{-}6$s |
| LPR-PDU | Yes | $p = 0.091756$ Hz $\mathbf{\Delta = 5.9e{-}5s}$ | $p = 0.01739$ Hz $\Delta = 2.5e{-}5$s | **p=0.783869 Hz** $\Delta = 4.1e{-}5$s |
|  | No | $p = 0.079935$ Hz $\Delta = 1.4e{-}5$s | $p = 0.03806$ Hz $\mathbf{\Delta = 0.000631s}$ | **p = 0.77687 Hz** $\Delta = 1e{-}6$s |
| MPR | Yes | $\bar{p} = 0.83315$ Hz | $\bar{p} = 0.83315$ Hz | $\bar{p} = 0.83315$ Hz |
|  | No | $\bar{p} = 4049$ Hz | $\bar{p} = 21845$ Hz | $\bar{p} = 995$ Hz |
| PRV | Yes | $\sigma^2 = 0.028007$ Hz$^2$ | $\sigma^2 = 0.028007$ Hz$^2$ | $\sigma^2 = 0.028007$ Hz$^2$ |
|  | No | $\sigma^2 = 1332497506$ Hz$^2$ | $\sigma^2 = 1332497506$ Hz$^2$ | $\sigma^2 = 1332497506$ Hz$^2$ |

The thresholds determined by this test can be seen in Table 2. The table shows, that some schemes are very similar for all attacks (e.g. MPR, PRV; LC for slowloris and slowhttptest) while other schemes show big differences for different attacks (e.g. LPR-PDU). MPR and PRV show extreme differences depending on if the TCP handshake is part of the evaluation or not. The high thresholds when ignoring the handshake might imply, that these schemes might not be applicable

**Table 3.** Evaluation results (first part) dependent on scheme, whether or not TCP handshake is evaluated, data set, attack (SL: slowloris, SH: slowhttptest, NG: slowlorisng) and thresholds; detection time is the mean and standard deviation of the detection times of the true positives in seconds.

| Schemes | TCP handshake | Data set | Attack | True positive | False positive | False negative | True negative | Balanced accuracy | Detection time t in s |
|---|---|---|---|---|---|---|---|---|---|
| LC | | SUEE8 | SL | 32 | 4959 | 17 | 3544 | 0.535 | $\bar{t}=0.84\ \sigma=1.35$ |
| | | | SH | 49 | 4959 | 0 | 3544 | 0.708 | $\bar{t}=12.86\ \sigma=8.81$ |
| | | | NG | 50 | 8502 | 0 | 1 | 0.5 | $\bar{t}=0.12\ \sigma=0.59$ |
| | | ICSI | SL | 32 | 19 | 17 | 544 | 0.81 | $\bar{t}=0.85\ \sigma=1.35$ |
| | | | SH | 49 | 19 | 0 | 544 | 0.983 | $\bar{t}=12.86\ \sigma=8.81$ |
| | | | NG | 50 | 562 | 0 | 1 | 0.501 | $\bar{t}=0.12\ \sigma=0.59$ |
| MPR | N | SUEE8 | SL | 49 | 7690 | 0 | 813 | 0.548 | $\bar{t}=2.61\ \sigma=5.10$ |
| | | | SH | 49 | 7690 | 0 | 813 | 0.548 | $\bar{t}=24.34\ \sigma=37.56$ |
| | | | NG | 50 | 7690 | 0 | 813 | 0.548 | $\bar{t}=4.39\ \sigma=6.68$ |
| | | ICSI | SL | 49 | 532 | 0 | 31 | 0.528 | $\bar{t}=2.61\ \sigma=5.10$ |
| | | | SH | 49 | 532 | 0 | 31 | 0.528 | $\bar{t}=24.33\ \sigma=37.56$ |
| | | | NG | 50 | 532 | 0 | 31 | 0.528 | $\bar{t}=4.39\ \sigma=6.68$ |
| | Y | SUEE8 | SL | 19 | 611 | 30 | 7892 | 0.658 | $\bar{t}=71.81\ \sigma=42.96$ |
| | | | SH | 49 | 611 | 0 | 7892 | 0.964 | $\bar{t}=108.73\ \sigma=52.65$ |
| | | | NG | 14 | 611 | 36 | 7892 | 0.604 | $\bar{t}=106.34\ \sigma=85.91$ |
| | | ICSI | SL | 19 | 153 | 30 | 410 | 0.558 | $\bar{t}=71.81\ \sigma=42.96$ |
| | | | SH | 49 | 153 | 0 | 410 | 0.864 | $\bar{t}=108.73\ \sigma=52.65$ |
| | | | NG | 14 | 153 | 36 | 410 | 0.504 | $\bar{t}=106.34\ \sigma=85.91$ |
| PRV | N | SUEE8 | SL | 49 | 7691 | 0 | 812 | 0.548 | $\bar{t}=1.07\ \sigma=1.36$ |
| | | | SH | 49 | 7691 | 0 | 812 | 0.548 | $\bar{t}=20.58\ \sigma=38.77$ |
| | | | NG | 50 | 7691 | 0 | 812 | 0.548 | $\bar{t}=1.60\ \sigma=1.50$ |
| | | ICSI | SL | 49 | 520 | 0 | 43 | 0.538 | $\bar{t}=1.07\ \sigma=1.36$ |
| | | | SH | 49 | 520 | 0 | 43 | 0.538 | $\bar{t}=20.58\ \sigma=38.77$ |
| | | | NG | 50 | 520 | 0 | 43 | 0.538 | $\bar{t}=1.60\ \sigma=1.50$ |
| | Y | SUEE8 | SL | 24 | 1431 | 25 | 7072 | 0.661 | $\bar{t}=1.46\ \sigma=1.19$ |
| | | | SH | 49 | 1431 | 0 | 7072 | 0.916 | $\bar{t}=82.18\ \sigma=44.05$ |
| | | | NG | 13 | 1431 | 37 | 7072 | 0.546 | $\bar{t}=2.00\ \sigma=0.00$ |
| | | ICSI | SL | 24 | 70 | 25 | 493 | 0.683 | $\bar{t}=1.46\ \sigma=1.19$ |
| | | | SH | 49 | 70 | 0 | 493 | 0.938 | $\bar{t}=82.18\ \sigma=44.05$ |
| | | | NG | 13 | 70 | 37 | 493 | 0.568 | $\bar{t}=2.00\ \sigma=0.00$ |

without the TCP handshake. For LPR-PDU, in addition to the best thresholds for each attack, we also evaluate the maximum values for each partial scheme (highlighted in the table in bold).

For every classification scheme, there are two things to consider. On the one hand, how precise the identification is of each scheme for each attack, measuring if the attack can be mitigated successfully without too many blocked benign clients. We again use the balanced accuracy to assess the quality of the scheme but report all false/true positive and false/true negative values as well. Furthermore, another very important aspect is the detection time, i.e. the mean time each attacker remains undetected. Slow attacks work by opening as many connections as possible and keeping them open as long as possible to ensure maximum impact. If all attackers can be identified correctly but the detection

**Table 4.** Evaluation results (second part) dependent on scheme, whether or not TCP handshake is evaluated, data set, attack (SL: slowloris, SH: slowhttptest, NG: slowloris-ng) and thresholds; detection time is the mean and standard deviation of the detection times of the true positives in seconds.

| Schemes | TCP handshake | Data set | Attack | True positive | False positive | False negative | True negative | Balanced accuracy | Detection time t in s |
|---|---|---|---|---|---|---|---|---|---|
| LPR | N | SUEE8 | SL | 49 | 641 | 0 | 7862 | 0.962 | $t = 211.26\ \sigma = 28.65$ |
| | | | SH | 49 | 403 | 0 | 8100 | 0.976 | $t = 210.21\ \sigma = 28.65$ |
| | | | NG | 50 | 3853 | 0 | 4650 | 0.773 | $t = 52.87\ \sigma = 51.39$ |
| | | ICSI | SL | 49 | 165 | 0 | 398 | 0.853 | $t = 211.25\ \sigma = 28.65$ |
| | | | SH | 49 | 107 | 0 | 456 | 0.905 | $t = 210.21\ \sigma = 0.01$ |
| | | | NG | 50 | 336 | 0 | 227 | 0.702 | $t = 52.87\ \sigma = 51.39$ |
| | Y | SUEE8 | SL | 49 | 1019 | 0 | 7484 | 0.94 | $t = 174.83\ \sigma = 34.78$ |
| | | | SH | 49 | 139 | 0 | 8364 | 0.992 | $t = 240.06\ \sigma = 0.07$ |
| | | | NG | 50 | 4242 | 0 | 4261 | 0.751 | $t = 38.77\ \sigma = 55.31$ |
| | | ICSI | SL | 49 | 185 | 0 | 378 | 0.836 | $t = 174.84\ \sigma = 34.78$ |
| | | | SH | 49 | 64 | 0 | 499 | 0.943 | $t = 240.06\ \sigma = 0.07$ |
| | | | NG | 50 | 349 | 0 | 214 | 0.69 | $t = 38.77\ \sigma = 55.31$ |
| PDU | N | SUEE8 | SL | 49 | 1884 | 0 | 6619 | 0.889 | $t = 46.09\ \sigma = 37.79$ |
| | | | SH | 49 | 3502 | 0 | 5001 | 0.794 | $t = 105.63\ \sigma = 42.73$ |
| | | | NG | 50 | 538 | 0 | 7965 | 0.968 | $t = 12.22\ \sigma = 14.01$ |
| | | ICSI | SL | 49 | 278 | 0 | 285 | 0.753 | $t = 46.09\ \sigma = 37.79$ |
| | | | SH | 49 | 396 | 0 | 167 | 0.648 | $t = 105.63\ \sigma = 42.73$ |
| | | | NG | 50 | 212 | 0 | 351 | 0.812 | $t = 12.21\ \sigma = 14.01$ |
| | Y | SUEE8 | SL | 49 | 4021 | 0 | 4482 | 0.764 | $t = 5.94\ \sigma = 33.78$ |
| | | | SH | 49 | 3407 | 0 | 5096 | 0.8 | $t = 5.88\ \sigma = 6.69$ |
| | | | NG | 49 | 3407 | 1 | 5096 | 0.79 | $t = 1.56\ \sigma = 1.49$ |
| | | ICSI | SL | 49 | 380 | 0 | 183 | 0.663 | $t = 5.94\ \sigma = 33.78$ |
| | | | SH | 49 | 352 | 0 | 211 | 0.687 | $t = 5.88\ \sigma = 6.69$ |
| | | | NG | 49 | 352 | 1 | 211 | 0.677 | $t = 1.56\ \sigma = 1.49$ |
| LPR-PDU | N | SUEE8 | SL | 49 | 217 | 0 | 8286 | 0.987 | $t = 211.26\ \sigma = 28.65$ |
| | | | SH | 49 | 197 | 0 | 8306 | 0.988 | $t = 210.21\ \sigma = 0.01$ |
| | | | NG | 50 | 315 | 0 | 8188 | 0.981 | $t = 55.85\ \sigma = 50.06$ |
| | | ICSI | SL | 49 | 102 | 0 | 461 | 0.909 | $t = 211.26\ \sigma = 28.65$ |
| | | | SH | 49 | 86 | 0 | 477 | 0.924 | $t = 210.21\ \sigma = 0.01$ |
| | | | NG | 50 | 164 | 0 | 399 | 0.854 | $t = 55.85\ \sigma = 50.06$ |
| | Y | SUEE8 | SL | 49 | 471 | 0 | 8032 | 0.972 | $t = 176.36\ \sigma = 35.93$ |
| | | | SH | 49 | 88 | 0 | 8415 | 0.995 | $t = 240.06\ \sigma = 0.07$ |
| | | | NG | 50 | 1509 | 0 | 6994 | 0.911 | $t = 39.21\ \sigma = 55.03$ |
| | | ICSI | SL | 49 | 134 | 0 | 429 | 0.881 | $t = 176.36\ \sigma = 35.93$ |
| | | | SH | 49 | 33 | 0 | 530 | 0.971 | $t = 240.01\ \sigma = 0.07$ |
| | | | NG | 50 | 270 | 0 | 293 | 0.76 | $t = 39.21\ \sigma = 55.03$ |

time is too high, the attack might still be successful. It might even be worth trading accuracy for lower detection times if necessary.

Table 3 shows the results for the long connection scheme (LC), the low mean packet rate scheme (MPR) and the low packet rate variance scheme (PRV). LC can be used to detect slowhttptest fast with a highly varying false positive rate between 3.4% and 58%. It cannot be used to detect the other attacks. For slowloris-ng, it behaves on the same level as a coin toss. MPR and PRV show similar results. They can detect slowhttptest but are close to useless for the

**Table 5.** Evaluation results for LPR-PDU when for each partial scheme the maximum threshold is chosen (bold values in Table 2).

| TCP handshake | Data set | Attack | True positive | False positive | False negative | True negative | Balanced accuracy | Detection time t in s |
|---|---|---|---|---|---|---|---|---|
| N | SUEE8 | SL | 49 | 1261 | 0 | 7242 | 0.926 | $\bar{t} = 20.35\ \sigma = 11.28$ |
| | | SH | 49 | 1261 | 0 | 7242 | 0.926 | $\bar{t} = 107.47\ \sigma = 38.59$ |
| | | NG | 50 | 1261 | 0 | 7242 | 0.926 | $\bar{t} = 52.87\ \sigma = 51.39$ |
| | ICSI | SL | 49 | 277 | 0 | 286 | 0.754 | $\bar{t} = 20.35\ \sigma = 11.28$ |
| | | SH | 49 | 277 | 0 | 286 | 0.754 | $\bar{t} = 107.47\ \sigma = 38.59$ |
| | | NG | 50 | 277 | 0 | 286 | 0.754 | $\bar{t} = 52.87\ \sigma = 51.39$ |
| Y | SUEE8 | SL | 49 | 1603 | 0 | 6900 | 0.906 | $\bar{t} = 14.83\ \sigma = 33.02$ |
| | | SH | 49 | 1603 | 0 | 6900 | 0.906 | $\bar{t} = 13.05\ \sigma = 7.75$ |
| | | NG | 50 | 1603 | 0 | 6900 | 0.906 | $\bar{t} = 39.21\ \sigma = 55.03$ |
| | ICSI | SL | 49 | 272 | 0 | 291 | 0.758 | $\bar{t} = 14.83\ \sigma = 33.02$ |
| | | SH | 49 | 272 | 0 | 291 | 0.758 | $\bar{t} = 13.05\ \sigma = 7.75$ |
| | | NG | 50 | 272 | 0 | 291 | 0.758 | $\bar{t} = 39.21\ \sigma = 55.03$ |

other attacks. For these three schemes, the TCP handshake has to be taken into account.

Tables 4 and 5 contain our results for the schemes low packet rate (LPR), packet distance uniformity (PDU), and the combination of both schemes. The results show, that all metrics can be used to detect attacks (except for rare cases, all attackers were found), however, the false positive rate varies significantly.

Low packet rate is a good classifier for the basic attacks slowloris and slowhttptest with a balanced accuracy of 0.96 to 0.98 for the SUEE8 data set. However, detection times of up to 210 s per client have to be considered. Packet distance uniformity is much faster but also less reliable than LPR for the basic attacks, it performs better than PTR when faced with the improved slowloris-ng attack. The combination of the aforementioned schemes shows much better results than the two schemes each alone. With a balanced accuracy between 0.854 (untrained data set) and 0.987 (trained data set) without TCP handshake and 0.76 (untrained data set) to 0.995 (trained data set) with TCP handshake, this method proves to be the most reliable scheme. However, as a combined method, it also inherits the high detection time of LPR with the best threshold pairs for each attack.

Up to here, we evaluated whether the schemes can work with the right thresholds for each attack. However, when defending a real network we do not know which attack the attacker will choose. For the most promising schemes (LPR, PDU, and LPR-PDU) we therefore also evaluated how these schemes hold up when the threshold is not the ideal one for these attacks.

Figure 2 shows extended balanced accuracy results for LPR, PDU, and LPR-PDU. For each threshold (or threshold pair) the diagrams show how good the classifiers are identifying the attackers in all three attacks. For LPR in the top two graphs, it can be seen that the best threshold for slowloris also works well against slowhttptest (with the same detection rate). The best threshold for slowhttptest, however, is unusable both for slowloris and slowloris-ng. As slowloris-ng has a

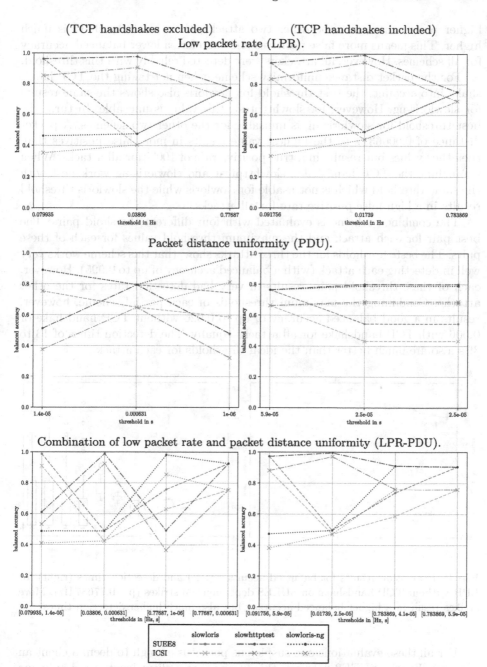

**Fig. 2.** Balanced accuracy for LPR, PDU, and LPR-PDU (top to bottom) without TCP handshake and with TCP handshake (left to right). Each with the best thresholds for slowloris, slowhttptest, and slowloris-ng (left to right) and for LPR-PDU additionally the results when for each partial scheme threshold the maximum value of the three is used.

higher packet rate than the other two attacks, their ideal threshold is much higher. This means more false positives and therefore a lower balanced accuracy for all schemes. However, all attackers were detected reliably with this threshold.

For the packet distance uniformity scheme, when not taking the TCP handshake into account, the best threshold for slowloris also shows the same results for slowloris-ng. However, for slowhttptest, this value is unusable. In turn, the best threshold for slowloris-ng is unusable for the other two schemes. A packet distance of 0.000631 s as the highest value results in more false positives than the other values but results in a true positive rate of 100% for all attacks. When we include the TCP handshake, slowhttptest and slowloris-ng work best with the same threshold which is not usable for slowloris while the slowloris threshold results in a high false positive rate for all attacks.

The combined scheme is evaluated with four different threshold pairs: The best pair for each attack and the maximum threshold values for each of these pairs. The best thresholds for the three attacks show, that this scheme works very well in detecting each attack (with a balanced accuracy of up to 0.995). However, each of these threshold pairs results in very bad detection rates for the other attacks. Combining the maximum thresholds of each partial scheme, however, results in a good balanced accuracy of up to 0.926 without TCP handshake or 0.906 with TCP handshake for all attacks equally. The detection times of 13 to 39 s also are much better than the ideal thresholds for each attack.

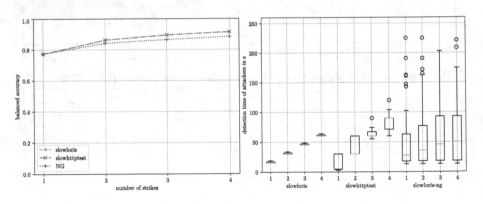

**Fig. 3.** Evaluation results for balanced accuracy (left) and detection times (right) for LPR without TCP handshake on SUEE8 dependent on strikes (p = 0.77687 Hz). More strikes result in a higher balanced accuracy but also much higher detection times.

For all these evaluations one suspicious packet is enough to deem a client an attacker. For the SUEE8 data set, this means that a client has to send only one suspicious packet in more than one week. The accuracy can be improved when several strikes, i.e. suspicious packets are necessary for an attacker classification. We conducted all tests with one, two, three, and four strikes. As an example, Fig. 3 shows our results for low packet rate without TCP handshake and a fixed threshold of 0.77687 Hz for all measurements. The left figure shows, that the balanced accuracy can be improved when the amount of strikes necessary for a detection is increased. However, as can be seen in the right figure, this extends the detection time extensively, from a mean of 16 s to 61 s for slowloris, from 12 s to 86 s for slowhttptest, and from 53 to 67 s for slowloris-ng, this means a 281%, 616% and 26% increase in detection time. Therefore, the comparably low increase in accuracy does result in impractical detection times.

## 4.4 Discussion

In line with our expectations, the schemes provide better results for the SUEE8 data set compared to the results of the ICSI data set. This is because the identification thresholds were determined using training data more similar to the former load. This might indicate the importance of taking the actual deployment network into account, further tests need to be conducted to come to a definitive conclusion. The evaluation shows varying results for the different schemes. In general, LC, MPR, and PRV are only able to detect slowhttptest. The TCP handshakes have to be taken into account when using these schemes. LC is both more accurate and faster than the other two. LPR, PDU, and the combined scheme LPR-PDU show much more potential. The best results in our measurements are achieved with LPR-PDU while also including TCP handshakes. We reached a balanced accuracy of 0.992 when using this scheme. The varying threshold values per attack introduce additional complexity for successful defenses. We recommend less aggressive thresholds that detect simpler attacks as a default, and then dynamically ramp up to more aggressive thresholds in case the initial mitigation is not successful.

## 5 Conclusion

Slow HTTP attacks differ quite a bit from flooding attacks and their identification and mitigation can lead to a high management effort of the network infrastructure. We developed several concepts based on light-weight flow-based analysis of network traffic that can identify attackers and help to exclude them from the network. Our analyses showed that a network-based defense approach against slow attacks is actually feasible and should be considered as part of a defense strategy for network providers. The accuracy of the schemes is not high enough to leave the system active all the time but it is very effective as part of a reactive defense system once ongoing attacks have been identified. The attack tools we used are only able to conduct attacks based on the HTTP protocol. However, as we did not use any scheme that is dependent on application layer data, our mechanisms should also be able to protect other TCP-based application layer protocols that are vulnerable to slow attacks.

Except for the number of strikes, where we also considered the detection time, we choose the best scheme and threshold solely based on the balanced accuracy. However, the detection time should be considered as well. For future work, we would like to implement a system, that can dynamically alter thresholds based on the current network data to increase robustness and adaptiveness of the system. With slow HTTP attacks, we are faced with the necessity to analyze large amounts of online traffic data efficiently. Detection time and accuracy of the mitigation system are in sharp contrast to each other and the right middle ground needs to be found. Therefore, for future work, we also plan to deepen our analysis concerning this compromise.

In this work, we also introduced slowloris-ng, a more sophisticated attack tool that is harder to detect by network operators due to its more randomized behavior. The effectiveness of attack tools for slow DDoS attacks relies on using a lot less resources than the system under attack. Slowloris-ng does require slightly more resources than slowloris for the same attack effectiveness (given no mitigation system is present) as the predictability of slowloris stems from its implementation optimized for highest impact. A formal analysis of the trade-off between attack effectiveness and detectability will be one of our next steps.

As part of our analysis, we compiled a new data set based on real-world traffic traces of one and eight days of benign traffic combined with attack traffic of three different attacks, marked in the data sets by their IP addresses. The data sets include traffic from nearly 10,000 unique IP addresses. We hope that by making these data sets publicly available without any restrictions, we can help others to both replicate our results and to enable the development of more efficient slow DDoS attack detectors.

**Acknowledgment.** We like to thank the Student Union of Electrical Engineering (Fachbereichsvertretung Elektrotechnik) at Ulm University and Philipp Hinz in particular for providing the necessary data. This work was supported in the bwNET100G+ project by the Ministry of Science, Research and the Arts Baden-Württemberg (MWK). The authors alone are responsible for the content of this paper.

# References

1. Slowloris HTTP DoS, Jun 2009. http://ha.ckers.org/slowloris/. Accessed 16 Dec 2017 via web.archive.org
2. Fayaz, S.K., Tobioka, Y., Sekar, V., Bailey, M.: Bohatei: flexible and elastic DDoS defense. In 24th USENIX Security Symposium (USENIX Security 15), pp. 817–832. USENIX Association, Washington (2015)
3. Fielding, R., et al.: Hypertext Transfer Protocol - HTTP/1.1. RFC 2616 (Draft Standard), June 1999
4. Hirakawa, T., Ogura, K., Bista, B.B., Takata, T.: A defense method against distributed slow HTTP DoS attack. In: 2016 19th International Conference on Network-Based Information Systems (NBiS), pp. 152–158. IEEE (2016)
5. Hong, K., Kim, Y., Choi, H., Park, J.: SDN-assisted slow HTTP DDoS attack defense method. IEEE Commun. Lett. **PP**(99), 1 (2017)
6. Jonker, M., Sperotto, A., van Rijswijk-Deij, R., Sadre, R., Pras, A.: Measuring the adoption of DDoS protection services. In: ACM IMC, pp. 279–285. ACM, New York (2016)
7. Lukaseder, T., Hunt, A., Stehle, C., Wagner, D., van der Heijden, R., Kargl, F.: An extensible host-agnostic framework for SDN-assisted DDoS-mitigation. In: IEEE LCN, pp. 619–622, October 2017

8. Lukaseder, T., Maile, L., Kargl,F.: SDN-assisted network-based mitigation of slow HTTP attacks. In: 1. KuVS Fachgespräch Network Softwarization - From Research to Application. Universitätsbibliothek Tübingen (2017)
9. Moustis, D., Kotzanikolaou, P.: Evaluating security controls against HTTP-based DDoS attacks. In: Fourth International Conference on Information Intelligence Systems and Applications (IISA) (2013)
10. Park, J., Iwai, K., Tanaka, H., Kurokawa, T.: Analysis of slow read DoS attack. In: 2014 International Symposium on Information Theory and its Applications, pp. 60–64, October 2014
11. Tayama, S., Tanaka, H.: Analysis of slow read DoS attack and communication environment. In: Kim, K.J., Joukov, N. (eds.) ICMWT 2017. LNEE, vol. 425, pp. 350–359. Springer, Singapore (2018). https://doi.org/10.1007/978-981-10-5281-1_38
12. Tripathi, N., Hubballi, N., Singh,Y.: How secure are web servers? An empirical study of slow HTTP DoS attacks and detection. In: ARES, pp. 454–463. IEEE (2016)
13. Voron, J.-B., Démoulins, C., Kordon,F.: Adaptable intrusion detection systems dedicated to concurrent programs: a petri net-based approach, pp. 57–66. IEEE Computer Society, Washington (2010)
14. Zdrnja, B.: Slowloris and Iranian DDoS attacks, Jun 2009. https://isc.sans.edu/diary/6622. Accessed 16 Dec 2017

# A Holistic Approach Towards Peer-to-Peer Security and Why Proof of Work Won't Do

Bernd Prünster[1](✉), Dominik Ziegler[2], Chrisitan Kollmann[3], and Bojan Suzic[4]

[1] Secure Information Technology Center – Austria (A-SIT), Graz, Austria
bernd.pruenster@a-sit.at
[2] Know-Center GmbH, Graz, Austria
dominik.ziegler@tugraz.at
[3] A-SIT Plus GmbH, Vienna, Austria
christian.kollmann@a-sit.at
[4] Institute of Applied Information Processing and Communications (IAIK),
Graz University of Technology, Graz, Austria
bojan.suzic@iaik.tugraz.at

**Abstract.** Separation of identity and location is one of the key properties of peer-to-peer networks. However, this separation can be abused to mount attacks against the network itself. Our contribution in this matter is twofold: First, we present a security-first design for P2P networking based on self-certifying identifiers. It provides message authenticity, integrity of routing tables, and authenticated communication, is resistant (and not only resilient) against many typical peer-to-peer-specific attacks, and guarantees uniform identifier distribution. The second aspect of our contribution disproves the often-quoted assumption that proof-of-work-based identifier generation can sufficiently hinder certain peer-to-peer attacks such as the Sybil attack. This finding seriously questions previously proposed proof-of-work-based defence mechanisms and leads to the only conclusion possible: Proof-of-work-based measures to limit arbitrary identifier generation do not stand the test of reality.

**Keywords:** Peer-to-peer networks · Network security
Decentralised routing · Authenticated communication
Self-certification · Proof of work

## 1 Introduction

Peer-to-peer (P2P) networks like *BitTorrent* [3], for example, enable the creation of logical overlays on top of heterogeneous networks by separating location from identity. Especially in fully decentralised P2P networks, validating the origin and authenticity of data can become a challenging endeavour. Much research effort has since been put into securing such systems [1,5,9,10,17,19,20]. Some proposed improvements succeed in their own domain—usually at the cost of

© ICST Institute for Computer Sciences, Social Informatics and Telecommunications Engineering 2018
R. Beyah et al. (Eds.): SecureComm 2018, LNICST 255, pp. 122–138, 2018.
https://doi.org/10.1007/978-3-030-01704-0_7

introducing additional complexity and overhead. Others (even recognised ones) do not stand the test of reality, as we have discovered.

We present a security-first approach towards P2P networking based on *self-certifying identifiers*, a concept inspired by *self-certifying pathnames* originally described by Mazières and Kaashoek [12]. We show that the combination of self-certifying identifiers and regulation of identifier generation (before joining the network) suffices to solve a variety of P2P-specific issues. Contrary to previous proposals [1,5,20], we show that this requires no complex governance models, external dependencies, or sophisticated, multi-layered signature schemes.

We provide both a requirements-driven security analysis as well as a performance evaluation of our approach. Our design targets *structured* overlay networks due to their efficient routing, low overhead, and guaranteed round trip times and does not impose any restrictions on possible applications running on top of P2P networks.

The second major aspect of our contribution deals with countermeasures against *Sybil* [4] and *eclipse* [17] attacks. We discovered that the often-made claim that a proof-of-work-based decentralised identifier generation process can defend against such attacks is simply not true under real-world constraints. Section 5 elaborates on this in detail.

The following section explains the problem we try to solve, discusses the shortcomings of previously proposed defence mechanisms and motivates why a holistic approach towards designing secure P2P systems is necessary.

## 2   Background

The heyday of peer-to-peer research dates back more than ten years, when not only *Kademlia* [11], *Chord* [18], and *CAN* [16] but also unstructured P2P networks were conceived. Back then, the device landscape and usage patterns were dramatically different from today's and security was often not considered a top priority. Still, most P2P-specific attacks have also been long known and some currently deployed systems are based on concepts established at that time. The ease of routing table poisoning or *distributed denial-of-service* (DDoS) attacks in P2P scenarios strongly suggest that security should be considered a first-class feature for networked applications. The following section provides a short summary of key P2P security issues and attacks.

### 2.1   Well-Known P2P Security Concerns

Routing information in (decentralised) P2P networks is provided by network participants and the correctness of this information is vital. Consequently, *routing table poisoning*—propagating false routing information through the network—constitutes a category of potentially devastating attacks. The *eclipse* attack [17] is one such attack, where attackers deliberately place nodes in close proximity to a target node (or target information) and refuse to respond to queries regarding the target, thus eclipsing it.

The so-called *Sybil* attack [4] describes an adversary generating multiple identities and posing as many unrelated entities to the network. This can be used to mount eclipse attacks. It can also influence consensus mechanisms, due to the illusion of independent actions, while in reality a single powerful party makes all decisions.

Honest nodes can also be tricked into overwhelming other nodes with queries, routing table updates, or responses, resulting in DDoS attacks. A specific variant of this attack, known as the *backscatter* attack [13], uses forged requests containing false sender information to provoke a vast amount of responses from honest nodes, all targeting a single victim.

Requests can also be involuntarily transmitted to malicious nodes, as soon as *Man-in-the-middle* (MITM) attacks can be mounted. This issue essentially boils down to inaccurate routing information and/or adversaries impersonating other nodes.

Still, P2P networks can be more resilient than centralised systems, due to their distributed nature. At the same time, many of the just described attacks arise precisely due to the lack of a single entity being able to detect and counter malicious activity. In general, networks lacking built-in defences against *message forgery* are susceptible to various attacks. The following section discusses previously proposed defence mechanisms.

## 2.2   Previous Work

A variety of hardening mechanisms targeting P2P-specific attacks have been proposed. *S/Kademlia* [1], for example, presents a concept to tackle eclipse attacks using a combination of self-certifying identifiers and mandating a proof-of-work for identifier generation, complemented with disjoint lookup paths. Section 5, however, demonstrates that this solution is not adequate anymore. Moreover, the authors also introduce additional traffic and complexity to node lookups, which we show becomes unnecessary, when redesigning routing procedures based on the full potential of self-certifying identifiers.

Much research has been done to try and conceive decentralised, widely-applicable P2P network designs. At the core of many proposals lie defences against Sybil and eclipse attacks. Some strategies against eclipse attacks assume working Sybil defences in place [17]. Levine, Shields, and Margolin [9] classify more than 90 approaches to defending against Sybil attacks into five categories: trusted certification, no solution, resource testing, recurring costs and fees, and trusted devices—with trusted certification being the only way to actually prevent Sybil attacks. Resource testing (sometimes also continuously, inducing recurring costs) is often proclaimed as a viable solution to deploy Sybil and eclipse-resilient P2P networks. This encompasses computing ability testing (proof-of-work), bandwidth testing, incorporating IP addresses, and storage testing—and always assumes somewhat resource-constrained attackers. Today, computing power, bandwidth, and storage is not distributed evenly. Consequently, imposing high bandwidth, storage, or CPU requirements can actually prevent widespread adoption of a system. Generally speaking, a smaller network is easier to over-power than a lager one. Thus, hindering adoption of a system can make it easier for attackers to gain signifiant influence on the network.

Li et al. [10] explain why social-network-graph-based solutions are only effective in controlled (lab) environments (based on the work by Viswanath et al. [19]) and illustrate why virtually all proof-of-work-based designs are also of limited use under real-world constraints. This also seriously questions the performance of schemes such as *SybilGuard* [20]. Li et al. argue for a "repaired" proof-of-work approach. This concept, however, also relies on assumptions, which simply do not reflect the current device landscape and the current cost of computing resources. Moreover, a clear evaluation of the performance impact of any proposed solution is crucial in order to judge its real-world applicability. Often, however, no such figures are available.

## 2.3 Open Issues

More important than previously tackled problems are the ones not discussed in this context. Eclipse attacks can be devastating to P2P networks, and Sybil attacks also cannot be dismissed in fully open, decentralised systems. However, countermeasures against one attack must not induce additional churn or significantly increase the overall traffic, as this can easily result in DDoS attacks. Moreover, inducing recurring computational costs or communication overhead to participate in a network is hard to justify with mobile users in mind. Arguing for a proof-of-work-based identifier generation without demonstrating how the difficulty of the problem being solved scales in relation to the overall network size simply fails to provide essential information required to build a working system.

The following section presents the requirements-driven architecture of our approach. We argue that introducing self-certifying identifiers, and imposing cryptographic signatures on all traffic can prevent many forms of attacks on P2P networks without introducing additional requirements or artificial constraints. We then provide a thorough security evaluation of our system in Sect. 4.

## 3 Architecture

This section elaborates on an architecture and protocol for implementing a structured P2P network based on a Kademlia-like routing mechanism and state-of-the-art cryptographic primitives.

Our design makes it actually impossible for nodes to produce false information and have the network accept it. It does so by ensuring that origin and contents of all messages are verifiable even without knowing their source. In short, we guarantee that (routing) information regarding a particular node also originated at this node. This effectively ensures that only valid routing information can spread through the network. To satisfy these claims, the following requirements must be fulfilled:

**R1 Decentralisation.** Maintaining the connection to the network must not require central instances.

**R2 Self-Certification.** Node identifiers must be self-certifying in order to prevent identity theft.

**R3 Uniform Identifier Distribution.** Identifier generation must be random, one-way, and unpredictable.

**R4 Message Authenticity.** It must not be possible to alter (routing) messages passed along the network.

**R5 Source and Destination Authenticity.** It must not be possible to spoof sender or recipient of messages.

**R6 No Dependency on Gossip.** No operation must be dependent on information about nodes produced by other nodes.

**R7 Routing Information Authenticity.** All information used for routing must be authentic at any time.

**R8 Resiliency Against DoS Attacks.** The overlay must me resilient against DoS attacks such as eclipse attacks, and backscatter attacks.

**R9 Secure Hash-Function-Based Identifiers.** Identifiers must be based on secure hash functions.

**R10 Low Overhead.** Memory consumption and computational overhead should be within realistic constraints even for networks consisting of millions of nodes.

**R11 Resiliency Against Sybil Attacks.** A single entity must not be able to (automatically) generate a large amount of identifiers.

### 3.1 System Model

We have identified the properties necessary to fulfill the previously discussed requirements and present the following descriptive model for decentralised, structured peer-to-peer networks:

- Each node in the network has an identifier independent of its network location.
- Each node generates an *elliptic curve* (EC) key pair.
- Creation of node identifiers must not be automatable (this follows from R11), i. e. it has to include information not automatically obtainable.
- This information must be verifiable offline to enable fully decentralised network operation (following R1). We require a signature over a node's public key created by a trusted authority (cf. [10]), obtainable only after completing a challenge-response procedure, such as *reCAPTCHA*[1].

---

[1] https://www.google.com/recaptcha/.

- An identifier is computed by calculating a cryptographic hash (such as *SHA-3-256* [15], following R9) over the authority-signed public key of a node's key pair (this follows from R2 and R3).
- Communication is message-based.
  - Each message contains a message code, indicating the type of the message.
  - Each message has to be signed by its sender, using the private key corresponding to the sender's identifier (following R4).
  - Each message contains the signed public key corresponding to the signing key (this follows from R5).
  - Each message contains a timestamp.
  - Each message contains a cryptographic nonce, called the *communication ID*.
  - Each message contains the identifier of the intended receiver (following R5).
- The authenticity of each incoming message is checked by verifying its signature.
- Nodes cannot "speak for" other nodes (following R6). Instead, information about the location of a node is communicated by forwarding messages originally sent by this node (following R7, messages are contained in routing table entries).
- A receiving node has to check, if it is the indented receiver of a message. This prevents misdirected responses and backscatter attacks (following R8).

| Byte | 0 | 1 | 2 | 3 | 4 | 5 | 6 | 7 | ... | 37 |
|---|---|---|---|---|---|---|---|---|---|---|
| 0 (0 · 38) | Code | Comm.ID | | | | Sender Public Key | | | | |
| 38 (1 · 38) | Authority Key ID | | | | | | | | | |
| 76 (2 · 38) | Detached Authority Signature (72 bytes) | | | | | | | | | |
| 114 (3 · 38) | IP Address | | | | Port | | Receiver ID | | | |
| 152 (4 · 38) | Timestamp | | | | | | | | | |
| ⋮ | Payload (variable) | | | | | | | | | |
| (n − 1) · 38 | | | | | | | | | | |
| n · 38 | ECDSA Signature (72 bytes) | | | | | | | | | |

**Fig. 1.** Message format

By tying identifiers to the possession of private keys, it becomes computationally infeasible to present a specific identifier to the network without possessing the associated private key—typically, a node will announce its location (IP address) and its identifier to the network upon joining.

Our message format (see Fig. 1) thus mandates that messages include a signed statement about their origin. This statement also doubles as the key, which is used to verify the signature. Consequently, nodes cannot assume a false identity. When queried for some node, the responding node also cannot fabricate false information, since the response is expected to contain the requested information in the form of a statement signed by the entity who originally issued it. Contrary to previous proposals [1,2], no additional messages and no further overhead are required to verify this information. This assumes certificates reflecting the authority key ID used in a particular message are rolled-out.

To prevent replaying of stale messages, the sequence of messages originating from a node is important. The timestamp is therefore considered *relative* in the sense that it is strictly monotonic increasing on a per-node basis. A message sent from node $A$ after a message sent from node $B$ can therefore still feature an earlier timestamp. In short, no common network time is required.

Finally, the communication ID is necessary to associate incoming responses to previously sent queries. The overhead introduced by this approach is discussed in the following section (in accordance with R10).

## 3.2  Low-Overhead, High-Performance Self-Certifying Identifiers

We based our work on the general idea presented by the *Host Identity Protocol* (HIP): "In HIP, the public key of an asymmetric key pair is used as the Host Identifier (HI). Correspondingly, the host itself is defined as the entity that holds the private key from the key pair" [14].

Identifiers are based on the *SHA-3* [15] cryptographic hash function and elliptic curve cryptography, enabling compact representations and reducing the overhead introduced by this concept. Signatures are created using the *Elliptic Curve Digital Signature Algorithm* (ECDSA) [8] based on 256-bit keys. By employing point compression, public keys can be represented by as little as 257 bits: 256 bits to represent the $x$ coordinate of the public key and one bit to indicate the sign of the $y$ coordinate. Aligning these 257 bits to byte boundaries still leaves seven bits to encode curve identifiers within a total size of 33 bytes. Using those seven bits to reference the underlying curve allows for a considerable degree of extensibility. Our design directly enables establishing authenticated communication channels, e. g. to perform an *Elliptic Curve Diffie-Hellman ephemeral* (ECDHE) key agreement. This inherently prevents man-in-the-middle attacks.

**Table 1.** System performance

| Number of OPs | ID Gen. | Signing | Verification |
|---|---|---|---|
| 100,000 | 8,385 ms | 10,268 ms | 31,648 ms |
| 500,000 | 41,245 ms | 50,609 ms | 157,823 ms |
| 1,00,0000 | 83,399 ms | 101,600 ms | 317,111 ms |
| Average/s | ≈12,000 ops | ≈9,900 ops | ≈3,200 ops |

We have evaluated the computational overhead of introducing self-certifying identifiers using a cloud computing instance. On *Hetzner*'s smallest and cheapest

CX11[2] cloud instance featuring one virtualised *Intel Skylake Xeon* CPU core, it is still possible to verify and sign thousands of messages each second, as shown in Table 1.

The following section explains our routing protocol in detail, and argues that the overhead introduced is minimal.

### 3.3 Authenticated Routing Protocol

Our routing protocol is based on the Kademlia *distributed hash table* (DHT) [11]. Therefore, we shall highlight only the differences to the original design.

Apart from the last seen time, the information required to construct routing table entries (node identifier, IP address and port, timestamp, . . . ), is already contained in messages defined by our design. Therefore, we can keep messages from other nodes as a whole to build up the local routing table. The messages remain small ($\approx 300$ bytes), thus only inducing a small overhead when compared to the original Kademlia design.

During a node lookup process, all nodes respond with messages contained in their routing tables. Therefore, receiving nodes can verify the authenticity of the messages, as explained in Sect. 3.2. Additionally, the responding node includes a fresh message, to enable the receiver to update its respective routing table entry. In accordance to [1], nodes must ensure disjoint lookup paths, to prevent eclipse attacks.

Mandating self-certifying identifiers essentially prevents forged messages from being introduced into the network. This way, all information received about the location of nodes is verifiably accurate. Identifiers themselves also cannot be forged, as they cannot be chosen deliberately and require the possession of a private key to be recognised. The following section provides a comprehensive security evaluation of our design.

## 4 Security Evaluation

In order to verify that our design does indeed provide the proclaimed security features, we performed a *Common Criteria for Information Technology Security Evaluation* (CC)-based [7] security evaluation.

We do not consider attacks on the implementation and assume correctness of all involved cryptographic primitives. We further consider the underlying network infrastructure (the IP network) to operate as expected. As our design features built-in mechanisms to prevent various attacks instead of countering them after the fact, we refrain from discussing *countermeasures* as defined by the CC methodology. Instead, we evaluate *system properties* for countering/preventing threats. Apart from this deviation, the evaluation adheres to the definitions of the CC evaluation methodology and identifies threats aimed at assets, as well as explicit assumptions, and security objectives. We did, however, introduce a separate section regarding threat mitigation. The outcome of this evaluation shows

---

[2] https://www.hetzner.com/cloud.

that the interdependence of some objectives, threats, and system properties are not an issue since no residual threats remain.

## 4.1   Assets

The following assets need to be protected to provide all desired security features:

[A1] **Message.** Messages form the main building block of our design and are used for building routing tables. This information must be protected from alterations but is not considered confidential.

[A2] **Private Key.** As the private key is tied to identifier and signature generation, it needs to be kept confidential and must not be shared among entities.

[A3] **Identifier.** Identifiers uniquely define nodes in the network and are used to contact other participants. Consequently, confidentiality is irrelevant, but uniqueness is imperative.

[A4] **Routing Table.** The routing table stores all information necessary to contact other nodes. This includes identifiers, IP addresses as well as messages and timestamps.

   As our design focuses on providing an overlay network without targeting any specific application, no further assets are relevant.

## 4.2   Assumptions

Our approach tries to prevent many attacks instead of countering them through tightly-regulated behavioural constraints. It therefore relies only on two single assumptions:

[AS1] **Uncompromised Trusted Authority.** The trusted authority signing keys operates as intended and is not compromised.

[AS2] **Secrecy of Private Key.** The proposed design requires messages to be signed using a cryptographic key, which ensures authenticity and integrity of all sent data. Keeping this key secret is thus crucial for the security of the overall system: Attackers obtaining the private key of a specific node can sign arbitrary messages and thus impersonate this node. However, as no purely technological measures exist to keep the private key secret, we therefore assume that appropriate measures are taken to keep the private key secret. The same holds for [AS1].

## 4.3   Security Objectives

Our design aims at providing the following security objectives:

[O1] **Message Integrity.** As all information is exchanged through messages, it must not be possible to tamper with messages, without recipients detecting this.

**[O2] Uniform Distribution of Identifiers.** A uniform distribution of node identifiers must be guaranteed to prevent attackers from being able to generate specific identifiers, e. g. to carry out eclipse attacks.

**[O3] Integrity of Routing Tables.** Accurate routing tables are integral to operating a P2P network.

**[O4] Message Order.** To process only up-to-date routing information, nodes shall detect and discard messages which contain information already processed at an earlier point in time.

**[O5] Reachability.** Assuming working transport, physical, and data link layers, this objective effectively boils down to answering node lookups.

**[O6] Authenticated Communication.** While establishing authenticated communication channels is not a P2P-specific feature, it is still considered an essential security objective.

## 4.4   Threats

We have identified the following threats based on known attacks aimed at peer-to-peer networks. Table 2 illustrates how these map to security objectives.

**[T1] Eclipse Attack.** Being able to generate specific identifiers, or identifiers close to a specific node enables eclipse attacks. This directly violates *[O2]*, and *[O5]*.

**[T2] Impersonation.** An adversary able to assume the identity of a specific node, can send arbitrary messages which then appear to be originating from the original node. This can lead to disruptions, violating *[O3]*, and *[O5]*; impersonation can be a consequence of violating *[AS2]*.

**[T3] Message Forgery.** An attacker could try to alter messages originating from other nodes in the network or compose messages which contain inaccurate information, violating *[O1]*, *[O3]*, and thus *[O5]*.

**[T4] Replay Attacks.** Replay attacks are defined as re-sending previously captured messages to disrupt the network and violate *[O4]*. This can lead to compromising *[O3]*, and *[O5]*.

**[T5] Routing Table Poisoning.** Routing table poisoning as a general attack describes deliberately inserting false information or malicious nodes into routing tables. This directly conflicts with *[O3]*, leading to compromising *[O5]*.

**[T6] Sybil Attacks.** Sybil attacks can disrupt a network in various way, from a DoS point of view, this violates *[O5]*. More generally speaking, a successful Sybil attack can lead to fatal disruption of the whole network.

**[T7] Backscatter Attacks.** The backscatter is a DDoS attack and violates *[O5]*.

**[T8] Man-in-the-Middle Attacks.** When trying to establish a communication channel, an attacker could try to fool a node into contacting their node instead of the intended target. This directly violates *[O5]* and *[O6]*.

### 4.5    System Properties

This section illustrates how most threats can be mitigated by one or more system properties. The security features of our system are the result of a combination of properties. Because of this, we first define all relevant system properties and separately elaborate on how threats are inhibited. Table 3 provides an overview of the results obtained as part of this security evaluation, illustrating which combinations of properties prevent certain threats. Our design features the following properties:

**[P1] Public-Key-Based, Self-Certifying Identifiers.** Identifiers are created by calculating a cryptographic hash over the authority-signed public key of a node's EC key pair. These form the basis for countering a variety of threats.

**[P2] Signed Messages.** As explained in Sect. 3, this makes it possible to unequivocally determine the origin and authenticity of a message.

**[P3] One-Way Derivation of Identifiers.** Using an unbiased hash function as final step during identifier generation ensures uniform identifier distribution.

**[P4] Message Timestamp.** Message timestamps enable stale messages originating from a specific node can be detected.

**[P5] Recipient Declaration in Messages.** By mandating messages to declare the intended recipient, incoming messages addressed to some other node can be detected and discarded.

### 4.6    Threat Mitigation

Typically, a combination of system properties is required to prevent a threat. Table 3 shows exactly how each threat is mitigated by a combination of system properties (and *[AS1]*).

**Table 2.** Mapping of threats to security objectives

|     | T1 | T2 | T3 | T4 | T5 | T6 | T7 | T8 |
|-----|----|----|----|----|----|----|----|----|
| O1  | ◯  | ◯  | ⊗  | ◯  | ◯  | ◯  | ◯  | ◯  |
| O2  | ⊗  | ◯  | ◯  | ◯  | ◯  | ◯  | ◯  | ◯  |
| O3  | ◯  | ⊗  | ⊗  | ⊗  | ⊗  | ◯  | ◯  | ◯  |
| O4  | ◯  | ◯  | ◯  | ⊗  | ◯  | ◯  | ◯  | ◯  |
| O5  | ⊗  | ⊗  | ⊗  | ⊗  | ⊗  | ⊗  | ⊗  | ⊗  |
| O6  | ◯  | ◯  | ◯  | ◯  | ◯  | ◯  | ◯  | ⊗  |

**Table 3.** Mapping of threats to system properties preventing them

|     | T1 | T2 | T3 | T4 | T5 | T6 | T7 | T8 |
|-----|----|----|----|----|----|----|----|----|
| P1  | ⊗  | ⊗  | ◯  | ◯  | ⊗  | ◯  | ◯  | ⊗  |
| P2  | ⊗  | ⊗  | ⊗  | ◯  | ⊗  | ◯  | ⊗  | ⊗  |
| P3  | ⊗  | ◯  | ◯  | ⊗  | ⊗  | ◯  | ◯  | ◯  |
| P4  | ◯  | ◯  | ◯  | ⊗  | ⊗  | ◯  | ◯  | ◯  |
| P5  | ◯  | ◯  | ◯  | ◯  | ◯  | ◯  | ⊗  | ◯  |
| AS1 | ⊗  | ◯  | ◯  | ◯  | ◯  | ⊗  | ◯  | ◯  |

All threats are effectively countered, given a trusted authority regulates identifier generation. During normal operation, the system is fully decentralised.

This, in conjunction with the system performance discussed in Sect. 3.3, demonstrates the applicability of our system under real-world conditions. At the same time, our design does not introduce additional complexity, such as auditing mechanisms, or external dependencies which were previously proposed as defences against eclipse attacks, e. g. [5,17]. This clearly presents an improvement over existing systems. Still, many (even widely-used) P2P designs suggest that fully decentralised identifier generation and satisfactory attack resilience are possible based on proof-of-work approaches—a claim we shall refute in the following section.

## 5    Proof of Work and Attack Resiliency

This section illustrates why proof-of-work-based defence mechanisms against eclipse and Sybil attacks fail to achieve their goals. We use our system's model as a baseline (i. e. worst case for attackers), replace regulated identifier generation with a proof-of-work approach and evaluate the difficulty and cost of certain attacks. The results clearly show that proof-of-work in itself has to be questioned. Assuming an unbiased hash function, the following network properties can be defined:

$$k \equiv \text{system-wide replication factor}$$
$$b \equiv \text{identifier length in bits}$$
$$S = 2^b \equiv \text{size of identifier space}$$
$$c \equiv \text{cost of generating a single identifier}$$
$$N \equiv \text{actual number of nodes in the network}$$
$$d = \frac{S}{N} \equiv \text{average shortest distance between nodes.}$$

Generally speaking, an (eclipse) attack targeting a single node requires the operation of *enough* attacker-controlled nodes *close* to the victim node. The relevant notion of *closeness* in this context amounts to malicious nodes being closer to the target than the closest honest node. Considering that any given distance to other nodes can occur only once from a given node's point of view, the probability of generating an identifier, which is closer to the target node than the closest neighbour, can be estimated as $\frac{1}{N}$ (following Eq. 1, given a sensible identifier space such as $2^{256}$).

$$p(\text{close}) = p(\text{dist} < d) = \sum_{i=1}^{d-1} p\left(\text{dist} = i\right) = \sum_{i=1}^{\frac{S}{N}-1} \frac{1}{S} \approx \frac{S}{N} \cdot \frac{1}{S} = \frac{1}{N} \quad (1)$$

As our design ensures disjoint lookup paths, $k$ malicious nodes will need to be placed and operated close to an attack target to successfully eclipse it [1]. The probability $p(\text{atk})$ of obtaining $k$ close identifiers in $n$ trials can be calculated according to Eq. 2: Generating identifiers can be modelled as a Bernoulli process (following the first term of Eq. 2). However, the probability of generating an identifier multiple times (which would not increase the chance of a successful attack) also needs to be compensated for (following the second term of Eq. 2).

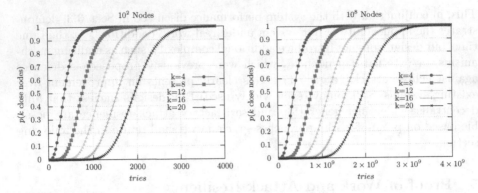

**Fig. 2.** Probability of generating $k$ identifiers close to a target for different network sizes

$$p(\text{atk}) = \underbrace{\left(1 - \sum_{i=0}^{k-1}\left(\binom{n}{i}\underbrace{\left(\frac{1}{N}\right)^i}\left(1-\frac{1}{N}\right)^{n-i}\right)\right)}_{\substack{p(\text{close})\\ \text{probability to generate }\geq k\text{ close IDs}}} \cdot \underbrace{\left(\prod_{i=1}^{k}\left(\frac{S}{N}-i+1\right)\right)\left(\frac{N}{S}\right)^k}_{p(\text{alldifferent})} \quad (2)$$

Considering the benchmark results from Sect. 3.2 and a price of 0.4 ct/h to achieve this performance[3], a single instance can process $\approx 2,400$ messages (request–response workflows) per second. A single lookup will lead to $\mathcal{O}(k)$ many messages to be processed. As $k$ is typically $\leq 20$, the running costs for operating $k$ malicious nodes can thus be virtually neglected, if the goal is to eclipse a single target.

More crucial is the cost of generating *enough close* identifiers. The plots shown in Fig. 2 illustrate the success probabilities of generating enough nodes to eclipse a single target for multiple network sizes, based on 256-bit identifiers. We can observe that the probability scales almost linearly with the number of generated identifiers between 0.1 and 0.9. Generating approximately $k \cdot N$ identifiers already results in a success probability of $>50\%$, while generating $2k \cdot N$ suffices to succeed almost certainly as further illustrated in Fig. 3.

When mapping these figures to a network consisting of $N$ nodes and the aforementioned prices of cloud computing resources, the actual cost of generating enough identifiers to eclipse a single node can be calculated. Matching the performance figures to current pricing leads to an estimated cost of 1 ct for generating 100 million identifiers. Consequently, the proof-of-work can be scaled to match different attacker budgets following Eqs. 3, and 4.

$$cost_{\text{base}} = p(\text{atk} > 95\%) = \frac{2k \cdot N}{100\text{M}} \text{ [ct]} \quad (3)$$

$$\text{len(PoW-prefix)} = \log_2\left\lceil\frac{B}{cost_{\text{base}}}\right\rceil \text{[bits]} \qquad B \dots \text{Budget [ct]} \quad (4)$$

---

[3] According to pricing information available at https://www.hetzner.com/cloud.

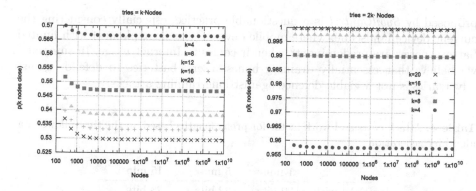

**Fig. 3.** Probability of generating $k$ identifiers close to a target after $k \cdot N$ and $2k \cdot N$ tries for different network sizes

Increasing the cost of identifier generation without keeping in mind the time it takes for legitimate users to generate identifiers can lead to identifier generation taking too long for the typical, honest user. Therefore, it is more sensible to calculate the cost of an attack, given the amount of time honest users are willing to wait during identifier generation. Equations 5–6 formalise this optimisation problem.

$$\max \quad cost_\text{base} \cdot factor = cost_\text{atk} \tag{5}$$

$$\text{s.t.} \quad \frac{1}{12000} \cdot 2^{\lceil \log_2 factor \rceil} \leq t_\text{IDgen} \tag{6}$$

To put these relations into context, we set $b = 256$, and $k = 20$ for a network consisting of $N = 1\text{M}$ nodes, while allowing a single identifier generation to take 1, 5, and 15 min, respectively. The results are depicted in Table 4 and scale linearly wrt. $N$. Clearly, hardening a fully decentralised P2P network solely using a proof-of-work based identified generation is not a viable solution, even though it is often praised as such [1,2,9]. This does raise some concerns, considering that our design imposes even tighter constraints than *S/Kademlia*, for example, and already restricts attackers as much as possible. Other designs, e. g. *SybilControl* [10], which mandate nodes to periodically solve proof-of-work challenges, also do not help against targeted attacks, as the cost of operating $k$ nodes is still negligible.

At the other end of the spectrum are long-running, global attacks. The limiting cost factor in this case is not generating identifiers, but operating enough nodes for a prolonged period of time. Considering the performance figures, and a price of 0.4 ct/h, a single instance can process $\approx 1{,}200$ messages per second[4]. Assuming 10 messages per second for a single operating node amounts to a cost of $\approx 33\,\text{€/h}$ to operate a million nodes. The time it takes to actually become resident in all nodes' routing tables is dependent on the churn rate and costs scale accordingly. Introducing an artificial overhead to increase running costs, as

---

[4] Each message requires two signatures to be verified.

proposed by *SybilControl* is a questionable practice, especially considering the
current device landscape, where mobile devices (like smartphones) with limited
battery power are predominant[5] when it comes to Internet usage. In summary,
we believe that essentially draining honest users' batteries to defend against
adversaries is not a viable defence against long-running attacks.

**Table 4.** Attack costs and work factor for prefix lengths based on the time allowed for
identifier generation

|  | 1 min | 5 min | 15 min |
|---|---|---|---|
| len(PoW-prefix) | 20 bits | 22 bits | 23 bits |
| $factor$ | 1,048,576 | 4,194,304 | 8,388,608 |
| $cost_{atk}$ | € 4,194.30 | € 16,777.22 | € 33,554.43 |

The only other (noteworthy) decentralised alternatives to centralised identifier generation are based on the graph of the nodes' social network. As mentioned
in Sect. 2, these approaches also do not stand the test of reality. Furthermore,
countermeasures such as those against eclipse attacks inside the Bitcoin network [6], are either already part of our system, or highly specific to the layout of
the Bitcoin network, and target P2P networks with low churn rates. Therefore,
P2P networks in general are still susceptible to eclipse and Sybil attacks, especially when targeting mobile users, who can cause considerable churn rates. This
effectively leaves centralised identifier generation as the only viable alternative.

## 6    Conclusion

This work presented a holistic approach towards P2P network security based
on self-certifying identifiers. A comprehensive common-criteria-based security
analysis as well as a performance evaluation demonstrate real-world applicability. Our authenticated routing protocol harnesses the full potential of self-
certifying identifiers without introducing additional overhead or imposing complex behavioural constraints. All in all, this presents an advancement over existing designs, as network operation itself is kept as simple as possible while at the
same time successfully defending against a variety of critical P2P attacks.

The second key finding presented in this work concerns proof-of-work-based
strategies, often claimed to be effective against Sybil and eclipse attacks. We
have demonstrated that such proposals simply do not hold up to real-world
constraints, given the current prices of cloud computing power. This raises some
concerns, since even proposals questioning proof-of-work as an adequate defence
mechanism tend to simply propose different proof-of-work approaches.

---

[5] https://www.statista.com/statistics/306528/share-of-mobile-internet-traffic-in-
global-regions/.

The only other (significant) approaches towards tackling the problem of decentralised identifier generation are based on the graphs of nodes' social networks. It has been shown, however, that these mechanisms assume certain properties, which are not present in real-world P2P networks. This leads to identifier generation based on a trusted authority being the only defence that is known [4] to work.

# References

1. Baumgart, I., Mies, S.: S/Kademlia: a practicable approach towards secure key-based routing. In: 2007 International Conference on Parallel and Distributed Systems, pp. 1–8, December 2007
2. Benet, J.: IPFS - Content Addressed, Versioned, P2P File System (DRAFT 3). July 2014. https://ipfs.io/ipfs/QmR7GSQM93Cx5eAg6a6yRzNde1FQv7uL6X1o4k7zrJa3LX/ipfs.draft3.pdf (visited on 07/04/2017)
3. Cohen, B.: The BitTorrent Protocol Specification, 11 October 2013. http://www.bittorrent.org/beps/bep_0003.html. Accessed 24 Apr 2017
4. Douceur, J.R.: The sybil attack. In: Druschel, P., Kaashoek, F., Rowstron, A. (eds.) IPTPS 2002. LNCS, vol. 2429, pp. 251–260. Springer, Heidelberg (2002). https://doi.org/10.1007/3-540-45748-8_24
5. Fantacci, R., et al.: Avoiding eclipse attacks on Kad/Kademlia: an identity based approach. In: 2009 IEEE International Conference on Communications, pp. 1–5, June 2009
6. Heilman,E., et al.: Eclipse attacks on bitcoin's peer-to-peer network. In: 24th USENIX Security Symposium (USENIX Security 15), pp. 129–144. USENIX Association, Washington, August 2015
7. International Organization for Standardization: ISO/IEC 15408–1:2008 Information technology - Security techniques - Evaluation criteria for IT security - Part 1: Introduction and general model. Geneva, Switzerland, 15 January 2014
8. Johnson, D., Menezes, A., Vanstone, S.: The elliptic curve digital signature algorithm (ECDSA). Int. J. Inf. Secur. 1(1), 36–63 (2001)
9. Levine, B.N., Shields, C., Margolin, N.B.: A survey of solutions to the sybil attack. Technical report 2006–052. University of Massachusetts Amherst, Amherst, October 2006
10. Li, F., et al.: SybilControl: practical sybil defense with computational puzzles. In: Proceedings of the Seventh ACM Workshop on Scalable Trusted Computing, pp. 67–78. ACM, Raleigh (2012)
11. Maymounkov, P., Mazières, D.: Kademlia: a peer-to-peer information system based on the XOR metric. In: Druschel, P., Kaashoek, F., Rowstron, A. (eds.) IPTPS 2002. LNCS, vol. 2429, pp. 53–65. Springer, Heidelberg (2002). https://doi.org/10.1007/3-540-45748-8_5
12. Mazières, D., Frans Kaashoek, M.: Escaping the evils of centralized control with self-certifying pathnames. In: Proceedings of the 8th ACM SIGOPS European Workshop on Support for Composing Distributed Applications, pp. 118–125. ACM, Sintra (1998)
13. Moore, D.: Inferring internet denial-of-service activity. ACM Trans. Comput. Syst. 24(2), 115–139 (2006)
14. Moskowitz, R., Nikander, P., Henderson, T.: Host identity protocol. RFC 5201, April 2008. http://www.rfc-editor.org/rfc/rfc5201.txt. Accessed 05/04/2017

15. National Institute of Standards and Technology: SHA-3 Standard: Permutation-Based Hash and Extendable-Output Functions. FIPS PIB 202, 4 August 2015
16. Ratnasamy, S., et al.: A scalable content-addressable network. In: Proceedings of the 2001 Conference on Applications, Technologies, Architectures, and Protocols for Computer Communications, SIGCOMM 2001, pp. 161–172. ACM, San Diego (2001)
17. Singh, A., et al.: Defending against eclipse attacks on overlay networks. In: Proceedings of the 11th Workshop on ACM SIGOPS European Workshop, EW 11. ACM, Leuven (2004)
18. Stoica, I., et al.: Chord: a scalable peer-to-peer lookup service for internet applications. In: Proceedings of the 2001 Conference on Applications, Technologies, Architectures, and Protocols for Computer Communications, SIGCOMM 2001, pp. 149–160. ACM, San Diego (2001)
19. Viswanath, B., et al.: An analysis of social network-based sybil defenses. In: Proceedings of the ACM SIGCOMM 2010 Conference, pp. 363–374. ACM, New Delhi (2010)
20. Yu, H., et al.: SybilGuard: defending against sybil attacks via social networks. In: Proceedings of the 2006 Conference on Applications, Technologies, Architectures, and Protocols for Computer Communications, SIGCOMM 2006, pp. 267–278. ACM, Pisa (2006)

# A Robust Intrusion Detection Network Using Thresholdless Trust Management System with Incentive Design

Amir Rezapour[✉] and Wen-Guey Tzeng

Department of Computer Science, National Chiao Tung University, Hsinchu, Taiwan
{rezapour,wgtzeng}@cs.nctu.edu.tw

**Abstract.** Intrusion detection networks (IDNs) have been developed to improve the detection accuracy of a single IDS, by collecting intrusion intelligence knowledge and learning experience from other IDSs. However, some malicious IDSs within an IDN can corrupt the whole collaborative network. In this paper, we propose a robust trust management system, where each IDS evaluates the trustworthiness of its neighbors by making direct observations on their recommendations over time. We present a *thresholdless clustering technique* that automatically discards malicious neighbors. Our clustering approach with its effective features only needs to assume that each IDS has at least one honest neighbor. Hence, we do not need to assume that the majority of the involved IDSs are honest. Furthermore, we design an incentive utility function to penalize free-riders.

**Keywords:** Trust management model · Intrusion detection network
Collaborative network

## 1 Introduction

Nowadays, intrusion detection systems (IDSs) have been a de facto standard in many networks aiming to defend against a variety of attacks. Traditional IDSs work in isolation and may be compromised by unknown or novel threats. In addition, recent network threats become more complicated and are progressively difficult to detect [19]. As a part of an effort to remedy this shortcoming, IDS collaboration is regarded as a powerful approach to improve the detection capability of an individual IDS.

Intrusion detection network (IDN) which consists of many IDSs has been developed with the objective of strengthening a single IDS by collecting intrusion intelligence knowledge and learning experience from other IDSs. Collaboration not only enhances the detection capability of an individual IDS, but also equips it with the ability to discover new types of intrusions. Yet, newly proposed IDNs related to this context [15,21] assume that all IDSs behave honestly. However, some compromised IDSs within an IDN can corrupt the whole collaborative network. For example, malicious IDSs can use betrayal attack, Sybil

© ICST Institute for Computer Sciences, Social Informatics and Telecommunications Engineering 2018
R. Beyah et al. (Eds.): SecureComm 2018, LNICST 255, pp. 139–154, 2018.
https://doi.org/10.1007/978-3-030-01704-0_8

attack, collusion attack and inconsistency attack, to degrade the effectiveness of IDN by sharing false information. Hence, designing a robust IDN that effectively accounts for the trustworthiness of each IDS becomes crucial against the abovementioned attacks to maintain the detection capability.

In this work, we use a central repository, such as *Dshield.org* [1], of shared security logs from voluntary IDSs. Every voluntary IDS submits a security log to a central server once it detects a threat. The submitted security logs (recommendations) are used to help involved IDSs (a.k.a neighbors) to preemptively mitigate threats. For example, the server can compile a customized blacklist for each IDS using the shared security logs.

We investigate a robust approach that ensures reliability of recommendations coming from the neighbors of an IDS. In a society, trust value between two individuals is obtained after observing their behavior over time. Therefore, the aim is to establish a trust management system, where each IDS evaluates the trustworthiness of its neighbors by directly observing their recommendations over time. Hence, the effect of malicious IDSs with useless recommendations can be mitigated since lower trust values are assigned to them.

The contributions of our work are four-fold. First, we design a satisfaction function of a neighbor by evaluating validity of its recommendations to measure the satisfaction level. Second, we introduce a *thresholdless clustering technique* that nonparametrically discards malicious neighbors. Third, we design an incentive utility function to promote cooperation between IDSs. Fourth, we evaluate our trust management system on both simulated and real-world collaborative IDS network. In the real-world environment, our trust management system improved our previous result [14] in predicting malicious IPs.

## 2   Related Work

Intrusion detection networks can be grouped into information-based and experience-based IDNs. In information-based technique [3,15,20,21], intrusion samples and firewall logs are shared to improve the detection capability of an individual IDS. In experienced-based technique [6,7,10], an IDS sends suspicious data samples to a set of collaborators for further analysis. Feedbacks from collaborators are then aggregated to assist the sender IDS for decision making.

Many results use direct and indirect recommendations between an IDS and its neighbors to assess the trust values. The intuition is that when no direct observation between an IDS and a neighbor is available, the opinion of other neighbors can be considered. Nielsen et al. [13] proposed a Bayesian trust model, where the model predicts trust values based on both outcomes of the latest interaction and the history of trust information. Ganeriwal et al. [8] introduced a classical beta reputation system where an IDS applies both direct and indirect observations over time to evaluate other's trust values. Sun et al. [17] make use of entropy-based probability model to address uncertainty in measuring trust values. In the absence of direct observations, the uncertainty is measured through propagating indirect recommendations. Srour et al. [16] introduced a reputation-based trust network consisting of multiple trust domains which help to recognize the trustworthiness of other peers using its own experience and recommendations gathered by other peers in the network.

Another line of the work uses game theory [2,11,18] to model and analyze trust management system. In particular, Tuan [18] found that if a trust management system is not incentive, the higher the number of IDSs in network, the less likely that an IDS report a malicious neighbor.

Our work differs from previous work as we design a customized trust management system for a specific *centralized* environment. To evaluate the trustworthiness of IDSs, a number of results rely both on direct and indirect recommendations from their neighbors. However, in this work, we would like the trust values to reflect the direct observation of an IDS over its neighbors. The intuition is that when a direct interaction between an IDS and a neighbor is *not* available, then such a neighbor is irrelevant to the IDS.

In contrast to prior results [2,6–8,10–12,16–18], our goal is to propose a thresholdless approach to filter out the malicious IDSs.

## 3 System Model

### 3.1 Network Model

In our model, each IDS $i \in \mathcal{V}$ communicates to other IDSs through a centralized infrastructure (e.x., *Dshield.org*), called CE. Here, CE is a trusted third party that serves the IDSs. It receives attack alerts from each IDS. The alerts will be used later to provide useful recommendations to the other IDSs.

CE measures the similarity between IDS $i$ and its neighbors $j$ using a relevant similarity function $\mathsf{Sim}(i,j) \in [0,1]$ [14]. In [14], we let the similarity function to be a conditional probability $P(i|j) = \frac{p(i,j)}{p(j)}$, where the joint probability $p(i,j)$ is the probability that both $i$ and $j$ report illicit activities within some intervals over the number of intervals. $p(j)$ is the marginal probability of $j$. $P(i|j)$ is the probability of IDS $i$ to be threatened given that its neighbor $j$ was attacked. Using similarity values, for each IDS $i \in \mathcal{V}$, CE constructs a list of neighbors as $\mathcal{N}_i = \{j \in \mathcal{V} - \{i\} : \mathsf{Sim}(i,j) > \epsilon\}$. When IDS $i$ and its neighbor $j$ are highly similar ($\mathsf{Sim}(i,j) \simeq 1$), it is very likely that IDS $i$ uses some of the attack alerts (recommendations) of neighbor $j$. This is because similar IDSs might have similar vulnerabilities and they might be targeted by similar attackers [15].

### 3.2 Attack Model

**Sybil Attack:** It occurs when a malicious neighbor creates and maintains several fake identities.

**Betrayal Attack:** It occurs when a malicious IDS attains a high trust value and suddenly begins to act dishonestly.

**Collusion attacks:** The collusion attack occurs when several malicious neighbors collaborate through providing useless recommendations in order to damage the QoS.

**Inconsistency Attack:** It occurs when a neighbor frequently switches its behavior between honest and dishonest in order to reduce the QoS.

## 4  Trust Management System

We first model the trust values of neighbors of a given IDS by observing their behavior and then use the decision model to extract honest neighbors. Figure 1 summarizes the components of our trust management system. Each component consists of variables, along with its parameters (if applicable) in brackets. Each IDS $i$ receives recommendations from its neighbors through security logs. Using the recommendations and previous blacklist, we compute the satisfaction levels of its neighbors. Next, we use the beta model to update its neighbors' views, incorporating new observations. We also embed an aging factor into beta variables. Finally, we compute the trust values of its neighbors $j \in \mathcal{N}_i$.

In the decision model, we first normalize the accumulated beta variables. Then, we extract honest neighbors using correlation and normalized accumulated beta variables. We further use the extracted honest neighbors to update the correlation variables. Finally, we use both trust values and the extracted honest neighbors to compile a new customized blacklist for each IDS $i \in \mathcal{V}$.

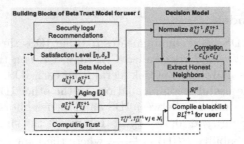

**Fig. 1.** The components of our trust management system.

### 4.1  Building Blocks of Beta Trust Model

**Satisfaction Level.** Our system uses a satisfaction function for each IDS to model the satisfaction levels of its neighbors. Suppose that a blacklist $BL_i^\tau$ that is compiled for IDS $i$ over time interval $\tau$, contains some attackers that are suggested by its neighbor $j$. Depending on the outcome, IDS $i$ would like to express how much it is satisfied with the list of the malicious IPs that are recommended by neighbor $j$. The satisfaction of neighbor $j$ held by IDS $i$ at time interval $\tau$ is given by

$$S_{i,j}^\tau = \begin{cases} \dfrac{\ln\left(\eta \dfrac{Hit(BL_i^\tau(j))}{max\left(|BL_i^\tau(j)|, AVG(BL_i^\tau)\right)} + 1\right)}{\ln(\eta+1)}, & \text{if } |BL_i^\tau(j)| > 0 \\ \delta_s, & \text{if } |BL_i^\tau(j)| = 0 \end{cases} \tag{1}$$

where $\eta > 0$ is a system parameter that controls the satisfaction curve. $|BL_i^\tau(j)|$ counts the number of the malicious source IPs in $i$'s blacklist that are suggested by neighbor $j$ at the end of the time interval $\tau$. $Hit(BL_i^\tau(j))$ counts the number of the malicious source IPs which are suggested by neighbor $j$ and actually attack IDS $i$. $AVG(BL_i^\tau)$ computes the average number of recommended malicious source IPs from neighbors of IDS $i$, i.e., $AVG(BL_i^\tau) = \frac{1}{|\mathcal{N}_i|} \sum_{j \in \mathcal{N}_i} |BL_i^\tau(j)|$ where $\mathcal{N}_i$ denote the set of $i$'s neighbors.

We also allow an IDS to be *silent* by not providing any recommendations. In order to discriminate silent IDSs from those malicious IDSs that provide useless recommendations, we reward silent IDSs with $\delta_s$.

**Trust Representation and Update.** Suppose a blacklist is compiled for IDS $i$ and its neighbor $j$ recommends some malicious source IPs. Depending on the result, IDS $i$ might assign the value 1 if the recommendation of neighbor $j$ is beneficial and 0 otherwise (e.g. in case $j$ is malicious or free-rider). IDS $i$ will then update neighbor $j$'s behavior, incorporating this new observation. Independently, IDS $j$ also creates its own view w.r.t. IDS $i$ over $BL_j$ and updates IDS $i$'s behavior. For simplicity, we will focus on the computation executed by IDS $i$ with the knowledge that the other IDSs in the system will follow similar computation after using their blacklists over a day.

Let $\theta$ be the view of neighbor $j$ to the eye of IDS $i$. Suppose that $\theta \in \Theta$ follows a beta distribution with parameters $\alpha_{i,j}^0$ and $\beta_{i,j}^0$ as $p(\theta) = \frac{\Gamma(\alpha_{i,j}^0 + \beta_{i,j}^0)}{\Gamma(\alpha_{i,j}^0) + \Gamma(\beta_{i,j}^0)}(\theta)^{\alpha_{i,j}^0 - 1}(1-\theta)^{\beta_{i,j}^0 - 1}$, where $\Gamma(.)$ is a gamma function. Initially, $\theta$ is an unknown parameter and takes all values between 0 and 1 uniformly random. To represent such uncertainty before receiving any recommendation from neighbor $j$, we can choose parameters $\alpha_{i,j}^0 = \beta_{i,j}^0 = 1$.

At time $\tau$, let $X_{i,j}^\tau \in \{0,1\}$ denote the binary rating of IDS $i$ on neighbor $j$ over a blacklist $BL_i^\tau$. Given $\theta$, we can model the probability that $X_{i,j}^\tau$ occurs in $\tau$'s interaction by $p(X_{i,j}^\tau|\theta) = \theta^{X_{i,j}}(1-\theta)^{1-X_{i,j}}$.

Once the blacklist expires, the posterior distribution of $\theta$ can be updated by applying Bayes' theorem by $p(\theta|X_{i,j}^\tau) \propto p(X_{i,j}^\tau|\theta)p(\theta) = (\theta)^{X_{i,j}^\tau + \alpha_{i,j}^0 - 1}(1 - \theta)^{\beta_{i,j}^0 - X_{i,j}^\tau}$.

A good point of using probabilistic model is that it requires IDS $i$ to maintain only two parameters to describe the behavior of neighbor $j$ and has very simple update steps once new recommendations are received as follows.

$$\alpha_{i,j}^{\tau+1} = \alpha_{i,j}^\tau + X_{i,j}^\tau \quad \beta_{i,j}^{\tau+1} = \beta_{i,j}^\tau + 1 - X_{i,j}^\tau \tag{2}$$

Now we consider the interactions between IDS $i$ and its neighbor as real-valued events with possible outcomes in the interval $[0,1]$. Generally, the soft assignment $(S_{i,j}^\tau)$ is more consistent in this context than the hard assignment $(X_{i,j}^\tau)$ as in real world scenarios the satisfaction reflects the quality of a service rather than its quantity. Ganeriwal et al. [8] showed that the binary observation $X_{i,j}^\tau$ in Eq. (2) can be replaced with the real-valued $S_{i,j}^\tau$ which is justified by using Dirichlet process for multi-values. Hence, the posterior beta distribution over real-valued observation is updated as follows[1].

$$\alpha_{i,j}^{\tau+1} = \alpha_{i,j}^{\tau} + S_{i,j}^{\tau} \quad \beta_{i,j}^{\tau+1} = \beta_{i,j}^{\tau} + 1 - S_{i,j}^{\tau} \tag{3}$$

**Aging.** We further incorporate an aging factor so that an IDS's trustworthiness is reevaluated continuously. It also provides resiliency against betrayal attack, where a neighbor behaves well for a long duration and then behave bad immediately. Hence, we embed an aging factor into the Eq. (3) as $\tilde{\alpha}_{i,j}^{\tau+1} = \lambda \cdot \tilde{\alpha}_{i,j}^{\tau} + S_{i,j}^{\tau}$, $\tilde{\beta}_{i,j}^{\tau+1} = \lambda \cdot \tilde{\beta}_{i,j}^{\tau} + 1 - S_{i,j}^{\tau}$, where $\lambda \in [0,1]$ controls the rate at which the old behaviors are discounted.

**Computing Trust.** A number of results [8,12,17] make use of posterior expectation of neighbor's behavior (Eq. (4) or Eq. (5)) and define a trust threshold to discard malicious neighbors. However, defining such a threshold requires a prior knowledge about IDS's behavior in different environments. Moreover, assigning a higher value might extremely limits the model with a few neighbors that can satisfy such a high threshold. Nevertheless, assigning a lower value will introduce useless recommendations to the IDSs. To remedy this shortcoming, we introduce our thresholdless clustering technique that automatically discards malicious neighbors.

We define the trust metric $T_{i,j}^{\tau+1}$ as IDS $i$'s prediction of the expected future behavior of neighbor $j$ at time interval $\tau + 1$ using the entropy function as

$$P_{i,j}^{\tau+1} = \mathbb{E}(Beta(\tilde{\alpha}_{i,j}^{\tau+1}, \tilde{\beta}_{i,j}^{\tau+1})) = \frac{\tilde{\alpha}_{i,j}^{\tau+1}}{\tilde{\alpha}_{i,j}^{\tau+1} + \tilde{\beta}_{i,j}^{\tau+1}} \tag{4}$$

$$T_{i,j}^{\tau+1} = \begin{cases} 1 - 0.5\mathcal{H}(P_{i,j}^{\tau+1}), & 0.5 \leq P_{i,j}^{\tau+1} \leq 1 \\ 0.5\mathcal{H}(P_{i,j}^{\tau+1}), & 0 \leq P_{i,j}^{\tau+1} < 0.5 \end{cases} \tag{5}$$

where $\mathcal{H} \in \{H_1(.), H_2(.), \ldots, H_\infty(.)\}$ with $\log n \geq H_1 \geq \cdots \geq H_\infty(.)$ is set of entropy functions. The choice of quantifying uncertainty using Shannon entropy has been introduced in earlier results [9,17].

### 4.2 Decision Model

**Extracting Effective Features.** In this section, we extract two effective features that discriminate between honest and malicious neighbors.

**Normalized Accumulated Satisfaction:** In our study, each IDS $i$ keeps a table of $\langle \tilde{\alpha}_{i,j}^{\tau+1}, \tilde{\beta}_{i,j}^{\tau+1} \rangle$ tuples of its neighbors that it has previously interacted with, where $\tilde{\alpha}_{i,j}^{\tau+1}$ and $\tilde{\beta}_{i,j}^{\tau+1}$ are the amount of trustworthy and untrustworthy of neighbor $j$, respectively. We consider those neighbors that continuously satisfy IDS $i$ as useful neighbors. Such IDSs would have $\tilde{\alpha}_{i,j}^{\tau+1} > \tilde{\beta}_{i,j}^{\tau+1}$. Otherwise, the

---

[1] The other possibility is to use quantification technique. However, it introduces a new parameter into the system.

neighbors are not useful and $\tilde{\alpha}_{i,j}^{\tau+1} < \tilde{\beta}_{i,j}^{\tau+1}$. Before applying clustering, the tuples are first normalized by using $\tilde{\alpha}_{i,j}^{\tau+1} + \tilde{\beta}_{i,j}^{\tau+1}$ to divide $\alpha_j^{\tau+1}$ and $\tilde{\beta}_{i,j}^{\tau+1}$ respectively.

**Correlation:** The next feature is dedicated to identify malicious neighbors within a given set of neighbors. For malicious neighbors, an effective strategy to harm the target IDS is to collude.

Suppose that the set of real honest and malicious neighbors denoted by $\mathcal{N}_i^H \subset \mathcal{N}_i$ and $\mathcal{N}_i^M \subset \mathcal{N}_i - \mathcal{N}_i^H$, respectively. Clustering can partition the set of IDS $i$'s neighbors into honest and malicious neighbors denoted by $\widehat{\mathcal{N}}_i^H \subseteq \mathcal{N}_i^H$ and $\widehat{\mathcal{N}}_i^M \subseteq \mathcal{N}_i^M$, respectively. We say a clustering technique is effective if $\widehat{\mathcal{N}}_i^H \cap \mathcal{N}_i^M = \emptyset$. Otherwise, colluders will succeed specially when they all appear in the same cluster as IDS $i$ and honest neighbors are in the other clusters.

We use correlation of the counts, for a pair of IDS and neighbor ($i \in \mathcal{V}, j \in \mathcal{N}_i$), that how often they appear together in the same and the opposite clusters. This feature excludes the influence of malicious neighbors ($i \in \mathcal{V}, j \in \mathcal{N}_i^M$) from honest neighbors ($i \in \mathcal{V}, j \in \mathcal{N}_i^H$). That is, the set of honest neighbors that continuously satisfying IDS $i$ would have relatively higher counts than the set of malicious neighbors. This indicates that a malicious neighbor can only appear as a honest neighbor only by withdrawing from collusion.

For each pair of IDS and neighbor ($i \in \mathcal{V}, j \in \mathcal{N}_i$), we maintain a counter $c_{i,j}^+$ that shows how many time periods they were together, and $c_{i,j}^-$ that how often they were in the opposite clusters. The correlation success probability $p_{i,j}^c$ can be estimated using beta distribution. We estimate the expected future correlation of neighbor $j$ held by IDS $i$ by $p_{i,j}^c = \mathbb{E}(Beta(\alpha_{i,j}^+, \beta_{i,j}^-)] = \frac{\alpha_{i,j}^+}{\alpha_{i,j}^+ + \beta_{i,j}^-}$.

**Our Clustering Approach for Extracting Honest Neighbors.** Algorithm 1 takes as input the feature vectors and neighbors $\mathcal{N}_i$ of IDS $i$ and proceeds as follows. First, it constructs a database $DB_i$ where each neighbor constitutes a row and values of the feature vector are used as attributes. In a next step, it invokes *Affinity Propagation* (AP) clustering method [5] which automatically specifies the number of clusters based on the input data. The cluster with the largest sum over the amount of trustworthy ($\sum_{j \in C_b} \frac{\alpha_b^{\tau+1}}{\alpha_j^{\tau+1} + \beta_j^{\tau+1}}$) is supposed to contain the strongest correlated honest neighbors. However, if the honest neighbors are minority and malicious neighbors are appear in the opposite cluster, then the simple summation over trustworthiness might become misleading. Therefore, we consider the *average* trustworthiness over the neighbors of a cluster as a more robust metric.

## 4.3   Utility with Incentive Design

After constructing trust management system, each IDS $i \in \mathcal{V}$ can leverage the trustworthiness and distrustworthiness of its neighbors to accept or reject their recommendation. We design an incentive utility function where the amount of recommendation that IDS $j$ provides to its neighbors is proportional to the

---

**Algorithm 1.** Extracting honest neighbors of IDS $i$

---

**Input**: *normalized accumulated satisfaction, correlation,* $\mathcal{N}_i$
**Result**: A set of extracted honest neighbors $\widehat{\mathcal{N}}_i^H \subseteq \mathcal{N}_i^H$

1  $DB_i = \langle \frac{\alpha_j^{\tau+1}}{\alpha_j^{\tau+1}+\beta_j^{\tau+1}}, \frac{\beta_j^{\tau+1}}{\alpha_j^{\tau+1}+\beta_j^{\tau+1}}, p_{i,j}^c \rangle \; \forall j \in \mathcal{N}_i$

2  $C_1, C_2, \ldots, C_z \leftarrow AP(DB_i)$

3  return $\text{argmax}_b(avg(C_b(\frac{\alpha_j^{\tau+1}}{\alpha_j^{\tau+1}+\beta_j^{\tau+1}})))$

---

trustworthiness and the amount of recommendation that is received from its neighbors. When an IDS decides to be silent and not provide any recommendations, then its neighbors will refuse to assist gradually. Therefore, *free-rider* neighbors are penalized through assigning a lower weight in the utility function.

Let $U_i^{\tau+1} : \mathbf{R}_{\widehat{\mathcal{N}}_i^H} \to \mathbb{R}$ represent the utility value obtained by IDS $i$ at time interval $\tau + 1$ by consuming the recommendations from $\widehat{\mathcal{N}}_i^H$.

$$U_i^{\tau+1} = \frac{\sum_{j \in \widehat{\mathcal{N}}_i^H} T_{i,j}^{\tau+1} \cdot T_{j,i}^{\tau+1} \cdot h_{j \to i}^{\tau+1}}{\sum_{j \in \widehat{\mathcal{N}}_i^H} h_{j \to i}^{\tau+1}} \tag{6}$$

where $h_{j \to i}^{\tau+1} \in \mathbb{R}_+$ is the recommendation's profit suggested by neighbor $j$ at time $\tau + 1$. $(T_{i,j}^{\tau+1} \cdot T_{j,i}^{\tau+1})^2$ is the weight on neighbor $j$'s recommendation. A higher weight is applied on neighbor $j$'s recommendation if neighbor $j$ and $i$ highly trust each other. In this event, IDS $i$ and $j$ are more generous to provide recommendations to each other. Any other way, if trust values are not proportional (e.g., $T_{i,j}^{\tau+1} > T_{j,i}^{\tau+1}$), neighbor $j$ limits its recommendation by assigning lower weight $(T_{i,j}^{\tau+1} \cdot T_{j,i}^{\tau+1})$.

Every IDS $i \in \mathcal{V}$ can maximize its utility as follows. Firstly, the utility function demands each IDS $i$ to choose a set of useful neighbors to maximize its utility. Secondly, it requires that such useful neighbors highly trust the IDS $i$, i.e., the weights $(T_{i,j}^{\tau+1} \cdot T_{j,i}^{\tau+1})_{\forall j \in \widehat{\mathcal{N}}_i^H}$ are high. The only possible solution to satisfy such a chain of dependency is that each IDS provides useful recommendation to its neighbors and hopes that in return, its neighbors also provide useful recommendations. This action also in return increases the trust values of its neighbors calculated by Eq. (5). The later can only be obtained by behaving well over a long period to build up high trust values. The former can be obtained by our clustering technique that effectively discards malicious neighbors and the utility function $U_i^{\tau+1}$ is computed using $\widehat{\mathcal{N}}_i^H$ instead of $\mathcal{N}_i$.

---

[2] Notice that $T_{j,i}^{\tau+1}$ is a private information of the IDS $j$. However, in our settings, the trust management system is centralized and a trusted third party (e.g., *Dshield.org*) honestly plays the roll of each IDS. Therefore, we have access to such private values.

# 5   Evaluation

## 5.1   Evaluation in Simulated Environments

**Simulation Setting.** The collaborative intrusion detection network, consisting of 30 IDSs $\mathcal{V} = \{1, 2, \ldots, 30\}$. Initially, we set the similarity values $\text{Sim}(i, j) = 1 \ \forall i \in \mathcal{V}, \ j \in \mathcal{N}_i$. To test trustworthiness of a neighbor $j \in \mathcal{N}_i$, its satisfaction level is randomly modeled from a $Beta(\alpha, \beta)$ distribution. We simulate an honest neighbor $j$ that always provides useful recommendations for IDS $i$ by setting $\alpha > \beta$. Otherwise, a dishonest neighbor $j$ is simulated by setting $\alpha < \beta$. The initial trust value of the neighbors $j \in \mathcal{N}_i$ are set to $Beta(1, 1) = 0.5$. We set the system parameter $\eta = 2$ and $\delta_s = 0.2$.

**Results for an Honest Environment.** In this experiment, we simulate the first 100 days to observe trust values of each neighbor, while all neighbors are honest. Moreover, the satisfaction level of all neighbors $j \in \mathcal{N}_i$ held by IDS $i$ are simulated by $Beta(20, 1)$.

Figure 2 shows trust values of a neighbor $j \in \mathcal{N}_i$ evaluated using different choices of aging factor $\lambda = \{0, 0.3, 0.99\}$. It shows that after 20–30 days trust values of the neighbor $j$ converges to the stable values. When $\lambda = 0$, the previous behaviors of the neighbor $j$ are ignored and the predicted trust values are highly fluctuating. In contrast, when $\lambda = 0.99$, the previous behaviors of the neighbor $j$ are highly incorporated into the predicted trust values and the red curve does not oscillate.

The black curve plots the trust value of a silent (free-rider) neighbor. As illustrated in Fig. 2, a silent neighbor's trust values slowly reduces with a long tail around $\delta_s$.

We observe that our clustering approach with different choices of $\lambda = \{0, 0.3, 0.99\}$ successfully group on average 23 neighbors in the same cluster as IDS $i$ starting from the second day even though their trust values are not very high. This decision is due to overall behavior of neighbors which are detected as well-behaving neighbors by providing useful recommendations. Such a rapid decision enables the IDSs to receive recommendations quickly and they no longer have to wait to reach a predefined threshold.

**Results for Malicious Environment.** The goal of this experiment is to measure the robustness of our trust model against attackers. Starting from day 101, neighbor $j \in \widehat{\mathcal{N}}_i$ switches to a malicious one, and therefore, IDS $i$'s satisfaction level reduces in each day. We instantiate the satisfaction level of the malicious neighbor $j$ held by IDS $i$ using $Beta(1, 20)$.

As illustrated in Fig. 2, trust values of neighbor $j$ held by IDS $i$ reduces after day 100. The aging factor $\lambda$ controls the reduction speed. Despite rapid or slow changes in trust values, our clustering approach successfully discards neighbor $j$ after 2 to 3 days. For example, when $\lambda = 0.99$, IDS $i$ discards neighbor $j$ after 3 days. The decision is based on observing a few useless recommendations of neighbor $j$. As illustrated in Fig. 2, trust values of the neighbor $j$ reduces significantly on day 101 over small choices of aging factor. If we were to use a predefined threshold, we could have discard neighbor $j$ on day 101. However, it is not logical to make such a decision by only observing one bad-behavior.

**Defense Against Betrayal Attack:** To further study the relationship between robustness of our trust model and betrayal attack, we randomly select 5 neighbors and have them to spread useless recommendations from day 110. In this experiment, we set $max(|BL_i^\tau(j)|, AVG(BL_i^\tau)) = 30$ in Eq. 1. That is, IDS $i$ will be fully satisfied if it receives 30 useful recommendations.

Figure 3 show trust values of the randomly selected neighbors held by IDS $i$ over different choices of $\lambda = \{0.3, 0.99\}$. The bars show the portion of the randomly selected neighbors that appear to be in the same cluster as honest IDSs. As shown in Fig. 3, since the randomly selected neighbors behaved well in the first 10 days, majority of them fall into the same cluster as honest IDSs. However, their portion reduces after they misbehave.

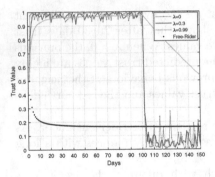 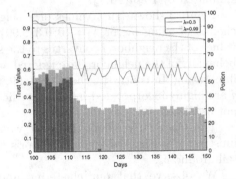

**Fig. 2.** In the first 100 days, trust values for honest neighbors converges using different aging factors. After day 100, trust values for malicious neighbor reduces over different aging factors.

**Fig. 3.** Convergence of trust values for malicious neighbors over betrayal attack. The red and blue bars show the portion of the randomly selected neighbors that appear in the same cluster as honest IDSs for $\lambda = 0.99$ and $\lambda = 0.3$, respectively. (Color figure online)

We observe that the impact of the reduction in a number of useful recommendations causes different interpretations. Depending on the aging factor $\lambda$, our trust model categorizes the behavior of the randomly selected neighbors as follows.

– When $\lambda = 0.99$, the randomly selected neighbors are treated as semi-trustworthy neighbors and their trust values are reduced. As presented in Fig. 3, a larger aging factor (red curve) highly incorporates their past well-behavior and reduces their misbehavior gradually. Therefore, the contribution

of the randomly selected neighbors decreases from day 111 and only some of appear in the same cluster as honest IDSs.
- When $\lambda = 0.3$, the randomly selected neighbors are treated as malicious neighbors, thus, they are discarded after 2 days. As illustrated in Fig. 3, a smaller aging factor (blue curve) quickly forgets the previous behaviors and reduces their misbehavior rapidly. In fact, the aging factor $\lambda$ provides such a resiliency against betrayal attack by reevaluating the trust values continuously. In addition, the recovery time is only 2 days as the trust values of malicious neighbors drop down and they are no longer in the same cluster as honest IDSs. Hence, from day 112, malicious neighbors are ignored and their influence is entirely eliminated.

**Defense Against Collusion Attack:** To demonstrate the robustness of our trust model against colluders, we consider the following scenario. We start by configuring a neighbor $j \in \widehat{\mathcal{N}}_i$ to switch to a malicious one by sending a few useless recommendations. We instantiate the satisfaction level of the malicious neighbor $j$ held by IDS $i$ using $Beta(1, 20)$. We increase the number of malicious neighbors until it reaches 28. We use utility function Eq. (6) to evaluate the influence of malicious neighbors on IDS $i$'s utility value. In Eq. (6), we let the recommendation's profit suggested by an honest neighbor $j$ to be $h_{j \to i}^{\tau+1} = Beta(20, 1)$, otherwise $h_{j \to i}^{\tau+1} = Beta(1, 20)$.

Figure 4 shows the utility values of the neighbors as a function of number of the colluding neighbors from 1 to 28. The blue curve remains almost the same regardless of number of the colluding neighbors. This indicates that our clustering approach is able to maintain a high utility value by correctly mitigating the effects of colluding neighbors. The improvement is done by assigning each IDS to the cluster with the highest *average* over the amount of trustworthy (for more details please refer to Sect. 4.2). Consequently, we do not need to assume that the majority of the neighbors are honest [6–11,16,17]. Our clustering approach with its *effective* features only needs to assume that each IDS has at least one honest neighbor. That is, as long as each IDS has one honest neighbor, the average trustworthy of the cluster that contains the honest neighbor stands relatively higher than other clusters. Since Algorithm 1 relies on a cluster with the largest average over the amount of trustworthy, the remaining clusters that contain malicious neighbors, no matter how large, are all discarded.

As seen in Fig. 4, the utility values of colluding neighbors (red curve) are strictly less than that of honest neighbors. In fact, their utility values drop drastically as the number of the colluding neighbors increases. Recall that we have 30 IDSs in our simulated environment and when the number of colluding neighbors changes, we have the following situations.

- When we have two colluding neighbors, each has up to 28 honest neighbors to choose with useful recommendations.
- When we have 28 colluding neighbors, each has up to two honest neighbors and the remaining neighbors are malicious.

Therefore, by increasing the number of colluding neighbors, the chance of receiving useful recommendation reduces. In addition, even though a colluding neighbor receives a useful recommendation from an honest neighbor, the profit of the received recommendation is weighted by the trust value of the honest neighbor. Since the trust value of the colluding neighbor held by the honest neighbor is low, the utility value of the colluding neighbor is always less than that of the honest neighbor.

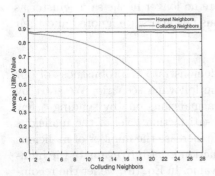

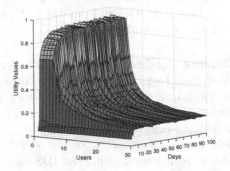

**Fig. 4.** Average utility value as a function of the number of the colluding neighbors. The blue and red curves plot the utility values of honest and malicious neighbors, respectively. (Color figure online)

**Fig. 5.** Utility values of the IDSs over 100 days. IDS 1 to 5 are honest and the rest are malicious neighbors that are behaving inconsistently.

**Defense Against Inconsistency Attack:** Recall that the inconsistency attack occurs when a neighbor frequently switches its behavior between honest and dishonest in order to reduce the QoS. In this experiment, we let 25 malicious IDSs collaboratively execute inconsistency attack. We simulate the behavior of inconsistent attackers more strategically. That is, a malicious neighbor sends a useless recommendation if and only if, it is in the same cluster as the targeted IDS. This prolongs the lifetime of the malicious neighbors for producing more damage. We give the description of malicious neighbors as follows.

1. Each malicious neighbor behaves well to appear in the same cluster as honest IDSs.
2. Once it appears in the same cluster as honest IDSs, it frequently switches to a malicious one by sending useless recommendations.
3. if the malicious neighbor is not in the same cluster as honest IDSs, go to 1.

Figure 5 shows the utility values of the IDSs over 100 days. IDS 1 to 5 are honest and the rest of them are malicious IDSs that behave with the aforementioned description. The utility values of the honest IDSs are strictly higher than that of malicious IDSs.

Previous works [8,16,17] rely on both direct and indirect recommendations between an IDS and its neighbors to assess the trust values. Since our target system works in a centralized environment, we did not compare our results with those that are not applicable in our environment.

**Sybil Attack.** A sybil attack [4] occurs when an intruder creates and maintains several distinct identities. The intruder uses fake contributors to gain higher influence for injecting useless recommendations. A trivial solution is to leverage an authentication mechanism (CA) and hope that registering fake contributor becomes more difficult. It worth nothing that if a CA is compromised, then sybil attack might become successful. *Dshield.org* does not require authentication to facilitate the contributors to engage into the system. In this situation, we would like to rely more on our trust model. Suppose many neighbors are registered as a new contributor. In this case, the result of Fig. 2 shows that it takes 2 days to gain enough trust and appear in the same cluster as the targeted IDS. Therefore, our model is robust against this attack. Moreover, the sybil attacker maintains some neighbors whose trust values are high and they are in the same cluster as the targeted IDS. If the intruder uses such neighbors to provide useless recommendation, then it is equivalent to betrayal attack.

Current studies [8,9,12,13,17] also fail to capture such a powerful sybil attacker. Perhaps a possible strategy is to leverage an authentication mechanism and a trust management system simultaneously to mitigate the effect of the sybil attacker [6,7,10,11]. We will follow this direction for future research.

### 5.2   Evaluation in a Real Environment

**The Dataset.** *Dshield.org* is a repository of firewalls and IDSs logs collected from a large number of IDSs over all the Internet. Every time an alarm is raised by an IDS's network, the IDS submits a log to the *Dshield.org* repository. The log contains IDS ID, target port, source IP, source port, Protocol ID, and time stamp. We use one month data (June 2017) that contains logs of 372 K IDSs and 2.4 M malicious source IPs.

**Setup.** We use a sampled dataset that contains logs of 562 active IDSs $\mathcal{V} = \{1, 2, 3, \ldots, 562\}$ and more than 391 K malicious source IPs. Initially, for each IDS $i \in \mathcal{V}$, we use the similarity function $\mathsf{Sim}(i, j)$ to build a set of neighbors $\mathcal{N}_i$. The initial trust value of the neighbors $j \in \mathcal{N}_i$ for all $i \in \mathcal{V}$ are set to $Beta(1, 1) = 0.5$. We set the system parameter $\eta = 2$, $\delta_s = 0.01$ and $\lambda = 0.99$.

Blacklists $BL_i^\tau \ \forall i \in \mathcal{V}$ are compiled at the end of each time interval $\tau$, and recompiled at the end of time interval $\tau + 1$. Hence, at the end of each time interval, we evaluate the effectiveness of the compiled blacklists. We use the prediction ratio, which is a ratio of the hit count $Hit(BL_i^\tau)$ over the number of the reported malicious source IPs from each IDS $i \in \mathcal{V}$ at time interval $\tau + 1$.

In our previous research [14], malicious source IPs are blacklisted using three predicators: *temporal attack predicator*, *victim similarity*, and *attacker correlation* models. In order to effectively incorporate the trust management system, we modify the *victim similarity* model in [14] and include trust values of both IDS $i$ and its neighbors $j \in \mathcal{N}_i$ as follows.

$$N_{a,i}^{\tau+1} = \frac{\sum_{j \in \mathcal{N}_i} (T_{i,j} * T_{j,i}) + \mathsf{Sim}(i,j) \cdot \mathsf{h}(tr_{a,j}(\tau, w))}{\sum_{j \in \mathcal{N}_i} (T_{i,j} * T_{j,i}) + \mathsf{Sim}(i,j)} \tag{7}$$

where $\mathsf{Sim}(i,j) \in [0,1]$ is a similarity function that outputs a higher value for strongly similar neighbors. $h(.)$ is a temporal attack predictor that estimates the probability that neighbor $j$ will be attacked by malicious source IP $a$ in time interval $\tau + 1$ given $tr_{a,j}(\tau, w)$, $w$ previous joint interactions of $j$ and $a$ up to time interval $\tau$.

**Prediction Performance.** Figure 6 compares the prediction ratios of our previous prediction algorithm [14] with and without trust management system. The x-axis is the test day, from 6 to 15. The y-axis is the average prediction ratio on the given day. The prediction ratios of the prediction algorithm without the trust management system (red curve) range from 21% to 24%. Whereas, the prediction ratios of the prediction algorithm with the trust management system (blue curve) range from 24% to 26%.

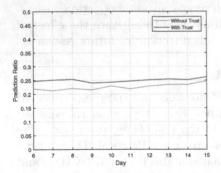

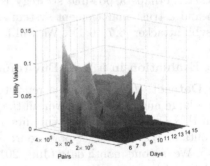

**Fig. 6.** The performance comparison of prediction algorithm [14] with and without trust management system. The first 5 days are used for training. (Color figure online)

**Fig. 7.** Utility values of IDS and neighbor pairs over 10 days.

We investigate the prediction ratio improvement across all IDSs. We observe that the discarded neighbors are not necessarily malicious as their recommendations are very useful for other IDSs. Since trust values are computed only based on individual interactions, each IDS $i$ can reflect its opinion over its neighbors $j \in \mathcal{N}_i$ using different trust values even though they share the same similarity, i.e., $\mathsf{Sim}(i,j) = \mathsf{Sim}(i,k) \ \forall j, k \in \mathcal{N}_i, \ j \neq k$. As a result, the smaller trust values in Eq. (7) assign relatively lower weights over irrelevant neighbors. Notice that the trust values here complement, but not replace the similarity function.

Overall, we observe that 30% of IDSs are free-riders, because all of the remaining IDSs reported them as a silent neighbor. They obtain a trust value of 0.066 after 10 iterations. A few neighbors are consistently sending useful recommendations and they always appear in the same cluster as their corresponding IDSs. Some neighbors are reported to be malicious by 52 IDSs, and some are reported by 155 IDSs. Totally, 69% of neighbors are reported to be malicious by some number of IDSs range from 52 to 155. Interestingly, only 2 to 20 IDSs reported that malicious neighbors have inconsistent behavior and the effect of all of them have been mitigated, thanks to the correlation feature.

Figure 7 shows the utility of IDS and neighbor pairs ($i \in \mathcal{V}, j \in \mathcal{N}_i$) over 10 testing days. 19% of pairs obtained a utility value in range $(0, 0.05]$. Only 17 IDSs maintained a utility value higher than 0.05 over all 10 testing days. We observed that the blacklist quality of these 17 victims are always higher than average prediction ratios in Fig. 6. This supports our hypothesis that the amount of recommendation that an IDS provides to its neighbors is proportional to the trustworthiness and the amount of recommendation that is received from its neighbors. When an IDS satisfies its neighbors, then the trustworthiness of its neighbors increases and it obtains a higher utility value in return.

# 6    Conclusions

We propose a trust management system which is robust against betrayal attack, Sybil attack, collusion attack and inconsistency attack. Our clustering approach with its effective features only needs to assume that each IDS has at least one honest neighbor. Hence, we do not need to assume that the majority of the IDSs are honest. Furthermore, we design an incentive utility function to penalize free-riders.

We analyze the performance our trust management system over both simulated and real-world collaborative IDS network. Experimental results show that our trust management system can effectively discard the malicious IDSs and increase the prediction ratios of our algorithm [14].

# References

1. Dshield dataset. https://www.dshield.org/
2. Alpcan, T., Basar, T.: A game theoretic approach to decision and analysis in network intrusion detection. In: Proceedings of 42nd IEEE Conference on Decision and Control, vol. 3, pp. 2595–2600. IEEE (2003)
3. Chen, S., Liu, D., Chen, S., Jajodia, S.: V-cops: a vulnerability-based cooperative alert distribution system. In: 22nd Annual Computer Security Applications Conference, ACSAC 2006, pp. 43–56. IEEE (2006)
4. Douceur, J.R.: The sybil attack. In: Druschel, P., Kaashoek, F., Rowstron, A. (eds.) IPTPS 2002. LNCS, vol. 2429, pp. 251–260. Springer, Heidelberg (2002). https://doi.org/10.1007/3-540-45748-8_24
5. Frey, B.J., Dueck, D.: Clustering by passing messages between data points. Science 315(5814), 972–976 (2007)

6. Fung, C.J., Baysal, O., Zhang, J., Aib, I., Boutaba, R.: Trust management for host-based collaborative intrusion detection. In: De Turck, F., Kellerer, W., Kormentzas, G. (eds.) DSOM 2008. LNCS, vol. 5273, pp. 109–122. Springer, Heidelberg (2008). https://doi.org/10.1007/978-3-540-87353-2_9

7. Fung, C.J., Zhang, J., Aib, I., Boutaba, R.: Robust and scalable trust management for collaborative intrusion detection. In: IFIP/IEEE International Symposium on Integrated Network Management, IM 2009, pp. 33–40. IEEE (2009)

8. Ganeriwal, S., Balzano, L.K., Srivastava, M.B.: Reputation-based framework for high integrity sensor networks. ACM Trans. Sens. Netw. **4**(3), 15:1–15:37 (2008)

9. Hongjun, D., Zhiping, J., Xiaona, D.: An entropy-based trust modeling and evaluation for wireless sensor networks. In: International Conference on Embedded Software and Systems, ICESS 2008, pp. 27–34. IEEE (2008)

10. Li, W., Meng, W., Kwok, L.F., IP, H.H.: Enhancing collaborative intrusion detection networks against insider attacks using supervised intrusion sensitivity-based trust management model. J. Netw. Comput. Appl. **77**(C), 135–145 (2017)

11. Marchang, N., Datta, R., Das, S.K.: A novel approach for efficient usage of intrusion detection system in mobile ad hoc networks. IEEE Trans. Veh. Technol. **66**(2), 1684–1695 (2017)

12. Nguyen, T., Seneviratne, A., Hoang, D., Nguyen, D.: Initial trust establishment for personal space IoT systems. In: IEEE Conference on Computer Communications Workshops (INFOCOM WKSHPS): MobiSec 2017 (2017)

13. Nielsen, M., Krukow, K., Sassone, V.: A Bayesian model for event-based trust. Electron. Notes Theor. Comput. Sci. **172**, 499–521 (2007)

14. Rezapour, A., Tzeng, W.G.: A robust algorithm for predicting attacks using collaborative security logs (2017). Manuscript

15. Soldo, F., Le, A., Markopoulou, A.: Predictive blacklisting as an implicit recommendation system. In: Proceedings of the 29th Conference on Information Communications, INFOCOM 2010, pp. 1640–1648. IEEE Press, Piscataway (2010)

16. Srour, L., Kayssi, A., Chehab, A.: Reputation-based algorithm for managing trust in file sharing networks. In: Securecomm and Workshops, pp. 1–10. IEEE (2006)

17. Sun, Y.L., Yu, W., Han, Z., Liu, K.J.: Information theoretic framework of trust modeling and evaluation for ad hoc networks. IEEE J. Sel. A. Commun. **24**(2), 305–317 (2006)

18. Tuan, T.A.: A game-theoretic analysis of trust management in P2P systems. In: First International Conference on Communications and Electronics, ICCE 2006, pp. 130–134. IEEE (2006)

19. Wu, Y.S., Foo, B., Mei, Y., Bagchi, S.: Collaborative intrusion detection system (CIDS): a framework for accurate and efficient IDs. In: Proceedings of the 19th Annual Computer Security Applications Conference, ACSAC 2003, p. 234. IEEE Computer Society, Washington, DC (2003)

20. Yegneswaran, V., Barford, P., Jha, S.: Global intrusion detection in the domino overlay system. In: NDSS (2004)

21. Zhang, J., Porras, P., Ullrich, J.: Highly predictive blacklisting. In: Proceedings of the 17th Conference on Security Symposium, SS 2008, pp. 107–122. USENIX Association, Berkeley (2008)

# A Metapolicy Framework for Enhancing Domain Expressiveness on the Internet

Gaurav Varshney and Pawel Szalachowski[✉]

SUTD, Singapore, Singapore
pawel@sutd.edu.sg

**Abstract.** Domain Name System (DNS) domains became Internet-level identifiers for entities (like companies, organizations, or individuals) hosting services and sharing resources over the Internet. Domains can specify a set of security policies (such as, email and trust security policies) that should be followed by clients while accessing the resources or services represented by them. Unfortunately, in the current Internet, the policy specification and enforcement are dispersed, non-comprehensive, insecure, and difficult to manage.

In this paper, we present a comprehensive and secure metapolicy framework for enhancing the domain expressiveness on the Internet. The proposed framework allows the domain owners to specify, manage, and publish their domain-level security policies over the existing DNS infrastructure. The framework also utilizes the existing trust infrastructures (i.e., TLS and DNSSEC) for providing security. By reusing the existing infrastructures, our framework requires minimal changes and requirements for adoption. We also discuss the initial results of the measurements performed to evaluate what fraction of the current Internet can get benefits from deploying our framework. Moreover, overheads of deploying the proposed framework have been quantified and discussed.

**Keywords:** Domain · DNS · TLS · Security policies · Certificates

## 1 Introduction

Domain names are a de facto standard way to identify computers, networks, services and other resources on the Internet. Domain security policies provide a way through which domain owners can specify the restrictions or rules that should be followed while accessing the computers, services or the resources represented by their domain names.

Currently, most of the domain security policies are either specified individually and published using the DNS infrastructure (e.g., SPF [10], DKIM [3], DMARC [13]—see Subsect. 2.3), or are specified at the domain web servers and communicated to *policy agents* [1] via dedicated HTTP headers (e.g., HSTS [7] or

---

[1] A policy agent is a software component that processes and enforces policies. It can be implemented within a user agent (such as a browser) or within a server software that supports a given policy.

© ICST Institute for Computer Sciences, Social Informatics and Telecommunications Engineering 2018
R. Beyah et al. (Eds.): SecureComm 2018, LNICST 255, pp. 155–170, 2018.
https://doi.org/10.1007/978-3-030-01704-0_9

HPKP [5]—see Subsect. 2.3). Finally, the obtained security policies are enforced by policy agents.

In some cases, the enforcement of security policies is not automated and requires user's involvement (i.e., users are making policy decisions). One example of such a case is accepting or denying a secure connection to a domain that presented an expired certificate. However, most of the security policies are standardized and governed by software vendors and Internet communities, and domains cannot influence this process and have to just follow these standards for specification of their security policies.

The current mechanisms of security policy specification and enforcement are unsatisfactory and the future Internet requires a higher level of domain expressiveness for the following reasons.

1. Users are not proficient enough to make security decisions when a policy agent requires that [4]. In the previous studies, it was observed that most of the users do not even notice the browser security indicators (like padlock icons), or they ignore warnings displayed to them by browsers and just *clickthrough* [4,12].

2. For scalability reasons, software vendors and the Internet community can only introduce global and generic policies without focusing on domain-specific policies. Obviously, global policies might not fit all domains as domains have different resources, services, and business models. One concrete example is a non-security-critical website (like a news or an informational website) that mostly displays a read-only content to its visitors and makes profits on ads. In such a case, the website may want to relax its security policies and display the content (and ads) to visitors, even if some security properties are not met (e.g., the website's certificate is expired). On the other hand, an e-banking website may need a stricter security policy that must generate an error and does not let its users interact with the website in a case of certificate errors. Domains are usually more aware of their security requirements and therefore they are the right candidates for policymakers. Unfortunately, the current policy specifications barely consider domain-specific requirements as of today.

3. Another consequence of policies implemented by software vendors is that these policies may be inconsistently enforced by different software implementations, especially, when a policy specification leaves some choices to developers. For instance, if browsers do not implement policy enforcement uniformly, it may cause a situation where users can switch from one browser to another in order to overcome a generated policy error (actually, such a behavior has been observed in the past). Hence any new framework of security policy specification could benefit from providing a way through which security policies can be specified and managed by domains with a relatively less involvement of software vendors, user agents, or even the users.

4. Downgrade attacks, like stripping of policy headers, is another problem. Policy headers can be manipulated by a Man-in-the-Middle (MITM) adversary, or at client-ends via modified implementation (like malicious browser extensions). Such a stripping of headers may lead to downgrade attacks, as an adversary can pretend to a client that the contacted domain does not deploy

the given enhancement or policy. Third party extensions such as *Modify headers for Google Chrome* [11] can be used to modify or strip off HTTP headers making it easier to compromise the security policies at the application layer itself. Downgrade attacks (arising from backward compatibility [20]) can be possible if an exploitable backward compatibility is provided by the user agents.

5. Already a set of security policies is getting expressed via domains (see Subsect. 2.3). Hence, the Internet security may get benefited if domains can easily express and manage more security policies in future.

For a better expressiveness of domain level security policies, we propose a metapolicy framework through which domains can specify and manage a comprehensive set of their security policies. The proposed framework leverages the DNS infrastructure for publishing and accessing metapolicies, and the trust infrastructures of TLS or DNSSEC to provide the necessary layer of security.

## 2    Background

### 2.1    Domain Name System

Domain Name System (DNS) [15] is a decentralized and hierarchical system which stores information about domains. Different types of information are stored in different resource records. Some of the DNS resource record types include A record that points a domain to an IPv4 address, CNAME record that points one domain to another domain, TXT record for storing human-readable textual information, or MX records for point to domain's mail exchangers. DNS is mostly known for resolution of domain names to IP addresses, however currently, the DNS is getting utilized for storage of email policies, information on domain certificates, and other domain related information. Publishing policies over DNS has an inherent benefit. As most of the times a DNS resolution precedes the communication with a domain, it is easy for the initiating party to fetch security policies prior to the connection. This also removes the need for communication with any other party (only DNS servers are contacted).

DNS Security Extensions (DNSSEC) [14] is an extension of DNS which provides security to the DNS records by adding cryptographic signatures on top of it. For each DNS zone a zone signing key (ZSK) pair and ZSK's private key is used to sign the DNS records (the corresponding signatures are stored in special RRSIG resource records). The ZSK public key is stored in the DNSKEY record. The DNSKEY record is also signed with the private key of another key pair known as Key Signing Keys (KSK). The chain of trust is followed till the root. This addition of signature on top of DNS records help in verifying the origin of the DNS records and in identifying if the records have been tempered during the transit via a MITM attack.

## 2.2  Transport Layer Security

Transport Layer Security (TLS) is a key protocol that provides confidentiality and data integrity on the Internet. The TLS handshake protocol is the initial phase of the TLS, and it provides a way through which the clients and the servers can verify each other identity via X.509 digital certificates [9] issued to them by trusted certification authorities (CAs).

X.509 public-key infrastructure (PKI) certificates are issued to domains (such as google.com) by trusted intermediate CAs (such as Google Internet Authority G3) forming trust chains. The certificate contains the details of the domain's identity and the domain's TLS certificate's public key. The information in the certificate is trusted as a trusted CA has signed it asserting its correctness. X.509 certificates are either signed by other intermediate CAs or the root CA and then a root CA (such as GlobalSign) may have a self-signed X.509 certificate that is stored by clients. The chain of trust can be verified till root CA to identify if the certificate issued to the domain is valid. Usually, only servers have their certificates (i.e., clients' identities are not verified by servers).

As communicating parties can verify their identifies, the TLS handshake protocol allows them to securely exchange secret session keys. The session key is then used for the encryption of data over a communication session between the clients and the servers.

## 2.3  Security Policies

Email and the TLS PKI are two key areas in which domains are currently expressing their security policies. Email policies are one of the oldest policies that rely upon the DNS infrastructure.

The Sender Policy Framework (SPF) [10] helps the receiving email server to identify whether the host from which the email has been originated is an authorized entity to send an email to the domain's owner. Spam and phishing emails can be filtered using this email policy. To deploy this policy the domain needs to add a TXT record in its DNS zone file, specifying authorized addresses (that can send emails on behalf of the domain).

DomainKeys Identified Mail (DKIM) [3] helps in verifying the authenticity of a given email. A domain supporting DKIM digitally signs the outgoing emails using a private key. The domain publishes the corresponding public key in the DKIM-specific DNS TXT records. A receiving email server accesses the public key from the DNS records of the email's originating domain. This public key is used to verify the digital signature of the email. DKIM aims to ensure that the email has not been modified in the transit and is signed by the correct outbound email server authorized to send email for that domain.

Domain Message Authentication Reporting and Conformance (DMARC) [13] is a policy system that allows domain owners to specify whether SPF or DKIM or both should be used while sending the emails for that domain and what the receiving email servers should do in the case of policy failures.

DNS-based Authentication of Named Entities (DANE) [8] is a TLS PKI policy system that provides a way to authenticate TLS entities without a CA. DANE introduces new TLSA records, that are published over DNS and signed are via DNSSEC. TLSA records provide domains a way through which they can specify which CAs can issue a valid TLS certificate for a domain and which TLS certificate to use for a specific service. If a browser supporting DANE get a TLS certificate for a domain which is not from the domain specified CA list, then it can display a warning to the user mentioning that the connection with the domain is insecure.

Certification Authority Authorization (CAA) [6] provides a mechanism by which domains can specify (over DNS) which CAs can issue certificates for them and their subdomains. It is required for a CA to retrieve a CAA record for a particular domain and follow the rules and restrictions before issuing a certificate for that domain.

Some policies are defined using HTTP headers, instead of employing the DNS infrastructure. For instance, HTTP Strict Transport Security (HSTS) [7] allows web operators to mandate access to their websites on HTTPS connections. Whenever a browser accesses a website for the very first time the website replies back with an HSTS header that specifies that the subsequent connections should be conducted over HTTPS. The browser caches this information and connects the website only via HTTPS even if the user types a URL with HTTP specified. Around 4.37% of the domains enforce HSTS and there has been an increase of around 69% in its usage in Q2 2017 [16].

Similarly, HTTP Public Key Pinning (HPKP) [5] is a policy mechanism that allows domains to express their keys or keys of their CAs using HTTP headers. Around 0.71% of domains on an average are expected to have enforced HPKP. There has been an increase of 42% in the use of HPKP in Q2 2017 [16]. However, browser vendors decided to obsolete HPKP due to operational issues [12].

The deployment of the presented policies was recently analyzed by Szalachowski and Perrig [19], and Amann et al. [2].

## 3   Requirements and Challenges

In the current Internet, there is no comprehensive and secure framework through which the security policies can be easily defined, managed, stored, and published by domain owners. We identify a set of requirements that such a security policy framework should follow to enhance the domain expressiveness on the Internet. These include:

1. **Easy Management:** The new policy specification framework or protocol must make it easy for domains to specify, manage, and publish various security policies at one place with a sufficient level of security from known threats.
2. **Security:** The protocol must provide security for policies, i.e., policy agents can verify their authenticity (i.e., that a given policy was indeed produced by the corresponding domain).

3. **Deployability:** The protocol must be easy to deploy, manage, and use. Moreover, policies should be disseminated and secured using the existing infrastructures to minimize operational and deployment costs.
4. **Recoverability:** The protocol should not end up in an unrecoverable state. It must provide suitable recovery mechanisms in the case of a policy misconfiguration.
5. **Adaptability:** The protocol must be adaptable in the sense that it can coexist with the currently deployed mechanisms without needing major changes.
6. **Availability:** Policies should be highly available and publicly accessible.

## 4    A High-Level Overview

To fulfill the above requirements we propose a comprehensive and secure metapolicy framework for specification and management of domain security policies. The framework allows the domains to specify, manage all the existing domain-level security policies as a metapolicy. Metapolicies are published in DNS and are secured using the existing TLS or DNSSEC PKI infrastructure.

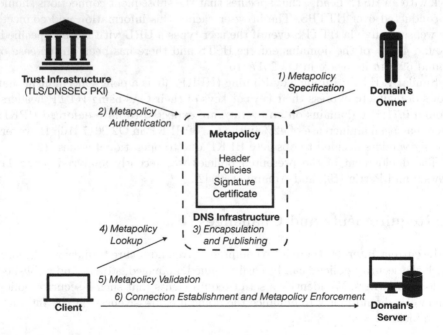

**Fig. 1.** A high-level overview of the metapolicy framework.

A high-level abstract overview of the proposed metapolicy framework is given in Fig. 1 and the sequential workflow is described as follows.

1. **Metapolicy Specification:** The domain-level policies are specified by the domain owners using the policy specification format of the metapolicy framework (details of the metapolicy format is given Sect. 5).
2. **Metapolicy Authentication:** The metapolicy is then signed using the domain's X.509 certificate private key or DNSSEC key. Since the domain's TLS certificate (or the DNSSEC key) can be verified, the domain binding with the metapolicy can be verified too.
3. **Encapsulation and Publishing:** Finally the signed metapolicy gets published in the DNS. To this end, the metapolicy has to be encoded as resource records. Publishing metapolicy in the DNS decreases the infrastructure cost and latency.
4. **Metapolicy Lookup:** Policies can then be queried by policy agents whenever a domain is going to be visited by a user (i.e., when a DNS resolution for a domain takes place).
5. **Metapolicy Validation:** The metapolicy's signature is verified using the domain's TLS certificate public key or the DNSSEC public key. All information required to validate the metapolicy is published as its part.
6. **Connection Establishment and Metapolicy Enforcement:** Once the metapolicy is verified the content of the metapolicy (individual security policies) are extracted and the specifications are enforced by the policy agents during the access to the domain's services and resources.

# 5   Details of the Framework

In the proposed framework all the domain security policies are included within a single metapolicy. Every metapolicy consists of:

- `Header`: This section contains metadata about the metapolicy.
- `Policies`: This section contains the actual content of the various security policies which are specified by the domain owner.
- `Signature`: This section contains a signature created using the domain's TLS certificate key or DNSSEC key over the metapolicy header and the policies section.
- `Certificate`: This section contains the domain's TLS certificate chain which is necessary to verify the authenticity of the created signature (i.e., whether the metapolicy was signed by the correct domain). When the metapolicy is signed with the DNSSEC key this field is empty, as the DNSSEC key of the domain can be obtained through the `DNSKEY` record.

The `Header` section contains the basic metadata about the metapolicy. In particular, it includes the following:

- `Domain` name on which the metapolicy is applicable. This is stored as a string.
- `Version` number of the metapolicy. The version increments when the metapolicy changes and an update happens. The version is represented as an integer. For example, a value of 1 in `Version` will represent the first version of the metapolicy.

- Valid From, Valid To dates in the $mm/dd/yyyy$ format to specify the time period in which the metapolicy is considered as valid. Time is expressed in the UTC standard.
- Parts specify the number of DNS TXT records (see below) that needs to be downloaded to get the contents of the complete metapolicy. If the complete metapolicy can be wrapped up in 512 bytes the value of Parts is set to 1 else it will always be greater than 1 and will correspond to the number of TXT records needed to store the complete metapolicy. This field is required to encapsulate and decapsulate metapolicies over DNS protocol.
- Subdomains section lists the subdomains which will also follow the specified policies. Hence inheritance is provided as the information of whether the subdomains will follow the domain policies can also be specified in the metapolicy. This section can store subdomain names as a comma-separated list (it can be also a *wildcard* domain).

The Policies section contains the actual content of domain security policies. Each policy has to specify these fields in the domain's metapolicy:

- ID specifies a unique RFC number of a specific security policy.
- Specification section contains the actual content of a policy.
- Fail section instruct the clients about what they should do if a policy failure happens (an error in a policy specification or an error during its enforcement). The failing function can be either hard, soft, or ignore instructing the policy agent, that if a policy failure happens, the client should either immediately terminate the connection (hard), or soft-fail (soft) and show a warning to the user, or just ignore this policy failure and proceed normally. Domains can also instruct clients to do error reporting to a set of email addresses in case of failures.

The Signature section stores the signature computed over the metapolicy Header and Policies sections. The key used for signing the metapolicy corresponds to the private key(s) of the domain's TLS certificate or domain's DNSSEC key.

The last section of the metapolicy is the Certificate section that stores the domain's X.509 certificate chain (i.e., domains certificate and certificates of intermediate CAs). This certificate chain is used by the policy agents for validation of the domain's TLS certificate and the signature of the metapolicy. The storage of all the certificates (required to establish the chain of trust) in the domain's metapolicy avoids the extra efforts of locating and downloading these certificates by the policy agents. When the metapolicy is authenticated with the DNSSEC key this section is empty.

Finally, the complete metapolicy is published via DNS. To do so, it has to be encapsulated into DNS resource records. A natural resource record type to store an arbitrary information is TXT. However, as shown by Szalachowski and Perrig [19] to transmit resource records reliably, they should not exceed 512 bytes. Therefore, if the total size of the metapolicy exceeds 512 bytes the metapolicy record is stored in parts up to 512 bytes each. The first part is published at _metapolicy.<domain_name> and the policy agents learn the number of parts by accessing the value of the Parts field from the metapolicy header (located in the first part). Other parts of a metapolicy are accessed by querying <part_number>._metapolicy.<domain_name> (e.g., 2._metapolicy.fb.com). An example policy is shown in Fig. 2.

```
Header:
    Domain: a.com
    Version: 1
    Valid From: 12/09/2016 UTC
    Valid To: 12/09/2018 UTC
    Parts: 1
    Subdomains: example.a.com, verbal.a.com
Policies:
    Id: 7288
    Specification: v=spf1 a include:aspmx.googlemail.com ~all
    Fail: hard, report@a.com

    Id: 6376
    Specification:v=DKIM1; k=rsa; p=TAMAfMAOGCSqGSIb3DQLOGE...
    Fail: soft, report@a.com

Signature: 9243152cd53fe3d1...

Certificate: MIIEBDCCAuygAwIBAgIDAjJ...
```

Fig. 2. An example of the metapolicy.

## 5.1  Metapolicy Lifetime

**Creation.** A domain creates its metapolicy by specifying the security policies in the format specified in Fig. 2. The domain then digitally signs the metapolicy with the private key(s) associated with its X.509 TLS certificate or with its DNSSEC private key. Finally, the signed metapolicy is published in the DNS as a series of TXT records.

**Querying and Enforcing Meta Policies.** Whenever a policy agent receives a request to connect to a domain it obtains the domain's metapolicy (if not cached) from the DNS TXT records of that domain. However, if the metapolicy for a domain has already been cached by the policy agent only the first DNS TXT record gets downloaded. The cached metapolicy is utilized and the complete metapolicy from the DNS does not get downloaded if the version of the metapolicy in the DNS is not higher than the version of the cached metapolicy.

Integrity and authenticity of the metapolicy content are guaranteed by the digital signature. To validate a metapolicy the policy agent must verify the `Signature` with the public key available from the domain's TLS certificate or DNSSEC. The client must also verify the domain's TLS certificate by validating the trust chain. If the signature verification succeeds the content of the specific security policies (identified by their ID) are fetched and enforced by the policy agent. Policy failures are handled and reported depending on the failing scenario specified (`Fail`).

A pseudocode that describes querying and enforcing of metapolicies is given in Algorithm 1.

**Updates and Recovery.** An update happens when at least one of the metapolicy section needs to be updated. The changes can be modifications of critical parameters (like adding or removing of security policies); update of the `Valid From` and `Valid To` field etc. In all cases, the metapolicy `Version` needs to be updated and a new signature must be calculated and placed in the `Signature` field of the metapolicy.

In the case when a cached metapolicy expires (i.e., the current date is greater than `Valid To`) the policy agent will fetch a new metapolicy published by the domain in the DNS. If by any chance the domain has not published a new metapolicy (a metapolicy with higher `Version`) the policy agent will use the cached metapolicy and report it to the domain. Because the policy agent queries the metapolicy header during each DNS query (i.e., each connection), it will download the newly published metapolicy once it finds that the `Version` number of the metapolicy in DNS is higher than that of the one stored in its local cache.

If the private key of the domain's TLS certificate or DNSSEC gets compromised or lost the last metapolicy published by the domain will still remain valid. This is because the policy agents can still verify the metapolicy using the domain's public key which will hold true until the TLS certificate corresponding to the compromised key gets revoked or a new DNSSEC key pair is generated and published. The certificate revocation does not affect the metapolicy framework because the policy agents who have already cached an old metapolicy will not be verifying the chain of trust again and whenever they find a higher version of metapolicy published in the DNS they will use the new chain of trust to validate the domain's new TLS certificate or DNSSEC key which is used to sign the metapolicy. Also, the metapolicy framework does not get affected when some of the intermediate CAs (in the domain's TLS certificate chain of trust) go out of business for the same reason. However, whenever a new TLS certificate is introduced the domain must remove the old certificate from the `Certificate` section and add the new certificate belonging to the new chain of trust. If with that change a domain's private/public keypair was changed, the domain must also update the old signature in the `Signature` section.

---

**Algorithm 1.** Querying and Enforcing Metapolicy

---

$M_{Domain}$: Domain's metapolicy
$S_{Policy}$: Metapolicy's signature
$DNS_{TXT}$: DNS TXT records storing the domain's metapolicy.
$DNS_{TXT\ Part\ 1}$: The first part of the metapolicy's DNS TXT record containing
the metapolicy's header information.
$M_{Domain}$(**Cache**): Client cached version of Domain's metapolicy specifications.
**Cache**: Client's/Server's local storage to store the metapolicy.
**Policy**: Stores the content of a security policy.
**Return**: Stores the execution status of the metapolicy querying and enforcement
operations.
**ID**: ID represents the RFC number of a specific security policy.
*Cached(X)*: Checks if the metapolicy for domain X is cached in the client's local
storage.
*FetchContent(X)*: Fetches the content of a security policy identified by ID X.
*Verify(X)*: Verify if the signature ($S_{Policy}$) of the metapolicy (represented by
X) is valid using the domain's TLS Certificate or DNSSEC key.
*Delete(X)*: Deletes the contents of the metapolicy X from the client's cache.
*Enforce(X)*: Enforce the specifications of policy X and return the execution
status as either success or failure (soft, hard, ignore).

**if** *Cached($M_{Domain}$)* **then**
    $M_{Domain} \leftarrow DNS_{TXT\ Part\ 1}$
    **if** $M_{Domain}(Cache) \rightarrow Version\ is\ equal\ to\ M_{Domain} \rightarrow Version$ **then**
        Policy $\leftarrow$ FetchContent(ID) (*From Cache*)
        Return $\leftarrow$ Enforce(Policy)
    **else**
        Delete($M_{Domain}$(Cache))
        $M_{Domain} \leftarrow DNS_{TXT}$
        **if** *Verify($S_{Policy}$) == Success* **then**
            Policy $\leftarrow$ FetchContent(ID)
            Cache $\leftarrow M_{Domain}$
            Return $\leftarrow$ Enforce(Policy)
        **else**
         |  Return $\leftarrow$ **hard**
        **end**
    **end**
**else**
    $M_{Domain} \leftarrow DNS_{TXT}$
    **if** *Verify($S_{Policy}$) == Success* **then**
        Policy $\leftarrow$ FetchContent(ID)
        Cache $\leftarrow M_{Domain}$
        Return $\leftarrow$ Enforce(Policy)
    **else**
     |  Return $\leftarrow$ **hard**
    **end**
**end**

---

# 6    Analysis

## 6.1    Security Analysis

We assume that the first connection to the DNS is not under attack because if that is the case then a MITM adversary could just censor all subsequent communication and clients would never reach a metapolicy. We also assume that the user's system and the policy agent are trusted and that the system is free from host-based malware. Study of the effects of malware on the security of the proposal is currently out of the scope of the current research work.

With the above assumptions the metapolicy framework can be compromised when: (1) the policy agents or user does a wrong decision in case of policy failures, or (2) when the key used to sign the metapolicy gets compromised or used PKI is compromised.

For the first case, as all the information resides within the metapolicy and is specified by the domain owners; the policy agents or the users are not involved in decision making during policy failures. Hence attacks arising from user's bad decision making or from provisions of backward compatibility cannot happen if the domain does not specify to take a user input or want the policy agents to fallback during a policy failure. The possibility of downgrade attacks also gets reduced with the use of our metapolicy framework because the policy agents can cache the metapolicy records.

An adversary able to compromise a domain's private key, or able to obtain a malicious certificate on behalf of the domain can create a malicious metapolicy. In such a case, the domain owner can initiate the recovery mechanisms, revoking the malicious public key and establishing a new metapolicy.

## 6.2    Deployability

As the proposed scheme uses the TLS or DNSSEC key(s) for signing the metapolicy, all the domains supporting DNSSEC or TLS can deploy the proposed metapolicy framework. To find out how many domains can possibly deploy our scheme we conducted an experiment over a dataset of 120 K top websites received from the Alexa top 1 million domains list [1]. We used the `tls-scan` library [17] to obtain these statistics. From our experiments, we identified that around 77.8% websites support TLS and 2.6% of the websites supports DNSSEC. Hence, a large fraction of websites can implement the metapolicy framework even today.

We also measured the percentage of domains which may get benefited via metapolicy framework. To calculate the same we conducted an experiment to obtain the number of websites that today implement a security policy that can be expressed by our metapolicy framework. The `host` command of Linux was used to fetch the records of various email and TLS policies from DNS. The outcomes of the experiment are given in Table 1. The obtained results indicate that majority of domains (around 76.3%) sets at least one security policy today.

**Table 1.** Number of websites supporting various domain policies

| Policy | Supporting websites | Percentage |
|--------|--------------------|------------|
| SPF    | 68213              | 56.00%     |
| DKIM   | 56704              | 46.60%     |
| DMARC  | 11973              | 9.80%      |
| DNSSEC | 3217               | 2.60%      |
| CAA    | 1213               | 0.99%      |
| DANE   | 34                 | 0.03%      |

**Table 2.** Number of domains supporting multiple security policies

| # of Policies | # of Domains | Percentage | # of Policies | # of Domains | Percentage |
|---------------|--------------|------------|---------------|--------------|------------|
| At least 1    | 92801        | 76.30%     | 1             | 53057        | 43.62%     |
| At least 2    | 39744        | 32.67%     | 2             | 31755        | 26.24%     |
| At least 3    | 7989         | 6.50%      | 3             | 7233         | 5.94%      |
| At least 4    | 756          | 0.62%      | 4             | 699          | 0.57%      |
| At least 5    | 57           | 0.05%      | 5             | 50           | 0.04%      |
| At least 6    | 7            | 0.01%      | 6             | 7            | 0.01%      |

## 6.3 Overheads

**Metapolicy Size.** Size of a TLS certificate chain is a dominant factor in the overall size of a given metapolicy. To find out how big this overhead is we conducted an experiment. During this experiment, we downloaded all certificate chains which are required for domain's TLS certificate validation for a domain set. We used the `openssl` tool for this purpose. The experiment was performed on the Alexa top 13k websites. We found that the average size of the of a certificate chain needed for a domain's TLS certificate validation is around 4.75 KB. Thus on average, a metapolicy protected with a TLS certificate will have to contain 4.75 KB for a certificate chain. (Note that policy agents do not have to store certificates of validated policies.)

To calculate the size of an average metapolicy we did an analysis of the results obtained in Subsect. 6.2. As shown in Table 2, around 33% of websites deploy at least two or more policies. With the results from Table 1 we can assume that on average policies implemented by domains will be either a SPF, DKIM or DMARC policy. We used this analysis to identify the size of an average metapolicy record. We created multiple metapolicy records with these three policies specified in it and stored domain's TLS certificate chain and a computed signature. We calculated the average size of metapolicy to be around 5.4 KB. Thus, on average, a metapolicy would require about 11 TXT records to be encoded.

**Latency.** Another overhead is the additional time needed for fetching a metapolicy. To calculate this overhead we performed an experiment sending DNS queries to calculate the time needed for fetching a single DNS TXT record. We identified that accessing it takes around 20 ms on an average, on a system having a network download speed of 13 Mbps. In the same setting obtaining additional 10 records, even sequentially (what is the worst case), increases the latency by 200 ms (for the records queried in parallel that should be around only 20 ms). Hence, the proposed metapolicy framework introduces an acceptable overhead on top of a normal DNS query for a metapolicy. However, once the metapolicy is cached only the first 512 bytes of the metapolicy (the first part) gets downloaded by the policy agents.

**Computational Overhead.** To identify the overheads of the certificate validation process (that will happen when the metapolicy's signature will be verified at the client) we used the `OpenSSL` library and the certificate chains obtained in the previous experiment. In our tests, we identified that it takes 4 ms on an average for the certificate chain and signature validation process. Hence the metapolicy verification introduces an acceptable overhead to a standard connection establishment.

## 7   Implementation

To implement a prototype of the proposed metapolicy framework, we used the Bind open source DNS server implementation. We configured a Bind to serve as a private DNS server. It ran under Ubuntu 16.04 equipped with Intel (R) Core (TM) i7-7600U CPU (2.8 GHz) with 8 GB of RAM. We created and published (in `TXT` records) an example metapolicy. We also prototyped a policy agent able to fetch and process metapolicies. Our experiments confirm the feasibility of our framework and deployability even with currently existing tools and libraries.

## 8   Related Work

Despite important of the topic, there has been a little work in the area of domain expressiveness over the Internet. In particular, we are not aware of any work which directly fits into our line of research work described in this paper. One example of domain expressiveness system is DMARC [13]. It is a policy system that allows domain owners to manage their email security policies (SPF and DKIM, specifically). DMARC, similarly to our system, uses DNS for publishing its policies. However, the scheme does not provide any security and has limited functionality.

Another related system is PoliCert [18] which enhances the security of the existing TLS PKI infrastructure by allowing domain owners to decide and define policies that govern the usage of their TLS certificates. The authors introduced the concept of subject certificate policies that provide domains a way to specify trusted CAs, their update criteria, error handling and private key loss mechanisms. To take care of a single CA compromise they introduced the concept of multiple signature certificates that allows multiple CAs to sign a certificate. PoliCert relies on verifiable public logs, thus it needs to introduce a new infrastructure.

# 9  Conclusions

In this paper, we presented a metapolicy framework for enhancing the domain expressiveness on the Internet. Our proposal provides domains a mechanism to define and manage domain related security policies themselves. All the metapolicies related to a domain and which the domains want to enforce can be mentioned in a metapolicy which is signed by the domain's private key corresponding to the domain's TLS certificate or DNSSEC key. The metapolicy is published as a series of DNS TXT records in the domain's DNS zone. Therefore, no new infrastructure is required, and our scheme can be deployed today.

The framework makes it easy for domains to manage the policy themselves. It also reduces the chances of a downgrade attack due to incorrect choices which can be made by a user or its user agent, because a fail-over mechanism as specified in the metapolicy has to be followed and neither the software or the user decides the fate of a policy failure. It also provides a simple way of management and specification of policies including the HTTPS related security policies likes HSTS or HPKP or Email related security policies including SPF, Sender ID, DMARC, DKIM or other security policies including the DANE or CAA. In future, we believe that more security policies can be expressed by domains through our proposed metapolicy framework.

**Acknowledgment.** We thank the anonymous reviewers whose feedback helped to improve the paper. This work is supported by SUTD SRG ISTD 2017 128 grant.

# References

1. Alexa. Alexa Top 1 Million Websites (2017). http://s3.amazonaws.com/alexa-static/top-1m.csv.zip
2. Amann, J., Gasser, O., Scheitle, Q., Brent, L., Carle, G., Holz, R.: Mission accomplished?: Https security after diginotar. In: Proceedings of the 2017 Internet Measurement Conference, pp. 325–340. ACM (2017)
3. Crocker, D., Hansen, T., Kucherawy, M.: DomainKeys Identified Mail (DKIM) Signatures. RFC 6376 (Internet Standard), September 2011
4. Egelman, S., Cranor, L.F., Hong, J.: You've been warned: an empirical study of the effectiveness of web browser phishing warnings. In: Proceedings of the SIGCHI Conference on Human Factors in Computing Systems, pp. 1065–1074. ACM (2008)
5. Evans, C., Palmer, C., Sleevi, R.: Public Key Pinning Extension for HTTP. RFC 7469 (Proposed Standard), April 2015
6. Hallam-Baker, P., Stradling, R.: DNS Certification Authority Authorization (CAA) Resource Record. RFC 6844 (Proposed Standard), January 2013
7. Hodges, J., Jackson, C., Barth, A.: HTTP Strict Transport Security (HSTS). RFC 6797 (Proposed Standard), November 2012
8. Hoffman, P., Schlyter, J.: The DNS-Based Authentication of Named Entities (DANE) Transport Layer Security (TLS) Protocol: TLSA. RFC 6698 (Proposed Standard), August 2012. Updated by RFCs 7218, 7671
9. Housley, R., Polk, W., Ford, W., Solo, D.: Internet x. 509 public key infrastructure certificate and certificate revocation list (crl) profile. Technical report (2002)

10. Kitterman, S.: Sender Policy Framework (SPF) for Authorizing Use of Domains in Email, Version 1. RFC 7208 (Proposed Standard), April 2014. Updated by RFC 7372

11. Kommareddi, A.: Modify Headers for Google Chrome (2017). https://chrome.google.com/webstore/detail/modify-headers-for-google/innpjfdalfhpcoinfnehdnbk glpmogdi

12. Kranch, M., Bonneau, J.: Upgrading https in mid-air: an empirical study of strict transport security and key pinning. In: NDSS (2015)

13. Kucherawy, M., Zwicky, E.: Domain-based Message Authentication, Reporting, and Conformance (DMARC). RFC 7489 (Informational), March 2015

14. Larson, M., Massey, D., Rose, S., Arends, R., Austein, R.: Dns security introduction and requirements (2005)

15. Mockapetris, P.V.: Domain names: Implementation specification (1983)

16. Pokeinthe.io. Analysis of the Alexa Top 1M sites, June 2017 (2017). https://pokeinthe.io/2017/06/13/state-of-security-alexa-top-one-million-2017-06/

17. Security Sauce. tls-scan (2017). https://github.com/prbinu/tls-scan

18. Szalachowski, P., Matsumoto, S., Perrig, A.: Policert: secure and flexible TLS certificate management. In: Proceedings of the ACM Conference on Computer and Communications Security (CCS), pp. 406–417, November 2014

19. Szalachowski, P., Perrig, A.: Short paper: on deployment of DNS-based security enhancements. In: Kiayias, A. (ed.) FC 2017. LNCS, vol. 10322, pp. 424–433. Springer, Cham (2017). https://doi.org/10.1007/978-3-319-70972-7_24

20. US-CERT. SSL 3.0 Protocol Vulnerability and POODLE Attack (2014). https://www.us-cert.gov/ncas/alerts/TA14-290A

# Adaptive Deterrence of DNS Cache Poisoning

Sze Yiu Chau[1](✉), Omar Chowdhury[2], Victor Gonsalves[1], Huangyi Ge[1],
Weining Yang[3], Sonia Fahmy[1], and Ninghui Li[1]

[1] Purdue University, West Lafayette, IN, USA
{schau,vgonsalv,geh,fahmy,ninghui}@cs.purdue.edu
[2] The University of Iowa, Iowa City, IA, USA
omar-chowdhury@uiowa.edu
[3] Google Inc., Mountain View, CA, USA
weiningy@google.com

**Abstract.** Many long-lived network protocols were not designed with
adversarial environments in mind; security is often an afterthought.
Developing security mechanisms for protecting such systems is often very
challenging as they are required to maintain compatibility with existing
implementations, minimize deployment cost and performance overhead.
The Domain Name System (DNS) is one such noteworthy example; the
lack of source authentication has made DNS susceptible to cache poisoning. Existing countermeasures often suffer from at least one of the
following limitations: insufficient protection; modest deployment; complex configuration; dependent on domain owners' participation. We propose CGuard which is an adaptive defense framework for caching DNS
resolvers: CGuard actively tries to detect cache poisoning attempts and
protect the cache entries under attack by only updating them through
available high confidence channels. CGuard's effective defense is immediately deployable by the caching resolvers without having to rely on
domain owners' assistance and is compatible with existing and future
solutions. We have empirically demonstrated the efficacy of CGuard. We
envision that by taking away the attacker's incentive to launch DNS
cache poisoning attacks, CGuard essentially turns the existence of high
confidence channels into a deterrence. Deterrence-based defense mechanisms can be applicable to other systems beyond DNS.

## 1 Introduction

At the inception of network protocol design and system development, designers
were oftentimes more focused on attaining scalability, instead of robustness in
adversarial environments. Security mechanisms were thus only introduced retro-
spectively after suffering damaging attacks. This requires security mechanisms
to be compatible with existing installations, manage overhead and deployment
cost, and remain incentive compatible at the same time. Such design restrictions
induce security mechanisms that are often ineffective in many corner cases or

© ICST Institute for Computer Sciences, Social Informatics and Telecommunications Engineering 2018
R. Beyah et al. (Eds.): SecureComm 2018, LNICST 255, pp. 171–191, 2018.
https://doi.org/10.1007/978-3-030-01704-0_10

require major infrastructural overhaul that risks widespread adoption. One pragmatic approach to remedy this often hopeless situation, is to aim for deterrence. The key idea behind practical deterrence-based defense mechanisms is to ensure that the attacker has to invest a substantial amount of resources to carry out a successful attack, hence removing the incentives for attackers to launch attacks. Such a principle is reminiscent of the classic deterrence theory [59]. In this paper, we *apply the principle of deterrence-based defense for the case of DNS*.

DNS is a critical part of the core Internet infrastructure. From the outset, DNS lacked a robust mechanism to authenticate DNS responses which enabled attackers to poison a caching resolver's cache of DNS entries by response spoofing—violating the integrity guarantees expected from DNS caches. Despite years of patching, DNS cache poisoning attacks still plague the DNS infrastructure [5,6,30,33]. As shown by recent reports, successful cache poisoning can further enable a variety of other attacks; *e.g.*, mail handling hijacks [53,58], drive-by downloads [13], and phishing [20,48,50].

The revelation of the *Kaminsky attack* in 2008 [35] was a wake-up call for the DNS community. Many software vendors started to implement source port randomization [15]—the effectiveness of which has been shown to be limited, particularly if the resolver is behind a Port Address Translator (PAT) that uses a deterministic port allocation scheme [2,28,34]. Efforts have also been made in further increasing the entropy of DNS packets [22,44]. This line of defense, however, faces a dichotomy of challenges: each proposal has its own corner cases that limit robustness; and using such mechanisms while remaining compatible with entities that do not support them requires significant management effort [7].

An alternative is to run the DNS protocol on top of TCP [RFC5966] instead of the connectionless UDP. TCP provides better DNS response authentication than UDP. However, as reported in previous studies [10,19,31,32,60,62] and also observed in our own experiments, DNS over TCP, if not deployed with carefully chosen optimizations (recommended but not mandated by [RFC7766]), incur a noticeable overhead and negatively impact overall DNS performance.

Another line of cache poisoning defenses (*e.g.*, DNSSEC, DNSCurve), employs cryptographic primitives to provide authenticity guarantees to DNS response. DNSSEC in particular has been considered to be the future of DNS. These solutions, however, have not seen prevalent adoption. The deployment of DNSSEC is currently very limited [54,57], and ICANN will not deploy DNSCurve in the root zone due to key distribution and management issues [17].

The central research question we seek to answer in this paper, is *whether it is possible to design a robust defense mechanism for resolvers—without cooperation from the domain owners—that is applicable irrespective of the deployment rate of new defenses (eg., DNSSEC)?* We focus our discussion on recursive resolvers, as they are higher-valued attack targets than stub resolvers (*i.e.*, resolvers running on a client machine) due to impact on more victims, and we argue that operators of recursive resolvers have an incentive in deploying reliable DNS services for their customers. We particularly focus on racing cache poisoning attacks carried out by off-path/blind attackers.

To this end, we propose an adaptive defense framework against DNS cache poisoning that we refer to as CGuard. In short, CGuard actively tries to detect attack attempts on cache entries and switches to a higher confidence channel for cache updates. Though mechanisms that switch to TCP during spoofing attacks have been described before [29,41], developing a robust but flexible adaptive defense involves subtle design decisions that, as we show through a case study, if not chosen carefully, can make the resolver vulnerable to an adaptation of Kaminsky attack.

CGuard provides strong guarantees and is readily deployable by operators of recursive resolvers. As a flexible framework, CGuard can be instantiated by configuring its detection sensitivity and providing a list of usable channels, ordered in preference. Since the various high-confidence channels are used only when CGuard detects an attack, it greatly limits any attacker's success probability while maintaining a good overall performance. This also allows the various proposed high confidence channels to potentially cover for each other in terms of both corner cases and availability.

We envision that by ensuring attacks have a low probability of success, the incentives for rational attackers to launch poisoning attacks could be removed, effectively turning CGuard into a deterrence, without having to always pay for the high overhead associated with the various high confidence channels.

**Contributions.** In summary, this paper makes the following two contributions. **First**, we show how previously proposed cache poisoning defenses, though well-designed, fall short in practice due to different reasons. **Second**, based on the lesson learned from an adaptive defense case study, we design the CGuard adaptive deterrence framework against racing cache poisoning attacks, and empirically evaluate its effectiveness based on a particular instantiation of CGuard that we implemented.

## 2    Background

We now give a brief primer on DNS, and establish some of the terminology and notations that are used throughout the rest of the paper. For a detailed taxonomy of DNS cache poisoning attacks, we refer the readers to [52].

DNS queries from users are typically sent to an upstream *recursive resolver*, which will fully answer the query (or give an error) by traversing the DNS domain tree and querying other name servers. When a valid response is received, it is used to answer the query and cached for future queries. DNS queries and responses typically go over UDP, though the standard also supports message exchange over TCP. A response over UDP is considered valid if the query information, including the transaction ID (TXID), query name, and query type, matches that of the query. As such matching heuristic is not strongly authenticated, this presents an opportunity for cache poisoning attacks [49].

Depending on their capabilities, cache poisoning attackers can be classified as *in-path*, *on-path*, and *off-path*. On-path attackers have the ability to observe DNS query packets, and therefore can easily create forged response packets that will be accepted. In-path attackers have the additional capability to delay and drop packets. These are usually powerful nation-state adversaries, often used in implementing censorship [23,40]. For DNS resolvers that operate outside the jurisdiction of such censors, however, connection controlling in-path and on-path attackers are much less likely. One is mostly concerned about *off-path* attackers who cannot observe but can query resolvers with domain names of their choosing. Protecting DNS resolvers against such off-path attackers is extremely important, as the number of parties who can potentially carry out off-path attacks could be very large. In addition, once a cache entry is poisoned, it can affect other clients that are configured to use the same resolver.

## 3 Assessing Proposed Defenses

We now discuss previously proposed defenses against cache poisoning, with a focus on their deployment challenges, availability, and corner cases.

### 3.1 Increasing Entropy

One school of thought on hardening DNS is to introduce more entropy on top of the 16-bit entropy provided by TXID.

**Source Port Randomization.** One possibility is to use random source ports for DNS UDP queries [2,15]. This defense is adopted by several major DNS implementations. Ideally, close to 16 bits of entropy would be added. However, network middleboxes (*e.g.*, the likes of firewalls, proxies and routers) that perform Port Address Translation (PAT), depending on their configurations, might reduce the randomness of UDP source ports used by resolvers behind them [2,34], and such resolver-behind-NAT scenario is reported to be quite common [26,28]. It has also been shown that if a DNS server and an attacker-controlled machine are behind the same NAT, then the attacker can force the NAT to make highly predictable choices of UDP ports, possibly removing any extra entropy [28].

**0x20 Encoding.** This mechanism rewrites the domain name in a DNS query by randomly using upper/lowercase letters [22]. If a domain name contains $k$ alphabetic characters, the entropy gain is $k$ bits. The method is less effective for domain names with few letters. To poison the entries for name servers of .com, attackers can send queries with domain names such as 853211.com in Kaminsky attacks [28]. Another deployment hurdle is that some name servers always respond with names in lowercase [7]. Some others, in violation of the DNS standards [RFC4343], try to match the exact case of the name in the query, hence fail to resolve. Google Public DNS's solution is to create a whitelist of name servers which is compatible with 0x20 encoding. Name servers in the whitelist constitute about 70% of all traffic [7].

**WSEC DNS.** Another proposal is to prepend a random nonce label to query QNAME [44]. This is possible because, in most cases, requests to the root or top-level domain (TLD) name servers will result in a referral to a name server lower in the hierarchy, instead of an actual answer with IP addresses. For example, asdf.www.msn.com should yield the same resource record (RR) as www.msn.com when querying the root or .com name servers. It has been argued that WSEC DNS is ineffective against Kaminsky attacks [28]. This is because the total number of characters in a domain name cannot exceed 255, thus attackers can query near 255-byte-long domain names to circumvent the mechanism. Furthermore, this defense applies only to requests where referrals are expected. The Google DNS team faced challenges in deciding when is such defense applicable [7].

**Randomizing Destination and Source IP Addresses.** Destination IP address can be randomized if there exists a pool of possible server addresses, and source IP address can be randomized at an NAT that can inspect and rewrite IP addresses. The actual entropy gain of these two proposals, however, are logarithmic to the number of servers and size of a network, hence often quite limited.

**Summary.** Proposals on increasing entropy are generally opportunistic, and there exist corner cases that would yield limited gains. Some mechanisms like WSEC DNS and 0x20 encoding require significant manual effort on tracking incompatible servers. Consequently, when we develop our adaptive approach, we do not use these mechanisms.

## 3.2  DNSSEC

DNSSEC (Domain Name System Security Extensions) digitally signs DNS RRs using public-key cryptography [RFC4033–4035]. Although DNSSEC was proposed back in 1997 [RFC2065] its adoption has been slow. The number of DNSSEC validating clients is growing, albeit slowly [4,12,38]. Meanwhile, the adoption rate on the domain side remains low. It has been shown that only around 1% of all the .com and .net domains are secured by DNSSEC [27,54,57]. The measurement of our experiment below shows similar findings. To enjoy the assurances of DNSSEC, domain owners are often required to take the initiative in configuring it. Misconfiguration can be used by DDoS reflection attacks [18,47], and can lead to loss of users [38]. A recent study showed that many DNSSEC-signed domains are also plagued by poor key generation practices [51]. There are no real technical reasons why DNSSEC should not be used, though cost and management issues exist that are deterring adoption.

**DNSSEC Support.** To test whether DNSSEC is deployed, for each authoritative name server address[1] we request the DNSKEY type record of the domains for which it is authoritative. If a domain has DNSSEC correctly deployed, the

---

[1] We obtained 18,075 unique IP addresses from 19,669 authoritative name servers of the top 20,000 domains as ranked by Alexa. Many of our subsequent experiments are also based on this data.

authoritative name servers should return a response with DNSKEY type and a RRSIG type RR. We then consider the authoritative name server as supporting DNSSEC if the signature validates. A domain is considered to support DNSSEC if all its authoritative name servers support DNSSEC. We observe that *among the top* 15,000 *domains, only* 1.1% *have DNSSEC support.*

**Summary:** DNSSEC availability is currently very limited but we will use it in our adaptive defense mechanism whenever applicable, as it has been standardized and the Internet community has been promoting its adoption [8,9,39].

### 3.3    DNS over TCP

Although TCP support is mandated by the standard, it is typically only used by resolvers as a fall-back mechanism when packets are long, or if a TCP connection has already been established and is open [RFC5966]. DNS over TCP enjoys both reliable transport and extra entropy. Specifically, the combined entropy from TXID and TCP sequence number is high enough to make off-path attack unappealing. We would like to quantify the overhead if all the resolutions are done over TCP.

**TCP Support.** For each authoritative name server address, using TCP as the transport protocol, we ask for the A records of the domains it is authoritative for. If a valid response is returned, then this authoritative name server address is considered to support TCP. If not, we send the same query again but through UDP, to verify that the server is responsive. In the end, 636 addresses did not respond to any TCP or UDP queries. *Out of the* 17,439 *authoritative name server addresses that responded,* 15,774 (90.4%) *support TCP. About* **85%** *of the top* 15,000 *domains have TCP support on all of their authoritative name servers.*

**TCP Overhead in Recursive Resolvers.** We empirically determine the overhead a recursive resolver incurs due to resolving queries iteratively through TCP. We extract domains whose authoritative name servers support TCP, and query for A records using the drill utility. For each domain, after measuring the latency with UDP, we clear the cache, reset the resolver software, and then measure the latency with TCP. This guarantees that the recursive resolver will perform iterative queries from the root for each measurement instance. In the end, the average time for UDP was 423 ms/domain and TCP was 834 ms/domain, over 17,340 domains. *On average, the total communication overhead for TCP is roughly twice of UDP, as shown in* Fig. 1. This result is consistent with the number reported in a recent work [62] (Fig. 7(b), with full TCP handshake and no connection reuse), which is unsurprising as each such DNS over TCP instance needs two round-trip times whereas UDP needs only one [62].

We note that various optimizations like connection reuse, pipelining and out-of-order processing that can improve the performance of DNS over TCP are also discussed in [62]. For the latter two, as noted in [62], major software have no/partial support, so we do not consider them here. For connection reuse, its effect depends on actual traffic pattern and server configurations. Also note that in [RFC7766], connection reuse and pipelining are recommended but not mandated for clients. Our experiments here can be thought of as stressing servers at a worst-case scenario.

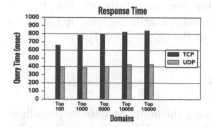

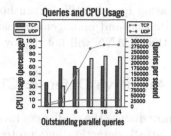

**Fig. 1.** Resolution latency between recursive and authoritative servers

**Fig. 2.** Service rate and CPU usage of an authoritative server

**TCP Overhead in Authoritative Name Servers.** We attempt to find empirically, from the point of view of an authoritative name server, how much overhead it will incur if all the resolvers use TCP for queries, without connection reuse.

We did an emulation study using a machine with Intel Core i5 2.5 GHz CPU and 8 GB RAM, running Unbound 1.5.4 configured as an authoritative name server (of a local zone). Client is another machine with Intel Core i7 2.2 GHz CPU and 16 GB RAM running a modified version of queryperf++ [56].

For both TCP and UDP, we vary the query window size (*i.e.*, number of parallel outstanding queries on the client side) to produce different volumes of traffic. For each window size, the average CPU usage of the authoritative name server for {TCP, UDP} is obtained by taking the mean of 600 data points measured over 1,200 s of queries. The results can be found in Fig. 2. As we allow more outstanding parallel queries, the service rate (queries responded per second) also increases, up to a point where it saturates. *Comparing to TCP, UDP yields a higher peak service rate.* When the window size is 2 for UDP and 6 for TCP, the service rate becomes comparable, and UDP exhibits a much lower (roughly half) CPU usage than that of TCP.

**Summary:** TCP support is widely available, though without the recommended optimizations, it negatively impacts overall DNS performance, which motivates the benefits of having an adaptive deterrence that uses the TCP channel. Given its standardized status and good general availability, we will use TCP in our adaptive defense mechanism whenever applicable.

### 3.4 Other Defenses

Other proposals including CoDNS [43], DoX [61], ConfiDNS [45] and Anax [11] require significant resources and changes to the DNS infrastructure in order to be deployed at DNS resolvers, making their adoption unlikely.

Another cryptographic mechanism is DNSCurve [14]. Though promising, it has not received wide deployment on authoritative name servers. Overhead is one of its discussed drawbacks, particularly because embedding cryptographic keys in names would render existing resolver caching mechanisms ineffective [36], increasing query traffic at authoritative name servers. Moreover, due to key distribution and management issues in potentially hostile regions, it has been said that ICANN will not deploy DNSCurve in the root zone [17].

## 4    Adaptive Defense: Challenges

We now discuss the challenges involved in making the adaptive defense paradigm (i.e., attack detection and protection) effective against Kaminsky-style racing cache poisoning attacks. Though adaptively switching to TCP during spoofing attack has been mentioned as a possible countermeasure before [29,41], to make such a defense robust and widely applicable is actually non-trivial. The intricacies are hidden in (1) the decision logic of when to use which channel, (2) the granularity of detection and protection, and (3) the availability of high confidence channels and a reasonable preference. Using a real world instantiation from Nominum [41] as a case study, we will explain the associated challenges and show how a simplistic implementation falls short in effectiveness. Our design decisions will be discussed in Sect. 5.

### 4.1    Preliminary

**Threat Model:** We consider an off-path or a blind attacker targeting a DNS caching resolver. The attacker can neither observe any outgoing query posed by the resolver nor has the capability to stop it. We also consider the attacker to have the knowledge of the deployed mechanism enabling him to adapt his attack strategy. We consider that the TXIDs are randomly generated and are unpredictable to the attacker. Finally, we assume that the attacker may control many edge hosts (e.g., a botnet) and have coordination capabilities resulting in a substantial amount of attack bandwidth.

**Mismatched DNS Response and Attack:** If a DNS resolver sends a DNS query $q$ and receives a response $r$ such that $r$ agrees with $q$ on all the deterministic fields but disagrees on one or more of the randomized fields (e.g., TXID, source port), then we call the response $r$ a **mismatched DNS response**.

At a first glance, it seems very enticing to consider receiving any mismatched DNS response to be a sign of active cache poisoning attack; we want to point out that a mismatched response can also occur in a benign setting. Suppose a resolver does not get a response to a pending DNS query within a threshold amount of time, and it sends out a new query with a new random TXID. While waiting for the response to the new query, the old response arrives, and the old response's TXID does not match the current pending query's TXID. This is plausible as UDP does not provide reliability guarantees.

**Kaminsky Attack:** Suppose an off-path attacker Adv intends to poison caching resolver R's DNS cache entry for `google.com`'s authoritative name server (e.g., `ns1.google.com`). Adv starts off by querying R with an inevitably non-existant domain of the form `dshmik.google.com` which is unlikely to be stored in R's cache, resulting in a cache miss. Without loss of generality, suppose the IP address of `google.com`'s name server `ns1.google.com` (e.g., 1.2.3.4) is stored in R's cache and random `TXID` is the only form of available entropy. In which case, R will query `ns1.google.com` to resolve the query.

Adv then races the legitimate name server's response by flooding R with fake DNS responses with spoofed source IP address 1.2.3.4 where it tries different values of `TXID`. Adv generated fake DNS responses contain a glue record which provides the IP address of `ns1.google.com` to be one of Adv's choice. If one of the fake responses submitted by Adv contains the correct `TXID` and it arrives before the legitimate response, R will cache the malicious glue record; poisoning it. Once poisoned, any future resolution of any subdomain of `google.com` (e.g., `docs.google.com`), Adv's name server is going to be consulted. If Adv cannot guess the correct `TXID`, he can restart the same attack with a different non-existant domain (e.g., `rksjtw.google.com`). This attack has the following two desirable characteristics over regular cache poisoning: (1) The attacker can start the attack without having to wait for a cache entry to expire; (2) The attacker does not have to pay any penalty (i.e., no waiting), even if he cannot submit a fake response with correct `TXID` before the legitimate response arrives.

**Nominum's Adaptive Defense:** In Nominum's approach implemented in their proprietary Vantio CacheServe product, whenever a resolver receives a mismatched DNS response for an outstanding DNS query, the resolver considers the query to be under attack and immediately switches to TCP for responding that pending query. For spoofing the DNS response, the attacker additionally has to guess the TCP sequence number increasing the overall entropy to around 48 bits (i.e., 32 bit TCP sequence number + 16 bits for `TXID`).

## 4.2   Attack Detection: Challenges

We now discuss the challenges a resolver has to overcome for effectively detecting an active cache poisoning attempt.

(1) **Attack Detection Settings:** A resolver can possibly attempt to detect an attack in a **local setting** or in a **global setting**. In the local setting, the resolver checks to see whether a particular unit is under attack. In case of a detected attack, only that unit is protected. In this setting, different protection units are considered independent. *Nominum's attack detection operates in the local setting.* Depending on the attack detection granularity (discussed next), it may be possible to bypass the detection mechanism in the local setting by slightly modifying the original Kaminsky attack.

In the global setting, however, when the resolver detects an attempted attack, it proactively starts protecting all the cache entries. Under the assumption that cache entry protection incurs some amount of additional overhead (e.g., network bandwidth, memory), even if only one query (or cache entry) is under attack, other queries will suffer, thus it is undesirable to always use this setting.

(2) **Granularity of Detection and Protection:** A fundamental challenge in successfully detecting cache poisoning attacks is to be able to correlate different attack instances. In the above example of Kaminsky attack, both dshmik.google.com and rksjtw.google.com queries are part of the attacker's goal of poisoning the name server (e.g., ns1.google.com) of google.com. This induces the critical design decision of the granularity of attack detection. The three alternatives are: (i) **per-query**, (ii) **per-domain**, and (iii) both **per-query** and **per-domain**.

In the per-query attack detection, whenever the resolver receives one or more mismatched responses for a pending DNS query, the query (answered in the Answer Section of the responses) is considered to be under attack. When a resolver, however, is detecting attack at per-domain granularity, it considers its zone to be under attack if the domain (and its subdomain) was in the records of the Additional Section of one or more mismatched DNS responses. Detecting attacks at both the per-query and per-domain granularity offers better protection. *Nominum's implementation detects attack at per-query granularity and it is susceptible to the following attack.*

**Bypassing Per-Query Attack Detection:** Detecting attacks at per-query level, with mismatch threshold of one, only limits an off-path, Kaminsky-style attacker to send one mismatched response for each attack query. After the first mismatched response, the resolver will start protecting the query (e.g., using TCP to resolve the query as in Nominum's implementation) thwarting all subsequent forged responses by the attacker. **However, it does not stop the attacker to start a new attack instance right away.** This is due to the fact that the resolver cannot correlate two attack instances dshmik.google.com and rksjtw.google.com, by only keeping track of queries. One can thus modify the original Kaminsky attack, which we dubb as **Parallel Kaminsky Attack (PKA)**, to send only one forged response (instead of many forged responses) for each non-existant DNS query.

Each PKA instance has a $\frac{1}{2^r}$ success probability when $r$-bit entropy is available to the resolver. For the traditional Kaminsky attack, on the contrary, if the attacker can send $n$ forged responses before the legitimate response arrives, the attacker's success probability is $\frac{n}{2^r}$. A PKA instance succeeds when the *single forged response* for the query happens to match. The attacker, however, does not need to wait until one attack has failed to carry out another attack. If the resolver has only a 16-bit entropy, either because source port randomization is not available or is severely limited, and the attacker can cause the server to send, *e.g.*, 500 queries/second, then it takes just a couple of minutes for PKA to succeed. With 30-bit entropy, it takes the attacker about 2 days to succeed. *Note that imposing rate limiting on outstanding queries of the same question (i.e., Birthday attack [42] protection) does not prevent PKA as the query for each PKA instance is different.*

(3) **Storing Attack History:** Irrespective of the attack detection setting and granularity, the affected domains, queries, or cache entries should be stored in some data structure so that the resolver can protect them. One of the main challenges is the resolver-side overhead and accuracy trade-off for storing attack information. If the resolver stores fully accurate attack information, the attacker can strategically make the overhead prohibitive whereas if the resolver stores attack information in a probabilistic data structure (e.g., bloom filter) its attack detection accuracy may deteriorate due to false positives. One possibility is to maintain a fixed-size cache which contains fully accurate attack information. This, however, signifies that past information may have to be evicted to accommodate new attack information, exposing an attack vector where an attacker can strategically try to remove entries from the attack history cache.

(4) **Lifetime of an Attack Entry:** The next natural question is how long does the resolver protect a query, a domain, or a cache entry under attack. This is similar to the time-to-live (TTL) field for DNS cache entries. Suppose the TTL of an attack entry is 2 min. In this case, a greedy attacker with the goal of poisoning one of the top 100, 000 domains can possibly carry out a **spray attack** on different domains. Such an attack could be carried out by posing the following queries in succession: $\langle random_1 \rangle$.`google.com`, $\langle random_2 \rangle$.`facebook.com`, $\langle random_3 \rangle$.`yahoo.com`, ... By the time attacker comes back to attacking `google.com` again, hopefully the 2 min are up; forcing the resolver to forget about the attack on `google.com`.

## 4.3   Protection: Challenges

Under the assumption that an effective attack detection mechanism is in place, the resolver has to establish a mechanism to protect a domain, a query, or a cache entry. The following are few possibilities with which a resolver can protect a domain, a query, or a cache entry.

(1) **Employ a High-Confidence Channel:** Although DNS was designed to run on top of UDP for scalability, some authoritative name servers expose high confidence channels such as TCP and DNSSEC. When a resolver detects an attack on a cache entry (or, a query), it can employ one of these high confidence channels to update the cache entry under attack. Along with the additional overhead imposed by these high confidence channels, one of the major obstacles of employing high confidence channels is their low adoption rate. *Nominum's implementation employ TCP as the high confidence channel.* Based on our measurements in Sects. 3.2 and 3.3, among Alexa's top 15, 000 domains, TCP availability is about 85% and DNSSEC availability is about 1%. This means more high-confidence channels are needed to provide protection to more domains.

(2) **No Caching:** When a resolver detects an attack on a cache entry, it may decide not to update the entry even if it is part of a possibly legitimate

response (e.g., glue record). This, however, leads to significant performance degradation due to the need to traverse the domain hierarchy even for benign cases.

**Summary: Why Nominum's Adaptive Defense Approach is inadequate?** Nominum's implementation does not achieve the full defense potential due to the following two limitations: (I) Due to their query level attack detection, they are susceptible to PKA; (II) They do not take into consideration the possibility of an authoritative name server not supporting TCP.

# 5  CGuard: An Effective Adaptive Defense

We now present our instantiation of the adaptive defense paradigm which we refer to as by **CGuard**. CGuard *proactively tries to detect racing cache poisoning attack attempts and switches to one of the available high confidence channels to update those cache entries that are under attack.* We detail CGuard's attack detection, the high confidence channels we currently consider, and the overall defense mechanism.

## 5.1  Attack Detection of CGuard

CGuard conservatively detects attack at both global and local setting. To prevent spray attacks across a large variety of different domains, if CGuard observes a total of mm_thresh (default value 10, configurable) mismatched responses over the last 10 min, it considers a system-wide attack and starts protecting all cache entries. In other case, CGuard detects attack at local setting using both per-domain and per-query granularities for attack detection. For storing attacks CGuard uses a set-associative cache with least-recently used (LRU) replacement policy. We use a non-cryptographic hash function to map a domain to its set in the attack cache. The life-time of each attack entry is attack_TTL with the default value being 15 min.

For a pending DNS query, *if CGuard receives a mismatched response, we conhis channel is applicable for a query whosesider the query, the additional* RR*s, and their associated zones* to be under attack. A DNS response can have additional RRs that the resolver did not *explicitly* ask for. These additional RRs can be viewed as prefetching of NS records (authoritative name server records) signifying that the authoritative name server of a domain has changed. For each RR in the additional section of a mismatched response, we consider that RR's domain (and if it is an NS record, then also its zone), to be under attack. This is based on the intuition that if the TXID would have matched, then the RR would have been cached, and hence it is safe to consider it under attack. Without considering the zone of the RRs to be under attack, the threat of PKA lingers as demonstrated by the following example.

**Example Attack Scenario.** Suppose an attacker Adv started a PKA instance by posing an A-type query for a non-existent domain xdRfggh.google.com.

Obviously, there is no A record in the resolver R's cache for that domain. Suppose R has not observed any attack so far. R starts traversing the domain hierarchy and observes that it has the following authoritative name server for the zone google.com in its cache: ns1.google.com. Suppose that R also has the name servers' A records in its cache and sends the query to it. Adv then sends a mismatched, forged response for xdRfggh.google.com; trying to poison the cache entry for ns1.google.com. A hypothetical attack detection mechanism that does not add the name servers' zone, will add the following domains to the attach cache: xdRfggh.google.com and ns1.google.com. In the next PKA instance, Adv sends an A record request for YUrrpom.google.com to R. R will ask ns1.google.com for the A record of the domain YUrrpom.google.com. However, this time around Adv gets lucky and correctly guesses the TXID. In this forged response, Adv also adds a new name server for google.com, say ns2.google.com, and provides a glue record for it. The glue records for ns1.google.com can be ignored as it is under attack. However, the glue record for ns2.google.com will be cached resulting in a cache poisoning. If we monitor whether a name server's zone is under attack, in the above example, we will check whether google.com is under attack—which it is—before we add an NS record for google.com and update the A record for ns2.google.com, hence thwarting the attack.

## 5.2  High Confidence Channels

CGuard uses high confidence channels to update a cache entry when that entry is affected by a detected attack. As an abstract framework, CGuard can be instantiated to use any desirable high confidence channels in a preferred order in actual deployment. As discussed in Sect. 3, various previously proposed defense proposals currently suffer availability issues and a lack of robustness given certain corner cases. We envision that by combining them in the CGuard way, the high confidence channels that stem from the various proposals can effectively cover for each other.

In our particular instantiation, we choose to use plain UDP as the base channel, as it has the best availability and performance. Alternative, one can choose to always use a base channel that is of higher confidence (e.g., TCP, 0x20 Encoding [22], etc.) at additional performance and management costs.

We now present the high confidence channels that we consider in our implementation of CGuard for the resolver to resolve DNS queries under active cache poisoning attack. For ease of management, we focus on leveraging existing standardized channels (i.e., UDP, TCP, and DNSSEC), though this is not an inherent restriction of the CGuard framework. We leave the incorporation and the subsequent evaluation of other high confidence channels (e.g., the likes discussed in Sect. 3, as well as the new proposed standards of DNS over TLS/DTLS [RFC7858, RFC8094]) as future work.

Having multiple such channels is vital as some of these channels are not supported by certain name servers. Based on our measurements in Sect. 3, 14.79% of Alexa's top 15,000 domains have authoritative name servers that support neither TCP nor DNSSEC. Consequently, we propose to leverage three high confidence channels in addition to TCP and DNSSEC. The first two are both based on the fact that the mappings between domain names and IP addresses of a large number of domains remain fairly stable over time; we call this the **domain name-IP stability** observation. One may question the mapping stability given the prevalence of CDNs (Content Delivery Networks). We note that not all CDNs perform DNS-based redirection. In fact, a large portion of CDNs leverage anycast-based services [1,21,24,37,46,55], where one IP address is shared by various hosts distributed in different locations. Comparing to DNS-based CDNs, anycast-based setups are generally considered to be more resilient to DDoS attacks and more compatible with public resolvers [16].

**UDP Double Query (UDQ).** One possible high confidence channel that leverages the *domain name-IP stability* observation, is for the resolver to simultaneously send out two queries with the same question over UDP. If answers to both queries match and there is no attack detected then we can accept the answers with high confidence. We call this channel "UDQ".

**UDQ Support.** This experiment is to determine when an authoritative name server is queried two consecutive times over UDP about the same domain, would the addresses it returns be the same. For each of the name servers we found, we send two A queries about a domain for which it is authoritative. Once the responses are received, we compare the IP addresses in the two responses. If the sets of IP addresses match exactly, the domain is said to support double query. We found **89.57%** *of Alexa's top* 15,000 *domains exhibit double query stability.*

**Long-Term Stability (LTS).** This channel is applicable for a query whose answer is already in the cache but the entry's TTL has expired. In such a case, one can send out a DNS query over UDP and if the answer (*i.e.*, IP address for A query) in the DNS response matches the value in the cache, then we can take that answer to be correct with high confidence. This is safe under the assumption that the DNS cache was *not* poisoned to begin with.

**LTS Support.** For measuring this, we keep querying name servers about domains for which they are authoritative over a period of 30 days (from Sept. 11, 2015 to Oct. 11, 2015). Our goal is to validate that the mappings between a domain and its addresses remain mostly stable over time. *We observed that for the top* 15,000 *domains,* **94.3%**, **92.7%**, *and* **88.8%** *of them have the exact same list of addresses after 7, 14, and 28 days, respectively.*

In addition to the main domains (*e.g.*, nih.gov), we also correlated with the data from DNSCensus 2013 [3]. We found 25502 existing subdomains (*e.g.*, dpcpsi.nih.gov), and measured the stability of their address over a period of two weeks (from May 4, 2016 to May 18, 2016). *About* **95%** *of them have the exact same list of addresses after 12 days.*

**Public Resolver over TCP (PR-TCP) as a Last Resort.** According to our experiments, 5.41%of Alexa top 15,000 domains do not support any of the aforementioned high confidence channels. In such cases, one possibility is to ask a somewhat trusted public resolver to resolve the query over TCP. We call this channel "PR–TCP". The rationale for not always using PR–TCP is that (1) simply delegating all queries to PR-TCP has additional privacy implications; (2) there may be conflict of interests between the recursive resolver provider and companies behind public resolvers like Google and Cisco; (3) always relying on public resolvers may negatively impact the optimality of DNS-based redirections in CDNs. We thus consider using PR–TCP only as a last resort.

**High Confidence Channel Preference.** Our preference criteria is jointly based on network delay and confidence level. LTS is our first choice as it has the lowest cost (the resolver has to send only one UDP query) while delivering a fairly high confidence. We then prefer DNSSEC as it can run on top of UDP and does not incur the connection establishment cost of TCP while delivering a higher confidence. Finally, TCP has a higher confidence than UDQ. Hence, we use the following preference in our mechanism: LTS > DNSSEC > TCP > UDQ.

If desired, CGuard can be flexibly instantiated with **other preferences** on the high confidence channels. For example, one might prioritize confidence level and use the channels in this order: DNSSEC > TCP > LTS > UDQ.

## 5.3 CGuard's Adaptive Defense: Putting It Altogether

We now briefly describe how CGuard's active, fine-grained attack detection and use of high confidence channels achieve a robust defense against racing cache poisoning attacks; removing the incentive of a rational attacker to attack a CGuard resolver and consequently achieving deterrence. Note that when we refer to the attack state of a CGuard resolver we mean CGuard's attack cache and global attack state (timestamps of most recent mm_thresh attacks).

When a CGuard resolver receives a client DNS query and the answer to the query is in the cache, CGuard responds with its cached result. In case of a cache miss, CGuard consults the attack state to see whether the system is either under global attack, or a particular query, domain or zone is under attack. In case of an attack, CGuard uses one of the high confidence channels to resolve this query and update its cache. If a domain's authoritative name server ns does not support a particular high confidence channel $hc_1$, it goes to the next available high confidence channel according to our priority (see Sect. 5.2) and in the process stores the information that ns does not support $hc_1$. When resolving for the same domain (or, its zone) in future, this information can be used to avoid walking the priority chain of high confidence channels. When such information expires in the cache, CGuard will once again walk through the chain of possible high confidence channels, which can be thought of as a passive probing of the domain for newly added high confidence channels. In the case that neither the query (domain or its zone) nor the whole system is under attack CGuard resumes its benign behavior by using UDP.

When CGuard receives a matched DNS response through a high confidence channel, it caches it and uses it to possibly respond to pending client queries. In case the response arrives through UDP (as in normal DNS operation), it consults the attack state to see whether to cache it. If the attack state does not point to attack to the query (or, its zone) or the system, it caches it; otherwise, it drops the packet and sends the query with a high confidence channel. In case of a mismatched response through UDP (as in normal DNS operation), CGuard updates the system's attack state.

# 6    Evaluation

**Setup.** For evaluation purposes, we use Unbound 1.5.4 as a recursive resolver, and also use it as an authoritative name server (of a local zone). Our version of CGuard was also implemented based on Unbound 1.5.4. Here we evaluate CGuard along two dimensions: (1) the overhead it incurs, and (2) how resistant it is to attacks. We emphasize that this is just a proof-of-concept implementation; it does not mean CGuard can only be implemented in Unbound. In fact, one should easily be able to implement CGuard in other software.

We use `pidstat` from `sysstat` [25] to capture statistics about CPU usage, and `pmap` for memory measurements. All readings are taken after waiting an initial short period of time for the system to stabilize.

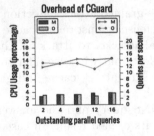

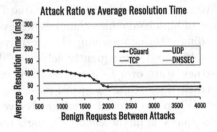

**Fig. 3.** Service rate and CPU usage of {Modified, Original} Unbound

**Fig. 4.**    Probabilistic    modeling    of CGuard's average resolution time

**CPU Overhead.** We evaluate the overhead of CGuard under normal operations by setting up both the original and modified Unbound as recursive resolvers, sharing the same configurations. We then issue queries using queryperf++ asking the resolver about A records of Alexa's top domains. We let this experiment run for 450 s separately for each setup. We collected the CPU usage and the service rate that the resolver delivered. The results are depicted in Fig. 3. As can be seen, CGuard does not incur significant overhead comparing to its unhardened counterpart in the benign case. We note that the actual service rate delivered by the resolver fluctuates due to environmental reasons including but not limited to non-deterministic network delay.

**Memory Overhead.** We also measured the memory usage of CGuard for benign cases and when under attack. We used the same setup as above and ran the 450-second query blasting experiment six times. We measured the memory usage of CGuard and the original Unbound. We use RSS to denote resident set size and VIRT to denote virtual memory. On average, after system initialization, the original Unbound consumes **22,727** kB RSS (**547,696** kB VIRT) while CGuard consumes a comparable **22,278** kB RSS (**547,638** kB VIRT). After handling all the queries, on average, the original Unbound consumes **43,000** kB RSS (**548,519** kB VIRT) and CGuard consumes **42,887** kB RSS (**548,570** kB VIRT), which shows that the memory overhead, if any, is negligible. We additionally ran 7 attacks on CGuard targeting different domains. When under attack, the memory usage of CGuard peaked at **44,180** kB RSS (**548,572** kB VIRT). We note that OS-level memory measurements can vary due to various environmental factors. The results here is not a proof of CGuard being more memory efficient but they show that the memory overhead is not heavy.

**Probabilistic Modeling.** To determine the average latency CGuard introduces, we probabilistically model its operation under varying volumes of attack traffic. The result in Fig. 4 depicts the average of 5 separate simulation runs. For simplicity, we assume the following key parameters: (a) latency (ms) for each channel: 30 for UDP, 60 for TCP, 300 for DNSSEC, 40 for UDP double query, and 55 for asking Google; (b) the probability of a domain supporting each channel: 100% for UDP, 85% for TCP, 85% for long-term stability, 85% for UDP double query, 1% for DNSSEC, and 100% for Google Public Resolver. As shown in Fig. 4, on average, CGuard has a much lower resolution time than always using DNSSEC, and when attacks occur only infrequently, it will also perform better than always using TCP without optimizations.

**Table 1.** Six runs of Parallel Kaminsky attack on (Original and Modified) Unbound 1.5.4 recursive resolver

|   |           | 1        | 2        | 3        | 4        | 5        | 6        |
|---|-----------|----------|----------|----------|----------|----------|----------|
| O | Instances | 2266     | 1331     | **3072** | 1884     | 2519     | 1674     |
|   | Result    | Poisoned | Poisoned | Failed   | Poisoned | Poisoned | Poisoned |
| M | Instances | **3072** | **3072** | **3072** | **3072** | **3072** | **3072** |
|   | Result    | Failed   | Failed   | Failed   | Failed   | Failed   | Failed   |

**Attack Resistance.** As Nominum's Vantio CacheServe is a proprietary product, we do not attempt to evaluate it. Instead, we launch PKAs on the original and modified Unbound, both configured as recursive resolvers, running on a single thread, and only 10 bit entropy is used in the TXID. Note that **not** using the full 16-bit gives an attacker an advantage in launching a successful attack since it is easier to match the TXID. To mitigate the influence of source port randomization, we forced Unbound to use a fixed source port. This resembles a scenario where the recursive resolver is behind a NAT.

We repeat the attack 6 times. Each time we stop the attack after at most $3 \times 2^{10} = 3,072$ instances. For each attack instance, we randomly generate a likely non-existent sub-domain of a victim domain and send a query about it to the resolver. Consequently, the recursive resolver is going to perform iterative queries in attempt to find an answer, which gives an attack window. We then send one forged DNS response to the resolver by spoofing the sender address to be one of the authoritative name servers. With the unprotected original Unbound, each attack instance has an independent probability of $\frac{1}{2^{10}}$ of being successful and hence the expected number of instances needed to have one success is simply $2^{10}$. The results of the 6 attack attempts can be found in Table 1. Across the 5 successful attempts, on average, it took $1,934$ instances for the attack to be successful, which is within 2 standard deviations from the theoretical expected value. When Unbound was hardened with CGuard, it detected the attack and did not allow the cache to be poisoned. Hence, all attack instances in all 6 runs failed. This shows the efficacy of CGuard in detecting and defending against cache poisoning.

**Threat of Performance Attack.** One might suspect that given an adaptive attacker, CGuard might be forced to continuously stay on system-wide attack mode. This is true, however, the outcome of such a case should be close to that of always using the heaviest high-confidence channel (say DNSSEC), with a small manageable detection and bookkeeping overhead. CGuard would then opportunistically fall back to low-confidence channels once the attacks are over.

## 7    Conclusion

We present CGuard that proactively detects whether cache entries are under active attack and protects them by using high confidence channels. CGuard complements existing cache poisoning solutions; unlike many existing solutions, DNS resolvers can enjoy CGuard's protection for a minimal deployment cost without having to rely on any substantial effort from domain owners. By incorporating multiple high confidence channels, CGuard also enables them to cover for each other in terms of availability and against some tricky corner cases. Our evaluation of CGuard—implemented in Unbound DNS resolver 1.5.4—demonstrates that CGuard is effective at thwarting DNS cache poisoning attacks and incurs minimal overhead under normal operation. We envision that by taking away the attacker's incentive to launch DNS cache poisoning attacks, CGuard essentially turns the existence of high confidence channels into a deterrence. Such a deterrence-based defense mechanism can be relevant to other applications.

Being a critical infrastructure of the Internet, DNS continues to attract efforts on making it more robust and trustworthy. Recent developments include the various documents produced by the DNS Private Exchange (dprive) workgroup. Motivated by the need for privacy and confidentiality against eavesdroppers, dprive recently proposed new standards on DNS over TLS/DTLS [RFC7858, RFC8094], which also adds resilience against cache poisoning attacks. As for future work, we intend to investigate the adoption of the TLS/DTLS-based high confidence channels in CGuard instantiations, and possibly evaluate their performance when compared with other channels.

# References

1. 5 Myths about Content Delivery Networks and the truths you should know. https://www.thatwhitepaperguy.com/downloads/5-CDN-Myths.pdf
2. Vulnerability Note VU 800113: Multiple DNS implementations vulnerable to cache poisoning. Technical report, US CERT Vulnerability Notes Database (2008)
3. DNS Census 2013 (2013). https://dnscensus2013.neocities.org
4. DNS, DNSSEC and Google's Public DNS Service (2013). http://www.circleid.com/posts/20130717_dns_dnssec_and_googles_public_dns_service/
5. Google's Malaysian domains hit with DNS cache poisoning attack (2013). http://www.tripwire.com/state-of-security/latest-security-news/googles-malaysian-domains-hit-dns-cache-poisoning-attack/
6. DNS poisoning slams web traffic from millions in China into the wrong hole (2014). http://www.theregister.co.uk/2014/01/21/china_dns_poisoning_attack/
7. Google Public DNS - Security Benefits (2014). https://developers.google.com/speed/public-dns/docs/security
8. CloudFlare Enables Universal DNSSEC for Its Millions of Customers for Free (2015). http://www.marketwired.com/press-release/cloudflare-enables-universal-dnssec-for-its-millions-of-customers-for-free-2072174.htm
9. DNSSEC name and shame! (2015). https://dnssec-name-and-shame.com/
10. Ager, B., Dreger, H., Feldmann, A.: Predicting the DNSSEC overhead using DNS traces. In: 40th IEEE CISS (2006)
11. Antonakakis, M., Dagon, D., Luo, X., Perdisci, R., Lee, W., Bellmor, J.: A centralized monitoring infrastructure for improving DNS security. In: Jha, S., Sommer, R., Kreibich, C. (eds.) RAID 2010. LNCS, vol. 6307, pp. 18–37. Springer, Heidelberg (2010). https://doi.org/10.1007/978-3-642-15512-3_2
12. APNIC Labs: Use of DNSSEC validation for world (2015). http://stats.labs.apnic.net/dnssec/XA
13. Assolini, F.: Attacks against Boletos (2014). https://securelist.com/attacks-against-boletos/66591/
14. Bernstein, D.J.: DNSCurve: usable security for DNS (2009). http://dnscurve.org/
15. Bernstein, D.J.: DNS forgery (2002). http://cr.yp.to/djbdns/forgery.html
16. Calder, M., Flavel, A., Katz-Bassett, E., Mahajan, R., Padhye, J.: Analyzing the performance of an anycast CDN. In: Proceedings of ACM IMC, pp. 531–537 (2015)
17. CCCen: An overview of secure name resolution [29c3] (2013). https://www.youtube.com/watch?v=eOGezLjlzFU
18. Catalin Cimpanu: Around four in five DNSSEC servers can be hijacked for DDoS attacks (2016). http://news.softpedia.com/news/around-four-in-five-dnssec-servers-can-be-used-in-ddos-attacks-507503.shtml
19. CommunityDNS: Performance testing of BIND, NSD and CDNS platforms on identical hardware (2010). http://communitydns.net/DNSSEC-Performance.pdf
20. Constantin, L.: DNS cache poisoning used in Brazilian phishing attack (2011). http://news.softpedia.com/news/DNS-Cache-Poisoning-Used-in-Brazilian-Phishing-Attack-212328.shtml
21. Czarny, M.: How anycast IP routing is used at MaxCDN (2013). https://www.maxcdn.com/blog/anycast-ip-routing-used-maxcdn/

22. Dagon, D., Antonakakis, M., Vixie, P., Jinmei, T., Lee, W.: Increased DNS forgery resistance through 0x20-bit encoding: security via LeET queries. In: Proceedings of the 15th ACM CCS, pp. 211–222 (2008)
23. Duan, H., et al.: Hold-on: protecting against on-path DNS poisoning. In: Securing and Trusting Internet Names (SATIN) (2012)
24. Flavel, A., et al.: FastRoute: a scalable load-aware anycast routing architecture for modern CDNs. In: 12th USENIX NSDI, pp. 381–394 (2015)
25. Godard, S.: sysstat - system Performance tools for the Linux operating system (2015). https://github.com/sysstat/sysstat
26. Guðmundsson, Ó., Crocker, S.D.: Observing DNSSEC validation in the wild. In: Securing and Trusting Internet Names (SATIN) (2011)
27. Herzberg, A., Shulman, H.: Retrofitting security into network protocols: the case of DNSSEC. IEEE Internet Comput. **18**(1), 66–71 (2014)
28. Herzberg, A., Shulman, H.: Security of patched DNS. In: Foresti, S., Yung, M., Martinelli, F. (eds.) ESORICS 2012. LNCS, vol. 7459, pp. 271–288. Springer, Heidelberg (2012). https://doi.org/10.1007/978-3-642-33167-1_16
29. Hubert, A., van Mook, R.: Measures for making DNS more resilient against forged answers, January 2009. https://www.rfc-editor.org/rfc/rfc5452.txt
30. Hussain, I.: Google.com.bd down (2016). http://www.dhakatribune.com/feature/2016/12/20/google-com-bd/
31. Huston, G.: Measuring DNSSEC use (2013). https://labs.apnic.net/presentations/store/2013-08-27-dnssec-apnic.pdf
32. Huston, G., Michaelson, G.: Measuring DNSSEC performance (2013). http://impossible.rand.apnic.net/ispcol/2013-05/dnssec-performance.pdf
33. Infoblox: Infoblox DNS Threat Index (2015). https://www.infoblox.com/sites/infobloxcom/files/resources/infoblox-white-paper-dns-threat-index-q2-2015-report.pdf
34. JUNIPER TechLibrary: Network address translation feature guide for security devices - disabling port randomization for source NAT (CLI Procedure) (2016). https://www.juniper.net/documentation/en_US/junos/topics/task/configuration/nat-security-source-port-randomization-disabling-cli.html
35. Kaminsky, D.: Black Ops 2008: It's The End Of The Cache As We Know It (2008)
36. Kaminsky, D.: DNSSEC Interlude 2: DJB@CCC — Dan Kaminsky's Blog (2011). http://dankaminsky.com/2011/01/05/djb-ccc/
37. Levine, M.: Measuring throughput performance: DNS vs. TCP anycast routing (2014). http://www.cachefly.com/2014/07/11/measuring-throughput-performance-dns-vs-tcp-anycast-routing/
38. Lian, W., Rescorla, E., Shacham, H., Savage, S.: Measuring the practical impact of DNSSEC deployment. In: USENIX Security, pp. 573–588 (2013)
39. Lindstrom, A.: DNSSEC implementation in Sweden (2012). https://www.antonlindstrom.com/2012/01/02/dnssec-implementation-in-sweden.html
40. Lowe, G., Winters, P., Marcus, M.L.: The great DNS wall of china, December 2007
41. Nice, B.V.: High performance DNS needs high performance security (2012). http://nominum.com/high-performance-dns-needs-high-performance-security/
42. NIST National Vulnerability Database: CVE-2002-2211 (2002). http://web.nvd.nist.gov/view/vuln/detail?vulnId=CVE-2002-2211
43. Park, K., Pai, V.S., Peterson, L.L., Wang, Z.: CoDNS: improving DNS performance and reliability via cooperative lookups. OSDI **4**, 14 (2004)
44. Perdisci, R., Antonakakis, M., Luo, X., Lee, W.: WSEC DNS: Protecting recursive DNS resolvers from poisoning attacks. In: IEEE/IFIP International Conference on Dependable Systems & Networks, DSN 2009, pp. 3–12. IEEE (2009)

45. Poole, L., Pai, V.S.: ConfiDNS: leveraging scale and history to improve DNS security. In: WORLDS (2006)
46. Prince, M.: A brief primer on Anycast (2011). https://blog.cloudflare.com/a-brief-anycast-primer/
47. Rashid, F.Y.: Poorly configured DNSSEC servers at root of DDoS attacks (2016). http://www.infoworld.com/article/3109581/security/poorly-configured-dnssec-servers-at-root-of-ddos-attacks.html
48. Raywood, D.: Irish ISP Eircom hit by multiple attacks that restrict service for users (2009). http://www.scmagazineuk.com/irish-isp-eircom-hit-by-multiple-attacks-that-restrict-service-for-users/article/140243/
49. Schuba, C.: Addressing weaknesses in the domain name system protocol. Ph.D. thesis, Purdue University (1993)
50. Seltzer, L.: Report claims DNS cache poisoning attack against Brazilian Bank and ISP (2009). http://www.eweek.com/c/a/Security/Report-Claims-DNS-Cache-Poisoning-Attack-Against-Brazilian-Bank-and-ISP-761709
51. Shulman, H., Waidner, M.: One key to sign them all considered vulnerable: evaluation of DNSSEC in the Internet. In: NSDI, pp. 131–144 (2017)
52. Son, S., Shmatikov, V.: The Hitchhiker's guide to DNS cache poisoning. In: Security and Privacy in Communication Networks, pp. 466–483 (2010)
53. Spring, J.: Probable cache poisoning of mail handling domains (2014). https://insights.sei.cmu.edu/cert/2014/09/-probable-cache-poisoning-of-mail-handling-domains.html
54. StatDNS: TLD zone file statistics (2016). http://www.statdns.com/
55. KeyCDN Support: Anycast (2016). https://www.keycdn.com/support/anycast/
56. Tatuya, J.: queryperf++ (2014). https://github.com/jinmei/queryperfpp
57. Verisign Labs: DNSSEC Scoreboard. http://scoreboard.verisignlabs.com/
58. Virus Bulletin: DNS cache poisoning used to steal emails (2014). https://www.virusbtn.com/blog/2014/09_12.xml
59. Wikipedia: Deterrence theory – Wikipedia, The Free Encyclopedia. https://en.wikipedia.org/w/index.php?title=Deterrence_theory
60. Yao, Y., He, L., Xiong, G.: Security and cost analyses of DNSSEC protocol. In: Yuan, Y., Wu, X., Lu, Y. (eds.) ISCTCS 2012. CCIS, vol. 320, pp. 429–435. Springer, Heidelberg (2013). https://doi.org/10.1007/978-3-642-35795-4_54
61. Yuan, L., Kant, K., Mohapatra, P., Chuah, C.N.: DoX: a peer-to-peer antidote for DNS cache poisoning attacks. In: IEEE ICC 2006, vol. 5 (2006)
62. Zhu, L., Hu, Z., Heidemann, J., Wessels, D., Mankin, A., Somaiya, N.: Connection-oriented DNS to improve privacy and security (extended). Technical Report ISI-TR-2015-695, Febuary 2015. http://www.isi.edu/~johnh/PAPERS/Zhu15c.html

# Mission-Oriented Security Model, Incorporating Security Risk, Cost and Payout

Sayed M. Saghaian N. E.$^{(\boxtimes)}$, Tom La Porta, Trent Jaeger, Z. Berkay Celik, and Patrick McDaniel

Department of Computer Science and Engineering,
The Pennsylvania State University, University Park, USA
{sms676,tlp,tjaeger,zbc102,mcdaniel}@cse.psu.edu

**Abstract.** One of the most difficult challenges facing network operators is to estimate risk and allocate resources in adversarial environments. Failure to properly allocate resources leads to failed activities, poor utilization, and insecure environments. In this paper, we explore an optimization-based approach to allocating resources called a *mission-oriented security model*. This model integrates security risk, cost and payout metrics to optimally allocate constrained secure resources to discrete actions called missions. We model this operation as a Mixed Integer Linear Program (MILP) which can be solved efficiently by different optimization solvers such as MATLAB MILP solver, IBM-CPLEX optimizer or CVX solver. We further introduce and explore a novel method to evaluate security risk in resource planning using two datasets—the Ponemon Institute cost of breach survey and CSI/FBI surveys of security events. Data driven simulations are used to validate the model robustness and uncover a number of insights on the importance of risk valuation in resource allocation.

## 1 Introduction

Operators of modern networks must allocate resources such as computation, bandwidth, storage capacity, or personnel to achieve operational goals in the face of adversaries. Consider the deployment of a file system service within a LAN–one could simply deploy an unauthenticated server, or use industry grade cryptography, multifactor authentication, multiple backups, and log every packet and filesystem event. These two deployments represent points in the spectrum in the cost/security/reliability space. In the absence of context, both deployments are equally appropriate. The key to secure operations is to make such a decision by understanding the needs and risks of the environment.

Indeed, today's operators make decisions about what is appropriate for an environment simply from intuition and experience—and often unconsciously assess and weigh the risks of the environment [3]. In this work, we seek to formalize this decision-making process. We develop a mathematically rigorous decision-making model to explore different policies by evaluating their effectiveness when

© ICST Institute for Computer Sciences, Social Informatics and Telecommunications Engineering 2018
R. Beyah et al. (Eds.): SecureComm 2018, LNICST 255, pp. 192–212, 2018.
https://doi.org/10.1007/978-3-030-01704-0_11

dealing with different risk characteristics. Using this model, we explore the inter-play between utilization, risk, and security and develop new insights on how to allocate resources in the face of adversaries with varying goals and strategies.

After reviewing operational best practices and work in decision theory, we have identified several essential elements of an operationally aware decision pro-cess: *risk, cost, payout* and *missions*. We provide intuitive definitions here (see Sect. 3 for formal definitions). Intuitively, the risk is a valuation of the harms that may occur, the damage they would cause, and the probability that the harms will occur. We refer to cost as the *security* cost. The cost is the required amount to spend to achieve some level of security. The payout is the value of performing an action (e.g., the "value" of an action to the environment)–which enables the decision process to prioritize actions by attempting to maximize profit.

Lastly, we refer to a mission as a series of actions that leads to an objective. A mission is defined by intent as well as how it is executed. With mission-oriented security, we consider the overall security of a system, not a single algorithm. Based on the risk level of a mission and the potential damage due to the risk, a mission might be allowed to continue even though there is a chance of being exposed to attacks or being compromised. When referring to a mission-oriented security model, we are referring to a mathematical model to make such decisions.

Note that often when considering the security of a system, people instinctively behave in a risk-averse fashion. However risk-averse approaches may sacrifice the total profit of the system, particularly when the probability of undesirable event occurrence or the damage due to these events are *relatively* small. On the other hand, a system that does not account or prepare for risk may suffer serious consequences, particularly when the probability of undesirable events is relatively large, or when the damage to the infrastructure or outcomes is extensive. Trading the contextual risk against the payout is a key to making good (optimal) decisions on resource allocations. We explore how this can be formally modeled throughout.

In general, there can be two different types of decision processes: deploy-ment and operational. As an example of a deployment decision, suppose we have three missions in an enterprise: providing email service, telnet access, and wireless access. Assume all these services are at risk for various attacks. Remedi-ation measures might include adding two-factor authentication for email service, adding a firewall and VPN for telnet access, or adding a VPN for wireless access. However, due to the limited number of available staff and infrastructure, we can only perform two out of the three remediations. The dilemma is that given attack characteristics corresponding to each of the missions, which of these missions should be assigned to our limited resource (staff). This kind of configuration or deployment decision is closely related to security planning.

As an example of an operational decision, assume a server in networked environment notes growing evidence of attacks (e.g., an adversary has found the IP address behind the firewall of a server in our server farm). Furthermore, there is a set of servers in our system which is more secure but slower. However, the cost of migrating processes to the secure server and the limited number of secure servers prevent us from moving all processes to those servers. The dilemma is which processes to migrate to the secure server, and if a process is not migrated, should we keep running that process or terminate it.

In the first part of this work, we define a cyber mission-oriented security model. We incorporate security risk, cost, and payout into our model, and consider a resource allocation problem where the objective is to jointly optimally allocate a secure constrained resource to missions and to decide whether to stop missions that do not receive the secure resources.

This formulation is the first step toward a larger body of analyses. To make the problem mathematically tractable, we explore three simple agility maneuvers: (i) assigning a mission to specially secured resources, (ii) continuing a mission, or (iii) stopping a mission. Our study can be extended to include more agility maneuvers such as reconfiguration, suspending a mission, etc.

We model the resource allocation problem as a Mixed Integer Nonlinear Program (MINLP) [6] where the objective function is to maximize the total profit gained from all missions. MINLP is a class of Nonlinear Programming which consists of both integer and continuous variables where the objective function or the constraints contain nonlinear terms. Our nonlinear programming problem can be linearized and transformed into a Mixed Integer Linear Program (MILP) by exploiting McCormick envelopes. Typically, a branch and bound algorithm is used to solve MILPs. Optimization solvers such as MATLAB MILP solver, IBM-CPLEX optimizer, or CVX commercial solver can efficiently provide a solution to a MILP. In this paper, we adopt MATLAB MILP solver to obtain an optimal resource allocation strategy. The main contributions of this paper are:

1. We introduce a mission-oriented security model that integrates security risk, cost and payout metrics, and develop a mathematical framework to optimally allocate constrained secure resources to missions.
2. We evaluate three different policies for allocating the constrained resources in facing with different risk profiles by using two datasets—the Ponemon Institute cost of breach survey and CSI/FBI survey of security events.
3. We investigate the sensitivity of our proposed framework with respect to under/over-estimating the probability of undesirable events.

We begin in the following section with a review of several key related work.

## 2   Related Work

In the sensor network domain, [11] proposed a framework to optimally allocate constrained resources (sensors) to missions such that the total profit is maximized when there exist uncertainties in users demands and their achievable profits. They assumed missions are always profitable and hence, should always be continued. However, in this work, missions might not always be profitable due to risks, and hence, we might have to terminate them. Furthermore, missions payouts and damages due to risks depend on if and how much of their request to use secure special resources is satisfied.

One challenge in today's development of security technology is misaligned incentives of different parties. For example, potential failure or security breach rises when a person or a software guarding a system faces a lower failure or compromise cost. The goal in information security economics [1,2] is to combine concepts from game theory, microeconomic theory and risk assessment with cryptography concepts to develop security technology. To protect a given set of information, [7] presented an economic model to derive the optimal amount to invest in security.

Unlike dependability and reliability of a computer system, there is not much work on quantitatively evaluating the security of a computer system. To evaluate the security of a system quantitatively, [16] surveyed model-based methods for evaluating dependability of a computer system. Furthermore, they discuss extending these methods to evaluate the security of a computer system.

A risk assessment method is a *qualitative* approach in which the likelihood of occurrence of undesirable events or their impacts are described qualitatively using terms like low, medium or high. Conversely, when the likelihood of occurrence of undesirable events and their consequences are expressed numerically, the risk evaluation method is called *quantitative* risk assessment [4]. Given a qualitative assessment of risk and complying with the ISO/IEC 27005 standard on risk management [12], European Network and Information Security Agency (ENISA) ranks different risks using the likelihood of a threat times its impact by assuming a scale from 1 to 5 (where 1 represents very low, whereas 5 denotes very high) for each of the likelihoods and impacts [5]. Clearly, the scaling values are relative values, and it is not clear how the resulted quantities for risk can be combined with other parameters such as cost or payouts in these methods.

Note that this work is highly related to the field of systems resilience [13] and agility [3,15]. Agility refers to an approach to achieving system resilience in which a defender reconfigure the system or the operation in response to a potential attack or perceived risk. In this work, we focus on formulations of the decision problem to reconfigure in response to various risks and threats.

# 3  Problem Statement

Figure 1 illustrates our mission-oriented security model. Missions are running on their own local server. However, these servers are under risk because of various potential cyber attacks. To mitigate these risks, the system may assign some of these missions to special secure resources that are immune from cyber attacks. In the beginning of each time frame, the set of available missions are competing for scarce secure resources. We want to determine how to allocate resources and whether to stop or continue the missions for the current time frame. In the next time frame, previously stopped missions with potentially different risk profiles will compete with a set of newly arrived missions. We do not allow preemption.

Informally, the problem is to determine which missions are assigned to the secure resources, to determine the amount of special resources assigned to the selected missions, and to decide whether to continue or stop the missions. In other

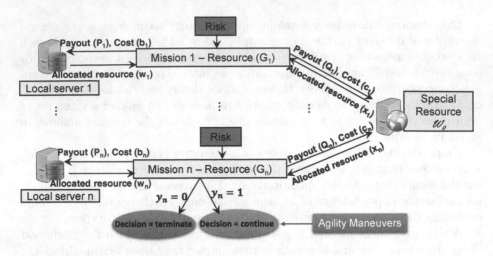

**Fig. 1.** Mission-oriented security model

words, we find the optimal strategy that maximizes the total profit achieved from the execution of all the missions.

Formally, assume there are $n$ missions $M_1, \ldots, M_n$ where for each mission, $M_i$ requires $G_i$ amount of resource. Initially, each mission is running on its own local server which has sufficient resources to support the mission. In a risk-free environment, $M_i$ achieves payout $P_i$ from its local resource/server if the local server fully allocates the entire requested amount of resources ($G_i$) to the mission. Further, the unit cost of allocating resources to $M_i$ by its local server is $b_i$.

Now due to security risks, each mission will request to use a global special resource/server that has only $\mathcal{W}_0$ amount of a special (secure) resource. Each mission $M_i$ is exposed to $l$ different types of attack; each attack type happens with probability of $\alpha_j^i$ (where superscript $i$ denotes the $i$-th mission, while subscript $j$ indicates the $j$-th attack type corresponding to $M_i$) and results in damage (loss of profit) of $d_j^i$. These types of attack are independent. They are potentially derived from different probability distributions.

For each mission $M_i$, risk is modeled as a set of triples [4]:

$$R_i = \{(s_1^i, \alpha_1^i, d_1^i), \ldots, (s_l^i, \alpha_l^i, d_l^i)\} \tag{1}$$

where $s_j^i$ is the $j$-th type of attack corresponding to $M_i$, $\alpha_j^i$ is the probability that this attack type happens, and $d_j^i$ is the damage due to that event.

Let $c_i$ be the unit cost of allocating the special resources to the $i$-th mission, $M_i$. If mission $M_i$ is fully allocated $G_i$ amount of the special resource (mission gets all the resources it needs), it achieves payout $Q_i$ with no loss due to risk. If we don't allocate any special resource to mission $M_i$, then mission $M_i$ is exposed to the entire potential damage as a result of risk. If a portion of the required special resource is assigned to mission $M_i$, only the remaining portion is exposed to risk. Table 1 provides the description of symbols used in the proposed framework for optimally allocating constrained secure resources to missions.

We assume payouts ($P_i$'s and $Q_i$'s) and potential damage are proportional (linear) to the amount of allocated resources. Formally, let $w_i$ and $x_i$ be the amount of allocated resources from the local resources and the special secure resources to mission $M_i$, respectively. Then, we define:

Partial payout from local server $= \frac{w_i}{G_i} P_i$,

Partial payout from special server $= \frac{x_i}{G_i} Q_i$,

Partial potential damage $= \frac{G_i - x_i}{G_i} \alpha_j^i d_j^i$,

where $w_i, x_i \leq G_i$.

We only have $\mathcal{W}_0$ amount of the special resource, and we would like to optimally allocate it amongst multiple missions in response to risk. We formalize the problem as follows:

1. Allocate resources ($w_i$'s, $x_i$'s) to missions optimally such that the total profit (payout minus cost minus damage due to risk) from all missions is maximized.
2. Decide to stop the missions ($y_i = 0$) or let them continue ($y_i = 1$):
   (a) if a mission stops, then it gains no profit and no damage.
   (b) if a mission continues, then it achieves partial payouts minus partial cost minus partial potential damage from risk.

# 4    Problem Formulation

We define profit as payout minus cost minus expected potential damage due to risk. We model the problem as a Mixed Integer Nonlinear Program (MINLP), where the objective function is to maximize the total profit gained from all the missions. Using our assumption regarding the linearity (in respect to the allocated resource) of partial payouts and damage, and by using techniques in Nonlinear Programming, we linearize our nonlinear programming problem and transform the problem into a Mixed Integer Linear Program (MILP). An optimal solution to the MILP can be found by using a branch and bound algorithm.

In Sect. 4.1, we construct a MINLP that formulates the problem. Using McCormick envelopes, we then linearize this MINLP in Sect. 4.2. The resulted MILP can be solved by using different solvers such as MATLAB MILP solver.

## 4.1    Objective Function

We consider a binary decision variable $y_i$ for each mission $M_i$; $y_i = 0$ indicates the mission is terminated, and the mission receives no profit and no damage. Whereas $y_i = 1$ indicates the mission $M_i$ is continued. Further, let $w_i$ and $x_i$ be the amount of the local and the special resource allocated to the $i$-th mission

**Table 1.** Symbols and parameters used in our resource allocation framework.

| Symbols | Descriptions |
|---------|--------------|
| $M_i$ | $i$-th mission |
| $s_j^i$ | $j$-th type of attack corresponding to $M_i$ |
| $\alpha_j^i$ | Probability that the event $s_j^i$ happens |
| $d_j^i$ | The damage as a result of occurrence of $s_j^i$ |
| $\mathcal{W}_0$ | Amount of available special resource |
| $G_i$ | Total requested resources by mission $M_i$ |
| $b_i$ | Unit cost of allocating local resources to $M_i$ by its local server |
| $c_i$ | Unit cost of allocating the special resource to mission $M_i$ |
| $P_i$ | Achieved payout by $M_i$ from its local resource if the local server allocates $G_i$ to $M_i$, when there is no risk to mission $M_i$ |
| $Q_i$ | Achieved payout by $M_i$ from the special resource if it is assigned $G_i$ amount of special resource |
| $w_i$ | Allocated resources from local resource to $M_i$ |
| $x_i$ | Allocated resources from special resource to $M_i$ |
| $y_i$ | $y_i = 0$ indicates to stop mission $M_i$ |
|  | $y_i = 1$ indicates to continue mission $M_i$ |

$M_i$, respectively. Then, the optimization problem is formulated by (2):

$$\underset{w,x,y}{\text{Min}} \quad \sum_{i=1}^{n} \overbrace{(b_i w_i + c_i x_i)}^{\text{cost}} -$$

$$\sum_{i=1}^{n} y_i \left[ \underbrace{\left( \frac{w_i}{G_i} P_i + \frac{x_i}{G_i} Q_i \right)}_{\text{payout}} - \sum_{j=1}^{l} \underbrace{\frac{G_i - x_i}{G_i} \alpha_j^i d_j^i}_{\text{potential risk damage}} \right] \qquad (2)$$

$$\text{s.t.} \quad \sum_{i=1}^{n} x_i \leq \mathcal{W}_0$$

$$w_i + x_i \leq G_i \qquad \text{for} \quad i = 1, \ldots, n$$

$$w_i, x_i \geq 0 \qquad \text{for} \quad i = 1, \ldots, n$$

$$y_i \in \{0, 1\} \qquad \text{for} \quad i = 1, \ldots, n$$

By construction and inherent nature of MINLP, this formulation returns a strategy that leads to the highest expected total profit.

## 4.2   Solving the Minimization Problem

We linearize the objective function in (2) by exploiting *McCormick envelopes*, and reformulate the problem as a *Mixed Integer Linear* Problem (MILP). McCormick envelopes are a convex relaxation technique that can be exploited to linearize MINLPs. In particular, if the objective function is a bilinear function, applying McCormick envelopes linearizes the objective function. The function $f(x, y)$ is a bilinear function if it is linear with respect to each variable $x$ and $y$ individually.

Let $f(x, y) = yg(x)$, where $y$ is a binary variable and $g(x)$ is a linear function with lower bound of $L$ and upper bound of $U$, i.e. $L \leq g(x) \leq U$. Then, one can linearize $f(x, y)$ by defining a new variable $z$ and exploiting McCormick envelopes. The function $f(x, y)$ is equivalent to:

$$z$$

$$\text{s.t.} \qquad Ly \leq z \leq Uy \qquad (3)$$

$$g(x) + U(y - 1) \leq z \leq g(x) + L(y - 1) \qquad (4)$$

We note that if $y = 0$, then $f(x, y) = 0$. Furthermore, from (3), $z$ must be 0 too. Moreover, if $y = 1$, then $f(x, y) = g(x)$. On the other hand, from (4), $z$ must be $g(x)$ as well. Hence, $f(x, y)$ is equivalent to $z$ with constraints (3) and (4).

By defining $D_i := \sum_{j=1}^{l} \alpha_j^i d_j^i$, $B_i := \frac{Q_i}{G_i} + \frac{1}{G_i} D_i$ and $A_i := \frac{P_i}{G_i}$, and by using McCormick envelopes, we can linearize (2) and obtain the following MILP:

$$\underset{w,x,y,z}{\text{Min}} \quad \sum_{i=1}^{n} (b_i w_i + c_i x_i - z_i + D_i y_i)$$

$$\text{s.t.} \quad \sum_{i=1}^{n} x_i \leq \mathcal{W}_0$$

$$\text{for} \quad i = 1, \ldots, n:$$

$$w_i + x_i \leq G_i \qquad (5)$$

$$y_i \in \{0, 1\}$$

$$w_i, x_i, z_i \geq 0$$

$$z_i \leq (P_i + Q_i + D_i) y_i$$

$$z_i \geq A_i w_i + B_i x_i + (P_i + Q_i + D_i)(y_i - 1)$$

$$z_i \leq A_i w_i + B_i x_i$$

To solve MILP, a branch and bound algorithm is typically used in different solvers such as MATLAB MILP solver, IBM-CPLEX optimizer, or CVX commercial solver. In this paper, we use MATLAB MILP solver.

To deploy our proposed decision making under security risk in practice, a method to assess risk quantitatively is required. We next formally define security risk and propose a novel quantitative risk assessment method.

## 5  Risk Evaluation

In this section, we first briefly review the definition of security risk and the expected damage from risk (Sect. 5.1). We then construct the elements of our proposed novel probabilistic risk assessment method based on the relative probability of the $j$-th attack type (Sect. 5.2.1) and the probability of experiencing a successful attack (Sect. 5.2.2).

### 5.1  Risk Definition

Probabilistic risk assessment [4] is an analysis that measures and evaluates risk systematically. It estimates the consequences of undesirable events and predicts the likelihood of such events. These approaches often use expert opinion or historical data to assess the likelihood of undesirable events and their consequences. This method of risk assessment aims to address three questions [14]:

1. What vulnerabilities are exposed? What are undesirable events? What are types of attacks experienced by a mission, system or enterprise?
2. What is the probability of occurrence of those events?
3. What are the consequences or potential impact of occurrence of those undesirable events? What is the damage due to those events?

Historical data can be used as test data to evaluate security systems as we discuss later. Furthermore, they form the basis of our proposed risk assessment framework. One might argue that historical data cannot be a valid sampling set to estimate future probabilities and consequences as they only refer to series of known past events. However, as reference [10] points out, although studies by the Computer Emergency Response Team Coordination Center (CERT/CC) show that risks do change with technological advances and human factors, the changes are small and infrequent, i.e., risk is largely stable over time.

Discussed previously, we model the risk of each $M_i$ as a set of triples in (1). In a probabilistic risk assessment approach, risk is related to two parameters. The first parameter is the likelihood of occurrence of undesirable events such as experiencing cyber attacks, or vulnerability exposure. The other parameter is the consequence of the occurrence of these events.

Following ISO/IEC 27005 [12], we define the expected loss due to the event $s_j^i$, the $j$-th type of attack corresponding to mission $M_i$ as: $\mathscr{L}_j^i := \alpha_j^i d_j^i$. However, there is very limited statistical information from studies on attacks experienced by enterprises. As a result, it is very difficult to quantify $\alpha_j^i$'s in practice. To be able to quantify risk, we define potential loss due to the $j$-th type of attack corresponding to mission $M_i$ as [21]:

$$\mathscr{L}_j^i := p_\tau^i p_j^i d_j^i \tag{6}$$

where $p_\tau^i$ is the probability that mission $M_i$ experiences a successful attack during time interval $\tau$ and $p_j^i$ is the *relative* probability of occurrence of the $j$-th type of attack, or threat. Table 2 provides the description of symbols used in the proposed risk assessment method.

The relative probability of the $j$-th attack type is defined as the likelihood that a mission is under the $j$-th type of attack given an intense assumption that the mission is in fact under an attack.

From (6), we can compute the total expected damage from risks for each of the missions from: $\mathscr{L}^i := \sum_{j=1}^{l_i} p_\tau^i p_j^i d_j^i$, where $l_i$ is the number of attack types corresponding to the $i$-th mission, $M_i$.

**Table 2.** Symbols and parameters used in the risk assessment method.

| Symbols | Descriptions |
|---|---|
| $p_\tau^i$ | Probability that $M_i$ experiences a successful attack during time interval $\tau$ when no secure resource is assigned to this mission |
| $p_j^i$ | Relative probability of occurrence of the $j$-th attack |
| $l_i$ | Number of attack types corresponding to $M_i$ |
| $\mathscr{L}_j^i$ | Potential loss due to the event $s_j^i$ |
| $\mathscr{L}^i$ | Total expected damage from risk for mission $M_i$ |
| $\mathscr{L}_{LogN}^i$ | Total expected damage from risk for mission $M_i$ when TBC is modeled by lognormal distribution |

## 5.2 Risk Assessment

To calculate the expected loss due to risk, we find the relative probabilities of attack types (Sect. 5.2.1) and the probability that missions experience a successful attack during a time interval (Sect. 5.2.2).

### 5.2.1 Computing Relative Probabilities

The relative probability of the $j$-th attack type can be computed based on available historical data. Given historical data from a previous time period, the relative probability of the $j$-th attack type corresponding to mission $M_i$ is computed from:

$$p_j^i = \frac{perc_j^i}{\sum_{k=1}^{l_i} perc_k^i} \tag{7}$$

where $perc_k^i$ is the percentage of times that mission $M_i$ experienced attack type $k$ during the last time period. Alternatively, depending on the available data set,

$perc_k^i$ can be defined as the percentage of enterprises that experienced the $k$-th type of attack during the last time period. Moreover, in case that an enterprise is supplied with its security expert's opinion rather than past data, $perc_k^i$ can be expressed based on the expert opinion, and be defined as the percentage of experts that think the enterprise will experience the attack type $k$.

### 5.2.2  Computing Probability of Experiencing an Attack

The probability of experiencing a successful attack during time interval $\tau$ can be modeled by different probability distributions. Let random variable $X$ represent the time between two consecutive attacks. Further, let $q^i(\tau)$ denote the probability that no successful attack has occurred in the time interval $\tau$ for mission $M_i$. Then:

$$q^i(\tau) = \Pr(X > \tau)$$
$$p_\tau^i = 1 - q^i(\tau) = F_X(\tau) \tag{8}$$

where $F_X$ is the Cumulative Distribution Function (CDF) corresponding to the random variable $X$ [17].

**Lognormal Distribution:** Authors in [9] conducted a large-scale study on the required time to compromise a computer system. According to their analysis on detected cyber intrusions on 260,000 computer systems over a period of three years, they find that lognormal distribution is the best fit to model the Time Between Compromises (TBC).

Assume $X$ has a lognormal distribution with parameters $\mu^i$ and $\sigma^i$: $X \sim ln\mathcal{N}(\mu^i, \sigma^i)$. Then,

$$p_\tau^i = \frac{1}{2}\left[1 + erf\left(\frac{ln\,(\tau) - \mu^i}{\sigma^i\sqrt{2}}\right)\right] \tag{9}$$

where erf is the error function. The parameters of lognormal distribution ($\mu^i$ and $\sigma^i$) can be estimated from the historical data.

## 6  Data and Simulation Results

We evaluate the mission-oriented security model through an example of seven missions competing for constrained secure resources. We first calculate a numerical value for the probability of experiencing a successful attack during 30 days (Sect. 6.1). We then present datasets of the Ponemon Institute cost of breach survey and CSI/FBI surveys of security event that we exploit to characterize the risk of missions (Sect. 6.2). We evaluate the performance of our proposed model and compare it with the performance of two other policies (Sect. 6.3). We further investigate the effect of different factors on the performance of the three different approaches (Sect. 6.4). Finally, we provide a sensitivity analysis that studies the effect of incorrectly estimating the probability of occurrence of attacks on the performance of our method (Sect. 6.5).

## 6.1 Computing the Probability of Experiencing a Successful Attack on the Local Servers $(p_\tau)$

We consider the probability of attack arrival over a month by setting the parameter $\tau$ in (9) to 30 days.

The study in [9] found that the Maximum Likelihood estimate of the lognormal parameters are $\hat{\mu} = 3.719$ and $\hat{\sigma} = 1.065$. Hence, assuming TBC has a lognormal distribution, from (9), the probability that $M_i$ experiences a successful attack when its resource requirements are satisfied from its local server is computed as:

$$p_\tau^i = \frac{1}{2}\left[1 + erf\left(\frac{ln\,(30) - 3.719}{1.065\sqrt{2}}\right)\right] = 0.3827$$

Recall that mission $M_i$ will not experience any successful attack if all of its resource requirements are satisfied from the secure server. If part of its resource requirements is satisfied from its local server, the damage due to a successful attack will only be proportional to the amount of resources allocated from the local server, i.e., only local server use induces damage.

## 6.2 Data and Experiments Settings for Ponemon Institute and CSI/FBI Surveys

We consider seven different missions with risk characteristics derived from the Ponemon Institute and CSI/FBI surveys, and conduct 100 iterations in which attack characteristics are simulated based on $p_\tau$ and risk vectors in Table 3. The special resource has only $W_0 = 3500$ units of resource while the amount of required resources ($G_i$'s) and payouts ($P_i$'s and $Q_i$'s) are drawn uniformly at random from ranges: $G_i \in U([1000, 1500])$ (for all missions).
$P_1 \in U([80000, 100000])$, $P_2 \in U([30000, 40000])$, $P_3 = U([40000, 60000])$,
$P_4 \in U([40000, 60000])$, $P_5 \in U([20000, 22000])$, $P_6 \in U([50000, 52000])$,
and $P_7 \in U([11000, 13000])$.
$Q_1 \in U([50000, 70000])$, $Q_2 \in U([15000, 25000])$, $Q_3 \in U([30000, 40000])$,
$Q_4 \in U([30000, 40000])$, $Q_5 \in U([12000, 15000])$, $Q_6 \in U([30000, 35000])$,
and $Q_7 \in U([7000, 10000])$.
Further, the unit cost of using the special resources is $c_i = 2$ for each mission, while the unit cost of the local resources is $b_i = 1$ for each mission.

### 6.2.1 Ponemon Institute Study

The Ponemon Institute conducted a survey [18] on the annual cost of cybercrime from 237 organizations in six different countries: United States $(M_1)$, Japan $(M_2)$, Germany $(M_3)$, United Kingdom $(M_4)$, Brazil $(M_5)$ and Australia $(M_6)$. We use their results to assess risk corresponding to six missions. We consider a scenario in which the data of each country contributes to the evaluation of risk for the six different missions $(M_1, \ldots, M_6)$.

Eight different types of attack have been identified by the Ponemon Institute study. The eight types of attack categorized by Ponemon Institute and the percentage of users who experienced these attacks are: Malware (98%), Phishing and Social Engineering (70%), Web-based attacks (63%), Malicious code (61%), Botnets (55%), Stolen devices (50%), Denial of services (49%), and Malicious insiders (41%). Organizations were asked if they have experienced these types of attack. Using (7), we calculate the relative probability of each attack type ($p_j^i$'s for $i = 1, \ldots, 6$ and $j = 1, \ldots, 8$). Furthermore, we use their results, and compute the monthly damage as a result of these types of attack for each mission. As an example, we can compute the relative probability of the Malware attacks (the first type of attack corresponding to missions $M_1, \ldots, M_6$) from (7) as: $p_1 = \frac{0.98}{0.98+0.70+0.63+0.61+0.55+0.50+0.49+0.41} = 0.2012$. Furthermore, the damage due to Malware attacks for mission $M_1$ (United States) for the fiscal year of 2016 was reported to be 0.13x17.36 million $= \$2,256,800$. Therefore, on average, the monthly damage as a result of Malware attacks for mission $M_1$ was $d_1 = \frac{2,256,800}{12} = 188,067$.

Table 3 summarizes risk parameters for each mission with the columns $M_1, \ldots, M_6$. From this data set, Malware attacks were the most common types of attack experienced by users, while Malicious code had the most severe damage.

### 6.2.2    CSI/FBI Survey

In a sequence of surveys [8,19,20] conducted yearly by the Computer Security Institute (CSI) and the Federal Bureau of Investigation (FBI), respondents from different industry organizations are asked the types of attack they experienced and the cost of those attacks to their organization. We use this dataset to evaluate security risk corresponding to another mission ($M_7$).

The latest CSI/FBI survey that we found which contains damage lost per attack type, per respondent is their 2003 survey [19]. 12 different types of attacks were identified by this survey. These attack types and percentage of respondents that experience each of these types of attack are: Denial of service (42%), Stolen devices (59%), Active wiretap (1%), Telecom fraud (10%), Unauthorized access by insiders (45%), Virus (82%), Financial fraud (15%), Insider abuse of Net access (80%), System Penetration (36%), Telecom Eavesdropping (6%), Sabotage (21%), and Theft of Proprietary Info (21%).

Likewise, we calculate the relative probability of each attack type ($p_j^7$'s for $j = 1, \ldots, 12$) for $M_7$ using (7). For example, the relative probability corresponding to DoS (the first type of attack corresponding to missions $M_7$) is $p_1 = 0.1005$. Moreover, the damage due to DoS attack was on average $d_1 = \frac{1,427,028}{12} = 118,919$ monthly. Refer to column $M_7$ of Table 3 for risk vectors of this mission.

Table 3. Risk characteristic from Ponemon Institute and CSI/FBI surveys.

| Relative probabilities/damage | Missions | | | | | | |
|---|---|---|---|---|---|---|---|
| | $M_1$ | $M_2$ | $M_3$ | $M_4$ | $M_5$ | $M_6$ | $M_7$ |
| $p_1^i$ | 0.2012 | 0.2012 | 0.2012 | 0.2012 | 0.2012 | 0.2012 | 0.1005 |
| $d_1^i$ | 188,067 | 139,833 | 124,133 | 78,108 | 79,050 | 57,333 | 118,919 |
| $p_2^i$ | 0.1437 | 0.1437 | 0.1437 | 0.1437 | 0.1437 | 0.1437 | 0.1411 |
| $d_2^i$ | 217,000 | 69,917 | 124,133 | 66,092 | 35,133 | 53,750 | 3,926 |
| $p_3^i$ | 0.1294 | 0.1294 | 0.1294 | 0.1294 | 0.1294 | 0.1294 | 0.0024 |
| $d_3^i$ | 173,600 | 146,825 | 111,067 | 102,142 | 87,833 | 46,583 | 29,375 |
| $p_4^i$ | 0.1253 | 0.1253 | 0.1253 | 0.1253 | 0.1253 | 0.1253 | 0.0239 |
| $d_4^i$ | 347,200 | 48,942 | 58,800 | 66,092 | 48,308 | 46,583 | 4,176 |
| $p_5^i$ | 0.1129 | 0.1129 | 0.1129 | 0.1129 | 0.1129 | 0.1129 | 0.1077 |
| $d_5^i$ | 43,400 | 34,958 | 13,067 | 18,025 | 8,783 | 7,167 | 2,605 |
| $p_6^i$ | 0.1027 | 0.1027 | 0.1027 | 0.1027 | 0.1027 | 0.1027 | 0.1962 |
| $d_6^i$ | 86,800 | 34,958 | 78,400 | 72,100 | 43,917 | 28,667 | 16,656 |
| $p_7^i$ | 0.1006 | 0.1006 | 0.1006 | 0.1006 | 0.1006 | 0.1006 | 0.0359 |
| $d_7^i$ | 231,467 | 90,892 | 104,533 | 138,192 | 79,050 | 68,083 | 27,383 |
| $p_8^i$ | 0.0842 | 0.0842 | 0.0842 | 0.0842 | 0.0842 | 0.0842 | 0.1914 |
| $d_8^i$ | 159,133 | 132,842 | 39,200 | 60,083 | 57,092 | 50,167 | 11,271 |
| $p_9^i$ | — | — | — | — | — | — | 0.0861 |
| $d_9^i$ | — | — | — | — | — | — | 4,684 |
| $p_{10}^i$ | — | — | — | — | — | — | 0.0144 |
| $d_{10}^i$ | — | — | — | — | — | — | 1,267 |
| $p_{11}^i$ | — | — | — | — | — | — | 0.0502 |
| $d_{11}^i$ | — | — | — | — | — | — | 17,877 |
| $p_{12}^i$ | — | — | — | — | — | — | 0.0502 |
| $d_{12}^i$ | — | — | — | — | — | — | 224,987 |
| Expected damage $(\mathscr{L}_{LogN}^i)$ | 70987 | 34894 | 33638 | 28745 | 21674 | 17585 | 12238 |

## 6.3 Performance Evaluation

### 6.3.1 Comparison of Different Policies

We compare our proposed MILP-based framework that maximizes the expected total profit with two other policies:

(a) **Risk-Averse Policy:** In this policy, we only continue missions whose request to use the secure resources can be fully satisfied. We stop the rest of the missions. Then, the secure resource allocation is a well-known *knapsack* problem where we have $n$ objects with values of $Q_i$, weights of $G_i$ and cost of $c_i$. The capacity of the knapsack is $W_0$. The optimal allocation of secure resources in this policy can be found by a greedy algorithm which serves the requests of the missions with a higher $\frac{Q_i}{c_i G_i}$ value first until the knapsack does not have enough capacity to store any other object.

(b) **Risk-Ignorant Policy:** In this policy, the risk is ignored. Hence, every mission is always continued, and the resource allocation is based on a simple Linear Program, a modified version of (2), where for each mission, $y_i = 1$ and the probability of occurrence of attacks $\alpha_j^i = 0$.

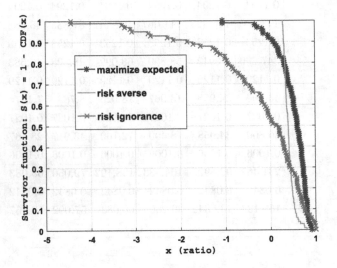

Fig. 2. Survivor functions of three policies

We present our results by showing the ratio of achieved total profit from these three policies over the maximum possible total profit. Based on the value of $p_\tau$ and the risk vectors shown in Table 3, we simulate the attack occurrences. The maximum possible total profit is achieved from a hypothetical scenario in which an oracle knows the attack occurrences ahead of time so that accordingly the assignment of the secure resources and the decisions to continue or stop missions are made with full knowledge. Note that in reality, we do not have such oracles, so the best we can achieve is to plan to maximize the expected total profit.

The average ratios are 0.52, −0.23 and 0.41 for our proposed approach, risk-ignorant, risk-averse policies, respectively. Moreover, the standard deviations of the ratios are 0.32, 1.11 and 0.1 for our proposed method, risk-ignorant, risk-averse policies, respectively. Figure 2 shows the survivor functions (1-CDF) of the ratios for 100 iterations.

**Insight 1.** *We observe that the risk-ignorant method might result in a negative total profit with a probability of about 0.50, while our proposed approach leads to a positive total profit with a probability of about 0.90.*

**Insight 2.** *The risk-averse policy almost never results in a ratio (achieved total profit over maximum possible total profit) close to one. In fact, the probability that the risk-averse approach exceeds a ratio of 0.5 is only 0.14, while our proposed approach results in a ratio of 0.5 or greater with a probability of 0.64.*

### 6.4  Affect of the Probability of Experiencing a Successful Attack on the Local Servers ($p_\tau$) and the normalized damage ($d_j^i/\min P_i$)n the performance

To investigate the effects of $p_\tau$ (probability of experiencing a successful attack on the local servers) and $d_j^i/\min P_i$ (damage per attack type normalized by the minimum possible payout from all the local servers) on the ratios (achieved total profit from the three polices over the maximum possible total profit), we perform two different simulations. In the first simulation, we still assume the probability of a successful attack follows the lognormal distribution ($p_\tau = 0.3827$), and investigate the affect of damage from attacks. In this experiment, we set all the attack types to have the same damage value ($d_j^i := D$) for a constant $D$. In Fig. 3a, we plot the average ratios from 100 iterations for each different values of $D$. We show the x-axis as $D$ values normalized by the minimum possible achievable payouts from all the local servers (11000).

In the second simulation, we fix the damage as in Table 3, but we vary the probability of a successful attack ($p_\tau$). We plot in Fig. 3b the average ratios from 100 iterations for each different values of $p_\tau$.

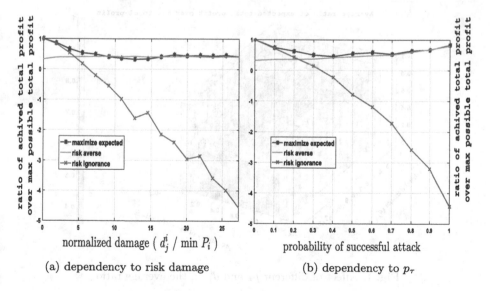

(a) dependency to risk damage          (b) dependency to $p_\tau$

**Fig. 3.** Effect of $p_\tau$ and $d_j^i/\min P_i$ on the ratios

**Insight 3.** *As can be seen from Fig. 3, when the probability of a successful attack* $(p_\tau)$ *or damage* $(D)$ *have small values, our algorithm performance matches the risk-ignorant performance and even outperforms it. On the other hand, when* $p_\tau$ *or* $D$ *are large, the performance of risk-ignorant policy drops drastically, while the performance of our algorithm matches the risk-averse policy performance.*

To conclude this subsection, we illustrate the average ratio of our proposed approach from 500 iterations for each different values of $p_\tau$ and $D$ using a bar plot (Fig. 4). For $p_\tau = 0$ or $d_j^i = 0$, maximizing the expected total profit (our MILP-based approach) matches maximizing the total possible profit, and hence the ratio is 1. Furthermore, when $p_\tau = 1$, the ratio is also close to 1. This observation leads to insight 4:

**Insight 4.** *In the situations where there exist no uncertainty on the occurrence of attacks (i.e. the chance of a successful attack is either 0 or 1), our proposed approach reaches the maximum achievable total profit.*

**Insight 5.** *Generally, the loss in the total profit achieved by our proposed policy is caused by uncertainty on the occurrence of successful attacks. Particularly, when the probability of a successful attack is roughly about 0.5, the lowest performance of our approach is caused. More precisely, based on different levels of damage due to the attack, Table 4 shows the probabilities of a successful attack that leads to the lowest performance of our proposed method.*

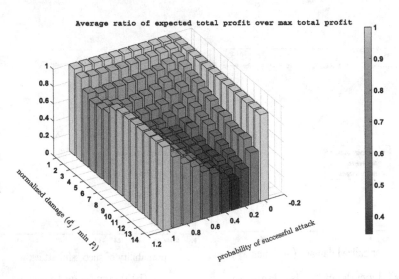

**Fig. 4.** Affect of different $p_\tau$ and $d_j^i$ on the average ratio

**Table 4.** Successful attack probabilities that cause the lowest performance of our proposed approach for the different level of damage due to the attack.

| $D$ | 13 | 12 | 11 | 10 | 9 | 8 | 7 | 6 | 5 | 4 | 3 | 2 | 1 |
|---|---|---|---|---|---|---|---|---|---|---|---|---|---|
| $p_\tau$ | 0.3 | 0.4 | 0.4 | 0.4,0.5 | 0.3,0.5 | 0.5 | 0.5,0.4 | 0.5,0.4 | 0.5,0.6 | 0.7 | 0.7 | 0.9 | 0.6,0.7 |

## 6.5  Sensitivity Analysis

In this scenario, we study the affect of incorrect estimation of the probability of occurrence of different attack types ($\alpha_j^i$) on the total profit. Over- or under-estimating this probability can result in non-optimal decisions:

(a) Decide to continue a mission while the optimal decision is to stop the mission, and vice versa.
(b) Decide to allocate the secure resources to a mission while the optimal decision is to only assign the local resources to that mission.

Consider the following scenario where there are three different types of mission: 10 missions have a low-level payout, 10 missions have a medium-level payout, and 5 missions have a high-level payout. The capacity of the secure special resources/server $\mathscr{W}_0 = 200$, and each mission requires $U([20\text{--}40])$ units of resource. The cost for each mission for using their local and the secure servers are $b_i = 1$ and $c_i = 2$, respectively. The payout of the high-level missions from their local server is in the range of $U([120\text{--}150])$ while their payout from the secure server is in $U([100\text{--}120])$. Further, the payout of the medium-level missions from their local server is in $U([100\text{--}120])$ while their payout from the secure server is in $U([80\text{--}100])$. The payout of the low-level missions from their local server is in $U([80\text{--}100])$ while their payout from the secure server is in $U([60\text{--}80])$. In this scenario, each mission is exposed to 10 different types of attack. The true probability of each type of attack for all missions is $\alpha_j^i = 0.25$. Table 5 summarizes the parameters for this scenario.

For each value of $\hat{\alpha}$ (estimated probability of occurrence of different attack types) and $d_j^i$ (damage due to those undesirable events), we run 500 iterations, and find the average error rate where the error rate is calculated by first finding the difference between the total profit when there is no error on the estimated probability ($\hat{\alpha}$) and the total profit when under/over-estimating $\hat{\alpha}$. Then, the absolute value of the difference is divided by the total profit when there is no error on the estimated probability. An error rate of greater than 1 indicates that the obtained total profit by miscalculating the probability of occurrence of attacks has a negative value. As expected the more we deviate from the true probability of occurrence of attacks the higher the error rate is. Figure 5 depicts the results when the true probability of occurrence of all types of attack is $\alpha_j^i = 0.25$.

**Table 5.** Data and parameters of the synthetic dataset.

| $\mathcal{W}_0 = 200$ | Missions | | |
| --- | --- | --- | --- |
| | $M_{\text{high}}$ | $M_{\text{med}}$ | $M_{\text{low}}$ |
| Number of missions | 5 | 10 | 10 |
| $G_i$ | U([20–40]) | U([20–40]) | U([20–40]) |
| $b_i$ | 1 | 1 | 1 |
| $c_i$ | 2 | 2 | 2 |
| Number of different types of attack | 10 | 10 | 10 |
| $\alpha_j^i$ | 0.25 | 0.25 | 0.25 |
| Estimated $\alpha_j^i$ | $\hat{\alpha}$ | $\hat{\alpha}$ | $\hat{\alpha}$ |
| $P_i$ | U([120–150]) | U([100–120]) | U([80–100]) |
| $Q_i$ | U([100–120]) | U([80–100]) | U([60–80]) |

**Insight 6.** *We observe that under-estimating the occurrence of different types of attack probabilities has more severe consequences than over-estimating them.*

**Insight 7.** *A counter-intuitive observation is that when over-estimating the probability of occurrence of different attack types, as the damage increases the error rate increases also. However, after the normalized damage reaches a certain level, the error rate starts to decrease.*

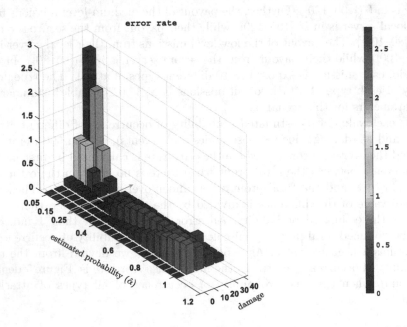

**Fig. 5.** Sensitivity to under/over-estimating the probability of occurrence of different types of attack. The green arrow shows the borderline of under- and over-estimation of the probability.

# 7    Limitations and Discussion

In this work, for mathematical simplicity, we assumed payouts ($P_i$'s and $Q_i$'s) and potential damage are proportional (linear) to the amount of allocated resources. In general, partial payouts and damage might have a nonlinear relation to the amount of allocated resources. However, these mathematical assumptions are prevalent, and usually, do not have a significant impact on the overall performance.

Another limitation of our framework is that we assumed the secure resources are immune from any successful attack, and hence, a mission whose request is fully satisfied from the secure server will not suffer from any attack. This might not be the case in real-world scenarios, and there could be a chance that the secure server is vulnerable to risk too. However, our model can be easily modified to address this scenario.

# 8    Conclusions

In this paper, we presented a mission-oriented security model—an optimization-based framework to allocating resources that integrates security risk, cost and payout metrics to optimally allocate constrained secure resources to discrete actions called missions. We modeled this deployment or adaptive decision problem as a Mixed Integer Linear Program (MILP) which can be solved efficiently by different optimization solvers such as MATLAB MILP solver. Additionally, we proposed a novel quantitative risk assessment technique to learn the attack rates and risk characteristic from historical data. We used this technique to maximize the expected total profit gained from all the missions. We evaluated our model using the existing risk surveys and validated the model robustness and uncovered a number of insights on the importance of risk valuation in resource allocation.

This work is an effort in developing techniques on how to allocate resources in the face of risk. The capability afforded by this model will allow us to explore different policies by evaluating their effectiveness when dealing with varying characteristics of risk. In the future, we will explore a wide range of environments and assess its ability to promote effectiveness to different adversarial assumptions.

**Acknowledgments.** Research was sponsored by the Army Research Laboratory and was accomplished under Cooperative Agreement Number W911NF-13-2-0045 (ARL Cyber Security CRA). The views and conclusions contained in this document are those of the authors and should not be interpreted as representing the official policies, either expressed or implied, of the Army Research Laboratory or the U.S. Government. The U.S. Government is authorized to reproduce and distribute reprints for Government purposes notwithstanding any copyright notation herein.

# References

1. Anderson, R., Moore, T.: The economics of information security. Science **314**, 610–613 (2006)
2. Anderson, R., Moore, T.: Information security economics – and beyond. In: Menezes, A. (ed.) CRYPTO 2007. LNCS, vol. 4622, pp. 68–91. Springer, Heidelberg (2007). https://doi.org/10.1007/978-3-540-74143-5_5
3. Celik, Z.B., et al.: Mapping sample scenarios to operational models. In: Military Communications Conference (MILCOM) (2016)
4. Cherdantseva, Y., et al.: A review of cyber security risk assessment methods for SCADA systems. Comput. secur. **56**, 1–27 (2016)
5. Dekker, M., Liveri, D.: Cloud security guide for SMEs-cloud computing security risks and opportunities for SMEs. European Union Agency for Network and Information Security (ENISA) (2015)
6. Floudas, C.A.: Nonlinear and Mixed-Integer Optimization: Fundamentals and Applications. Oxford University Press, Oxford (1995)
7. Gordon, L.A., Loeb, M.P.: The economics of information security investment. ACM Trans. Inf. Syst. Secur. (TISSEC) **5**, 438–457 (2002)
8. Gordon, L.A., Loeb, M.P., Lucyshyn, W., Richardson, R.: 2006 CSI/FBI computer crime and security survey (2006). www.lfca.net/ReferenceDocuments/2006CSI-FBISurvey.pdf. Accessed 11 Jan 2018
9. Holm, H.: A large-scale study of the time required to compromise a computer system. IEEE Trans. Dependable Secur. Comput. **11**, 2–15 (2014)
10. Hoo, K.J.S.: How Much is Enough? A Risk Management Approach to Computer Security. Stanford University, Stanford (2000). Consortium for Research on Information Security and Policy
11. Hu, N., La Porta, T., Bartolini, N.: Self-adaptive resource allocation for event monitoring with uncertainty in sensor networks. In: IEEE Mobile Ad Hoc and Sensor Systems (MASS) (2015)
12. Information technology - Security techniques - Information security risk management (2017). http://www.iso27001security.com/html/27005.html. Accessed 11 Jan 2018
13. Jajodia, S., Ghosh, A.K., Swarup, V., Wang, C., Wang, X.S.: Moving tArget Defense: Creating Asymmetric Uncertainty for Cyber Threats, vol. 54. Springer, New York (2011). https://doi.org/10.1007/978-1-4614-0977-9
14. Kaplan, S., Garrick, B.J.: On the quantitative definition of risk. Risk Anal. **1**, 11–27 (1981)
15. McDaniel, P., et al.: Security and science of agility. In: ACM Workshop on Moving Target Defense (2014)
16. Nicol, D.M., Sanders, W.H., Trivedi, K.S.: Model-based evaluation: from dependability to security. IEEE Trans. Dependable Secur. Comput. **1**, 48–65 (2004)
17. Papoulis, A., Pillai, S.U.: Probability, Random Variables, and Stochastic Processes. Tata McGraw-Hill Education, New York City (2002)
18. Ponemon Institute: Cost of cyber crime study and the risk of business innovation (2016). http://www8.hp.com/us/en/software-solutions/ponemon-cyber-security-report/. Accessed 11 Jan 2018
19. Richardson, R.: Issues and trends: 2003 CSI/FBI computer crime and security survey (2003). www.lfca.net/ReferenceDocuments/2003-CSI-FBI-Survey.pdf. Accessed 11 Jan 2018
20. Richardson, R.: 2010/2011 computer crime and security survey (2010)
21. Schneidewind, N.F.: Cyber security prediction models. In: Systems and Software Engineering with Applications (2005)

# On the Feasibility of Fine-Grained TLS Security Configurations in Web Browsers Based on the Requested Domain Name

Eman Salem Alashwali[1,2(✉)] and Kasper Rasmussen[1]

[1] University of Oxford, Oxford, UK
{eman.alashwali,kasper.rasmussen}@cs.ox.ac.uk
[2] King Abdulaziz University (KAU), Jeddah, Saudi Arabia
ealashwali@kau.edu.sa

**Abstract.** Most modern web browsers today sacrifice optimal TLS security for backward compatibility. They apply coarse-grained TLS configurations that support (by default) legacy versions of the protocol that have known design weaknesses, and weak ciphersuites that provide fewer security guarantees (e.g. non Forward Secrecy), and silently fall back to them if the server selects to. This introduces various risks including downgrade attacks such as the POODLE attack [15] that exploits the browsers silent fallback mechanism to downgrade the protocol version in order to exploit the legacy version flaws. To achieve a better balance between security and backward compatibility, we propose a mechanism for fine-grained TLS configurations in web browsers based on the sensitivity of the domain name in the HTTPS request using a whitelisting technique. That is, the browser enforces optimal TLS configurations for connections going to sensitive domains while enforcing default configurations for the rest of the connections. We demonstrate the feasibility of our proposal by implementing a proof-of-concept as a Firefox browser extension. We envision this mechanism as a built-in security feature in web browsers, e.g. a button similar to the "Bookmark" button in Firefox browsers and as a standardised HTTP header, to augment browsers security.

## 1 Introduction

The Transport Layer Security (TLS) protocol [8,20] is one of the most important and widely used protocols to date. It is used to secure internet communications for billions of people everyday. TLS provides a secure communication channel between two communicating parties. At the beginning of each new TLS session, the client and server must agree on a single common TLS version and ciphersuite to be used in that session. These are extremely important parameters as they define the security guarantees that the protocol can provide in a particular session. TLS supports various protocol versions and ciphersuites. Each ciphersuite

© ICST Institute for Computer Sciences, Social Informatics and Telecommunications Engineering 2018
R. Beyah et al. (Eds.): SecureComm 2018, LNICST 255, pp. 213–228, 2018.
https://doi.org/10.1007/978-3-030-01704-0_12

is a string that defines the cryptographic algorithms that will be used in a particular session. Generally, these algorithms include[1]: the Key-Exchange, Digital Signature, Symmetric Encryption, Authenticated Encryption (AE), and Hash. Clients[2] and servers tend to support legacy versions, e.g. TLS 1.1 and TLS 1.0, and weak, less secure, or unrecommended ciphersuites, e.g. non-Forward Secrecy (non-FS), non-Authenticated Encryption (non-AE)[3], or weak Hash algorithms, mainly to provide backward compatibility with legacy servers. For example, a recent analysis of IPv4 internet scan dataset shows that embedded web servers in networked devices tend to use legacy TLS versions compared to top domain web servers [21]. To accommodate such servers, web browsers tend to support legacy versions and weak ciphersuites to be able to connect to such legacy servers. The same goes for updated servers. They support legacy versions and weak ciphersuites so as not to lose connections from legacy clients.

## 1.1   Motivation

In the near future, the coming version of TLS, TLS 1.3, which is currently work in progress [20], will become a standard. Ideally, mainstream browsers[4] will deploy it and offer it as the default version. TLS 1.3 provides significant improvements in security and performance over its predecessors. However, experience has shown that ordinary web servers may take years till they get upgraded to support the latest TLS version. This is especially true in embedded web servers as we mentioned earlier. For this reason, web browsers tend to maintain support for legacy TLS versions and weak ciphersuites and silently (without warning or indicator) fall back to them if the server they are trying to connect to does not support the latest version or the strongest ciphersuite. This is the case in all mainstream web browsers today. It is not inconceivable that this will remain the case after the deployment of the coming version, TLS 1.3, despite numerous known weaknesses including design flaws in the current version, TLS 1.2. For example, legacy versions up to TLS 1.2 do not authenticate the server's selected version and ciphersuite at early stage of the handshake. This flaw allows various attacks that result in breaking the protocol's main security guarantees as shown in [3,6], for example.

There are several TLS attacks that exploit the support for legacy versions or weak ciphersuites by one or both of the communicating parties during the TLS handshake. This family of attacks is known as downgrade attack, where an

---

[1] TLS 1.2 and TLS 1.3 ciphersuite strings have different format and define different set of algorithms. See [8] and [20] for more details.

[2] In our paper, TLS clients are represented by web browsers. We will use the terms client, web browser, or browser interchangeably.

[3] In our context, non-AE refers to ciphersuites that do not provide confidentiality, integrity, and authenticity simultaneously. For example the CBC MAC-then-encrypt ciphersuites which are susceptible to padding oracle attacks [25,28].

[4] Throughout the paper, mainstream browsers refer to the following tested versions: Chrome version 63.0.3239.108, Firefox 57.0.2, Internet Explorer 11.125.16299.0, Edge 41.16299.15.0, and Opera 49.0.2725.64.

active network attacker forces the communicating parties to operate in a mode that is weaker than they would prefer and support, in order for him to perform attacks that would not have been possible in the strong mode. For example, [3,5–7,15], among others.

The tension between security and backward compatibility in cryptographic protocols is historical. Backward compatibility seems inevitable in internet protocols such as TLS due to the global and heterogeneous nature of the connected devices over the internet, in addition to the heavy reliance on the internet services in people's daily lives. From the client's perspective (which is our focus in this paper), if a browser is configured with optimal TLS configurations, i.e. it only negotiates the latest version of TLS, e.g. TLS 1.3, and a handful of the strongest ciphersuites that satisfy *both* FS and AE properties, this can be the strongest client but can render many ordinary websites on legacy servers unreachable due to compatibility issues. Obviously, this will lead to a difficult user experience. On the other hand, if the client supports legacy versions, e.g. TLS 1.0 and weak or non preferred ciphersuites, e.g. non-FS or non-AE as is the case in all mainstream web browsers today, the browser silently falls back to one of the legacy versions or weak ciphersuites to connect to those legacy servers that do not support the latest version or the strongest ciphersuites.

To maintain a balance between the two extremes, the browser needs to distinguish between various contexts and apply fine-grained TLS configurations. That is, the browser enforces optimal configurations for connections going to sensitive domains, and default ones for the rest of the connections.

To this end, we try to answer the following question: *How can we guide the browser into making an informed decision on whether to enforce optimal or default TLS configurations?*

## 1.2   Contribution

Our contribution is twofold: First, we propose a light-weight mechanism for fine-grained TLS security configurations in web browsers. Our mechanism allows browsers to enforce optimal TLS security configurations for connections going to sensitive domains while maintaining default configurations for the rest of the connections. It represents a middle-ground between optimal TLS configurations that might render many ordinary websites unreachable and default configurations that might be abused by attackers to perform downgrade attacks. Our mechanism can detect and prevent a class of dangerous downgrade attacks and server misconfigurations. Furthermore, it does not require a new Public Key Infrastructure (PKI) nor third parties such as Certificate Authorities (CAs). Second, we examine the feasibility of our mechanism by implementing a proof-of-concept as a Firefox browser extension. In addition, we present the extension architecture.

## 1.3  Organisation

The rest of the paper is organised as follows: In Sect. 2 we provide a brief background. In Sect. 3 we summarise some related work. In Sect. 4 we describe our system and threat models, and goals. In Sect. 5 we present our proposed mechanism. In Sect. 6 we briefly describe some other server-based TLS configurations advertisement methods. In Sect. 7 we list some limitations. Finally, in Sect. 8 we conclude.

# 2  Background

## 2.1  TLS Version and Ciphersuite Negotiation

We now briefly describe the version and ciphersuite negotiation in both TLS 1.2 [8] and TLS 1.3 (draft-24) [20]. We base our description on the current version, TLS 1.2, and if there is any difference in TLS 1.3 we mention it explicitly. As depicted in Fig. 1, at the beginning of a new TLS handshake the client (Initiator $I$) must send a ClientHello (CH) message to initiate a connection with the server (Responder $R$). The ClientHello contains several parameters including: First, the client's TLS supported versions which is sent as a single value that represents the maximum supported version ($vmax_I$) while in TLS 1.3, it is sent as a list of supported versions ($[v_1, ..., v_n]$) in the "supported_versions" extension. The $vmax_I$ is still included in TLS 1.3 ClientHello for backward compatibility and its value is set to TLS 1.2. Second, a list of supported ciphersuites ($[a_1, ..., a_n]$). Third, a list of the client's supported extensions ($[e_1, ... ,e_n]$) is sent at the end of the message. In TLS 1.3 the extensions must at least include the "supported_versions" $[v_1, ..., v_n]$, while in TLS 1.2, the extensions are optional.

Upon receiving a ClientHello, the server decides which version and ciphersuite will be used in the session and responds with a ServerHello (SH). The ServerHello contains several parameters including: First, the server's selected TLS version ($v_R$) based on the client's supported versions. Second, the selected ciphersuite ($a_R$) based on the client's proposed list. If the server does not support any of the client's proposed versions or ciphersuites, it responds with a handshake failure alert. However, if the server selected a version lower than the client's maximum version, all mainstream web browsers today fall back silently to a lower version (up to TLS 1.0).

## 2.2  TLS Downgrade Attack

In recent years, several downgrade attacks have been shown practical. For example, the version downgrade in the Padding Oracle On Downgraded Legacy Encryption (POODLE) attack [15], the "Version rollback by ClientHello fragmentation" [7], and the ciphersuite downgrade (from RSA to non-RSA) in a variant of the DROWN attack [5].

The aforementioned attacks share a pattern: First, the client supports either a legacy version (SSL 3.0 or TLS 1.0) or non preferred or weak ciphersuite (RSA)

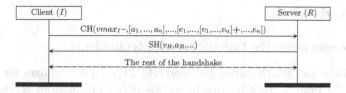

**Fig. 1.** Simplified message sequence diagram illustrating the version and ciphersuite negotiation in the TLS `Hello` messages. Parameters followed by "−" are deprecated in TLS 1.3 while those followed by "+" are newly introduced in TLS 1.3. The unmarked parameters are mutual to both versions.

and silently falls back to them. Second, the attacks circumvent the handshake transcript authentication mechanism (in the `Finished` MACs) that is placed to detect any modifications in the protocol messages (including the version or ciphersuite). Clearly, these attacks could have been prevented if the client does not support legacy versions or weak ciphersuites. In these cases, the client will refuse to proceed the handshake with a version or ciphersuite that it does not support, as illustrated in Fig. 2. One might argue that this is what all browsers should do: disable all legacy versions and unrecommended ciphersuites that provide fewer security guarantees (e.g. non-FS) and never accept them from any server. Experience shows that disabling legacy versions and exclusively offering the strongest ciphersuites is a complex decision for browser vendors. Browser vendors scarifies optimal TLS security configurations to some degree to provide backward compatibility for their users who might need to connect to legacy servers as we mentioned earlier. However, in this paper, we do not argue for or against. Rather, we explore the solutions space to augment browsers security while maintaining usability and backward compatibility. Our mechanism augments browsers security for connections to sensitive domains that are capable of providing optimal TLS configurations (but also support legacy configurations for legacy clients) by providing the browser with prior knowledge about these sensitive domains. This is an improvement over the "one-size-fits-all" TLS security policy in all mainstream web browsers which renders some downgrade attacks undetected.

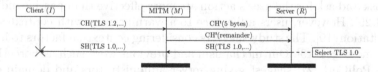

**Fig. 2.** Illustration of a version downgrade attack attempt based on the "Version rollback by ClientHello fragmentation" attack scenario [7] when the client does not support legacy TLS versions.

# 3   Related Work

## 3.1   Browsers Security Enhancement Mechanisms

In [12] Jackson and Barth introduce "ForceHTTPS", a mechanism for enforcing strict HTTPS policy. Websites opt-in to this policy either from the server side by advertising a special HTTP response header, or from the client side by the user. The strict policy converts any plain HTTP URL to HTTPS and performs stricter TLS certificate validation than the default one. The mechanism blocks any opted-in website that violates the policy. Our work is similar in spirit to [12], and can be viewed as an extension to [12], at a finer level. Our mechanism is for enforcing optimal TLS *configurations* (TLS version and ciphersuites) using a different technique (whitelisting). Unlike a decade ago, nowadays enforcing TLS is not sufficient. We aim for methods to enforce optimal TLS. Experience has shown the practicality of TLS version and ciphersuite downgrade attacks that circumvent design-level downgrade protection mechanisms (e.g. by exploiting implementation bugs). These attacks abuse the support of legacy versions or ciphersuites by one or both parties, which result in breaking TLS main security guarantees as in [5, 7, 15].

In [27] Szalachowski et al. propose PoliCert which introduces the idea of policy certificate which includes optional parameters to specify the minimum TLS security level that the client should enforce and the error handling mechanism. Our idea of enforcing fine-grained TLS configurations complements and provides a new perspective for a relevant concept. However, there are subtle differences between the two work. For example, unlike [27], our proposal does not require a new PKI nor CAs. It is a light-weight mechanism that can be adopted by browser vendors as an additional layer of security.

Overall, we are not aware of an existing light-weight mechanism or browser extension that proposes or implements our concept in this paper.

## 3.2   Warning Messages in Web Browsers

Previous work shows that users tend to ignore passive security indicators such as the padlock and the Extended Validation (EV)[5] indicators [13, 23].

On the other hand, it has become clear that active warnings that interrupt the user's task and ask for the user's action are more effective than passive indicators [4, 10, 23, 29]. However, users adherence to a warning vary with context such as site reputation [19]. The study suggests considering contextual factors to improve warning messages [19]. Our mechanism and previous work such as ForceHTTPS [12] and PoliCert [27] suggest giving server administrators and domain owners means to advertise strict TLS security policies and error handling which can help protect users from making bad security decisions.

---

[5] Extended Validation is a passive browser indicator that appears in the address bar only for websites which have strongly verified identity.

Warning messages should be avoided in benign situations to avoid the "habituation" effect that results from seeing the warning too often such that users underestimate the risk behind it [26].

These studies give useful insights that will be considered in the usability aspect of our mechanism.

# 4 Our System and Threat Models, and Goals

Our system model consists of TLS client and server trying to establish a TLS connection. TLS proxies[6] (middleboxes) are out of our system's model scope. Both parties support multiple TLS versions and ciphersuites with various security levels. The TLS client is represented by mainstream web browsers. It supports and prefers the latest TLS version and the strongest ciphersuite. However, for backward compatibility, it also supports legacy versions and weak ciphersuites, and silently falls back to them if the server selected a legacy version or weak ciphersuite. The client implements the "downgrade dance" mechanism that makes the browser fall back to a lower version and retry the handshake if the initial handshake failed for any reason as is the case in the POODLE attack [15]. Ideally, updated web browsers today do not support completely broken cryptographic algorithms (ciphersuites). However, they do support ciphersuites that provide fewer security guarantees such as those with non-FS key-exchange or non-AE. The assumption that the browser supports weak, unrecommended, or plausibly broken ciphersuites is realistic and can happen in the future. Classical cryptographic algorithms do not last forever. Algorithm design flaws can be found, and advances in computation powers enable solving hard problems such as prime factorisation. For example, several algorithms were supported through years of speculations about their insecurity until they got officially deprecated such as the RC4 algorithm [18].

In terms of threat model, our model assumes that the client and server are honest peers. The adversary has full control over the communication channel and can drop, modify, inject, or redirect messages in the channel.

In terms of system goals, our proposal tries to mitigate the risks that can result from the browsers silent fallback to a legacy TLS version or weak ciphersuite which puts the client at the risk of:

1. Falling victim to downgrade attacks by a man-in-the-middle that exploits the client support for legacy versions or ciphersuites. For example, the case of version downgrade in the POODLE attack [15] which allows the attacker to exploit flaws in the legacy version to decrypt secret data.

---

[6] A proxy (also known as middlebox) is an entity that can be placed between a client and server for various purposes such as interception or packet inspection. It splits the TLS connection between the client and server so that the client and server are in fact connecting to the proxy and not directly to each other.

2. Connect to misconfigured servers for important services such as ebanking and egovernment websites, or important services that are not necessarily maintained by large service providers or experts who are up-to-date with advances in security. For example, an organisation's web mail server.

# 5  Our Proposal

## 5.1  Overview

Our proposal tries to tackle the challenge of providing a high level of security for connections to sensitive websites while maintaining backward compatibility with ordinary websites in TLS implementations in web browsers. To this end, we propose a mechanism for fine-grained TLS configurations. That is, optimal TLS configurations are enforced for connections to sensitive domains, while default configurations are enforced for the rest of the connections. To do this, the browser needs guidance to distinguish between different contexts. We achieve this by providing the browser with prior knowledge through a pre-defined list of sensitive domain names, e.g. ebanking, egovernment, ebusiness portals, etc. that guides the browser into whether to enforce the optimal TLS configurations or the default ones. See Fig. 3 for an overview of our proposed mechanism.

To realise the idea, we implemented a proof-of-concept as a Firefox browser extension. For the extension's implementation, we built a hybrid Firefox extension using WebExtensions API [17] and Add-on SDK [16]. We run the extension in Firefox Developer edition version 56.0b3 (32-bit). The overall concept seems straight-forward but implementing it required non-trivial effort to overcome WebExtensions API limitations to perform low-level functions such as the configurations re-writing and error messages customisation.

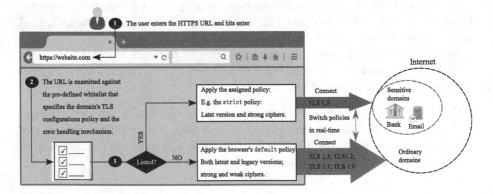

**Fig. 3.** Illustration for our proposed fine-grained TLS configurations mechanism applied on the TLS versions (omitting the ciphersuites for simplicity).

## 5.2  Subscribing to the Mechanism

Websites (domains) can subscribe to our mechanism by two methods. The first method is a client-side method which targets two groups of users: First, security-conscious users who want to protect their sensitive connections, e.g. connections to email and ebanking websites, from the threats described in the system goals in Sect. 4. Second, Information Technology (IT) administrators in organisations such as banks, universities, etc. who can whitelist some sensitive domains in their employees PCs and laptops so that any connection from their devices to these domains is initiated using optimal TLS configurations. Similar to any client-side security feature, the mechanism requires some level of awareness about its benefits to incentivize users to use it.

The second subscription method is a server-side method through an HTTP response header. The server administrator needs to configure the server to send the mechanism's specific header. Upon receiving, our extension adds the domain name that has sent the header to the whitelist. This method does not require user intervention but assumes an authentic first connection that contains the HTTP header, also known as Trust On First Use (TOFU). This is a well understood prerequisite for all header-based policies such as HSTS [11], Content Security Policy (CSP) [24] and Public-Key Pinning (PKP) [1]. Therefore, the user must make the first connection to these website that advertise the mechanism's header using a trusted network. In addition, unlike the client-side method where the policy can be enforced before the first HTTPS request is sent, in the server-side subscription method, the policy can only be enforced after a first request is sent (to get the server response header first).

## 5.3  Architecture

Our Firefox extension's components can be described as follows:

**Pre-Defined TLS Configuration Policies.** The policies govern the TLS configurations that will be enforced before an HTTPS request is sent. The TLS configurations space for our policies is the set of versions and ciphersuites that exist in Firefox Developer edition version 56.0b3. That is, in terms of versions: TLS 1.3, TLS 1.2, TLS 1.1, and TLS 1.0, and in terms of ciphersuites: 15 ciphersuites that provide different levels of security guarantees which include FS, non-FS, AE, and non-AE ciphersuites. There is a consensus among the security community that FS and AE ciphersuites provide stronger security guarantees than non-FS or non-AE. Therefore, for our set of ciphersuites in Firefox we can define strong cipehrsuites as those that provides *both* FS and AE, while weak ciphersuites as those that do not support FS or AE or both, as they provide fewer security guarantees. Similarly, if there are known or plausibly broken primitives in any cipehrsuite (this can happen in the future), it can not be added to the set of strong ciphersuites.

For our proof-of-concept, we define two TLS configuration policies and hard code them in the extension: `strict` which represents the optimal TLS configurations, and `default` which represents the default configurations. The `strict` policy is the strictest class which supports only TLS 1.3[7], and only the TLS 1.3 ciphersuites that provide *both* AE and FS. Second, the `default` policy (default configurations) is equivalent to the Firefox Developer edition version 56.0b3 default configurations which support TLS 1.3, TLS 1.2, TLS 1.1 and TLS 1.0, and 15 different ciphersuites including FS, non-FS, AE, and non-AE ciphersuites. See Table 1 for our proof-of-concept TLS policy levels.

The number of policy levels is a design decision. We could have defined more levels if desired. For example, we could have defined a level for each version of TLS. The more levels, the more granularity is achieved. However, more granularity means more warning messages since the essence of our mechanism is to either warn the user before falling back to a lower policy or block the user from proceeding to the website (depending on the error handling mechanism that is assigned to that domain as we will elaborate later), unlike the browser's default behaviour that silently falls back to a lower version or weaker ciphersuite without warning which can render some downgrade attacks or misconfigured important servers undetected. We try to maintain a balance between security and usability and decided to define two levels policy where there is a significant shift in the provided security guarantees, and present only one warning message to the user in case of policy violation.

**Table 1.** Our extension's built-in policies.

| Policy level | TLS version | Ciphersuites |
|---|---|---|
| Strict | TLS 1.3 | *Both* FS and AE |
| Default | TLS 1.3; TLS 1.2; TLS 1.1; TLS 1.0 | FS; AE; non-FS; non-AE |

**Pre-Defined Domain Names List.** The domain names list combined with the TLS policy that is assigned to each domain name is used to provide the browser with the prior knowledge that guides it into which TLS policy should be enforced for each examined HTTPS request. In our proof-of-concept, the domain names list takes the domain names from two sources: either manually as an input from the user, or automatically by extracting the domain name from the URL that sent the mechanism's specified HTTP header. The domains are entered in the form of "example.com". We do not allow duplicate domain names. Therefore, a domain's TLS policy can not be over-written unless after removing the existing

---

[7] We hypothetically and proactively assume TLS 1.3 is the highest version in our TLS policy levels' definitions. This will be the case when TLS 1.3 becomes a standard soon. However, in practice (and in our proof-of-concept) the highest possible version is still TLS 1.2.

record. By default, the domain names are added to the strictest TLS policy that enforces optimal TLS configurations which is the `strict` policy. However, if the connection using the optimal TLS configurations could not be established due to lack of server support for the requested configurations, the user is presented with a warning message. Depending on the error handling mechanism (will be explained next) that is assigned to that particular domain, the user will be either blocked from proceeding to the website, or warned and allowed to relax the domain's TLS policy to a lower one (from `strict` to `default` in our case).

**Pre-Defined Error Handling Mechanism.** In general, there are three main strategies for error handling in web browsers: blocking, active warning, and passive warning. Blocking is a conservative approach that blocks the user from proceeding to the website. It should be used when the attack is certain. This approach is adopted by the "ForceHTTPS" mechanism which considers violating the strict TLS policy by an opted-in website as an attack [12]. On the other hand, the active warning strategy is less conservative. It temporarily blocks the user to warn him, but it allows him to click-through (bypass) the error through one or multiple clicks. This strategy is used in the self-signed certificate warning in most browsers today. Finally, the passive warning strategy shows an indicator which can be negative or positive indicator without interrupting the user's task, e.g. the padlock icon. As stated earlier, previous studies suggest that active warnings are more effective than passive ones, but need to be used with caution not to cause the "habituation" effect.

In our browser extension, the error handling mechanism specifies the type of the error message that will be presented to the user in case of TLS policy violation. Each whitelisted domain has a TLS policy and an error handling mechanism assigned to it. We define two error handling mechanisms: `blocking` and `active warning`. The error mechanism depends on the subscription method (client-side or server-side) which implies the level of confidence on the server's ability to meet optimal TLS configurations.

- If the domain subscription is client-side through a user, the user has the choice to assign either `blocking` or `active warning` error handling to the domain. By default, the error handling mechanism for client-side subscription is set to `active warning`. However, if the user (e.g. IT administrator) has high level of confidence that the added domain should be able to meet the `strict` TLS policy (e.g. bank or enterprise server), he can select the `blocking` error handling mechanism to block the user from proceeding to the website if the TLS server response violated the policy.
- If the domain subscription is server-side through an HTTP response header, the mechanism automatically assign the `blocking` error handling mechanism for the advertising domain. Servers that advertise the mechanism's header must first ensure that they are capable of meeting the `strict` TLS policy requirements. They must be aware that their users will be blocked from reaching the server if the `strict` TLS configurations policy has been violated. This is a conservative approach towards highly secure connections and

reduced decision making effort on users, in the same direction of HSTS policy [11]. We adopt it when the confidence of the server's TLS capabilities is high (i.e., when the knowledge comes from the server side) to avoid denial of service.

**HTTP Observers.** The extension employs three observers (listeners) running in the background (as long as the extension is running):

1. **HTTP Before Send Request Observer.** This observer examines every HTTPS request that goes through the main address bar. The URL is either manually entered in the address bar by the user or automatically through URL redirection or through clicking on links. The examination occurs *before* the request is sent, against the pre-defined domain names list. If the examined URL (e.g. mail.example.com/etc) belongs to any of the whitelisted domains (e.g. example.com), the extension enforces the TLS policy that is assigned to that domain. If the requested URL does not belong to any of the whitelsited domains, the extension enforces the browser's default policy. After the policy enforcement, the request is sent. Note that the browser re-writes the configurations in real-time. Therefore, if the next URL does not belong to a whitelisted domain, the default policy will be re-enforced again.

2. **HTTP Response Header Observer.** This observer examines every HTTP response header against a pre-defined header that we name it "strict-transport-security-config". A server that wishes to subscribe to our strict TLS policy must send this header in its HTTP response. Upon receiving, the browser interprets this as a request to add the domain to the whitelist in the strict configurations policy with a blocking error handling. Advertising security policies through the HTTP response header has been employed in the literature in other policies such as HSTS [2,11] to enforce HTTPS to protect against TLS stripping attacks, CSP [24] to enforce trusted sources for page content scripts to protect against script injection attacks, and PKP header [1] to bind specific public keys to a website to protect against forged certificates. However, as stated earlier, the header advertisement method assumes a TOFU, i.e. the header is sent from an authentic server and not a man-in-the-middle. In addition, ideally such headers also contains a maximum-age parameter that specifies an age after which the header is expired, and the server needs to re-subscribe through the next header (in our mechanism header expiration implies removing the domain from the whitelist). For simplicity, in our proof-of-concept, our header consists of a name field only, without any fine-grained header parameters such as the maximum-age.

3. **HTTP Error Observer.** This observer is triggered when the request can not be processed due to lack of common TLS version or ciphersuite between the client and server. Our extension builds on the browser's built-in error detection mechanism but we customise the browser error page if the error occurred for one of the whitelisted domains. Our extension detects the version or ciphersuites mismatch errors by observing the

loaded documents (i.e. tabs) Uniform Resource Identifier (URI). We match every loaded tab's URI against defined patterns that represent the Firefox's version and ciphersuites mismatch errors URIs. In particular, we check if the loaded tab URI starts with "about:neterror" and contains either "SSL_ERROR_UNSUPPORTED_VERSION" or "SSL_ERROR_NO_CYPHER_OVERLAP". Note that these patterns are vendor-specific. If a match is found, the extension extracts the URL that caused the error from the tab URI. Then, it examines the just extracted URL against the whitelist. If the URL belongs to a whitelisted domain name, the extension updates the tab with our extension's customised error page according to the error handling mechanism that is assigned to the domain name.

**Error Message.** As described earlier, if the browser could not complete the handshake due to lack of common TLS version or ciphersuite with the server, a customised error page is shown to the user. Our mechanism employs two approaches for error handling: `blocking` and `active warning`. The browser selects the strategy based on the error handling mechanism that is assigned to the domain in the whitelist as described earlier in this section (see "Pre-Defined Error Handling Mechanism").

In all cases, the error message is shown when the suspicious is higher than normal, based on the prior knowledge the browser has obtained either from the user or from the server about the sensitivity of the domain. It presents the user with a short message describing the reason of the error. If the error handling mechanism is `active warning` the message also contains two buttons. The first button is labeled "Restore Defaults", and the second one is "Close". The first button will relax the domain's policy to the `default` policy and will try to connect again, through one click. This approach is similar to the Firefox built-in approach for handling version or ciphersuite mismatch error which presents "Restore Defaults" button that restores the Firefox's default TLS versions and ciphersuites and reconnect, through one click. However, there is an intrinsic difference between our `active warning` error handling mechanism and the Firefox built-in mechanism. In our mechanism, the "Restore Defaults" button will change the configurations of the concerned domain only, and will not affect any other domain that the user may desire a `strict` TLS policy for. Thanks to our fine-grained TLS configurations concept that enables this feature. On the other hand, the "Restore Defaults" in the built-in Firefox warning will change the global configurations which will relax the configurations at a coarse-grained level and the new configurations will affect every connection.

Our warning message design is an initial prototype. Indeed, a further study with a focus on the usability aspect in addition to a user study needs its own space and we leave this for future work.

# 6  Other Methods for Policy Advertisement

There are other server-side policy advertisement methods that can be employed. In this section, we briefly describe some methods.

- **Domain Name System (DNS) Record.** The DNS [14] in conjunction with DNSSEC [9] (the latter is to provide authentication) can include records for policy advertisement. This method has been proposed in HTTPSSR [22], a mechanism that advertises TLS support by a domain name through a DNS record, to protect against stripping attacks. If DNS in conjunction with DNSSEC is used for TLS configurations advertisement, it eliminates the TOFU issue and allows the configurations to be effective before the first connection request is sent since the DNS query is performed before the TLS request is sent. However, DNSSEC adoption might still be a barrier to rely on DNS for policy advertisement as noted in [12].
- **Certificates.** The use of certificates to advertise policies has been proposed in PoliCert [27]. PoliCert proposes a separate certificate for policies that has optional parameter that informs the browser about the server's desired TLS minimum security level. The policy certificate method eliminates the TOFU issue since the certificate is signed by a trusted-third-party. However, it inherits the trusted-third-party complexity such as the cost since the domain owner needs to sign the policy by multiple CAs. Furthermore, similar to the HTTP header advertisement method, the policies can not be enforced before the first request is sent as the certificate needs to be received in a first connection.

## 7   Limitations

In our proof-of-concept implementation there are few limitations: First, we used Add-on SDK (which is deprecated starting from Firefox 57.0) to perform the configurations re-writing which is not supported in Webextensions API. However, our present purpose is to demonstrate the feasibility of the concept. The configurations re-writing will not represent an issue if the mechanism got implemented at the browser source code level. Second, we do not consider measuring the performance at this stage. It can be measured if the mechanism is implemented at the browser source code level. As stated earlier, our scope in this paper is to propose and test the feasibility of the concept.

## 8   Conclusion and Future Work

Motivated by the experimental deployment of the coming version of TLS, TLS 1.3, we look at the problem of providing backward compatibility with legacy servers while maintaining security in web browsers. We propose a mechanism for fine-grained TLS security configurations in web browsers to augment browsers security and reduce the attack surface that exploits the client support for legacy versions, and non preferred or weak ciphersuites. Our proposal enables web browsers to learn about websites sensitivity and enforce optimal TLS configurations when connecting to sensitive websites while enforcing default configurations when connecting to the rest of the websites. This is an improvement over the "one-size-fits-all" coarse-grained TLS configurations mechanism that is used in all mainstream web browsers today. Our mechanism represents a middle-ground between optimal TLS configurations that might render many ordinary websites unreachable and default configurations that might be abused by attackers. We present our tool's architecture and examine the feasibility of our proposal by implementing a proof-of-concept as a Firefox browser extension. We envision this mechanism as a built-in security feature in modern web browsers and as a standardised HTTP header that augment browsers security. Future work will focus on the usability aspect in addition to exploring new methods for server-based policy advertisement.

**Acknowledgment.** The authors would like to thank Prof. Karthikeyan Bhargavan and Prof. Andrew Martin for useful feedback, Nicholas Moore for useful discussions on javascript, William Seymour and John Gallacher for proofreading.

# References

1. Public key pinning extension for HTTP (2015). https://www.rfc-editor.org/rfc/rfc7469.txt
2. HSTS preloaded list submission (2017). https://hstspreload.org/
3. Adrian, D., et al.: Imperfect forward secrecy: how Diffie-Hellman fails in practice. In: Proceedings of Conference on Computer and Communications Security (CCS 2015), pp. 5–17 (2015)
4. Akhawe, D., Felt, A.P.: Alice in warningland: a large-scale field study of browser security warning effectiveness. In: Proceedings of USENIX Security Symposium, pp. 257–272 (2013)
5. Aviram, N., et al.: DROWN: breaking TLS using SSLv2. In: Proceedings of USENIX Security Symposium, pp. 689–706 (2016)
6. Beurdouche, B., et al.: A messy state of the union: taming the composite state machines of TLS. In: Proceedings of IEEE Symposium on Security and Privacy (SP), pp. 535–552 (2015)
7. Beurdouche, B., Delignat-Lavaud, A., Kobeissi, N., Pironti, A., Bhargavan, K.: FLEXTLS a tool for testing TLS implementations. In: Proceedings of 9th USENIX Workshop on Offensive Technologies (WOOT) (2014)
8. Dierks, T., Rescorla, E.: The transport layer security (TLS) protocol version 1.2 (2008). https://tools.ietf.org/html/rfc5246
9. Eastlake, D.: Domain name system security extensions (1999). https://tools.ietf.org/html/rfc2535
10. Egelman, S., Cranor, L.F., Hong, J.: You've been warned: an empirical study of the effectiveness of web browser phishing warnings. In: Proceedings of Human Factors in Computing Systems (SIGCHI), pp. 1065–1074 (2008)
11. Hodges, J., Jackson, C., Barth, A.: HTTP strict transport security (HSTS) (2012). https://tools.ietf.org/html/rfc6797
12. Jackson, C., Barth, A.: ForceHTTPS: protecting high-security web sites from network attacks. In: Proceedings of 17th International Conference on World Wide Web (WWW 2008), pp. 525–534 (2008)
13. Jackson, C., Simon, D.R., Tan, D.S., Barth, A.: An evaluation of extended validation and picture-in-picture phishing attacks. In: Dietrich, S., Dhamija, R. (eds.) FC 2007. LNCS, vol. 4886, pp. 281–293. Springer, Heidelberg (2007). https://doi.org/10.1007/978-3-540-77366-5_27

14. Mockapetris, P.: Domain names - implementation and specification (1987). https://www.ietf.org/rfc/rfc1035.txt
15. Möller, B., Duong, T., Kotowicz, K.: This POODLE bites: exploiting the SSL 3.0 fallback (2014). https://www.openssl.org/~bodo/ssl-poodle.pdf
16. Mozilla: Add-on SDK (2017). https://developer.mozilla.org/en-US/Add-ons/SDK
17. Mozilla: Browser extensions (2017). https://developer.mozilla.org/en-US/Add-ons/WebExtensions
18. Popov, A.: Prohibiting RC4 cipher suites (2015). https://tools.ietf.org/html/rfc7465
19. Reeder, R., Felt, A.P., Consolvo, S., Malkin, N., Thompson, C., Egelman, S.: An experience sampling study of user reactions to browser warnings in the field. In: Proceedings of ACM CHI Conference in Human Factors on Computing Systems (2018)
20. Rescorla, E.: The transport layer security (TLS) protocol version 1.3 draft-ietf-tls-tls13-24 (2018). https://tools.ietf.org/html/draft-ietf-tls-tls13-24
21. Samarasinghe, N., Mannan, M.: Short paper: TLS ecosystems in networked devices vs. web servers. In: Kiayias, A. (ed.) FC 2017. LNCS, vol. 10322, pp. 533–541. Springer, Cham (2017). https://doi.org/10.1007/978-3-319-70972-7_30
22. Schechter, S.: Storing HTTP security requirements in the domain name system (2007). https://lists.w3.org/Archives/Public/public-wsc-wg/2007Apr/att-0332/http-ssr.html
23. Schechter, S.E., Dhamija, R., Ozment, A., Fischer, I.: The emperors new security indicators. In: Proceedings of IEEE Symposium on Security and Privacy (SP), pp. 51–65 (2007)
24. Stamm, S., Sterne, B., Markham, G.: Reining in the web with content security policy. In: Proceedings of 19th International Conference on World Wide Web (WWW 2010), pp. 921–930 (2010)
25. Sullivan, N.: Padding oracles and the decline of CBC-mode cipher suites (2016). https://blog.cloudflare.com/padding-oracles-and-the-decline-of-cbc-mode-ciphersuites/
26. Sunshine, J., Egelman, S., Almuhimedi, H., Atri, N., Cranor, L.F.: Crying wolf: an empirical study of SSL warning effectiveness. In: Proceedings of USENIX Security Symposium, pp. 399–416 (2009)
27. Szalachowski, P., Matsumoto, S., Perrig, A.: PoliCert: secure and flexible TLS certificate management. In: Proceedings of Conference on Computer and Communications Security (CCS), pp. 406–417 (2014)
28. Vaudenay, S.: Security flaws induced by CBC padding—applications to SSL, IPSEC, WTLS. In: Knudsen, L.R. (ed.) EUROCRYPT 2002. LNCS, vol. 2332, pp. 534–545. Springer, Heidelberg (2002). https://doi.org/10.1007/3-540-46035-7_35
29. Wu, M., Miller, R.C., Garfinkel, S.L.: Do security toolbars actually prevent phishing attacks? In: Proceedings of Human Factors in Computing Systems (SIGCHI), pp. 601–610 (2006)

# Applied Cryptography

# Neural Network Based Min-entropy Estimation for Random Number Generators

Jing Yang[1,2,3], Shuangyi Zhu[1,2,3], Tianyu Chen[1,2(✉)], Yuan Ma[1,2], Na Lv[1,2,3], and Jingqiang Lin[1,2]

[1] Data Assurance and Communication Security Research Center,
Chinese Academy of Sciences, Beijing, China
{yangjing,zhushuangyi,tychen,yma,nlv14,linjq}@is.ac.cn
[2] State Key Laboratory of Information Security, Institute of Information
Engineering, Chinese Academy of Sciences, Beijing, China
[3] School of Cyber Security, University of Chinese Academy of Sciences,
Beijing, China

**Abstract.** Random Number Generators (RNGs) are essential for cryptographic systems and communication security. A cryptographic application is prone to have a serious security risk if the entropy source that generates the random number cannot provide sufficient randomness (unpredictability) as expected. The min-entropy is usually employed to evaluate the unpredictability, which measures the difficulty of guessing the most likely output of RNGs. Recently, predictors for min-entropy estimation are proposed in the NIST 800-90B (90B), which attempt to predict the next sample in a sequence based on all previous samples. However, these predictors have shortfalls in evaluating random number with long dependence and multivariate due to huge time complexity (i.e., high-order polynomial time complexity). From the concept of predictors, we provide several suitable and efficient predictors based on neural networks for min-entropy estimation. The neural networks apply to approximating the Probability Distribution Function (PDF) and have a linear complexity of the sample space. Compared to the 90B's predictors, the experimental results on various simulated source demonstrate that our proposed predictors have a comparable accuracy, and the execution efficiency has a significant improvement. Furthermore, when the sample space is over $2^2$ and sample size is over $10^8$, the 90B's predictors cannot give the estimated result. Instead, our proposed predictors still can provide an accurate result.

**Keywords:** Random number · Neural network · Entropy estimation Predictor

## 1 Introduction

Random numbers are widely used in numerous cryptographic applications and cryptosystems, such as the session key generation in communications, digital

© ICST Institute for Computer Sciences, Social Informatics and Telecommunications Engineering 2018
R. Beyah et al. (Eds.): SecureComm 2018, LNICST 255, pp. 231–250, 2018.
https://doi.org/10.1007/978-3-030-01704-0_13

signature generation, and key exchange. The generated approaches are usually divided into two categories: Pseudo/deterministic Random Number Generator (PRNG) and True/non-deterministic Random Number Generator (TRNG). In general, PRNGs utilize a deterministic algorithm to generate random numbers via stretching a seed. The security essentially depends on the truly unpredictable seed produced by a TRNG (i.e., entropy source).

If the entropy source cannot provide sufficient unpredictability as expected, the cryptographic applications would be vulnerable, as in [6,10,23]. Hence, the entropy source's unpredictability shall be quantified to ensure the security. At present, several major standardization organizations recommend to adopt the concept of *entropy* to quantify the randomness (unpredictability) of the outputs of an entropy source, such as the criterions ISO 18031 [12] and AIS 31 [16]. There are many types of methods for measuring entropy, including Shannon entropy, Rényi entropy, min-entropy, *etc.* Min-entropy is a very conservative measure, which means the difficulty of guessing the most-likely output of the entropy source [22].

However, the entropy estimation is a challenging task because the common assumptions may not be consistent with the real conditions and the distribution of the outputs is unknown. Nowadays, entropy estimation has two realizations: stochastic model (white-box testing) and statistical test (black-box testing). A suitable stochastic model can achieve a theoretical proof for the security of entropy sources, as in [1,3,17,19,25]. But the modeling, which is based on the specific structure of an entropy source and an appropriate assumption on the entropy source's behavior, is always difficult and complex, and even some structures of entropy source still do not have a suitable model [7,24]. Relatively, statistical test focuses on the statistical properties of the generated outputs regardless of the knowledge of entropy sources, so it has an extensive use on the evaluation of entropy sources.

Statistical tests published in [21] only detected the statistical properties like uniformity or independence of the tested sequence, rather than quantify the unpredictability of tested sequence. Furthermore, Zhu *et al.* [27] found that their second-level tests are flawed due to the inconsistency between the assessed distribution and the assumed one. The second NIST SP 800-90B (called 90B in the text below) [22] put forward ten approaches to estimate min-entropy, and they are divided into three classes. The first class is based on the frequency, and the min-entropy is calculated according to the probability of the most-likely output value. The approach usually gives the overestimated result. The second class is based on entropic statistics presented by Hagerty and Draper [11]. However, Zhu *et al.* [26] proved that this kind of approaches may underestimate the entropy source. The third class is based on predictors presented by Kelsey *et al.* [15], and has a better performance than the other two classes. The predictor refers to a machine learning algorithm that attempts to predict each sample in a sequence and updates its internal state based on all observed samples. However, the execution efficiency of these predictive models is influenced significantly due to the increase of the sample space. It is analysed that the complexity of 90B's predictors have high order linear relationship with the size of sample space. As stated in [22], the key difficulty of making these estimates is the large data required to resolve the dependencies of the samples, so they limited the sample space to a small value, such as 6 bits in the Markov estimate and 8 bits in the MultiMMC prediction estimate. Also, every predictor is only designed to predict samples from sources with a certain statistical property, which constrains the applications of the predictors.

In this work, we aim to propose several suitable and efficient predictors for min-entropy estimation of entropy sources utilizing the neural network. The fully-connected neural network (FNN), a representative neural network model, is widely used to approximate some Probability Distribution Functions (PDFs) and predicts the next output via inputting sufficient previous samples. Also, the recurrent neural network (RNN), is another powerful tool and widely applies to time series forecasting. For this reason, we adopt the two predictive models based on neural networks mentioned above to design the predictors for entropy estimation. After a large number of experiments, compared to the work in [15], we find that the proposed predictive models not only have the comparable accuracy but also have an outstanding executing efficiency because of the linear relationship between the time complexity and the sample space. Furthermore, when the sample space and sample size are large, the 90B's predictors cannot estimate the entropy, while our proposed predictors can calculate the estimated results.

To verify the effect of the proposed predictors, many of the experiments described in the rest of this paper are carried out on various types of simulated sources with the known probability distribution.

In summary, we make the following contributions.

- We adopt neural networks to achieve the min-entropy estimation for the first time in view of two reasonable assumptions for the outputs of an entropy source, (1) the outputs are viewed as time series, and (2) the current output is related to historical observations.
- We analyze the computational complexity of our proposed predictors compared with that of 90B. The analysis results indicate that the complexity of our proposed predictors is a linear relationship with the sample space rather than high order corresponding to 90B's. Therefore, our proposed predictors can work on the estimation of long dependence and multivariate random number.
- We provide a set of experiments to compare the performance of our predictors against that of the 90B's predictors in [15] on many classes of simulated sources, where the correct entropy is known. In the experimental results, our proposed predictive models give the same good estimated results as 90B's predictors. Also, the mean execution time performance improves significantly, when the sample space and the sample size grow.

The rest of paper is organized as follows. In Sect. 2, we introduce fundamental definitions about entropy estimators and basic knowledge about several typical neural networks. In Sect. 3, we provide two predictors based on neural networks for min-entropy estimation. Furthermore, we implement our proposed predictive models and give the experimental results in Sect. 4. We finally conclude our work in Sect. 5.

## 2    Preliminaries

In this section, we introduce fundamental concept of entropy estimation, including min-entropy and predictive models based estimators defined in the 90B. After that, we describe two predictive models based on neural networks, which contribute to the design of new predictors in the following section.

### 2.1    Existing Entropy Estimation

The 90B describes the properties that an entropy source must have to make it suitable for use by cryptographic random bit generators, as well as the tests used to validate the quality of the entropy source [22]. The core mathematical thought of the 90B is based on the concept of entropy. The assessment method is the *min-entropy* which is a conservative way to ensure the quality of random number in the worst case for some high-security applications, such as the seed of PRNGs.

**Min-entropy.** The 90B [22] gave the definition of min-entropy: let the next output generated from an i.i.d. entropy source be a random variable $X$, which the values are contained in a finite set $S = \{z_1, z_2, \cdots, z_s\}$ ($s \in \mathbb{Z}^*$ denotes the size of sample space), with the probability $\Pr(X = z_i) = p_i$ ($i = 1, 2, \cdots, s$). The min-entropy of the output is:

$$H_{min} = \min_{1 \le i \le s} (-\log_2 p_i)$$
$$= -\log_2(\max_{1 \le i \le s} (p_i)).$$

If the min-entropy is $h$ for the variable $X$, then the probability of occurrence of any particular value observed is no greater than $2^{-h}$. The maximum possible value for min-entropy of an i.i.d. random variable with $s$ distinct values is $\log_2(s)$, which is satisfied when the random variable follows a uniform probability distribution, namely, $p_1 = p_2 = \cdots = p_s = \frac{1}{s}$.

For the non-i.i.d. source, such as Markov process, Barker and Kelsey provided a calculation method of min-entropy in [22]. A stochastic process $\{X_i\}_{i \in \mathbb{N}}$ that takes values from the finite set $S$ defined above is known as a first-order Markov chain, if

$$\Pr(X_{m+1} = x_{m+1} | X_m = x_m, X_{m-1} = x_{m-1}, \cdots, X_0 = x_0)$$
$$= \Pr(X_{m+1} = x_{m+1} | X_m = x_m)$$

for any $m \in \mathbb{Z}^*$ and all $x_0, x_1, \cdots, x_m, x_{m+1} \in S$. In a $d^{th}$-order Markov process, the transition probabilities have the property that

$$\Pr(X_{m+1} = x_{m+1} | X_m = x_m, X_{m-1} = x_{m-1}, \cdots, X_0 = x_0)$$
$$= \Pr(X_{m+1} = x_{m+1} | X_m = x_m, \cdots, X_{m-d+1} = x_{m-d+1}).$$

The initial probabilities of the process are $p_i = \Pr(X_0 = i)$, and the transition probabilities are $p_{ij} = \Pr(X_{m+1} = j | X_m = i)$. The min-entropy of a Markov process of length $L$ is defined as

$$H_{min} = -\log_2\big( \max_{x_1, \cdots, x_L} p_{x_1} \prod_{j=1}^{L} p_{x_{j-1} x_j} \big).$$

The approximate value of min-entropy per sample can be obtained by dividing $H$ by $L$.

## 2.2  Predictive Models for Min-entropy Estimation

Kelsey et al. [15] utilized several machine learning models served as predictors to improve the accuracy of entropy estimations. A predictor's performance can be expressed as a probability, and it provides a lower bound on the best performance an attacker could get predicting the sources outputs. That is to say, an attacker will never do worse than the predictor (he could just reuse it directly), but he may do better. These improved results were absorbed into the second NIST SP 800-90B.

**Prediction Based Type Estimators.** Each predictor attempts to predict the next sample in a sequence according to a certain statistical property of previous samples, and provides an estimated result based on the probability of successful prediction. Each predictor consists of a set of subpredictors and chooses the subpredictor with the highest rate of successful predictions to predict the subsequent output.

Below we introduce the specific mechanisms of these predictors, which are originally proposed in [15].

- *Multi Most Common in Window Predictor (MultiMCW)*. The MCW subpredictor predicts the most common value that occurred in a sliding window of the most recently observed $w$ samples. The MultiMCW predictor contains several MCW subpredictors parameterized by the window sizes of its subpredictors $w$, where $w \in \{63, 255, 1023, 4095\}$.
- *Lag predictor (Lag)*. The Lag subpredictor predicts the value that occurred $N$ samples back in the sequence. The Lag predictor contains several Lag subpredictor. The range of the parameter $N$ is set from 1 to 128.
- *Multi Markov Model with Counting (MultiMMC)*. The MMC subpredictor predicts the most common value followed the previous $N$-sample string. The MultiMMC predictor contains several the MMC subpredictors. The range of the parameter $N$ is set from 1 to 16.

– *LZ78Y*. It predicts the value that most often has followed the previous from 1 to $N$ sample string so far, where $N = 16$ in this predictor.

**Min-entropy Estimation.** As for each predictor, they calculated the global predictability and local predictability with the upper bound of the 99% confidence interval, and then derived the global and the local entropy estimates, respectively. Finally, the final entropy estimate for this predictor was the minimum of the global and the local entropy estimates.

To estimate the entropy of a given entropy source, each predictor offered a predicted result after testing the output produced by the source and provided an entropy estimate based on the probability of successful prediction. After obtaining the estimates from the predictors, the final entropy estimate of the source was taken as the minimum of all the estimations.

If no predictor is applied that can detect predictable behavior; then the entropy estimate will be overly generous. Because a set of predictors that use different approaches be applied, and the lowest entropy estimate is taken as the final entropy estimate. They can guarantee that the predictor that is most effective at predicting the sources outputs determines the entropy estimate.

### 2.3   Several Predictive Models Based on Neural Network

There has been increasing attention to using neural networks to model and forecast time series. Neural networks have been found to be an alternative method when compared to various traditional time series models [2,5,18]. Below we introduce two neural networks to help us design predictive models, FNN and RNN, respectively.

**FNN.** In 1991, De Groot and Wurtz presented a detailed analysis of univariate time series forecasting using FNN for two nonlinear time series [9]. FNNs are used to approximate some PDFs [8]. For an instance, a classifier $y = F(x)$ maps an input $x$ to a category $y$. A fully-connected network describes a mapping $y = G(x; \theta)$ and learns the value of the parameters $\theta$ that result in the best function approximation. The principle of FNN is depicted in Fig. 1.

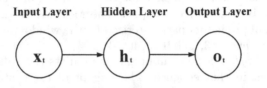

**Fig. 1.** Fully-connected neural network.

For each time step from $t = 1$ to $t = n$ ($n \in \mathbb{Z}^*$ denotes the sample size), the FNN applies the following forward propagation equations.

$$
\begin{aligned}
\mathbf{h}_t &= f(\mathbf{b} + \mathbf{W}\mathbf{x}_t) \\
\mathbf{o}_t &= \mathbf{c} + \mathbf{V}\mathbf{h}_t \\
\hat{\mathbf{y}}_t &= g(\mathbf{o}_t)
\end{aligned}
\tag{1}
$$

The formulas that govern the computation happening in an FNN are as follows.

- $\mathbf{x}_t$ is the input at time step $t$ and is a vector composed of the previous inputs (i.e., $\mathbf{x}_t = [x_{t-k}, ...x_{t-1}]$, where $k$ refers to the step of memory).
- $\mathbf{h}_t$ is the hidden state at time step $t$, where the bias vectors $\mathbf{b}$ and input-to-hidden weights $\mathbf{W}$ are derived via training. The number of hidden layers and the number of hidden nodes per layer are defined before training, which called hyperparameters in neural networks. In this paper, we set the number of hidden layers as 2, and the number of hidden nodes per layer are 10 and 5, respectively.
- $\mathbf{o}_t$ is the output at step $t$, where the bias vectors $\mathbf{c}$ and hidden-to-output weights $\mathbf{V}$ are derived via training.
- $\hat{\mathbf{y}}_t$ is our predictive output at time step $t$, which would be a vector of probabilities across our sample space.
- The function $f(\cdot)$ is a fixed nonlinear function called activation function, and the function $g(\cdot)$ is output function used in the final layer of a neural network. Both functions belong to hyperparameters defined before training.

The models are called feedforward because information flows through the approximate function from input $\mathbf{x}_t$, through the internal computations used to update the model to define $f(\cdot)$, and to the output $\hat{\mathbf{y}}_t$ finally. Besides, there is no feedback connection, namely the outputs of the model are fed back into itself.

**RNN.** If adding the feedback connections to the network, then it is called RNN, which can also be used for time series forecasting [4,13,14]. In particular, the RNN records the information that has been calculated so far, and use it for the calculation of the present output. The principle of RNN is depicted in Fig. 2.

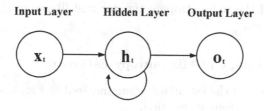

**Fig. 2.** Recurrent neural network.

For each time step from $t = 1$ to $t = n$, the RNN applies the following forward propagation equations:

$$\mathbf{h}_t = f(\mathbf{b} + \mathbf{W}\mathbf{h}_{t-1} + \mathbf{U}\mathbf{x}_t)$$
$$\mathbf{o}_t = \mathbf{c} + \mathbf{V}\mathbf{h}_t \qquad\qquad (2)$$
$$\hat{\mathbf{y}}_t = g(\mathbf{o}_t)$$

The formulas that govern the computation happening in an RNN are as follows.

- $\mathbf{x}_t$ is the input at time step $t$ and is one-hot vector. For example, if $x_t = 1$ and the sample space $S = \{0, 1\}$, then $\mathbf{x}_t = [0, 1]$.
- $\mathbf{h}_t$ is the hidden state at time step $t$. It's the "memory" of the network. $\mathbf{h}_t$ is calculated based on the previous hidden state $\mathbf{h}_{t-1}$ and the input at the current step $\mathbf{x}_t$. $\mathbf{b}$, $\mathbf{U}$ and $\mathbf{W}$ respectively denote the bias vectors, input-to-hidden weights, and hidden-to-hidden connection into the RNN cell.
- $\mathbf{o}_t$ is the output at step $t$. $\mathbf{c}$ and $\mathbf{V}$ respectively denote the bias vectors and hidden-to-output weights.
- $\hat{\mathbf{y}}_t$ is our predictive output at time step $t$, which would be a vector of probabilities across our sample space.
- Similarly, the function $f(\cdot)$ is an activation function and $g(\cdot)$ is an output function, which are defined before training.

## 3   Entropy Estimator Based on Neural Network

Kelsey *et al.* [15] proposed some predictive models for min-entropy estimation. However, there are some problems in these predictors. On the one hand, every predictor is only designed to predict samples from sources with a certain statistical property successfully. On the other hand, the complexity of the algorithm explodes with the increment of sample space. Therefore, it cannot be well applied to the entropy evaluation of other unknown behavior and multivariate sequences. Relatively, the neural network is able to approximate the various PDFs, and the complexity of neural network is increased slower (linear relationship) as the sample space increases. Based on the above analysis, the predictor based on neural networks has wider applicability. Motivated by [15], we propose predictive models based on neural network for min-entropy estimation. Next, we describe the general strategy of the min-entropy estimator and illustrate the choices of the key hyperparameters.

### 3.1   General Strategy of Min-entropy Estimator

The general strategy of the estimator is summarized in Fig. 3, which consists of model training and entropy estimation.

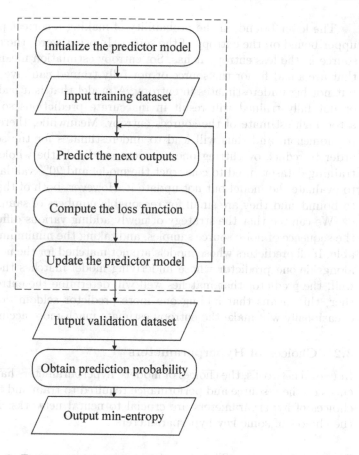

**Fig. 3.** Entropy estimator based on neural network.

**Model Training.** The procedure of model training is listed as the following Steps.

1. Choose one model (FNN or RNN) and set the hyperparameters of the model.
2. Input the training dataset and predict the current output according to the forward propagation equations.
3. Observe the true outputs and compute the loss function.
4. Compute the gradient and update the model.
5. Repeat the above steps until the model training is completed.

**Entropy Estimation.** After finishing the model training, input the validation dataset and then follow the same approach that the 90B uses for min-entropy estimation but not update the model (i.e., evaluate the accuracy of each predictor, including global predictability and local predictability. After obtaining the estimates from the predictors, the final entropy estimate of the source is taken as the minimum of the two estimators).

The lower bound on the probability of making a correct prediction gives an upper bound on the entropy of the source. In other word, the more predictable a source is, the less entropy it has. So, entropy estimation means that the models that are a bad fit for the source or not fully trained can give big overestimates, but not big underestimates in entropy. A model that is a bad fit for the source or not fully trained will result in inaccurate predictions so that will lead to a too-high estimate of the sources entropy. Meanwhile, there exists overfitting phenomenon, and thus will lead to underestimates for the sources entropy. In order to reduce overfitting phenomenon, we divide the whole dataset into 80% training datasets used to construct the model and 20% validation datasets used to evaluate the model but not update it. However, both of these effects are easy to bound, and they are small for reasonable numbers of samples.

We can see that the strategy of newly adding various different predictors to the sequence of noise source samples, and taking the minimum estimate, is workable. If all predictors whose models are not matched for the noise source are used alongside one predictor whose underlying model matches the sources behavior well, the predictor that matches well will determine the entropy estimate. Further, this means that adding one more predictor seldom does any harm, and occasionally will make the entropy estimate much more accurate.

## 3.2   Choices of Hyperparameters

In neural networks, the choices of models' hyperparameters have significant influences on the resource and performance required to train and test. Therefore, the choices of hyperparameters are crucial to neural networks. Next, we illustrate the choices of some key hyperparameters.

**Step of Memory.** The step of memory determines the number of previous samples used for predicting the current output. Generally speaking, the larger the value, the better the performance. However, the computational resources (memory and runtime) increase as the step of memory grows. In this paper, we set the step of memory as 20 by trading off performance and resource. That is to say, as for the FNN, the input at time step $t$ is the previous 20 observed values, and as for the RNN, the hidden layer contains 20 unfolded hidden units.

**Loss Function.** The loss function refers to the function that can measure the difference between the predicted values and the true values. The total loss for a given sequence of $\mathbf{x} = \{x_1, ..., x_n\}$ values paired with a sequence of $\mathbf{y} = \{y_1, ..., y_n\}$ values would then be just the sum of the losses over all the time steps. For example, if $L_t$ is the negative log-likelihood of $y_t$ given $x_1, ..., x_t$, then

$$
\begin{aligned}
L(\{x_1, ... x_n\}, \{y_1, ... y_n\}) \\
= \sum_t L_t \\
= - \sum_t \log_2(p_{model}(y_t | x_1, ... x_t)),
\end{aligned}
\tag{3}
$$

where $p_{model}(y_t|x_1,...x_t)$ is given by reading the entry for $y_t$ from the model's output vector $\hat{\mathbf{y}}_t$. The models are trained to minimize the cross-entropy between the training data and the models' predictions (i.e., Eq. (3)), which is equivalent to minimizing the mean squared error (i.e., the average of the squares of the errors or deviations).

**Learning Rate.** To control the effective capacity of the model, we need to set the value of learning rate in the appropriate range. The learning rate determines how fast the parameters ($\theta$) move to its optimum value. If the learning rate is especially large, the parameters are likely to cross the optimal value, but if the learning rate is too small, training is not only slower but may become permanently stuck with a high training error. So the learning rate is crucial to the performance of the model. We pick the learning rate approximately on a logarithmic scale, i.e., the learning rate taken within the set $\{0.1, 0.01, 10^{-3}, 10^{-4}, 10^{-5}\}$. At the beginning of model training, we set the learning rate as larger value to faster reach the optimum value. Then, we set the smaller value as the number of training increases for not crossing the optimal value. The specific settings are as follows:

---

**Algorithm 1.** setting of learning rate

---
1: **if** *training number* < *training dataset size*/3 **then**
2:     *learning rate* ← $\{0.1, 0.01\}$
3: **else if** *training number* < *training dataset size*/1.5 **then**
4:     *learningrate* ← $\{0.01, 10^{-3}, 10^{-4}\}$
5: **else**
6:     *learningrate* ← $\{10^{-4}, 10^{-5}\}$
7: **end if**

---

**Activation Function.** In general, we must use a nonlinear function to describe the features. Most neural networks do so using an affine transformation controlled by learned parameters, followed by a fixed nonlinear function called an activation function. Activation function plays an important role in neural networks. After many attempts (i.e., we compare the efficiency and performance by means of the exhaustive method manually), we choose the tanh($\cdot$) and relu($\cdot$) as activation functions for FNN and RNN, respectively. They can be expressed as

$$\tanh(x) = \frac{e^x - e^{-x}}{e^x - e^{-x}} \tag{4}$$

It compresses the real-valued input to a range of $-1$ to $1$, and the mean of its output is zero, which is suitable for activation function. The zero-centered training dataset contributes the convergence speed of model training.

$$\text{relu}(x) = \max(0, x) \tag{5}$$

It is linear and gets the activation value required the only one threshold. There exist the following advantages. For one thing, it solves vanishing gradient problem of Back Propagation Through Time (BPTT) algorithms for the reason that the derivative of relu($\cdot$) is 1. For another thing, it greatly improves the speed of calculation for the reason that only judging whether the input is greater than 0 is needed.

**Output Function.** The output function is used in the final layer of a neural network. The time series predictors are considered as a solution to a multiclass classification problem, so we take softmax($\cdot$) as the output function, which can be expressed as

$$y_i = \text{softmax}(z_i) = \frac{e^{z_i}}{\Sigma_{i=1}^s e^{z_i}} \qquad (6)$$

where the $s$ is the size of sample space, softmax($z_i$) denotes the probability of output is $z_i$ and satisfies that $\Sigma_{i=1}^s y_i = 1$, i.e., the sum of the probability of all outputs is equal to 1. Such networks are commonly trained under a cross-entropy regime (i.e., the loss function mentioned above).

## 4    Results and Analysis

Our proposed entropy estimators can be applied to both simulated data and real-world data and follow the same procedure (only input the random sequence to be tested and then output the estimated min-entropy). To determine whether our proposed predictive models are effective for the min-entropy estimation, we train our predictive models on a number of simulated data, i.e., the correct entropy can be obtained by the known distribution of outputs to validate our proposed predictive models. Then, the performances are discussed in the subsections below. We have also compared our results with 90B's predictor entropy estimators presented in [15] and recorded the execution time. Similar to 90B [22], our predictors in these experiments compute an upper-bound of min-entropy estimation at the significance level $\alpha = 0.01$.

### 4.1    Performance on Simulated Data

Datasets of simulated sequences are produced using the following distribution families adopted in [15], and we append several new distribution families like the last two classes.

- *Discrete Uniform Distribution.* The samples are equally-likely, which come from an i.i.d. source.
- *Discrete Near-Uniform Distribution.* All samples are equally-likely except one, which come from an i.i.d. source. A certain sample has a higher probability than the rest.

- *Normal Distribution Rounded to Integers.* The samples are subject to a normal distribution and rounded to integer values, which come from an i.i.d. source.
- *Time-varying Normal Distribution Rounded to Integers.* The samples are subject to a normal distribution and rounded to integer values, but the mean of the distribution moves along a sine curve to simulate a time-varying signal.
- *Markov Model.* The samples are generated using a $d^{th}$-order Markov model, which come from non-i.i.d. source.
- *M-sequence.* A maximum length sequence, which is a type of pseudorandom binary sequence (see [20]).
- *Non-uniform Distribution by Post-Processing Using LFSR.* The samples are processed using a Linear Feedback Shifting Register (LFSR), which come from i.i.d. source (see [20]).

For every class listed above, we generate a set of 60 consecutive sequences of $10^6$ samples, and estimate min-entropy using our predictors and 90B's predictors [22]. For each source, the correct min-entropy, $H_{min}$, is derived from the known probability distribution.

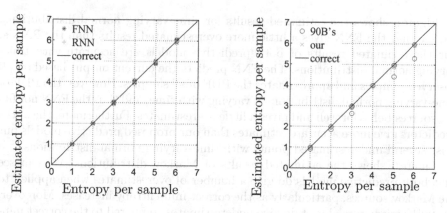

**Fig. 4.** Estimated results for uniform distributions. The left subfigure: comparison of estimated results obtained by the two proposed predictors and the correct entropy. The right subfigure: comparison of the lowest estimated results given by 90B's predictors, the lowest estimated results given by our predictors and the correct entropy.

Figure 4 describes the estimated results for the simulated sources with uniform distributions. The left subfigure shows the estimated results of two predictive models in this work, and the right subfigure shows the results of the lowest estimation given by the 90B's predictor estimators and our predictive models. We see that both of two predictive models give the estimated results that are consistent with the correct entropy with uniform distribution, so the final estimated results also coincide with the theoretical entropy. However, the plot in the right shows that there are several points where the 90B's predictors give underestimates, perhaps the overfitting occurs.

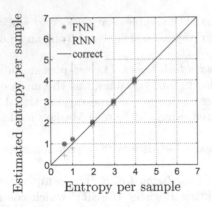 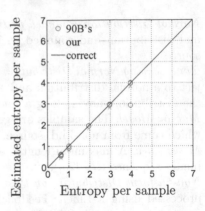

**Fig. 5.** Estimated results for time-varying normal distributions. The left subfigure: comparison of estimated results obtained by the two proposed predictors and the correct entropy. The right subfigure: comparison of the lowest estimated results given by 90B's predictors, the lowest estimated results given by our predictors and the correct entropy.

Figure 5 shows the estimated results for time-varying normal distributions. We see that the FNN gives a little more overestimated results than the RNN's, but the estimated results of both predictive models are accurate with time-varying normal distributions. The FNN predicts the current output based on all observed samples and approximates the PDF of all samples. However, the PDF of time-varying normal distributions is varying with time, and thus the FNN not fits the sources behavior well and gives a little overestimates. Furthermore, the 90B's predictors give more accurate estimates than our proposed predictive models but exist several underestimated points with time-varying normal distributions.

Figure 6 shows the estimated results of Markov distributions. We can see that both predictive models do give a number of overestimates when applied to the Markov sources, particularly as the correct min-entropy increases. Moreover, the 90B's predictors almost do give underestimates compared to the correct min-entropy, while estimated results given by our predictors are more accurate than those given by the 90B's predictors.

To further compare the performance of our predictive models with the 90B's predictors, we apply our predictive models and 90B's predictors to m-sequence and non-uniform distribution sequence by post-processing using LFSR, which are the typical pseudo-random sequence and post-processing sequence, respectively. It is further confirmed that the high stage m-sequence and non-uniform distribution sequence by post-processing using LFSR are able to pass NIST SP 800-22 statistical tests [21]. The estimated results are listed in Table 1 and 2, and the lowest entropy estimate for each stage is shown in bold font.

As for m-sequence and non-uniform distribution by post-processing using LFSR, the MultiMMC predictor given by 90B gives most accurate entropy estimate results. But when the stage of m-sequence and LFSR are greater than 16, the MultiMMC predictor cannot give accurate entropy estimation for the reason

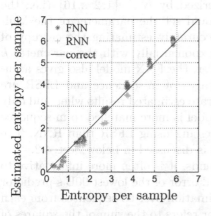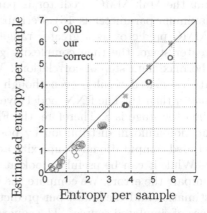

**Fig. 6.** Estimated results for Markov distributions. The left subfigure: comparison of estimated results obtained by the two proposed predictors and the correct entropy. The right subfigure: comparison of the lowest estimated results given by 90B's predictors, the lowest estimated results given by our predictors and the correct entropy.

**Table 1.** Estimated results for M-sequence ($H_{min} = 0.000$).

| Stage | 8 | 10 | 12 | 14 | 16 | 18 | 20 |
|---|---|---|---|---|---|---|---|
| MultiMCW | 0.991 | 0.996 | 0.988 | 0.990 | 0.993 | 0.999 | 1.001 |
| Lag | 1.157 | 1.155 | 1.083 | 1.020 | 1.041 | 1.019 | 1.010 |
| MultiMMC | **0.000** | **0.000** | **0.000** | **0.000** | **0.000** | 1.003 | 1.000 |
| LZ78Y | 1.048 | 1.076 | 1.021 | 1.021 | 1.010 | **1.002*** | **0.998*** |
| FNN | **0.000** | **0.000** | **0.000** | **0.000** | **0.000** | **0.000** | **0.000** |
| RNN | 0.003 | 0.933 | 0.976 | 0.966 | 0.965 | 0.970 | 0.915 |

**Table 2.** Estimated results for non-uniform distribution by post-processing using LFSR ($H_{min} = 0.152$).

| Stage | 8 | 10 | 12 | 14 | 16 | 18 | 20 |
|---|---|---|---|---|---|---|---|
| MultiMCW | 0.440 | 0.582 | 0.743 | 0.719 | 0.998 | 0.996 | 0.997 |
| Lag | 0.582 | 0.743 | 0.683 | 0.680 | 0.992 | 0.995 | 0.999 |
| MultiMMC | **0.152** | **0.153** | **0.158** | **0.180** | **0.233** | 0.996 | 0.997 |
| LZ78Y | 0.567 | 0.582 | 0.766 | 0.680 | 0.996 | **0.994*** | **0.995*** |
| FNN | **0.138** | **0.140** | **0.148** | **0.142** | **0.149** | **0.147** | **0.144** |
| RNN | 0.140 | 0.966 | 0.962 | 0.968 | 0.963 | 0.965 | 0.965 |

that the MultiMMC predictor is parameterized by $N \in \{1, 2, ...16\}$ (i.e., the maximum parameter is 16). Perhaps we could set the parameter of the MultiMMC predictor as a greater range for accurately estimating the entropy of greater stage, the time complexity grows exponentially with the parameter $k$ (the maximum step of correlation). Moreover, the FNN model also gives accurate estimated results, even though the stages of m-sequence and LFSR are greater than 16. The RNN model gives accurate estimated results when and only when the stage is 8. Therefore, the FNN model is more matched to m-sequence and non-uniform distribution by post-processing using LFSR than RNN. The detailed computational complexity analysis is discussed in below Sect. 4.2.

While it can be useful to look at the trends, it is often more informative to compare the errors. We compute the squared error of the lowest 90B's predictor estimation and the lowest our predictor estimation over 60 sequences from each class of simulated sources. The squared error refers to the sum of the squares of the errors or deviations for each class of simulated sources.

**Table 3.** Squared error for the lowest 90B's predictors and the lowest our predictors estimates by simulated source class.

| Simulated data class | 90B's predictor | Our work | | |
|---|---|---|---|---|
| | | FNN | RNN | Our predictor |
| Uniform | 1.5349 | 0.1357 | 0.0328 | **0.1111** |
| Near-uniform | 0.1050 | 0.1362 | 0.0136 | **0.0825** |
| Normal | 0.0410 | 0.0698 | 0.0035 | **0.0337** |
| Time-varying normal | **1.1301** | 3.0296 | 1.7534 | 1.7534 |
| Markov | 17.0816 | 2.6415 | 4.7969 | **4.7706** |

As illustrated in Table 3, all squared errors are low for both proposed predictive models. Overall, the squared error for the RNN predictive model is slightly lower than that for the FNN predictive model, except for the cases of the Markov sources, m-sequence and non-uniform distribution by post-processing using LFSR. Better performance on the RNN predictive model may be due to the following reasons. On the one hand, RNNs add the feedback connections to the network, i.e., they not only consider the relationship between the current output and the previous observations but also the relationship among previous observations. On the other hand, RNNs one-hot-encode the training dataset for better forecasting categorical data. As for Markov sources, m-sequence and non-uniform distribution by post-processing using LFSR, the current output is only related to previous observations, which fits the FNN well, and thus the FNN predictive model has more accurate estimates. Compared with the 90B's predictors, the squared error for our proposed predictors is also lower than that for 90B's predictors, except for the case of the time-varying normal sources because our proposed predictive models focus on the relationship of the overall training dataset. However, the time-varying normal source is the time series of different distribution with time, and thus the FNN gives commonly overestimates. By contrast, the 90B's predictors predict the current output while updating its model to not give commonly overestimates. In a word, this suggests that our proposed predictive models have comparable performance compared with the 90B's predictors.

## 4.2 Complexity Analysis

We derive the following computational complexity through analyzing the implementation code. In which the parameter $n$ is sample size, the parameter $s$ is the size of sample space and the parameter $k$ denotes the maximum step of correlation (i.e., the step of the memory of our predictors) which is set as a constant in 90B's predictors and our predictors. In addition to the theoretical analysis of the computational complexity, we also present the experimental results regarding the predictors' performance. To this end, we implement our predictors and 90B's using Python 3.5, and all the following tests are conducted on a computer with Intel Core i5 CPU and 16 GB RAM (Table 4).

**Table 4.** Comparison on mean execution time with 90B's predictor estimate.

| $\{n, s\}$ | 90B's predictor | Our predictor | $\{n, s\}$ | 90B's predictor | Our predictor |
|---|---|---|---|---|---|
| $\{10^6, 2^1\}$ | 553 $s$ | 696 $s$ | $\{10^8, 2^1\}$ | 47,458 $s$ | 9,584 $s$ |
| $\{10^6, 2^2\}$ | 511 $s$ | 702 $s$ | $\{10^8, 2^2\}$ | $--$ $s$ | 9,911 $s$ |
| $\{10^6, 2^3\}$ | 560 $s$ | 707 $s$ | $\{10^8, 2^3\}$ | $--$ $s$ | 11,451 $s$ |
| $\{10^6, 2^4\}$ | 591 $s$ | 725 $s$ | $\{10^8, 2^4\}$ | $--$ $s$ | 12,582 $s$ |
| $\{10^6, 2^5\}$ | 634 $s$ | 738 $s$ | $\{10^8, 2^5\}$ | $--$ $s$ | 13,105 $s$ |
| $\{10^6, 2^6\}$ | 752 $s$ | 750 $s$ | $\{10^8, 2^6\}$ | $--$ $s$ | 15,808 $s$ |
| $\{10^6, 2^7\}$ | 890 $s$ | 782 $s$ | $\{10^8, 2^7\}$ | $--$ $s$ | 18,155 $s$ |
| $\{10^6, 2^8\}$ | 1,250 $s$ | 818 $s$ | $\{10^8, 2^8\}$ | $--$ $s$ | 23,070 $s$ |

We consider the scale of the problem depends on the sample space and sample size. Through the analysis of the code, the complexity of the 90B's predictors mainly comes from the MultiMMC predictor and is of order $O(s^k \cdot n)$, which is linear time complexity of $n$ and $k$-order polynomial time complexity of $s$. While, the complexity of our predictor is of order $O(s \cdot n)$, which is linear time complexity of $s$ and $n$. It can be seen that the complexity of our predictors is much lower than that of the 90B. From the listed mean execution time with different scales ($\{n, s\}$), it can be seen that the mean execution time of our predictors is increasing slower than that of the 90B's predictors with $s$ on the case $n = 10^6$. When $s = 2^6$, the mean execution time of 90B's predictor exceeds our predictor. In particular, when $n = 10^8$, the mean execution time given by 90's predictors is far more than our predictors regardless of the size of sample space and is too long (over three days) to calculate the estimated results on the case $s \geq 10^2$. It is important to note that the MultiMMC predictor in [22] requires $s^k \ll n$, otherwise, which cannot give accurate estimated results from the aspect of statistic (i.e., when the $s$ increases, the MultiMMC predictor requires large sample size to estimate the entropy accurately).

### 4.3    General Discussion

The thought of the proposed estimation methods is to approximate the original PDF for all the samples. Therefore, for the entropy estimation of random numbers whose generation process is stationary, our estimation is more suitable in comparison with the estimation in 90B. Compared to the FNN, the RNN model adds the feedback connections to the network and means that not only previous observations but also the relationship among previous observations are taken into consideration. As a whole, the RNN gives more accurate estimations than the FNN. However, as for the case that the current output is only related to previous observations like Markov distributions, it is enough that the FNN model rather than the more complex RNN is applied to make a very accurate estimation.

## 5    Conclusion

Entropy estimation provides a crucial evaluation for the security of RNGs. The predictor serves as a universal sanity check for entropy estimation. In this work, on the basis of two neural networks: FNN and RNN, we provide two predictors to achieve the min-entropy estimation for entropy sources. In order to validate the accuracy of estimated results, we collect various types of simulated sources, whose correct entropy of the source can be derived from the known probability distribution. The experimental results demonstrate that the entropy estimation obtained by our proposed predictors are comparable to that of the 90B. In addition, the computational complexity of ours is obviously lower than that of the 90B with the growing sample space in theoretical analysis. Particularly, the 90B's cannot calculate out a result due to the huge time complexity when the sample space $s$ overs $2^2$ with the parameter of maximum step $k = 16$. Our proposed predictors apply to predicting the outputs of entropy sources with large sample space and long dependence. Thus the predictors have wider applicability compared to the 90B's.

**Acknowledgments.** This work was partially supported by National Natural Science Foundation of China (No. 61602476 and No. 61772518), and Cryptography Development Foundation of China (No. MMJJ20170205).

# References

1. Amaki, T., Hashimoto, M., Mitsuyama, Y., Onoye, T.: A worst-case-aware design methodology for noise-tolerant oscillator-based true random number generator with stochastic behavior modeling. IEEE Trans. Inf. Forensics Secur. 8(8), 1331–1342 (2013)
2. Aras, S., Kocakoç, I.D.: A new model selection strategy in time series forecasting with artificial neural networks: IHTS. Neurocomputing 174, 974–987 (2016). https://doi.org/10.1016/j.neucom.2015.10.036
3. Baudet, M., Lubicz, D., Micolod, J., Tassiaux, A.: On the security of oscillator-based random number generators. J. Cryptol. 24(2), 398–425 (2011)
4. Cai, X., Zhang, N., Venayagamoorthy, G.K., Wunsch II, D.C.: Time series prediction with recurrent neural networks trained by a hybrid PSO-EA algorithm. Neurocomputing 70(13–15), 2342–2353 (2007). https://doi.org/10.1016/j.neucom.2005.12.138
5. Donate, J.P., Li, X., Sánchez, G.G., de Miguel, A.S.: Time series forecasting by evolving artificial neural networks with genetic algorithms, differential evolution and estimation of distribution algorithm. Neural Comput. Appl. 22(1), 11–20 (2013). https://doi.org/10.1007/s00521-011-0741-0
6. Dorrendorf, L., Gutterman, Z., Pinkas, B.: Cryptanalysis of the random number generator of the windows operating system. ACM Trans. Inf. Syst. Secur. 13(1), 10:1–10:32 (2009)
7. Golic, J.D.: New methods for digital generation and postprocessing of random data. IEEE Trans. Comput. 55(10), 1217–1229 (2006)
8. Goodfellow, I., Bengio, Y., Courville, A.: Deep Learning. MIT Press, Cambridge (2016). http://www.deeplearningbook.org
9. de Groot, C., Würtz, D.: Analysis of univariate time series with connectionist nets: a case study of two classical examples. Neurocomputing 3(4), 177–192 (1991). https://doi.org/10.1016/0925-2312(91)90040-I
10. Gutterman, Z., Pinkas, B., Reinman, T.: Analysis of the linux random number generator. In: 2006 IEEE Symposium on Security and Privacy (S&P 2006), 21–24 May 2006, Berkeley, California, USA, pp. 371–385 (2006)
11. Hagerty, P., Draper, T.: Entropy bounds and statistical tests. https://csrc.nist.gov/csrc/media/events/random-bit-generation-workshop-2012/documents/hagerty_entropy_paper.pdf
12. ISO/IEC JTC 1/SC 27, Berlin, Germany: ISO/IEC 18031: Information technology - Security techniques - Random bit generation (2011)
13. Jain, A., Kumar, A.M.: Hybrid neural network models for hydrologic time series forecasting. Appl. Soft Comput. 7(2), 585–592 (2007). https://doi.org/10.1016/j.asoc.2006.03.002
14. Menezes Jr., J.M.P., Barreto, G.A.: Long-term time series prediction with the NARX network: an empirical evaluation. Neurocomputing 71(16–18), 3335–3343 (2008). https://doi.org/10.1016/j.neucom.2008.01.030
15. Kelsey, J., McKay, K.A., Sönmez Turan, M.: Predictive models for min-entropy estimation. In: Güneysu, T., Handschuh, H. (eds.) CHES 2015. LNCS, vol. 9293, pp. 373–392. Springer, Heidelberg (2015). https://doi.org/10.1007/978-3-662-48324-4_19
16. Killmann, W., Schindler, W.: AIS 31: Functionality Classes and Evaluation Methodology for True (Physical) Random Number Generators. Version 3.1. T-Systems GEI GmbH and Bundesamt fr Sicherheit in der Informationstechnik (BSI), Bonn, Germany (2001)

17. Killmann, W., Schindler, W.: A design for a physical RNG with robust entropy estimators. In: Oswald, E., Rohatgi, P. (eds.) CHES 2008. LNCS, vol. 5154, pp. 146–163. Springer, Heidelberg (2008). https://doi.org/10.1007/978-3-540-85053-3_10

18. Luna-Sanchez, J.C., Gómez-Ramírez, E., Najim, K., Ikonen, E.: Forecasting time series with a logarithmic model for the polynomial artificial neural networks. In: The 2011 International Joint Conference on Neural Networks, IJCNN 2011, San Jose, California, USA, 31 July–5 August 2011, pp. 2725–2732 (2011). https://doi.org/10.1109/IJCNN.2011.6033576

19. Ma, Y., Lin, J., Chen, T., Xu, C., Liu, Z., Jing, J.: Entropy evaluation for oscillator-based true random number generators. In: Batina, L., Robshaw, M. (eds.) CHES 2014. LNCS, vol. 8731, pp. 544–561. Springer, Heidelberg (2014). https://doi.org/10.1007/978-3-662-44709-3_30

20. Menezes, A., van Oorschot, P.C., Vanstone, S.A.: Handbook of Applied Cryptography. CRC Press, Boca Raton (1996)

21. NIST: The NIST Statistical Test Suite (2010). http://csrc.nist.gov/groups/ST/toolkit/rng/documents/sts-2.1.2.zip

22. Turan, M.S., Barker, E., Kelsey, J., McKay, K., Baish, M., Boyle, M.: (Second Draft) NIST special publication 800-90B: recommendation for the entropy sources used for random bit generation, January 2016. https://csrc.nist.gov/CSRC/media/Publications/sp/800-90b/draft/documents/sp800-90b_second_draft.pdf

23. Vanhoef, M., Piessens, F.: Predicting, decrypting, and abusing WPA2/802.11 group keys. In: 25th USENIX Security Symposium, USENIX Security 16, Austin, TX, USA, 10–12 August 2016, pp. 673–688 (2016)

24. Wieczorek, P.Z., Golofit, K.: Dual-metastability time-competitive true random number generator. IEEE Trans. Circuits Syst. **61**–**I**(1), 134–145 (2014). https://doi.org/10.1109/TCSI.2013.2265952

25. Yang, J., Ma, Y., Chen, T., Lin, J., Jing, J.: Extracting more entropy for TRNGs based on coherent sampling. In: Deng, R., Weng, J., Ren, K., Yegneswaran, V. (eds.) SecureComm 2016. LNICSSITE, vol. 198, pp. 694–709. Springer, Cham (2017). https://doi.org/10.1007/978-3-319-59608-2_38

26. Zhu, S., Ma, Y., Chen, T., Lin, J., Jing, J.: Analysis and improvement of entropy estimators in NIST SP 800-90B for Non-IID entropy sources. IACR Trans. Symmetric Cryptol. **2017**(3), 151–168 (2017)

27. Zhu, S., Ma, Y., Lin, J., Zhuang, J., Jing, J.: More powerful and reliable second-level statistical randomness tests for NIST SP 800-22. In: Proceedings Advances in Cryptology - ASIACRYPT 2016 - 22nd International Conference on the Theory and Application of Cryptology and Information Security, Hanoi, Vietnam, 4–8 December 2016, Part I, pp. 307–329 (2016)

# Improved Quantum Key Distribution Networks Based on Blom-Scheme

Ya-Qi Song[1,2,3] and Li Yang[1,2,3(✉)]

[1] State Key Laboratory of Information Security, Institute of Information Engineering, Chinese Academy of Sciences, Beijing 100093, China
yangli@iie.ac.cn
[2] Data Assurance and Communication Security Research Center, Chinese Academy of Sciences, Beijing 100093, China
[3] School of Cyber Security, University of Chinese Academy of Sciences, Beijing 100049, China

**Abstract.** With the mature implement of point-to-point quantum key distribution (QKD) system, QKD networks become the focal points of the research. In general, QKD network is a simple extension of point-to-point QKD systems. An $N$-user QKD network is constructed with $O(N^2)$ point-to-point QKD systems, which consumes a great deal of resources. We first propose an improved QKD network based on Blom-scheme, which reduces the number of point-to-point QKD systems from $O(N^2)$ to $O(N)$ and maintains unconditional secure. Then we develop it to a multiple-centre network. Moreover, as denial-of-service is a normal and effective attack on quantum communication system, we creatively construct a network architecture based on block design against the attack. Our network architecture can reduce the cost of the quantum channels greatly and improve the survivability compared to the existing QKD networks.

**Keywords:** Quantum key distribution · Key distribution network
Unconditional secure · Denial-of-service · Block design

## 1 Introduction

Key distribution is a crucial primitive in cryptographic system. If the key cannot be distributed securely, the system is vulnerable whatever encryption algorithm is used. The security of most conventional key distribution systems is based on computation assumptions. For instance, Diffie-Hellman key distribution scheme [1] is based on the intractability of the discrete logarithm on classical computers. With the development of quantum computing, the security of cryptography based on computation assumptions may be under threat.

For unconditional security, the eavesdropper Eve is only restricted by the laws of physics rather than computation assumptions. Fortunately, quantum cryptography provides a new way and quantum key distribution (QKD) has

© ICST Institute for Computer Sciences, Social Informatics and Telecommunications Engineering 2018
R. Beyah et al. (Eds.): SecureComm 2018, LNICST 255, pp. 251–270, 2018.
https://doi.org/10.1007/978-3-030-01704-0_14

been proved to be unconditional secure [2–7]. In 1984, the first and the most famous QKD protocol [8] was proposed, which is usually referred to as BB84 scheme. It was inspired by the earlier idea of Wiesner [9]. In 1991, Ekert [10] presented a QKD scheme referred to as Ekert91 using entangled states. Then Bennett et al. [11] described a simpler EPR-type QKD scheme and proved that EPR-type QKD protocols are equivalent to BB84-type protocols. Bennett [12] also proposed a QKD protocol using two nonorthogonal states. In the same year, Bennett et al. [13] first completed the experiment demonstration of QKD. The field of QKD has been developed quickly since then.

The early research of QKD mainly focused on the communication between two users. With the development of technology, people pay more attention to the way of constructing the communication network containing multiple users. Some countries and regions, such as China, USA, Europe, and Japan, have deployed QKD networks these years. The first experiment of QKD network was realized by Townsend in 1997 [14]. The scheme enables a single controller on the network to establish the secret key with each network user other than establish the key between each pair of ordinary users. DARPA (Defense Advanced Research Projects Agency) quantum network [15] set up by USA is the world's first quantum cryptography network, which contains six QKD nodes in 2004. The second QKD network [16] was realized based on the quantum router structure transferred through the commercial telecommunication fiber network in Beijing, China. The QKD network designed by the European project SECOQC (SEcure COmmunication based on Quantum Cryptography) contains eight point-to-point links with six different QKD systems [17]. In 2010, Chen et al. [18] demonstrated an all-pass quantum communication network for four nodes in Hefei, China. A live video conference using one-time-pad encryption through a high-speed QKD network was realized in Tokyo [19]. The Hefei-Chaohu-Wuhu wide area QKD network spreading three cities and two areas ran for more than five thousand hours [20]. The world's first secret quantum communication trunk line, Beijing-Shanghai trunk line, starts trials in 2017. The key rate of the line is higher than 20 kbps and more than two thousand kilometers of quantum communication backbone network has been completed.

There remain two difficulties of constructing QKD network for multiple users. Firstly, each point-to-point QKD system needs emission apparatus, detection apparatus and one quantum channel. QKD network is an extension of point-to-point QKD system. If a network contains $N$ users, there are $N(N-1)/2$ point-to-point QKD systems. It is a waste of resources to realize multi-user communication just by the point-to-point QKD system. Secondly, QKD can easily be attacked by denial-of-service (DoS). In quantum communication system, there are kinds of DoS attacks. For free space quantum channel, Eve could set up obstacles in channel to intercept the signal transmission. For optical fiber channel, polarization of the states in fibers is susceptible to disturbances resulting from birefringence. If Eve applies forces on the fiber, as a result of the stress birefringence the polarization may be changed. Then the quantum bit error rate of the signal transmission may greater than the threshold of the post-processing of

QKD scheme, which leads the parties of the scheme to restart again and again or give up the communication. The attacks which interrupt communication directly or make large quantum bit error rate beyond the threshold can compel the parties to terminate the protocol. These attacks mainly aim at quantum devices or quantum channels, which can be named as quantum denial of service (QDoS).

**Our Contributions.** So far research and implement of QKD networks have been mainly based on point-to-point QKD systems. How to reduce the number of point-to-point QKD systems, improve the scalability of the network, resist QDoS attack, and ensure the unconditional security are the problems this paper wants to resolve. Our contributions are:

- We novelly combine quantum cryptography with conventional cryptography and propose a QKD network based on Blom-scheme [21]. Compared to general QKD networks, our protocol can reduce the number of point-to-point QKD systems from $N(N-1)/2$ to $N$.
- Relaxing the assumption of a trusted authority, we put forward an improved multi-centre QKD network that unless all of the centres cooperate, none can get the key shared by the users.
- When the system is attacked by QDoS, there are four types connection of each pair of users in total. We propose different key distribution schemes for the corresponding connection of users.
- We give a structure of key distribution network based on block design to resist QDoS attack to some extent.

## 2  Background

### 2.1  Blom-Scheme

Blom [21] proposed an unconditional secure key distribution system based on MDS code. There are $N$ users in the system. As long as less than $k$ users in the system cooperate, the system is unconditional secure. Select a prime number $q$, which satisfies $q > N$. Let $G$ denotes a $k \times n$ matrix over a finite field $GF(q)$, which is known by all users in the system. Any $k$ columns of matrix $G$ are linearly independent. The trusted authority generates a random $k \times k$ symmetric matrix $D$ over the finite field $GF(q)$. The trusted authority calculates $P \equiv (DG)^T$ and distributes the $i^{th}$ row to user $U_i$. The key matrix is $K \equiv PG$, which is $N \times N$ symmetric matrix and $K_{ij} = K_{ji}$. The process of the generation of the key is shown in Fig. 1. For a pair of users, such as user $U_i$ and user $U_j$, user $U_i$ $(U_j)$ multiplies the $i^{th}$ $(j^{th})$ row of the matrix $P$ and the $j^{th}$ $(i^{th})$ column of matrix $G$ to calculate key $K_{ij}$ $(K_{ji})$. Since

$$
\begin{aligned}
K &= P \cdot G \\
&= (DG)^T \cdot G = G^T \cdot D^T \cdot G \\
&= G^T \cdot D \cdot G = (P \cdot G)^T,
\end{aligned}
\tag{1}
$$

then $K_{ij} = K_{ji}$.

In practice, matrix $G$ is usually a Vandermonde matrix generated by $s$,

$$
G = \begin{bmatrix}
1 & 1 & \cdots & 1 \\
s & s^2 & \cdots & s^N \\
s^2 & s^4 & \cdots & s^{2N} \\
\vdots & \vdots & \ddots & \vdots \\
s^{k-1} & (s^2)^{k-1} & \cdots & (s^N)^{k-1}
\end{bmatrix}, \tag{2}
$$

where $s$ is a primitive element over $GF(q)$. It is no need for each user to store the whole matrix $G$. For user $U_i$, he just stores the $i^{th}$ row of matrix $P$ and the $s^i$. When calculating the session key with user $U_j$, they first exchange $s^i$ and $s^j$. Then they know the $j^{th}$ and $i^{th}$ column of matrix $G$ to calculate the key.

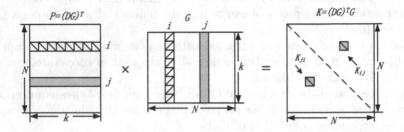

**Fig. 1.** The computational process in Blom-scheme of the key shared by users $U_i$ and $U_j$. The key matrix $K$ is symmetric and $K_{ij} = K_{ji}$.

If $m < k$ users cooperate, they know $m$ rows of matrix $K$. Because matrix $K$ is a symmetric matrix, they know $m$ elements in each row of matrix $K$. But they have no idea about any other elements in these rows. However, each row of matrix $K$ is a codeword generated by $G$. Knowing less than $k$ elements does not reveal any information about any other element. Therefore, if less than $k$ users cooperate they get no information about an unknown key. If $k$ or more users cooperate, they know the whole matrix $K$ because $k$ elements in a codeword determine the codeword.

## 2.2    Related Work of QKD Protocol

BB84 scheme is one of the most used QKD protocols. The following part is the detailed description of BB84 scheme in the polarization-coding system.

1. Alice generates a random sequence of polarization bases, where $B_0 = \{|0\rangle, |1\rangle\}$ represents the basis of rectilinear polarizations, $B_1 = \{|+\rangle, |-\rangle\}$ represents the basis of diagonal polarization. She chooses a random basis string and a random bit string. Then she sends a train of qubits in four states according to her choice, where $|0\rangle$ and $|+\rangle$ stand for a binary bit 0, $|1\rangle$ and $|-\rangle$ stands for a binary bit 1.

2. As Bob receives the states, he randomly selects the measurement basis $B_0$ or $B_1$ for each qubit. Then he records his measurement bases and results.
3. Alice publishes her bases value with identity information. Bob authenticates Alice's identity and then compares the basis value of each received qubit and discards the data with the different bases. Then the remaining bits are the raw keys.
4. To test for the existence of Eve, Alice and Bob pick some of the bits to compare their values and compute the quantum bit error rate. If the quantum bit error rate is below a certain agreed threshold value, they apply classical post-processing protocols, for instance error correction and privacy amplification to obtain the final key. If the quantum bit error rate is beyond the threshold, they restart the transmission.

## 2.3   The Related Work of QKD Networks

QKD is unconditional secure in theory. However, limited by the development of technology, there are kinds of attacks on QKD system in practice. In general, the system of the quantum communication system consists of five parts: light source, coding, channel, decoding and detection. The optical devices and the electronics devices in each part may be imperfect, which leads the information of the key vulnerable to Eve. There are many researchers concentrating on the attack and defense of practical QKD system.

For light source, as practical single-photon sources are limited to the technique and have yet to be realized, most QKD systems use the weak coherent pulses (WCPs) instead. If Eve performs photon-number-splitting (PNS) attack [22], she would get all information of key. Fortunately, The method called decoy-state [23–25] can resist PNS attack. In the coding of QKD, some of the modulators based on the electro-optical crystals. Eve could perform phase-remapping attack [26,27] to obtain the full information of the key causing 14.6% quantum bit error rate, which is less than 20%, the threshold of the post-processing. This attack mainly aims at the bidirectional QKD systems, such as the plug & play system and the Sagnac system. The unidirectional system is not vulnerable to phase-remapping attack. In the decoding stage, Bob randomly selects one of two bases to measure each state actively or passively. For QKD system with passive state modulation, Li et al. [28] proposed a wavelength-dependent attacking protocol based on the wavelength dependent property of beam splitter. For QKD system with active state modulation, there is no effective attack at present. In practical system, the efficiency of two detectors may be slightly different. Eve could obtain a part of information by fake state attack [29–31] and time-shift attack [32]. These can be resisted by careful examination of the detectors efficiency. However, there is few solution to the attack on the channels. The attack may take place at any point of the channel. Unless the whole channel is kept from Eve's access, she can apply the attack.

Compared to eavesdrop the communication without detection, it is easier to damage the communication. Quantum denial of service (QDoS) is an attack that the attacker seeks to prevent the quantum protocol from being executed successfully. On the one hand, Eve can cut off the channel, bend the optical fiber and apply other attacks that break the quantum devices and quantum channels down. On the other hand, Eve can make the legal parties detect the existence of the eavesdropper intentionally. Then the legal parties have to terminate the protocol. In Sects. 5 and 6, we propose key distribution schemes according to the different type of the users' connection and design a network based on block design against QDoS attack to some extent.

## 3 A QKD Network Based on Blom-Scheme

The related technology is mature to implement point-to-point QKD system. It is a trend to develop multi-user QKD networks. A problem of QKD network implement is that there are $C_N^2$ point-to-point QKD systems to construct an $N$-user QKD network even ignoring other relay stations. As is well-known, the cost of quantum channel is high. When implementing a wide-range QKD network, $O(N^2)$ quantum channels and point-to-point QKD systems are costly. Moreover, the general QKD networks lack of flexibility and extensibility. When introducing new users to the network, another quantum channel and point-to-point QKD system should be established between every new user and every existing user.

In previous studies, researches generally apply QKD scheme to other types of cryptographic protocols or applications but seldom considering combine the same type of cryptographic protocol in conventional cryptography and quantum cryptography. We creatively put forward a practical hybrid key distribution scheme that combines QKD with Blom-scheme. The reason of employing Blom-scheme is that there are only $N$ secure channels needed for $N$-user communication network and it is an unconditional secure key distribution scheme as long as less than $k$ users cooperate and the data can be transmitted safely from the trusted authority to each user. Therefore, constructing QKD network based on Blom-scheme can reduce the number of quantum channels and point-to-point QKD systems from $O(N^2)$ to $O(N)$ and maintain the unconditional security of the whole system. The specific scheme is described as follows.

**Scheme 1 QKD network based on Blom-scheme**

1. *Number the users from $U_1$ to $U_N$. Select a prime number $q$ satisfied $q > N$. The matrix $G$ is a $k \times N$ Vandermonde matrix according to Eq. (2), where $s$ is a primitive element over the finite field $GF(q)$. Although matrix $G$ is public over network, it is no need to store the whole matrix for each user. For instance, user $U_u$ just stores the element $s^u$.*
2. *The trusted authority executes QKD scheme with each user. Let $QK_l^{(u)}$ denotes the $l^{th}$ key shared by the authority and user $U_u$ via QKD.*
3. *The trusted authority generates a random $k \times k$ symmetric matrix $D$ over the finite field $GF(q)$, then calculates $P = (DG)^T$. The authority encrypts the $u^{th}$ row of the matrix $P$ with the QKD keys $QK^{(u)}$ through one-time pad encryption to get the ciphertext $c^{(u)} \equiv \left( c_1^{(u)} \; c_2^{(u)} \; ... \; c_N^{(u)} \right)$, where the $l^{th}$ bit of*

*the ciphertext is*

$$c_l^{(u)} = P_{ul} \oplus QK_l^{(u)}, l = 1, 2, ..., N,$$

*and $P_{ul}$ is the element in Row $u$ and Column $l$ of the matrix $P$. Then the authority sends the ciphertext $c^{(u)}$ to user $u$.*

4. *User $U_u$ decrypts the ciphertext with the corresponding QKD keys to get the $u^{th}$ row of the matrix $P$.*
5. *If user $U_u$ and user $U_v$ want to establish the session key, they exchange their column generator of matrix $G$. Then user $U_u$ ($U_v$) multiplies the uth (vth) row of the matrix $P$ and the $v^{th}$ ($u^{th}$) column of the matrix $G$ to calculate key $K_{uv}$ ($K_{vu}$).*

**Security.** The above scheme is a combination of Blom-scheme, QKD and one-time pad encryption. Blom-scheme is unconditional secure in the following conditions: (i) each row of the matrix $P$ must be safely sent from the authority to the corresponding users; (ii) less than $k$ users cooperate to attack the system. A one-time pad encryption is perfectly secure as long as the keys are not be reused. QKD system is proved to be unconditional secure in theory and it is composably secure [5–7], which implies that the keys generated by QKD scheme can be safely used in one-time pad encryption. Therefore, Item (i) can be guaranteed in Scheme 1. When $k = N - 1$, if less than $N - 1$ users cooperate they get no information about an unknown key. It means that no matter internal attackers or external attackers, they cannot get any other keys they should not know by setting $k = N - 1$. In conclusion, Scheme 1 is also unconditional secure. In practical applications, the size of matrix $G$ can be set up larger to ensure the scalability for new users.

Compared to general QKD network and Blom-scheme, the advantages of our scheme are as follows.

1. Comparison with QKD network. If a $N$-user key distribution network is constructed simply by establishing point-to-point QKD system between each pair of users, there are $N(N - 1)/2$ quantum channels. In our scheme, the quantum channels are only established between the trusted authority and the users, where there are only $N$ quantum channels. The cost of quantum channels of the our system is much less than that of using QKD scheme only. Using wavelength-division multiplexing technology may further reduced the cost of establishing the quantum channels.
   Moreover, the quantum emission apparatus and detection apparatus are set up in both parties in point-to-point QKD system . In Scheme 1, the detection apparatus can be set up in the authority's site while the emission apparatus are set up in each user's site, which simplifies the system.
2. Comparison with Blom-scheme. The original Blom-scheme is unconditional secure if each row of the matrix $P$ is secretly delivered to the corresponding user. One-time pad encryption is needed to ensure the security of data transmission. However, every time execute Blom-scheme, there are a number of keys for the encryption. It is unrealistic to provide a quantity of extra keys

to keep the system operating. Fortunately, QKD system can generate endless keys only with a few initial authentication keys and it is composably secure. Therefore, our scheme is unconditional secure and it can operate perennially only by expending a few of initial keys.

3. Scalability. Using onefold QKD scheme, when increase the number of users to $N + X$, another $X(X + 2N - 1)/2$ quantum channels should be added to the original $N$-user system. New quantum channels are established to connect each of the new node with all of the pre-existing nodes. In our scheme, the number of added quantum channels is equal to the number of new users in the network. It enhances the flexibility and scalability of the system.

## 4     A Multi-centre QKD Network

In Scheme 1, the authority is trusted and immune to attack. Because matrix $P$ and matrix $G$ are known by the authority, he has all information of the keys. Once the authority is untrusted or attacked by Eve, the security of each user's key is threatened. In this section, relaxing the assumption of a trusted authority, we put forward an improved QKD network by introducing multiple centres. The centres are the weakened authorities and can be attacked. Suppose there are $t$ centres and $N$ users. The model of the improved key distribution system is shown in Fig. 2. And the scheme is described as follows.

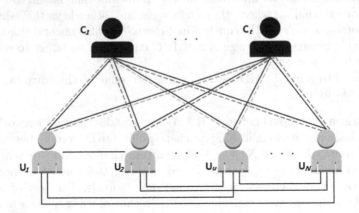

**Fig. 2.** The model of the improved QKD network containing $t$ centres and $N$ users. Let $C_1,..., C_t$ denote the centres, $U_1,..., U_N$ denote the users. The solid lines represent the classical channels while the dotted lines represent the quantum channels.

### Scheme 2 A multi-centre QKD network

1. *Number the users from $U_1$ to $U_N$. Number the centres from $C_1$ to $C_t$. Select a prime number $q$, which satisfies $q > N$. The matrix $G$ is a $k \times N$ Vandermonde matrix over a finite field $GF(q)$. Each user stores the column generator of matrix $G$.*

2. *Each centre executes Protocol 1 with $N$ users. Note that the symmetric matrix $D^{(i)}$ is generated by Centre $C_i$ randomly and $D^{(i)} \neq D^{(j)}$ for $i \neq j$. Then centre $C_i$ calculates $P^{(i)} = [D^{(i)}G]^T$ and sends the ciphertext of $P_u^{(i)}$ which is encrypted with QKD keys to $U_u$, where $P_u^{(i)}$ is the $u^{th}$ row of $P^{(i)}$.*
*Then user $U_u$ decrypts to get $P_u^{(i)}$. When a pair of users, such as $U_u$ and $U_v$, want to establish the session key, they exchange their column generator of matrix $G$. Then user $U_u$ $(U_v)$ multiplies $P_u^{(i)}(P_v^{(i)})$ and the $v^{th}$ $(u^{th})$ column of the matrix $G$ to obtain key $K_{uv}^{(i)}$ $(K_{vu}^{(i)})$. For $i = 1, 2, ..., t$, there is $K_{uv}^{(i)} = K_{vu}^{(i)}$.*

3. *Users $U_u$ and $U_v$ exclusive or (XOR) all the $K_{uv}^{(i)}$ and $K_{vu}^{(i)}$ for $i = 1, 2, ...t$. Their session key is $K_{uv} = K_{uv}^{(1)} \oplus K_{uv}^{(2)} \oplus ... \oplus K_{uv}^{(t)}$ $(K_{vu} = K_{vu}^{(1)} \oplus K_{vu}^{(2)} \oplus ... \oplus K_{vu}^{(t)})$.*

**Security.** Scheme 2 is unconditional secure as long as less than $k$ users or less than $t$ centres cooperate. Then we demonstrate the security from three aspects. Firstly, $K_{uv} = f(K_{uv}^{(1)}, K_{uv}^{(2)}, ..., K_{uv}^{(t)}) = K_{vu}^{(1)} \oplus K_{vu}^{(2)} \oplus ... \oplus K_{vu}^{(t)}$ is a $(t-1)$th-order correlation-immune Boolean function. Correlation immune Boolean function is defined as follows.

***Correlation Immune Boolean Function*** [33]. Let $X_1, X_2, ..., X_n$ be a sequence of independent identically distributed binary random variables, each taking on the values 0 or 1 independently with probability $1/2$. The $n$-variable Boolean function $f(x_1, x_2, ..., x_n)$ is $m$th-order correlation-immune if for each choice of indices $i_1, i_2, ..., i_m$ with $1 \leq i_1 < i_2 < \cdots < i_m \leq n$, the random variable $Z = f(X_1, X_2, ..., X_n)$ is statistically independent of the random vector $(X_{i_1}, X_{i_2}, ..., X_{i_m})$.

A $n$-variable Boolean function $f(x_1, x_2, ..., x_n)$ is $(n-1)$th -order correlation-immune if and only if $f(x_1, x_2, ..., x_n) = x_1 + x_2 + \cdots + x_n$. Then $K_{uv}$ is a $(t-1)$th order correlation-immune Boolean function that the value of $K_{uv}$ is statistically independent of any $t - 1$ $K_{uv}^i$, $i = 1, 2, ..., t$. That is, if less than $t$ centres cooperate, they get no information about the users' key. Secondly, Blom-scheme is proved to be $(k-1)$-secure. It means that for each $K_{uv}^{(i)}$ if less than $k$ ordinary users cooperate, they get no information about it. Thirdly, even if the centres join up with ordinary users, for example $t - 1$ centres and $k - 1$ users cooperate, they have no information about an unknown key.

# 5   QKD Networks Against QDoS Attack to Some Extent

The QKD network with one trusted authority proposed in Sect. 3 reduces the cost of quantum channels and point-to-point QKD systems from $O(N^2)$ to $O(N)$. The improved QKD network with multiple centres in Sect. 4 solves the difficulty that the centre may be untrusted and can be attacked by Eve. There still exists a problem that QKD can easily be attacked by QDoS.

**QDoS Attack.** In computing, the intent and impact of DoS attack is to prevent or impair the legitimate use of computer or network resources [34]. DoS is typically accomplished by sending a large number of superfluous requests to the targeted machine in order to overload systems and keep the resource unavailable to the users. QDoS is an attack aimed at quantum cryptographic system where the attacker seeks to prevent the quantum protocol from being executed successfully. It can be typically accomplished by breaking the quantum devices and quantum channels down, intentionally making more quantum bit error rate than the threshold to make the legal parties detect the existence of the eavesdropper, and so on.

The attack and defense of practical QKD system are described in Sect. 2.3. It can be seen that there are kinds of defenses against the attacks aimed at light source, coding, decoding and detection. There is few solution to the attack on the channels. The attack may take place at any point of the channel. Therefore, to make a point-to-point QKD system immune to the QDoS attack, it is necessary to keep the whole quantum channel from Eve's attack. In a wide-range QKD network, it is unrealistic to keep all of the quantum channels from Eve's attack. But it is practicable to protect only a few short quantum channels. In this section, we propose QKD networks against QDoS to some extent with an assumption that some quantum channels can be protect well.

In the QKD network with only one authority, the damage of any quantum channel leads that a user is excluded the network and cannot share the session key with other users. Introducing multi-centres may resist the QDoS attack to some extent. To improve Scheme 2 to an anti-QDoS protocol, establish quantum channels between each pair of centres and the centres have the capacity to execute QKD protocol with each other if necessary. The main idea of anti-QDoS scheme is that when point-to-point QKD system of center $C_i$ and user $U_u$ has been destroyed, the other centres act as the relay nodes to connect user $U_u$. But it requires that each pair of centres can be protected from QDoS attack. Assume that all centres are near from each other and the quantum channel between them can be protected well.

When Eve applies QDoS attack, the communication conditions of each pair of users $U_u$ and $U_v$ can be divided into four types: (i) the nodes and quantum channels cannot construct a connected graph; (ii) Users $U_u$ and $U_v$ are in the same connected subgraph and both of them are linked to $t$ centres; (iii) the users are in the same connected subgraph and there are no common centres linked to them; (iv) the users are in the same connected subgraph and they are linked to $t_0$ centres in common, where $1 \leq t_0 < t$. The corresponding key distribution schemes are as follows.

1. The nodes and quantum channels cannot construct a connected graph. Then the users in different subgraph cannot share keys.
2. Users $U_u$ and $U_v$ are in the same connected subgraph and both of them are linked to $t$ centres. The connection is same as the model shown in Fig. 2. They implement Scheme 2 and it is no need to execute QKD for each pair of centres.

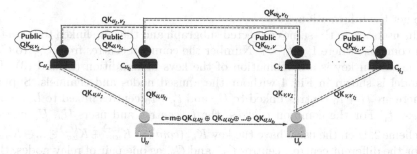

**Fig. 3.** A communication model of a particular QDoS attack for $t$-centre and $n$-user key distribution system. The model shows the communication of any two users that are linked to no centres in common. Let $C_{u_1}, ..., C_{u_{t_1}}$ and $C_{v_1}, ..., C_{v_{t_1'}}$ denote the centres linked to users $U_u$ and $U_v$, respectively. Assume $t_1 \leq t_1'$. The centres $C_{v_{t_1+1}}, C_{v_{t_1+2}}, ..., C_{v_{t_1'}}$ do not participate in the communication of $U_u$ and $U_v$ and only the participating centres are shown in this figure. The session key is $K_{uv} = QK_{u,u_1} \oplus ... \oplus QK_{u,u_{t_1}}$.

3. The users are in the same connected subgraph and there are no common centres linked to them. The model is shown in Fig. 3, where the unused nodes and channels do not appear. Let $t_1$ and $t_1'$ denote the number of centres linked to $U_u$ and $U_v$, respectively. Assume $t_1 < t_1'$. As users $U_u$ and $U_v$ are linked to different centres and each pair of centres can execute QKD protocol, any pair of centres linked to the users could act as the quantum relay nodes. Firstly, number the centres linked to $U_u$ from $C_{u_1}$ to $C_{u_{t_1}}$. Then select $t_1$ centres from those linked to $U_v$ and number them from $C_{v_1}$ to $C_{v_{t_1}}$, and the other $t_1' - t_1$ centres are invalid. For each $i = 1, 2, ..., t_1$, centres $C_{u_i}$ and $C_{v_i}$ as one pair of relay nodes. The relay nodes XOR the QKD keys of upstream and downstream and publish the results. That is, centre $C_{u_i}$ calculates $QK_{u,v_i} = QK_{u,u_i} \oplus QK_{u_i,v_i}$ then publishes $QK_{u,v_i}$, where $QK_{u,u_i}$ is the QKD key generated by user $U_u$ and centre $C_{u_i}$, $QK_{u_i,v_i}$ is the QKD key generated by centre $C_{u_i}$ and centre $C_{v_i}$. Similarly, centre $C_{v_i}$ calculates $QK_{u_i,v} = QK_{u_i,v_i} \oplus QK_{v_i,v}$ and publishes $QK_{u_i,v}$. To set up session between users $U_u$ and $U_v$, user $U_u$ encrypts the message $m$ with all of the QKD keys $QK_{u,u_i}$, and the ciphertext is $c = m \oplus QK_{u,u_1} \oplus QK_{u,u_2} \oplus ... \oplus QK_{u,u_{t_1}}$. When $U_v$ receives the ciphertext $c$, he uses the published XOR keys and his QKD keys as the decryption key and calculates

$$
\begin{aligned}
c &\oplus (QK_{u,v_1} \oplus ... \oplus QK_{u,v_{t_1}}) \\
&\oplus (QK_{u_1,v} \oplus ... \oplus QK_{u_{t_1},v}) \\
&\oplus (QK_{v,v_1} \oplus ... \oplus QK_{v,v_{t_1}}) \\
= m &\oplus (QK_{u,u_1} \oplus QK_{u,v_1} \oplus QK_{u_1,v} \oplus QK_{v,v_1}) \\
&\oplus ... \oplus (QK_{u,u_{t_1}} \oplus QK_{u,v_{t_1}} \\
&\oplus QK_{u_{t_1},v} \oplus QK_{v,v_{t_1}}) \\
= m &
\end{aligned}
\tag{3}
$$

to get the information.

4. The users are in the same connected subgraph and they are linked to $t_0$ centres in common, where $1 \leq t_0 < t$. Number the common centres from $C_{c_1}$ to $C_{c_{t_0}}$. The session key is a combination of the keys in Condition (2) and (3). The model is shown in Fig. 4 without the unused nodes and channels. Suppose there are $t_1 + t_0$ centres linked to $U_u$ and $t'_1 + t_0$ centres linked to $U_v$, where $t_1 < t'_1$. For the common centres, the $t_0$ centres and users $U_u$, $U_v$ execute Scheme 2, then the users have the key $K_{uv}(com) = K_{uv}^{(c_1)} \oplus K_{uv}^{(c_2)} \oplus ... \oplus K_{uv}^{(c_{t_0})}$. For the different centres, centres $C_{u_i}$ and $C_{v_i}$ as one pair of relay nodes, then the users have the key $K_{uv}(dif) = QK_{u,u_1} \oplus QK_{u,u_2} \oplus ... \oplus QK_{u,u_{t_1}}$. The session key of users $U_u$ and $U_v$ is $K_{uv} = K_{uv}(com) \oplus K_{uv}(dif)$.

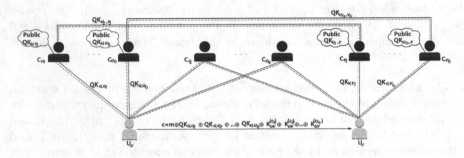

**Fig. 4.** A communication model of a particular QDoS attack for $t$-centre and $n$- user key distribution system. The model shows the communication of any two users that are linked to $t_0$ centres in common, where $1 \leq t_0 < t$. Let $C_{c_1},...,C_{c_{t_0}}$ denote the common centres linked to users $U_u$ and $U_v$. Assume $t_1 \leq t'_1$. The session key is $K_{uv} = QK_{u,u_1} \oplus ... \oplus QK_{u,u_{t_1}} \oplus K_{uv}^{(c_1)} \oplus ... \oplus K_{uv}^{(c_{t_0})}$.

**Security.** Similarly to the security analysis of Schemes 1 and 2, we analyze the security of the anti-QDoS scheme. The scheme in Condition (2) is $(t-1)$-secure. It is unconditional secure when less than $t$ centres cooperate. The scheme in Condition (3) is $(t_1-1)$-secure. And the scheme in Condition (4) is $(t_1+t_0-1)$-secure.

In Condition (3), each pathway distributes a pair of QKD keys for $U_u$ and $U_v$ as a part of the final session key. In general, to select two relay nodes connecting $U_u$ and $U_v$, there are $t_1 \cdot t'_1$ different choices, where $t_1$ is the number of centres linked to $U_u$ and $t'_1$ is the number of centres linked to $U_v$. For the relay nodes in each pathway, both of them can calculate the QKD keys transmitted through the pathway. Therefore, even if the session key is the sum of $t_1 \cdot t'_1$ QKD keys, the scheme in Condition (3) is still $(t_1-1)$-secure. Furthermore, each QKD key cannot be reused, it means that if centre $C_{u_i}$ and $t'_1$ centres linked to $U_v$ as the relay nodes, $C_{u_i}$ should execute $t'_1$ times QKD protocol with $U_u$. Therefore, the scheme in Condition (3) is not only ensure $(t_1-1)$-secure but also save the resources of QKD keys.

# 6  Key Distribution Network Using Block Design

A block design is a set together with a family of subsets whose members have some properties. The block design has been widely used in different types of networks, such as wireless sensor networks [35], broadcast encryption design [36], wireless ad hoc networks [37], optical network [38] and so on. The previous application of block design mainly focus on coding and the way of distributing the keys. In this section, we apply the block design to network architecture. To construct a structure of network based on the schemes proposed in the previous sections, the connection of users and centers should satisfy some properties that each centre is connected with some users and each user connected with at least one centres. The specific connection can be implemented by block design. Particularly, we propose a network structure based on Symmetric Balanced Incomplete Block Design (SBIBD).

A Balanced Incomplete Block Design (BIBD) is a typical block design which arranges $v$ different objects into $b$ blocks. Each block contains $k$ ($k > 0$) different objects, each object occurs in $r$ ($r > 0$) different blocks, and every pair of objects occurs together in $\lambda$ ($\lambda > 0$) blocks. In general, a BIBD is denoted as $(v, k, \lambda)$ or $(v, b, r, k, \lambda)$, which satisfies $bk = vr$ and $\lambda(v - 1) = r(k - 1)$. A block design is called SBIBD when $b = v$ and $r = k$, which has four properties: (i) each block contains $k = r$ objects, (ii) each object occurs in $r = k$ blocks, (iii) every pair of objects occurs in $\lambda$ blocks, (iv) every pair of blocks has $\lambda$ objects in common. Suppose a block design $D = (v, k, \lambda)$ is an arrangement of $|S| = v$ objects into $|B| = b$ blocks, where $B = \{B_1, B_2, ..., B_b\}$ and each block contains $k$ objects. The complement blocks $\bar{B}_i = S - B_i$ constitute its Complementary Design $\bar{D}$ with $(v, b, b - r, v - k, b - 2r + \lambda)$, where $1 \leq i \leq b$. If $D = (v, k, \lambda)$ is a SBIBD, the Complementary Design $\bar{D}$ is also a SBIBD [39].

Finite Projective Plane is subset of SBIBD. Finite Projective Plane consists of a points set P and a lines set. Each line is a subset of $P$ and consists of the points. The order of the Finite Projective Plane $\pi$ is $n$ if each line contains $n + 1$ points. The Finite Projective Plane $\pi$ of order $q$ ($q \geq 2$) has four properties: (i) each line contains exactly $q + 1$ points. (ii) each point occurs on exactly $q + 1$ lines, (iii) there are $q^2 + q + 1$ points, (iv) there are $q^2 + q + 1$ lines. Regard the lines as blocks and points as objects. Then Finite Projective Plane $\pi$ of order $q$ is a SBIBD with parameters $(q^2 + q + 1, q + 1, 1)$. We list the parameters of a SBIBD $D$ and its Complementary Design $\bar{D}$ which are constructed with the Finite Projective Plane of order $q$ in Table 1.

**Table 1.** The parameters of a SBIBD $D$ constructed with the Finite Projective Plane of order $q$ and its Complementary Design $\bar{D}$.

| Design | $v$ | $b$ | $r$ | $k$ | $\lambda$ |
|---|---|---|---|---|---|
| $D$ | $q^2 + q + 1$ | $q^2 + q + 1$ | $q + 1$ | $q + 1$ | $1$ |
| $\bar{D}$ | $q^2 + q + 1$ | $q^2 + q + 1$ | $q^2$ | $q^2$ | $q^2 - q$ |

In Sect. 5, we present key distribution schemes for users with different kinds of connections. In this section, we construct a key distribution network using block design based on the schemes in Sect. 5. To reduce the total length of the quantum channel, the centres can be set up in the geographical centre of the network. In this condition, the centres are far from the peripheral nodes and it is difficult to maintain the connectedness of the nodes. Therefore, it is necessary to divide several layers for the network, where the users of the higher layer act as the centres and the users of the lower layer act as the ordinary users in the schemes of Sect. 5. For SBIBD-type network, the number of each layer's users should be same. The detailed steps of constructing the network as follows.

1. **Preparation.** According to the distance between the users and the centre, divide $N$-user network into $m$ layers. The users of the first layer are the nearest from the geographical centre while the users of the $m^{th}$ layer are the farthest. The parameters $m$ and $n$ satisfies $(m-1)n < N \leq mn$. There are $n \equiv q^2 + q + 1$ users in the $1^{st} \sim (m-1)^{th}$ layers and $N - (m-1)n$ users in the $m^{th}$ layer, where the integer $q > 1$. Supplement the $m^{th}$ layer from $N - (m-1)n$ to $n$ objects. Number the users of each layer from 1 to $q^2 + q + 1$.

2. **Session keys shared by the users in the 1$^{\text{st}}$ layer.** Each pair of users in the first layer has a point-to-point QKD system and the short distance makes it can be protected from QDoS. The users in the first layer share keys via QKD. The keys distributed through this layer are unconditional secure.

3. **Session keys shared by the users in the other (2$^{\text{nd}}$ $\sim$ m$^{\text{th}}$) layers.** Generate blocks $B = \{B_1, B_2, ..., B_{q^2+q+1}\}$ based on SBIBD. Then its Complementary Design $\bar{D} = (q^2 + q + 1, q^2, q^2 - q)$ is $B' = \{B'_1, B'_2, ..., B'_{q^2+q+1}\}$. Arrange the $n = q^2 + q + 1$ users of each layer with $\bar{D}$ into $n$ blocks. Each block contains $k = q^2$ objects and every pair of objects occurs in $\lambda = q^2 + q$ blocks.

   Each user in block $B'_i$ is set up a point-to-point QKD system with user $U_i^{hi}$ in the higher layer. For any pair of users, denoted as $U_u$ and $U_v$, both of them are linked with $r = q^2$ higher-layer users, where there are $\lambda = q^2 - q$ higher-layer users in common. Regard the common higher-layer users as $C_{c_1}, ..., C_{c_{t_0}}$, the different higher-layer users connected with $U_u$ as $C_{u_1}, .., C_{u_{t_1}}$, the different higher-layer users connected with $U_v$ as $C_{v_1}, .., C_{v_{v_1}}$ to execute the scheme described in the Condition (4) of Sect. 5, where $t_0 = q^2 - q$ and $t_1 = t'_1 = q$. The keys distributed in the $2^{nd} \sim m^{th}$ layers are secure as long as less than $q^2$ nodes cooperate.

4. **Session keys shared by the users in different layers.** Each user executes QKD scheme with $k = q^2 \geq 4$ users in the higher layer and they can set up communication directly with QKD keys.

   For those users who are not directly connected with quantum channels, they generate the session key with the help of other users. Assume there is no quantum channel connected user $U_s$ with the higher layer user $U_t^{hi}$. But user $U_s$ shares QKD keys $QK_{su}, ..., QK_{sv}$ with some of the higher layer users $U_u^{hi}, ..., U_v^{hi}$, respectively. Because the users in the same layer can share the session keys with each other by the former steps, then user $U_t^{hi}$ shares keys

$K_{tu}, .., K_{tv}$ with users $U_u^{hi}, ..., U_v^{hi}$. These relay-operated users, for example, user $U_u^{hi}$ and $U_v^{hi}$ calculate $K_{sut} = QK_{su} \oplus K_{tu}$ and $K_{svt} = QK_{sv} \oplus K_{tv}$ and publish them over the internet. Note that $QK_{su}, QK_{sv}, K_{tu}$ and $K_{tv}$ are all new and never used as the session key. The session keys of users $U_s$ and $U_t^{hi}$ are $K_{st} = QK_{su} \oplus ... \oplus QK_{sv}$ and $K_{ts} = (K_{sut} \oplus K_{tu}) \oplus ... \oplus (K_{svt} \oplus K_{tv})$. It can be seen that $K_{st} = K_{ts}$. The key establishment between the users in nonadjacent layers is similar.

Because the higher-layer users linked to user $U_s$ directly play the role of relay nodes and the number of them is $r = q^2$, the key distributed in different layers is secure as long as less than $q^2$ nodes cooperate.

An example is given to describe the construction. Assume there are $N = 21$ users in the network to share session keys with each other. Divide the users into $m = 3$ layers and each layer contains $n = 7$ users. The division of the layers is shown in Fig. 5.

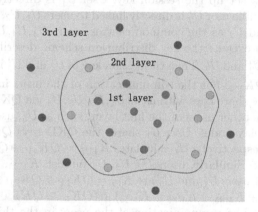

**Fig. 5.** An example of divide the network into different layers. Arrange $N = 21$ users into $m = 3$ layers and each layer contains $n = 7$ users.

For the set $S = \{1, 2, 3, 4, 5, 6, 7\}$, the Finite Projective Plane of order $q = 2$ is $D(7, 3, 1)$, which is shown in Fig. 6. The blocks of the design $D$ are:

$$B_1 = \{3, 5, 6\}; \quad B_2 = \{3, 4, 7\}; \quad B_3 = \{2, 5, 7\};$$
$$B_4 = \{2, 4, 6\}; \quad B_5 = \{1, 6, 7\}; \quad B_6 = \{1, 4, 5\};$$
$$B_7 = \{1, 2, 3\}.$$

Then, the blocks of the Complementary Design $D'(7, 4, 2)$ are:

$$B_1' = \{1, 2, 4, 7\}; \quad B_2' = \{1, 2, 5, 6\}; \quad B_3' = \{1, 3, 4, 6\};$$
$$B_4' = \{1, 3, 5, 7\}; \quad B_5' = \{2, 3, 4, 5\}; \quad B_6' = \{2, 3, 6, 7\};$$
$$B_7' = \{4, 5, 6, 7\}.$$

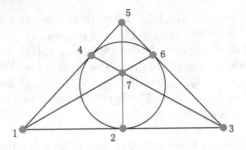

**Fig. 6.** The Finite Projective Plane of order $q = 2$ to construct a SBIBD with $v = b = 7$.

Number the users in the first layer as $U_1, U_2, ..., U_7$, the users in the second layer as $U_1', U_2', ..., U_7'$, the users in the third layer as $U_1'', U_2'', ..., U_7''$. The users in the first layer execute QKD with each other. The users in the second and third layer are arranged with design $\bar{D}$. Any pair of users in second or third layer, such as users $U_1'$ and $U_2'$ set up the session key. User $U_1'$ is directly linked to users $U_1, U_2, U_3$ and $U_4$ while user $U_2'$ is directly linked to users $U_1, U_2, U_5$ and $U_6$. Then regard users $U_1$ and $U_2$ as the common centres, users $U_3, U_4, U_5$ and $U_6$ as the different centres to execute the key distribution scheme described in Condition (4) of Sect. 5 with $U_1'$ and $U_2'$. Then the session key of $U_1'$ and $U_2'$ is $K_{1'2'} = K_{1'2'}^{(1)} \oplus K_{1'2'}^{(2)} \oplus QK_{1'3} \oplus QK_{1'4}$. For the communication of the users in different layers, user $U_1'$ can directly share keys with users $U_1, U_2, U_3, U_4$ via QKD. When user $U_1'$ share keys with the other users of the first layer, such as $U_5$, users $U_1, U_2, U_3, U_4$ plays the role of relay nodes. User $U_1$ shares the QKD keys $QK_{11'}$, $QK_{15}$ with users $U_1'$ and $U_5$, respectively. $U_1$ calculates $K_{1'15} = QK_{11'} \oplus QK_{15}$ and publish it over the network. Similarly, users $U_2, U_3, U_4$ publish $K_{1'25}$, $K_{1'35}$ and $K_{1'45}$. The session keys of users $U_1'$ and $U_5$ are $K_{15} = QK_{11'} \oplus QK_{21'} \oplus QK_{31'} \oplus QK_{41'}$ and $K_{51} = (K_{1'15} \oplus K_{1'25} \oplus K_{1'35} \oplus K_{1'45}) \oplus (QK_{15} \oplus QK_{25} \oplus QK_{35} \oplus QK_{45})$, where $K_{15} = K_{51}$. The communication of the users in the third layer and the users in the first layer is similar with the former method. Because both the user $U_i''$ in the third layer and the user $U_j$ in the first layer share keys with all of the users in the second layer. The users in the second layer could act as the relay nodes.

**Comparison.** Then we compare the traditional QKD network with our network from the cost of quantum channels and the survivability. If establish a key distribution network among $N$ users only based on QKD scheme, there are $QS(QKD) = N(N - 1)/2$ point-to-point QKD systems. In contrast, there are $QS(SBIBD) = n(n - 1)/2 + k(N - n)$ point-to-point QKD systems in the network based on SBIBD. The difference of the number of QKD systems between two kinds of network is

$$QS(SBIBD)/QS(QKD)$$
$$= [n(n-1)/2 + kN - kn] / [N(N-1)/2]$$
$$= \frac{n(n-2k-1)}{N(N-1)} + \frac{2k}{N-1} \tag{4}$$
$$< \frac{2k}{N-1}$$

" $<$ " holds because $n - 2k - 1 = q^2 + q - 2q^2 = q(1-q) < 0$. In the example, $N = 21, n = 7, k = 4, q = 2$, then $QC(SBIBD)/QC(QKD) < 40\%$. It can be seen that the network based on SBIBD can greatly reduce the cost of quantum devices and quantum channels.

There are kinds of invulnerability measurements of he network. We focus on compare the survivability of two network architectures. As the number of the quantum channels are different, we compare the survivability by the proportion of link connectivity in all quantum channels. Link connectivity is the minimum number of branches which must be removed from a connected graph $G$ in order to disconnect it. The link connectivity of N-users traditional QKD network is $N - 1$ while the link connectivity of the network based on SBIBD is $2k$. The difference of the survivability between two kinds of network is

$$Sur(QKD)/Sur(SBIBD)$$
$$= \frac{N-1}{N(N-1)/2} \cdot \frac{n(n-1)/2 + kN - kn}{2k}$$
$$= 1 + \frac{nq(1-q)}{2kN} \tag{5}$$
$$< 1,$$

where " $<$ " holds because $q \geq 2$. In the example, $N = 21, n = 7, k = 4, q = 2$, then $Sur(QKD)/Sur(SBIBD) = 11/12$. It can be seen that the survivability of the network based on SBIBD is better than that of traditional QKD network.

Therefore, our network not only reduces the complexity of the system but also improves the survivability against QDoS.

## 7 Discussion

In this paper, we proposed QKD networks based on Blom-scheme. There may be a question that why we choose Blom-scheme rather than other symmetric key distribution schemes. This is because Blom-scheme is unconditional secure and the combination of QKD and Blom-scheme can still maintain unconditional security of the networks. In addition, there are only $N$ channels in Blom-scheme, which reduces the number of quantum channels and point-to-point systems of the QKD networks.

There may be another question that since Blom-scheme is unconditional secure, why we develop QKD scheme. It is because there is a difficulty in practical application of Blom-scheme. A trusted authority is there to send $k$ elements of a finite field $GF(q)$ to each user over a secure channel. Extra keys are necessary for the channel security. As long as execute Blom-scheme, whether for key update of new users addition, there are a number of encryption keys for secure data transmission. It is unrealistic to provide a quantity of extra keys. The combination of QKD and Blom-scheme ensures the security of the data distributed from the trusted authority to each user only by a few initial keys for QKD identity authentication.

## 8    Conclusion

In this paper, we present a QKD network based on Blom-scheme, which combines the advantages of QKD scheme and Blom-scheme. The QKD network not only keeps the virtue of QKD that can operate perennially with a few initial keys but also reduces the number of quantum channels from $O(N^2)$ to $O(N)$. Relaxing the assumption of the trusted authority, we improve the QKD network with multiple centres. As QDoS attack is one of the most effective attacks in quantum communication network, we propose different key distribution systems fro different connection of users under the QDoS attack. Finally, we construct a network based on block design with simplified system and better survivability compared to general QKD network. As SBIBD is a particular block design, we are planning to construct the key distribution network based on other types of block design for different application in the future study.

**Acknowledgements.** This work was supported by National Natural Science Foundation of China (Grant No. 61672517), National Cryptography Development Fund (Grant No. MMJJ20170108) and the Fundamental theory and cutting edge technology Research Program of Institute of Information Engineering, CAS (Grant No. Y7Z0301 103).

## References

1. Diffie, W., Van Oorschot, P.C., Wiener, M.J.: Authentication and authenticated key exchanges. Des. Codes Cryptogr. **2**, 107–125 (1992)
2. Mayers, D.: Quantum key distribution and string oblivious transfer in noisy channels. In: Koblitz, N. (ed.) CRYPTO 1996. LNCS, vol. 1109, pp. 343–357. Springer, Heidelberg (1996). https://doi.org/10.1007/3-540-68697-5_26
3. Lo, H.K., Chau, H.F.: Unconditional security of quantum key distribution over arbitrarily long distances. Science **283**, 2050 (1999)
4. Shor, P.W., Preskill, J.: Simple proof of security of the BB84 quantum key distribution protocol. Phys. Rev. Lett. **85**, 441 (2000)
5. Renner, R.: Security of quantum key distribution. Int. J. Quantum Inf. **6**, 1–127 (2008)
6. Ben-Or, M., Horodecki, M., Leung, D.W., Mayers, D., Oppenheim, J.: The universal composable security of quantum key distribution. In: Kilian, J. (ed.) TCC 2005. LNCS, vol. 3378, pp. 386–406. Springer, Heidelberg (2005). https://doi.org/ 10.1007/978-3-540-30576-7_21

7. Renner, R., König, R.: Universally composable privacy amplification against quantum adversaries. In: Kilian, J. (ed.) TCC 2005. LNCS, vol. 3378, pp. 407–425. Springer, Heidelberg (2005). https://doi.org/10.1007/978-3-540-30576-7_22
8. Bennett, C.H., Brassard, G.: Quantum cryptography: public key distribution and coin tossing. In: Proceedings of IEEE International Conference on Computers Systems and Signal Processing, pp. 175–179 (1984)
9. Wiesner, S.: Conjugate coding. ACM Sigact News 15, 78–88 (1983)
10. Ekert, A.K.: Quantum cryptography based on Bell's theorem. Phys. Rev. Lett. 67, 661 (1991)
11. Bennett, C.H., Brassard, G., Mermin, N.D.: Quantum cryptography without Bell's theorem. Phys. Rev. Lett. 68, 557 (1992)
12. Bennett, C.H.: Quantum cryptography using any two nonorthogonal states. Phys. Rev. Lett. 68, 3121 (1992)
13. Bennett, C.H., Bessette, F., Brassard, G., Salvail, L., Smolin, J.: Experimental quantum cryptography. J. Cryptol. 5, 3–28 (1992)
14. Townsend, P.D.: Quantum cryptography on multiuser optical fibre networks. Nature 385, 47–49 (1997)
15. Elliott, C., Colvin, A., Pearson, D., Pikalo, O., Schlafer, J., Yeh, H.: Current status of the DARPA quantum network. arXiv preprint quant-ph/0503058 (2005)
16. Chen, W., et al.: Field experiment on a star type metropolitan quantum key distribution network. IEEE Photonics Technol. Lett. 21, 575–577 (2009)
17. Peev, M., et al.: The SECOQC quantum key distribution network in Vienna. New J. Phys. 11, 075001 (2009)
18. Chen, T.Y., et al.: Metropolitan all-pass and inter-city quantum communication network. Opt. Express 18, 27217–27225 (2010)
19. Sasaki, M., et al.: Field test of quantum key distribution in the tokyo QKD network. Opt. Express 19, 10387–10409 (2011)
20. Wang, S., et al.: Field and long-term demonstration of a wide area quantum key distribution network. Opt. Express 22, 21739–21756 (2014)
21. Blom, R.: An optimal class of symmetric key generation systems. In: Beth, T., Cot, N., Ingemarsson, I. (eds.) EUROCRYPT 1984. LNCS, vol. 209, pp. 335–338. Springer, Heidelberg (1985). https://doi.org/10.1007/3-540-39757-4_22
22. Huttner, B., Imoto, N., Gisin, N., Mor, T.: Quantum cryptography with coherent states. Phys. Rev. A 51, 1863–1869 (1995)
23. Hwang, W.Y.: Quantum key distribution with high loss: toward global secure communication. Phys. Rev. Lett. 91, 057901 (2003)
24. Wang, X.B.: Beating the photon-number-splitting attack in practical quantum cryptography. Phys. Rev. Lett. 94, 230503 (2005)
25. Ma, X., Qi, B., Zhao, Y., Lo, H.K.: Practical decoy state for quantum key distribution. Phys. Rev. A 72, 012326 (2005)
26. Fung, C.H.F., Qi, B., Tamaki, K., Lo, H.K.: Phase-remapping attack in practical quantum-key-distribution systems. Phys. Rev. A 75, 032314 (2007)
27. Xu, F., Qi, B., Lo, H.K.: Experimental demonstration of phase-remapping attack in a practical quantum key distribution system. New J. Phys. 12, 113026 (2010)
28. Li, H.W., et al.: Attacking a practical quantum-key-distribution system with wavelength-dependent beam-splitter and multiwavelength sources. Phys. Rev. A 84, 062308 (2011)
29. Makarov, V., Hjelme, D.R.: Faked states attack on quantum cryptosystems. J. Mod. Opt. 52, 691–705 (2005)
30. Makarov, V., Anisimov, A., Skaar, J.: Effects of detector efficiency mismatch on security of quantum cryptosystems. Phys. Rev. A 74, 154 (2007)

31. Makarov, V., Skaar, J.: Faked states attack using detector efficiency mismatch on SARG04, phase-time, DPSK, and Ekert protocols. Quantum Inf. Comput. **8**, 0622–0635 (2007)
32. Zhao, Y., Fung, C.H.F., Qi, B., Chen, C., Lo, H.K.: Quantum hacking: experimental demonstration of time-shift attack against practical quantum-key-distribution systems. In: 2009 APS March Meeting, pp. 4702–4705 (2009)
33. Siegenthaler, T.: Correlation-immunity of nonlinear combining functions for cryptographic applications (corresp.). IEEE Trans. Inf. Theory **30**, 776–780 (1984)
34. Long, N., Thomas, R.: Trends in denial of service attack technology. CERT Coordination Center (2001)
35. Çamtepe, S.A., Yener, B.: Combinatorial design of key distribution mechanisms for wireless sensor networks. In: Samarati, P., Ryan, P., Gollmann, D., Molva, R. (eds.) ESORICS 2004. LNCS, vol. 3193, pp. 293–308. Springer, Heidelberg (2004). https://doi.org/10.1007/978-3-540-30108-0_18
36. Stinson, D.R., Van Trung, T.: Some new results on key distribution patterns and broadcast encryption. Des. Codes Cryptogr. **14**, 261–279 (1998)
37. Camarda, P., Fiume, O.: Collision free MAC protocols for wireless ad hoc networks based on BIBD architecture. JCM **2**, 1–8 (2007)
38. Yang, C.C.: Optical CDMA passive optical network using prime code with interference elimination. IEEE Photonics Technol. Lett. **19**, 516–518 (2007)
39. Anderson, I.: Combinatorial Designs: Construction Methods. Ellis Horwood, Chichester (1990)

# Implementation of High Throughput XTS-SM4 Module for Data Storage Devices

Liang Zheng[1,2,3], Changting Li[1,2,3], Zongbin Liu[2,3], Lingchen Zhang[2,3(✉)], and Cunqing Ma[2,3]

[1] School of Cyber Security, University of Chinese Academy of Sciences, Beijing 100049, China
[2] Data Assurance and Communication Security Research Center, Beijing, China
[3] State Key Laboratory of Information Security, Institute of Information Engineering, CAS, 100093 Beijing, China
{zhengliang,lichangting,liuzongbin,zhanglingchen,macunqing}@iie.ac.cn

**Abstract.** Though SM4 was originally designed for data security and protection in WLAN, it demonstrates high application value in many other data transmission and protection scenarios. In this paper, we present a novel architecture of XTS-SM4 module design for data storage devices, in which we adopt fully unrolled pipeline to adapt SM4 to high throughput requirement. In addition, efforts have been done to optimize the area of Sbox and control quantity of registers. We have also managed to make the module's interface as elegant as possible to simplify user's operation. According to synthesis results with TSMC 28 nm cell library, our implementation scheme has achieved a highest throughput of 33.68 Gbps with an efficiency of 325.12 Mbps/(Kgate). Comparing with other XTS-AES designs in the same technology, our XTS-SM4 scheme gains at least twice better throughput/area efficiency.

**Keywords:** SM4 · XTS · Data at rest protection
Hardware implementation

## 1 Introduction

In the past few years, with the popularity of portable equipment, e.g. laptop, tablet PC and smartphone, more and more personal or sensitive data are stored in such mobile devices. Data at rest stored in these devices are facing unprecedent threat of being accessed unauthorizedly, because these devices are easy to get lost and functions of applications installed in them are usually complicated and unauthenticated [7]. Though varieties of cloud services providers have offered free space to attract users to upload their data in the cloud, as there is not a

The work is supported by a grant from the National Key Research and Development Program of China (Grant NO. 2016YFB0800500).

© ICST Institute for Computer Sciences, Social Informatics and Telecommunications Engineering 2018
R. Beyah et al. (Eds.): SecureComm 2018, LNICST 255, pp. 271–290, 2018.
https://doi.org/10.1007/978-3-030-01704-0_15

satisfactory cloud security solution and recent scandals of data leakage has also undermined user's faith in cloud [2,14], backing up data in a local storage is still the first choice for most users. With the increasing significance of securing data at rest, the IEEE Security in Storage Working Group (SISWG) has standardized the XTS mode of the Advanced Encryption Standard (AES) in the IEEE 1619-2007 standard [10]. XTS stands for XEX-based tweaked codebook mode with ciphertext stealing, which is based on Xor-Encrypt-Xor construction [11] and meanwhile uses ciphertext stealing [15] to handle data in size that is not divisible by block size. Generally, data at rest protection should possess three properties:

1. The data should remain confidential.
2. Data retrieval and storage should be fast operations.
3. Encryption should not waste disk space.

The first property is the fundamental requirement on any safe cryptographic algorithm and the XEX mode applied in XTS further strengthen the encrypted data's resistance to cryptanalysis. The second property demands the data encryption to acquire high throughput. As with the third property, ciphertext stealing ensures that ciphertext is exactly in the same size with the plaintext even the size of the plaintext is not an integer multiple of the cipher block size. In conclusion, XTS-AES exactly satisfies the above demands and provides more protection against unauthorized manipulation of the encrypted data than the other approved confidentiality-only modes. Therefore, this mode has even been approved by the US National of Standards and Technology (NIST) for US government use [5].

SM4 (formerly SMS4) is a block cipher promulgated by Chinese National Security Agency for WLAN Authentication and Privacy Infrastructure in 2006 [4] and was formally approved by The Office of Security Commercial Code Administration (OSCCA) as industry standard in 2012. SM4 adopts unbalanced Feistel network [13] and is proved to have pretty high resistance to differential cryptanalysis [9]. One of SM4's advantage is that its decryption and encryption process can share the same logic circuit and same keys (but in reverse order), which makes SM4 more cost-effective than AES thereby have more advantages in resource limited scenarios. To apply SM4 to storage encryption, we aim to design and implement a high-throughput XTS-SM4 module with elegant interface. To our knowledge, this is the first paper that elaborates hardware implementation of XTS-SM4, and our challenge is how to simplify the handling of the XTS interface and how to make our module's area smaller with a full pipeline design in our implementation.

In conclusion, our contributions are summarized as follows:

1. In our design, a full pipeline is applied, which enables processing of a new block at every clock cycle. According to synthesis results with TSMC 28 nm cell library, our implementation scheme has achieved a highest throughput of 33.68 Gbps with an efficiency of 325.12 Mbps/(Kgate).
2. To minimize the area, we reduce the number of registers and optimize the area of Sbox by using tower field $GF(2^8) \rightarrow GF(((2^2)^2)^2)$. Compared with the scheme of XTS-AES, our scheme has great advantages in area.

3. Besides, the XTS interface behavior is carefully designed to simplify user's operation, which makes our module more flexible and easy to use.

The remainder of this paper is organized as follows. Section 2 gives a simple introduction of the SM4 algorithm and XTS mode. Then we elaborate our implementation scheme in Sect. 3. The XTS-SM4 implementation and performance comparison with other familiar designs is demonstrated in Sect. 4. Finally, we conclude in Sect. 5.

# 2 Background

## 2.1 SM4 Algorithm

SM4 is block cipher with 8-bit Sbox, 128-bit key and 128-bit block size [4]. It is an unbalanced Feistel network as Fig. 1 demonstrates. SM4 performs 32 rounds with different 32-bit round keys ($rk_i$) to process one block. The 32 round keys are generated in turn by the key expansion process with the original 128-bit key. While doing encryption or decryption, the input 128-bit plaintext will be divided into four 32-bit words. In every round, a new word will be created by nonlinear transformation. The algorithm structures of decryption and encryption are the same, only the order of using round keys is inverse.

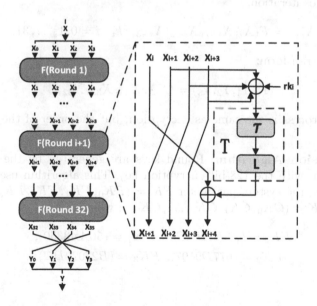

**Fig. 1.** Flow chart of SM4 algorithm.

**Round Function:** Suppose the input four words of the $i^{th}$ round function are $(X_i, X_{i+1}, X_{i+2}, X_{i+3}) \in (Z_2^{32})^4$ ,and the round key is $rk_i \in Z_2^{32}, i = 0, 1, \ldots, 31,$

then the round function $F$ can be expressed as

$$F(X_i, X_{i+1}, X_{i+2}, X_{i+3}, rk_i) = X_i \oplus T(X_{i+1} \oplus X_{i+2} \oplus X_{i+3} \oplus rk_i). \quad (1)$$

**Mixed Substitution:** $T : Z_2^{32} \to Z_2^{32}$ is an invertible transformation which is composed of a nonlinear transform $\tau$ and a linear transform $L$, namely $T(\cdot) = L(\tau(\cdot))$. Where the nonlinear transform $\tau$ consists of four parallel Sboxes. Suppose the input of $\tau$ is $A = (a_0, a_1, a_2, a_3) \in (Z_2^8)^4$ and the output is $B = (b_0, b_1, b_2, b_3) \in (Z_2^8)^4$, then

$$B = (b_0, b_1, b_2, b_3) = \tau(A) = (Sbox(a_0), Sbox(a_1), Sbox(a_2), Sbox(a_3)). \quad (2)$$

Regarding the linear transform $L$, its input is $\tau$'s output, suppose its output is $C \in Z_2^{32}$, then

$$C = L(B) = B \oplus (B \lll 2) \oplus (B \lll 10) \oplus (B \lll 18) \oplus (B \lll 24). \quad (3)$$

where $\lll$ represents left circular shift in a 32-bit vector.

**Encryption Process:** Suppose the input plaintext is $(X_0, X_1, X_2, X_3) \in (Z_2^{32})^4$, the output ciphertext is $(Y_0, Y_1, Y_2, Y_3) \in (Z_2^{32})^4$ and round keys $rk_i \in Z_2^{32}, i = 0, 1, \ldots, 31$, then the encryption process is as follows:

(1) 32 times iteration:

$$X_{i+4} = F(X_i, X_{i+1}, X_{i+2}, X_{i+3}, rk_i), i = 0, 1, \ldots, 31. \quad (4)$$

(2) Converse transform:

$$(Y_0, Y_1, Y_2, Y_3) = (X_{35}, X_{34}, X_{33}, X_{32}). \quad (5)$$

Decryption process is the same as encryption, but the order of the round keys is reversed.

**Key Expansion Algorithm:** Round keys are generated by the key expansion algorithm with the 128-bit encryption key. This algorithm uses two kinds of parameters, the system parameter $FK = (FK_0, FK_1, FK_2, FK_3)$ and fixed parameter $CK = (CK_0, CK_1, CK_2, \ldots, CK_{31})$, where:

$$FK_0 = (A3B1BAC6), \ FK_1 = (56AA3350),$$
$$FK_2 = (677D9197), \ FK_3 = (B27022DC). \quad (6)$$

and

$$CK_i = (ck_{i,0}, ck_{i,1}, ck_{i,2}, ck_{i,3}) \in (Z_2^8)^4,$$
$$ck_{i,j} = (4i + j) \times 7 (mod\ 256). \quad (7)$$

Suppose the encryption key $MK = (MK_0, MK_1, MK_2, MK_3 \in (Z_2^{32})^4$, then round keys are calculated as follows:

1)

$$(K_0, K_1, K_2, K_3) = (MK_0 \oplus FK_0, MK_1 \oplus FK_1,$$
$$MK_2 \oplus FK_2, MK_3 \oplus FK_3). \tag{8}$$

2)

$$rk_i = K_{i+4} = K_i \oplus T'(K_{i+1} \oplus K_{i+2} \oplus K_{i+3} \oplus CK_i), i = 0, 1, ..., 31. \tag{9}$$

where the mix substitution $T'$ resembles $T$ used in encryption, but the linear transform $L$ is replaced by another linear transform:

$$L'(B) = B \oplus (B \lll 13) \oplus (B \lll 23). \tag{10}$$

## 2.2 XTS Mode

XTS is a mode of AES designed for the cryptographic protection of data on storage devices that use of fixed length data units [10]. Therefore, the available inputs for XTS include only the data to be stored on the disk, then encryption key and some metadata such as the sector index and the block number in the sector. XTS mainly applies Phli Rogaway's XEX tweakable block cipher and ciphertext stealing to satisfy disk encryption requirements [11]. The encryption workflow of XTS mode is demonstrated in Fig. 2, decryption process is analogous.

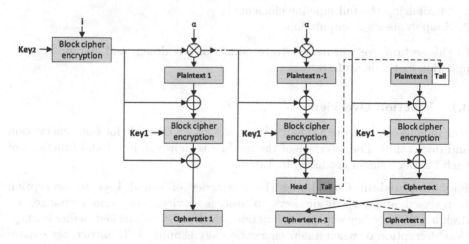

**Fig. 2.** XTS encryption diagram

**XEX Mode:** This mode allows efficient processing of consecutive blocks in one data unit. For each data unit, a non-negative integer, usually a combination of the sector address and index of the block within the sector that we call it "tweak", is assigned and used to provide aleatory to the cipher stream. In this mode, a ciphertext $C$ is obtained as follows:

1) $X = Encrypt(I, Key_2) \otimes \alpha^j,$

2) $C = Encrypt(P \oplus X, Key_1) \oplus X.$  (11)

where $P$ is the plaintext, $Key_1$ is raw data key, $Key_2$ is tweak key, $I$ is the sector index, $j$ is the number of the block within the sector, multiplication $\otimes$ and addition $\oplus$ are performed in $GF(2^{128})$ and $\alpha$ is the primitive element defined by polynomial $x^{128} + x^7 + x^2 + x + 1$.

**Ciphertext Stealing (CTS):** Suppose the last block of data $P_n$ to be processed is smaller than the cipher block and $P_{n-1}$ is the penultimate data block, then the processing of the last two blocks in CTS is described as follows:

1) $E_{n-1} = En/De(P_{n-1}, Key) = (Head \parallel Tail),$

2) $C_n = Head,$  (12)

3) $C_{n-1} = En/De(P_n \parallel Tail, Key).$

## 3    Implementation Scheme

We aim to implement a XTS-SM4 module core to achieve a better throughput/area efficiency, and our design obeys the following three principles ranked by priority:

1. Minimizing the consumption of area;
2. Maximizing the full pipeline efficiency;
3. Simplify user's manipulation.

In this section, we will demonstrate details of our design and elaborates optimization methods we have taken.

### 3.1    Function Overview

Our module implements SM4 algorithm in XEX/XTS mode for both encryption and decryption. The interface of the module is shown in Fig. 3 and functions of each interface signal are listed in Table 1.

**Key Expansion:** Considering the use order of round keys in decryption is reversed and encryption keys in storage devices are seldom change, we design a discrete key expansion function which must be invoked before encryption/decryption or when a new encryption key is applied. To invoke key expansion function, just prepare the encryption key at port *Key* and set *KxpStart* for one clock cycle. After key expansion having been done, the output signal *KxpDone* will be set.

**Changing IV and Selecting Function:** Before processing a new data unit, the data's logic index, which we use as an input IV, should be encrypted by

**Table 1.** Descriptions of interface signals

| Signal | Direction | Description |
|--------|-----------|-------------|
| clk | Input | Clock signal |
| rstn | Input | Asynchronously reset signal, active low |
| KxpStart | Input | Starts key expansion signal |
| ChgIV | Input | Change IV and function signal. When this signal is set, the data's logic index, selected function and the tweak key will be locked into the module |
| ValidIn | Input | Valid input signal. This signal indicates that valid data are available at Din[127:0] |
| FunSel | Input | Function select signal: 0 is encryption, 1 is decryption |
| Din[127:0] | Input | Input data (plain or cipher text) |
| IBL[3:0] | Input | Input invalid block length (in bytes) |
| IV[127:0] | Input | Logic index (e.g. sector index) |
| Key[127:0] | Input | When KxpStart is set, the encryption key ($Key_1$) is prepared at this port; when ChgTwk is set, the tweak $Key_2$ is input from here |
| Ready | Output | Ready signal. When key expansion and tweak encryption have all been done, this signal will be set |
| KxpDone | Output | Key expansion done signal |
| CTSFlag | Output | Ciphertext stealing flag. This signal indicates the module is doing ciphertext stealing |
| IdleFlag | Output | Idle flag. This signal indicates there is no data being processed in the module |
| ValidOut | Output | Valid input signal. This signal indicates that the processed data are available at Dout[127:0] |
| Dout[127:0] | Output | Output data (encrypted ciphertext or decrypted plaintext) |
| OIBL[3:0] | Output | Output invalid block length (in bytes) |

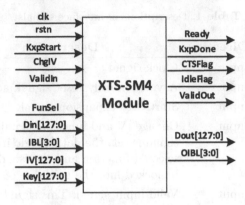

**Fig. 3.** XTS-SM4 module interface

the tweak key beforehand. Usually, when the data's logic index has been known, the operation (encryption or decryption) has also been determined. Therefore, in our design, changing IV and selecting function are done simultaneously. To do this, the user input the chosen function and tweak key from port *FunSel* and *Key* respectively, then set the *ChgIV* signal to high level for one clock cycle.

After key expansion and changing IV have both been done, the output signal *Ready* will be set, which indicates that the module has already been prepared for encryption or decryption. Both key expansion and changing IV are permitted only when *IdleFlag* is set, or the current processing will be malfunctioned.

**Encryption/Decryption:** Because we adopt a 32-stage pipeline in the SM4 core, our design is able to process a new block at every clock. The input valid data is indicated by *ValidIn* signal and, similarly, the output valid data is indicated by *ValidOut* signal. Our module does not need a dedicated input signal to invoke CTS deliberately. Instead, we use a 4-bit *IBL* signal to indicate invalid block length of current input data. *IBL* always stays in 0, until the last data block is less than 16 bytes. For example, if the input $LBL = 4$, it indicates that current input data is the last block and the lower 4 bytes of it is invalid. In this case, CTS will start automatically. If $LBL = 0$, it means the input block is 16 bytes, then the module will just work as if in XEX mode.

## 3.2 Implementation Details

The overview architecture of our XTS-SM4 module is shown in Fig. 4, which demonstrates major circuit logics and registers, as well as the dataflow in the module.

### • Consideration of Area Minimization
To Minimize area, we manage to avoid using unnecessary registers or memories in the module. We store the 32 round keys in a 32-bit wide memory. Because we utilize a 32-stage pipeline to boost the throughput, and 31 128-bit data buffer registers are required to separate adjacent stages.

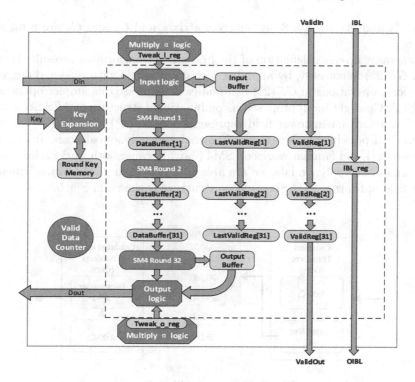

**Fig. 4.** Overview architecture of the XTS-SM4 module

According to XTS mode, the calculated tweak would Xor with the input and the encrypted/decrypted data respectively, therefore two 128-bit tweak registers at the SM4 core's input and output is demanded. In XTS mode, the order of the last blocks is reversed after CTS, hence a 128-bit output buffer is needed. Besides, as the last block need to wait for the penultimate block to be processed completely, an input data is also inevitable. In addition, we use some state trace registers or counters to record information of current valid data being processed in the pipeline.

In summary, the total sequential storage elements that we use in the XTS-SM4 module are 35 128-bit registers, two 31-bit registers, one 4-bit register, one 5-bit counter, one $32 \times 32$-bit round key memory and few other 1-bit registers (less than ten).

- **Optimization for Sbox**

According to SM4 algorithm, in the key expansion module and every round of SM4, there are 4 parallel Sboxes, i.e. totally 132 Sboxes in our full pipelined XTS-SM4 module. Like AES, the efficiency of SM4 hardware implementation mainly depends on its Sbox implementation. The Sbox function can be represented by the following expression [1]:

$$Sbox(x) = A_2(A_1 \cdot x + C_1)^{-1} + C_2 \tag{13}$$

where $A_1$ and $A_2$ are $8 \times 8$-bit binary matrixes and $C_1$ and $C_2$ are 8-bit row vectors.

Generally, inverse calculation of the first affine transformation result $A_1 \cdot x + C_1$ in $GF(2^8)$ is not easy, by applying a composite field with repeated degree 2 extensions, operations in $GF(2^8)$ can finally be expressed in simpler operations in $GF(2)$. Canright in [3] proposed a combinational structure of AES Sbox with inversion algorithm in tower field representation $GF(2^8) \rightarrow GF(((2^2)^2)^2)$ and analyzed all possible combinations of normal and polynomial basis. Imran and Mehreen in [1] did familiar works on SM4 Sbox. Because both works selected the same irreducible polynomials, we are able to merge their works to implement a tower field optimized SM4 Sbox whose structure is shown in Fig. 5.

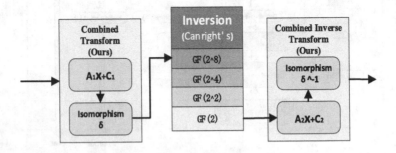

**Fig. 5.** Structure of SM4 Sbox

Specifically, we use the normal basis (conjugate pair basis (0x94, 0x95), (0x51, 0x50) and (0x5C, 0x5D) in $GF(2^4)$, $GF(2^2)$ and $GF(2)$ respectively) given by Imran and Mehreen to reconstruct the base transformation matrix $\sigma$ and inverse transformation matrix $\sigma^{-1}$, then we combine them respectively with the first and the second affine transformation $A_1 \cdot x + C_1$ and $A_2 \cdot x + C_2$ and optimize the circuit design with MiniSat SAT solver. Thus, we recompose the Verilog code offered by Canright into SM4 Sbox code. The modified Verilog code is provided in Appendix A and performance comparison is demonstrated in Table 2.

**Table 2.** Performance comparison of Sbox

| Performance | Optimized Sbox | Sbox implemented by LUT |
|---|---|---|
| Area/$\mu m^2$ | 81.27 | 180 |
| Equivalent gate number | 215 | 476 |
| Power consumption/$mW$ | 0.06 | 0.04 |

- **IV Encryption**

As shown in Fig. 6, the first tweak to Xor with the first block data is calculate by the key expansion module cooperatively with the first encryption core of the pipeline during the changing IV process (the key expansion module works parallelly one clock before the encryption core). It is the encrypted result of the input IV by the tweak key. During the process, two tweak registers and the input buffer are reused as median values or round key's buffers. After encryption, the result will be assigned to both input and output tweak registers.

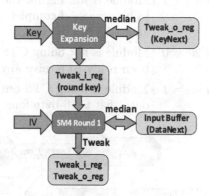

**Fig. 6.** Tweak calculation diagram

• **CTS Implementation**
There are two difficulties in CTS implementation:

1. The invoking of CTS would block the pipeline, because the last block need to be padded with the processed result of the penultimate block. During the waiting process, there cannot be any valid input.
2. According to the IEEE standard, CTS swaps the last two blocks, i.e. makes the truncated processed penultimate block to follow the processed full final block, which will influent the use order of the tweaks.

To cope with the first difficulty, we design two 1-bit output signals *CTSFlag* and *Ready* to demonstrate the module's data receiving state in Table 3. When signal *CTSFlag* is set, it indicates the module is doing CTS. In our design, the module can only process one CTS each time, therefore, the last block which is less than 16 bytes can only be input when *Ready* = 1 and *CTSFlag* = 0, while, to increase the pipeline's efficiency, 16-byte blocks can always be input as long as *Ready* = 1.

In CTS mode shown Fig. 7, the order of the last two blocks will be swapped and the use order of tweaks will also be influenced by this swap, therefore, we adopt a 128-bit data buffer and a 128-bit tweak register in both the module's input and output to implement CTS. In addition, three combinational circuits that respectively calculate the next input tweak, the previous input tweak and the next output tweak are prepared.

**Table 3.** Description of [ReadyCTSFlag]

| Truth value | Optimized Sbox |
|---|---|
| $Ready = 0$, $CTSFlag = 0$ | Module has not been ready: key expansion or changing IV has not been done, no input is allowed |
| $Ready = 0$, $CTSFlag = 1$ | Module is waiting for the penultimate to be processed completely, no input is allowed |
| $Ready = 1$, $CTSFlag = 0$ | Module is not doing CTS and has been ready to receive any data |
| $Ready = 1$, $CTSFlag = 1$ | Module is doing CTS but can receive data that is 16-byte long |

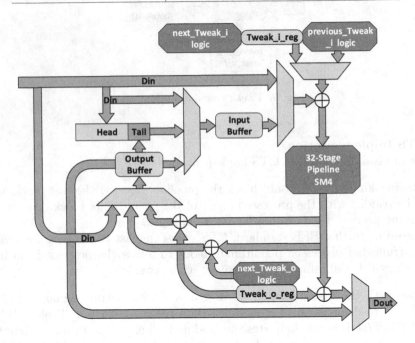

**Fig. 7.** Architecture of CTS data strobe

During normal encryption and decryption, i.e. encrypting 16-byte data only in XEX mode, valid data input from *Din* will be delivered directly to Xor with the tweak value in the input tweak register and enter the pipeline. Then the next tweak value calculated by the combinational circuit will be loaded into the input tweak register. As for the output, processed data from the SM4 core will Xor with the output tweak and be output directly without buffering. Similarly, the output tweak register will then be automatically renewed by the next tweak value.

In our design, if all the blocks are 16 bytes, CTS will not be triggered by this data unit and the order of the last two blocks will not be swapped. When there comes a valid data block less than 16 bytes (which also indicates that this is the last block), CTS starts automatically. In XTS mode, operations on data and tweaks in decryption is more complicated than that in encryption, therefore we will describe these two processes separately.

**(1) Encryption in XTS mode:** The processing in the input is roughly the same as normal encryption. However, when the last block comes, it will be cached in the input data buffer and wait for the penultimate block to be processed completely. The processed penultimate block, after being Xored with the current output tweak, will be stored in the *Output Buffer*. Then the padded last block (higher bytes of the *Input Buffer* and lower bytes of the *Output Buffer*) will Xor with current input tweak and get into the pipeline. The processed last block will be output directly and cached penultimate block in the *Output Buffer* will follow one clock later. Thus, the encrypted last two blocks are swapped.

**(2)  Decryption in XTS mode:** In decryption, the last block should Xor with the penultimate tweak and vice versa. But our module will not tell which input is the penultimate tweak until the last block comes. To solve this problem, we firstly cached every valid input data in the *Input Buffer*. Then we use a 31-bit register *ValidReg* (refer to Fig. 4) to indicate valid data processing in the pipeline and another 31-bit register *LastValidReg* to indicate the position of the last valid data. Therefore, when perceive the last block, the module cancels the last valid data in the pipeline by Xoring register *ValidReg* with *LastValidReg*. Then the cached penultimate block (in *Input Buffer*) Xors with current tweak and re-enters the pipeline. The input tweak register holds its value this time (does not load the next tweak). Then the last block input from *Din* will be firstly cached in the output buffer (for the input data buffer is still occupied by the penultimate block), and then delivered to *Input Buffer* at the next clock. The following processes are almost the same as encryption, except that the processed penultimate clock from the pipeline will Xor with the next output tweak value and the padded last block will Xor with the previous tweak value calculated by the combinational circuit before entering the pipeline.

## 4    Implementation Results

In this section, we will demonstrate synthesis results of our module for both FPGA implementation and ASIC implementation. First, we implement our design on Xilinx Kintex-7 KC705 Evaluation Platform. According to utilization and timing reports given by Xilinx Vivado 2016.3, our design utilizes 8583 LUTs, 5601 Flip Flop registers and 527 IOBs and achieves 193.69 MHz with a highest throughput of 24.76 Gbps (as Table 4 shows). As we did not find any previous hardware implementation of XTS-SM4, we list some other results of full pipelined SM4 and XTS-AES on FPGAs for comparison in Table 5.

We also synthesize our module with TSMC 28nm and 90nm CMOS libraries and compare it with other two XTS-AES designs (in which the XTS3-64 is a

**Table 4.** Performance comparison on FPGA

| Algorithm | Device | LUT | FF | IOB | BRAM | CLB | Frequency (MHz) | Throughput (Gbps) |
|---|---|---|---|---|---|---|---|---|
| XTS-SM4 (ours) | xc7k325 tffg900 | 8583 | 5601 | 527 | / | / | 193.69 | 24.76 |
| SM4 [8] | xc4vlx100 | / | / | 386 | 128 | 9500 | 190.00 | 24.32 |
| SM4-GCM [16] | 5vlx50t | 16712 | 21921 | / | / | / | 173.82 | 22.25 |
| XTS-AES (encrypt)[12] | xc5vlx50 3ff676 | 12172 | 12458 | 418 | 27 | / | 279.82 | 35.82 |

[1]LUT-Look Up Table; FF-Flip Flop; IOB-Input/Output Blocks; BRAM- Block Select RAM; CLB-Configurable Logic Blocks.

commercial IP core designed by the IPCores Inc). Results are demonstrated in Table 5. To make a fair comparison, we set parameters the same as [17] ($0.6ns$ clock uncertainty, $1.5ns$ clock network delay and $2.5ns$ input external delay). Timing and area reports are available in Appendix B. Through the experimental comparison, we can conclude that our XTS-SM4 scheme not only has smaller area, but also has a higher throughput compared with the existing data storage scheme.

**Table 5.** Performance comparison on ASIC

| Algorithm | Technology | Area ($\mu m^2$) | Equivalent Gates ($kgates$) | Frequency ($MHZ$) | Throughput ($Gbps$) | Throughput/Area ($Mbps/Kgate$) |
|---|---|---|---|---|---|---|
| XTS-SM4 (ours) | TSMC 28 nm CMOS | 39158 | 103.59 | 263 | 33.68 | 325.12 |
|  | TSMC 90nm CMOS | 289778 | 102.67 | 250 | 32.00 | 311.68 |
| XTS-AES [17] | UMC 90nm CMOS | 940564 | 203.15 | 262 | 33.53 | 165.05 |
| XTS3-64 [6] | TSMC 90nm | / | 140.50 | 215 | 13.70 | 97.51 |

## 5   Conclusion

In this paper, we present a high-performance implementation of XTS-SM4 for data storage devices. According to implementation results on both FPGA and ASIC, we can see that the implemented XTS-SM4 gains a better throughput/area efficiency than XTS-AES. Even compared with other full pipelined SM4 implementation, our design is still competitive. Our future work will focus on inserting pipelines to Sbox by applying tower filed to further reduce critical path thereby improve throughput.

# A  Optimized SM4 Sbox description in Verilog

```
module bSbox ( A, D );
input [7:0] A;
output [7:0] D;
wire [7:0] B, C;
wire R1, R2, R3, R4, R5;
wire T1, T2, T3, T4, T5, T6;
```

/*change basis from $GF(2^8)$ to $GF(2^8)/GF(2^4)/GF(2^2)$ combined with the first affine transformation*/

```
assign R1 = A[7] ∧ A[3];
assign R2 = A[5] ∧ A[3] ;
assign R3 = A[4] ∧ A[2] ;
assign R4 = A[6] ∧ A[2] ;
assign R5 = A[0] ∧ R3 ;
assign B[7] = A[1] ∧ A[0] ∧ R2 ;
assign B[6] = A[6] ∧ R1 ∧ R5 ;
assign B[5] = R4 ;
assign B[4] = A[1] ∧ R4 ;
assign B[3] = R2 ∼ ∧ R3 ;
assign B[2] = A[1] ∧ R1 ;
assign B[1] = A[5] ∼ ∧ R1 ;
assign B[0] = A[7] ∼ ∧ R5 ;
```

/*inverse in $GF(2^8)/GF(2^4)$, using normal basis $[d^{16}, d]$ by Canright Algorithm*/

```
GF_INV_8 inv( B, C );
```

/*change basis back from $GF(2^8)/GF(2^4)/GF(2^2)$ to $GF(2^8)$ combined with the second affine transformation*/

```
assign T1 = C[7] ∧ C[4] ;
assign T2 = C[3] ∧ C[1] ;
assign T3 = C[3] ∼ ∧ T1 ;
assign T4 = C[0] ∧ T2 ;
```

assign T5 = C[5] ∧ T4 ;

assign T6 = C[2] ∼ ∧ T5 ;

assign D[7] = ∼ C[1] ;

assign D[6] = C[6] ∧ C[4] ∧ T6 ;

assign D[5] = C[7] ∧ T4 ;

assign D[4] = C[5] ∧ T3 ;

assign D[3] = C[2] ;

assign D[2] = T5 ;

assign D[1] = T1 ∧ T6 ;

assign D[0] = T3 ;

endmodule

# B    Synthesis Report of TSMC 28nm Library

## Area report of TSMC 28nm Library

\* \* \* \* \* \* \* \* \* \* \* \* \* \* \* \* \* \* \* \* \* \* \* \* \* \* \* \* \* \* \* \* \* \* \* \* \* \* \* \* \* \* \* \* \* \*\*

| Report : | area |
| --- | --- |
| Design : | SM4_TOP_PIPE |
| Version: | J-2014.09-SP1 |
| Date : | Wed Sep 13 09:52:28 |

\* \* \* \* \* \* \* \* \* \* \* \* \* \* \* \* \* \* \* \* \* \* \* \* \* \* \* \* \* \* \* \* \* \* \* \* \* \* \* \* \* \* \* \* \* \*\*

Library(s) Used: ts28nchslogl35hdl140f_ffbc0p99vn40c

(File:/home/shyw/work/SM4_XTS_0905/tsmc_28nm/db/ts28nchslogl35hdl140f_ffbc0p99vn40c.db)

Number of ports:                     531

Number of nets:                      44322

Number of cells:                     43926

Number of combinational cells: 38333

Number of sequential cells:      5593

Number of macros/black boxes: 0

Number of buf/inv:                   6628

Number of references:            96

Combinational area:       27177.947842
Buf/Inv area:             1707.048024
Noncombinational area:    11980.205776
Macro/Black Box area:     0.000000
Net Interconnect area:    undefined

Total cell area:          39158.153618
Total area:               undefined

## Timing report of TSMC 28nm Library

\* \* \* \* \* \* \* \* \* \* \* \* \* \* \* \* \* \* \* \* \* \* \* \* \* \* \* \* \* \* \* \* \* \* \* \* \* \* \* \* \* \* \* \* \* \* \* \* \* \*\*

Report :                  timing
                          -path full
                          -delay max
                          -max_paths 1000
Design :                  SM4_TOP_PIPE
Version:                  J-2014.09-SP1
Date :                    Wed Sep 13 09:52:27 2017

\* \* \* \* \* \* \* \* \* \* \* \* \* \* \* \* \* \* \* \* \* \* \* \* \* \* \* \* \* \* \* \* \* \* \* \* \* \* \* \* \* \* \* \* \* \* \* \* \* \*\*

Operating Conditions:     FFBC0P99VN40C
Library:                  ts28nchslogl35hdl140f_ffbc0p99vn40c
Wire Load Model Mode:     enclosed

Startpoint:               IBL[3] (input port clocked by clk)
Endpoint:                 DataIn_reg_1__4_ ( rising edge-triggered flip-flop
                          clocked by clk)
Path Group:               clk
Path Type:                max

| Des/Clust/Port | Wire Load Model | Library |
| --- | --- | --- |
| SM4_TOP_PIPE | ZeroWLM | ts28nchslogl35hdl |
| | | 140f_ffbc0p99vn40c |

| Point | Incr | Path |
| --- | --- | --- |
| clock clk (rise edge) | 0.00 | 0.00 |
| clock network delay (ideal) | 1.50 | 1.50 |
| input external delay | 2.50 | 4.00 f |
| IBL [3] (in) | 0.00 | 4.00 f |
| U40664/X (SEP_NR4_8) | 0.02 | 4.02 r |
| U40662/X (SEP_ND2_S_10) | 0.01 | 4.03 f |
| U40661/X (SEP_ND2_10) | 0.01 | 4.03 r |
| U40916/X (SEP_INV_1) | 0.02 | 4.05 f |
| U35897/X (SEP_INV_2) | 0.02 | 4.07 r |
| U41271/X (SEP_OAI222_1) | 0.03 | 4.10 f |
| U41285/X (SEP_EN2_V2_1) | 0.03 | 4.13 f |
| U41297/X (SEP_EN3_1) | 0.02 | 4.15 r |
| U39626/X (SEP_EO2_1P5) | 0.03 | 4.18 f |
| U40676/X (SEP_EO2_2) | 0.02 | 4.20 r |
| U39541/X (SEP_EO2_1P5) | 0.02 | 4.22 f |
| U41557/X (SEP_INV_1) | 0.01 | 4.23 r |
| U41559/X (SEP_EO2_1P5) | 0.02 | 4.25 f |
| U41561/X (SEP_NR2_G_1) | 0.01 | 4.26 r |
| U41564/X (SEP_EO2_1P5) | 0.02 | 4.29 f |
| U41565/X (SEP_EN3_3) | 0.04 | 4.32 f |
| U39434/X (SEP_INV_1) | 0.01 | 4.33 r |
| U41576/X (SEP_NR2_G_1) | 0.01 | 4.33 f |
| U41584/X (SEP_EO2_1P5) | 0.02 | 4.36 r |
| U35633/X (SEP_ND2B_V1U_1) | 0.01 | 4.37 r |
| U40699/X (SEP_INV_1) | 0.01 | 4.37 f |

| | | |
|---|---|---|
| U40698/X (SEP_NR2_G_1) | 0.01 | 4.39 r |
| U40648/X (SEP_EO2_1P5) | 0.02 | 4.41 f |
| U37893/X (SEP_EO2_1P5) | 0.02 | 4.43 r |
| U42559/X (SEP_ND2B_V1DG_1) | 0.01 | 4.44 f |
| U42561/X (SEP_EN2_V2_1) | 0.03 | 4.47 f |
| U42590/X (SEP_EO3_3) | 0.04 | 4.51 f |
| U44195/X (SEP_INV_1) | 0.01 | 4.52 r |
| U44266/X (SEP_AOI22_1) | 0.01 | 4.53 f |
| U35976/X (SEP_EO3_0P5) | 0.05 | 4.58 f |
| U40782/X (SEP_EO3_1) | 0.04 | 4.62 r |
| U35900/X (SEP_EO3_1) | 0.02 | 4.65 f |
| U40781/X (SEP_AO2BB2_1) | 0.02 | 4.67 f |
| U47959/X (SEP_AOI22_1) | 0.01 | 4.68 r |
| DataIn_reg_1__4_/D (SEP_FDPRBQ_V2_1) | 0.00 | 4.68 r |
| data arrival time | | 4.68 |
| | | |
| clock clk (rise edge) | 3.80 | 3.80 |
| clock network delay (ideal) | 1.50 | 5.30 |
| clock uncertainty | -0.60 | 4.70 |
| DataIn_reg_1__4_/CK (SEP_FDPRBQ_V2_1) | 0.00 | 4.70 r |
| library setup time | -0.02 | 4.68 |
| data required time | | 4.68 |
| | | |
| data required time | | 4.68 |
| data arrival time | | -4.68 |
| | | |
| slack (MET) | | 0.00 |

# References

1. Abbasi, I., Afzal, M.: A compact S-Box design for SMS4 block cipher. In: Park, J., Arabnia, H., Chang, H.B., Shon, T. (eds.) IT Convergence and Services, vol. 107. Springer, Dordrecht (2011)
2. Bhatia, T., Verma, A.K.: Data security in mobile cloud computing paradigm: a survey, taxonomy and open research issues. J. Supercomput. **73**(6), 1–74 (2017)
3. Canright, D.: A very compact Rijndael S-box. Tech. Rep. Collect. (Jan), 4–5 (2005)
4. Chinese Commercial Cryptography Administration Office: Sepecification of SM4 block cipher algorithm (2010). http://dacas.cn/sharedimages/ARTICLES/SMAlgorithms/SM4.pdf
5. Dworkin, M.J.: SP 800–38E. Recommendation for block cipher modes of operation: the XTS-AES mode for confidentiality on storage devices. National Institute of Standards & Technology (2010)
6. IP Cores. Inc.: XTS3 family of cores, IEEE P1619 XTS-AES cores. http://www.ipcores.com/xts_aes_p1619_ip_core.htm
7. James, P.: Securing data at rest. In: Australian Information Security Management Conference, pp. 94–103 (2004)
8. Jin, Y., Shen, H., You, R.: Implementation of SMS4 block cipher on FPGA. In: International Conference on Communications and Networking in China, pp. 1–4 (2006)
9. Lv, S., Su, B., Wang, P., Mao, Y., Huo, L.: Overview of SM4 algorithm. J. Inf. Secur. Res. 995–1007 (2016). http://ris.sic.gov.cn/CN/Y2016/V2/I11/995
10. 1619–2007 - IEEE Standard for Cryptographic Protection of Data on Block-Oriented Storage Devices. In: IEEE Approved Draft Std P1619/d18, October, pp. c1–32 (2007)
11. Rogaway, P.: Efficient instantiations of tweakable blockciphers and refinements to modes OCB and PMAC. In: Lee, P.J. (ed.) ASIACRYPT 2004. LNCS, vol. 3329, pp. 16–31. Springer, Heidelberg (2004). https://doi.org/10.1007/978-3-540-30539-2_2
12. S Ahmed, M.N.: Efficient AES-XTS Pipelined Implementation on FPGA. http://sirsyeduniversity.edu.pk/ssurj/rj/file/article/WSDDHXCVVN.pdf
13. Schneier, B., Kelsey, J.: Unbalanced Feistel networks and block cipher design. In: Gollmann, D. (ed.) FSE 1996. LNCS, vol. 1039, pp. 121–144. Springer, Heidelberg (1996). https://doi.org/10.1007/3-540-60865-6_49
14. Sethi, K., Majumdar, A., Bera, P.: A novel implementation of parallel homomorphic encryption for secure data storage in cloud. In: International Conference on Cyber Security and Protection of Digital Services pp. 1–7 (2017)
15. US Department of Commerce: NIST: Recommendation for Block Cipher Modes of Operation: Three Variants of Ciphertext Stealing for CBC Mode (NIST SP 800–38A)
16. Zhao, M., Shou, G., Hu, Y., Guo, Z.: High-speed architecture design and implementation for SMS4-GCM. In: International Conference on Communications and Mobile Computing, pp. 15–18 (2011)
17. Zi-Lei, L.I., Liu, Z.L., Huo, W.J., Zou, X.C.: A High-Throughput Hardware Implementation of XTS-AES Encryption Algorithm. Microelectronics & Computer **28**(4), 95–90 (2011)

# Detecting and Defending Against Certificate Attacks with Origin-Bound CAPTCHAs

Adil Ahmad[1]([⊠]), Faizan Ahmad[2], Lei Wei[3], Vinod Yegneswaran[4],
and Fareed Zaffar[2]

[1] Purdue University, West Lafayette, USA
ahmad37@purdue.edu
[2] Lahore University of Management Sciences (LUMS), Lahore, Pakistan
[3] Apple Inc., Cupertino, USA
[4] SRI International, Menlo Park, USA

**Abstract.** Published reports have highlighted various attacks on secure Public Key Infrastructure (PKI)-based SSL/TLS protocols. A well-known example of such an attack, that exploits a flaw in the Certificate Authority (CA) model of the PKI, is the compelled Man-in-the-Middle (MITM) attack, in which governments or affiliated agencies compel a CA to issue false but verifiable certificates for popular websites. These certificates are then used to hijack secure communication for censorship and surveillance purposes. Such attacks significantly undermine the confidentiality guarantees provided by SSL and the privacy of Internet users at large.

To address this issue, we present Origin-Bound CAPTCHAs (OBCs), which are dual CAPTCHA tests that elevate the difficulty of launching such attacks and make their deployment infeasible especially in cases of mass surveillance. An OBC is linked to the public key of the server and by solving the OBC, the client can use the certificate to authenticate the server and verify the confidentially of the link. Our design is distinguished from prior efforts in that it does not require bootstrapping but does require minor changes at the server side. We discuss the security provided by an OBC from the perspective of an adversary who employs a human work force and presents the findings from a controlled user study that evaluates tradeoffs in OBC design choices. We also evaluate a software prototype of this concept that demonstrates how OBCs can be implemented and deployed efficiently with 1.2-3x overhead when compared to a traditional TLS/SSL implementation.

**Keywords:** Compelled-certificate attacks
Man-in-the-middle attacks · CAPTCHAs

© ICST Institute for Computer Sciences, Social Informatics and Telecommunications Engineering 2018
R. Beyah et al. (Eds.): SecureComm 2018, LNICST 255, pp. 291–308, 2018.
https://doi.org/10.1007/978-3-030-01704-0_16

# 1   Introduction

Research in cryptographic security schemes has come a long way in making communication on the Internet more robust and secure. While the underlying cryptographic protocols are provably secure and theoretically sound, most attacks on the Internet take place due to implementation bugs and exploitation of factors such as false certificates, untrustworthy plugins, and vulnerable browsers. The problem of false certificates has plagued Internet for a long time, and there has been a concerted effort from major companies to mitigate this using solutions like certificate blacklisting. A Certificate Revocation List (CRL) is programmed into all browsers but needs to be constantly updated, a fact that most users remain completely oblivious to. Even with constant updates, there are numerous certificates that are uncaught.

An important and common certificate-based attack is the **compelled** Man-in-the-Middle attack [27]. The current PKI model, used for server validation, relies on the legitimacy of the Certificate Authority (CA). Therefore, when a CA issues certificates to an entity, users trust that entity without worrying about the integrity of the certificate. This poses a serious risk because attackers have, in the past, hijacked certificates from certificate authorities and launched massive attacks. A detailed analysis of the risks and problems associated with current PKI has been provided by Roosa et al. [25].

The problem of false but verifiable certificates is a significant issue undermining contemporary Internet security. There have been several reports highlighting the theft of verifiable certificates from CAs. Comodo is one of the CAs to publicly acknowledge the theft of certificates of various high-profile sites including the highly coveted google.com [4]. Another example is DigiNotar, a Dutch CA, which took a month to acknowledge that its certificates had been stolen, which resulted in the Dutch government seizing its operations [26]. Nation states have also been suspected to compel Certificate Authorities to issue SSL certificates which can then be used to carry out automated MITM attacks. Such reports are highly disturbing because if government agencies control CAs, then mass surveillance becomes trivially deployable.

Consider, for example, the case in which an attacker gets hold of verified certificates and wants to hijack communication between a legitimate client and server. The attacker can simply impersonate the legitimate server, using the verified certificate. Such MITM attacks are extremely dangerous because they enable the adversary to (*i*) passively eavesdrop, (*ii*) tamper with information, and (*iii*) coerce the user into sharing sensitive information. Both the user and the legitimate server may remain oblivious due to the stealthy nature of such attacks. The attacker obtains the data from the user, forwards to the server by pretending to be a user, and then transmits any response it gets from the server to the user. Also, this attack can easily be perpetrated in an *automated* fashion to eavesdrop on the browsing activities of a large group of people for surveillance and censorship purposes.

In recent years, a number of efforts [15,16,20,31] have tried to mitigate the problem of a compelled MITM but as yet there is no solution that is (*i*) easily deployable, (*ii*) user-friendly, (*iii*) does not rely on trusted third-parties, and (*iv*) significantly reduces the attack capability of the attacker. One of the major concerns with previous designs is that it may reveal a surveillance attack is taking place, but does not hamper capabilities of the attacker. Our work tries to address this problem with a CAPTCHA (Completely Automated Public Turing Test to Tell Computers and Humans Apart)-based solution that we believe addresses all of the above requirements with only minor modifications to the systems in place and a moderate usability cost.

A CAPTCHA, introduced by von Ahn et al. [30], is a program that makes a human solvable test that goes beyond the capabilities of current computers. The idea is for the server to challenge any communicating endpoint with a test which, if solved, allows the server to confidently assume it is interacting with an actual human being. Traditionally, servers have used CAPTCHAs to validate that the clients are real humans and not bots programmed by an attacker to perpetrate Denial-of-Service (DoS) attacks. The race to develop improved and resilient CAPTCHAs is an active area of research. This has also stimulated adversarial research into developing automated CAPTCHA solvers. Although Machine Learning (ML)-based attacks have proven to be effective on leading text-based CAPTCHAs [11], there is also new research into novel CAPTCHA designs that resist automated and human-solver relay attacks [18,19,24].

In this paper, we make the following contributions:

1. Present the Origin-Bound CAPTCHA (OBC), which is a novel CAPTCHA designed to validate the legitimacy of the server. It consists of a dual-CAPTCHA test that has an embedded proof telling the user whether or not the OBC and the certificate originated from the same server.
2. Provide a detailed security analysis of the OBC and demonstrate that it is infeasible for an attacker to solve a large amount of CAPTCHAs because it would require hiring a large human workforce.
3. Provide the findings of our user study to demonstrate the usability tradeoffs our design has to make in order to mitigate the impact of such attacks.
4. Provide a reference implementation and show that OBC is deployment-friendly in an incremental way.

The paper is divided into 10 sections. Section 2 discusses the related work in this area. In Sect. 3, we dissect the attack, and in Sect. 4, we explain the design considerations. Section 5 explains how an OBC is created, and Sect. 6 deals with a detailed security analysis of the design. We document the findings of our user study in Sect. 7, discuss our reference implementation in Sect. 8, and show the performance overhead incurred in Sect. 9. We discuss the limitations of the approach and potential avenues for future work in Sect. 10.

## 2    Related Work

Significant effort has been dedicated to finding and mitigating the effects of MITM attacks. Designs that have been considered include better CA models, more secure client-authentication using channel-IDs, reviewing historical data of visited sites, and using trusted third-parties.

Researchers in [16,23] attempt to tackle the problem by improving the Certificate Authentication model to account for all certificates currently in circulation. Some [28,29] have attempted to introduce publicly verifiable logs and monitoring solutions to mitigate problems with current PKI models. For these designs, bootstrapping and deployment in the current Internet ecosystem continue to be a huge concern, which is not likely to be the case with our proposal. Others have tried to strengthen client-authentication by using TLS-based Channel IDs [10,20], but such a design has been shown to be susceptible to other kinds of MITM attacks [22].

Perhaps the most closely related work is Certlock [1] – a system that employs a similar plugin-based approach to deal with compelled certificate attacks. The key difference between their system and ours is that Certlock relies on prior historical data of visited websites to detect anomalous behavior. In contrast, our system requires no bootstrapping. Other prior work has dealt with solving the issue of server impersonation by employing enhanced server verification techniques such as multi-path probing, pinning, etc. [16,31]. The Perspectives [31] and DoubleCheck [9] systems use notary servers to address such SSL MITM attacks. However, these systems rely on sharing browsing information to a trusted third party. Our approach does not have this requirement. The Heise SSL Guardian system detects weak SSL certificates [3]. Other work in this field includes the Multi-Factor Authentication (MFA) that saves user information from being accessible to the adversary in case of password leakages through MITM attacks. This method is currently employed by many top companies [5] in their applications but is rarely used by the end-users because it is veryinconvenient. Recent work [21] has also focused on ways to improve the two-step verification, but it remains an unpopular means of authentication.

Furthermore, prior work [17] has also drawn attention to the utility of server-bound CAPTCHAs, addressing the problem of CAPTCHAs being redirected to other websites. Their technique fails to protect users from a compelled MITM attack. The authors of [17] bind the IP and URL address to CAPTCHAs, which fails to control the attack.

## 3    Threat Model

In this section, we describe the main focus of the work, a targeted attack on unsuspecting users by snooping on their normal browsing activity. This kind of attack can only be perpetuated by an ISP-level attacker or an attacker that has hijacked a router along the pathway that a user or a group of users use to connect to the Internet. While discussing the attack, we make the following assumptions:

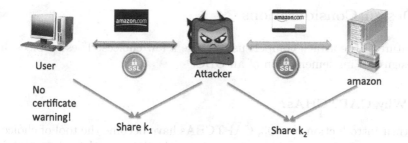

**Fig. 1.** Illustration of a compelled MITM attack between the User and Amazon using false certificates

1. The adversary targets *all or a major chunk* of users in his/her domain through automated attacks for surveillance purposes.
2. The adversary possesses the ability to perform *DNS/IP hijacking* and *Deep Packet Inspection (DPI)*.
3. The adversary has access to *false but verified certificates* through colluding CAs.

An adversary is able to intercept traffic between two communicating entities, redirect the traffic to its machines, and is able to read the transmissions through deep packet inspection and transmit them in a reasonable amount of time. The adversary needs to be able to respond in a timely manner, otherwise the connection will be dropped from the client or the server side due to timeouts. If the traffic is unencrypted, this becomes a trivial matter for an adversary with the abilities mentioned above.

However, if the attacker obtains access to verified certificates, he can just as easily read the contents of an encrypted connection. To do so, he must intercept incoming packets, redirect them to his machines using DNS/IP hijacking, send back the verified certificate through DPI, and simultaneously create a connection with the intended server. As such, the adversary merely needs to act as a conduit for the communication between the client and the server, and he can easily snoop on private data since he is the one who has an established shared secret with both the user and the server. The client remains unaware of the attacker because it received a verified certificate. The server, having received valid credentials, also has no reason to suspect foul play. Also, this attack can easily be carried out through automated scripts. The attacker simply directs all relevant traffic to its machines, performs the aforementioned procedure and dumps all intercepted data without having to maintain a human presence. Figure 1 explains this attack.

Traditional CAPTCHAs, widely used to distinguish bots and human users, also fail in detecting this attack. Instead of solving the CAPTCHAs, the adversary can simply redirect the CAPTCHA to the user and ask him/her to solve it. There have been reports of certain adult websites being used by attackers to make users solve CAPTCHAs for them. Researchers in [17] address that problem by using URL/IP binding on CAPTCHA content to ascertain the server address where the CAPTCHA was created.

# 4   Design Considerations

The nature of the attack compels us to make a few choices. These choices drive the design and implementation of an OBC.

## 4.1   Why CAPTCHAs?

Since their introduction in 2003, CAPTCHAs have become the tool of choice for e-commerce websites to facilitate user authentication and defend against DoS attacks. According to an estimate [7], more than 614,000 websites use various kinds of CAPTCHAs. We present two main arguments while making a case for CAPTCHAs as a tool to defend against compelled certificate attacks.

**Familiarity.** The extensive use of CAPTCHAs on the Internet means that users now possess a sense of familiarity with the software. Users have grown accustomed to solving CAPTCHAs in order to prove to the server that they are humans and not bots. Therefore, it would therefore be easier for them to adopt a similar solution to test the legitimacy of their connection rather than employ a new scheme. CAPTCHAs also offer an attractive range of possibilities such as text-based CAPTCHAs and audio/video CAPTCHAs, which improve both usability and accessibility of our scheme.

**Security.** CAPTCHAs have been proven to provide reasonable security against automated attacks. In the past, various attacks (especially ML-based) have been demonstrated against CAPTCHAs but have always been thwarted by trivial tweaking of the CAPTCHA modules. The current *state-of-the-art* are complex modules such as reCAPTCHA, that balance usability and resilience, using intelligent image distortion techniques to make it really hard for ML-based algorithms to crack them. Hence, the attacker must employ a human workforce or conscript unaware users in order to solve the CAPTCHAs. In short, the battle between CAPTCHA generators and solvers is a perennial arms race that we expect to continue for the forseeable future [11].

**Limitation.** People find it quite cumbersome to solve CAPTCHAs and it could be a major deterrent for some of them. However, we believe potential advantages gained through privacy preservation outweigh the trouble that solving CAPTCHAs would create. Also, newer proposals such as [13] illustrate ways to make it easier for people to solve CAPTCHAs without compromising the security of a CAPTCHA and can easily be used with OBC.

## 4.2   Proposed Modifications

Our work does not make changes to the TLS protocol and instead relies on simple modifications at the servers. The only modification required is that the server concurrently transmits an OBC with its certificate upon the initiation of a TLS-handshake and asserts the solution provided by the client before establishing the connection. At the client end, an installed browser plug-in intercepts the OBC and prompts the user to solve it. If the verification steps related to the Origin Bound CAPTCHA (mentioned in the next section) are successful, the client can authenticate the legitimacy of the connection and send his/her sensitive information securely.

We believe that to successfully avert an ISP-level attacker from snooping, there has to be some support from the server side. Our scheme would increase client trust on the servers, much like other schemes such as Multi-Factor Authentication.

## 5   Our Approach

An OBC is a dual-CAPTCHA test with the purpose of server validation, at the client side, in order to prevent compelled certificate attacks. The server is responsible for creating an OBC that it transmits back to the client as part of the SSL-handshake response. The user solves the CAPTCHAs and verifies it against the certificate being provided to authenticate the remote server. If the legitimacy is established, the user sends back the solution and, if not, terminates the connection and restarts the process. From here onward we refer to a legitimate SSL-enabled webserver as a *server* and a legitimate end-host as a *user*.

Our approach is tailored to fit the following assumptions:

1. We employ a ***passive detection*** technique in which we test the legitimacy of the connection only when transmitting sensitive information, e.g., username/passwords etc. and expect cryptographic protocols to take in afterwards.
2. We assume the attacker is not able to obtain the secret key corresponding to the public key of the server by breaking the cryptosystem. However, the user is able to obtain a verified certificate for any site that the user desires although the certificates will not be the same as those of the server that creates the OBC.

**Intuition.** The basic insight of our approach is to bind the content of the CAPTCHA to the identity of the server, so that the user solving the CAPTCHA is able to verify that the certificate that the user received during the SSL handshake indeed belongs to the server the user is communicating with. The CAPTCHA becomes non-transferable in some sense because the attacker risks being detected if he simply forwards the CAPTCHA to the user to solve, but would need to deploy a human being to solve by himself. While older CAPTCHAs can be solved by ML-based attacks [11], there is newer research that suggests new CAPTCHAs will be designed to resist existing attacks [19], including those that resist human-solver relay attacks. With hundreds of thousands of such CAPTCHAs needed to be manually solved in a short time (for many users), this becomes a non-trivial task for the attacker as we explain in Sect. 6.3.

**Construction.** Suppose the authentic certificate of the server endorses the public key $PK$. An OBC consists of two traditional CAPTCHAs $A$ and $B$ whose contents are derived from H($PK \parallel s$) and $s$, in which 'H' is a hash function, $s$ is a short random salt and $\parallel$ is concatenation function. In this scheme, $A$ is a CAPTCHA for $s$, displayed as characters in hexadecimal format. For usability reasons, we choose $s$ to be about 20 bits (5 characters shown in hexadecimal format). On the other hand, $B$ is a CAPTCHA for the value of H($PK \parallel s$) and only the first 6 characters in hexadecimal, i.e., 24 bits, of the hash value, are displayed.

We assume a browser plug-in is installed on the user's machine. The plug-in records the public key $PK'$ endorsed by the certificate that is verified during the SSL handshake process. Before the user is asked to input his login credential, the server sends the CAPTCHA to the user to solve. The add-on obtains the solution of the two CAPTCHAs, which we denote by the two strings as $a$ and $b$, and verifies if the first six characters of H($PK' \parallel a$) equal $b$. If this condition is not satisfied, it raises an alarm to the user and closes the connection. If the attacker used a $PK'$ different from $PK$ during the SSL handshake there is high probability the hash value would not verify. This would occur if the attacker intercepted the SSL-handshake request and replied with his/her own certificate without changing the CAPTCHAs sent by the server.

**Step-by-Step.** We now describe the above construction as a series of communication events between a user Alice and a service provider (server) Bob. An enumerated description of the aforementioned construction is shown below.

1. Alice attempts to initiate a SSL-handshake with Bob.
2. Bob acknowledges the handshake and returns his certificate with an OBC.
3. The browser plugin stores the CAPTCHAs $A$ and $B$ from the accompanying OBC.
4. First, Alice is prompted to solve CAPTCHA $A$.
5. Alice solves $A$, and the resulting value $a$ is stored by the installed plug-in.
6. Now, Alice is prompted to solve $B$ by the plugin.
7. Alice solves $B$, resulting in $b$, and the following relation is compared:

$$First\ 6\ digits\ of\ H(PK \parallel a) == b \tag{1}$$

8. If the relation holds, the credentials are sent forward alongwith the solution to the OBC. Otherwise, the user is notified his connection might not be secure.

In the next few sections, we provide a security and usability analysis of this approach.

## 6   Security Analysis

In this section, we explain in detail how the MITM attack is carried out and how our work counters it. We also explain why a manual attack on a large number of people is almost impossible if OBC is employed, the semantics of the hash function we use, and the probability of encountering a collision.

## 6.1    Detecting an Attack

Consider the attack mentioned in Sect. 3, i.e. an attacker tries to hijack a connection between a client and a server by presenting parallel realities to each of them. The capabilities of the attacker are that it controls a router along the pathway, can do arbitrary DNS/IP hijacking and has a false but verified certificate for the site that the user wants to initiate an SSL connection with. However, using OBCs, it becomes non-trivial to fool the client to think that you are the valid server and not the attacker. We provide an illustration of this in Fig. 2.

Suppose an attacker wants to hijack communication between User and Amazon. Using the router he has on the pathway between User and Amazon, he finds out the User is trying to contact Amazon. Therefore, he creates a connection with the User saying he is Amazon and he creates a connection with Amazon claiming to be the User. Since Amazon is using our technique, it sends the attacker an OBC that the attacker dutifully relays to the User. The User solves the OBC and verifies the relation provided by Eq. 1. However, the certificate the attacker sent to the User during the initial handshake will have a different public key $PK'$, and the relation will not be satisfied. Therefore, the browser plug-in will realize there is something wrong with the connection and will terminate the connection with the User's consent.

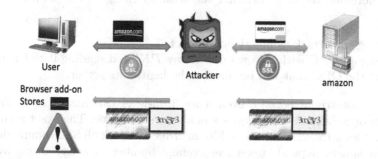

**Fig. 2.** Workflow illustrating how the MITM attack between the User and Amazon is detected with OBCs

## 6.2    Cryptoanalysis and Implementation Considerations

We use the SHA-256 hash function for the computation of the 6-digit hash $h$ of the salt $s$ and public key $PK$, i.e., $h = H(PK \parallel s)$. We first calculate the probability of a hash collision such that the public key provided by a malicious attacker has a combined hash with the salt $s$, $h'$, that collides with the hash $h$ provided by the server. The probability $q(n)$ that the attacker generates a random public key that hashes $s$ to $h' = h$ is given by, where $n = 1$ and $d = 16^6$, we obtain $q = 5.96 \times 10^{-8}$.

More concerning, however, is the probability that the server issues the same OBC to multiple clients. For any hash function–assuming random hash values with a uniform distribution, a collection of $n$ different data blocks and a hash function that generates $b$ bits–the probability $p$ that there will be one or more collisions is bounded by the number of pairs of blocks multiplied by the probability that a given pair will collide. For example, setting $b = 24$, we observe that to maintain a probability lower than $2^{-10}$ that there is a collision between two hashes, with the currently implemented 300-s expiry interval for each hash pair, the server should open up new connections with clients at a rate no faster than 109 connections per second.

If we use 5 and 6 Base-64 digits for the salt and hash, respectively, in place of the hexadecimal digits currently implemented, the rate for new connections to maintain the same probability goes up to 134217728. To avoid server-side storage overhead when dealing with multiple connections, we employ action tokens as a method of providing end users a reasonable time window to solve the OBC. However, if we keep track of issued and unsolved-yet-currently valid CAPTCHAs on the server, it is possible to reduce the probability of collision to 0 while enforcing a limit on the number active OBCs served.

### 6.3   Employing a Human Workforce

As described obove, OBC provides reasonable security against attacks on its design. Therefore, the only way that the attacker can get away with the attack is by:

- Initiating the attack as mentioned in Sect. 3.
- Creating an OBC with his own public key $PK'$ and sending it to the user.
- Solving the OBC that will be sent by the legitimate server.

This is non-trivial because even a medium-level ISP has to solve literally thousands of SSL-handshake requests in a very small time. The exact number of people that an attacker will have to hire in order to hijack all SSL communication within his sphere depends upon the average number of active users, average number of SSL connections initiated in a time interval, the average rate of solving CAPTCHAs, and the error rate of solving CAPTCHAs. Studies [30] have shown it takes about 10 s on average for a person to solve a CAPTCHA. Another factor that needs to be accounted for is the connection timeout limit, which is normally set to 1 min in a popular browser such as Google Chrome. For a 2-min interval, neglecting the exact start and end time for the SSL connections, the relation given below holds.

$$N_{people} = \frac{N_{avg} \times N_{users} \times N_{ssl} \times 2}{12 \times r_{error}^2} \tag{2}$$

In the equation, $N_{avg}$ represents the average percentage of people active, $N_{users}$ represents the total number of users registered with the ISP, $N_{ssl}$ represents the average number of SSL connections, and $r_{error}$ represents the error rate (which is a value between 0 and 1). We assume that takes about 10 s for a person to solve a CAPTCHA and if he/she works tirelessly for 2 min, about 12 CAPTCHAs can be solved. The error rate is squared because both the attacker and the user can make a mistake while solving CAPTCHAs. Here, we assume that all SSL connections are OBC-enabled.

To understand the equation, consider a 2-min interval in which the first minute is spent requesting SSL handshakes which must be solved within the next minute otherwise the connection will be terminated by the browser. So, any connection created between $T = 0$ and $T = 60$ will have to be responded to by $T = 60$ to $T = 120$. To simplify the equation, we neglect the exact start times and apply the worse case, which means that any connection created between $T = 0$ and $T = 60$ has to be responded to by $T = 120$.

Let us consider the case of a small ISP with about 100,000 registered users and also suppose each user uses only a single device at a time and the percentage of active users is 5%. Furthermore, suppose each active user initiates only a single SSL connection in the interval. Without considering any error, more than 800 people will be required to work tirelessly to hijack all the encrypted communication within an isolated 2-min interval for a small ISP. The number will rise exponentially as the number of users and/or the error rate increases. Hence, we believe employing a human workforce is a non-trivial barrier for medium-to-large large ISP environments.

## 7   Usability Analysis

To better understand the usability of OBCs, we conducted a two-week user study in our institution (Lahore University of Management Sciences) that involved 150 subjects. Our study was approved by our institute's Institutional Review Board (IRB). All participants consented to their participation in the study and data was sanitized to ensure that personal private information would not be disclosed to the public. We did not mass-distribute the study and limited it to the confines of our academic institution.

Our user study was conducted online using a website that was only accessible within the institute's network. All the participants were consenting adults between the ages of 18–35 years old and *non-native* English speakers. One caveat of our study is that it was fully conducted in a university environment and thus the results may be less indicative of a wider userbase (since younger students may be more technology savvy than the general public).

To participate in the study, users were first instructed to visit the OBC user study website link and provided with a survey that must be completed without pauses to ensure the consistency of our results. We conducted the study with two main CAPTCHA libraries, captchas.net [14] and Securimage PhP Captcha [2]. Both these libraries are popular, open-source, and have continued support from the developers.

**Fig. 3.** User study depictions for design 1 (left) and design 2 (right)

We outline below the specific goals of our user study:

- To measure out how long it takes for users to solve an OBC.
- To measure the error rate for users in solving an OBC.
- To evaluate various design choices and ascertain user preferences.

### 7.1 Introductory Message

The user were provided the following information at the start page:
"This is a study on the efficiency of CAPTCHAs. CAPTCHAs are commonly used to prevent automated attacks on webservers. This study will take 5–10 min. Please complete this study in a single pass and complete the survey provided at the end."

### 7.2 CAPTCHA Tests

We considered two main design choices for an OBC:

1. Two small CAPTCHAs of 6 characters, i.e., Captchas $A$ and $B$.
2. One large CAPTCHA of 12 characters (formed by joining both CAPTCHAs $A$ and $B$ together).

Our main goal was to measure the time taken, error rate, and user preference for each design. For design 1, we simply showed the participants two CAPTCHAs side by side as in Fig. 3. To calculate the time taken, we started a timer in the background as soon as the user started typing on the provided box. We set timers for individual CAPTCHAs as well as a timer that stopped when both boxes were filled and the user moved onto the next test. Figure 3 (right) depicts design 2, in which the user was asked to fill the 12 character CAPTCHA to ascertain the same insights we wanted from design 1. Here, it should also be mentioned that we used both libraries for each design, and users solved five OBCs for each library and for each design, which totals to 30 distinct (twenty 6-character + ten 12-character) CAPTCHAs per-user.

### 7.3 Survey

After completing the CAPTCHA tests, the users were asked to complete a simple survey that posed some simple questions about which design they preferred and which library of CAPTCHAs was easier for them.

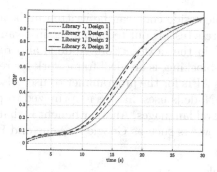

**Fig. 4.** CDF graphs for completion times for CAPTCHAs using design 1 and design 2

**Table 1.** Statistics from user study

|              | Design 1 |        | Design 2 |        |
| ------------ | -------- | ------ | -------- | ------ |
|              | Lib 1    | Lib 2  | Lib 1    | Lib 2  |
| Avg. time (s) | 18      | 17.5   | 16       | 15.3   |
| Err. rate (%) | 31.7    | 25.1   | 37.56    | 33.52  |

## 7.4  Results

Figure 4 shows the cumulative distribution function (CDF) o f completion times with designs 1 and 2. The CDFs were quite similar to each other with design 2 performing slightly better, which is as expected since the users don't have to switch between solving two CAPTCHAs and are simply solving a larger CAPTCHA. Table 1 provides a summary of the average completion times for users with all designs and the error rates that we encountered with the individual designs.

Our results indicate solving CAPTCHAs incurs a high error rate; the accuracy of our tests, which converged at a mean of 69%, is similar to previous studies [12] involving multiple CAPTCHAs and non-native English speakers. The accuracy is consistently within the range of 65–75%, which indicates there is still a fair amount of work to be done to make CAPTCHAs more solvable for humans.

Our results also show the vast majority i.e., almost 75%, of our subjects prefer design 2 (one long CAPTCHA) over design 1 (two smaller CAPTCHAs). Furthermore, the error rate does not necessarily increase by a significant margin when we move from design 1 to design 2, which makes design 2 seem even more practical for large-scale deployment.

## 8  Implementation

To evaluate our technique, we developed a reference client-server module using Node.js [6], a popular server-side JavaScript environment. Node.js was chosen for rapid prototyping since it allows us to run a webserver without using Apache, and both server and client-side code can be written in JavaScript. The Node.js module was used for stress testing our technique against vanilla-TLS, the results of which are presented in the next section. Node.js also relies on event-driven programming and non-blocking, is an ideal framework for real-time applications and provides numerous APIs for the programmer to use. Also, the V8 JavaScript runtime engine, which Node.js uses, has been optimized to provide performance similar to that of low-level languages. Another benefit is that Node.js works with a variety of modern browsers such as Google Chrome and Firefox.

## 8.1  The OBC Stack

The OBC implementation stack consists of two main modules: the browser plugin and an OBC-enabled server.

**OBC-Enabled Server.** We have used the term "OBC-enabled Server" to simply distinguish servers that have an OBC-patch[1] installed from the ones that do not. The difference in the working of an OBC-enabled server and a non-OBC server is that the latter sends an OBC to the client to solve and waits for the solution to the OBC before confirming the TLS/SSL handshake. The server tags the outgoing webpage with an OBC tag to signal to the client plugin that an OBC-enabled connection is about to be initiated.

**Browser Plugin.** The plugin is a non-intrusive add-on to the client's browser and is similar to various common extensions such as AdBlock etc. It serves the following functions:

- Checks TLS-response to ascertain an OBC-enabled connection
- Redirects an OBC onto a seperate page and asks the user to solve it
- Captures user's response and recreates the relationship proven by Eq. 1.
- Informs the user about the legitimacy of the connection

In our implementation, we used a Firefox plugin, but it can be easily implemented in any modern browser. The plugin's main role is to hide the semantics of the operations from the User and simply present the him/her with a ready-to-solve page embedded with an OBC and an MITM alert, in case the relationship does not hold.

## 8.2  OBC Workflow

The workflow of the OBC reference implementation is as follows. The user attempts to initiate a TLS connection with an OBC-enabled server. The server replies with the certificate and an OBC. The client plugin observes that an

---

[1] An "OBC-patch" could mean a change to the TLS protocol or installation of a shim layer that works in tandem with the TLS-protocol and is responsible for dealing with the OBC. We are in favor of the latter approach.

OBC-enabled connection is underway, prepares itself by storing the certificate, and consequently the public key (PK) of the contacting server.

The server sends a page on which an 'OBC' is embedded and the plugin simply presents that to the user. The user solves the OBC and the solution is extracted by the browser plugin. The plugin ascertains the conditions established in Eq. (1). The only way those relations will not be fulfilled are if:

- There is a certificate-attack being carried out.
- The user solved the CAPTCHAs incorrectly.

Newer forms of CAPTCHAs have been shown to have solution error rates less than 10% [13] and therefore we have opted not to recheck the solutions. In case of an error, we simply assume the worst-case and reset the connection. A new OBC is then requested from the server and the whole process is repeated.

## 9  Performance Analysis

In this section, we compare the performance of an OBC-enabled webserver with a traditional SSL webserver. The webserver used for the comparison is a Core i7 PC with 16 GB RAM and internal SSD memory. The following graph depicts the time taken in case of varying number of connections. We have ignored the network latency and focused solely on the stress it induces on the PC.

As shown in Fig. 5, the overhead of using an OBC increases as the number of concurrent connections established increase. With 10 concurrent connections, the performance of OBC TLS and vanilla TLS are comparable. As the number of concurrent connections increases to 100, the response time of the OBC TLS server increases to 4.5 s (this is a 3× overhead in comparison with the vanilla TLS server response time of 1.5 s). The overhead can be attributed to increased computations the server has to perform to create the CAPTCHAs to send to the clients. However, a few additional details need to be considered.

- The prototype implementation is unoptimized. In these experiments, the CAPTCHAs are created each time a connection is attempted. The time it takes to create a CAPTCHA is significant when compared to other trivial computations of the TLS protocol. If we can have a pre-computed local database of CAPTCHAs from which servers can simply extract, the overhead will reduce significantly. This is a straightforward extension we will pursue in future work.
- In most datacenters [8], effective load-balancing ensures that load is distributed amongst servers in such a manner that the overall instantaneous stress on a single server system is minimized.
- Finally, the benefits of using an OBC in guaranteeing reasonable security far surpass the induced overhead in many situations.

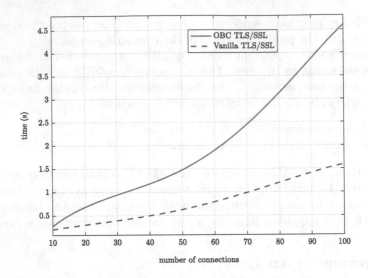

**Fig. 5.** Comparison between OBC and vanilla TLS

## 10    Limitations and Future Work

There is one scenario in which OBCs would fail. Suppose an attacker tries to simply get username/passwords for users connecting to a social networking site like Facebook or Twitter using fake certificates. As soon as the username and passwords are harvested, the attacker can simply end the transmission and allow the retry connection to go through unsnooped. In such instances, the plugin should be redesigned to warn users when there is a certificate mismatch between the original and retried connection. However, we believe such an attack is infeasible for mass surveillance on the internet, which is the main focus of this work.

CAPTCHAs are a necessary drawback of our system to make mass surveillance infeasible for ISP-level attackers. We hope that future research in improvements to CAPTCHA schemes will benefit our system and make it more accessible to normal users. We aim to further investigate how the OBC approach could be deployed on the Internet with the least number of modifications. We would like to improve the OBC stack by introducing stored databases of CAPTCHAs that would raise the performance of an OBC-enabled TLS/SSL quite close to that of vanilla TLS/SSL connections. We would also add support for other kinds of CAPTCHAs and also investigate if a modification of OBCs can be used to prevent other MITM attacks.

## 11    Conclusion

This paper presented the design and implementation of OBCs, a browser plugin-based solution against compelled MITM attacks. The simple and promising solution relies on CAPTCHAs, but requires no certificate pinning, bootstrapping, trusted notaries or third parties. We presented a detailed description of our design and conducted a user study to assess design tradeoffs. To validate our approach, we developed a simple prototype implementation that demonstrates how OBCs can deployed without prohibitive performance penalties. We believe if OBCs are deployed ubiquitously, they can render compelled MITM attacks ineffective, at least temporarily, and raise the bar by forcing adversaries to invest in human resources for CAPTCHA solving. We hope our approach can benefit from improvements in CAPTCHA design and inspire the development of alternate solutions against compelled MITM attacks, that do not rely on CAPTCHAs.

**Acknowledgements.** We would like to thank all the anonymous reviewers of the program committee for their valuable insights on the paper. This work was partially funded by the National Science Foundation (NSF) under Grant No. CNS-1514503. Any opinions, findings, and conclusions or recommendations expressed in this material are those of the author(s) and do not necessarily reflect the views of NSF.

# References

1. CertLock - SecureW2. https://www.securew2.com/products/certlock/
2. Securimage PHP Captcha. https://www.phpcaptcha.org/
3. Heise SSL Guardian: Protection against unsafe SSL certificates (2008). www.h-online.com/security/features/Heise-SSL-Guardian-746213.html
4. Comodo report of incident (2011). https://www.comodo.com/ComodoFraud-Incident-2011-03-23.html.
5. Google 2-Step Verification, September 2016. https://www.google.com/landing/2step/
6. Node.js, July 2016. https://www.nodejs.org/en/
7. Sites using CAPTCHAS, July 2016. https://wappalyzer.com/categories/captchas
8. Abts, D., Felderman, B.: A guided tour of data-center networking. Commun. ACM **55**(6), 44–51 (2012)
9. Alicherry, M., Keromytis, A.D.: DoubleCheck: multi-path verification against man-in-the-middle attacks. In: IEEE Symposium on Computers and Communications, ISCC 2009, pp. 557–563. IEEE (2009)
10. Balfanz, D., Hamilton, R.: Transport layer security (TLS) channel IDs. IETF Draft (2013)
11. Bursztein, E., Aigrain, J., Moscicki, A., Mitchell, J.C.: The end is nigh: generic solving of text-based CAPTCHAs. In: 8th USENIX Workshop on Offensive Technologies (WOOT 2014) (2014)
12. Bursztein, E., Bethard, S., Fabry, C., Mitchell, J.C., Jurafsky, D.: How good are humans at solving CAPTCHAs? A large scale evaluation. In: IEEE Symposium on Security and Privacy, pp. 399–413 (2010)
13. Bursztein, E., Moscicki, A., Fabry, C., Bethard, S., Mitchell, J.C., Jurafsky, D.: Easy does it: more usable CAPTCHAs. In: Proceedings of the 32nd Annual ACM Conference on Human Factors in Computing Systems, pp. 2637–2646. ACM (2014)
14. captchas.net: Free captcha-service. http://captchas.net/
15. Dietz, M., Czeskis, A., Balfanz, D., Wallach, D.S.: Origin-bound certificates: a fresh approach to strong client authentication for the web. Presented as part of the 21st USENIX Security Symposium (USENIX Security 2012), pp. 317–331 (2012)

16. Evans, C., Palmer, C., Sleevi, R.: Public key pinning extension for HTTP. Technical report (2015)
17. Ferraro Petrillo, U., Mastroianni, G., Visconti, I.: The design and implementation of a secure CAPTCHA against man-in-the-middle attacks. Secur. Commun. Netw. **7**(8), 1199–1209 (2014)
18. Gao, H., et al.: Robustness of text-based completely automated public turing test to tell computers and humans apart. IET Inf. Secur. **10**(1), 45–52 (2016)
19. Gao, S., Mohamed, M., Saxena, N., Zhang, C.: Emerging image game CAPTCHAs for resisting automated and human-solver relay attacks. In: Proceedings of the 31st Annual Computer Security Applications Conference. ACSAC (2015)
20. Karapanos, N., Capkun, S.: On the effective prevention of TLS man-in-the-middle attacks in web applications. In: 23rd USENIX Security Symposium (USENIX Security 2014), pp. 671–686 (2014)
21. Karapanos, N., Marforio, C., Soriente, C., Capkun, S.: Sound-proof: usable two-factor authentication based on ambient sound. In: 24th USENIX Security Symposium (USENIX Security 2015), pp. 483–498 (2015)
22. Karlof, C., Shankar, U., Tygar, J.D., Wagner, D.: Dynamic pharming attacks and locked same-origin policies for web browsers. In: Proceedings of the 14th ACM Conference on Computer and Communications Security, pp. 58–71. ACM (2007)
23. Kim, T.H.J., Huang, L.S., Perring, A., Jackson, C., Gligor, V.: Accountable key infrastructure (AKI): a proposal for a public-key validation infrastructure. In: Proceedings of the 22nd International Conference on World Wide Web, pp. 679–690. ACM (2013)
24. Osadchy, M., Hernandez-Castro, J., Gibson, S., Dunkelman, O., Pérez-Cabo, D.: No bot expects the DeepCAPTCHA! Introducing immutable adversarial examples, with applications to CAPTCHA generation. IEEE Trans. Inf. Forensics Secur. **12**(11), 2640–2653 (2017)
25. Roosa, S.B., Schultze, S.: Trust darknet: control and compromise in the internet's certificate authority model. IEEE Internet Comput. **17**(3), 18–25 (2013)
26. Shultze, S.: Diginotar hack highlights critical failures of our SSL web security model, September 2011. https://freedom-to-tinker.com/blog/sjs/diginotar-hack-highlights-critical-failures-our-ssl-web-security-model
27. Soghoian, C., Stamm, S.: Certified lies: detecting and defeating government interception attacks against SSL (short paper). In: Danezis, G. (ed.) FC 2011. LNCS, vol. 7035, pp. 250–259. Springer, Heidelberg (2012). https://doi.org/10.1007/978-3-642-27576-0_20
28. Syta, E., et al.: Keeping authorities "honest or bust" with decentralized witness cosigning. arXiv preprint arXiv:1503.08768 (2015)
29. Szalachowski, P., Matsumoto, S., Perrig, A.: PoliCert: Secure and flexible TLS certificate management. In: Proceedings of the 2014 ACM SIGSAC Conference on Computer and Communications Security, pp. 406–417. ACM (2014)
30. von Ahn, L., Blum, M., Hopper, N.J., Langford, J.: CAPTCHA: using hard AI problems for security. In: Biham, E. (ed.) EUROCRYPT 2003. LNCS, vol. 2656, pp. 294–311. Springer, Heidelberg (2003). https://doi.org/10.1007/3-540-39200-9_18
31. Wendlandt, D., Andersen, D.G., Perrig, A.: Perspectives: improving SSH-style host authentication with multi-path probing. In: USENIX Annual Technical Conference, vol. 200 (2008)

# Web Security

# FrameHanger: Evaluating and Classifying Iframe Injection at Large Scale

Ke Tian[1(✉)], Zhou Li[2], Kevin D. Bowers[2], and Danfeng (Daphne) Yao[1]

[1] Virginia Tech, Blacksburg, VA, USA
{ketian,danfeng}@cs.vt.edu
[2] RSA Laboratories, Bedford, MA, USA
{zhou.li,kevin.bowers}@rsa.com

**Abstract.** Iframe is a web primitive frequently used by web developers to integrate content from third parties. It is also extensively used by web hackers to distribute malicious content after compromising vulnerable sites. Previous works focused on page-level detection, which is insufficient for Iframe-specific injection detection. As such, we conducted a comprehensive study on how Iframe is included by websites around Internet in order to identify the gap between malicious and benign inclusions. By studying the online and offline inclusion patterns from Alexa top 1M sites, we found benign inclusion is usually regulated. Driven by this observation, we further developed a *tag-level* detection system named FrameHanger which aims to detect injection of malicious Iframes for both online and offline cases. Different from previous works, our system brings the detection granularity down to the tag-level for the first time without relying on any reference. The evaluation result shows FrameHanger could achieve this goal with high accuracy.

## 1 Introduction

The past decade has seen the strong trend of content consolidation in web technologies. Nowadays, a web page delivered to a user usually contains content pulled from many third-parties. A typical web primitive employed by website developers for this purpose is Iframe tag, which automatically renders web content in a container within a webpage. It gains popularity since the dawn of web and is still one major technique driving the Internet economy. Although Iframe facilitates the third-party content rendering, it introduces potential abuse. A recent take-down operation against Rig Exploit Kit shows Iframe is the major "glue" for its infrastructure [8]. After an attacker gains control over a vulnerable website, Iframe is usually injected into a webpage to make the site a gateway to attacker's infrastructure. Every time a user visits the compromised wepage, she is redirected to other website that hosts malicious payload.

Although malicious Iframe usage could be dangerous, Iframe injection characteristics and its countermeasure are not well studied. To fill this gap, we performed a large-scale analysis on *Alexa top 1 million* websites to understand how

© ICST Institute for Computer Sciences, Social Informatics and Telecommunications Engineering 2018
R. Beyah et al. (Eds.): SecureComm 2018, LNICST 255, pp. 311–331, 2018.
https://doi.org/10.1007/978-3-030-01704-0_17

Iframe is injected in both offline (embedded through Iframe tag) and online (generated through JavaScript) scenarios. We find Iframe inclusion is widely used by legitimate site owners. In particular, offline inclusion is more popular comparing to online inclusion, covering 30.8% of the pages returned to our crawler. A closer look into these Iframes shows a large portion of them point to several giant IT companies serving advertisements, social networks and web analytics. Techniques used extensively for injecting malicious Iframes have limited adoption in legitimate websites, like hidden style (except by several well-known third-parties) and obfuscation. On the downside, the support for browser policies, like CSP and `X-Frame-Options`, is still insufficient among site owners, though these policies could contain the damage caused by Iframe injection.

Because of the limited website protection, Iframe injection has already become a powerful weapon in hacker's arsenal [8]. Injected Iframes in compromised websites can point to arbitrary attacker's infrastructure for malware propagation. Therefore, we believe a system capable of pinpointing and classifying the Iframe injection and is very important in guarding the safety of web users and integrity of websites.

In this paper, we propose a new detection system named `FrameHanger` to mitigate the threat from Iframe injection. The system is composed of a static analyzer against offline injection and a dynamic analyzer against online injection. To counter the obfuscation and environment profiling heavily performed by malicious Iframe scripts, we propose a new technique called *selective multi-execution*. After an Iframe is extracted by `FrameHanger`, a machine-learning model is applied to classify its intention. We consider features regarding Iframe's style, destination and context. The evaluation result shows the combination of these features enables highly accurate detection: 0.94 accuracy is achieved by the static analyzer and 0.98 by the dynamic analyzer.

While prior works can detect webpages tampered by hackers [16,18,21,31, 32,34], they either work at coarse-grained level (page- or URL-) or require a clean reference to perform differential analysis. On the contrary, `FrameHanger` is able to spot the malicious Iframe at *tag-level* without the dependency on any reference. As such, by applying `FrameHanger`, finding Iframe injection should become less labor-intensive and error-prone. We release source code of components of `FrameHanger`, in hopes of propelling the research on countering web attacks [3]. The contributions of the paper are summarized as follows:

- We propose a new *tag-level* detection system `FrameHanger` for malicious Iframe injection detection by combining selective multi-execution and machine learning. We design multiple contextual features, considering Iframe style, destination and context properties.
- We implement the prototype of `FrameHanger`, which contains a static analyzer and a dynamic analyzer. The experimental results demonstrate the high precision of `FrameHanger`, i.e., 0.94 accuracy for offline Iframe detection and 0.98 for online Iframe detection.
- We carried out a large scale study on Iframe injection, in both legitimate and malicious scenarios.

## 2   Background

In this section, we give a short introduction about Iframe tag, including its attributes and capabilities first. Then, we describe how Iframe is abused by network adversaries to deliver malicious content.

### 2.1   Iframe Inclusion

HTML Frame allows a webpage to load content, like HTML, image or video, independently from different regions within a container. There are four types of Frame supported by mainstream browsers, including `frameset`, `frame`, `noframe` and `iframe`. Except Iframe, all the others were deprecated by the current HTML5 standard. In this work, we focus on the content inclusion through Iframe.

**Iframe Attributes.** How Iframe is displayed depends on a set of tag attributes. Attribute `height` and `width` determine the size of Iframe. The alignment of content inside Iframe can be configured by `marginheight`, `marginwidth` and `align`. For the same purpose, the developer can assign CSS properties into `style`, which provides more handlers for tuning the Iframe display. For instance, the position of Iframe within the webpage can be adjusted through two properties of `style` (`top` and `position`). When the Iframe has a parent node in the DOM tree, how it is displayed is influenced by the parent. The origin of Iframe content is determined by `src` attribute, which is either a path relative to the root host name (e.g., /iframe1.html) or an absolute path (e.g., http://example.com/iframe1.html). Figure 1 gives an example about what an Iframe tag looks like.

**Browser Policies.** One major reason for the adoption of Iframe inclusion is that its content is isolated based on browser's Same Origin Policy (SOP) [9]. Bounded by its origin, the code within an Iframe is forbidden to access the DOM objects from other origins, which reduces the damage posed by third parties. However, the threat is not mitigated entirely by this base policy. All DOM operations are allowed by default within the Iframe container. To manage the access at finer grain, three mechanisms have been proposed:

- `sandbox` **attribute.** Starting from HTML5, developers can enforce more strict policy on Iframe through the `sandbox` attribute, which limits what can be executed inside Iframe. For instance, if a field `allow-scripts` is disabled in `sandbox`, no JavaScript code is permitted to execute. Similarly, submitting HTML form is disallowed if `allow-forms` is disabled.
- **CSP (Content Security Policy).** CSP provides a method for site owner to declare what actions are allowed based on origins of the included content. It is designed to mitigate web attacks like XSS and clickjacking. For one website, the policy is specified in the `Content-Security-Policy` field (or `X-Content-Security-Policy` for older policy version) within server's response header. CSP manages Iframe inclusion through attributes like `frame- ancestors`, which specifies the valid origin of Iframe.

- X-Frame-Options. This is also a field in the HTTP response header indicating whether an Iframe is allowed to render. There are three options for
X-Frame-Options: SAMEORIGIN, DENY and ALLOW-FROM.

```
1  <p><span style="position: absolute; top: -1175px; width: 312px; height:
   306px;"> npz
2  <iframe src="http://gfd.JOSEPHANDRITO.COM/?
   q=wHnQMvXcJwDGFYbGMvrESqNbNknQA0OPxpH2_drWdZqxKGni0Ob5UU
   Sk6FSCEh3&amp;que=border.102ky68.406r3r5s3&amp;biw=border.111tk83.4
   06j4t3y2&amp;ct=border&amp;fix=border.98yv62.406y1w9o4&amp;oq=h9_Eq
   LbZROALjiBOJcwJnnY5fVQlA8qisi0iAyhDKicTQ-ByMZg91z6LRVvQ-2w"
   width="258" height="261"></iframe>
3  yqpwc </span>htkz</p>
4  <noscript>
5  <!DOCTYPE html >
6  <html lang="es">
7  <head>
8       <base href="http://www.selfprinting.es/" />
9  </noscript>
```

**Fig. 1.** An example of offline Iframe injection. Line 1–4 are added by attacker. The
Iframe can only be detected in the HTML source code. Visitors are unable to see this
Iframe from the webpage.

```
1  </script>
2  <body> </body>
3  <script type="text/javascript">
4  var hhfcdro = "iframe"; var mbusui = document.createElement(hhfcdro); var
   qqdbctd = ""; mbusui.style.width = "8px"; mbusui.style.height = "12px";
   mbusui.style.border = "0px"; mbusui.frameBorder = "0";
   mbusui.setAttribute("frameBorder", "0"); document.body.appendChild(mbusui);
   qqdbctd = "http://one.bestwingsinmemphis.com/?
   qtuif=2139&ct=soul&q=w3nQMvXcJxfQFYbGMvPDSKNbNkzWHViPxoqG9Mil
   dZ-qZGX_k7HDfF-
   qoV_cCgWR&oq=xfFf7tZNAOyikWJfQlznlxeUltBpfimj0PRyR_K1pKFrByJZA9
   H-qKlJLd_mhj2"; mbusui.src = qqdbctd; </script>
5  </body>
6  </html>
```

**Fig. 2.** An example of online Iframe injection. Line 3–4 are added by attacker. The
Iframe is injected by running JavaScript code. Visitors are unable to notice the injection
and see the Iframe from the webpage.

Though these primitives could help mitigate the threat from malicious
Iframe, we found they were not yet widely used, as shown in Sect. 3.3. What's
more, when the attacker is able to tamper the response header in addition to
page content, all these policies can be disabled.

## 2.2   Malicious Iframe Injection

The capabilities of Iframe are bounded by different browser policies like SOP,
but it is still extensively used by attackers to push malicious content to visitors, according to previous research [34] and reports [6,8]. In many cases, after
attacker compromises a website and gains access, an Iframe with src pointing
to a malicious website is injected to webpages under the compromised site. Next
time when a user visits the compromised site, her browser will automatically

load the content referred by the malicious Iframe, like drive-by-download code. In fact, it is not unusual to find a large number of websites hijacked to form one malware distribution network (MDN) through Iframe Injection [34]. So far, there are mainly two mechanisms used widely for Iframe injection and we briefly describe them below.

**Offline Iframe Injection.** In this case, the attacker injects the Iframe tag to the compromised webpage without any obfuscation. Figure 1 illustrates one real-world example. To avoid visual detection by users, the attacker sets `top` field of `style` to a very large negative value (`-1175px`). Instead of setting `style` in the Iframe tag, the attacker chooses to set it on the parent `span` node. Also interesting is that the injected Iframe appears at the very beginning of the HTML document, a popular pattern also mentioned by previous works [31]. The URL in `src` points to a remote site which aims to run Rig Exploit code in browser [6].

**Online Iframe Injection.** To protect the Iframe destination from being easily matched by URL blacklist, attacker generates Iframe on the fly when the webpage is rendered by user's browser. Such runtime generation is usually carried out by script injected by attacker, like JavaScript code. We call such code *Iframe script* throughout the paper. Figure 2 illustrates one example. The code within the script tag first creates an Iframe tag (`createElement`) and adds it to the DOM tree (`appendChild`). Then, it sets the attributes of Iframe separately to make it invisible and point to malicious URL.

The sophistication of this example is ranked low among the malicious samples we found, as the malicious URL is in plain text. By applying string functions of JavaScript, the URL can be assembled from many substrings in the runtime. Recovering the Iframe URL will incur much more human efforts. Even worse, attacker can use off-the-shelf or even in-house JavaScript obfuscator [7,22,38] to make the entire code unreadable and impede the commonly used analyzers. We show examples of advanced destination-obfuscation in Sect. 6.3.

# 3 Large-Scale Analysis of Iframe Inclusion

To get better understanding of how Iframe is included by websites around Internet, we crawled a large volume of websites and analyzed their code and runtime behaviors. Below we first describe our data collection methodologies. Then, we characterize the category, intention and sophistication of inclusion in both offline and online scenarios.

## 3.1 Data Collection

We choose the sites listed in Alexa top 1 million[1] as our study subject. For each site, our crawler visits the homepage and passes the collected data to a DOM parser and an instrumented browser for in-depth analysis. Some previous works

---

[1] http://s3.amazonaws.com/alexa-static/top-1m.csv.zip.

use different strategies for web measurement, e.g., crawling 500 pages per site in Alexa top 10K list [33]. In this study, we are also interested in how less popular sites include Iframe, therefore we use the entire list of Alexa 1M.

We built the crawler on top of Scrapy [10], an application framework supporting customized crawling jobs. We leverage its asynchronous request feature and are able to finish the crawling task within 10 days. For each site visited, our crawler downloads the homepage and also saves the response header to measure the usage of browser policies. We use an open-source library *BeautifulSoup* to parse the DOM tree and find all Iframe tags to measure offline inclusion. For online inclusion, we let a browser load each page and capture the dynamically generated Iframe through `MutationObserver` (detailed in Sect. 5.2). This approach allows us to study Iframe generated by *any* scripting code (JavaScript, Adobe Flash and etc.) within the entire page. In total, we obtained 860,873 distinct HTML pages (we name this set $P$) and their response headers. In total we spent 5 h analyzing offline Iframes and 148 h analyzing online Iframes. The ratio of websites returning valid to our crawler (86%) is slightly lower than a previous work also measuring Alexa top 1M sites (91%) [23]. We speculate the difference is caused by the crawler implementation: their crawler is built on top of an off-the-shelf browser and they set the timeout to 90 s.

To notice, we did not perform deep crawling (e.g., visiting pages other than the homepage, simulating user actions and attempting to log in) for each studied website. Our "breadth-first" crawling strategy aligns with previous works in large-scale web measurement [23]. Though deep crawling could discover more Iframe inclusions, it will take much more execution time.

## 3.2    Distribution of Iframes

**Popularity of Iframe Inclusion.** Table 1 presents the statistics of Iframe inclusion in the surveyed pages. In short, the usage of Iframe is moderate in the contemporary Internet world: only 31.6% pages include Iframe[2], whereas more than 92% pages have script tags. To notice, our instrumented browser captures any type of online Iframe inclusion, including that caused by script tags, which means script inclusion is rarely intended to insert Iframe.

**Table 1.** Statistics for the 860,873 webpages ($P$). We count the pages that embed Iframe and their ratio. We also count the pages embedding script tag.

|                          | Offline Iframe | Online Iframe | Script tag |
|--------------------------|----------------|---------------|------------|
| # pages                  | 265,087        | 16,292        | 799,673    |
| Percent                  | 30.8%          | 2%            | 92.9%      |
| # pages with external `src` | 229,558     | 6,016         | 587,946    |
| Percent                  | 26.7%          | 0.7%          | 68.3%      |

---

[2] Only Iframe with `src` is considered in the measurement study.

**Table 2.** Top 6 external domains referenced through offline inclusion. The percent is counted over $P_{OffEx}$.

| Domain | # Pages | Category | Percent |
|---|---|---|---|
| googletagmanager.com | 102,207 | Web analytics | 44.52% |
| youtube.com | 52,308 | Social web | 22.79% |
| facebook.com | 37,466 | Social web | 16.32% |
| google.com | 7,564 | Search engines | 3.29% |
| vimeo.com | 6,943 | Streaming | 3.02% |
| doubleclick.net | 3,838 | Advertisement | 1.67% |

**Table 3.** Top 5 external domains referenced through online inclusion. The percent is counted over $P_{OnEx}$.

| Domain | # Pages | Category | Percent |
|---|---|---|---|
| doubleclick.net | 3,269 | Advertisement | 54.34% |
| facebook.com | 213 | Social web | 3.54% |
| youtube.com | 172 | Social web | 2.85% |
| ad-back.com | 170 | Advertisements | 2.82% |
| prom.ua | 153 | Business & Economy | 2.54% |

Specifically, we found 30.8% pages include Iframe in the offline fashion, whereas only 2% include Iframe during runtime. We speculate such prominent difference is resulted from the separation of interfaces from third-party services. As an example, Google provides two options for using its web-tracking services [4]: placing an Iframe tag or a script tag. When the developer chooses the latter, the tracking code directly collects the visitor's information and no Iframe is created.

Then, we investigate the pages with offline Iframes which we name as $P_{Off}$. As expected, most pages (86.6% over $P_{Off}$) use offline Iframe to load content from external source (external hostname). For the remaining pages, though most of destinations are relative paths, we still find a large number of paths like file://*, javascript:false and about:blank, which would not load HTML content. It turns out file://* is used to load file from user's local hard-disk and and the latter two is used as placeholder which is assigned by script after a moment[3]. Among the 16,292 pages including Iframe in online fashion (named $P_{On}$), only 6,016 (36.9%) point to external destination (named $P_{OnEx}$). Non-standard paths described above are extensively used in online Iframes.

**Characterization of Iframe Destinations.** Tables 2 and 3 list the domain name of most popular destinations in terms of referenced pages. For each domain,

---

[3] The update of src might be triggered by user's action, like moving mouse. User actions are not simulated by our system so the update might be missed.

we obtained domain report from VirusTotal and used the result from Forcepoint ThreatSeeker to learn its category. In the offline case, services from the giant companies like Google and Facebook dominate the destinations. The number 1 domain is `googletagmanager.com`, a web analytics provided by Google. In the online case, while `doubleclick.net` takes 54.3% of $P_{OnEx}$, the percent for remaining domains are all small, 3.5% at most for `facebook.com`. Next, we compute the distribution of web categories regarding external destination. The result is shown in Fig. 3. It turns out the distribution is quite different for offline and online case: social network and web analytics are the two main categories in offline case while advertisement Iframe is used more often in online case.

**Comparison to Script Inclusion.** Finally, we compare the Iframe inclusion and script inclusion in terms of amount and categories. Previous work has studied the offline script inclusion and showed that most script are attributed to web analytics, advertisement and social network, which is consistent with our findings here. Still, there are two prominent differences. *(1)* The number of script tags is an order of magnitude more than Iframe tags (8,802,569 vs 561,048 from the crawled 860,873 pages). *(2)* The Iframe usage per site is quite limited. As shown in Fig. 4, more than 60% webpages with Iframe inclusion only embed 1 Iframe, whereas at least 2 script tags are seen for 90% webpages doing script inclusion.

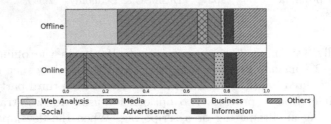

**Fig. 3.** Categories of offline and online Iframe destinations.

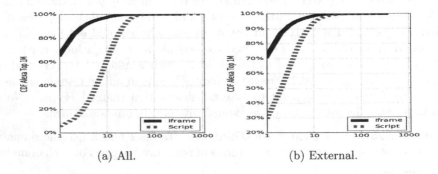

(a) All.                    (b) External.

**Fig. 4.** ECDF of number of offline Iframe and script tag per site.

**Table 4.** Usage of CSP.                    **Table 5.** X-Frame-Options usage.

| Site count | CSP | X-CSP |
|---|---|---|
| frame-src | 1,637 | 251 |
| frame-ancestor | 3,049 | 307 |
| child-src | 1,062 | 86 |

| Site count | X-Frame-Options | Ratio |
|---|---|---|
| SAMEORIGIN | 95,897 | 89.2% |
| DENY | 9,547 | 8.88% |
| ALLOW-FROM | 1,200 | 1.12% |

## 3.3  Usage of Browser Policies

Site developers can leverage policies defined by browser vendors to control the threat posed by Iframes from third-party or unknown destinations. We are eager to know how the policies are enforced. To this end, we measure the usage of CSP, X-Frame-Options and sandbox. The result is elaborated below.

Regarding the usage of CSP, we found only 18,329 websites (2.1%) specify CSP or X-CSP and less than half of them use Iframe-related fields (see Table 4). CSP has much better adoption than X-CSP and we speculate it is caused by the deprecation of X-CSP in the latest specification.

On the other hand, the adoption of X-Frame-Options is much better, as 107,553 websites make use of this feature (see Table 5). The reason is perhaps that X-Frame-Options is more compatible with outdated browsers [13]. Yet, on closer look, this result turns out to be quite puzzling. First, only 1.12% sites use the ALLOW-FROM option, meaning that most of the site owners make no differentiation on Iframe destinations. Second, a non-negligible amount of sites make mistakes that disable this policy: 979 sites use conflict options at the same time (e.g., both SAMEORIGIN and DENY are specified) and 1,338 sites misspell the options (DANY:6, SAMEORGIN:12, ALLOWALL:1,320). In the end, 86% percent of websites do not use either CSP or X-Frame-Options, suggesting there is a long way ahead for their broad adoption.

It is a good practice to restrict the capabilities of Iframe through sandbox attribute, but we found it only appears in 0.37% Iframes (2,104 out of 561,048).

## 3.4  Iframe Features

In this subsection, we take a close look at how Iframe tag is designed and included. In particular, we measured the style attribute of Iframe tag and the statistics of Iframe script.

**Iframe style.** Though the original purpose of Iframe is to split webpage's visible area into different regions, we found many Iframes are designed to be invisible to visitors, through the use of style attribute. Specifically, we found 31.0% of the Iframes are hidden for offline inclusion, in terms of size (e.g., width:0 and height:0) and visual position. However, when excluding 3 popular domains (googletagmanager.com, doublclick.net and yjtag.jp), only 3.8% Iframes are hidden. Similarly for online inclusion, 64.1% Iframes are hidden, but 80.2%

among them are belong to 2 domains (`doubleclick.net` and `ad-back.net`). The result shows web analytics and advertisements are the major supporters for hidden Iframe.

**Iframe Script.** Through the use of script, the destination of Iframe can be obfuscated, which could hinder existing web scanners or human analysts. We are interested in whether obfuscation is heavily performed by legitimate scripts and the answer turns out to be negative. We search the destination of all dynamically generated external Iframe among the script from the 6,016 pages (see Table 1) and found the match of domain name in 5,326 pages (88%). This result suggests developer usually has no intention to hide the destination. More specifically, among the 3,269 pages embedding `doublelcick.net` Iframe (see Table 3), match is found in 3,237 pages (>99%). One may question why developers choose Iframe script when it is only used in a light way. It turns out the purposes are merely delaying the assignment of destination and attaching more information to URL (e.g., add random nonce to URL parameter). This pattern significantly differs from the malicious samples where destination-obfuscation is extensively performed, which motivates our design of selective multi-execution (Sect. 5.2).

### 3.5  Summary

In conclusion, 30.8% sites perform offline injection and 2% perform online injection. Iframe is mainly used for social-network content, web analytics and advertisements. Several giant companies have taken the lion's share in terms of Iframe destination. The adoption of browser policies related to Iframe is still far from the ideal state and even writing policy in the correct way is not always done by developers.

## 4  Detecting Iframe Injection

Iframe is used extensively to deliver malicious web code, e.g., drive-by-download scripts, to web visitors of compromised sites since more than a decade ago [34]. How to accurately detect malicious Iframe is still an open problem. The detection systems proposed previously work at *page-*, *URL-* or *domain-level.* Given that many Iframes could be embedded by an individual page, *tag-level* detection is essential in saving the analysts valuable time for attack triaging. To this end, we propose `FrameHanger`, a detection system performing tag-level detection against Iframe injection. We envision that `FrameHanger` can be deployed by a security company to detect Iframe injection happening on any compromised website. In essence, `FrameHanger` consists of a static crawler to patrol websites, a static analyzer to detect offline injection and a dynamic analyzer to detect online injection. In what follow, we provide an overview of `FrameHanger` towards automatically identifying Iframe injection (the crawler component is identical to the one used for measurement study) and elaborate each component in next section. The system framework is illustrated in Fig. 5.

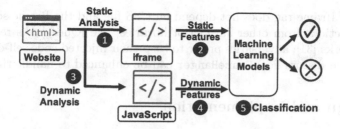

Fig. 5. The framework of FrameHanger.

*(1)* **Static Analyzer.** When a webpage passes through crawler, static analyzer parses it to a DOM tree (step ❶). For each Iframe tag identified, we create a entry and associate it with features derived from tag attributes, ancestor DOM nodes and the hosting page (step ❷).

*(2)* **Dynamic Analyzer.** An Iframe injected at the runtime by JavaScript code can be obfuscated to avoid its destination being easily exposed to security tools (e.g., URL blacklist) or human analysts. Static analyzer is ineffective under this case so we developed a dynamic analyzer to execute each extracted JavaScript code snippet with a full-fledged browser and log the execution traces (step ❸). While there have been a number of previous works applying dynamic analysis to detect malicious JavaScript code (e.g., [26]), these approaches are designed to achieve very high code coverage, but suffering from significant overhead. Alternatively, we optimize the dynamic analyzer to focus on Iframe injection and use a lightweight DOM monitor to reduce the cost of instrumentation. When an Iframe tag is discovered in the runtime, the features affiliated with it and the original Iframe script are extracted and stored in the feature vector similar to static analyzer (step ❹).

*(3)* **Classification.** Every Iframe tag and Iframe script is evaluated based on machine-learning models trained ahead (step ❺). We use separate classifiers for offline and online modes, as their training data are different and feature set are not entirely identical. The detection result is ordered by the prediction score and analysts can select the threshold to cap the number of Iframes to be inspected.

**Adversary Model.** Our goal in this work is to detect injected Iframes within the webpages of *compromised sites*. When the sites are fully controlled and used for malicious purposes, Iframe detection is more challenging as manipulation is much easier for attackers (e.g., changing the Iframe context). The systems designed to capture malicious domains/URLs/pages are better choices for this scenario. We focus on Iframe tag and Iframe script and build detection models around them. Not all methods leading to Iframe injection are covered by FrameHanger. For instance, Iframe can be added by Adobe Flash or Java Applet. Given that these content are now blocked by default on many browsers, we believe these options are less likely adopted by adversaries. We assume malicious Iframe tag and Iframe script are self-contained, without additional dependencies (e.g., the style attribute of Iframe tag does not depend on CSS file and the Iframe script does not use functions from other JavaScript libraries, like jQuery). As revealed by previous works [31], adversaries prefer to keep their injected code self-contained. In Sect. 7, we discuss how `FrameHanger` can be enhanced to handle these cases.

# 5   Design and Implementation

In this section, we elaborate the features for determining whether an Iframe is injected. To effectively and efficiently expose the Iframe injected in the runtime by JavaScript, we developed a lightweight dynamic analyzer and describe the implementation details.

## 5.1   Detecting Offline Iframe Injection

By examining online reports and a small set of samples about Iframe injection, we identified three categories of features related to the style, destination and context of malicious Iframe, which are persistently observed in different attack campaigns. Through the measurement study, we found these features are rarely presented in benign Iframes. All of the features can be directly extracted from HTML code and URL, therefore `FrameHanger` is able to classify Iframe immediately when a webpage is crawled. We describe the features by their category.

**Style-Based Features.** To avoid raising suspicion from the website visitors, the malicious Iframe is usually designed to be hidden, as shown in the example of Sect. 2. This can be achieved through a set of methods, including placing the Iframe outside of the visible area of browser, setting the Iframe size to be very small or preventing Iframe to be displayed. All of these visual effects can be determined by the `style` attribute of the Iframe tag. As such, `FrameHanger` parses this attribute and checks each individual value against a threshold (e.g., whether `height` is smaller than 5px) or matches it with a string label (e.g., whether `visibility` is `hidden`). As a countermeasure, attacker can create a parent node above the Iframe (e.g., `div` tag) and configure `style` there. Therefore, we also consider the parent node and the node above to extract the same set of features. We found style-based features could distinguish malicious and benign Iframe, as most of the benign Iframes are not hidden, except the ones belong to well-known third parties, like web analytics, as shown in Sect. 3.4. These benign but hidden Iframes can be easily recognized with the help of public list, like EasyList [1] and EasyPrivacy [2], and pre-filtered.

**Destination-Based Features.** We extract the lexical properties of the `src` attribute from the Iframe tag to model this category. `FrameHanger` only considers the properties from external destination, as this is the dominant way to redirect visitors to other malicious website, suggested by a large corpus of reports (e.g., [6]). For attacker, using relative path requires compromising another file or uploading a malicious webpage, which makes the hacking activity more observable. An Iframe without valid `src` value does not do any harm to visitors. The lexical properties FrameHanger uses is similar to what has been tested by previous works on URL classification [32], and we omit the details.

**Context-Based Features.** Based on our pilot study, we found attacker prefers to insert malicious Iframe code into abnormal position in HTML document, e.g., the beginning or end of the document. In contrast, site developers often avoid such positions. For this category, we consider the distance of the Iframe to positions of our interest and the distance is represented by number of lines or levels in DOM tree. Exploiting the code vulnerability of website, like SQL injection and XSS, is a common way to gain control illegally. Websites powered by web templates, like WordPress, Joomla and Drupal, are breached frequently because the related vulnerabilities are easy to find. We learn the template information from the META field of header and consider it as a feature. Finally, we compare the Iframe domain with other Iframe domains in the page and consider it more suspicious when it is different from most of others.

## 5.2  Detecting Online Iframe Injection

When the Iframe is injected by obfuscated JavaScript code, feature extraction is impossible by static analyzer. Deobfuscating JavaScript code is possible, but only works when the obfuscation algorithm can be reverse-engineered. Dynamic analysis is the common approach to counter obfuscation, but it can be evaded by environment profiling [27]: e.g., the malicious code could restrict its execution on certain browsers based on **useragent** strings. To fix this shortcoming, force execution [24,26] and symbolic execution [27,35] are integrated into dynamic analysis. While they ensure all paths are explored, the overhead is considerable, especially when the code contains many branches and dependencies on variables.

Based on our large-scale analysis of Iframe script in Alexa top 1M sites and samples of malicious Iframe scripts, we found the existing approaches can be optimized to address the overhead issue without sacrificing detection rate. For legitimate Iframe scripts, obfuscation and environment profiling is rarely used. For malicious Iframe scripts, though these techniques are extensively used, only popular browser configurations are attacked (e.g., Google Chrome and IE). Therefore, we can choose different execution model according to the complexity of code: when the script is obfuscated or wrapped with profiling code, FrameHanger sends the code to multi-execution engine using a set of popular browser configurations; otherwise, the script is executed within a single pass. When an Iframe injection is observed (i.e., new node added to DOM whose tag name is Iframe), the script (and the Iframe) will go through feature extraction and classification.

**Pre-filtering.** At first step, FrameHanger uses the DOM parser to extract all script tags within the page. In this work, we focus on the Iframe injected by *inline script* (we discuss this choice in Sect. 7). The script that has no code inside or non-empty **src** attribute is filtered out.

The next task is to determine whether the code is obfuscated or the running environment is profiled. It turns out though deobfuscation is difficult, learning whether the code is obfuscated is a much easier task. According to previous studies [25,41], string functions (e.g., `fromCharCode` and `charCodeAt`), dynamic evaluation (e.g., `eval`) and special characters are heavily used by JavaScript obfuscators. We leverage these observations and build a set of *obfuscation indicators* to examine the code. Likewise, whether environment profiling is performed can be assessed through a set of *profiling indicators*, like the usage of certain DOM functions (e.g., `getLocation` and `getTime`) and access of certain DOM objects (e.g., `navigator.userAgent`). In particular, a script is parsed into abstract syntax tree (AST) using Slimit [5] and we match each node with our indicators.

**Code Wrapping and Execution Monitoring.** Since we aim to detect Iframe injection at the tag level, `FrameHanger` executes every script tag separately in a *script container*, which wraps the script in a dummy HTML file. When the attacker distributes the Iframe script into multiple isolated script tags placed in different sections, the script code might not be correctly executed. However, such strategy might break the execution in user's browser as well, when a legitimate script tag is executed in between. Throughout our empirical analysis, code splitting is never observed, which resonates with findings from previous works [31].

Each script container is loaded by a browser to detect the runtime creation of Iframe. We first experimented with an open-source dynamic analysis framework [36] and instrument all the JavaScript function calls. However, the runtime overhead is considerable and recovering tag attributes completely is hindered when attacker plays string operations extensively. Therefore, we moved away from this direction and explore ways to directly catch the injected Iframe object. Fortunately, we found the mainstream browsers provide an API object named `MutationObserver`[4] to allow the logging of all sorts of DOM changes. Specifically, the script container first creates a `MutationObserver` with a callback function and then invokes a function `observe(target,config)` to monitor the execution. For the parameter `config`, we set both options `childList` and `subtree` to `true` to catch the insertions and removals of the DOM children's and their descendants. When the callback function is invoked, we perform logging when the input belongs to `mutation.addedNodes` and its name equals "`iframe`". All attributes are extracted from the newly created Iframe for the feature exaction later. Because only one script tag exists in the script container, we are able to link the Iframe creation with its source script with perfect accuracy. We found this approach is much easier to implement (only 32 lines of JavaScript code in script container) and highly efficient, since `MutationObserver` is supported natively and the monitoring surface is very pointed.

**Execution Environment.** We choose full-fledged browser as the execution environment. To manage the sequence of loading script containers, we leverage an automatic testing tool named Selenium [11] to open the container one by one in a new browser window. All events of our interest are logged by the browser logging API, e.g., `console.log`. The logger saves the name of hosting page, index of script tag and Iframe tag string (if created) into a local storage.

---

[4] https://developer.mozilla.org/en-US/docs/Web/API/MutationObserver.

We also override several APIs known to enable logic bomb, e.g., `setTimeout` which delays code execution and `onmousemove` which only responds to mouse events, with a function simply invoking the input. When a container is loaded, we keep the window open for 15 s, which is enough for a script to finish execution most of time. Depending on the pre-filtering result, single-execution or multi-execution will be preformed against the container. For multi-execution, we use 4 browser configurations (IE, Chrome, FireFox, Internet Explorer and Safari) by maneuvering `useragent`[5].

Changing `useragent` instead of actual browser for multi-execution reduces the running overhead significantly. However, this is problematic when the attacker profile environment based on browser-specific APIs. As revealed by previous works [31], `parseInt` can be used to determine whether the browser is IE 6 by passing a string beginning with "0" to it and checking whether the string is parsed with the octal radix. In this case, changing `useragent` is not effective. Hence, we command Selenium to switch browser when such APIs are observed.

**Feature Extraction.** Similar to static analyzer, we consider the features related to style, destination and the context, but extract them from different places. The destination and style features come from the generated Iframe while the context features come from the script tag. The number and meanings of features are identical.

# 6 Evaluation

In this section, we present the evaluation on `FrameHanger`. We first examine the accuracy of static and dynamic analyzer on a labeled dataset and then perform an analysis on the importance of features. Next, we measure the performance overhead of `FrameHanger`. Finally, we show cases of destination-obfuscation discovered by our study.

**Dataset.** We obtained 17,273 webpages detected by a security company through either manual or automated analysis. To notice, the malicious Iframe tag or script was not labeled by the company. To fill this missing information, we first extracted all Iframe tags and scanned their destination with VirusTotal. An Iframe tag triggers at least 2 alarms is included in our evaluation dataset. Similarly, all Iframe scripts were executed and labeled based on the response from VirusTotal regarding the generated Iframe tags. To avoid the issue of data bias, we select only one Iframe or script per unique destination, which leaves us 1,962 and 2,247 malicious samples for evaluating static and dynamic analyzers.

The benign samples come from the 229,558 tags and 6,016 scripts used for the measurement study. If we include all of them for training, the data will be very unbalanced. Therefore, we perform down-sampling to match the size of malicious set. Any sample triggering alarm from VirusTotal was removed.

---

[5] `useragent` strings extracted from http://useragentstring.com/.

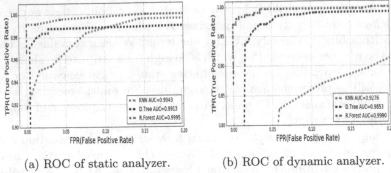

(a) ROC of static analyzer.          (b) ROC of dynamic analyzer.

**Fig. 6.** ROC curve for the static and dynamic analyzer of `FrameHanger`.

## 6.1 Effectiveness

We tested 3 different machine-learning algorithms on the labeled dataset, including KNN (K-nearest neighbors), D. Tree (Decision Tree) and R. Forest (Random Forest). 10-fold cross validation (9 folds for training and 1 for testing) is performed for each algorithm, measured by AUC, accuracy and F1-score.

Figure 6a and b present the ROC curve for static and dynamic analyzer. To save space, the result with over 0.2 False Positive Rate is not shown. R. Forest achieves the best result in terms of AUC. In addition, the accuracy and F1-score are (0.94, 0.93) for static analyzer, and (0.98,0.98) for dynamic analyzer. R. Forest has shown its advantage over other machine-learning algorithms in many security-related tasks and our result is consistent with this observation. We believe its capability of handling non-linear classification and over-fitting is key to its success here.

**Feature Analysis.** We use feature importance score of R. Forest [12] to evaluate the importance of features. For the offline detection, the most important features belong to the context category, with 0.025 mean and 0.001 variance. For the online detection, the most important features belong to destination category, with 0.030 mean and 0.002 variance. It turns out the importance varies for the two analyzers, and most features have good contribution to our model.

## 6.2 Runtime Overhead

We ran `FrameHanger` on a server with 8 CPUs (Intel(R) Xeon(R) CPU 3.50 GHz), 16 GB memory and Ubuntu 14.04.5. The time elapse was measured per page. For static analyzer, it takes 0.10 s in average (0.018 s variance) from parsing to classification, suggesting `FrameHanger` is highly efficient in detecting offline injection. For dynamic analyzer, the mean overhead is 17.4 s but the variance is as high as 386.4 s. The number of script tags per page and the code sophistication per script (e.g., obfuscation) are the main factors accounting for the runtime overhead. In the mean time, we will keep optimizing the performance on dynamic analyzer.

(a) Iframe destination in string of ASCII values. (b) Iframe destination assembled using `fromCharCode`.

**Fig. 7.** Obfuscations detected by the dynamic analyzer of `FrameHanger`.

### 6.3 Destination Obfuscation

Obfuscating destination is an effective evasion technique against static analysis. We are interested in how frequent this technique is used for real-world attacks. To this end, we compute the occurrences of obfuscation indicators in the 2,247 malicious Iframe scripts. The result suggests its usage is in deed prevalent: as an evidence, 1,247 has JavaScript function `fromCharCode` and 975 have `eval`.

Detecting destination obfuscation is very challenging for static-based approach, but can be adequately addressed by dynamic analyzer. Figure 7a and b show examples of obfuscated Iframe scripts. We summarize two categories of obfuscation techniques from attack samples. *(1)* lightweight obfuscation and *(2)* heavyweight obfuscation. In the lightweight obfuscation, attackers only hide the destination with ASCII values. Figure 7a is an example of lightweight obfuscation. The static approach is able to find the "iframe" string but hard to infer the destination. More common cases are the heavyweight obfuscation, where both the "iframe" string and the destination are obfuscated. Figure 7b is the example of heavyweight obfuscation. Figure 7b applies `fromCharCode` to concatenate the destination string. Attackers hide the Iframe payload with ASCII values or string concatenation or even masquerade the string function with DOM property. However, these samples were picked up by our dynamic analyzer and the Iframes were exposed after runtime execution.

### 6.4 Summary

We summarize our experimental findings. *(1)* `FrameHanger` achieves high precision of detection, i.e., 0.94 accuracy for offline Iframe detection and 0.98 for online Iframe detection. *(2)* `FrameHanger` encseounters moderate runtime overhead, 0.10 s for offline detection and 17.4 s for online detection. *(3)* `FrameHanger` successfully captures obfuscations in online Iframe injection, which is prevalent used by real-world attackers.

## 7 Discussion

We make two assumptions about adversaries, including their preferences on Iframe tag/script and self-contained payload. Invalidating these assumptions is possible, but comes with negative impact on attackers' themselves. Choosing other primitives like Adobe Flash subjects to content blocking by the latest browsers. Payload splitting could make the execution be disrupted by legitimate code running in between. On the other hand, FrameHanger can be enhanced to deal with these cases, by augmenting dynamic analyzer with the support of other primitives, and including other DOM objects of the same webpage.

FrameHanger uses a popular HTML parser, BeautifulSoup, to extract Iframe tag and script. Attacker can exploit the discrepancy between BeautifulSoup and the native parsers from browsers to launch parser confusion attack [14]. As a countermeasure, multiple parsers could be applied when an parser error is found. Knowing the features used by FrameHanger, attackers can tweak the attributes or position of Iframe for evasion (e.g., making Iframe visible). While they may succeed in evading our system, the Iframe would be more noticeable to web users and site developers.

Our dynamic analyzer launches multi-execution selectively to address the adversarial evasion leveraging environment profiling. We incorporate a set of indicators to identify profiling behaviors, which might be insufficient when new profiling techniques are used by adversary. That said, updating indicators is a straightforward task and we plan to make them more comprehensive. Multiple popular browser profiles are used for multi-execution. Attackers can target less used browsers or versions for evasion. However, it also means the victim base will be drastically reduced. FrameHanger aims to strike a balance between coverage and performance for dynamic analysis. We will keep improving FrameHanger in the future.

## 8   Related Works

**Content-Based Detection.** Detecting malicious code distributed through websites is a long-lasting yet challenging task. A plethora of research focused on applying static and dynamic analysis to detect such malicious code.

Differential analysis has shown promising results in identifying compromised websites. By comparing a website snapshot or JavaScript file to their "clean-copies" (i.e., web file known to be untampered), the content injected by attacker can be identified [16,31]. Though effective, getting "clean-copies" is not always feasible. On the contrary, FrameHanger is effective even without such reference. In addition to detection, researchers also investigated how website compromise can be predicted [37] and how signatures (i.e., Indicators of Compromise, or IoC) can be derived [19]. FrameHanger can work along with these systems. To expose the IFrame injected in the runtime by JavaScript code, we develop a dynamic analyzer to execute JavaScript and monitor DOM changes. Different from previous works on force execution and symbolic execution [24,26,27,35], our selective multi-execution model is more lightweight with the help of content-based pre-filtering. Previous works have also investigated how to detect compromised/malicious landing pages using static features [18,34]. Some features (e.g., "out-of-place" IFrames) used by their systems are utilized by FrameHanger as well. Comparing to this work, our work differs prominently regarding the detection goal (**FrameHanger** pinpoints the injected IFrame) and the integration of static and dynamic analysis (**FrameHanger** detects online injection).

**URL-Based Detection.** Another active line of research in detecting web attacks is analyzing the URLs associated with the webpages. Most of the relevant works leverage machine-learning techniques on the lexical, registration, and DNS features to classify URLs [15,20,30,32]. In our approach, URL-based features constitute one category of our feature set. We also leverage features unique to IFrame inclusion, like IFrame style. To extract relevant features, we propose a novel approach combining both static and dynamic analysis.

**Insecurity of Third-Party Content.** Previous works have studied how third-party content are integrated by a website, together with the security implications coming along. Nikiforakis et al. studied how JavaScript libraries are included by Alexa top 10K sites and showed many of the links were ill-maintained, exploitable by web attackers [33]. Kumar et al. showed a large number of websites fail to force HTTPS when including third-party content [28]. The study by Lauinger et al. found 37.8% websites include at least one outdated and vulnerable JavaScript libraries [29]. The adoption of policies framework like CSP has been measured as well, but incorrect implementation of CSP rules are widely seen in the wild, as shown by previous studies [17,39,40]. In this work, we also measured how third-party content were included, but with the focus on IFrame. The result revealed new insights about this research topic, e.g., the limited usage of CSP, and reaffirms that more stringent checks should be taken by site owners.

## 9 Conclusion

In this paper, we present a study about Iframe inclusion and a detection system against adversarial Iframe injection. By measuring its usage in Alexa top 1M sites, our study sheds new light into this "aged" web primitive, like developers' inclination to offline inclusion, the concentration of Iframe destination in terms of categories, and the simplicity of Iframe script in general. Based on these new observations, we propose a hybrid approach to capture both online and offline Iframe injections performed by web hackers. The evaluation result shows our system is able to achieve high accuracy and coverage at the same time, especially when trained with R. Forest algorithm. In the future, we will continue to improve the effectiveness and performance of our system.

## References

1. The easylist filter lists. https://easylist.to/. Accessed 10 Oct 2017
2. The easyprivacy filter lists. https://easylist.to/easylist/easyprivacy.txt. Accessed 10 Oct 2017
3. Framehanger released version. https://github.com/ririhedou/FrameHanger

4. Google tag manager quick start. https://developers.google.com/tag-manager/quickstart. Accessed 10 Oct 2017
5. A javascript minifier written in python. https://github.com/rspivak/slimit. Accessed 10 Oct 2017
6. Malvertising campaigns involving exploit kits. https://www.fireeye.com/blog/threat-research/2017/03/still_getting_served.html. Accessed 10 Oct 2017
7. Obfuscation service. https://javascriptobfuscator.com/. Accessed 10 Oct 2017
8. RSA shadow fall. https://www.rsa.com/en-us/blog/2017-06/shadowfall. Accessed 10 Oct 2017
9. Same original policy. https://developer.mozilla.org/en-US/docs/Web/Security/Same-origin_policy. Accessed 10 Oct 2017
10. Scrapy cralwer framework. https://scrapy.org/. Accessed 10 Oct 2017
11. Selenium automates browsers. http://www.seleniumhq.org/
12. Tree-based importance score. http://scikit-learn.org/stable/auto_examples/ensemble/plot_forest_importances.html. Accessed 10 Oct 2017
13. X-frame-options or CSP frame-ancestors? https://oxdef.info/csp-frame-ancestors/. Accessed 10 Oct 2017
14. Argyros, G., Stais, I., Jana, S., Keromytis, A.D., Kiayias, A.: SFADiff: automated evasion attacks and fingerprinting using black-box differential automata learning. In: Proceedings of CCS (2016)
15. Blum, A., Wardman, B., Solorio, T., Warner, G.: Lexical feature based phishing URL detection using online learning. In: Proceedings of AISec (2010)
16. Borgolte, K., Kruegel, C., Vigna, G.: Delta: automatic identification of unknown web-based infection campaigns. In: Proceedings of CCS (2013)
17. Calzavara, S., Rabitti, A., Bugliesi, M.: Content security problems?: evaluating the effectiveness of content security policy in the wild. In: Proceedings of CCS (2016)
18. Canali, D., Cova, M., Vigna, G., Kruegel, C.: Prophiler: a fast filter for the large-scale detection of malicious web pages. In: Proceedings of WWW (2011)
19. Catakoglu, O., Balduzzi, M., Balzarotti, D.: Automatic extraction of indicators of compromise for web applications. In: Proceedings of WWW (2016)
20. Choi, H., Zhu, B.B., Lee, H.: Detecting malicious web links and identifying their attack types. In: Proceedings of USENIX Conference on Web Application Development (2011)
21. Cova, M., Kruegel, C., Vigna, G.: Detection and analysis of drive-by-download attacks and malicious JavaScript code. In: Proceedings of WWW (2010)
22. Curtsinger, C., Livshits, B., Zorn, B.G., Seifert, C.: ZOZZLE: fast and precise in-browser JavaScript malware detection. In: Proceedings of USENIX Security (2011)
23. Englehardt, S., Narayanan, A.: Online tracking: a 1-million-site measurement and analysis. In: Proceedings of CCS (2016)
24. Hu, X., Cheng, Y., Duan, Y., Henderson, A., Yin, H.: JSForce: a forced execution engine for malicious JavaScript detection. CoRR, abs/1701.07860 (2017)
25. Kaplan, S., Livshits, B., Zorn, B., Seifert, C., Curtsinger, C.: "NOFUS: Automatically Detecting"+ String. fromCharCode (32)+ "ObFuSCateD ".toLowerCase()+ "JavaScript Code". Technical report MSR-TR-2011-57, Microsoft Research, May 2011
26. Kim, K., et al.: J-force: forced execution on JavaScript. In: Proceedings of WWW (2017)
27. Kolbitsch, C., Livshits, B., Zorn, B., Seifert, C.: Rozzle: de-cloaking internet malware. In: Proceedings of Security and Privacy (Oakland) (2012)
28. Kumar, D., et al.: Security challenges in an increasingly tangled web. In: Proceedings of WWW (2017)

29. Lauinger, T., Chaabane, A., Arshad, S., Robertson, W., Wilson, C., Kirda, E.: Thou shalt not depend on me: analysing the use of outdated JavaScript libraries on the web. In: Proceedings of NDSS (2017)

30. Le, A., Markopoulou, A., Faloutsos, M.: PhishDef: URL names say it all. In: Proceedings of INFOCOM (2011)

31. Li, Z., Alrwais, S. Wang, X., Alowaisheq, E.: Hunting the red fox online: Understanding and detection of mass redirect-script injections. In: Proceedings of Security and Privacy (Okaland) (2014)

32. Ma, J., Saul, L.K., Savage, S., Voelker, G.M.: Learning to detect malicious URLs. ACM Trans. Intell. Syst. Technol. (TIST) **2**(3), 30 (2011)

33. Nikiforakis, N., et al.: You are what you include: large-scale evaluation of remote JavaScript inclusions. In: Proceedings of CCS (2012)

34. Provos, N., Panayiotis, M., Rajab, M.A., Monrose, F.: All your iFRAMEs point to us. In: Proceedings of USENIX Security (2008)

35. Saxena, P., Akhawe, D., Hanna, S., Mao, F., McCamant, S., Song, D.: A symbolic execution framework for JavaScript. In: Proceedings of Security and Privacy (Okaland) (2010)

36. Sen, K., Kalasapur, S., Brutch, T., Gibbs, S.: Jalangi: a selective record-replay and dynamic analysis framework for JavaScript. In: Proceedings of ESEC/FSE (2013)

37. Soska, K., Christin, N.: Automatically detecting vulnerable websites before they turn malicious. In: Proceedings of USENIX Security (2014)

38. Stock, B., Livshits, B., Zorn, B.: KIZZLE: a signature compiler for exploit kits. In International Conference on Dependable Systems and Networks (DSN), June 2016

39. Weichselbaum, L., Spagnuolo, M., Lekies, S., Janc, A.: CSP is dead, long live CSP! on the insecurity of whitelists and the future of content security policy. In: Proceedings of CCS (2016)

40. Weissbacher, M., Lauinger, T., Robertson, W.: Why is CSP failing? Trends and challenges in CSP adoption. In: Stavrou, A., Bos, H., Portokalidis, G. (eds.) RAID 2014. LNCS, vol. 8688, pp. 212–233. Springer, Cham (2014). https://doi.org/10. 1007/978-3-319-11379-1_11

41. Xu, W., Zhang, F. Zhu, S.: Jstill: mostly static detection of obfuscated malicious JavaScript code. In: Proceedings of AsiaCCS (2013)

# Xilara: An XSS Filter Based on HTML Template Restoration

Keitaro Yamazaki$^{(\boxtimes)}$, Daisuke Kotani(iD), and Yasuo Okabe

Kyoto University, Yoshida-Honmachi, Sakyo, Kyoto 606-8501, Japan
yamazaki@net.ist.i.kyoto-u.ac.jp, kotani@media.kyoto-u.ac.jp,
okabe@i.kyoto-u.ac.jp

**Abstract.** Cross Site Scripting (XSS) is one of the most fearful attacks against web applications because of its potential damage to users. XSS filter is one of existing mitigation technologies against XSS by monitoring communication between servers and clients to find attack codes in HTTP requests. However, some complicated attacks can bypass such XSS filters, e.g., attack codes are encoded with base64 or others, and attacks may not include attack codes in HTTP requests, such as Stored XSS. This paper proposes a new XSS filter, Xilara, to detect XSS attacks including such complicated ones by a new approach: monitoring HTML document structures in HTTP responses instead of the requests. A key idea is that normal responses have very similar HTML document structures because they are usually generated by the same program (HTML template) and some parameters (untrusted data), but once an XSS attack succeeds, the structure of an HTML document changes due to the attack codes in the untrusted data. As a preparation, Xilara collects normal HTTP responses, and restores HTML templates. To detect XSS attacks, Xilara regards the response is harmful if an HTML document in the response is not an instance of the restored template. Our evaluation using XSS vulnerabilities reported in the real world shows that Xilara can detect XSS attacks whose attack codes are difficult to be detected by existing XSS filters, as well as performance comparison between Xilara and existing XSS filters.

## 1 Introduction

Cross Site Scripting (XSS) is one of the most fearful attacks towards web applications [1]. Attackers abuse XSS for various purposes such as accessing to sensitive user data, controlling the browser, or deceiving users by presenting fake information. The sensitive user data includes session data which is an identification of the user in the application. It is important to protect users from XSS, but there are still many vulnerable applications because bugs are always in applications.

There have been several protection and mitigation technologies against XSS. We focus on an XSS filter, which detects XSS by monitoring network communication between clients and servers, because it can be introduced to systems independently of the implementation of web applications. Some web browsers

© ICST Institute for Computer Sciences, Social Informatics and Telecommunications Engineering 2018
R. Beyah et al. (Eds.): SecureComm 2018, LNICST 255, pp. 332–351, 2018.
https://doi.org/10.1007/978-3-030-01704-0_18

have built-in XSS filters [2,3], and some web application firewalls provide XSS filter functions [4]. However, since existing XSS filters try to find attack codes in HTTP requests to detect XSS, attackers can sometimes bypass the detection mechanisms by carefully crafting and sending attack codes. An example of such attacks are to use base64 to encode attack codes, and use Stored XSS where the HTML document in an HTTP response is contaminated by attack codes that has been stored in servers.

In this paper, we propose a new XSS filter, Xilara, to detect XSS attacks including such complicated ones. Xilara is designed based on an idea that XSS attacks can be detected by checking the structures of the HTML documents in responses.

A typical XSS vulnerability occurs when an application constructs an HTML document with an HTML template (a structure of HTML documents) and data including valid HTML fragments from untrusted sources. If we can separate the HTML template and data accurately, we can detect XSS attacks through comparison of the structure of many HTML documents in responses.

Xilala first collects HTML documents in non-harmful HTTP responses, and restores HTML templates from the collected documents by existing methods for data extraction from multiple HTML documents. Then, to detect XSS attacks, Xilara confirms whether the structure of an HTML document in an HTTP response can be generated from the restored template, and regards the response is harmful if the structure of the document does not match with the template. Xilara can be applied not only to Reflected XSS but also to Stored XSS and can be used independently of an application code.

We implemented Xilara and conducted experiments to evaluate the performance of Xilara. We collected data of XSS attacks reported in the real world and compared the XSS detection capability of Xilara with that of existing XSS filter. The results show that, Xilara detected 94.5% of the XSS attacks but produced false positive detections on 20.6% of the non-attacked HTTP responses. Also, Xilara can detect all of the attacks which have base64-encoded attack codes though an existing XSS filter cannot detect any of these attacks. In addition, we show that Xilara can check whether the response is harmful not with little overhead in terms of the response time to users.

In the following of this paper, Sect. 2 describes our research background. Section 3 introduces related works for XSS. Sections 4 and 5 describes our proposed method and its implementation. Section 6 describes an evaluation of Xilara and its results. Section 7 shows a discussion, and Sect. 8 gives conclusion.

## 2 Background

### 2.1 XSS

XSS is an attack that injects a malicious script into a target web application. When this attack is successfully executed, an attacker can send a malicious JavaScript code to other clients accessing the target application and execute the code on their web browsers. By using XSS, the attacker can temper the web application's content and grab access tokens owned by other users.

Many web applications accept data submitted from users, but in some cases, data for attacks are submitted. We call these data submitted from users as untrusted data. OWASP classifies XSS [5] by the place where untrusted data is processed and whether untrusted data is permanently stored or not, as shown in Table 1.

**Table 1.** Class of XSS

|  |  | Untrusted data is used at | |
|---|---|---|---|
|  |  | Server | Client |
| Data persistence | Stored | Stored server XSS | Stored client XSS |
|  | Reflected | Reflected server XSS | Reflected client XSS |

The Server-side XSS occurs when a web application includes untrusted data in an HTML document and sends it to the user. The web application should process untrusted data as text or attribute values in the HTML document, but when it simply concatenates the string representing HTML fragments and untrusted data, XSS occurs. The Client-side XSS occurs when a JavaScript code provided by the web application to web browser mishandles the untrusted data. In this case, an attacker crafts untrusted data to create unintended HTML elements through those APIs and adds HTML elements to execute malicious JavaScript.

Reflected XSS occurs when untrusted data in an HTTP request is not processed correctly in the process of generating HTTP response or in the JavaScript code in the web application. Stored XSS occurs when untrusted data sent from the user is permanently stored in a database, log files in the web server, a database in the web browser, etc. and when the web application does not properly handle these data.

In this paper, we deal with Server-side XSS, and the XSS in the following examples and subsequent sections represents Server-side XSS except explicitly mentioned.

## 2.2  HTML Template

This section explains an HTML template, which is a concept used in this research. Many web applications use HTML templates to create HTML. For example, Ruby on Rails, which is a popular web application framework, uses an HTML template called ERB [6], and Flask uses an HTML template called Jinja [7].

In the same web page, data is encoded in the same way [8]. The representation of HTML document generation method is called HTML template in this research. Many web applications generate an HTML document by replacing the variables in HTML templates with data.

There are some algorithms such as RoadRunner [9], ExAlg [8] and DEPTA [10] which restore HTML templates from the multiple outputs of web pages. Though these algorithms are designed to extract data from web pages constructed from databases, they generate HTML templates during the extraction process.

RoadRunner receives multiple HTML documents generated from the same HTML template and outputs a program called wrapper which extracts data from an HTML document without any knowledge of the web page structure. Since this program represents the encoding method of data in the web page, it is an HTML template. RoadRunner defines the wrapper with prefix markup languages which abstract the structure that appears in general web pages, and it is represented by the XML mainly consisting of the following elements.

<tag> HTML element. *<p class="a">* will be represented as *<tag element="p" attrs="class:a">*.

<and> [T1, ..., Tn]. A template which is a set of n templates (T1, ..., Tn).

<plus> [T1, ..., T1]. A template which is a set of consecutive templates *T1*.

<hook> (T1)?. A template which has optional template *T1*. *T1* sometimes appears in this template and sometimes doesn't appear.

<variant> Template indicating that the content of its child element is variable.

<subtree> This template represents that it is impossible for RoadRunner to generate the template at this node.

# 3   Related Works

There are roughly three types of countermeasures to prevent or mitigate Server-side XSS attacks. One is to install XSS filters between web application servers and clients. Second is to modify application codes to detect XSS. The third is to modify the web browser to detect XSS. We introduce these types of existing countermeasures for XSS and compare them with our research.

## 3.1   XSS Filter in Web Application Firewalls

Some web application firewalls (WAF) have XSS filters using regular expression and blacklists for example in Javed and Schwenk [11]. People can easily install this XSS filter because it can be used independently from the web application. In their work, the HTTP request is considered as an attack when it matches the following regular expression. OWASP ModSecurity Core Rule Set[1] is one of the well-known filters including such regular expression.

```
1   /(?:=|U\s*R\s*L\s*\(\)\s*[^>]*\s*S\s*C\s*R\s*I\s*P\s*T\s*:/i
```

These mitigations are effective when they can detect attack codes in HTTP requests, however, these are not effective when an attacker hides attack codes in HTTP requests using a complicated converting process of the application.

---

[1] https://modsecurity.org/crs/.

For example, Kettle [12] reported that an attacker can bypass these mitigation techniques when an application uses some WAF and a web browser has built-in XSS filter. Another example can be found in an application which converts untrusted data given from outside as hexadecimal numbers into a UTF8 encoded string and displays it[2], and XSS filters introduced above cannot detect attacks against this web application. Our proposed method checks an HTTP response so that it can detect the attacks. Also, in the dataset used for the experiment of our research, we found a case where an attacker encodes attack codes in base64 format and a web application decodes[3]. In this case, an attack code[4]

j48c3ZnL29ubG9hZD1wcm9tcHQoL3hzc3Bvc2VkLyk

is included in the HTTP Request, so regular expression implemented in above WAF cannot detect the attack.

## 3.2 XSS Protection Installed in an Application

Another method is to modify an application code, and this method is relatively hard to be introduced because it is necessary to update the application code by hand or it is applicable only to applications developed in specific programming languages. However, it is possible to detect and process the untrusted data accurately because this method is implemented inside the application code.

A basic protection method of Server XSS is to escape HTML special characters in untrusted data when these data are going to be combined with strings representing HTML structure. For example, < in untrusted data should be converted to &lt; so that it is treated as a character in HTML documents. However, there are still many vulnerable applications because sanitizing all untrusted data comprehensively is difficult in some cases.

In addition, there are methods using a policy configured in web application servers to validate the HTTP response. The policy is used to prevent web browsers from loading the codes not intended by the administrator of the application. Using Content Security Policy (CSP) [13], it is possible to specify the location or hash value of valid JavaScript codes by creating a policy. Noncespaces [14] and Document Structure Integrity [15] can detect attacks by assigning random numbers to trusted HTML elements and its attribute names. xJS [16] isolates legitimate client-side JavaScript codes from the codes comes from untrusted data. However, since these methods require specific configuration for each application, it is necessary to rewrite the code of the application in some cases, which is a great burden to the server administrator. Therefore, they are not necessarily said to be used widely and properly [17].

---

[2] This example comes from a real application that converts the external input value by calling the function (*utf8HexDecode*) in the following URL. https://sourceforge.net/p/subsonic/code/4715/tree/trunk/subsonic-main/src/main/java/net/sourceforge/subsonic/util/StringUtil.java#l410.

[3] https://www.openbugbounty.org/reports/113400/.

[4] This is an base64 encoded attack code of "$>< svg/onload = prompt(/xssposed/)$.

Since our method is an filter-based XSS mitigation mechanism, there is no restriction to the programming language used by the web application and no modification to its source code to install the filter. Therefore, compared with these XSS protection mechanisms, an operator of the web application who is not the developer of it can install our XSS filter easily.

### 3.3    Web Browser Built-In XSS Filter

There are mitigation mechanisms implemented in web browsers. IE 8 using XSS filter [2], and Google Chrome using XSS Auditor [3]. These filters detect the attack codes in the HTTP request and prevent the attack if the HTTP response also includes similar attack codes.

These mitigation mechanisms have the same issue with the XSS filter in WAF. They cannot detect XSS attacks when the attack codes are not included in HTTP request and when an attacker hides the attack codes in HTTP requests using a complicated converting process of the application. However, these mechanisms can use the same HTML parser installed in the web browser, and it improves the accuracy of the detection.

## 4    Our Approach

We focused on the following features that appear when a Server-side XSS attack successes against a web application.

- Many web applications use HTML templates that describe how to encode data in HTML documents when constructing HTML dynamically.
- To execute JavaScript code on the victim's browser, attackers often inject new HTML elements and HTML element attributes into HTML documents.
- After attackers succeed in the injection, the structure of the HTML document becomes different from the structure of the HTML documents encoded by HTML template with expected data.

In particular, we focused on the difference between the structure of HTML documents that the application usually generates with HTML template and that the application constructs after an attacker succeeds in XSS attacks. For example, normal structure of HTML documents generated by web application shown in Fig. 1 will be that of Fig. 2. The application receives an ID from a query parameter in the URI and has vulnerability against Reflected XSS. When one of the user accesses to the attack URI (e.g. http://example.com/? id=ATTACKSTRING), the structure of the HTML document will be that of Fig. 3. Xilara detects XSS by checking whether the observed structure of HTML documents can be generated from HTML templates.

We propose a new XSS filter, Xilara (XSS filter based on HTML template restoration), which restores HTML templates from HTTP responses and detects the XSS by using them. Figure 4 represents the overview of Xilara. Xilara consists of the following three stages.

```
1   <html>
2     <h1>Sample Vuln app</h1>
3     <p>
4        Hello, <?php echo $_GET['id'] ?>
5     </p>
6   </html>
```

**Fig. 1.** An example source code that has Reflected XSS vulnerabilities, written by PHP.

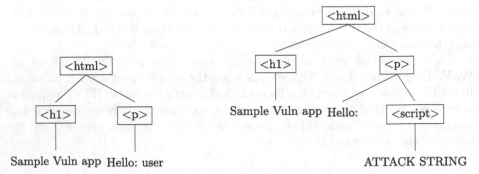

Sample Vuln app Hello: user

**Fig. 2.** HTML tree constructed with normal HTTP requests

**Fig. 3.** HTML tree constructed when an XSS attack is executed

**HTML Collection Stage.** Xilara collects HTTP responses from the web server for some periods.

**HTML Template Restoration Stage.** Xilara tries to restore the HTML template used by the web application from the HTTP response.

**XSS Detection Stage.** Xilara uses the restored HTML template to detect observed HTTP responses are contaminated by XSS attacks.

### 4.1 HTML Template

In this paper, we define an HTML template as a tuple consisting of the following nodes.

**Tag.** This node represents an HTML element that has a list of HTML element names and pairs of an attribute name and its value. There are two types of attribute: variable and fixed. The Tag template $t$ whose $t.name$ is $p$ and $t.attributes$ is *[class= "a"]* (value is fixed) is encoded in HTML $<p\ class= "a">$. Furthermore, the Tag node has an HTML template as a child element, and the parent-child relationship between the Tag nodes represents the parent-child relationship in the HTML element in the HTML document.

**Loop.** This node represents that at least one HTML template (*T1*) appears consecutively. An HTML template *T1* is a child element of the Loop node.

**Optional.** This node represents that one template (*T1*) sometimes appears and sometimes does not appear. An HTML template *T1* is a child element of the Optional node.

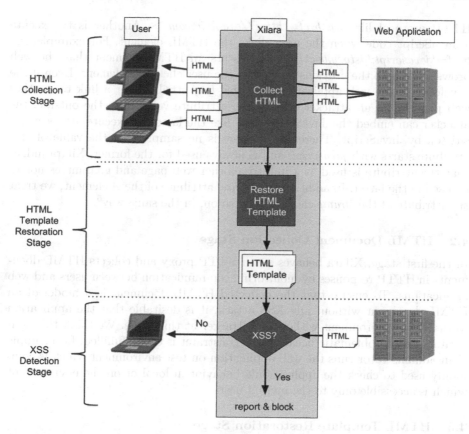

**Fig. 4.** Approach overview of Xilara

**Ignore.** This node represents an element that could not restore an HTML template. This node has no child elements.

**Null.** This node represents an empty node. This node has no child elements.

This definition is similar to the definition of HTML templates in RoadRunner (see Sect. 2.2), but we add the type of attribute value to Tag node to find whether the attribute value is variable or not for each Tag element.

To deal with XSS attacks using attribute values of HTML elements, Xilara classifies a specific attribute of the Tag node of the HTML templates in more detail by the attribute value. If an attacker can set an arbitrary value of *onerror*, *onload* attribute, *href* attribute of *A* HTML element, and so on, the attacker can conduct XSS attack. For example, attacker establishes the attack by setting attribute values like *onerror="ATTACK STRING"* or *href="javascript:ATTACK STRING"*. It is difficult to detect whether the value of *onerror* or *onload* attribute is a malicious code or not because there is no clue for detection. We focus on two patterns of *href* attribute of the *A* HTML element. One is to use as a link to another web page using the

HTTP protocol like *<a href="http://example.com">*. Another is to execute a JavaScript code when the user clicks the HTML element. For example, *<a href="javascript:history.back()">* represents an HTML element that the web browser backs to the previous page after the user clicks the element. Even if the developer of the web application uses this *href* attribute for a link to another web page, when an attacker can set the attribute value from the outside, the attacker can embed the JavaScript code like the latter to execute attack codes written by JavaScript. Therefore, if there is no sample that the value of this attribute starts with *javascript:* and is always used for the former, Xilara judges that the attribute is used as a link to another web page and guarantees not to be used in the latter. In addition to the *href* attribute of the *A* element, we treat *src* attribute of the *iframe* element, and so on, in the same way[5].

## 4.2 HTML Document Collection Stage

In the first stage, Xilara behaves as an HTTP proxy and collects HTML documents in HTTP responses by monitoring communication between users and web applications. To ensure that the collected HTML document is a model of an HTML document without any XSS attack, it is desirable that the application works in an environment without an attacker at this stage. We think this constraint is not problematic because this constraint is easily fulfilled, for example if an administrator runs the web application on test environment which is commonly used to check the application's behavior in local or on the environment which is accessible only to the invited user.

## 4.3 HTML Template Restoration Stage

At this stage, Xilara restores the HTML template from the HTML documents collected at the previous stage. To restore HTML templates, Xilara applies existing algorithms such as ExAlg and RoadRunner. Template nodes in the HTML template outputted by these algorithms are corresponding to Tag node, Loop node, Optional node, and so on. Therefore, we can convert from the HTML template outputted by these algorithms into the HTML template handled in Xilara. Xilara generates the HTML template in consideration of whether each value of some attributes starts with *javascript:* as described in Sect. 4.1. An detailed implementation of the conversion is described in Sect. 5.

## 4.4 XSS Detection Stage

In this stage, the application works in the real environment where external attackers can access to the applications. Xilara behaves as a reverse HTTP proxy

---

[5] We found these attributes in https://html5sec.org/ have the same characteristics. *formaction* attribute in *button* element/*poster* attribute in *video* element/*href* attribute in *math, a, base, go, line* element/*xlink:href* attribute in any element/*background* attribute in *table* element/*value* attribute in *param* element/*src* attribute in *embed, img, image, script* element/*action* attribute in *form* element/*to, from* attribute in *set, animate* element/*folder* attribute in *a* element.

and monitors communication between clients and servers. Xilara detects the XSS by checking whether HTML documents that the application server sends to users are instances of the HTML template restored at the previous stage. Algorithm 1 shows how to judge whether or not an observed HTML document is an instance of the HTML template.

---

**Algorithm 1.** Check if an HTML document is an instance of an HTML template

**Require:** $HTMLRoot$: HTML Tree, $TemplateRoot$: HTML Template
1:   $nodePairQueue := [[HTMLRoot, TemplateRoot]]$
2: **while** $nodePairQueue$ has element **do**
3:     $nodePair :=$ first element of $nodePairQueue$
4:     $html := nodePair[0]$
5:     $template := nodePair[1]$
6:     **if** $!checkNode(html, template)$ **then**
7:         **continue**
8:     **end if**
9:     **if** The children of $html$ and that of $template$ should be checked **then**
10:        Append node pairs which should be checked into $nodePairQueue$.
11:        **continue**
12:     **end if**
13:     **if** The next siblings of $html$ and that of $template$ should be checked **then**
14:        Append node pairs which should be checked into $nodePairQueue$.
15:        **continue**
16:     **end if**
17:     **if** The next node of $html$ and that of $template$ should be checked **then**
18:        Append node pairs which should be checked into $nodePairQueue$.
19:        **continue**
20:     **end if**
21:     **return** True
22: **end while**
23: **return** False

---

Algorithm 1 receives an HTML document and an HTML template and checks if the root node of HTML document can be an instance of the root node of HTML template by using a deep-first search. First, this algorithm checks the attribute and name of an HTML document node and an HTML template node with function $checkNode$ described in Algorithm 2. Next, it checks the children of an HTML document node and an HTML template node. Similarly, it checks the next sibling nodes of an HTML document node and an HTML template node and next sibling nodes of parent nodes of them. Finally, if the HTML document node can be the instance, the algorithm returns *True*.

If the HTML document is an instance of the HTML template, Xilara forwards the HTTP response to the user without any further actions. If it is not an instance, Xilara alerts the administrator to the detection of an XSS attack, and sends an error message or the original HTTP response to the user according to the configuration of Xilara set by the administrator.

---

**Algorithm 2.** Check if properties of *html* are same with that of *template*

---

1: **procedure** CHECKNODE(*html*, *template*)
2:     **if**  name of *HTMLNode* $\neq$ name of *TemplateNode* **or** *HTMLNode* has attributes not included in *TemplateNode*  **then**
3:         **return** False
4:     **end if**
5:     **while** not an end of attributes of *TemplateNode* **do**
6:         *tAttr* := next attribute of *TemplateNode*
7:         *hAttr* := attribute of *HTMLNode* which has same name of *tAttr*
8:         **if** name of *tAttr* = *id* or *class* **then**
9:             **if** *tAttr* has fixed value **and** value of *hAttr* $\neq$ value of *tAttr* **then**
10:                 **return** False
11:             **end if**
12:         **else if** *tAttr* receives both an URI and a JavaScript code **then**
13:             **if** the values of *tAttr* do not start with *javascript:* **and** value of *hAttr* start with *javascript:* **then**
14:                 **return** False
15:             **end if**
16:         **end if**
17:     **end while**
18:     **return** True
19: **end procedure**

---

## 5    Implementation

This section describes the design of Xilara for each stage in detail.

### 5.1    HTML Collection Stage

In the HTML Collection Stage, Xilara acts as an HTTP reverse proxy. As the input, Xilara receives the hostname and port number of the destination web application and port number where the reverse proxy accepts connections. After startup, Xilara observes HTTP requests and HTTP responses between clients and web application servers, and saves the pair of the URI in an HTTP request and contents in the corresponding HTTP response. Also, to prevent Xilara from saving non-HTML content such as images, Xilara saves the pair of the URI and the contents only if *Content-Type* in an HTTP response header is *text/html*.

To collect many HTTP responses, administrators can introduce some existing automatic web crawling techniques. For example, Heydon and Najork proposed a scalable web crawler [18], and Galan et al. [19] proposed a multi-agent XSS scanner that discovers the input locations and sends HTTP requests[6]. Administrators can also manually generate HTTP requests by using the web application as its user.

---

[6] In this case, injected data should not be malicious.

## 5.2 HTML Template Restoration Stage

If the web application uses multiple HTML templates, Xilara should classify each collected HTML documents by its source HTML template. Usually, web applications use different HTML templates if a requested URI is different. Some web applications use URI routing patterns indicating that all URIs that match the same pattern are related to the same HTML template. Xilara receives the collection of regular expressions as URL routing patterns from the owner of the web application. If Xilara receives no URI routing patterns, Xilara considers that URIs that has the same pathname are related to the same HTML template. In this way, Xilara groups HTML documents constructed from the same HTML template.

When RoadRunner restores the HTML template, RoadRunner may parse the HTML document in a different way that real web browser does. These differences occur when the document does not follow the rules of HTML specifications (e.g., closing HTML element without corresponding open HTML element). If Xilara uses a different parse result than that of the web browser, the attacker can exploit the difference to successfully add attributes of HTML elements only recognized by the web browser. To avoid this problem, Xilara parses the HTML document using *DOMParserAPI* on *Google Chrome* and encodes it to a string representing an HTML document. Strictly speaking, since different web browsers parse an HTML document differently, Xilara should conduct this process for all web browsers, but in our first implementation, Xilara only considers *Google Chrome*.

Then, Xilara uses RoadRunner to restore an HTML template from HTML documents in the same group. RoadRunner receives HTML documents and preferences file. The initial preferences of RoadRunner are set to match the HTML elements whose attribute values of *id* and *class* are same, and it is defined in the *attributeValues* setting. However, this setting prevents HTML template from being restored because some web applications set these attribute values dynamically. Therefore, we disable this setting. Instead, after restoring the HTML template, Xilara investigates the values of *id* and *class* attributes of each Tag node of the HTML template. If the attribute value is always the same, Xilara considers the attribute value as constant. Xilara investigates the possible values of these attributes by collecting the attribute values for each Tag node through checking the correspondence between Tag nodes in the HTML template and HTML elements in the input HTML documents. Xilara uses *nodePair* matched finally in Algorithm 1 and to collect the correspondence.

Since the output of RoadRunner is an XML document composed of the elements described in Sect. 2.2, Xilara converts the output of RoadRunner to the HTML template used by Xilara with the following rule.

$< tag > \rightarrow Tag$ A <tag> node is converted to a Tag node having the same element name, attributes and child elements.

$< and > \rightarrow Tuple$ An <and> node which is a set of HTML templates is converted into a tuple containing its child elements.

$< plus > \rightarrow Loop$ A <plus> node is converted to a Loop node having the same child elements.

$< hook > \rightarrow Optional$ A <hook> node is converted to an Optional node having the same child elements.

$< subtree > \rightarrow Ignore$ A <subtree> node is converted to an Ignore node having the same child elements.

### 5.3 XSS Detection Stage

At this stage, Xilara behaves as an HTTP reverse proxy like the HTML collection stage, and ignores the response when the *Content-Type* header in HTTP response is not *text/html*. Xilara parses each HTML document through *Google Chrome* as in the HTML template restoration stage. After that, Xilara searches the corresponding HTML template from the URI in the HTTP request and checks whether the HTML document is an instance of the HTML template or not.

## 6    Evaluation

### 6.1 Depth Evaluation with Specific Vulnerabilities

To evaluate the processing speed and XSS detection capability of Xilara, we conducted manual evaluation experiments with one web applications and two WordPress plugins. The targeted applications are shown in Table 2. For experiments, we used MacBook Pro 2016 with 2.9 GHz Intel Core i5 CPU and 8 GB memory.

**Table 2.** Applications and vulnerabilities used for experiments

| Application | Version | CVE or vuln info |
|---|---|---|
| Webmin | 1.678 | CVE-2014-0339 |
| Count Per Day | 3.5.4 | https://wpvulndb.com/vulnerabilities/8587 |
| AffiliateWP | 2.0.9 | https://wpvulndb.com/vulnerabilities/8835 |

We obtained 4 to 6 HTTP responses of each page where the XSS vulnerability exists through simulation of the typical use for each application, which causes a change of URI parameters and data in databases. We then restored the HTML template and tested whether Xilara can detect the XSS with the HTTP response created by the proof of concept (PoC) of the vulnerability. In addition, we tested whether Xilara detected XSS in normal HTTP responses by mistakes.

As a result of the experiment, we were able to detect attacks on Webmin and Count Per Day. However, Xilara could not detect the attack on AffiliateWP. This is because RoadRunner fails to restore an HTML template of AffiliateWP and the *subtree* appears in the template where the attack code is inserted. Normal responses were not detected as XSS in all applications. We confirmed that RoadRunner had some problems with restoring *Optional* HTML templates.

Table 3 shows the average times of vulnerable pages (calculated ten times) and the average times which Xilara takes to parse a HTML document and check XSS attacks. The result shows that the processing time of Xilara is moderate or low.

**Table 3.** Xilara performance result

| Application | Response time | Xilara overhead |
|---|---|---|
| Webmin | 423.46 ms | 14.16 ms |
| Count Per Day | 109.72 ms | 27.5 ms |
| AffiliateWP | 186.84 ms | 21.4 ms |

## 6.2 Large-Scale Evaluation with Vulnerable Website Dataset

Next, we conducted experiments using more web applications to investigate the differences of the behavior between Xilara and another XSS filter. We used the OpenBugBounty[7] as a dataset. As a part of responsible disclosure, OpenBug-Bounty lists web pages containing XSS vulnerabilities and the attack URI including attack codes against the pages. Experiments were carried out by the following procedure.

1. Collect reports that are still valid from OpenBugBounty.
2. Create normal requests and collect HTTP responses.
3. Check whether Xilara can detect XSS attacks.
4. Check whether another XSS filter can detect attacks for each report.

We describe the detail of each step and results in the following sections.

**Data Collection from OpenBugBounty.** First, we collected an XSS dataset from OpenBugBounty. At November 26, 2017, the number of reports was 179,702, and 74,888 reports were published as XSS reports. Since it takes time to investigate all the reports in this experiment, we use only reports whose ID ends with 0.

Furthermore, we checked whether each vulnerability exists even now. We collected HTTP responses by accessing the attack URI, and confirmed the vulnerability by monitoring the execution of JavaScript functions such as *alert, prompt, confirm* after rendering the HTTP responses on *Google Chrome*. As a result, 4,601 reports have vulnerabilities not fixed at the time of collecting the dataset. We proceeded the experiment using these 4,601 reports.

---

[7] https://www.openbugbounty.org/.

**HTML Collection Stage.** Next, to create an HTML template and to verify XSS filters do not erroneously detect XSS attacks from a normal HTTP response, we created normal HTTP requests by removing malicious codes from the attack URI of each report. In most cases, if a web application has XSS vulnerability and XSS attack codes are included in query parameters, the web application considers the value of the query parameters are variable and applies to the HTML template. Therefore, if the value of query parameters in the URI matched one of the two regular expressions in Fig. 5, we considered that the query parameters were used for the attack and replaced the value of the query parameter with numerals so that we could fetch an HTML document constructed without attack codes. The first regular expression in Fig. 5 matches with HTML elements such as `"><script>alert(1)</script>` whose text includes an attack JavaScript code. The second regular expression matches with HTML elements such as `"><img src=x onerror=alert(1)>` whose attribute value includes an attack JavaScript code. After we discovered the attack codes in URIs, we changed the value of the parameter to five numbers from 1 to 5. We sent HTTP requests with replaced URIs and obtained the corresponding HTTP responses. As a result, we got all HTTP responses for 3,408 reports.

```
1   /(['"]?[^>]*>)*<[^>]+>[^<]*(alert|confirm|prompt)
        [^<]*(<\/[^>]+>)?/ig
2   /(['"]?[^>]*>)*<[^>]+(alert|confirm|prompt)([^>]+>)?/ig
```

**Fig. 5.** Attack patterns we consider

Furthermore, we confirmed that some attack codes were encoded in special formats. For example, in eight reports, attack codes were encoded with base64. In one report, attack codes were displayed with hexadecimal digits. We also changed the value of the parameter used for each of these attacks and collected HTTP responses.

We continued our experiments using these 3,417 reports.

**XSS Detection with Xilara.** We restored the HTML template from four HTML documents with parameters 1 to 4 collected in the HTML collection stage. We succeeded to restore the HTML template in 3,295 reports.

Then, we checked whether Xilara could detect XSS attacks in HTTP responses generated from attack URIs and whether Xilara detects no XSS in HTTP responses collected in the previous stage.

**XSS Detection with Other XSS Filters.** To compare Xilara with existing XSS filters, we investigated whether ModSecurity [4] with OWASP ModSecurity CRS can detect reported attacks. We compared Xilara with ModSecurity because it is server-side and well-known XSS detection method. We used *libapache2-modsecurity* (version 2.7.7) as a ModSecurity implementation with Apache (version 2.4.18-2ubuntu 3.5). We enabled *SecRuleEngine* option for ModSecurity and used default settings for other options. Also, we used OWASP ModSecurity CRS version 3 and enabled the rules[8] to block the HTTP requests when ModSecurity detects XSS.

We replaced the hostname and port number in the attack URI to those of the Apache server and checked whether ModSecurity blocks HTTP requests or not after we sent HTTP requests of the attack URI.

**Evaluation Result.** We compared the XSS detection rates and XSS misdetection rates between Xilara and ModSecurity with OWASP ModSecurity CRS.

Row 1 and 2 in Table 4 shows XSS detection rates against 3417 attack URIs. In total, Xilara detected XSS attacks in 3,230 attack URIs. Xilara could not detect XSS attacks in 121 HTML documents because it could not restore the HTML template, and Xilara could not detect XSS attacks in 66 HTML documents though it could restore the HTML template. ModSecurity could detect 99.6% of the attacks in attack URIs because we used the attack URIs which matched the patterns in Fig. 5. However, ModSecurity could not detect all of the nine attacks in which attack codes were encoded with base64 or hexadecimal. Xilara detected eight of these attacks and Xilara failed to restore the HTML template correctly in one of these attacks.

Row 3 and 4 in Table 4 shows the XSS detection rates against $3,417*4 = 13,668$ normal HTTP responses (and HTTP requests) which were used to create HTML template and 3,417 normal HTTP responses (and HTTP requests) which were used for verification. Xilara detected XSS by mistakes in 1,640 HTML documents though they were used to construct HTML templates. Xilara detected XSS by mistakes in 703 HTML documents which were used for verification.

**Table 4.** XSS detection rates against attack URIs and normal HTTP responses

|  | Xilara | ModSecurity with CRS |
|---|---|---|
| All attacks (3,417 attacks) | 94.5% | 99.6% |
| Attacks using some encodings (9 attacks) | 88.9% | 0% |
| Template source responses (13,668 responses) | 12.0% | 0.18% |
| Verification responses (3,417 reseponses) | 20.6% | 0.18% |

# 7 Discussion

## 7.1 Adaptive Attacker Against Xilara

We discuss adaptive attacker against Xilara and attacks that cannot be detected by Xilara. Xilara detects XSS attacks using the result of matching of restored

---

[8] REQUEST-941-APPLICATION-ATTACK-XSS.conf      and      REQUEST-949-BLOCKING-EVALUATION.conf.

templates and the HTML documents. It means if an attacker can craft HTML documents for XSS attack that matches the template, the attacker can bypass Xilara. For example, if an attacker can control the content of the *li* element of the template *<loop><li /></loop>* and the attacker sets it as *text1</li><li>text2*, the number of *li* elements will be changed, but Xilara cannot detect this change.

In the above example, an attacker can increase the number of *li* elements. However, an attacker cannot execute arbitrary scripts on the vulnerabile page. For an attacker to avoid Xilara and run scripts, the template that such problems have should be an HTML element or attribute that can include a context for executing JavaScript (in this paper, we call a JavaScript execution context). In addition, this context should not be a fixed value and should exist after the part where the attacker can control in the document. There are following patterns of HTML document structures where an attacker can avoid detection.

**JavaScript execution context in Loop.** If Loop node includes a JavaScript execution context that is not a fixed value as shown in Fig. 6 and if the attacker can inject HTML elements, the attacker can avoid the filter by sending *text1<script>attack string</script></li><li>*.

**JavaScript execution context in Optional.** If Optional node includes a JavaScript execution context that is not a fixed value as shown in Fig. 7 and the attacker can inject HTML elements, the attacker can avoid the filter by sending *text1<script>attack string</script>*. This attack is available only if a *script* element in Optional node does not appear.

**Attacker controlled JavaScript execution context.** If the attacker can directly control the text in a *script* element or attribute values in the JavaScript execution context, the attacker can insert attack codes without changing the HTML document structure. In some cases, the attacker can also bypass general protection methods that use HTML escaping.

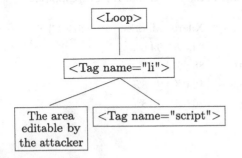

**Fig. 6.** A template including a dynamic JavaScript code in Loop

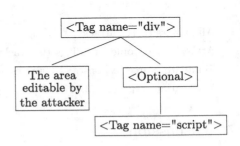

**Fig. 7.** A template including a dynamic JavaScript code in Optional

## 7.2   Limitations of Xilara and Its Use Case

There are some limitations to use Xilara. One is that Xilara should work in an environment without an attacker at the HTML collection stage. Another is that administrators of Xilara should prepare the URL routing patterns if the web application uses multiple HTML templates, unless the URIs of the application that has the same pathname are always related to the same HTML template. The third is that administrators of Xilara should run Xilara as an HTTP reverse proxy.

We suppose that the administrator of the web application can use Xilara because he or she can prepare environments without an attacker and Xilara does not require the source code of the application. In other words, the administrators of Xilara should not always be a developer of the application.

Xilara's performance of XSS detection will depends on the accuracy of HTML templates restoration, and some cases the templates cannot cover all possible cases. In this case, the administrator may be able to handle the situation by analyzing alerts made by Xilara and updating the templates manually.

This paper is focused on XSS attacks to HTML documents, but our scheme could be used in other similar attacks such as injection to some resource files including user-controllable data if the responses have a specific structure. In this case, implementation of three stages in Fig. 4 must be replaced with appropriate ones that support another data structure.

## 7.3   Deployment Consideration

Xilara has some performance overhead in the processing time as shown in Table 3. Although this overhead is moderate or low, this overhead could be a problem in frequently accessed web applications. In this case, we can easily scale out the XSS detection stage in Xilara by adding servers because this stage works only with the HTML templates, which have been prepared in the previous stages.

Current large web applications often use Content Delivery Networks (CDN) to cache static resources, and not all accesses comes to the web application servers. Xilara needs to check the output of the web applications which is modified by user input (untrusted data), and HTTP requests that will require such output will be forwarded to the backend servers that executes the codes of the web application (the origin server). By placing Xilara between the cache servers in CDN and the origin servers, Xilara can detect or mitigate some XSS attacks.

# 8   Conclusion

In this paper, we propose a new XSS filter, Xilara, to address the issue that attackers can bypass existing XSS filters that check attack codes in HTTP requests by carefully crafting and sending the attack codes. Our key idea is that the harmful HTML documents in HTTP responses have different structures than usual, and this difference can be detected because many web applications generates HTML documents in HTTP responses with very similar structures by the same programs. Xilara uses an HTML template, and we define our HTML template model. Our HTML template model distinguishes some HTML attributes with its value to detect XSS attacks that exploit those attribute values. Xilara observes an HTML structure in normal HTTP responses and restores HTML templates using RoadRunner developed for data extraction from multiple HTML documents. We implement Xilara as a HTTP reverse proxy between clients and servers, and Xilara can coexist with the existing XSS filters.

We also conducted experiments to evaluate the performance of Xilara. We collected the XSS attack dataset from OpenBugBounty and confirmed that Xilara detected 94.5% of the XSS attacks but judged XSS attacks mistakenly on 20.6% of the non-attacked HTTP responses. Xilara can also identify the attacks that use some encodings though an existing XSS filter cannot detect any of these attacks. In addition, our experiment shows that overhead of Xilara in each request is moderate or low.

Future works include more extensive evaluation of Xilara using various kinds of XSS vulnerabilities that current XSS filters are hard to detect, and investigation of relationship between the accuracy and false positive rates of XSS attack detection and the accuracy of HTML template restoration through quantitative evaluation, e.g., crawling web pages and test the accuracy of restored HTML templates.

# References

1. Wichers, D.: OWASP top-10 2013. OWASP Foundation, February 2013
2. Ross, D.: IE 8 XSS filter architecture/implementation (2008). https://blogs.technet.microsoft.com/srd/2008/08/19/ie-8-xss-filter-architecture-implementation/
3. Bates, D., Barth, A., Jackson, C.: Regular expressions considered harmful in client-side XSS filters. In: Proceedings of the 19th International Conference on World Wide Web, pp. 91–100. ACM (2010)
4. Trustwave: Modsecurity: open source web application firewall (2004). https://www.modsecurity.org/
5. Wichers, D.: Types of cross-site scripting. https://www.owasp.org/index.php/Types_of_Cross-Site_Scripting
6. Dave, T., David Heinemeier, H.: Agile web development with rails. Citeseer (2005)
7. Lokhande, P., Aslam, F., Hawa, N., Munir, J., Gulamgaus, M.: Efficient way of web development using Python and Flask (2015)
8. Arasu, A., Garcia-Molina, H.: Extracting structured data from web pages. In: Proceedings of the 2003 ACM SIGMOD International Conference on Management of Data, pp. 337–348. ACM (2003)
9. Crescenzi, V., Mecca, G., Merialdo, P., et al.: RoadRunner: towards automatic data extraction from large web sites. VLDB 1, 109–118 (2001)
10. Zhai, Y., Liu, B.: Structured data extraction from the web based on partial tree alignment. IEEE Trans. Knowl. Data Eng. 18(12), 1614–1628 (2006)
11. Javed, A., Schwenk, J.: Towards elimination of cross-site scripting on mobile versions of web applications. In: Kim, Y., Lee, H., Perrig, A. (eds.) WISA 2013. LNCS, vol. 8267, pp. 103–123. Springer, Cham (2014). https://doi.org/10.1007/978-3-319-05149-9_7

12. Kettle, J.: When security features collide (2017). http://blog.portswigger.net/2017/10/when-security-features-collide.html

13. Stamm, S., Sterne, B., Markham, G.: Reining in the web with content security policy. In: Proceedings of the 19th International Conference on World Wide Web, pp. 921–930. ACM (2010)

14. Van Gundy, M., Chen, H.: Noncespaces: using randomization to enforce information flow tracking and thwart cross-site scripting attacks. In: NDSS (2009)

15. Nadji, Y., Saxena, P., Song, D.: Document structure integrity: a robust basis for cross-site scripting defense. In: NDSS, vol. 2009, p. 20 (2009)

16. Athanasopoulos, E., Pappas, V., Krithinakis, A., Ligouras, S., Markatos, E.P., Karagiannis, T.: xJS: practical XSS prevention for web application development. In: Proceedings of the 2010 USENIX Conference on Web Application Development, p. 13. USENIX Association (2010)

17. Weichselbaum, L., Spagnuolo, M., Lekies, S., Janc, A.: CSP is dead, long live CSP! On the insecurity of whitelists and the future of content security policy. In: Proceedings of the 2016 ACM SIGSAC Conference on Computer and Communications Security, pp. 1376–1387. ACM (2016)

18. Heydon, A., Najork, M.: Mercator: a scalable, extensible web crawler. World Wide Web 2(4), 219–229 (1999)

19. Galán, E., Alcaide, A., Orfila, A., Blasco, J.: A multi-agent scanner to detect stored-XSS vulnerabilities. In: 2010 International Conference for Internet Technology and Secured Transactions (ICITST), pp. 1–6. IEEE (2010)

# Local Storage on Steroids: Abusing Web Browsers for Hidden Content Storage and Distribution

Juan D. Parra Rodriguez[(✉)] and Joachim Posegga

University of Passau, Innstraße 43, Passau, Germany
{dp,jp}@sec.uni-passau.de

**Abstract.** Analysing security assumptions taken for the WebRTC and postMessage APIs led us to find a novel attack abusing the browsers' persistent storage capabilities. The presented attack can be executed without the website's visitor knowledge, and it requires neither browser vulnerabilities nor additional software on the browser's side. To exemplify this, we study how can an attacker use browsers to create a network for persistent storage and distribution of arbitrary data.

In our proof of concept, the total storage of the network, and therefore the space used within each browser, grows linearly with the number of origins delivering the malicious JavaScript code. Further, data transfers between browsers are not restricted by the Same Origin Policy, which allows for a unified cross-origin browser network, regardless of the origin from which the script executing the functionality is loaded from.

In the course of our work, we assess the feasibility of a real-life deployment of the network by running experiments using Linux containers and browser automation tools. Moreover, we show how security mechanisms against third-party tracking, cross-site scripting and click-jacking can diminish the attack's impact, or even prevent it.

**Keywords:** Web security · WebRTC · postMessage
Browser security · Content Security Policy

## 1 Introduction

So far, the Web security community has invested significant efforts to research the impact of single API calls introduced by HTML5 standards on the client side. For instance, Lekies et al. described how using local storage for content caching results in script injection, and how to prevent it [25]. Also, in the case of the postMessage API, which allows two windows to have cross-origin communication within the browser, Hanna et al. illustrated how the lack of origin[1] validation leads to execution of undesired functionality in real life Web sites [20]. Last but

---

[1] Two JavaScript execution contexts have the same origin only if they have the same IP or fully qualified hostname, and if they use the same protocol and port.

© ICST Institute for Computer Sciences, Social Informatics and Telecommunications Engineering 2018
R. Beyah et al. (Eds.): SecureComm 2018, LNICST 255, pp. 352–371, 2018.
https://doi.org/10.1007/978-3-030-01704-0_19

not least, Provos et al. detected that the dynamic creation of zero pixel frames through scripts is a common attack vector used for drive-by downloads [35].

In spite of the significant efforts invested to secure each API, undesired consequences arising from client-side API combinations remain uncharted. So, we explore two particular aspects of browser APIs. On the one hand, we show that using the postMessage API, local storage, and the dynamic creation of Iframes leads to a transparent[2] increase of the total storage available for a website in the visitor's browser, i.e. beyond the storage quota. On the other hand, we show how WebRTC data channels aggravate the situation by allowing cross-origin data transfers among browsers. Thus, the combination of both factors comprises a novel attack vector in which the visitor's browser is coerced, not only to store data permanently but also to transmit such data directly to other browsers without the user's knowledge. This kind of attack could be catalogued as a browser resource abuse problem, which is orthogonal to more known Web attacks, e.g. cross-site scripting, since it does not pertain to the user's data or session.

The presented attack has *two* interesting properties. *First*, the attack relieves the server from the responsibility (and performance overhead) associated with hosting and distributing the content. This is a direct consequence of storing the content in browsers and transferring it over direct browser-to-browser links. *Second*, an attacker keeps the site's visitor oblivious to the malicious behaviour, i.e. storage and distribution of unknown content, since no warnings or messages are presented to the user. This lack of awareness on the user's side is particularly concerning when data stored in his/her browser is used for illegal purposes. Another concerning aspect is the use of computational resources in detriment of the user, e.g higher electricity costs and decreasing lifespan of a computing system, without his consent. This kind of abuse has lead to a court settlement between the state of New Jersey and a company doing Bitcoin mining on browsers to monetize Web sites [22].

Our **contributions** can be summarized as follows: *(1)* we describe a novel attack whereby the persistent storage and networking capabilities of the browser are abused for the attacker's benefit, yet without requiring any additional software or vulnerability exploitation on the client's browser or operating system. *(2)* we enumerate the security assumptions from the browser APIs (postMessage, Iframe creation and WebRTC) which led to the browser abuse vector. *(3)* We implement a proof of concept browser network which has long-term storage capabilities, and transfers data over peer-to-peer links between browsers, and bypasses the Same Origin Policy, without making the user aware of its existence. *(4)* We evaluate the proof of concept through a set of experiments by automating real-life browsers in a controlled environment while modifying the number of visitors, the time between visits, and the visitor return rate[3]. *(5)* From a more constructive perspective, we discuss how existing security measures, taken by the browser's user or Web developers, can prevent the attack.

---

[2] The mechanism described here does not require the user's consent.

[3] Number of visitors who returned to the website in a given period of time.

This paper is organized as follows. We describe our attack in Sect. 2. Sections 3 and 4 describe the proof of concept implementation and its evaluation. Afterwards, we present a discussion of countermeasures in Sect. 5 followed by related work in Sect. 6. Lastly, we present our conclusions in Sect. 7.

## 2   The Attack

This section clarifies the attacker model, the benefits for the attacker, as well as the technical details exploited; however, this section is written under the assumption that users have not deployed any security mechanisms in the browser or on their sites, e.g. CSP policies. Throughout this paper, we will refer to the attacker model presented here. Later on, Sect. 5 presents countermeasures available today.

### 2.1   Attacker Model

We assume an attacker slightly less powerful than the Web attacker formalized by Akhawe et al. [5]. A Web attacker can execute JavaScript code in the victim's browser according to the browser's policies. Also, the attacker can host malicious servers which do not need to comply with Web standards. Moreover, a Web attacker can obtain valid domain names and certificates for his servers.

In our attacker model, the attacker is capable of executing a *script abusing the browser's storage, i.e.* **Abusive Script**, when a *website is intentionally opened by a visitor, i.e.* **Intended Site**. This can be achieved through an advertisement network, or script injection techniques. Further, the JavaScript context where the Abusive Script is executed, as well as its origin, are totally irrelevant for the attack. To increase the browser's storage without the user's knowledge, the attacker needs to host an Abusive Script in several origins. This can be easily achieved by using free domains; also, if the attacker owns a domain already, he could generate many sub-domains or use several ports in one domain to deliver the script[4]. The final storage space available for the attacker will be the number of origins hosting his script multiplied by the storage quota imposed by the browser. Nonetheless, unlike the Intended Site, the Abusive Script does not need to be intentionally opened by the user.

To communicate data between browsers, the attacker needs access to a server to negotiate browser-to-browser connections. Notably, this server only intervenes during the connection session establishment, but it is not used to transfer data between browsers. The attacker creating the network is slightly weaker than a Web attacker because all servers comply with Web standards, and the script context where the attacker's code is loaded is irrelevant for the attack.

---

[4] All are separate Origins According to RFC 6454.

## 2.2 Attack Details

For the sake of clarity, Fig. 1 depicts the attack where three different browsers opened Intended Sites including Abusive Scripts in different ways. First of all, the figure shows Intended Sites including Abusive Scripts from two different origins, i.e. Origin1 and Origin2. Further, cross-site scripting injection (Browser 3) would allow the Abusive Script to access the JavaScript execution context of the Intended Site. On the contrary, Intended Sites are shown in Browser 1 and 2 load the Abusive Script in a different context, e.g. inside an Iframe. The latter occurs when the Abusive Script is present in an advertisement and is therefore isolated from the Intended Site context due to the Same Origin Policy. Now, we mention how to achieve the Abusive Script's execution, the irrelevance of the Same Origin Policy for the attack, how to increase the browser quota, the browser-to-browser channels, and summarize the complete attack.

**Abusive Script Execution.** Although script injection through additional software is possible, we analyse techniques without requiring browser plug-ins, vulnerability exploitation or additional software on the client's side.

An attacker can deliver the Abusive Script through an advertisement network. This has been demonstrated by Grossman et al. [19] and has been used to do crypto-mining without the visitors' knowledge [40]. Although in this case, the Abusive Script would be included inside an Iframe in the Intended Site, as seen in Browser 1 and 2 in Fig. 1, this does not interfere with the attack. Further, it does not matter whether the advertising executing the Abusive Script is delivered through legitimate advertising networks or advertising injectors [41].

Scripts can also be included in sites by either leveraging forgotten inclusions, or by modifying popular libraries or CMS Widgets. Nikiforakis et al. [32] showed a number ways allowing to execute malicious code, e.g. using stale IPs or domains that are still included but forgotten. Particularly, the authors found out that 56 domains used in the 47 top Alexa Web sites were available for registration at the time. Also, thousands of sites were affected after by two Content Management System plugins performing crypto-mining without the user's knowledge [12,28].

Last but not least, cross-site scripting is a particularly promising way to infect Web sites, given that by 2013 more than 6000 unique vulnerabilities were found across the Alexa top 500 Web sites (9.6% of the analysed sites) [26].

**Irrelevance of the Same Origin Policy.** The attacker's goal is to execute the Abusive Script and abuse the local storage space and networking capabilities of the browser; hence, accessing the DOM or the JavaScript context of the Intended Site is not a prerequisite for the attacker. Thus, as it can be seen in Fig. 1, the Same Origin Policy isolation between the Intended Site and the Abusive Script is not hindering the attacker.

Data can be sent to browsers which loaded the Abusive Script from any origin. Thus, cross-origin communication is allowed, not only among different Intended Sites but also between different Abusive Script origins too. This is

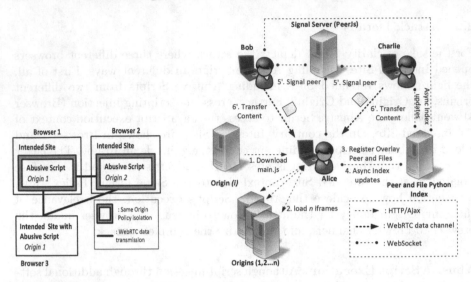

**Fig. 1.** Attack's overview        **Fig. 2.** Proof of concept diagram

possible because according to the security architecture proposed[5] for WebRTC dataChannels [36], enforcing the Same Origin Policy between browser-to-browser channels does not provide any additional security. This design decision was based on two reasons: data channels do not inject code into other origins, and data can always be forwarded through the severs. Although these two statements are true, enabling cross-origin communication over peer-to-peer links is problematic because the direct channel empowers the developer to move data from one browser to another without the user's knowledge regardless of the origin from which the code was loaded from. What is worse, this happens without burdening the server with the data transfer. The latter is of utmost importance for the scalability of the attack since, although data could be relayed through a server, this would impose a heavy toll on the performance of the server, therefore making the proposed attack less attractive.

**Increasing the Local Storage Limit.** From the local storage perspective, a 5 MB quota is enforced per origin, unless the user opts-in to increase it for a particular origin. The quota prevents a single origin from abusing the browser's local storage. From this point of view, letting a script create an Iframe is not problematic because, unless the Iframe and the parent window share the same origin[6], data loaded inside the Iframe (and its JavaScript execution context) is out of reach of the script creating it due to the Same Origin Policy. Although this separation of script contexts is helpful for data isolation, it can be misused to increase the local storage used on the browser.

---

[5] This is a IETF-draft which means this is still work in progress.

[6] Windows can also set their origin to be a super origin, i.e. mysite.company.com can set its origin as company.com to share the same origin with other pages.

The technique used to bypass the quota enforcement for a particular website uses *Iframes with different origins to store data in their local storage, i.e.* **Storage Iframes**. Given that each Storage Iframe has a different origin, each one of them has 5 MB of local storage. A Similar approach has been used to show how information can be placed within the user's browser by Aboukhadijeh [1,9]. So far, this technique allows an attacker to store information in several Iframes, but how to access such information as one centralized database is not yet solved.

An attacker can solve this problem by using the PostMessage API to communicate data from several Storage Iframes controlled by him. According to the postMessage specification [30], the assumptions dictate that, as long as developers validate the origin of the messages exchanged and their proper encoding, no vulnerabilities can be exploited. The rationale behind these validations is to prevent Web sites from acting on commands sent by malicious windows and to avoid script injection. Unfortunately, as this fails to consider two origins colluding against the browser, the Abusive Script obtains a quota equivalent to the number of Storage Iframes spawned by it multiplied by the browser storage quota. In other words, postMessages are used as an asynchronous intra-browser messaging system to exchange control commands and data between the Storage Iframe and the Abusive Script, shown as "broker" in each browser in Fig. 3.

**Inter-browser Cross-Origin Communication.** Inter-browser communication is paramount if the attacker wants to instruct browsers to share data with each other. This functionality relies on the WebRTC dataChannels [31] which requires an initial negotiation phase. Such initialization phase is solved by the implementation of the *Interactive Connectivity Establishment* protocol (ICE) [23]. In particular cases, when browsers are behind a router with *Network Address Translation* (NAT), a server providing *Session Traversal Utilities for NAT* (STUN) [38] allows them to discover their public IP address and port. In most cases a short intervention of a STUN server is enough to enable browsers to communicate with each other directly. The previous protocols are covered by a server accessible by the attacker, as mentioned in Sect. 2.1. Nevertheless, in some cases, it may be impossible to establish a direct connection between two peers who are behind two different NAT routers. Then, an additional relay server implementing the *Traversal Using Relay NAT* protocol (TURN) [27] is needed for the communication.

**Putting It All Together** In order to put together an attack in which data stored in a browser is available across the whole cross-origin browser network, the attacker needs to extend the increase of the Local Storage use with browser-to-browser connectivity. As a result, each Storage Iframe hosts an **overlay peer**, i.e. *a WebRTC enabled frame*. Also, the Storage IFrame needs to receive control commands, through postMessage API, not only to share data from Local Storage but also to connect to other peers, retrieve and send data from them, etc. Figure 3 reflects an example in which two browsers visit one origin each, where the Abusive Script is hosted. Further, this figure shows the Storage Iframe hosted on three different origins, i.e. Origin1, Origin2, Origin3.

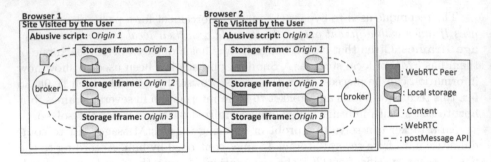

**Fig. 3.** Attack schematics

# 3  Proof of Concept

We have built a proof of concept where every browser opening a website containing an Abusive Script replicates files present in a unified browser network. In our implementation there is no central server hosting the files; instead, every browser can register files in the network and they will be automatically replicated by other browsers. Further, every browser spawns several storage frames, i.e. 10 Origins equivalent to 50 MB in our case, and attempts to replicate as many files as possible. The replication process stops when every file in the network is replicated locally, or when there is no space left in any Storage Iframe. Also, content transfers happen over browser-to-browser WebRTC connections.

Although the mapping between peers and files in the network could have been distributed across the browser network, e.g. using a Distributed Hash Table [14], this neither strengthens nor weakens our argumentation on the security issues raised by the attack. Likewise, our prototypical implementation requires files to have at most 5 MB when they are encoded in base 64. Also, we have tested our implementation with Chrome 43.0.2357.81, and Firefox 38.0.

Based on Fig. 2, the remainder of this section describes the components and the message exchange in our proof of concept. The **components** are:

*Abusive Script*: Our "broker" uses the postMessage API adopting a hierarchical approach where the Abusive Script commands each Storage Iframe to execute actions, e.g. retrieve a file from another peer, and receives callbacks with the status of the task. This provisions the Abusive Script with an overview of files stored locally, and ensures files are replicated at most once per browser.

*Signalling Server*: We used a local installation of the PeerJS Server. This open-source server, in combination with the Peer client library, provides a high-level API allowing to send signals to peers in the network and to establish WebRTC channels among them.

*Peer and File Index*: this is a Python server used to track which files are stored in which peer as well as which peers are currently in the overlay network. Whenever a browser joins the network a WebSocket is opened to this server. We used WebSockets to receive and broadcast notifications from and to the peers when the index has changed, etc. Also, when a WebSocket connection is closed the server can safely assume that a given browser (and all its Overlay Peers) left the network. Also, for visualization purposes, this server offers a simple HTML page to upload files to a Storage Iframe, retrieve files from other browsers, and query an updated index of peers and files.

The **message exchange** between the different components mentioned before is depicted by Fig. 2. In this set-up, we show how Bob and Charlie have already joined the network; thus, they are already registered in the *Peer and File Index*, and they already stored locally some files required by the peers in Alice's browser.

The first step corresponds to when Alice opens an Intended Site containing an Abusive Script. The second step takes place when the Abusive Script generates $n$ different invisible Storage Iframes, where $n$ is the number of origins serving the code. The registration of the Storage Iframe as a peer in the network is shown in the third step. At this point, in the fourth step, the Abusive Script will command each Storage Iframe to download files from several peers. Once a Storage Iframe, inside Alice's browser, receives a command from the Abusive Script requiring the acquisition of a file from a specific peer, it will start the transfer between browsers. This process starts when Alice's browser uses the PeerJS implementation to negotiate the connection details to establish the WebRTC channel with the specific Iframe in Bob's and Charlie's browsers[7]. Once the signalling process succeeds, a direct connection between Alice and Bob, and another one between Alice and Charlie can be established, so the content can be transferred directly. Once Alice receives a new file, her browser will communicate this to the *Peer and File Index* server. Also, arrows labelled as *Async index updates* in Fig. 2 show the WebSockets asynchronous full-duplex updates between peers and the index server.

Each Abusive Script follows a simple replication approach. When there is space in a Storage Iframe, the Abusive Script instructs a Storage Iframe to replicate the file with the least amount replications in the network that has not been stored in the browser. This guarantees that when nodes leave and files are being less replicated, they are copied to other nodes before they perish.

# 4    Evaluation

We do not pretend to cover an extensive performance evaluation of the proof of concept. Instead, we merely want to establish a set of conditions under which the attack works and argue for its plausibility in a real-world deployment. Thus, there are two concerns that we need to address. First of all, the browser network should keep files available in spite of the high churn produced by browsers joining and leaving the Intended Site. Also, network overhead imposed on servers, e.g. the signalling server, should be negligible compared to the network use on the browser's side. This would guarantee that the network can scale without requiring high computational resources from the attacker. To this end, we collect log files and network traffic from several experiments. The main goal is to calculate

---

[7] Steps 5 and 6 are denoted with an apostrophe to represent that they are executed in parallel.

how long is a file available in the network during an experiment run and also to assess the network load on the servers and browsers forming the browser network. Moreover, every component was restarted between experiments to ensure that sequential runs do not interfere with each other.

## 4.1  Set-Up

We have used Docker [15] Linux containers to ensure that tests have exactly the same initial state (docker image). As shown by Fig. 4, we used docker containers to execute the so-called *selenium controller*. The controller is a custom-made multi-threaded Java application providing a REST API. This application receives commands, including actions such as open a website, close the window, or wait a certain time before the next instruction, through HTTP. These actions are executed on a Chromium browser inside the docker instance through a Selenium driver [39]. To run a headless Chromium browser, we used Xvfb as an X server to simulate a terminal without using hardware for it.

Having a generic selenium client proved to be very useful to execute several tests without re-building the containers for every test case. In addition to the containers for the selenium controller, an apache2 (hosting the Intended Site, the Abusive Script, and the Storage Frames), a Peer and Index server, as well as a PeerJS server were run in separate containers, in the same host machine.

On the bottom of Fig. 4, the *orchestrator* represents a Python program sending actions to every selenium controller used for the experiment. This is a multi-threaded Python application implementing an HTTP server to receive callbacks from the selenium controllers, once they have finished a task. The Orchestrator implements the waiting times between browser visits and specifies which Chromium profile should be used for the browser session to be opened from the selenium controller. Specifying a certain profile empowers the Orchestrator to ensure that elements stored in the local storage for the given profile are available in the browser session executed by Selenium. For example, if the orchestrator wants to simulate a visitor that comes for the first time to a website, a clean profile without any cookies, local storage items, or any other previous information is used. Conversely, loading a Selenium session with a specific profile, which has already been used by a browser session which visited the network's site, would contain all the stored files in local storage and is therefore used to represent a returning visitor. The profiles are represented as folders in the case of Chromium and Chrome. Moreover, the host machine used was a Lenovo T430S with 16 GB RAM memory and an Intel(R) Core(TM) i7-3520M CPU @ 2.90 GHz processor with Ubuntu 12.04 LTS.

## 4.2  Browsers' Behaviour

A selenium controller has the possibility to do one-time visits, or a returning visit depending on the profile used, see Sect. 4.1. Therefore, we generate instructions to simulate returning and non-returning visits. We divide the set of browsers into two sets accordingly. In this way, a returning controller will always return

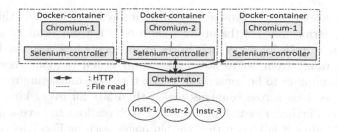

**Fig. 4.** Overall measurement set-up for 3 browsers

with its previous state during the whole experiment. On the contrary, a selenium controller doing visits equivalent to a one-time visit also returns to the Web site following the same pattern, but it loads a fresh profile every time. Since the latter kind of selenium controller represents a one-time, or "non-returning" visitor, it is also called non-returning selenium controller (or browser) from now on. For each returning or non-returning selenium controller, the process to generate the *visit length*, i.e. time in which the browser keeps the Intended Site open, and the *time between visits*, i.e. time until the browser comes back, is generated using a random number generator, see Fig. 5. Thus, the time of the experiment is filled with sequences of visits followed by waiting times between visits. The visit length is depicted in the grey-shaded areas for each browser, while the time between visits is represented by white sections.

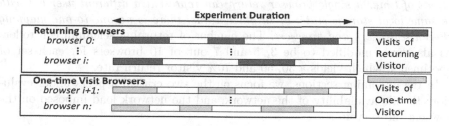

**Fig. 5.** Visits simulation

## 4.3 Measurements

Figure 6 shows the data sources required for our evaluation in grey-shaded boxes. The data sources were: a network (tcpdump) capture including all the traffic during the experiment, and the log files where the peer and index server counts the number of replications per file, i.e. a simple array.

The content hosted by the network is comprised of 33 pictures with an average size of 1 MB each, i.e. a total of 33 MB. This size ensures that 33 MB can be stored in one browser (using up to 50 MB of Local Storage) once they have been encoded in base 64. Although exploring how the network reacts when not all files can be stored in one browser would be interesting, we omit this analysis because the performance of the browser network is not our primary goal.

The *visit length* for every visit in the experiments has been randomly generated in a range from 30 to 50 s using NumPy [33] random generator. We consider this number to be conservative since there are marketing reports showing average sessions across countries higher than 50 s for every kind of website category [13]. Further, research has reported Web sessions to have a mean value of 74 min [7]; also, it is known that certain pages such as Facebook, have users with sessions ranging from a few to several tens of minutes [8]. The duration of every experiment is 5 min.

As mentioned in Sect. 4.1, returning visits are achieved by instructing a selenium controller to load a Chromium profile containing information from a previous visit. Moreover, to have files in the browser network, each selenium controller acting as a returning client has a profile containing its initial state. Therein lie all the files to be replicated in the browser network. This profile is copied to the docker instance at the beginning of every experiment in order to keep a consistent initial state across the different runs of the tests. Browsers acting as first visitors don't use these profiles and have no information in local storage, cookies, or browsing cache.

We vary two parameters during our experiments, namely the time between visits, and the number of selenium controllers returning to the website, i.e. using a Chrome profile containing data from their previous visits. Further, the *time between visits* is generated randomly within the ranges [10–40], [110–140] and [210–240] s. Note that *even though we use returning browsers with relatively short periods of time, a single browser return can represent a different user but with the same local storage state; or in other words, there is no one-to-one mapping between real users and browsers.* The number of returning selenium controllers has also been modified to be 3, 5 and 7 out of 10 browsers for each set of experiments, which yields a 30, 50 and 70% visitor return rate.

In the upcoming sections, we focus on the two critical aspects under evaluation: the file availability of the network, and the network load imposed on the browsers and servers.

**File Availability.** The analysis of the index file, generated by the *Peer and File Index* server consisted on verifying the timestamps and state of the index to calculate the percentage of the time for the experiment run in which each file was available. Then, the average value and standard deviation for the array of percentages was calculated using Python NumPy [33].

As shown in Fig. 7, the availability is strongly influenced by the time between visits; on the contrary, it is noticeable that the percentage of returning visits impacts to a lesser extent. With the shortest time between visits (10–40 s), the mean availability for the files is 95.7%, 93.2%, and 87.8% for 70%, 50% and 30% of return rate respectively; furthermore, in all the cases the standard deviation lies between 3.0% and 3.1%.

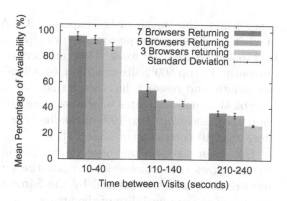

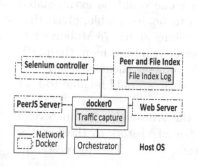

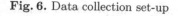

**Fig. 6.** Data collection set-up

**Fig. 7.** Attack evaluation with *visit lengths* between 30–50 s (5 min experiments)

We can safely conclude that when 3 out of 10 browsers are controlled by the returning selenium controller, there is a 30% visitor return rate. This can be directly extrapolated to visitor return rate calculated for Web sites per month, or per day without any loss of generality. Moreover, considering that a recent marketing report [13] states that return visitor rates commonly lie between 25 and 52%, achieving a visitor rate of 30% for an Intended Site is realistic from the returning visitor perspective.

Further, regarding the comeback rate our browser network has two advantages. The first advantage in favour of the attacker is that he does not need to ensure a high return rate for every Origin used by the network, e.g. Origins used to store the Storage Iframes. As long as an Intended Site is visited, the Abusive Script will spawn invisible frames which can point to any domain without the user's knowledge. The second advantage is that, although a 30% return visitor ratio is feasible to achieve, the requirements for the browser network are less restrictive. The attacker could place the Abusive Script in several Intended Sites, such that whenever they are visited, they spawn *n* Storage Frames owned by the attacker. Since the Same Origin Policy is not affecting our network, the browser will always join the same network, i.e. returning to it, in spite of visiting a different Intended Site, or even when the Abusive Script is from a different Origin. Therefore, the return rate required for the attack is not that of a single Intended Site, but rather the return rate of all the Intended Sites serving the Abusive Scripts combined.

Given that we have already covered the visit length and the visitor return rate, it is key to assess whether the concurrent sessions opened by browsers during our experiment is feasible in real-world Web sites. To this end, we do an approximate estimation of this based on average values. First of all, we calculate the average number of visits per browser as the duration of the experiment divided by the sum of the average time of a visit and the average waiting time between visits. This yields a total of 8.75 visits per browser with the shortest wait between visits (10–40 s). Thus, it follows that for 10 browsers, we have 87.5 visits every 5 min (the length of the experiment). Assuming a uniform distribution of visits and using the pigeonhole principle this value could be extrapolated to 176.400 visitors per week. This number seems to be acceptable, given that currently the top 500th site according to Alexa's ranking [6] has 78 Million visits per month, and research has shown that even several years ago more than 20% of typical commercial sites had more than 10.000 browser clients concurrently connected, and from 4 to 10% of randomly selected sites would be able to host more than 1000 concurrent nodes [7].

Like with the previous observation, placing the Abusive Script in several origins allows the attacker to increase the number of visitors to the browser network since it is not covered by the Same Origin Policy. This increases the chances of the applicability of the attack.

To summarize, we can extrapolate the effectiveness of the presented attack when the following assumptions are met. First of all, every file can be stored in one browser, i.e. the attacker has deployed JavaScript code in sufficient domains. Second, the attacker is capable of placing Abusive Script in at least one domain achieving a return rate of at least 30% for all domains combined. Third, Web sites' visitors have sessions in the range between 30 and 50 s.

**Network Analysis.** Raw network traffic has been collected from every experiment. The raw capture file, containing all the bytes exchanged between entities of the browser network, was processed after the experiment has finished by a Python script using the dpkt [16] package to count the bytes aggregated by source and destination IP. We use this information to analyse properties of the browser network. For readability reasons, the information is not shown on a per-entity basis, but instead we focus on interaction between three groups of entities: the group of returning browsers, the group of browsers executing the one-time visits, and the group of servers including the index and peer server, the Web server, and the PeerJs server. The nature of the network analysis requires representing the network traffic for each experiment run individually. Due to the similarity between network captures, we chose one experiment to analyse the traffic, i.e. time between visits in [10–40] with 5 selenium controllers returning. In Fig. 8 we depict the average amount of data (in MB) transmitted between the group represented by the row of the matrix to the group represented by the column of the matrix; also, darker colours represent less amount of data. Based on this, it is observed that browsers executed by selenium clients send a very small amount of data to servers. It is also clear that browsers exchange the highest amount of data in the browser network, as expected. Another interesting fact is that returning browsers send more data to non-returning browsers than returning browsers, this happens because non-returning browsers have a clean local storage every time they join, and therefore attempt to replicate files constantly. Due to HTTP Headers, static content must not be retrieved again (when it has not changed). This is clearly observable because returning browsers send and receive fewer data to/from servers in comparison to browsers controlled by non-returning selenium controllers. Last but not least, returning browsers send

a considerable amount of bytes to non-returning browsers, which is not recipro-
cal. Figure 8 shows that non-returning browsers receive 23.39 (18.9 + 4.49) MB
from returning and non-returning browsers on average. Moreover, non-returning
browsers deliver 6.97 (2.48 + 4.49) MB to returning and non-returning browsers
in average. Nonetheless, the fact that they deliver almost 5 (out of 6.97) MB
to other non-returning browsers, is a sign of their contribution towards keeping
files replicated.

| | returning selenium | non-returning selenium | servers |
|---|---|---|---|
| returning selenium | 15.57 | 18.90 | 0.13 |
| non-returning selenium | 2.48 | 4.49 | 0.22 |
| servers | 0.55 | 1.17 | 0.00 |

**Fig. 8.** Average data (in MB) transmitted with 5 returning selenium controllers - time
between visits in [10–40] s

## 5   Countermeasures

In this section, we cover how security-aware Web developers and browser's users
can employ third-party tracking protection and Content Security Policy (CSP)
directives available today to thwart the attack. Also, the countermeasure discussion is continued by analysing relevant proposals for CSP that would help
against the attack but have not been adopted yet.

**Third-Party Tracking:** Previous research has shown that Internet users are
constantly under surveillance when sites include third-party functionality on the
Web [17]. Thus, browser vendors let users prevent third-party sites from tracking
them [11,18], i.e. use cookies or any other permanent storage mechanism. This
implies that users can prevent the Abusive Script in Fig. 1 to use their local
storage because it is a third-party site included by the Intended Site.

**CSP:** The Content Security Policy (CSP) specification is a tool for developers
and Web masters to restrict functionality and limit privileges of resources loaded
from their sites, through headers in the HTTP response. Restrictions include,
but are not limited to whitelisting sources from which content or scripts can
be loaded, which resources can execute scripts, or whether their environment
should be sandboxed. It must be noted, that CSP is not meant to supersede
proper output encoding and input validation, but it offers a second line of defense
implemented by browsers when a Web application has been compromised.

CSP contains a `sandbox` directive offering the same functionality offered
by the HTML5 attribute under the same name for Iframes [43]. Both mechanisms would ensure that an Iframe cannot execute JavaScript unless the
`allow-scripts` used. And even if the `allow-scripts` keyword is used, sandboxed Iframes are assigned to a random origin making all same-origin checks
fail, which in turn does not allow them to use Local Storage or cookies.

To prevent click-jacking, a developer can use the CSP `frame-ancestors` keyword to ensure that a particular site can only be embedded in resources loaded from a list of origins. If a security-aware Web master specifies a restrictive list of frame ancestors for his site, this would prevent an attacker who has compromised the site from including this particular site as a Storage Frame in the Abusive Script. In more practical terms, this means that an attacker injecting the Storage Frame code in *Origin1* depicted in Fig. 1, cannot include *Origin1* in his Abusive Frame due to the frame ancestors list. However, if an attacker would host the Storage Frame on his own server, the attack would still work.

The `script-src` CSP directive specifies which scripts can be executed from a particular site. Thus, with a restrictive policy allowing to include only secure scripts, which cannot be compromised by the attacker, it becomes impossible for the attacker to execute his Abusive Script or the Storage Frame functionality. In practice, this mechanism has faced several challenges, i.e. it has been already shown that 94% of all policies deployed with CSP can be bypassed due to unsafe exceptions [44]; however, the authors also proposed a new keyword, i.e. `strict-dynamic` which is part of the current CSP draft, to ease the definition of CSP script source policies.

**Pending CSP Proposals:** Now we cover CSP extensions limiting the studied attack which have been proposed but are either not implemented, or have been discussed but are not included in CSP yet.

Hanna et. al have shown that developers tend to forget place proper origin validations when there are scripts collaborating and exchanging messages over the PostMessage API [20]. In 2011, one of the authors proposed to address this issue by providing a declarative way to specify which sites can interact with other origins (whitelist) as part of CSP, and this has been discussed over the Web security standardization mailing list already [3]. Recently (5 years after the initial discussion), a new issue has been created to decide where and how enforcement on PostMessages would be meaningful for existent Web applications [4]. Although this discussion revolves around CSP3, PostMessage API enforcement has not been included yet. If a Web master or developer would be able to specify with which origins can a Web application interact with using PostMessages, the mechanisms to increase the Local Storage limit could be hindered from distributing and serving all the content over the broker shown in Fig. 3.

Early warnings pointing out that WebRTC can be used for data exfiltration are visible as an issue for CSP created in 2014 [42,46]. Later, certain sites started abusing the WebRTC API to transfer data without the user's knowledge or control. Thus, there is a new thread for discussion on the latest CSP specification [24], still open, but created 2 years after the initial issue. If users would be able to restrict with which origins can a site communicate using WebRTC data channels, the cross-origin feature provided by the invisible DataStore would be removed from the attack. However, this feature is not part of the CSP3 [45] draft.

# 6    Related Work

Using Local Storage to store information on the client without the user's knowledge has been introduced by Bogaard et al. [10]. Their work focused on placing a single file on a Web server and distributing pieces of this file to several browsers. Then, the Web developer would deploy a different application to retrieve the content to the server again. The attack studied shares the motivation to keep the user uninformed, but it neither builds a browser network nor circumvents Local Storage quotas through PostMessages. From the storage abuse perspective, Feross discovered that a single website could instruct Local Storage to store data in many subdomains. This lead to abuse the users' disk, filling it until the browser crashes or the whole disk is occupied [1,9]. This relates to our quota bypass mechanism as both rely on using different origins to increase the quota. However, we have enhanced this approach to make the data accessible to the Abusive Script, by implementing letting several origins collaborate through an asynchronous message channel, the broker shown in Fig. 3 implemented through the postMessage API. There have been previous browser networks using WebRTC to deliver static content. For example, PeerCDN [21] is a WebRTC-based Content Distribution Network (CDN) using the visitor's browser to share the website's static HTML content with other browsers. Owners of the company claim to achieve a 90% bandwidth reduction for the server hosting the site. Zhang et al. implemented another browser-based CDN called Maygh [47]. Maygh relies not only on WebRTC, but also on Real Time Media Flow Protocol (RTMFP), i.e. a closed source protocol accessible from Flash plug-ins. The authors examined the performance and the applicability of the CDN network by conducting experiments where simulated browsers would visit the website using the CDN. They conclude a reduction of 75% on bandwidth use on the operator of the website's side. Further, to avoid abusing the clients, the CDN network ensures that users do not upload more than 10 MB to the CDN. From a slightly different perspective, there is research work to transmit video streams between browsers using WebRTC [29,34,37] to ease the burden imposed on servers hosting the video streams. And there is a tool designed to implement a similar protocol to Torrent within browsers called WebTorrent [2].

Although these three approaches execute JavaScript code to distribute content, there are important differences between the previously mentioned approaches and ours. First of all, content and the video distribution networks do not use the browsers as a storage system to put and retrieve information unrelated to what they are consuming. Instead, these approaches replicate the content matching what is being rendered to the visitor of the website. Also, these content distribution networks, do not collude against the user bypassing the storage restriction as the attack described here does. Also, they do not leverage data channels across different origins, which is part of the attack presented.

# 7   Conclusion

Cross-window and browser-to-browser communication channels provided by the postMessage API WebRTC, respectively, bring more flexibility to Web developers; however, adding new communication channels to an already highly complex security model is problematic. Specifically, we show that despite extensive research on new APIs added to the browser [20,25], there are combinations of browser APIs posing threats to browsers. An attacker serving malicious code, e.g. through an advertisement network, can access persistent storage mechanisms in browsers beyond the intended quota per site. Furthermore, circumventing the local storage enforcement can be combined with coercing the visitor's browser to communicate stored data through browser-to-browser links, even when the site's origins of sites loaded by browsers differ. Thus, an attacker can create a browser network for data storage and distribution in a hidden manner. As discussed in Sect. 2.1, the attacker requires neither access to the DOM nor access to the JavaScript execution context of the compromised website, i.e. Intended Site.

The attack we presented has several key differences with respect to "common" Web attack scenarios. On the one hand, the attacker abuses the resources available to the browser instead of targeting a Web application, e.g. to compromise the user's credentials. On the other hand, the attack presented here goes beyond a single misbehaving script. Instead, several colluding scripts are loaded by the initial Abusive script. This goes against some of the typical assumptions of the current Web security model and is visible in three dimensions: Iframe isolation, cross-window communication, and cross-browser communication. The issue with Iframes pertains to the local storage origin-based isolation, which is useful for data access control but enables the storage quota explosion. For cross-window communication, the PostMessage assumes that a window should protect itself against other rogue windows sending malicious messages. This fails to consider two malicious windows cooperating to abuse the browser (instead of attacking the window receiving messages). A similar principle applies to cross-browser communication. Although it seems that browser-to-browser channels do not pose a threat to the user as they cannot steal information from other JavaScript contexts, they can be used to create an overlay network of browsers to host potentially malicious information. Aside from saving computation resources, an attacker can force browsers to store information used for criminal activities, while avoiding the risk associated with hosting and distributing the information himself. In other words, an attacker can complicate forensic analysis greatly by distributing his malicious information across browsers, yet being able to retrieve it when needed.

Although resource abuse cases have not been included in the security model, we also show how mechanisms initially intended against click-jacking, third-party tracking and cross-site scripting can be used to prevent the attack. With this paper, we expect to raise awareness about resource abuse through browsers to ensure that existing countermeasures stay in place.

**Acknowledgements.** This research has been supported by the EU under the H2020 AGILE (Adaptive Gateways for dIverse muLtiple Environments), grant agreement number H2020-688088.

# References

1. Aboukhadijeh, F.: The Joys of HTML5: Introducing the new HTML5 Hard Disk Filler API. www.filldisk.com/. Accessed 15 Apr 2018
2. Aboukhadijeh, F.: Webtorrent (2014). https://github.com/feross/webtorrent. Accessed 15 Apr 2018
3. Akhawe, D.: CSP and PostMessage. https://lists.w3.org/Archives/Public/public-web-security/2011Dec/0020.html. Accessed 15 Apr 2018
4. Akhawe, D.: Do we want a directive to control postMessage explicit channels outbound?. https://lists.w3.org/Archives/Public/public-web-security/2011Dec/0020. html. Accessed 15 Apr 2018
5. Akhawe, D., Barth, A., Lam, P.E., Mitchell, J., Song, D.: Towards a formal foundation of web security. In: Proceedings of the 2010 23rd IEEE Computer Security Foundations Symposium, CSF 2010, pp. 290–304. IEEE Computer Society, Washington, DC (2010). https://doi.org/10.1109/CSF.2010.27
6. Alexa Traffic Ranking and visitor statistics for 7 years. http://www.rank2traffic. com/. Accessed 15 Apr 2018
7. Antonatos, S., Akritidis, P., Lam, V.T., Anagnostakis, K.G.: Puppetnets: misusing web browsers as a distributed attack infrastructure. ACM Trans. Inf. Syst. Secur. **12**(2), 12 (2008)
8. Athanasopoulos, E., et al.: Antisocial networks: turning a social network into a botnet. In: Wu, T.-C., Lei, C.-L., Rijmen, V., Lee, D.-T. (eds.) ISC 2008. LNCS, vol. 5222, pp. 146–160. Springer, Heidelberg (2008). https://doi.org/10.1007/978-3-540-85886-7_10
9. Web Code Weakness allows Data Dump on PCs (2008). http://www.bbc.com/ news/technology-21628622. Accessed 15 Apr 2018
10. Bogaard, D., Johnson, D., Parody, R.: Browser web storage vulnerability investigation HTML5 localStorage object. In: Proceedings of the International Conference on Security and Management, pp. 1–7, July 2012
11. Clear, enable, and manage cookies in Chrome. https://support.google.com/ chrome/answer/95647. Accessed 15 Apr 2018
12. Cimpanu, C.: Cryptojacking Script Found in Live Help Widget, Impacts Around 1,500 Sites. https://www.bleepingcomputer.com/news/security/cryptojacking-script-found-in-live-help-widget-impacts-around-1-500-sites/. Accessed 25 Nov 2017
13. Clicktale: Web-Aanalytics Benchmark Q2 (2013). https://research.clicktale.com/ web_analytics_benchmarks.html. Accessed 15 Apr 2018
14. Dias, D.: WebRTC Explorer. https://github.com/diasdavid/webrtc-explorer. Accessed 15 Apr 2018
15. Docker. https://www.docker.com/. Accessed 15 Apr 2018
16. Dpkt package. https://pypi.python.org/pypi/dpkt. Accessed 15 Apr 2018
17. Englehardt, S., et al.: Cookies that give you away: the surveillance implications of web tracking. In: Proceedings of the 24th International Conference on World Wide Web, WWW 2015, pp. 289–299. International World Wide Web Conferences Steering Committee, Republic and Canton of Geneva, Switzerland (2015). https:// doi.org/10.1145/2736277.2741679

18. Disable third-party cookies in Firefox to stop some types of tracking by advertisers. https://support.mozilla.org/en-US/kb/disable-third-party-cookies. Accessed 15 Apr 2018

19. Grossman, J., Johansen, M.: Million Browser Botnet. https://www.blackhat.com/us-13/briefings.html. Accessed 15 Jan 2018

20. Hanna, S., Shin, E.C.R., Akhawe, D., Boehm, A., Saxena, P., Song, D.: The emperor's new APIs: on the (in) secure usage of new client-side primitives. In: Workshop on Web 2.0 Security and Privacy, W2SP (2010)

21. Hiesey, J., Aboukhadijeh, F., Rajah, A.: PeerCDN (2013). https://peercdn.com/. Accessed 15 Apr 2018

22. Hoffman, J.J.: New Jersey Division of Consumer Affairs Obtains Settlement with Developer of Bitcoin-Mining Software Found to Have Accessed New Jersey Computers Without Users' Knowledge or Consent. http://www.njconsumeraffairs.gov/News/Pages/05262015.aspx. Accessed 15 Apr 2018

23. Rosenberg, J.: RFC 5245: Interactive connectivity establishment (ICE): A protocol for network address translator (NAT) traversal for offer/answer protocols. RFC 5245, April 2010. https://tools.ietf.org/html/rfc5245. Accessed 15 Apr 2018

24. Kesteren, A.V.: WebRTC RTCDataChannel can be used for exfiltration. https://github.com/w3c/webappsec-csp/issues/92. Accessed 15 Apr 2018

25. Lekies, S., Johns, M.: Lightweight integrity protection for web storage-driven content caching. In: Workshop on Web 2.0 Security and Privacy, W2SP (2012)

26. Lekies, S., Stock, B., Johns, M.: 25 million flows later: large-scale detection of DOM-based XSS. In: Proceedings of the 2013 ACM SIGSAC Conference on Computer & Communications Security, CCS 2013, pp. 1193–1204. ACM, New York (2013). https://doi.org/10.1145/2508859.2516703

27. Mahy, R., Matthews, P.: RFC5766: Traversal using relays around NAT (TURN): Relay extensions to session traversal utilities for NAT (STUN). RFC 5766, IETF, April 2010. https://tools.ietf.org/html/rfc5766

28. Maunder, M.: WordPress plugin banned for crypto mining. https://www.wordfence.com/blog/2017/11/wordpress-plugin-banned-crypto-mining/. Accessed 15 Jan 2018

29. Meyn, A.J.R., Nurminen, J.K., Probst, C.W.: Browser to browser media streaming with HTML5. Master's thesis. Aalto University (2012). https://aaltodoc.aalto.fi/handle/123456789/6094

30. Mozilla Developer Network (MDN) - Window.postMessage(), April 2015. https://developer.mozilla.org/en-US/docs/Web/API/Window/postMessage. Accessed 15 Apr 2018

31. Narayanan, A., Jennings, C., Bergkvist, A., Burnett, D.C.: WebRTC 1.0: Real-time Communication Between Browsers. W3C working draft, W3C, September 2013. http://www.w3.org/TR/2013/WD-webrtc-20130910/

32. Nikiforakis, N., et al.: You are what you include: large-scale evaluation of remote JavaScript inclusions. In: Proceedings of the 2012 ACM Conference on Computer and Communications Security, CCS 2012, pp. 736–747. ACM, New York (2012). https://doi.org/10.1145/2382196.2382274

33. NumPy. http://www.numpy.org/. Accessed 15 Apr 2018

34. Nurminen, J., Meyn, A., Jalonen, E., Raivio, Y., Marrero, R.G.: P2P media streaming with HTML5 and WebRTC. In: 2013 IEEE Conference on Computer Communications Workshops (INFOCOM WKSHPS), pp. 63–64, April 2013. https://doi.org/10.1109/INFCOMW.2013.6970739

35. Provos, N., Mavrommatis, P., Rajab, M.A., Monrose, F.: All your iFRAMEs point to us. In: Proceedings of the 17th Conference on Security Symposium, SS 2008, pp. 1–15. USENIX Association, Berkeley (2008)
36. Rescorla, E.: IETF-draft: WebRTC Security Architecture, March 2015. https://tools.ietf.org/html/draft-ietf-rtcweb-security-arch-11. Accessed 15 Apr 2018
37. Rhinow, F., Veloso, P.P., Puyelo, C., Barrett, S., Nuallain, E.O.: P2P live video streaming in WebRTC. In: 2014 World Congress on Computer Applications and Information Systems, WCCAIS, pp. 1–6, January 2014. https://doi.org/10.1109/WCCAIS.2014.6916588
38. Rosenberg, J., Mahy, R., Matthews, P., Wing, D.: RFC5389: Session traversal utilities for NAT (STUN). RFC 5389, RFC Editor, October 2008. https://tools.ietf.org/html/rfc5389
39. SeleniumHQ: Browser Automation. http://www.seleniumhq.org/. Accessed 15 Apr 2018
40. Telegraph, T.: YouTube shuts down hidden cryptojacking adverts. http://www.telegraph.co.uk/technology/2018/01/29/youtube-shuts-hidden-crypto-jacking-adverts/. Accessed 15 Jan 2018
41. Thomas, K., et al.: Ad injection at scale: assessing deceptive advertisement modifications. In: Proceedings of the 2015 IEEE Symposium on Security and Privacy, SP 2015, pp. 151–167. IEEE Computer Society, Washington, DC (2015). https://doi.org/10.1109/SP.2015.17
42. Thomson, M.: CSP for WebRTC. https://lists.w3.org/Archives/Public/public-webappsec/2014Aug/0162.html. Accessed 15 Apr 2018
43. W3CScools: HTML Iframe sandbox Attribute. https://www.w3schools.com/tags/att_iframe_sandbox.asp. Accessed 15 Apr 2018
44. Weichselbaum, L., Spagnuolo, M., Lekies, S., Janc, A.: CSP is dead, long live CSP! On the insecurity of whitelists and the future of content security policy. In: Proceedings of the 2016 ACM SIGSAC Conference on Computer and Communications Security, CCS 2016, pp. 1376–1387. ACM, New York (2016). https://doi.org/10.1145/2976749.2978363
45. West, M.: Content Security Policy Level 3. https://www.w3.org/TR/2016/WD-CSP3-20160913/. Accessed 15 Apr 2018
46. West, M.: WebRTC via 'connect-src'? https://www.w3.org/2011/webappsec/track/issues/67. Accessed 15 Apr 2018
47. Zhang, L., Zhou, F., Mislove, A., Sundaram, R.: Maygh: building a CDN from client web browsers. In: Proceedings of the 8th ACM European Conference on Computer Systems, EuroSys 2013, pp. 281–294. ACM, New York (2013). https://doi.org/10.1145/2465351.2465379

# ATCS Workshop

# A Review and Costing of Lightweight Authentication Schemes for Internet of Things (IoT): *Towards Design of an Authentication Architecture for Smart Home Applications*

Attlee M. Gamundani[1(✉)], Amelia Phillips[2],
and Hippolyte N. Muyingi[1]

[1] Faculty of Computing and Informatics, Computer Science Department,
Namibia University of Science and Technology, Windhoek, Namibia
{agamundani, hmuyingi}@nust.na
[2] CIS and Computer Science, Departments Cyber Security and Forensics BAS
Lead, Highline College, Seattle, USA
aphillips@highline.edu

**Abstract.** Internet of Things (IoT) authentication for resource-constrained devices thrives under lightweight solutions. The requirements of the lightweight solutions are that, they have to meet the processing, storage and limited resource base of the resource-constrained devices. There are a number of lightweight solutions advanced for IoT under different domains. To provide feasible authentication solutions for smart home security calls for focus on key attributes that suit the domain in question. This paper is positioned to give a review of some existing lightweight authentication schemes, guide the selection and design of best possible solutions that can be applied to smart home environments. From the costing of randomly selected lightweight authentication techniques, the least costly solution is recommended for adoption.

**Keywords:** Authentication · Architecture · Cost · Lightweight
IoT · Smart home

## 1 Introduction

The strength and weakness of many security solutions is anchored on authentication as it grants access to various components of any system. The varied nature of the appliances in a smart home setup presents a huge challenge towards IoT authentication especially considering a setup where remote access is enabled [1]. To further support the challenge of incorporating security protocols in IoT components [2] highlights that, it is a challenge due to their extreme constrained resources.

Coming up with the best authentication scheme for resource-constrained devices is one of the biggest challenges. Existing solutions applied under similar constrained environments sometimes do not meet the strictly constrained device resource capabilities in terms of computational power and storage facility. The need therefore to

© ICST Institute for Computer Sciences, Social Informatics and Telecommunications Engineering 2018
R. Beyah et al. (Eds.): SecureComm 2018, LNICST 255, pp. 375–390, 2018.
https://doi.org/10.1007/978-3-030-01704-0_20

evaluate existing lightweight solutions advanced even outside the smart home domain, will inform the design of lightweight solutions that suits strictly constrained devices.

**Contribution:** This paper gives a costing on a comparison basis of various IoT authentication architectures. The costing is done on the basis of the hash algorithm used, the intensity of string concatenation and exclusive or operations. These parameters were selected, without loss of generality, on the basis that, they may affect the performance of resource-constrained devices.

The best authentication approach for smart home applications is proposed based on the comparison results from the randomly selected lightweight authentication protocols without focus on their domain of application as depicted in Table 12.

The paper gives a quick overview of several lightweight authentication architectures. From the pool of identified lightweight authentication architectures the ones closely linked to the architectural setup of a smart home environment were selected.

The key observation presented in this paper is that, the lightweight stature of authentication schemes may differ based on the domain of application but the principal design goals are the same. It is therefore safe to consider one solution from a different domain and customise it for another domain. We maintain that, if the principal design goals of the scheme to be adopted are maintained, the functional specifications should be returned. Furthermore, the original security design goals of the protocol should be preserved. If that condition cannot be met, then customisation should be discarded thereof.

**Organisation:** Section 2 is a summary of the threat landscape for smart home applications. Section 3 gives an overview of IoT security with the motivation of placing authentication in light of security design. Section 4 takes a detailed look at IoT authentication by first highlighting some of the existing lightweight IoT authentication schemes then zooming into lightweight authentication schemes that have been applied to smart home applications. Guided by the observations from Sects. 4 and 5 gives comparisons of lightweight solutions based on the costing of the algorithms. Section 6 finally presents some recommendations for smart home security solution designs. The conclusion is aptly packed in Sect. 7.

## 2   Threat Landscape for Smart Home Applications

In general, the threats inherent to IoT devices anywhere else are typically the same threats one would find in a smart home setup. The smart home domain may have setbacks of not having formal security design setups and that mainly depend on the expertise level of the inhabitants. If at manufacturer level, certain devices don't have robust security solutions embedded in them, that will contribute to the vulnerabilities a smart home domain is likely to suffer.

For consideration of a threat landscape for the purposes of this paper, the Dolev-Yao attack model [3] is considered. The possible attacks such as eavesdropping, message injects, replay, spoofing, insider and outside attacks are all deemed possible actions by the attacker. These attacks may be perpetrated with the motive to gain access to sensitive data, gain unauthorised control of smart home devices and propagate denial of service and service degradation.

## 3   IoT Security

The general approach to IoT security is one that carefully pays attention to the resource-constrained attributes of the various applications and devices/things. Third party platforms are sometimes used to design security solutions due to computational and storage limitations for robust solutions. The need for end-to-end security therefore becomes of paramount importance.

A typical IoT environment and implementation may involve various communication and networking protocols and designs. This is further supported by the work of [4], on multi-protocol security framework. For example we can consider wireless network connectivity and the Radio Frequency Identification (RFID) tags being applied for the same platform. As part of the fundamental security requirements for wireless communications, resilience towards message forgery and non-repudiation are key [5]. RFID systems as poised by [6] may cause security and privacy risks. Advancing security to RFID may call for cloud-based security solutions, hence remote authentication. An argument for proposing RFID cloud based authentication may be under the supposition that, the backend server is dependable as supported by [7] when they looked at a solution which was meant for secure cloud based RFID systems.

Home area networks as mainly enabled by wireless sensors and actuators which are generally resource constrained and depend on open standard protocols [8]. This setup alone deems IoT security design a complex task to execute for effective results. Clearly, when it comes to IoT security, authentication as the first line of defence demands attention like any other key security activities. Many if not all of the security solutions will depend on how properly the authentication part is crafted.

## 4   IoT Authentication

As summarized by [9], the key operations for authentication as observed from [10–12] are key establishment, message authentication code and handshake. It can therefore be highlighted that these are the three vital ingredients for effective authentication.

A close look at various solutions presented and applied for IoT authentication platforms, signals the varied nature of such solutions. Common among the various solutions as will be covered in this section, despite the domain of application is their lightweight nature, which of course has varying degrees depending on areas of implementation.

The first selection on lightweight IoT authentication schemes in general have been randomly on the following key categories: - two-factor authentication based, use of pseudonyms, hardware and bio based, network based, Physically Unclonable function (PUF) based, three-factor authentication based and cloud computing application focused. These were general trends observed from recent work on lightweight authentication schemes. The second selection on lightweight IoT authentication for smart home applications were mainly populated based on a random selection which satisfied the condition, A = {IoT, Lightweight, Authentication, Smart Home}.

## 4.1 Lightweight IoT Authentication Schemes in General

This section will give an overview of selected authentication schemes in groups of the classifications already highlighted above. For the scheme selected from any classification for further comparisons in Sect. 5, a costing of the scheme will be done. The main focus will be on the authentication function, without focusing on the key establishment phase and any other procedures before or after authentication.

### A. Two- Factor Authentication Schemes

Two-factor authentication (2FLIP) solutions as applied in Vehicular Ad Hoc Network (VANET) communication presented by [5] focused on privacy-preserving. The presented 2FLIP operates by employing a certificate authority that is decentralized making use of two-factor authentication which is biologically password protected [5]. For message signing, a number of very lightweight hashing processes coupled with fast message authentication-code were applied [5].

### B. Pseudonym Technique Based Schemes

Pseudonyms are another popular technique employed for lightweight solutions as can be observed from the following three examples:

(a) The proposed $k$-pseudonym by [13] presents an anonymous authentication protocol that functions on the premise of a shared secret key where $k$-pseudonym set, are send by the user including an open real identity as well as other $k - 1$ pseudonyms. After the authentication server exchanges shared keys with each of the users in the set and verifies the authentication information, it can determine the real user and complete the authentication [13]. (b) A lightweight mutual authentication protocol also preserving anonymity, through use of a unique selection of pseudorandom numbers towards attaining fundamental security objectives was proposed by [14], for RFID setups which encompassed a tag, readers and a backend server [15]. Readers and tags realize mutual authentication as proposed by [14] through a combination of a pseudorandom number generator as well as an XOR computation. (c) A similar authentication scheme that made use of pseudonym identities is presented by [16] where the scheme, provided security by discharging sessions through lightweight overhead. Diminishing the count for exchanged messages, helped significantly reduce the cumulative computation load and the communication for Vehicle to Grid (V2G) connection, particularly for Electric Vehicles (EVs).

Considering the resource constraints for low-cost RFID tags, and as presented by [6] that several researchers focused more on proposing protocols that are based on hash functions and pseudo-random number generators. The enhanced lightweight authentication protocol henceforth proposed by [6] was aiming at meeting the security demands of low-cost RFID systems and improve computational cost and search efficiency at the backend database [15]. This was an attempt to counter some of the general approach limitations. The cost analysis of the presented solution as summarised in Table 1 is relatively reasonable in terms of the lightweight features employed.

**Table 1.** Cost analysis of Zhang's protocol [6]

|  | Device (tag) | Database |
|---|---|---|
| Hash $(x)$ | 3 | 3 |
| XOR $(y)$ | 3 | 3 |
| $\|(z)$ | 2 | 2 |
| Total cost | $3x + 3y + 2z$ | $3x + 3y + 2z$ |

## C. Network Based Schemes

An interesting trend among the authentication schemes is their ability to authenticate among the communicating things. Typical to that functionality is the lightweight authentication protocol between sensors in stationary and mobile node proposed by [17] which is suitable for constrained entities. The proposed protocol by [17] can ensure some security and privacy features such as anonymity, untraceability etc. The performance analysis based on costing of the protocol as depicted in Table 2 is relatively reasonable, but will require some adjustments at device level if applied to seriously constrained devices that may have little to no computational capacity.

**Table 2.** Cost analysis of Janbabaei et al.'s protocol [17]

|  | Device | Server |
|---|---|---|
| Hash $(x)$ | 4 | 5 |
| XOR $(y)$ | 5 | 7 |
| $\|(z)$ | 8 | 9 |
| Total cost | $4x + 5y + 8z$ | $5x + 7y + 9z$ |

Central to some of the solutions is their pursuit to observe anonymity, which closely relate towards addressing the privacy concerns. An authentication scheme such as a realistic authentication scheme advanced for WSN, promising key security attributes such as user privacy, unreachability, forward/backward confidentiality and perfect forward confidentiality, which was proposed by [18] in their work aimed at real-time application security for data access in WSN which is closely related to setups typical to IoT environments. Table 3 details the performance analysis based on the costing of the protocol.

**Table 3.** Cost analysis of Gope et al.'s protocol [18]

|  | Device (smart card) | Server |
|---|---|---|
| Hash $(x)$ | 12 | 10 |
| XOR $(y)$ | 6 | 5 |
| $\|(z)$ | 13 | 19 |
| Total cost | $12x + 6y + 13z$ | $10x + 5y + 19z$ |

The authentication scheme for information hiding towards prevention of DoS attacks in software defined network control channel is presented by [19], which is an architecture that offloads overall network control from the end nodes to a central controller. Yet for group authentication as well as group session, [20] proposes on the client side, a key generation that is lightweight authenticated via a dynamic group as enabled by the various members in the IoT environments. Table 4, gives a summary of the costing analysis, the analysis is based on equivalent operations for hashing and XOR where encryption/decryption and nonce are used respectively.

**Table 4.** Costing analysis of Huang et al.'s protocol [20]

|  | Device (node $i$) | Proxy server |
|---|---|---|
| Encryption $(x)$ | 3 | 6 |
| nonce($y$) | 1 | – |
| $\|(z)$ | 3 | 5 |
| Total cost | $3x + y + 3z$ | $6x + 5z$ |

## D. Hardware and Bio Based Schemes

In the work by [21], an authentication framework that is scalable and less complex was proposed for low-power IoT applications and environments. The applications under consideration were those capable of using physical layer information gained from previous verified communications as part of shared secrecy between two parties. The assumption that each terminal individually made use of half-duplex radio and independent noises to generate a key meant that the extracted bit sequences were ultimately non-identical after a quantification process [21]. As argued by [21] proper authentication was attained as a result of bit mismatches which required certain key properties to be applied for their handling. Similarly, [22] proposed an authentication scheme based on the ability of the card and reader to generate identical pairwise keys, not their shared secret keys. The identical pairwise keys were generated using their own private key methods gotten from the same source.

Nevertheless, the same capabilities of authenticating among the things in IoT is apparent in an object authentication framework proposed by [23] which utilize specific device information referred to here as fingerprints, for authenticating the objects in the IoT environment. The authentication is attained by effectively tracking the environmental effects towards the object's fingerprints, which can be detected through the distinction between supposed attacks and identifiable fingerprint changes [23]. On the other hand, the authentication scheme presented by [24] enabled the sensor and the remote server to authenticate mutually thereby achieving communication security. While, [25] proposed an authentication protocol based on Kerberos for both authentication and authorization, whose performance analysis mainly based on the costing being used for other schemes so far, is presented in Table 5. From the costing in Table 5, it is clear that optimisation was done on the gateway level as compared with the device level.

**Table 5.** Cost analysis of Khemissa et al.'s protocol [24]

|            | Sensor node | Remote user | Gateway |
|------------|-------------|-------------|---------|
| Hash $(x)$ | 2           | 2           | 1       |
| XOR $(y)$  | 3           | 4           | 1       |
| $\|(z)$    | 1           | 1           | 0       |
| Total cost | $2x + 3y + z$ | $2x + 4y + z$ | $x + y$ |

On the other hand [26], proposed a Pre-Shared Key (PSK) chaining system functioning on the basis of a lightweight pre-shared key enabling and offering defence against key attacks at minimal cost. Through generation of a series of arbitrary PSKs and not utilizing secret exchanges the system provides new PSK from the series of the envisaged secure session.

### E. Physically Unclonable Function (PUF) Based Schemes

Challenge-response authentication schemes enabled through Physically Unclonable Function are another popular approach towards lightweight authentication. The work by [27] proposed a PUF that operate on carbon nanotube technologies. A hardware and software co-verification authentication scheme, a resource–efficient PUF-based security protocol is presented by [28], and is based on elliptic curve cryptography. The cost analysis of the protocol reveals that, the protocol is expensive on the device level as compared with the provider side, hence will require optimisation if adopted for use on strictly constrained devices. In the work of [29] PUF is recommended to prevent fake injection into the chain, which is quite an important aspect to consider if overall security is to be advanced in IoT applications (Table 6).

**Table 6.** Cost analysis of Hossain et al.'s protocol [28]

|            | IoT           | IoT Identity Provider (IIP) |
|------------|---------------|-----------------------------|
| Hash $(x)$ | 7             | 5                           |
| XOR $(y)$  | 2             | 4                           |
| $\|(z)$    | 5             | 6                           |
| Total cost | $7x + 2y + 5z$ | $5x + 4y + 6z$             |

Another work on PUF is demonstrated by [30], where an authenticated sensing procedure is presented to identify man-in-the middle attacks and robust against eavesdropping. The scheme presented by [31] uses a server-managed challenge/response pair lockdown protocol which was an improvement of previous similar approaches.

A close analysis of PUF-based authentication done by [32], points to a key viewpoint that many PUF-based authentication solutions proposed, though equipped with unique features and astounding functioning assertions, there is need for practical implementation and a measure of even simple performance figures. On the contrary, PUF has been proposed in PUF-enabled tag to prevent tag cloning [33].

## F. Cloud Computing Application Based Schemes

A unique approach on RFID authentication is proposed by [7], where a cloud based RFID authentication scheme aimed at providing tag location privacy is proposed. A performance analysis of [6] and [7], clearly show that Zhang's protocol scales way better on the device level, which is one of the focus for lightweight solutions, to reduce as much computation as necessary on the device level. Since there was a proposal to use a cloud server, we strongly feel that could have been maximally be used to reduce the computation cost at the device level on [7] 's protocol (Table 7).

**Table 7.** Cost analysis of Karthi et al.'s protocol [7]

|            | Device (Tag) | Tag reader | Cloud server |
|------------|--------------|------------|--------------|
| Hash $(x)$ | 2            | 3          | 0            |
| XOR $(y)$  | 6            | 6          | 0            |
| $\|(z)$    | 16           | 22         | 4            |
| Total cost | $2x + 6y + 16z$ | $3x + 6y + 22z$ | $4z$ |

Three interrelated lightweight authentication schemes are Shen et al. [34], Yang et al.'s [35] ID-based user authentication scheme for cloud computing and Yang et al.'s [36] user authentication scheme on multi-server environments for cloud computing. These schemes are related in that Shen et al.'s [34] protocol is an improvement of Yang et al.'s [35, 36] protocols and they are all applied in the cloud environment setup (Table 8).

**Table 8.** Cost analysis of Yang et al. [35, 36] and Shen et al. [34]' protocols. Key: A - user side B - server side

|            | Yang et al. [35] | | Yang et al. [36] | | Shen et al. [34] | |
|------------|------|------|------|------|------|------|
|            | A    | B    | A    | B    | A    | B    |
| Hash $(x)$ | 4    | 4    | 2    | 2    | 1    | 1    |
| XOR $(y)$  | 6    | 6    | 4    | 4    | 1    | 1    |
| $\|(z)$    | 4    | 4    | 6    | 6    | 1    | 1    |
| Total cost | $4x + 6y + 4z$ | $4x + 6y + 4z$ | $2x + 4y + 6z$ | $2x + 4y + 6z$ | $x + y + z$ | $x + y + z$ |

## G. Three-Factor Authentication Schemes

To wrap up this section, now focus on three-factor authentication schemes. The BISC authentication algorithm uses three-factor authentication when performing identity confirming credentials from three varying authentication factors – (knowledge, possession and inherent) categories [37]. In the sense of BISC the three-factor authentication combines biometrics information with colour and smart card to provide security-enhanced user authentication [37]. The three-factor authenticated scheme proposed by Amin et al. [38], for IoT networks was further improved by [39] and [40] addressing some of the identified weaknesses such as 'smart card loss attack' user identity and password guessing attacks. Our costing analysis of the three protocols as reflected in Table 9, indicate varying improvements on the overall protocol costs.

**Table 9.** Cost analysis of Amin et al. (A) [38], Arasteh et al. (B) [39] and Jiang et al. (C) [40] protocols

| | Ui (user) | | | Gateway (GWN) | | | Sensor node (Si) | | |
|---|---|---|---|---|---|---|---|---|---|
| | A | B | C | A | B | C | A | B | C |
| Hash (x) | 12 | 5 | 8 | 15 | 8 | 12 | 5 | 5 | 5 |
| XOR (y) | 8 | 5 | 6 | 7 | 7 | 5 | 3 | 2 | 3 |
| ‖(z) | 20 | 13 | 17 | 31 | 20 | 29 | 14 | 4 | 16 |
| Total cost | $12x + 8y + 20z$ | $5x + 5y + 13z$ | $8x + 6y + 17z$ | $15x + 7y + 31z$ | $8x + 7y + 20z$ | $12x + 5y + 29z$ | $5x + 3y + 14z$ | $5x + 2y + 4z$ | $5x + 3y + 16z$ |

## 4.2 Lightweight IoT Authentication for Smart Home Applications

With homes becoming smarter and more complex as well as technologically dependent, the call for robust and less to no human mediation reliant security solutions, are now critical as summed up by [41]. The use of two-phase authentication is popular among many smart home solutions for security designs [42–44]. A context-aware authentication framework for smart homes, that utilize contextual information such as the user's location, profile, calendar, request time and access behaviour patterns to enable access to home devices is presented by [45], which does not require additional user intervention. Pairing-based cryptography was advanced by [8] for ensuring bootstrapping security for Home Area Networks (HAN) wireless devices based on IBC. We performed a costing of [41], as summarised in Table 10, and there is an indication of the need for more optimisation to cater for seriously constrained devices in the smart home.

**Table 10.** Performance analysis of Linatti et al.'s protocol [41]

| | Device | Home gateway (HG) |
|---|---|---|
| Hash (x) | 8 | 11 |
| XOR (y) | 7 | 8 |
| ‖ (z) | 12 | 13 |
| Total cost | $8x + 7y + 12z$ | $11x + 8y + 13z$ |

Enhanced Secure Device Authentication (ESDA) scheme for HAN in smart grids is also presented by [46]. The Secure Intuitive and Low Cost Device Authentication (SILDA) mechanism for HANs was resilient against insider incidents, man-in-the-middle and impersonation attacks [46]. The SILDA has its problems surfacing in the management of symmetric keys to make the authentication procedure complex as during the process of establishing a secure communication channel, there is room to launch some malicious attacks by the attacker such as replay and unknown key sharing attacks [46].

'Near Field Communication (NFC) tag, secured password system and fingerprint authentication' are some of the highlighted options for authentication as proposed by [47], a six layered smart Home Security System (HSS). A secure lightweight authentication scheme was proposed by [48], aimed at tag based services in NFC, effectively prevented such attacks as DoS, phishing, spoofing and data modification.

In the proposed solution by [42], an Authentication, Access Control, Assurance (AAA) - based mechanism which uses the RADIUS protocol [49], is presented. The focus of [42]'s solution was on the isolation of such functions as management, forwarding, control and routing away from the actual operations for example, access points and routers. As a solution, the REST-based scheme which was externally hosted on the cloud platform ran a resource graph as a replica of the home network, is presented by [42]. For authentication purposes, contained in each home is the RADIUS server whose sole responsibility is to authenticate local users against given identifications for example passwords for having access to home networks [42]. Other key attributes taken into account by the architecture are roles and time to ensure adequate authentication validation [42].

As observed by [50], the use of network-level solutions has been supported by many researchers, on the premise that, they can be key in detecting possible attacks which subsequently help in the prevention of possible attacks towards IoT devices in smart home setups. In their proposed solution, [50] did a comparison of flow-based versus packet based towards an analysis of techniques for network-level monitoring solutions in IoT. They found out that flow-based monitoring has the potential to offer more security benefits especially towards packet-based monitoring, but at relatively low processing costs.

As suggested by [9] DAoT functions by utilizing feedback control scheme as a way of dynamically selecting an energy-efficient authentication policy. With DAoT, focus is on the device identification for accessing the network, hence more efficient and cost-effective [9]. The authentication of IoT devices as presented in this scheme, is possible through device ID verification by the target device, which is considered to be secure [9].

In the work of [51], they looked at a lightweight solution to secure and preserve user anonymity through roaming services in global mobility networking primitives, one-way hash functions and XOR operations were made environments. To ensure that their solution best suit mobile devices, which were battery powered, cryptographic use of. Table 11 is the summary of the costing for the protocol.

**Table 11.** Performance analysis of Gope et al.'s protocol [51]

|              | Device (smart card) | Server (home agent) |
| ------------ | ------------------- | ------------------- |
| Hash $(x)$   | 9                   | 11                  |
| XOR $(y)$    | 8                   | 9                   |
| $\|(z)$      | 15                  | 17                  |
| Total cost   | $9x + 8y + 15z$     | $11x + 9y + 17z$    |

An android application requiring two factor authentication is presented by [52], which makes use of biometric security features such as facial recognition and a personalized five digit pin code, gives control of access to the application. This clearly shows some of the similarities as already discussed under Sect. A.

# 5 Comparison of IoT Authentication Schemes Based on Costing

In this section, the various selected lightweight solutions are compared on the basic architectural attributes of hash functions (x), XOR (y) and concatenation (z). Based on the comparison given in Table 12, our recommendation is that, the possible authentication techniques to adopt for smart home applications are those that do not have high cost but at the same time, they need to satisfy the fundamental security solution requirements. The basis for choosing a typical scheme to apply in a smart home environment will be the consideration of the device features and the computational capabilities. Most of the IoT devices and sensors finding themselves in smart home environments are typically constrained in terms of storage space, computational capacity and memory size.

The costing comparison represented in Table 12, was mainly done considering the device level authentication phase. The reason for considering the device level was mainly on the basis that, it is the constrained element in the whole IoT setup for smart home applications.

**Table 12.** Device level costing comparison of various protocols

| Hash (x) | 3 | 2 | 4 | 2 | 3 | 12 | 7 | 5 | 5 | 5 | 8 | 9 | 2 | 1 | 4 |
|---|---|---|---|---|---|---|---|---|---|---|---|---|---|---|---|
| XoR(y) | 3 | 6 | 5 | 3 | 1 | 6 | 2 | 2 | 3 | 3 | 7 | 8 | 4 | 1 | 6 |
| ‖(z) | 2 | 16 | 8 | 1 | 3 | 13 | 5 | 4 | 14 | 16 | 12 | 15 | 6 | 1 | 4 |
| Protocols | Zhang[25] | Karthi et al[7] | Janbabaei et al[17] | Khemissa et al[24] | Huang et al[20] | Gope et al[18] | Hossain et al[28] | Arasteh et al[39] | Amin et al[39] | Jiang et al[40] | Linatti et al[41] | Gope et al[51] | Yang et al[35] | Shen et al[34] | Yang et al[36] |

What is out of the scope of this paper, but also critical to consider when looking at comparison of authentication architectures, which we strongly believe will bring an in-depth dimension to the classification of the various authentication techniques is what was covered by [53]. The classification done by [53] depicts two distinct approaches, firstly according to how the authentication process is performed, which they classified into centralized and distributed, which was tallied against hierarchical and flat based. Secondly, they performed a classification according to the characteristics of the authentication process and the attributes employed. The comparisons of the selected authentication techniques by [53] based on the evaluation model and their resistance to some identified security attacks, brings a comprehensive approach towards evaluation and subsequently selecting the best features to incorporate when designing an authentication architecture.

# 6 Recommendations for Smart Home Solutions

To guide the choice of solutions, for smart homes, from the comparisons done in Table 12, it will be ideal to consider all the dimensions of the authentication protocol to be advanced from functional specifications to their resilience towards some known attacks as well as their resource requirements.

It will be important to consider the identity of the objects for a holistic authentication solution. Uniquely identifying the objects or things in IoT will help, but this aspect is out of the scope of this paper. We strongly believe digital signatures will play an important role in this regard and introducing agent based trusted solutions would enhance the authentication solutions to be advanced to IoT platforms especially in smart homes.

From the comparison done in Table 12, we picked Huang et al. [20], Khemissa et al. [24] and Shen et al.'s [34] protocols as probable best options based on their costing values. We did further comparisons as depicted in Table 13, of the three based on the threats they address. This comparison was focused on the threat landscape highlighted in Sect. 2.

**Table 13.** Device level costing comparison of various protocols

| | Dictionary attack | Man-in-the-middle attack | Replay attack | Modification attack | Impersonation attack | DoS attack | Forward security |
|---|---|---|---|---|---|---|---|
| *Khemissa et al*[24] | ✔ | ✔ | ✔ | ✔ | ✔ | ✔ | |
| *Huang et al*[20] | ✔ | ✔ | ✔ | ✔ | | | |
| *Shen et al*[34] | ✔ | ✔ | ✔ | ✔ | ✔ | | ✔ |
| *Threats addressed* | | | | | | | |

It is imperative to note that addressing all the threats using one solution may not be practical, especially with the backdrop of lightweight requirements. We may conclude based on this analysis that Shen et al. [34] can suitably be adopted for solutions in smart home applications.

# 7   Conclusion

Outlined in this paper was coverage of the different authentication architectures that can be found in the IoT domain, this is by no way an exhaustive list of the various approaches being developed and implemented as this area is receiving wide attention from various angles. A relook at existing authentication protocols will help in improving on newer designs and addressing some of the shortfalls of similar and previous versions. As security remains an evolving discipline, rigid approaches and standardizations for measuring some of the solutions on the ground may not be feasible, henceforth, it will be ideal to have an outline of fundamental features to be incorporated in typical solutions.

As the focus of the paper was to identify the best lightweight authentication approaches for smart homes, it will be ideal to consider a number of key aspects when selecting a solution to advance towards design of authentication techniques for smart homes. There are crosscutting dynamics in the various authentication approaches already in use and borrowing the best features from one solution and combining with the other will surely give a recipe for a secure solution.

This paper employed costing of probable authentication architectures for consideration hence helping in the decision of selecting a less cost effective solution to propose for lightweight applications.

**Acknowledgments.** The support from the Digital Forensics and Information security research cluster, the Faculty of Computing and Informatics and the NUST community's support are highly appreciated for the progress of this research work.

# References

1. Witkovski, A., Santin, A., Abreu, V., Marynowski, J.: An IdM and key-based authentication method for providing single sign-on in IoT. In: 2015 IEEE Global Communications Conference, GLOBECOM 2015, IdM (2015)
2. Arafin, M.T., Gao, M., Qu, G.: VOLtA: voltage over-scaling based lightweight authentication for IoT applications. In: Proceeding Asia South Pacific Design Automation Conference, ASP-DAC, pp. 336–341 (2017)
3. Dolev, D., Yao, A.: On the security of public key protocols. IEEE Trans. Inf. Theory **29**(2), 198–208 (1983)
4. Ray, B.R., Chowdhury, M.U., Abawajy, J.H.: A multi-protocol security framework to support internet of things. In: Deng, R., Weng, J., Ren, K., Yegneswaran, V. (eds.) SecureComm 2016. LNICST, vol. 198, pp. 257–270. Springer, Cham (2017). https://doi.org/10.1007/978-3-319-59608-2_14
5. Wang, F., Xu, Y., Zhang, H., Zhang, Y., Zhu, L.: 2FLIP: a two-factor lightweight privacy-preserving authentication scheme for VANET. IEEE Trans. Veh. Technol. **65**(2), 896–911 (2016)
6. Zhang, R.: An enhanced lightweight authentication protocol for low-cost RFID systems. In: Proceeding 2016 IEEE International Conference on Electronic Information and Communication Technology, ICEICT 2016, ICEICT, pp. 29–33 (2017)

7. Karthi M., Harris, P.: A realistic lightweight authentication protocol for securing cloud based RFID system Surekha, pp. 168–171 (2016)
8. Jacobsen, R.H., Mikkelsen, S.A., Rasmussen, N.H.: Towards the use of pairing-based cryptography for resource-constrained home area networks. In: Proceeding—18th Euromicro Conference Digital System Design, DSD 2015, pp. 233–240 (2015)
9. Kim, Y.P., Yoo, S., Yoo, C.: DAoT: dynamic and energy-aware authentication for smart home appliances in Internet of Things. In: 2015 IEEE International Conference on Consumer Electronics, ICCE 2015 (2015)
10. Saied, Y.B., Olivereau, A., Zeghlache, D., Laurent, M.: Lightweight collaborative key establishment scheme for the internet of things. Comput. Netw. **64**, 273–295 (2014)
11. Denning, T., Kohno, T., Levy, H.M.: Computer security and the modern home. Commun. ACM **56**(1), 94 (2013)
12. Kothmayr, T., Schmitt, C., Hu, W., Brünig, M., Carle, G.: DTLS based security and two-way authentication for the internet of things. Ad Hoc Netw. **11**(8), 2710–2723 (2013)
13. Li, X., Liu, H., Wei, F., Ma, J., Yang, W.: A lightweight anonymous authentication protocol using k-pseudonym set in wireless networks. In: 2015 IEEE Global Communications Conference, GLOBECOM 2015 (2015)
14. Rahman, M., Sampangi, R.V., Sampalli, S.: Lightweight protocol for anonymity and mutual authentication in RFID systems. In: 2015 12th Annual IEEE Consumer Communications and Networking Conference, CCNC 2015, pp. 910–915 (2015)
15. Ray, B.R.R., Abawajy, J., Chowdhury, M., Alelaiwi, A.: Universal and secure object ownership transfer protocol for the internet of things. Future Gener. Comput. Syst. **78**, 838–849 (2018)
16. Abdallah, A., Shen, X.: Lightweight authentication and privacy-preserving scheme for V2G connections. IEEE Trans. Veh. Technol. **66**(3), 2615–2629 (2017)
17. Janbabaei, S., Gharaee, H., Mohammadzadeh, N.: Lightweight, anonymous and mutual authentication in IoT infrastructure. In: 2016 8th International Symposium on Telecommunications, IST 2016, pp. 162–166 (2017)
18. Gope, P., Hwang, T.: Authentication protocol for securing real-time application data access in wireless sensor networks. IEEE Trans. Ind. Electron. **63**(11), 7124–7132 (2016)
19. Abdullaziz, O.I., Chen, Y.J., Wang, L.-C.: Lightweight authentication mechanism for software defined network using information hiding. In: 2016 IEEE Global Communications Conference, GLOBECOM 2016—Proceeding, pp. 0–5 (2016)
20. Huang, J.-J., Juang, W.-S., Fan, C.-I., Tseng, Y.-F., Kikuchi, H.: Lightweight authentication scheme with dynamic group members in IoT environments. In: Proceedings of the 13th International Conference on Mobile and Ubiquitous Systems: Computing Networking and Services—MOBIQUITOUS 2016 (2016)
21. Shen, C., Li, H., Sahin, G., Choi, H.A.: Low-complexity scalable authentication algorithm with imperfect shared keys for internet of things. In: 2016 IEEE International Conference on Communications Workshops, ICC 2016, pp. 116–121 (2016)
22. Yang, M.L., Narayanan, A., Parry, D., Wang, X.: A lightweight authentication scheme for transport system farecards. 2016 IEEE International Conference on RFID Technology and Applications, RFID-TA 2016, pp. 150–155 (2016)
23. Sharaf-Dabbagh, Y., Saad, W.: On the authentication of devices in the Internet of things. In: WoWMoM 2016—17th International Symposium on A World of Wireless, Mobile and Multimedia Networks, pp. 1–3 (2016)
24. Khemissa, H., Tandjaoui, D.: A novel lightweight authentication scheme for heterogeneous wireless sensor networks in the context of internet of things. In: 2016 Wireless Telecommunications Symposium (WTS), pp. 1–6 (2016)

25. Zhang, N., Wu, X., Yang, C., Shen, Y., Cheng, Y.: A lightweight authentication and authorization solution based on Kerberos. In: Proceedings of 2016 IEEE Advanced Information Management, Communicates, Electronic and Automation Control Conference, IMCEC 2016, pp. 742–746 (2017)

26. Han, J.: Chaining the secret: lightweight authentication for security in pervasive computing. In: 2016 International Conference on Pervasive Computing and Communication Workshops, PerCom Work, pp. 0–2 (2016)

27. Liu, Y., Liu, L., Zhou, Y., Hu, S.: Leveraging carbon nanotube technologies in developing physically unclonable function for cyber-physical system authentication. In: Proceeding—IEEE INFOCOM, September 2016, pp. 176–180 (2016)

28. Hossain, M., Noor, S., Hasan, R.: HSC-IoT: a hardware and software co-verification based authentication scheme for internet of things. In: Proceeding—5th IEEE International Conference on Mobile Cloud Computing, Services, and Engineering, MobileCloud 2017, pp. 109–116 (2017)

29. Ray, B.R., Chowdhury, M.U., Abawajy, J.H.: Secure object tracking protocol for the internet of things. IEEE Internet Things J. 3(4), 544–553 (2016)

30. Gao, Y., Ma, H., Abbott, D., Al-Sarawi, S.F.: PUF sensor: exploiting PUF unreliability for secure wireless sensing. IEEE Trans. Circ. Syst. I: Reg. Pap. 1–12 (2017)

31. Yu, M.-D.M., et al.: A lockdown technique to prevent machine. IEEE Trans. Multi-Scale Comput. Syst. 2(3), 146–159 (2016)

32. Schaumont, P., Moriyama, D., Gulcan, E., Aysu, A.: Compact and low-power ASIP design for lightweight PUF-based authentication protocols. IET Inf. Secur. 10(5), 232–241 (2016)

33. Li, G., Xu, X., Li, Q.: LADP: a lightweight authentication and delegation protocol for RFID tags. In: International Conference on Ubiquitous and Future Networks, ICUFN, August 2015, pp. 860–865 (2015)

34. Shen, J., Liu, D., Chang, S., Shen, J., He, D.: A lightweight mutual authentication scheme for user and server in cloud. In: Proceeding—2015 1st International Conference on Computational Intelligence Theory, Systems and Applications, CCITSA 2015, pp. 183–186 (2016)

35. Yang, J.H., Lin, P.Y.: An ID-based user authentication scheme for cloud computing. In: 2014 Tenth International Conference on Intelligent Information Hiding and Multimedia Signal Processing, pp. 98–101 (2014)

36. Yang, J.-H., Chang, Y.-F., Huang, C.-C.: A user authentication scheme on multi-server environments for cloud computing. In: ICICS 2013—Conference 9th International Conference on Information, Communications & Signal Processing, pp. 1–4 (2013)

37. Shaju, S.: BISC authentication algorithm : an efficient new authentication algorithm using three factor authentication for mobile banking (2016)

38. Amin, R., et al.: Design of an anonymity-preserving three-factor authenticated key exchange protocol for wireless sensor networks. Comput. Netw. 101, 42–62 (2016)

39. Arasteh, S., Aghili, S.F., Mala, H.: A new lightweight authentication and key agreement protocol for Internet of Things. In: 2016 13th International Iranian Society of Cryptology Conference on Information Security and Cryptology, pp. 52–59 (2016)

40. Jiang, Q.I., Zeadally, S., He, D.: Lightweight three-factor authentication and key agreement protocol for internet-integrated wireless sensor networks, vol. 5 (2017)

41. Iinatti, J., Member, S., Ha, P.H.: Smart home environments. IEEE Trans. Inf. Forensics Secur. 12(4), 968–979 (2017)

42. Silverajan, B., Luoma, J.P., Vajaranta, M., Itapuro, R.: Collaborative cloud-based management of home networks. In: Proceedings 2015 IFIP/IEEE International Symposium on Integrated Network Management, IM 2015, pp. 786–789 (2015)

43. Margulies, J.: Garage door openers: an internet of things case study. IEEE Secur. Priv. **13**(4), 80–83 (2015)
44. Daramas, A., Pattarakitsophon, S., Eiumtrakul, K., Tantidham, T., Tamkittikhun, N.: HIVE: home automation system for intrusion detection. In: Proceeding 2016 5th ICT International Student Project Conference, ICT-ISPC 2016, pp. 101–104 (2016)
45. Ashibani, Y., Kauling, D., Mahmoud, Q.H.: A context-aware authentication framework for smart homes (2017)
46. Shen, T.: Home area networks in smart grids, pp. 2444–2447 (2016)
47. Morsalin, S., Islam, A.M. J., Rahat, G.R., Pidim, S.R.H., Rahman, A., Siddiqe, M.A.B.: Machine-to-machine communication based smart home security system by NFC, fingerprint, and PIR sensor with mobile android application. In: 2016 3rd International Conference on Electrical Engineering and Information Communication Technology, iCEEiCT 2016 (2017)
48. Baek, J., Youm, H.Y.: Secure and lightweight authentication protocol for NFC tag based services. In: Proceeding—2015 10th Asia Joint Conference on Information Security, pp. 63–68 (2015)
49. Rigney, C., Willens, S., Rubens, A., Simpson, W.: RFC 2687 - remote authentication dial in user service (RADIUS). J. Chem. Inf. Model. **53**(9), 1689–1699 (2013)
50. Sivanathan, A., Sherratt, D., Gharakheili, H.H., Sivaraman, V., Vishwanath, A.: Low-cost flow-based security solutions for smart-home IoT devices. In: 2016 IEEE International Conference on Advanced Networks and Telecommunications Systems, ANTS 2016 (2017)
51. Gope, P., Hwang, T.: Lightweight and energy-efficient mutual authentication and key agreement scheme with user anonymity for secure communication in global mobility networks. IEEE Syst. J. **10**(4), 1370–1379 (2016)
52. Pienaar, J.P., Fisher, R.M., Hancke, G.P.: Smartphone: the key to your connected smart home. In: Proceeding - 2015 IEEE International Conference on Industrial Informatics, INDIN 2015, pp. 999–1004 (2015)
53. Saadeh, M., Sleit, A., Qatawneh, M., Almobaideen, W.: Authentication techniques for the internet of things: a survey. In: Proceeding—2016 Cybersecurity Cyberforensics Conference, CCC 2016, pp. 28–34 (2016)

# A Survey of Big Data Security Solutions in Healthcare

Musfira Siddique[1], Muhammad Ayzed Mirza[1], Mudassar Ahmad[1(✉)],
Junaid Chaudhry[2], and Rafiqul Islam[3]

[1] Department of Computer Science, National Textile University, Faisalabad, Pakistan
musfirasiddique@ymail.com, ayzed@ntu.edu.pk, mudassar.utm@gmail.com
[2] Cyber Security Faculty, Cyber Intelligence and Security Department College of
Security and Intelligence, Embry-Riddle Aeronautical University Prescott, Prescott,
AZ, USA
chaudhrj@erau.edu
[3] School of Computing and Mathematics, Charles Sturt University, Bathurst, NSW
2795, Australia
mislam@csu.edu.au

**Abstract.** Today data is a strategic asset and organizational goal is
to maximize the value of their information. The concept of big data is
now treated from different points of view covering its implications in
many fields remarkably including Healthcare. Healthcare data is progressively being digitized and the Healthcare era is expansively using
new machineries. Thus the medical data is increasing day by day has
reached a momentous size all over the world. Although this data is being
addressed as the basic to offer treasured insights and sinking cost, the
security and privacy issues are so irresistible that medical industry is not
capable to take full benefit of it. Privacy of Healthcare is a significant
feature overseen by medical acts thus, the data must be secured from
dwindling into the wrong hands or from being hacked. Due to the growing threats of loss and outflows from personal data and augmented acceptance of cloud technologies it is important to secure current Healthcare
big data domain. This paper aims to present the state-of-the-art security
and privacy issues in big data as pragmatic to Healthcare industry and
discuss some available data privacy, data security, users' access control
mechanisms and approaches.

**Keywords:** Big data · Cloud · Healthcare · Security · Analytics

## 1 Introduction

Big data is data sets that are so voluminous and complex that cannot be analyzed with traditional computing techniques. Big data philosophy encompasses
unstructured, semi-structured and structured data, however the core concentration is on unstructured data [1]. Data that is unstructured or time sensitive
or simply very large cannot be handled by relational database engines. Quite

© ICST Institute for Computer Sciences, Social Informatics and Telecommunications Engineering 2018
R. Beyah et al. (Eds.): SecureComm 2018, LNICST 255, pp. 391–406, 2018.
https://doi.org/10.1007/978-3-030-01704-0_21

simply, big data reflects the changing world we live in. The more the variations are taken and documented as data as the more things alternate. Take Facebook as an example, Facebook handles almost 40 billion photos from its user base it also handles audio and video data, per second. There are many Twitter tweets handled per second and also YouTube data is generating enormously. Other examples are Cloud and web data, social media data, time and location data, scientific instruments and sensors data. Data has grown speedily, as of 2012, every day 2.5 exabytes ($2.5 \times 1018$) of data are generated. By 2025, International Data Corporation (IDC) predicts there will be 163 zettabytes of data. Big data is often characterized by its three V's. The extreme volume of data, the wide variety of data types and the velocity at which the data must be processed [2]. And some even extend this to five Vs and currently its extended to ten Vs shown in Fig. 1 and defined as follows [3–8]:

## 1.1   V's of Big Data

- **Volume:** Volume is the amount of data. While volume specifies more data, the data is generated from web, sensors, social media etc. It refers to the amount of data generated after every second and classify as records, tables and files.
- **Velocity:** Velocity is the fast rate at which data is received and possibly proceeded. It is the in and out flow of data, the data upload and download time and data at motion. It includes Batch velocity, near time data, Real time Data and Social media data.
- **Variety:** Variety is the many forms of data. Like Structured, Unstructured, semi-structured and multi-structure data types. Data such as text, audio, and video need supplementary processing to both originate denotation and the subsidiary metadata.
- **Variability:** In bigdata's context, variability refers to different things. One is inconsistencies/outliers in data. It is also variable due to multitude dimensions of variables resulting from various data sources and dissimilar data types. It also refers to variable frequency of bigdata to be loaded into database.
- **Veracity:** Veracity refers to the confidence to trust in data. This one is the unfortunate part of bigdata. As most of the other characteristics are in increasing trend but it drops. It refers more to the provenance or reliability of the data source, its context, and how meaningful it is to the analysis based on it. It helps us to determine the risk associated with the analysis or decision made based on a particular dataset.
- **Validity:** Much like veracity, validity refers to how correct and valid/accurate data is to be used for the task. Scientist's approximately 60% of time is consumed to refine the data for what they conduct analysis. The analytical advantage from bigdata is only as good as its primary data. There is a need to have a good data governance practices to ensure consistent data class and metadata.
- **Vulnerability:** Everybody is cautious regarding data security. Bigdata has also got new security concerns. If bigdata is breached it would be a colossal

data breach. E.g. AshleyMedison hack in 2015 and in May 2016, 167 million LinkedIn profiles and 360 million user passwords of MySpace hack had been reported in the past. So it is a question mark against bigdata vulnerability.

– *Volatility:* Data volatility belongs to the data life, how old data should have to be kept before it is considered as irrelevant. Or can say the data-age when data is not useful. Due to huge amount of data in bigdata data volatility is considered as an important and considerable point. Otherwise organizations don't bother to keep data for the life time archives and in live databases without hindering the performance. Rules for data availability, need and clear relationship of data with business process are to be defined for rapid and cost-effective retrieval of information. Bigdata magnifies the complexity the storage cost and retrieval process that's why data volatility is needed.

– *Visualization:* It includes the data visualization tools and techniques. Developing a meaningful visualization from the huge multitude variables and their complex relationships of big data. It's not an easy task to visualize that huge and complex data. The traditional ways of graphing and plotting are not sufficient, so different ways of representing data is needed. It may include data clustering, tree maps, sunbursts, parallel coordinates, circular network diagrams, or cone trees.

– *Value:* The most important of all is value, is the data into money it denotes the scientific value attributed to this data.

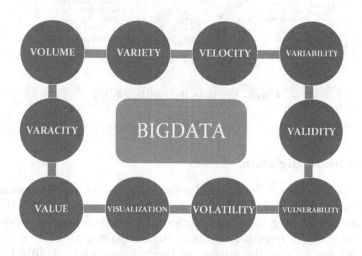

**Fig. 1.** Vs of big data

The importance of big data doesn't revolve around how much data you have, however what you do with it. You can take data from any source and it to find answers that enable cost reductions, time reductions, new product development and optimized offerings, and smart decision making. Data in its raw form has no value. Data needs to be processed in order to be of valuable. Processing information like this illustrates why big data has become so important. Unstructured data needs enormous storage and processing, the Internet is increasing the raw data day by day that needs to be processed [9].

There are many major issues related to big data. Big data analysis is one of them, which is the process to uncover hidden patterns and unknown correlations for actual decision making and better strategic moves. Others are big data Security issues, big data management, Data Visualization, Data integration, Transition of big data to the cloud, new ways and technologies to protect big data, Mining Big data, Processing issues, Gaining maximum value from big data and predictive analytics. Some hot topics related to big data are Real time big data analytics, IOT and Big data, big data security, big data in health care and many more [10,11].

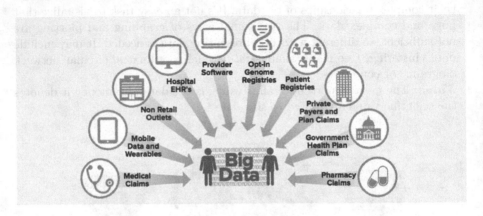

Fig. 2. Big data in Healthcare [12]

## 1.2   Healthcare Big Data

Generally the Healthcare data includes the patient data and elementary information, clinical data and doctors' data. However now a days the Healthcare era is expansively using new machineries such as apprehending devices, sensors, electronic health records and mobile computing etc. Thus the medical data is increasing day by day the volume of Healthcare data is rapidly increasing. Healthcare data is generating from internal and external sources like biometric data, genetics, blood pressure, electronic medical records, remote sensors data and social media data. All the electronic Healthcare data, patient medical records, surgeries results, medical images data, sensors data and all other medical related data is added into Healthcare database and increasing its size to a great extent [13]. This Healthcare data requires better real time analysis for meaningful information.

Big data analytics has many benefits in Healthcare as it embeds better decision making and reduce cost, it gives benefits to doctors and Healthcare providers, perceiving dispersal diseases earlier, fraud detection, and evidence based medicine and many more. Figure 2 reflects the bigdata involvement in healtcare system [12].

Healthcare data includes many challenges like Comfort of understanding unstructured data and its use, mining hypothetically valuable information from data in order to minimize faults, scalability, Reduction of cost in scrutinising genomics data and mixing this type of data with other information is of great importance, by using many sensors recording patients' interactive data is of great complexity. Above all the vital challenge in perspective of Healthcare domain is the Security issue in Healthcare systems.

Security of the Healthcare Information System is the key concern from the day one. Individual's information must be protected from loss and from hackers attack by using different physical security mechanism and techniques like encryption, authentication, cryptographic algorithms etc. The main root of the security issue is the use of Cloud in Healthcare systems as all the data storage is on cloud and it provides different storage and processing facilities. Hence we should tackle the security problem of Healthcare systems.

## 2   State-of-the-Art

Nowadays the backbone to the current storage devices is big data and Cloud Computing. As E-Health has grown rapidly and its databases contains voluminous data. The security and privacy preservation is the key concern in this respect. Cloud computing security is very important. The quality of Healthcare should be increased by its security. They proposed a secure e-health framework using hadoop Map reduce data that provides security for Healthcare. Proposed a new framework, Multi Authority Attribute based Encryption (MA-ABE) for securely transferred the PHI to health services after security checks. The encryption technique, Cipher Policy Attribute Based (CP-ABE) was used in it. The research concentrations are with safeguarding health care from outbreaks by illegal users and also detects the intimidations in health care. Accuracy, efficiency and consistency are the performance parameters in the proposed solution. To store the patient medical information securely any organization can use this application as it used the best encryption technique. Also the efficiency of this system is saleable as compared to existing system [14].

The modern Health Information Technology (HIT) electronically preserve and transfer data globally in seconds and offers quality of service to Healthcare. Thus by given the Electronic Medical Records (EMR) to every service provider the main problem with the modern EMRs is that they are potentially centralized. Patients' health information reclamation is a challenge. The aptitude to generally access all patient Healthcare information in an appropriate fashion is of highest importance. Health information must be available and obtain- able to

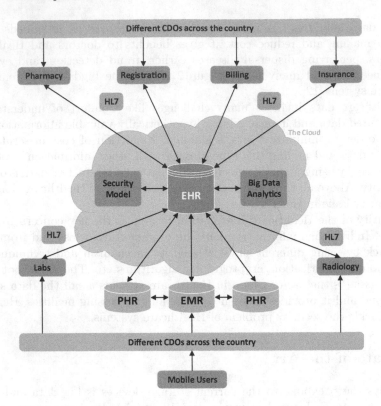

**Fig. 3.** A framework for secure Healthcare system [15]

everyone tangled in the system. Thus, in order to deliver high-quality Health-care to the patients they serve a high level of data integration, and sharing among different Healthcare specialists and organizations is essential. Among different Healthcare providers, practitioners and patients the proposed framework offers high level of integration, availability and sharing of data between them. The detailed framework is shown in Fig. 3. Mobile Cloud permits rapid Internet access and endowment of EHRs from everyplace and at any time by altered platforms. The proposed framework employs big data analytics to find useful insights that help specialists proceeds acute decisions in the right time. It applies a set of security constraints and access control that guarantee integrity, confidentiality, and privacy of medical information [15].

Gunamalai et al. proposed a method of security and privacy of Personal Medical Records and Digital Imaging and Communication in Medicine (DICOM) images in the Cloud environment. DICOM discourses dissemination and inspecting medical images and also is a typical rule for medical imaging. The penalty area is to enable numerous medical centers to admittance individuals' data for treatment in a protected method. The structure untraceably implants remote patient data like name and exclusive ID in the medical images. Access Governor is done via two-way authentication. In Two way authentication firstly the user log on by entering correct id and password and secondly the user has to enter the key sent to him after login on his mobile with in a given time period. Thus in this way the user will be verified and get access to cloud data storage. By using Column based encryption Healthcare centres can encrypt their PMR and images to allow granule access. By using column based encryption the user who know the encrypted password can access the specific columns' data. Column Based Encryption (CBE) permits discerning division of data amongst medical centers [16].

Security of patient data is vital in cloud based big data cooperative structure where they offer a platform for sharing and exchanging information exist in different clouds for numerous errands. There is a proposed scheme which is a two phase security protocol that uses pairing based cryptography. Secret data is shared by computing a secret session key which is dynamically generated for every new data-exchange session by computing a pairing in elliptic curve. Hence each new session is no dependent on the previous one. It also gives security against man-in-the-middle attack. Response time, memory and availability are the performance parameters in the proposed solution [17].

Medical content security need is increasing by the extended use of Healthcare management systems. The authors proposed an authentication based access control mechanism for medical content DICOM. The confidentiality of the DICOM in public cloud is ensured by the Access control mechanism. It also provides the integrity of the user detail in Healthcare system [18].

As the EMR of patient need to be accessed by the Healthcare experts. For the ease of access the EMRs need to be stored at Healthcare cloud in big data storages. However the key concern with the Healthcare cloud is its security as the patients sensitive information needs to be secure because data stealing outbreaks are well-thought-out to be one of the vital security breaks Clouds Healthcare data. By using a decoy technique with fog computing facility they present a methodology to prevent patient MBD in Healthcare cloud. Decoy files retrieved at the start thus, as to make system secure by hiding the original file. It uses a double security technique by the encryption of genuine file to prevent system from attackers. Key generation time, accuracy and availability are the performance parameters in the proposed solution. As a result, the proposed methodology guarantees that the MBD of users are 100% protected and reduces the process [19].

Big data contains voluminous amount of data which is growing rapidly day by day. However the booming of big data also hinges on fully accepting and handling newly rising safety and confidentiality trials. The security and privacy preservation of big data is the key concern. New extracted information will be unpersuasive if data is not reliable, while if confidentiality is not well addressed, people may be disinclined to share their data. This have introduced an efficient and privacy-preserving cosine similarity computing protocol in response to the efficiency and privacy requirements of data mining in the big data era. Although have analyzed the privacy and efficiency challenges in general big data analytics to shed light on the privacy research in big data, significant research efforts should be further put into addressing unique privacy issues in some specific big data analytics. Encrypt/decrypt time, speed and de-identification are the performance parameters in the proposed solution [20,21].

The modern Health Information Technology (HIT) electronically preserve and transfer data globally in seconds and offers quality of service to Healthcare. Thus by given the EMR to every service provider the main problem with the modern EMRs is that they are potentially centralized. Patients' health information reclamation is a challenge. The aptitude to generally access all patient Healthcare information in an appropriate fashion is of highest importance. The first contribution of this research is the provision of an overall picture on big data and Healthcare data for non-expert readers. The other one is the adoption of a holistic view to build an organized Healthcare model for protecting patient data. The model provides high-level integration and sharing of EHRs. The suggested framework as shown in Fig. 4 applies a set of security constraints and access control that guarantee integrity, confidentiality and privacy for medical data [22].

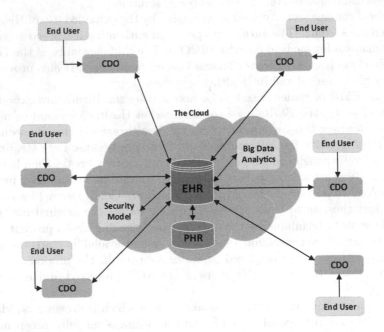

**Fig. 4.** A framework for distributed Health system [22]

Security is a key concern in Remote Patient Monitoring framework as there is a little evidence on this problem's solution. The authors proposed a new security framework for Patient Remote Monitoring devices which is a wide-ranging model. They projected NFC technology to tackle the problem of multi user device patient identification. Firstly a patient identifies using NFC no and take their

**Table 1.** Comparison of different security mechanism

| Sr. No | Author | Problem tackled | Security mechanism | Performance parameters |
|---|---|---|---|---|
| 1 | B. Prasanna et al. | Big data and Cloud security | CP-ABE scheme | Response time, accuracy |
| 2 | Ahmed E. Youssef | Mobile cloud security, | AES and RC4 encryption | Key generation time, response time, encrypt/decrypt time |
| 3 | Gunamalai et al. | Information security | Two way authentication and CBE | Tate pairing time, memory |
| 4 | Mehedi et al. | Big data and Cloud | Pairing based cryptography | Confidentiality, integrity |
| 5 | Subhasri et al. | Security | Authentication based access control mechanism | Response time, memory requirement, accuracy |
| 6 | Hadeal Abdul aziz et al. | Big data security in | Fog computing with pairing based cryptography | Key generation time, integrity, speed |
| 7 | Sathya et al. | Collaborative environment | Triple DES | Integrity, confidentiality, availability |
| 8 | Bikash Kanti Sarkar | DICOM content | AES and RC4 encryption | Authentication, availability |
| 9 | Brian Ondiege et al. | Security in cloud | NFC for identification | Authentication, availability |
| 10 | Chao YANG et al. | Big data and Cloud | triple encryption method | Encrypt/decrypt time, memory |
| 11 | Rui Zhang, Ling Liu | Big data Cloud security | Attribute-based Composite, encryption | Response time, memory requirement, accuracy |
| 12 | Ali Gholami and Erwin Laure | Cloud security | NFC for identification, DES etc | Integrity, confidentiality, availability |
| 13 | B. Vinoth Kumar et al. | Patient monitoring security (IOT and Cloud) | AES and DES encryption | Key generation time, memory used, availability |
| 14 | Weiwei LIN et al. | Data security WBANs | Multi biometric based key generation scheme | Confidentiality, integrity |
| 15 | Farrukh Aslam Khan et al. | Remote patient monitoring security | NFC for identification | Integrity, confidentiality, availability |

B.P reading. Then system checks if that patient exists and able to send its reading, thus it will continue its procedure. The also enable capability system which allows only registered devices to send their readings via secure communication protocol. They uses the performance parameters like accuracy, availability and memory used [23].

As Healthcare data is increasing rapidly and it need better storage, for this purpose cloud is used. However the security of the data in cloud is a threat. To address this problem the authors proposed a Novel Triple Encryption method. In the triple encryption scheme, HDFS files are encrypted by using the hybrid encryption based on DES and RSA, and the user's RSA private key is encrypted using IDEA. The triple encryption scheme is implemented and integrated in Hadoop-based cloud data storage. Encrypt/decrypt time, memory and availability are the performance parameters in the proposed solution. Results of experiment show that the triple encryption scheme is feasible, it meets the reading and writing characteristics of HDFS and can enhance the confidentiality of default HDFS [24]. Table 1 shows a summarized comparison of different security algorithms proposed by different researchers.

## 3   Big Data Security Solutions in Healthcare

The main security models discussed in this paper are related to big data Healthcare and cloud, big data and IOT in Healthcare and securing patient data in cloud and big data architectures.

### 3.1   Cloud and Big Data in Healthcare

Cloud computing is a shared pool of configurable computing resources. Now a days for handling of Healthcare data and Healthcare information classifications cloud computing in comprehensively used [13]. As Healthcare organizations has been moved to electronic platform today from where it gathers amply of data. The significant amount of data need to be stored and processed. Cloud computing is best suited for Healthcare domain. It provides many benefits as it makes data sharing easy and more handy for the user, it provides cost reduction operations. However with the electronic medical records there is a chance of data loss and other information loss. Cloud computing sideways with Big Data tools has Initiate use in Curative Imaging, clinic organization and Healthcare Information Systems, public health and individual's self-service applications. With the rising use of cloud computing tools in Healthcare it is authoritative that, security of Healthcare data in the cloud is a key concern that needs to be well-kept-up sideways with secure the cloud computing.

*Fog Computing Facility with Pairing-Based Cryptography*
Fog computing, is an evolving model that offers storing, dispensation, and communication amenities nearer to the end user. Providing data and tapping them on the upper hand of a network to be closer to the user are well-thought-out amongst the main tasks of fog computing. The proposed method as shown in Fig. 5 provide the user's multimedia data security by using fog computing. A well-organized tri-party genuine key covenant protocol has been proposed based on paring cryptography among the user, the DPG, and the OPG. This is an illusion technique as it provides the attacker a decoy gallery rather than the original one. As shown in figure when the user log on whether it is an attacker

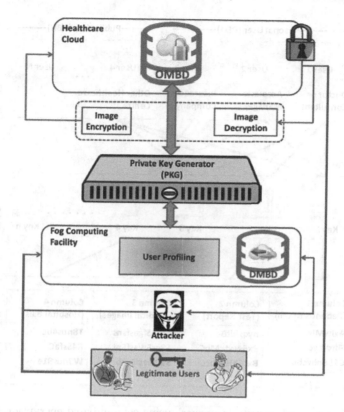

**Fig. 5.** Proposed security framework using fog computing facility [19]

or legitimate user it will be shown the DMBD which is a decoy gallery. Then the second step will be the verification of the legitimate user as he knows that DMBD is fake thus, he will access original OMBD by verifying himself. Thus in this way the original MBD will remain safe from hackers. The algorithms used are DMBD algorithm, Key exchange algorithm, user profiling algorithm and photo encryption and decryption algorithm [19].

### Two Way Authentication and Column Based Encryption
Authentication is a process of identifying the user who has stances the rights to access and modify data on cloud. In Two way authentication firstly the user log on by entering correct id and password and secondly the user has to enter the key sent to him after login on his mobile with in a given time period. Thus in this way the user will be verified and get access to cloud data storage. By using Column based encryption Healthcare centers can encrypt their PMR and images to allow granule access. By using column based encryption the user who know the encrypted password can access the specific columns' data. Hence it allows many Healthcare centers to access patients' data for treatment in a secure way. Figure 6 shows a scenario in which multiple centers can access multiple columns by using the secret key [16].

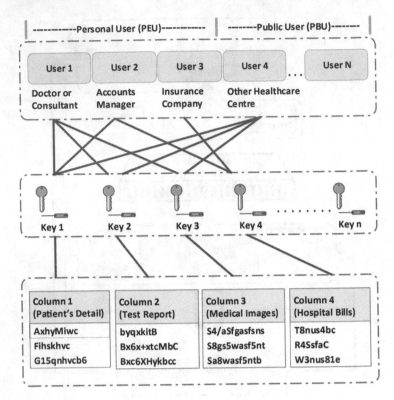

**Fig. 6.** Proposed security framework using column based encryption [16]

## 3.2  IOT and Big Data in Healthcare

To monitor the medical disorder of patient Wireless Body Area Networks or WBANs are used by using miniature sensor bulges entrenched to the human body. Wireless Sensor Network (WSN) is developed by these sensor bulges. From the human body the biological information is sent to a regulator device either devoted to the human body or in the 90 locality wirelessly. Then for more analysis the gathered data is sent to isolated servers or cloud of a hospital/Healthcare center. WBANs can be used for blood flow, ECG, pulse rate, blood pressure, body temperature etc. It is vigorous to guarantee precision and veracity of such Healthcare data [29–31]. Hereafter security and privacy of WBANs must be safeguarded. Security must be preserved for WBANs in the attached sensors to the body, isolated servers where WBAN data is pushed, communication medium.

*Multi Biometric Based Key Generation Process for Securing WBANs*
In patient monitoring the patients' data is gathered though the sensors attached to the patients' body and sent to the remote servers for further actions. Multi biometric scheme is used for securely generate the key. It is useful for secure inter sensor communication. Features are selected from ECG and EEG values and quantized hence divide in blocks and exchanged by applying key hashing. At

the receiving end the key generation algorithm is applied for extraction of information and then both the sensor nodes use this key for secure communication [23]. The flow of security framework is shown in Fig. 7. In patient monitoring the patients' data is gathered though the sensors attached to the patients' body and sent to the remote servers for further actions. Multi biometric scheme is used for securely generate the key. It is useful for secure inter sensor communication. Features are selected from ECG and EEG values and quantized hence divide in blocks and exchanged by applying key hashing. At the receiving end the key generation algorithm is applied for extraction of information and then both the sensor nodes use this key for secure communication. Then for more analysis the gathered data is sent to isolated servers or cloud of a hospital/Healthcare center. WBANs can be used for blood flow, ECG, pulse rate, blood pressure, body temperature etc. It is vigorous to guarantee precision and veracity of such Healthcare data. Hereafter security and privacy of WBANs must be safeguarded. Security must be preserved for WBANs in the attached sensors to the body, isolated servers where WBAN data medium.

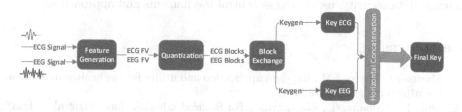

**Fig. 7.** Proposed security framework using multi biometric based key generation [23]

## 4  Discussion

In this paper, i have examined the security and privacy challenges in big data, by deliberating some existing mechanisms and techniques for achieving security and privacy in which Healthcare administrations are likely to be highly beneficial. The security challenges mainly include the security of patient data on cloud, the secure sharing of data in cloud collaborative environments, protect the patient medical records, sensors data security in remote patient monitoring systems, and information security. Many techniques were used to tackle these challenges like triple encryption, pairing based cryptography, CP-ABS mechanism, fog computing, two way authentication and Column based encryption and authentication based access control mechanism. From all of these Fog computing Technique with Pairing based Cryptography, two way authentication and CBE have shown better results. Future work may include to take one of these mechanism and apply it on some dataset to improve the security on cloud.

## 5    Conclusion

While Big Data technologies are improving day by day this also means that the volume of data along with the rate at which data is flowing into enterprises today is increasing. Healthcare data is progressively being digitized now a days the Healthcare era is expansively using new machineries such as apprehending devices, sensors, electronic health records and mobile computing etc. Thus the medical data is increasing day by day has reached a momentous size all over the world. Although this data is being addressed as the basic to offer treasured insights and sinking cost, the security and privacy issues are so irresistible that Medical industry is not capable to take full benefit of it. Privacy of Healthcare is a significant feature overseen by Medical Acts thus, the data must be secured from dwindling into the wrong hands or from being hacked. Due to the growing threats of loss and outflows from personal data and augmented acceptance of cloud technologies it is important to secure current Healthcare big data domain. This paper aims to present the state of- the-art security and privacy issues in big data as pragmatic to Healthcare industry and discuss some available data privacy, data security, users' access control mechanisms and approaches.

## References

1. Martınez Sesmero, J.M.: Big data application and utility for the healthcare system. FarmHosp **39**(2), 69–70 (2015)
2. Shin, D., Sahama, T., Gajanayake, R.: Secured e-health data retrieval in DaaS and big data. In: Proceedings of the 2013 IEEE 15th International Conference on e-Health Networking, Applications and Services, (Healthcom 2013), pp. 255–259. IEEE, Lisbon, Portugal, October 2013
3. Chang, V.A.: Amodel to compare cloud and non-cloud storage of big data. Future Gener. Comput. Syst. **57**, 56–76 (2016)
4. Huang, T., Lan, L., Fang, X., An, P., Min, J., Wang, F.: Promises and challenges of big data computing in health sciences. Big Data Res. **2**(1), 2–11 (2015)
5. Firican, G.:The 10 Vs of Big Data, TDWI, 8 February 2017. https://tdwi.org/articles/2017/02/08/10-vs-of-big-data.aspx. Accessed 23 Apr 2018
6. Chen, C.L.P., Zhang, C.Y.: Data-intensive applications, challenges, techniques and technologies: a survey on big data. Inf. Sci. **275**, 314–347 (2014)
7. Logica, B., Magdalena, R.: Using big data in the academic environment. Procedia Econ. Financ. **33**, 277–286 (2015)
8. Agrawal, D., El Abbadi, A., Arora, V.,et al.: Mind your Ps and Vs: a perspective on the challenges of big data management 6 wireless communications and mobile computing and privacy concerns. In: Proceedings of the 2015 International Conference on Big Data and Smart Computing, (BIGCOMP 2015), pp. 1–6, Republic of Korea, February 2015
9. Sabar, N.R., Abawajy, J., Yearwood, J.: Heterogeneous cooperative co-evolution memetic differential evolution algorithm for big data optimization problems. IEEE Trans. Evol. Comput. **21**(2), 315–327
10. Jina, X., Waha, B., Chenga, X., Wanga, Y.: Significance and challenges of big data research. Big Data Res. **2**, 59–64 (2015)

11. Mirza, M.A., Habib, M.A.: Optimized energy ingestion in IoT enabled sensor nodes: a survey. J. Softw. Eng. Intell. Syst. **2**(3), 3 (2017). E-ISSN: 2518–8739
12. Big data in HealthCare. https://www.google.com/imgres?imgurl=http
13. Widmer, A., Schaer, R., Markonis, D., Müller, H.: Gesture interaction for content-based medical image retrieval. In: Proceedings of the 4th ACM International Conference on Multimedia Retrieval, pp. 503–506. ACM, New York (2014)
14. Jina, X., Waha, B., Chenga, X., Wanga, Y.: E-health for security and privacy in health caresystem using hadoop map reduce. Big Data Res. **2**, 59–64 (2015)
15. Youssef, A.E.: A framework for secure healthcare systems based on big data analytics in mobile cloud computing environments. Int. J. Ambient Syst. Appl. (IJASA) **2**(2) (2014)
16. Gunamalai, C., Sivasubramanian, S.: Novel method of security and privacy for personal medical record and DICOM images in cloud computing. ARPN J. Eng. Appl. Sci. **2**, 59–64 (2015)
17. Masud, M., Hossain, M.S.: Secure data-exchange protocol in a cloud-based collaborative health care environment. Big Data Res. **2**, 59–64 (2017)
18. Subhasri, P., Padmapriya, A.: Authentication based access control mechanism for ensuring privacy of DICOM contents in public cloud. Aust. J. Basic Appl. Sci. **11**(10), 128–136 (2017)
19. Al Hamid, H.A., Mizanur, Sk. Md.: A security model for preserving the privacy of medical big data in a healthcare cloud using a fog computing facility with pairing-based cryptography. IEEE Access **2**, 59-64 (2016)
20. Sathya, S., Sethukarasi, T.: Efficient privacy preservation technique for healthcare records using big data. In: International Conference On Information Communication And Embedded System (ICICES 2016) (2016)
21. Victor, N., Lopez, D., Abawajy, J.H.: Privacy models for big data: a survey. Int. J. Big Data Intell. **3**(1), 61–75
22. Sarkar, B.K.: Big data for secure healthcare system: a conceptual design. Big Data Croos Mark **2**, 59–64 (2017)
23. Ondiege, B., Clarke, M., Mapp, G.: Exploring a new security framework for remote patient monitoring devices. Big Data Res. **2**, 59–64 (2017)
24. Yang, C., Lin, W., Liu, M.: A novel triple encryption scheme for hadoop-based cloud data security. In: 2014 Fourth International Conference on Emerging Intelligent Data and Web Technologies (2014)
25. Zhang, R., Liu, L.: Security models and requirements for healthcare application clouds. In: 2017 Fourth International Conference on Emerging Intelligent Data and Web Technologies (2017)
26. Gholami, A., Laure, E.: Security and privacy of sensitive data in cloud computing: a survey of recent developments, vol. 2. Springer (2016)
27. Vinoth Kumar, B., Ramaswami, M., Swathika, P.: Data security on patient monitoring for future healthcare application. Int. J. Comput. Appl. **163**(6), 0975–8887 (2017)
28. Khan, F.A., Alia, A., et al.: A cloud-based healthcare framework for security and patients' data privacy using wireless body area networks. In: The 2nd International Workshop on Communications and Sensor Networks (ComSense-2014) (2014)
29. Chaudhry, J.A., Tariq, U., Amin, M.A., Rittenhouse, R.G.: Sinkhole vulnerabilities in wireless sensor networks. Int. J. Secur. Appl. **8**(1), 401–410 (2014)
30. Rittenhouse, R.G., Chaudry, J.A., Lee, M.: Security in graphical authentication. Int. J. Secur. Appl. **7**(3), 347–356 (2013)

31. Jabbar, S., Ahmad, M., Malik, K.R., Khalid, S., Chaudhry, J., Aldabbas, O.: Designing an energy-aware mechanism for lifetime improvement of wireless sensor networks: a comprehensive study. Mobile Netw. Appl. **23**, 1–14 (2018)
32. Malik, K.R., Farhan, M., Habib, M.A., Khalid, S., Ahmad, M., Ghafir, I.: Remote access capability embedded in linked data using bi-directional transformation: issues and simulation. Sustain. Cities Soc. **38**, 662–674 (2018)

# Malware Detection for Healthcare Data Security

Mozammel Chowdhury[1(✉)], Sharmin Jahan[2], Rafiqul Islam[1],
and Junbin Gao[3]

[1] School of Computing and Mathematics, Charles Sturt University,
Bathurst, Australia
{mochowdhury, mislam}@csu.edu.au
[2] Department of Biochemistry and Molecular Biology,
Jahangirnagar University, Dhaka, Bangladesh
sharmin.biochemist@yahoo.com
[3] School of Business, The University of Sydney, Sydney, Australia

**Abstract.** In recent years, malware attacks against data and information is
considered as a serious cyber threat in the industries and organizations. Cyber
criminals attempt to attack and gain access to computer networks or systems of
many organizations especially in the healthcare industry by malicious software
or malware to breach or manipulate sensitive data, or to make illegal financial
transactions. Healthcare organizations nowadays preserve huge sensitive data
into virtual and cloud environments. As a result, targeted attacks on healthcare
data have become more common in recent years. Hence, protecting the medical
data is a big concern in the healthcare industry. This paper proposes an effective
approach for malware detection and classification using machine learning
techniques. The proposed scheme can uncover targeted attacks and stop spear
phishing attacks on healthcare records by detecting advanced malware and
attacker behavior and deliver custom sandbox analysis to identify malware. In
this work, we employ dynamic features in order to achieve high accuracy in
malware detection. Experimental results support the superior performance and
effectiveness of the proposed method over similar approaches.

**Keywords:** Malware · Healthcare data · Cyber security · API call
Machine learning

## 1 Introduction

Modern healthcare industry offers levels of healthcare and treatments through extensive
information sharing and transfer of health resources by using information and communications technology. The healthcare industry however, is vulnerable to cyber-
attacks and data breaches. Healthcare providers deal with patients' information and
medical records, intellectual property from medical trials, and financial and health
insurance information which are a treasure trove for cybercriminals. The Internet-
connected healthcare information system often can fend off cyberattacks due to
insufficient security and protection. Hence, malware and ransomware attacks on
healthcare data have become more common in recent years. Cyber attacks in the

© ICST Institute for Computer Sciences, Social Informatics and Telecommunications Engineering 2018
R. Beyah et al. (Eds.): SecureComm 2018, LNICST 255, pp. 407–416, 2018.
https://doi.org/10.1007/978-3-030-01704-0_22

healthcare industry has amplified 125% in the last five years at an average cost of $2.2 million per data breach [1]. Because of the sensitive nature of medical records, privacy, security, and confidentiality are considered as the key issues [31].

Healthcare cybersecurity is a growing concern all over the world. Hacking and IT security incidents steadily has risen in the last few years and numerous healthcare organizations fought for defending their healthcare systems [32]. It is apparent that, healthcare data is more valuable and hence targeted by hackers. In 2013, the Identity Theft Research Center (ITRC) reported that, around 43% of medical data was hacked by the cyber criminals in the USA [2].

In 2014, about 4.5 million medical records were stolen by the cyber criminals from the Community Health Systems in the USA. The criminals used a very sophisticated malware to breach the records that was evade by the antivirus software. Brian Dye, the senior vice president of Symantec's told in an interview with Wall Street Journal in May 2014, that "antivirus is dead. Signature-based antimalware solutions are no longer effective, and organizations must consider advanced malware detection tools to improve their healthcare security options" [2]. Eventually, the question may arise that how hackers are evading antivirus solutions? In fact, they use a remote access tool (RAT), a malware for getting access to the system. Therefore, antivirus developer should update their versions to identify RATs on the internet.

In 2015, data breaches occurred remarkably in the healthcare industry and in fact, more health records were attacked by the hackers compared to previous 6 years. 113 million records were attacked by the criminals and 78.8 million health records were stolen in a single cyberattack [2].

2016 and 2017 were two record breaker years for data breaches [3]. Department of Health and Human Services' Office for Civil Rights reported that 118 data breaches were occurred in 2018 (up to April) resulting 894,874 healthcare records stolen [4].

The number of cyber-attacks in the healthcare organizations is increasing and cyber attackers are developing more sophisticated malware tools for gaining access to the sensitive medical data and illegal ransoming [33, 34]. As a result, healthcare organizations must secure their medical devices and networks to prevent them from uprising cyber-attacks.

This research aims to propose an efficient malware detection technique based on analyzing dynamic features. The key features of this paper are listed below:

- We use Windows API (Application Programming Interface) dynamic features to detect malware.
- In order to achieve a higher detection rate, we use a refinement technique to select the best ones among the extracted features.
- We employ machine learning algorithm for malware classification.
- We use a large malware dataset to precisely evaluate the performance of our proposed scheme.

## 2 Related Work

Researchers have proposed various anti-malware techniques to defend malware attacks [5–9]. There are two most popular techniques for malware detection, such as: Signature-based and Anomaly-based detection method. In the signature-based malware detection techniques, the signature or fingerprint of a malware executable file is analyzed. The analyzed signature is then compared with a database of recognized malicious files. Signature based method is widely used to achieve high detection rate in case of known malware whose signatures are present in the database [10, 29, 30]. However, signature-based technique cannot protect systems from zero-day malware attacks. Using the obfuscation technique malware developers are creating new malware without changing the essence of malware. These new malwares are the variant of known malware and easily can bypass the detectors. Anomaly or behaviour based malware detection techniques work with normal and anomalous behaviour of the program to decide the maliciousness. The key feature of anomaly-based malware detection technique is its ability to recognize new malwares or prevent zero-day attacks. The anomaly-based malware detection methods generally use API call information, rather than byte sequence matching [11]. The anomaly-based detection methods use the behavior patterns of the malware files and provides better performance compared to signature-based methods. However, anomaly-based methods suffer from high false alarm rate.

The malware characteristics or features can be searched or extracted by analyzing the malware executables in two ways: statically or dynamically. In static analysis, a number of useful features are extracted from the unpacked static version of the malware executables by dissecting the components of the binary file without executing it. However, dynamic analysis executes the packed malware files within a controlled setting known as 'sandbox' [12] so that it cannot contaminate the environment. The main benefits of static analysis are that they are harmless since they do not require to execute the malware files. Moreover, static analysis methods are usually fast as they can analyze all the execution paths of the binary files. However, static analysis methods can be emvade by various obfuscation techniques, because obfuscation techniques become more sophisticated nowadays [13]. Additionally, static analysis methods are unable to detect new malware attacks as the signatures are unknown [14]. On the other hand, dynamic analysis methods perform well for obfuscated malware and they can provide good classification accuracy as they execute the binary files and show the actual behavior of the executable malware files. However, dynamic analysis techniques suffer from numerous limitations. They are able to analyze a single execution path and they require more processing time because, each malware file need to be executed within a controlled environment [15].

The effectiveness of the malware detection techniques generally depends on the malware features that are to be learnt in training phase to classify malware and benign precisely. The malware detectors may have limitations of getting high false alarm rate if we cannot select and classify the features properly. To skirt these limitations of the existing malware detection methods and to achieve higher detection accuracy, we propose an efficient detection technique using dynamic features.

## 3   Proposed System Architecture

The major components of the proposed malware detection system are shown in Fig. 1. Our proposed scheme is comprised of the following major parts: (i) Pre-processing of malware executable files, (ii) Extracting malware features, (iii) Refinement/selection of extracted features, (v) Features classification, and (vi) Malware detection.

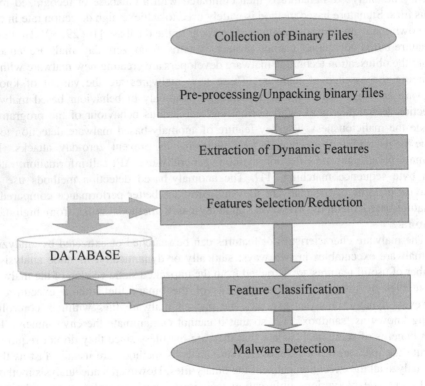

**Fig. 1.** Major steps of the proposed malware detection system.

### 3.1   Pre-processing

Malware executable files are normally raw files stored as binary code. Therefore, we have preprocessed them to make them usable. At first, the executables are unpacked in a virtual machine (VM) which is a restricted environment. To unpack the executable files, the most popular tool PEid [16] is used in this work.

### 3.2   Feature Extraction

For malware detection and classification, we extract the features by analyzing executable files using dynamic analysis [17–21]. Dynamic analysis technique executes malware binary files and monitors their behaviors. Dynamic analysis technique compares the behavior patterns of the unknown malware with that of the known malware and thus detects the unknown malware that shows similar behavior to the known ones. There are two eminent methods commonly used for dynamic analysis: control flow analysis and API call analysis [22, 23]. In this work, we extract Windows API calls from both malware and cleanware executable files.

The API calls are observed during the execution of the malware binary files. The API calls collected by dynamic analysis are used to generate behavioral patterns. The API call information can be processed by simple statistics such as frequency counting [17] and data mining or machine learning technique [20, 21].

In this experiment, we set up a virtual machine environment called "VirtualBox" [25] to execute and monitor both malicious and cleanware samples. To trace and import API call sequences during execution, we hook the programs using a trace tool HookMe [24]. 32-bit Windows XP is adopted as the operating system of the virtual machine because most malware files can easily be executed under the Windows XP platform. The maximum monitoring period is set to 30 s as default value for tracing each API calls. Experimentally we find that 30 s are enough for capturing all necessary log data.

After the execution of malware files and logging the Windows API calls, the API call features are extracted from the log files and represented in vector notation to fed into the classifier. The API features are comprised with API functions and parameters. The function names and parameters are separate entities those may individually affect the capacity of malware detection and classification.

### 3.3 Feature Selection/Refinement

After extracting API features from the malware executable files, Class-wise document frequency (DCFS) [26] is used for selecting the most relevant API calls that leads to achieve higher detection accuracy.

### 3.4 Malware Classification and Detection

Malware classification and detection process is done in two phases: training and testing. For training the classifier, a set of malwares and clean ware files is fed into the classifier. The classifier is trained by a learning algorithm. The classifier is trained with the data samples given to the system. For testing the classifier system, a set of new malwares and clean ware files are fed into the classifier. For experimentation, we built a program to interface with the machine learning algorithms in the Waikato Environment for Knowledge Analysis (WEKA) [27] for data classification. We perform experiment to evaluate the accuracy of the system employing four basic classifiers in the WEKA including: Support Vector Machine (SVM), Naïve Bayes, Decision Tree (J48), and Random Forest.

## 4 Experimental Results and Discussion

In this section, experimental results are reported and analyzed. We use a collected dataset consisting of malware and cleanware files to perform the experiments. The API call sequences are used for malware detection and classification.

### 4.1  Data Set

We develop a dataset of 52,185 recent executable files gathered from numerous malware and benign files. The number of malware files is 41,265 and the remaining are cleanware files. The malware files are taken from Heaven [28] and the cleanware files are collected from two online sources: Download.com and Softpedia.com. The malware executable files are of different types including, Trojans, root kits, worms, backdoors, and hack tools.

### 4.2  Experimental Evaluation

For experimentation, we use a virtual environment to execute and monitor both malicious and cleanware samples to extract the Windows API call features. We attain a total of 172,641 API call sequences from the samples. We then refine the collected features using Class-wise document frequency (DCFS) measure and select the top relevant API calls. We select top 100 API calls for each sample class. We generate a feature vector of 1's and 0's (1 if the API call is present, 0 if it is not) with these selected API calls for each sample.

To test the performance of the proposed approach, we use machine learning algorithms in the WEKA platform. We have used four common machine learning classifiers including, Random Forest, Decision Tree (J48), Naïve Bayes, and Support Vector Machine (SVM) to test the dataset. The WEKA generally uses Attribute-Relation File Format (ARFF) database. This file format lists all file features and their type (such as, numeric, nominal, string, etc.). We therefore, convert the malware and cleanware samples into WEKA format. We fed the training set into the WEKA platform to train the classifiers and then test their effectiveness using the test dataset.

In this work, a k-fold cross validation is done to validate each classifier. Empirically, we find that in case of k = 10, the classifier gives better accuracy. Therefore, the dataset is randomly partitioned into 10 different subsets of learning and testing samples. Thus, 90% of the total samples are used for training and the rest 10% are used for testing. For each step in the validation process, the classifier is trained with the training samples.

To estimate the performance of the classifiers, we measure the following evaluation metrics:

$$Accuracy = \frac{TP + TN}{TP + FP + TN + FN} \tag{1}$$

$$TPR = \frac{TP}{TP + FN} \tag{2}$$

$$FPR = \frac{FP}{FP + FN} \tag{3}$$

where,

*TP* (true positive) = Total number of malware files properly recognized as malware,

*FP* (false positive) = Total number of malware files inaccurately recognized as cleanware,

*TN* (true negative) = Total number of cleanware files accurately recognized as cleanware,

*FN* (false negative) = Total number of cleanware files inaccurately recognized as malware,

TPR = True Positive Rate also known as sensitivity, and FPR = False Positive Rate.

Figure 2, and Tables 1 and 2 represent the experimental results in terms of Accuracy, TPR and FPR, respectively. For every classifier, the results are improved by refinement of the dynamic features using DCFS algorithm. The best overall results are obtained by SVM, trained with Normalized Polynomial Kernel. Experimental results validate that machine-learning classifiers can achieve high performance in detection of unknown malware.

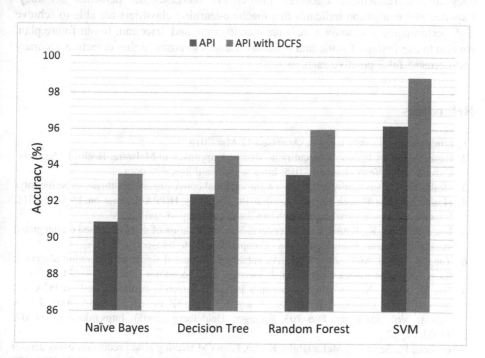

**Fig. 2.** Accuracy results (in %) of the malware classifiers using API features (without refinement) and API with DCFS (with refinement)

**Table 1.** TPR results of the malware classifiers (with and without refinement)

| Methods | API | API with DCFS |
|---|---|---|
| Naïve Bayes | 0.912 | 0.931 |
| Decision tree | 0.931 | 0.942 |
| Random forest | 0.944 | 0.953 |
| SVM | 0.971 | 0.991 |

**Table 2.** FPR results of the malware classifiers (with and without refinement)

| Methods | API | API with DCFS |
|---|---|---|
| Naïve Bayes | 0.07 | 0.062 |
| Decision tree | 0.04 | 0.034 |
| Random forest | 0.06 | 0.053 |
| SVM | 0.03 | 0.027 |

## 5  Conclusion

An efficient method for malware detection has been proposed in this paper using machine learning technique. We explore the disparity of parameters and their consequences on the performance of the algorithm. Our approach uses the dynamic features integrating a refinement algorithm that clearly increases the detection accuracy. Experimental evaluation indicates that machine-learning classifiers are able to achieve high performance in unknown malware classification and detection. In our future plan, we aim to use fusion of static and dynamic features to attain higher detection accuracy and decrease false positive rates as well.

## References

1. http://www.malwarebytes.com. Accessed 12 Mar 2018
2. Paster, M.: Why healthcare security needs a new approach to Malware. Health IT Security-Cybersecurity News, January 2015. http://www.healthitsecurity.com
3. Healthcare Cybersecurity: https://www.hipaajournal.com/category/healthcare-cybersecurity/
4. Healthcare Data Breach Report: April 2018, posted by HIPPA Journal on 18 May 2018. https://www.hipaajournal.com/healthcare-data-breach-report-april-2018/
5. Islam, R., Tian, R., Batten, L.M., Versteeg, S.: Classification of malware based on integrated static and dynamic features. J. Netw. Comput. Appl. **36**, 646–656 (2013)
6. Tang, K., Zhou, M.T., Zuo, Z.-H.: An enhanced automated signature generation algorithm for polymorphic malware detection. J. Electron. Sci. Technol. China **8**, 114–121 (2010)
7. Xu, X., Wang, X.: An adaptive network intrusion detection method based on PCA and support vector machines. In: Li, X., Wang, S., Dong, Z.Y. (eds.) ADMA 2005. LNCS (LNAI), vol. 3584, pp. 696–703. Springer, Heidelberg (2005). https://doi.org/10.1007/11527503_82
8. O'Kane, P., Sezer, S., McLaughlin, K., Im, E.: SVM training phase reduction using dataset feature filtering for malware detection. IEEE Trans. Inf. Forensics Secur. **8**(3), 500–509 (2013)
9. Hadžiosmanović, D., Simionato, L., Bolzoni, D., Zambon, E., Etalle, S.: N-gram against the machine: on the feasibility of the N-Gram network analysis for binary protocols. In: Balzarotti, D., Stolfo, Salvatore J., Cova, M. (eds.) RAID 2012. LNCS, vol. 7462, pp. 354–373. Springer, Heidelberg (2012). https://doi.org/10.1007/978-3-642-33338-5_18
10. Chowdhury, M., Rahman, A., Islam, R.: Protecting data from malware threats using machine learning technique. In: IEEE Conference on Industrial Electronics and Applications (ICIEA 2017), Siem Reap, Cambodia, 18–20 June 2017

11. Chowdhury, M., Rahman, A., Islam, R.: Malware analysis and detection using data mining and machine learning classification. In: Abawajy, J., Choo, K.-K.R., Islam, R. (eds.) ATCI 2017. AISC, vol. 580, pp. 266–274. Springer, Cham (2018). https://doi.org/10.1007/978-3-319-67071-3_33

12. Devesa, J., Santos, I., Cantero, X., Penya, Y.K., Bringas, P.G.: Automatic behaviour-based analysis and classification system for malware detection. In: Proceedings of the 12th International Conference on Enterprise Information Systems (ICEIS) (2010)

13. Okane, P., Sezer, S., McLaughlin, K.: Obfuscation: the hidden malware. IEEE Secur. Priv. **9** (5), 41–47 (2011)

14. Moser, A., Kruegel, C., Kirda, E.: Limits of static analysis for malware detection. In: Proceedings of the 23rd Annual Computer Security Applications Conference (ACSAC '07), pp. 421–430, December 2007

15. Cavallaro, L., Saxena, P., Sekar, R.: On the limits of information flow techniques for malware analysis and containment. In: Zamboni, D. (ed.) DIMVA 2008. LNCS, vol. 5137, pp. 143–163. Springer, Heidelberg (2008). https://doi.org/10.1007/978-3-540-70542-0_8

16. PEid Unpacker. http://www.peid.info/

17. Tian, R., Islam, M.R., Batten, L., Versteeg, S.: Differentiating malware from cleanware using behavioural analysis. In: Proceedings of the 5th International Conference on Malicious and Unwanted Software (MALWARE 2010), Nancy, France, pp. 23–30 October 2010

18. Shankarapani, M., Kancherla, K., Ramammoorthy, S., Movva, R., Mukkamala, S.: Kernel machines for malware classification and similarity analysis. In: Proceedings of the International Joint Conference on Neural Networks (IJCNN '10), pp. 1–6, July 2010

19. Shankarapani, M.K., Ramamoorthy, S., Movva, R.S., Mukkamala, S.: Malware detection using assembly and API call sequences. J. Comput. Virol. **7**(2), 107–119 (2011)

20. Ahmed, F., Hameed, H., Shafq, M.Z., Farooq, M.: Using spatio-temporal information in API calls with machine learning algorithms for malware detection. In: Proceedings of the 2nd ACM Workshop on Security and Artificial Intelligence, pp. 55–62, November 2009

21. Qiao, Y., Yang, Y., Ji, L., He, J.: Analyzing malware by abstracting the frequent item sets in API call sequences. In: Proceedings of the 12th IEEE International Conference on Trust, Security and Privacy in Computing and Communications (TrustCom '13), pp. 265–270, July 2013

22. Rajagopalan, M., Hiltunen, M.A., Jim, T., Schlichting, R.D.: System call monitoring using authenticated system calls. IEEE Trans. Dependable Secure Comput. **3**(3), 216–229 (2006)

23. Abadi, M., Budiu, M., Erlingsson, U., Ligatti, J.: Control-flow integrity. In: Proceedings of the 12th ACM Conference on Computer and Communications Security, pp. 340–353, November 2005

24. Tian, R., Islam, R., Batten, L., Versteeg, S.: Differentiating malware from cleanware using behavioural analysis. In: International Conference on Malicious and Unwanted Software: MALWARE 2010, pp. 23–30 (2010)

25. VirtualBox. https://www.virtualbox.org

26. http://msdn.microsoft.com/enus/library/aa383749%28VS.85%29.aspx. January 2010

27. Weka library. Data mining software in Java. http://www.cs.waikato.ac.nz/ml/weka

28. VX Heaven collection. VX Heaven website. http://vx.netlux.org

29. Huda, S. et al.: Hybrids of support vector machine wrapper and filter-based framework for malware detection, Future Gener. Comput. Syst. **55**, 376–390

30. Sharmeen, S., Huda, S., Abawajy, J.H., Ismail, W.N., Hassan, M.M.: Malware threats and detection for industrial mobile-IoT networks. IEEE Access **6**, 15941–15957 (2018)

31. Jahan, S., Chowdhury, M., Islam, R.: Robust user authentication model for securing electronic healthcare system using fingerprint biometrics. Int. J. Comput. Appl. (2018). https://doi.org/10.1080/1206212X.2018.1437651

32. Jahan, S., Chowdhury, M., Islam, R., Gao, J.: Security and privacy protection for ehealth data. In: Doss, R., Piramuthu, S., Zhou, W. (eds.) FNSS 2018. CCIS, vol. 878, pp. 197–205. Springer, Cham (2018). https://doi.org/10.1007/978-3-319-94421-0_16

33. Jahan, S., Chowdhury, M., Islam, R., Chaudhry, J.: Securing healthcare data using biometric authentication. In: Lin, X., Ghorbani, A., Ren, K., Zhu, S., Zhang, A. (eds.) SecureComm 2017. LNICST, vol. 239, pp. 123–132. Springer, Cham (2018). https://doi.org/10.1007/978-3-319-78816-6_10

34. Jahan, S., Chowdhury, M., Islam, R.: Robust fingerprint verification for enhancing security in healthcare system. In: Image and Vision Computing New Zealand conference (IVCNZ 2017), 4–6 December 2017, Christchurch, New Zealand (2017)

# Secure Communication on NoC Based MPSoC

Gaurav Sharma[1], Soultana Ellinidou[1(✉)], Veronika Kuchta[2],
Rajeev Anand Sahu[1], Olivier Markowitch[1], and Jean-Michel Dricot[1]

[1] Cyber Security Research Center, Université Libre de Bruxelles, Brussels, Belgium
{gsharma,soultana.ellinidou,rajeev.sahu,olivier.markowitch,
jdricot}@ulb.ac.be
[2] Monash University, Melbourne, Australia
veronika.kuchta@monash.edu

**Abstract.** The increasing integration on latest MPSoC devices invites various security threats. To execute a sensitive application, a combination of IP cores on an MPSoC platform creates a security zone. This security zone must be protected. In this paper, we attempt to achieve the secure communication among these security zones supported by a two party key agreement protocol. Furthermore, we extend this idea to cover both varieties of security zones: continuous as well as disrupted.

**Keywords:** Multi-Processor System on Chip · Key Agreement
NoC · Security zone

## 1 Introduction

The recent multi-fold increase in number of Intellectual Property (IP) cores on an Multi-Processor System-on-Chip (MPSoC) integrates more flexibility and promises better performance. These IP cores can be general purpose processor, memory or some dedicated processor following special requirement of the application. The Network-on-chip (NoC) is now the *de facto* way of on-chip communication for any scalable MPSoC system. The on-chip communication must be secure however NoC itself inserts many security challenges. The foundation of NoC communication is routers and links. The router receives the packets from the IP cores and links assist to reach these packets to other routers on the routing path, which is decided by the underlying routing algorithm.

The applications related to Internet of Things (IoTs) are continuously striving the need of such MPSoC units to fulfill varying needs of the market. With the increasing demand for MPSoCs, security issues are being addressed more attentively. The major classification of attacks [5] on MPSoC platform are: (a) denial of Service, (b) change of system behavior and (c) extract sensitive data from memory location. The threat model and related work for NoC based MPSoC is described in the following section.

© ICST Institute for Computer Sciences, Social Informatics and Telecommunications Engineering 2018
R. Beyah et al. (Eds.): SecureComm 2018, LNICST 255, pp. 417–428, 2018.
https://doi.org/10.1007/978-3-030-01704-0_23

In order to execute a sensitive application on MPSoC platform, the operating system allocates some of the trusted IP cores. The wrapping of these IP cores into a physical zone is known as security zone. The shape of this security zone can be continuous or disrupted as per the availability of the cores. On an MPSoC, the distribution of threads to different IP cores forces them to exchange the sensitive information. The plaintext communication on the NoC leads to the breach of information.

## 2  Threat Model and Related Work for NoC Based MPSoC

The sensitive information flow on the interconnect (bus or NoC) leaves the system vulnerable to various threats. Most of the real-time applications do not support any encryption or authentication strategy to protect this information. The applications running on an MPSoC based platform can be equally prone to attacks. The interface to external devices makes the IP cores more vulnerable to attacks. Moreover, frequent reconfiguration and wireless communication causes the situation more opportunistic. Additionally, running an untrusted application can turn the IP core behavior malicious. The infected IP cores extracts sensitive information stored locally and forwards this to some external entity. The basic assets of any secure communication are confidentiality, integrity, authentication and availability. In order to cover these security primitives, NoC based MPSoC categorizes the threats accordingly. However, access control is an additional primitive to care about, in this scenario. Here, we are not considering any of the side channel attacks as well as physical attacks.

The threat model in MPSoC covers mainly three attacks as following:

- **Denial of service attack:** In order to make the NoC resources unavailable to legitimate IP cores, an attacker may launch several attacks. The possible approaches to waste resources are replay, incorrect path, deadlock and livelock.
- **Extraction of secret information:** The attacker attempts to read some secure memory on an IP core or a shared memory. This information might be extremely critical, such as cryptographic keys used for encryption.
- **Hijacking:** In this attack, an attacker tries to write some data in a secure memory area in order to change the system behavior. The attack can be launched by using buffer overflow or reconfiguring the internal registers.

In the recent literature, some additional threats were introduced when NoC supplied to SoC integrator has a hardware Trojan embedded in it [12]. In order to activate this hardware Trojan, a malicious circuit is inserted during the design of the IP block or a malicious program can activate the Trojan later at runtime. The possible attacks due to infected router are:

- **Snooping of sensitive data (Confidentiality):** The information flow between any two IP cores must be confidential and accessible to them only.

- **Corrupt the data (Integrity):** During the routing of information, no malicious IP core is allowed to modify the messages. The integrity constraints must provide end to end security.
- **Spoofing (Authentication):** The destination IP core can verify the identity of source IP core.
- **Denial of service:** The denial or distributed denial of service can make the resources unavailable to legitimate IP cores.

Here, in this proposal, we are particularly interested about the confidentiality, integrity and authentication. However, there are many ways to approach the security in MPSoC platforms depending upon the application. Some of them (not independent to each other) can be listed as follows:

- Creation of security zones and protecting them via some firewall around it
- Secure packet routing among these zones (encapsulating the route within security zone)
- Secure memory access to IP cores
- Secure communication among these zones with some key agreement approach

In the following subsections, we briefly discuss the state of the art of these security solutions:

## 2.1 Creation of Security Zones

If the security zone is continuous, the existing solutions present a firewall to prevent the traffic from other malicious neighboring nodes. However, the disrupted security zones are difficult to manage. Additionally, the security zones must be dynamic in nature such that the IP cores can be added or removed at run-time. The addition of a core happens when some overheated IP core is replaced with an idle IP core. Moreover, one part of the security zone needs to communicate with rest of the parts securely.

The security policy implemented in these firewalls is integrated in Network Interface (NI) and it filters the data forwarded and received by the IP cores of security zone. These firewalls can be either static or dynamic. The static firewall has fixed access rules [8] while the reconfigurable firewalls update the security policy regularly [7,9,17]. The IP cores inside a security zone trust each other.

## 2.2 Secure Routing on MPSoC

The execution of any sensitive application attempts to spread the application on multiple IPs for better efficiency. These IP cores need to communicate frequently. As the IP cores involved in security zone are trusted to each other, a continuous security zone can be protected with firewalls on the boundary. Unfortunately, if the IPs are not adjacent to each other, they need to exchange the messages on the communication fabric. The infected IP on this routing path can extract some sensitive information. This sensitive path communication by disruptive security zones must be confidential and no infected IP must be able to extract information from it. The confidentiality or integrity of the communicated data is provided with the encryption and hashing of the data. Whenever a malicious IP is on the sensitive path, an adaptive routing can be a viable solution to find another path.

The primary objective is to maximize the encapsulation of sensitive path inside a security zone. The adaptive routing should be free from deadlock, livelock and starvation. In 2016, Fernandes et al. [6] presented a security aware routing approach for NoC based MPSoCs. Their approach uses Segment Based Routing (SBR) algorithm to find the route between source IP and destination IP. However, the solution has a performance impact but it avoids those routes which include routers attached with infected IPs. The existing security zone solutions attempt to avoid the routers attached with malicious IP cores. The adaptive routing at this point may choose another route which is longer and more risk sensitive. Sepulveda et al. [14] introduced the concept of risk aware routing. The risk factor depends on the malicious activities of the infected IP, and whenever the security rules are violated, a notification is communicated to the security manager. The presented solution Global Risk-Aware NoC Architecture (GRA-NoC) searches a new route as the risk exceeds the threshold value.

Later, Sepulveda et al. [13] proposed another security aware routing approach in zone based MPSoC. The Region Based Routing (RBR) is used at design time while at runtime Non-minimal Odd Even (NOE) routing is followed. The routing decision must be driven by the risk value of the hop.

## 2.3  Protected Memory Access

In order to protect the memory access, the firewall is implemented in the Network Interface (NI). The security rules can be either enforced at the NI of source IP core or at the destination IP core (which is memory in this case). Both the approaches have their own pros and cons. The implementation at source IP core causes area overhead while at memory IP, dealing a huge number of access requests is challenging. Furthermore, in order to validate the source, authentication at destination IP is additional burden.

The other NoC security requirements include confidentiality, availability, integrity and non-repudiation. In order to achieve confidentiality and integrity, encryption and message integrity codes can be used. The resource availability can be ensured with detection and prevention of Denial of Service (DoS). The non-repudiation protects the infected IPs to send messages on behalf of the legitimate IPs.

## 2.4  Intrazone Key Agreement on MPSoC

In the previous work, the researchers primarily focused on creating an envelope surrounding the IP cores, involved in security zone. The firewall is installed to filter the traffic based on security rules. The security policy can be upgraded during runtime. The firewall based approach is limited to the creation of continuous security zones only. These IPs become unreachable for other IP cores and hence it degrades the overall system performance. The disruptive security zones are forced to communicate on sensitive path. The communication among these zones must be protected against confidentiality and integrity. Moreover, a session key is needed to enable such secure communication among these IP cores.

To derive the session key among these IP cores, the initial solutions attempt to achieve pair-wise communication security [4,18]. However, they do not support group-wise confidential communication. In 2014, Sepulveda et al. [17] presented elastic security zones for 3D-MPSoC with group-wise shared secret establishment protocols. Later, another feasible solution was suggested in [15] which employs the use of hybrid group key agreement protocol. As a common standard in Internet, asymmetric system is used for session key establishment and a symmetric algorithm for data encryption thereafter. Their work [15] implemented two different approaches. The first approach is based on key pre-distribution and assumes that a pool of keys is already distributed to IPs at design time and a key is negotiated at runtime. The other approach counts on Diffie-Hellman and derives the shared secret as a function of secrets of all the participating IP cores. The major limitation of these approaches is lack of scalability and efficiency.

In a further enhancement, Sepulveda et al. [16] implemented three hierarchical group-wise key agreement protocols. A comparative analysis between flat and hierarchical key agreement protocols ensures the superiority of latter one. In their approach, all the IP cores are assumed to store a private key at design time and a Global Manager (GM) is supposed to keep all the private keys to securely communicate with them. The idea to store all the private keys at a single point (at GM) makes the whole architecture compromised if GM is compromised.

From the above discussion, it is easy to perceive that intrazone security has been addressed well but interzone security is still at large. Moreover, there is no solution which considers the communication security when these security zones are part of a pipeline process. In this paper, our concern is more related to provide a secure communication infrastructure to forward the data in a hierarchical manner. In the next section we present an application to highlight the aim of this research.

# 3 Endoscopy: General Overview

The health care industry is full of such complex diagnostic machines where the inaccuracy of some medical procedures can lead to serious consequences. The data security breach can be life threatening for a patient. Endoscopy machine is one of the common examples. The endoscopy machine is comprising of a variety of different processors to accomplish a specific task. The tasks can be broadly divided into five categories: light source, camera head for taking pictures/videos, Camera Control Unit (CCU) for image enhancement and image adjustment, image management and display. Generally, these machines use pipeline of tasks, initiating with taking the image, process the image and then recognize the disease. These different tasks can be performed with cluster of processors and they need to exchange data securely. The change in image data while transferring it to other components, will lead to faulty output and therefore, the algorithms used for recognition will make a wrong decision to identify the disease [1]. The current state of art suggests multiple Xilinx FPGAs for each component, to fulfill the need. The different components and flow of data is depicted in Fig. 1.

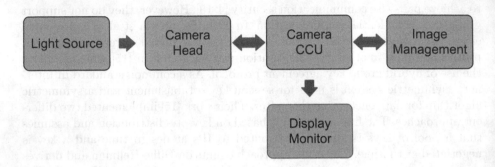

**Fig. 1.** Various clusters of IP cores for endoscopy machine

The camera head forwards the images to CCU for further processing. In order to enhance the image quality, image enhancement and image adjustment is performed. The image enhancement includes noise reduction, edge enhancement and wide dynamic range corrections to provide clear images. Furthermore, the user controlled image adjustments are accomplished with the support of digital zoom, video scalar for appropriate aspect ratio and static image capture. Additionally, in order to manage the data flow and CCU functions, a processor is needed.

The post-processing image treatment includes rotation, on-screen display and picture-in-picture display. An operating system with a custom GUI is also part of this unit. The input/output devices such as mouse, keyboard, ethernet are all connected here and vulnerable to various threats.

In endoscopy machines, the current state of the art explores full scope of implementing machine learning and deep learning for medical image processing. The implementation of machine learning and computer vision algorithms for a huge collection of images, will assist in polyp detection. The complexity and scalability requirements of these machines motivate the use of on-chip IP cores connected via NoC.

The communication among camera IP cores, CCU, display and image management unit IP cores must be protected with confidentiality and integrity. To ensure this, encrypted communication should be exchanged. The session key (derived for a specific period of time) can be input for a lightweight encryption algorithm such as PRESENT or ChaCha20.

Keeping in mind, here we present a generalized solution to enable secure communication among all these components. The security zones can derive a session key by running the presented key exchange algorithm. The Fig. 2 depicts three secure zones. In particular, the cameras IP on endoscopy machine can be running on zone 1, CCU on zone 2 and zone 3 may represent image management. A session key is exchanged between camera zone and CCU zone and another session key is needed between CCU and image management zone. There will be an anchor node in each of the zones and it will be responsible for the key derivation.

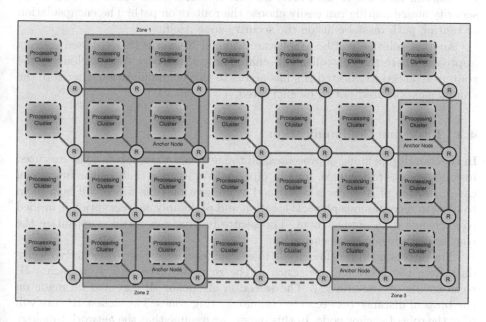

**Fig. 2.** Three secure zones in an MPSoC platform

# 4 Proposed Solution

The above discussed application is just an example to convey the need of secure communication among various components of the system. Our objective in this paper is to present a general solution adaptable to any such systems. The presented solution will enhance the communication security among these zones via a key agreement protocol.

The running application can decide whether the data is sensitive and need the communication security. The applications running on more than one security zones (as explained in the previous section), need to forward the processed data to other zones for further processing. All such zones which are created at runtime, choose an anchor IP core, responsible for interzone communication. The anchor node selection method is described in a later subsection. The intrazone and interzone communication security has been discussed separately in the following subsections:

## 4.1   Intrazone Communication

As per the application requirement, at the time of system integration, we can easily appoint the IP cores for various tasks. The best strategy is to cluster these IP cores continuously. The communication among these IP cores will be via the routers attached to these IP cores. To ensure the confidentiality of this communication, no other IP core must be able to extract this communication. The security aware routing can easily choose the routers on path. The encapsulation of routing path must be inside the security zone itself.

Another solution can be a Software Defined Networks (SDN) based routing approach where the controller will enable only the secure routes. None of the routers attached to infected IPs has access to this communication, therefore the communication need not to be encrypted.

## 4.2   Interzone Communication

In the overall pipelining of processes, all the involved zones forward the executed instruction sets to the next zone in pipeline. We assume that a clear functional categorization of IP cores is performed at integration time which will help them to place at a continuous physical location and preferably, no encryption is needed to exchange data among them. The secure routing can easily encapsulate the routing path inside the security zone.

The next zone in pipeline needs to exchange a session key to securely receive data from the previous zone. Each of the zones involved selects an anchor IP to negotiate the session key. The selection of anchor IP core can be made on the basis of distance between the communicating zones. The closest IP core will play the role of anchor node. In this paper, we assume that the network topology is 2-D mesh. Let the coordinates of IPs in zone 1 and zone 2 are $(sr, sc)$ and $(dr, dc)$ respectively. The closest distance between any pair of IP cores can be computed by the following rule:

$$|D_{closest}| = \begin{cases} (dc - sc) & \text{if } sr = dr \\ (dr - sr) & \text{if } sc = dc \\ (dr - sr) + (dc - sc) & \text{otherwise} \end{cases}$$

Here, $(sr, sc)$ and $(dr, dc)$ represent the coordinates for source IP core and destination IP core respectively. The $sr$, $dr$, $sc$ and $dc$ are source row, destination row, source column and destination column. If there are more than one IP core pairs with the same closest distance, the pair can be chosen randomly. These selected IP cores (source and destination) become anchor nodes for secure data exchange.

The anchor nodes will negotiate the key with two party key exchange algorithm. Rather than running a complex group key exchange protocol, all the communication will be through the anchor node only. The anchor node, representing the zone, communicates with other anchor nodes. The protocol adopted here is an identity-based one-round two-party key agreement protocol. For more details about the concept of identity-based cryptosystem and the security model related to authenticated key agreement, we refer ID-2PAKA [2]. We assume that all the public keys can be easily derived by the IP core, using the identity information. The key agreement protocol comprises of three phases: Setup, Extract and Key Agreement. The protocol is as follows:

# 5   PF-ID-2PAKA Protocol

The Private Key Generator (PKG), which is a trusted entity, generates the private keys for each IP core, corresponding to their identity. The system parameters derived from the setup phase, are used to run the extract and key agreement phase. The three algorithms are as follows:

1. **Setup:** Let $\mathbb{E}/\mathbb{F}_p$ be an elliptic curve $\mathbb{E}$ over a finite field $\mathbb{F}_p$, $\mathbb{G}$ be a cyclic additive group of prime order $q$ and $P$ is the generator of group $\mathbb{G}$. For a given security parameter $k$, PKG chooses two hash functions $H_0$ and $H_1$ such that $H_0 : \{0,1\}^* \to \mathbb{Z}_n^*$ and $H_1 : \{0,1\}^* \times \{0,1\}^* \times \mathbb{G} \times \mathbb{G} \times \mathbb{G} \times \mathbb{G} \to \{0,1\}^k$. The PKG chooses a random number $s \in \mathbb{Z}_n^*$ as a master key and computes $P_{pub} = s \cdot P$. Then, PKG publishes the system parameters as $param = \{\mathbb{F}_p, \mathbb{E}/\mathbb{F}_p, \mathbb{G}, P, P_{pub}, H_0, H_1\}$ and keep master key $s$ secret.

2. **Extract:** For a given PKG's master key $s$, IP core's identity $ID_i$ and system parameters $param$, PKG computes private-key for each identity $ID_i$. PKG chooses a random number $r_i \in \mathbb{Z}_n^*$ and computes $R_i = r_i \cdot P$, $h_i = H_0(ID_i)$ and $s_i = (r_i + h_i \cdot s) \bmod n$. The IP core can validate its correctness by checking whether $s_i \cdot P = R_i + h_i \cdot P_{pub}$. The PKG generates a private/public-key pair $\{s_i, R_i\}$ for each IP core and sends it through a secure channel.

3. **Key Agreement:** After receiving the private keys, the anchor IP cores A and B with identities $ID_A$ and $ID_B$, private-keys $s_A$ and $s_B$ and public values $h_A$ and $h_B$ initiate the key agreement phase explained below:

   (a) The anchor node A randomly chooses $t_A \in \mathbb{Z}_n^*$, sets $t_A$ as its ephemeral-private-key and computes $T_A = t_A \cdot P$

   (b) A computes a message $M_1 = \{ID_A, R_A, T_A\}$ and sends it to B

   (c) Similarly, the anchor node B randomly chooses $t_B \in \mathbb{Z}_n^*$, sets $t_B$ as its ephemeral-private-key and computes $T_B = t_B \cdot P$

   (d) B computes a message $M_2 = \{ID_B, R_B, T_B\}$ and sends to A

   (e) Upon receiving $M_1$ and $M_2$, both A and B compute their shared secrets as follows:

   (i) A computes $K_{AB}^1 = (s_A + t_A)(T_B + R_B + h_B \cdot P_{pub})$ and $K_{AB}^2 = t_A \cdot T_B$ and the session-key as $sk = H_1(ID_A \| ID_B \| T_A \| T_B \| K_{AB}^1 \| K_{AB}^2)$.

   (ii) B computes $K_{BA}^1 = (s_B + t_B)(T_A + R_A + h_A \cdot P_{pub})$ and $K_{BA}^2 = t_B \cdot T_A$ and the session-key as $sk = H_1(ID_A \| ID_B \| T_A \| T_B \| K_{BA}^1 \| K_{BA}^2)$.

   (iii) A and B both hold the same session-key $sk$.

The above protocol is secure in extended Canetti-Krawczyk (eCK) model which is the strongest security model presented by Ni et al. [11]. The leakage of private key does not reveal the session key. Moreover, the protocol is pairing-free and it uses only three point multiplications which is quite acceptable for on-chip communication. To minimize the computational cost, each IP core computes $h_A \cdot P_{pub}$ and stores it permanently. A scalar point multiplication usually takes around 2 ms at Pentium IV 3GHZ processor with 512 M bytes memory [3].

If the adversary is able to intercept and modify the communicated messages, a key offset attack can be launched on the above protocol. In this attack, both the participating parties will derive the different session key and the key integrity property is violated. To protect from this flaw, an additional signature verification can be used to securely communicate $T_A$ and $T_B$. The signature can be Schnorr digital signature, for example. Hence the anchor IP core with identity $ID_A$ also computes $\sigma_A = t_A + s_A \cdot H_2(ID, R_A, T_A)$, where $H_2 : \{0,1\}^* \times \mathbb{G} \times \mathbb{G} \rightarrow \{0,1\}^k$ and then sends this computed signature with rest of the tuple $(ID_A, R_A, T_A)$ to B. Upon receiving the tuple $(ID_A, R_A, T_A, \sigma_A)$, B verifies the authenticity of sender by checking whether $\sigma_A \cdot P = T_A + (R_A + h_A \cdot P_{pub})H_2(ID, R_A, T_A)$.

# 6     ID Based Setting and Security Features

All the IP cores possess a core identifier, assigned at the integration time and a private key provided by the on-chip PKG. The PKG maintains a list of all the IP core identifiers. Realizing the identity-based setup, it generates and assigns private keys to IP cores corresponding to their identities. The private key is stored in Non Volatile Memory (NVM) or SRAM, backed up by a small battery. The public key can be derived from the core identifier and some additional information, which may include node location coordinates on 2-D mesh architecture. The IP core must be equipped with the capability of encryption/decryption and hashing. These modules are implemented in the NI as a hardware block, for better efficiency. The PKG is a fully trusted entity and is implemented on a trusted IP core. Moreover, this IP core can be tamper-proof to protect the keys. The eCK security model of ID-2PAKA protocol allows private key and ephemeral secret key reveal in certain settings. In an authenticated key exchange protocol, two parties exchange information and compute a secret key as a function of at least four pieces of secret information: their own long-term and ephemeral keys and the other party's static and ephemeral keys. For two communicating parties, an adversary can reveal any subset of these four secret values. However, it should not include both the long-term and ephemeral secrets of one of the parties.

The continuous security zones do not pose much security threats as the communication is among the security zone routers. The additional measure can be a firewall around these zones. Furthermore, a security aware routing can provide the facility to encapsulate the path inside the zone itself. The major threat which is not well explored, is interzone communication. Sometimes, the allocation of threads to idle IP cores may be random but it should be preferred to create a continuous security zone. If the security zone is disrupted, some group key agreement approaches have been suggested to group those IP and pose them as a cluster. However, these approaches are expensive in terms of computations also, almost all the structures are realized over the PKI-based setup which itself is cost-inefficient with respect to identity-based setup. The verification and storage of all the public keys is a complex task and therefore, in this paper we preferred identity-based cryptosystem where the public key can be derived from the identity itself and there is no need to store any public keys.

In order to secure interzone communication, confidentiality and integrity must be maintained during the transfer of data from one zone to another. The authenticated key agreement protocol derives a session key between anchor nodes of two communicating zones. Moreover, the hash function $H_1$ used in the derivation of session key can be SHA-256 which outputs a key of 256-bits. The least significant 128-bits can be used for encryption algorithm while the rest 128 most significant bits can be used to provide integrity. A compact hardware implementation of lightweight block cipher PRESENT and a lightweight hash function SPONGENT has been presented in [10]. Our work can be considered as complimentary to the work in [10] and hence, the confidentiality and integrity property is maintained during the communication. Additionally, the anchor node may be a bottleneck sometimes to negotiate the session establishment and carry out the communication. However, considering the NoC routing strategies (eg., shortest path), this approach is still highly recommended to avoid multiple session establishment by different IP cores.

## 7   Conclusion

In this paper, we focused on a lightweight solution for zone to zone communication security. The sensitive applications need encryption before forwarding the data to other components on-chip. A two party key exchange algorithm assists to derive a session key for encryption during the communication. The encryption can be performed with any lightweight cipher such as ChaCha20 or PRESENT. We leave this choice to the vendor, depending upon the application requirements. The encryption and decryption block can be easily implemented at the NI of sender and receiver IP cores. The future work will include the real-time analysis of this solution on an MPSoC platform.

## References

1. Endoscope System Architecture Challenges. https://www.embedded-vision.com/platinum-members/xilinx/embedded-vision-training/documents/pages/using-xilinx-fpgas-solve-endoscope-. Accessed 18 Feb 2018
2. Bala, S., Sharma, G., Verma, A.K.: PF-ID-2PAKA: pairing free identity-based two-party authenticated key agreement protocol for wireless sensor networks. Wirel. Pers. Commun. 87(3), 995–1012 (2016)
3. Debiao, H., Jianhua, C., Jin, H.: An ID-based proxy signature schemes without bilinear pairings. Ann. Telecommun. - annales des télécommunications 66(11–12), 657–662 (2011)

4. English, T., Popovici, E., Keller, M., Marnane, W.P.: Network-on-chip interconnect for pairing-based cryptographic IP cores. J. Syst. Arch. **57**(1), 95–108 (2011)
5. Evain, S., Diguet, J.-P.: From NoC security analysis to design solutions. In: IEEE Workshop on Signal Processing Systems Design and Implementation, pp. 166–171. IEEE (2005)
6. Fernandes, R., Marcon, C., Cataldo, R., Silveira, J., Sigl, G., Sepúlveda, J.: A security aware routing approach for NoC-based MPSoCs. In: 2016 29th Symposium on Integrated Circuits and Systems Design (SBCCI), pp. 1–6. IEEE (2016)
7. Fernandes, R., Oliveira, B., Sepúlveda, J., Marcon, C., Moraes, F.G.: A non-intrusive and reconfigurable access control to secure NoCs. In: 2015 IEEE International Conference on Electronics, Circuits, and Systems (ICECS), pp. 316–319. IEEE (2015)
8. Fiorin, L., Palermo, G., Lukovic, S., Catalano, V., Silvano, C.: Secure memory accesses on networks-on-chip. IEEE Trans. Comput. **57**(9), 1216–1229 (2008)
9. Grammatikakis, M.D., et al.: Security effectiveness and a hardware firewall for MPSoCs. In: 2014 IEEE 6th International Symposium on Cyberspace Safety and Security High Performance Computing and Communications, 2014 IEEE 11th International Conference on Embedded Software and Systems (HPCC, CSS, ICESS), pp. 1032–1039. IEEE (2014)
10. Hatzivasilis, G., Floros, G., Papaefstathiou, I., Manifavas, C.: Lightweight authenticated encryption for embedded on-chip systems. Inf. Secur. J.: Glob. Perspect. **25**(4–6), 151–161 (2016)
11. Ni, L., Chen, G., Li, J.: Escrowable identity-based authenticated key agreement protocol with strong security. Comput. Math. Appl. **65**(9), 1339–1349 (2013)
12. Rajesh, J.S., Chakraborty, K., Roy, S.: Hardware Trojan attacks in SoC and NoC. In: Bhunia, S., Tehranipoor, M. (eds.) The Hardware Trojan War, pp. 55–74. Springer, Cham (2018). https://doi.org/10.1007/978-3-319-68511-3_3
13. Sepulveda, J., Fernandes, R., Marcon, C., Florez, D., Sigl, G.: A security-aware routing implementation for dynamic data protection in zone-based MPSoC. In: 2017 30th Symposium on Integrated Circuits and Systems Design (SBCCI), pp. 59–64. IEEE (2017)
14. Sepulveda, J., Flórez, D., Fernandes, R., Marcon, C., Gogniat, G., Sigl, G.: Towards risk aware NoCs for data protection in MPSoCs. In: 2016 11th International Symposium on Reconfigurable Communication-centric Systems-on-Chip (ReCoSoC), pp. 1–8. IEEE (2016)
15. Sepúlveda, J., Flórez, D., Gogniat, G.: Reconfigurable group-wise security architecture for NoC-based MPSoCs protection. In: 2015 28th Symposium on Integrated Circuits and Systems Design (SBCCI), pp. 1–6. IEEE (2015)
16. Sepulveda, J., Flórez, D., Immler, V., Gogniat, G., Sigl, G.: Efficient security zones implementation through hierarchical group key management at NoC-based MPSoCs. Microprocess. Microsyst. **50**, 164–174 (2017)
17. Sepulveda, J., Gogniat, G., Flórez, D., Diguet, J.-P., Zeferino, C., Strum, M.: Elastic security zones for NoC-based 3D-MPSoCs. In: 2014 21st IEEE International Conference on Electronics, Circuits and Systems (ICECS), pp. 506–509. IEEE (2014)
18. Young, C.-P., Chia, C.-C., Chen, L.-B., Huang, J.: On-chip-network cryptosystem: a high throughput and high security architecture. In: IEEE Asia Pacific Conference on Circuits and Systems, APCCAS 2008, pp. 1276–1279. IEEE (2008)

# Online Radicalisation Along a Continuum: From When Individuals Express Grievances to When They Transition into Extremism

Yeslam Al-Saggaf[✉]

School of Computing and Mathematics, Charles Sturt University,
Boorooma Street, Wagga Wagga, NSW 2678, Australia
yalsaggaf@csu.edu.au.com

**Abstract.** The aim of this paper is to propose a methodology to understand the grievances that radical groups could invoke to win the sympathy of youth, differentiate radicalised from non-radicalised individuals using signatures of personality and identify indicators of transition from radicalisation into extremism. The grievances of youth, techniques for identifying radicalised youth and indicators of transition to extremism have not been studied before. This is also the first time that a methodology for tracing radicalisation along a continuum (from when youth express grievances, to when they become radicalised, to when they transition into extremism) has been proposed. The methodology makes a significant contribution to the available strategies for studying online radicalisation.

**Keywords:** Online radicalisation · Extremism · Terrorism · Grievances
Machine learning algorithms for text classification
Stylometric signatures of personality · Critical slowing down near tipping points

## 1 Introduction

Radicalisation of vulnerable individuals poses a significant threat to human lives. Social media sites are increasingly being used as a medium for radicalisation [1–9]. The ubiquity of social media sites, especially among the youth who integrate social media sites as part of their daily existence and to a much higher intensity than many adults, has provided radical groups with a communication channel where they can identify, inform, influence and indoctrinate young people [10]. Social media sites, which reach across the divide of time and space, have provided terrorists with a platform to promote their propaganda to a mass audience of potential sympathisers and recruits [10] who were not possible to reach previously.

Radical groups can invoke a number of narratives to win the sympathy of vulnerable individuals [11] but recent studies by Torok [8] and Al-Saggaf [1] have found that the online radicalisation discourse appeals especially to grievances confirming Borum's [12] earlier conclusions. Borum's [12] notes that invoking grievances is the first step in the radicalisation process. Other narratives for winning sympathy include a shared identity in a diaspora grounded in a perception of victimhood – that Western

© ICST Institute for Computer Sciences, Social Informatics and Telecommunications Engineering 2018
R. Beyah et al. (Eds.): SecureComm 2018, LNICST 255, pp. 429–440, 2018.
https://doi.org/10.1007/978-3-030-01704-0_24

governments and media are conspiring to undermine them [10] and damage their image - consolidating the view that a clash of civilisations between the East and the West is inevitable. Upal [13] highlighted another pretext radical groups can use to win sympathy. According to Upal, a narrative which acknowledges that a group is currently not doing well, reminds the group of its glorious past, and promises that making a change to a group's shared beliefs will restore that glory in the future not only resonates well with some vulnerable people, but is more persuasive than other narratives. Torok's [8] and Al-Saggaf's [1] studies indicate that the grievances are context specific i.e. not generic applying to people broadly. There is no study in the literature that investigated the grievances from a specific context. This paper is a step in the direction of answering this call for such research. Therefore, the first research question is:

*RQ1: What are the grievances that radical groups could invoke to win the sympathy of youth?*

There is a limited but increasing body of research that used big data to understand radicals' use of social media for recruitment [see, for example, 3, 6, 9, and 14]. Bermingham, Conway and McInerney [3], for example, who crawled a YouTube group and applied social network analysis and sentiment analyses on the group's interactions, argued their approach has the potential to unearth content and interaction aimed at radicalisation of those with little or no apparent prior interest in violent extremism. Wadhwa and Bhatia [9] who experimented with investigative data mining to detect the dynamic behaviour of the radical groups in Twitter, concluded that their approach has the potential of informing the understanding of important topics, such as sympathy with extremist ideology as discussed within a large dataset. Meanwhile, Scanlon and Gerber [6] who used machine learning and time-series analysis to forecast cyber-recruitment activity within a Western extremist discussion forum, concluded that the automatic forecasting of violent extremism and cyber-recruitment are possible using their approach.

But, there is no study in the literature that focusses on identifying radicalised individuals in social media using neurolinguistics, and no study in the literature that focussed on when radicalised individuals transition into violent extremism ostensibly because of the risks associated with these kinds of studies [5]. The literature, however, indicates that it is possible to identify radicalised individuals in social media using a neurolinguistics algorithm. Kernot, Bossomaier, and Bradbury's [15–18 and 28, 29] work show that they have been able to create a stylistic fingerprint of a person's personality, i.e. his/her personal signature, from his/her writing style. Using a neurolinguistics algorithm, RPAS, a multi-faceted text analysis technique that draws on a writer's personality, in combination with multiple regression analysis and cross-validation, the authors have been able to correctly separate the works of known writers from the works of other writers. This suggests that by creating a stylometric signature from an individual's writing it is possible to differentiate radicalised individuals from non-radicalised individuals. The second research question is therefore:

*RQ2: Can a neurolinguistics algorithm differentiate radicalised individuals from non-radicalised individuals?*

The literature also indicates that it is also possible to identify the indicators of a tipping point at which radicalised individuals become violent extremists. Research on tipping points can provide clues about sudden changes in an individual's behaviour.

Scheffer et al. [19] argue that certain generic indicators can be used to detect if a system is close to change abruptly in response to changing conditions. Scheffer et al. [19] believe that critical slowing down near tipping points precedes abrupt transitions and this can provide an early-warning signal for critical transitions. This has the potential for identifying with precision when radicalised individuals transition into violent extremism. The third research question is therefore:

*RQ3: Can critical slowing down near tipping points identify when radicalised individuals transition into violent extremism?*

This paper is significant because it is the first time that a methodology to trace individuals along the continuum of radicalisation (i.e., from when they express grievances, to when they become radicalised, to potentially when they transition into violent extremism) has been proposed. The novelty of this methodology comes primarily from the use of a neurolinguistics algorithm and the critical slowing down near tipping points technique along with a mix of other approaches, such as qualitative interviews and machine learning algorithms for text classification, all of which have never been used together before. In addition to advancing knowledge with regards to understanding the grievances that radical groups could invoke to win the sympathy of youth, the use of stylometric signatures of personality to differentiate radicalised individuals from non-radicalised individuals and the critical slowing down near tipping points for identifying when radicalised individuals transition into violent extremism, makes a significant contribution to the available strategies for studying online radicalisation.

## 2  Background

### 2.1  Radicalisation and Terrorism

The terrorism threat is the biggest threat to human life. Radical groups have succeeded in recruiting hundreds of people who are currently fighting with them in Syria, a number which could have reached thousands if the 'wannabe' fighters had not been stopped at the borders of their home countries. Radical groups have also succeeded in recruiting dozens of home grown terrorists, who on a number of occasions succeeded in destroying innocent lives. This sections differentiates between radicalisation and terrorism and highlights one theory that can be used to understand terrorism.

The term radicalisation is widely used, yet there is no consensus on what it actually means [12]. For Borum [12], radicalisation is not a one-off event; it is a process. He defines radicalisation as "the processes by which people come to adopt beliefs that not only justify violence but compel it, and how they progress -or not- from thinking to action" [12, p. 8]. Radicalisation is not the same as terrorism. Radicalisation refers to the process of developing the extremist ideology; whereas terrorism refers to the process of engaging in terrorist (violent) activities [12]. Borum noted that those with an extremist ideology may not engage in terrorist activities; likewise, those who engage in terrorist activities may not necessarily possess a firm understanding of the radical ideologies which they use to justify their actions. Thus, ideology and action can be distinct from each other [12].

Research into online radicalisation has drawn from a number theories that benefited from academic scholarship in the field of Social Psychology but the most relevant one is Bandura's [32] theory of selective moral disengagement. In this theory, Bandura suggests that for individuals to commit actions that would not be committed by another individual with the same moral standards, they must disengage from their moral self-sanctions through one or more mechanisms of moral disengagement. Bandura lists these mechanisms as moral justification (i.e., the individual believes the immoral actions serve moral or socially worthy purposes), euphemistic labelling (e.g., labelling a genocide as a 'cleansing'), advantageous comparison (i.e., the individual uses contrast to make their actions seem less harmful); displacement of responsibility (i.e., the individual blames their actions on authority figures/the organisation), diffusion of responsibility (i.e., the individual diffuses responsibility for their actions across the group), disregard or distortion of consequences (i.e., the individual disregards or distorts the impact of their actions), dehumanisation (i.e., the individual strips their victims of human qualities), and attribution of blame (i.e., the individual blames their actions on the victim).

## 2.2   Radicalisation and Social Media

The terrorists' adoption of social media sites to radicalise vulnerable individuals is a key concern. Before the advent of social media, terrorists' attempts to radicalise vulnerable individuals via online communities achieved limited success, as evidenced by fewer and smaller magnitude terrorist activities compared to the multiple, large attacks post the social media era. One reason for this is radicals were not alone in the online communities in which they were operating [20]. The results of one study showed that there were voices louder than theirs in these online communities, which to some extent drowned their voices out [21, 34]. Other reasons for the limited success of these types of campaigns were that the radicals were either busy fighting in Iraq, killed during that war, serving time in jail or because the online communities' moderators regularly removed their contributions [20]. Even those contributions that escaped the moderators culling tended to be met with heavy criticism from other online community members [22].

However, the widespread adoption of social media sites has completely changed the environment in which radicals operate. Social media sites like YouTube, Facebook, Twitter, Instagram and Snapchat have allowed them to create their own channels to spread their messages and advance their agenda instead of, as before, competing with others for attention over shared media [23]. The revelation that extremists now use the secure messaging App 'Telegram', which emerged while investigating those responsible for the November 2015 Paris attacks, highlights radicals' technological sophistication and their ability to take advantage of the high-tech resources at their disposal. With more than two billion daily active users on Facebook [24], recruiting sympathisers via social media has never been easier [25]. What exacerbates the situation is that in social media 'birds of a feather flock together'. A study by Del Vicario et al. [26] found that users tend to congregate online in communities of interest, and tend to ignore news or information that does not align with their views and beliefs. This results in reinforcement of their current mindsets, and leads to the formation and spread of biased narratives fed by segregation, misinformation, and paranoia.

## 2.3  Radicalisation and Youth Grievances

According to Borum [12], individuals may become radicalised as a result of a personal grievance (i.e., harm or injustice inflicted upon them or a loved one); a political grievance (i.e., harm or injustice inflicted upon their group); social or emotional bonds they have with members of the radical group; being lured, expecting that joining will be exciting/glamorous and/or increase their social status/power; and/or due to experiencing a life event (e.g., loss of a loved one) that removes barriers to participation. This theory is supported by Al-Saggaf [1] who conducted a crawl of radicals' content on Twitter in order to find out why some people become attracted to radicalisation. Results showed that the individuals may have become attracted to radicalisation due to believing that injustice had been inflicted upon them by their country's Secret Police and Royal Family (i.e., having a personal grievance) and wanting to seek revenge.

A number of studies have also identified grievances as a tool leveraged by extremists for recruitment. A study by Ramswell [27] showed that extremists utilise and leverage issues within the socio-economic (e.g., focusing on the lack of economic opportunities), political (e.g., focusing on being invaded by the US), religious (e.g., focusing on the importance of adhering/being loyal to Sharia law) and cultural sphere (e.g., focusing on Islam being disrespected/threatened by the West) to recruit members. Additionally, a study by Torok [8] found that the persecution of Muslims and interference in Muslim lands, anti-Islamic attitudes of Western society, military action in Iraq, inaction of Western governments in Syria, and perceived targeting of the Muslim community were all issues heavily discussed on Facebook pages and internet sites recruiting members and/or promoting or supporting extremism.

## 2.4  Radicalisation and Neurolinguistics

Several strategies have been employed to study online radicalisation, including social network analysis and sentiment analysis [3], investigative data mining [9] and machine learning and time series analysis [6 and 14] but there is no model or algorithm available that can separate radicalised individuals from non-radicalised individuals. Several researchers have proposed and tested methods of differentiating between authors from their writing, which could be used to differentiate radicalised individuals from non-radicalised individuals using their social media posts.

In a recent study, Kernot et al. [15] used the RPAS text analysis technique to create stylistic signatures of the works of Shakespeare, Kyd, and Marlow and compare them to the 19 scenes within Edward III to suggest the authorship. Results showed that Kyd was the likely author of 14 scenes of Edward III, with Shakespeare the likely author of the rest. In another study, Kernot et al. [16] used RPAS text analysis to create stylistic signatures of the works of Shakespeare, Marlowe, Raleigh, Barnfield, and Griffin, as well as the 21 Passionate Pilgrim poems, in order to identify the likely authorship of 12 of the unknown poems. They found that nine of the poems were likely written by Shakespeare, two were likely written by Griffin (or an unknown poet), and one was likely written by Delaney (whose work was not examined). According to the authors, RPAS can not only be applied to classic literature but can also be applied to 'radicalisation' and used to identify the authors of anonymous 'radical' social media posts.

Not only can text analysis be used to distinguish authors, it can also be used to identify changes within their writing style over time. Later in 2017, Kernot et al. [17] used RPAS again to analyse Shakespeare's *Sonnets,* a collection of 154 poems written by Shakespeare in three distinct 'voices' (a feminine voice, a masculine voice, and a deliberately disjoined and contradictory voice), to see whether it was possible to distinguish between them. Results showed that RPAS was able to distinguish between the three voices. Building on this work, Bradbury et al. [28] used the RPAS to separate the authors of anonymous 'radical' social media posts from non-radical posts and found the technique can differentiate these posts with precision.

## 2.5  Radicalisation and the Critical Slowing Down Near Tipping Points

The literature also indicates that it is possible to identify the indicators of a tipping point at which radicalised individuals become violent extremists. Kernot et al. [17] also used the above technique to identify changes within the writers writing style over time. In a recent study, Kernot et al. [18] used two elements of RPAS (i.e., richness and sensory adjectives) to analyse the works of Iris Murdoch and PD James in order to see whether Murdoch's thoughts and language were impacted by depression and apathy as revealed in her writing style 12 years before she was formally diagnosed with Alzheimer's disease. Results showed that Murdoch's works displayed higher lexical repetition in the 12 years prior to her diagnosis, and that low olfactory word use and increased use of sensory-based adjectives might be a sign of the early onset of Alzheimer's. These findings, once again, can be applied to 'radicalisation' and be used to identify changes within the individual during the radicalisation process, specifically as radicalised individuals transition into extremism.

In a recent study, Bradbury, Bossomaier, and Kernot [28] used open source data to look at whether there exists a 'tipping point' where an individual's 'identity' can rapidly shift from one state to another and, if so, whether an individual's identity will show a critical slowing down before changing state. They found that 'identity' can vary in response to external factors (e.g., the death of a loved one) and that it can tip from one state to another. Additionally, it does show a critical slowing down before crossing this threshold. A 'critical slowing down' is defined as a subtle change in identity before and after a tipping point. Another study by Kernot, Bossomaier, and Bradbury [29] examined the 45 novels written by Iris Murdoch and PD James to see if an individual's 'identity' changes over time due to life events and natural ageing. They found that life events such as depression, anxiety, and Alzheimer's can be identified outside of natural ageing through a tipping point phenomenon. The authors suggested that this, too, could be applied to the problem of radicalisation, to identify 'identity' shifts within suspected radicals.

## 3  Methodology

To address the above three research questions, this paper proposes conducting qualitative interviews, crawling social media, applying machine learning for text classification algorithm, and using the RPAS text analysis and the critical slowing down techniques. Following the above three research questions, the plan is divided into three (3) stages where in each stage one of the research questions will be addressed. The data collection and data analysis will commence after gaining ethics approval from CSU's Ethics in Human Research Committee. The research methodology is detailed below. A summary of this methodology is depicted in Fig. 1 below.

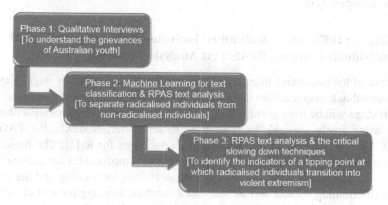

**Fig. 1.** Summary of approach

## 3.1 Stage 1: Understand the Grievances of Youth Using Qualitative Interviews

To understand the grievances that radical groups could invoke to win the sympathy of youth, semi-structured in-depth interviews will be conducted with youth aged 18 years and above. Since most terrorism incidents took place in capital cities and to ensure travel costs are kept to a minimum, the interviews will be conducted in capital cities. Councils and Schools as well as Student Unions at universities, and community leaders will be contacted to seek their assistance with recruiting participants for the interviews. Every effort will be made to choose participants who are representative of demographic characteristics, e.g. age, gender, geographic location, educational level, and employment status. Sixty (60) interviews will be conducted in total to ensure a representative sample is obtained and theoretical saturation is reached. To ensure responses are truthful and in line with the ethics in human research, interviewees will not be asked about their personal grievances; rather their perceptions about existing grievances within their communities. Participants will be cautioned in the informed consent forms that any advocacy for specific terrorism acts prescribed under relevant legislation would need to be reported to authorities. To protect participants' anonymity and maintain their confidentiality, they will be de-identified by removing all their identifying information and replacing their names with unique IDs. All interviews will be audio–recorded, transcribed verbatim and analysed using thematic analysis. QSR NVivo 11 will be used. The unit of analysis will be each individual interview document. First, interview documents will be read several times so the researchers can familiarise themselves with the data. Next, free nodes (i.e. nodes not organised or grouped) will be created based on keywords in the interview documents. Similar text within the interview documents will be located and assigned to these nodes. The nodes will act as 'buckets' in the sense that they will hold all the data related to a specific node. At the end of the creation of the free nodes, the free nodes will be further divided into tree nodes, i.e., broader categories will be developed to group the free nodes. This will create a hierarchy with which it will be possible to make sense of the data and facilitate interpretation.

## 3.2   Stage 2: Differentiate Radicalised Individuals from Non-radicalised Individuals Using the RPAS Text Analysis Technique

The output of the qualitative interviews stage will be the input for this stage. Keywords and phrases that transpired from the analysis of the expression of grievances during the previous stage will be used to crawl YouTube (for comments on videos), Facebook and Twitter using freely available tools such as IssueCrawler, NodeXL, the TAGs App [33], TCAT and TwitteR and SocialMediaLab packages for R [1]. The reason these sites have been chosen is because the majority of social media users are active on them. The extracted corpus will be split into two datasets; one for training and the other for testing. The training dataset will be fed into a machine learning for text classification algorithm, along with a random sample of ordinary social media messages, to train a model to distinguish aggrieved messages from ordinary social media messages. The trained model will then be applied on the testing dataset and another random sample of ordinary social media messages to measure the model's accuracy. The model will be retained if it achieved a 90% or above prediction accuracy. The retained machine learning for text classification model will then be used to classify all retrieved social media messages into aggrieved or non-aggrieved.

Using Regular Expressions tools in R, the usernames contained in the aggrieved messages will be extracted. Using TCAT and TwitteR and SocialMediaLab packages for R along with the usernames extracted in the previous step, the profile of these users will be built. The information collected in this step will include their biographies/ descriptions, latest posts, status updates and tweets, their location, their likes/favorites/ shares/re-tweets, and what latest status updates are liked/favorited/shared/re-tweeted as well as with whom they interacted (mentioned) in their latest posts, status updates and tweets, and who interacted with (mentioned) them. Their networks will also be constructed using the 'igraph' package in R to understand the characteristics of their networks.

Existing social media messages obtained from known radicals will be compared against the dataset developed in previous step using the RPAS text analysis technique to correctly separate aggrieved individuals from radicalised individuals. RPAS creates a stylometric signature from an individual's writing focussing on four indicators: Richness (R), the number of unique words used by an author, associated with education and age; Personal Pronouns (P), the pronouns used, associated with gender and self; Referential Activity Power (A), based on identifiers of depression; and Sensory (S) measures (visual, auditory, haptic olfactory and gustatory) from adjectives that correspond to the use of the senses [28]. By focusing on subtle characteristics hidden in a person's writing style, a person's personality can be revealed [28]. RPAS will be used in this step in conjunction with the Linguistic Inquiry and Word Count (LIWC) text program for measuring emotions in writing; multiple regression analysis and cross-validation. The usernames of the individuals classified by RPAS as radicalised will be stored in a dataset.

## 3.3 Stage 3: Identify the Indicators of a Tipping Point at Which Radicalised Individuals Transition into Violent Extremism Using the Critical Slowing Down Technique

The messages posted on YouTube, Facebook and Twitter by the anonymised usernames of the individuals, classified by RPAS in the previous step as radicalised, will be collected from these sites using IssueCrawler, NodeXL, the TAGs App, TCAT and TwitteR and SocialMediaLab packages for R over a year and stored in a dataset. While gathering the messages posted by the anonyms radicalised usernames following the process outlined in previous step, these anonymised individuals will be closely monitored for sudden changes in behaviour. Once a tipping point has been identified for an individual in which his/her behaviour tipped from one state to another, the dynamics before the behaviour abruptly changed will be studied using the critical slowing down technique. The idea is that as an individual's behaviour approaches a tipping point, i.e. before it tips from one state to another, such as from radicalised to extremism, it will show indicators of critical slowing down and these can provide an early-warning signal of a transition [28]. To apply this technique to the collected data, one of the RPAS elements, Referential Activity Power, which scores an individual from their writing across four categories, will be used focusing only on two categories namely that verbal expression have sensate characteristics and can reflect experiencing a sensation (concreteness) and a person's language can capture an emotional experience (imageability) [28]. Low scores on these two dimensions reflect a person's low sense of self, which can suggest a psychological disturbance. The dynamics near a tipping point will be studied using the skewness, which is a measure of the asymmetry in the distribution of a time series data, and time shifting, which is correlating the time series with itself at one step in time lag, in the elements of the Referential Activity Power [28]. Due to the sensitive nature of data, anonymisation of data will occur at the collection stage. Users will be de-identified by removing all their identifying information and replacing the usernames with unique IDs, which will represent them throughout. This will be done for historical and live data.

## 3.4 Summary of Methodology

Stage 1 will shed light on the grievances that radical groups could invoke to win the sympathy of youth using qualitative interviews with individuals aged 18 years and above. In Stage 2 the keywords and phrases that emerged from the analysis of the expression of grievances in Stage 1 will be used to crawl social media to then train a model to distinguish aggrieved messages from ordinary social media messages. The usernames contained in the aggrieved messages will be used to extract every piece of information available about the aggrieved individuals and this information will be compared against information obtained from known radicals [1] using the RPAS text analysis technique to correctly separate aggrieved individuals from radicalised individuals. In Stage 3, the social media messages posted by individuals classified by RPAS in the previous step as radicalised will be collected over year while closely monitoring the radicalised individuals for sudden changes in behaviour. Once a tipping point has been identified for an individual, the dynamics before the behaviour abruptly changed will be studied using the critical slowing down technique to identify the indicators of a transition from radicalised to extremist.

## 4  Discussion

The research addresses a significant problem. The threat of terrorism is real and continues to spread and diversify [30]. Terrorism poses a significant threat to nations' national securities [30]. With the ability of the internet to cross borders, geographic isolation is no longer the buttress that it once was and any country on the planet is vulnerable to terrorism. Of the 7.3 billion worldwide, more than two billion are daily active users on Facebook [24], of whom a large group are children and young adults. There is a need for research that focusses on the youth, who are the terrorists' main target, to address the reasons why some young people become attracted to the terrorist agenda [10]. Security and law enforcement agencies are monitoring social media sites where radicalised individuals 'meet' and are aware of the need to counter the extremist narrative on sites, but as Upal [13] notes, the efforts so far have not been informed by a thorough understanding of the potential sympathisers' identities, cultures and grievances. This paper is a step in the direction of answering these calls for research by first understanding the grievances of youth.

This project will advance knowledge about online radicalisation in two ways. (1) Since the grievances from a specific context have not been studied before, this research will make a significant contribution to filling this gap in the literature. (2) Online radicalisation has not been studied before along a continuum. This research will fill an important information need namely the indicators associated with the transitions from when individuals express grievances, to when they become radicalised, to potentially when they transition into violent extremism.

The novelty of this project comes primarily from the use of a neurolinguistics algorithm and the critical slowing down near tipping points technique along with a mix of other approaches, such as qualitative interviews and machine learning algorithms for text classification, all of which have never been used together before. This is also the first time that an attempt will be made to trace individuals along the continuum of radicalisation using naturally occurring big data. In their review of the literature on Facebook, Wilson, Gosling and Graham [31] noted that studying how users choose to portray themselves in their personal profiles presents an excellent opportunity for social scientists to study, as these profiles elicit accurate impressions. Wilson et al. [31] asked social scientists, who underappreciated social media profiles as a source of data, to take advantage of this unprecedented opportunity to study the social phenomenon in its natural setting where it occurs. This paper is a step in the direction of answering this call.

# 5   Conclusion

No study in the literature investigated the grievances from a specific context and online radicalisation has not been studied before along a continuum making this paper a significant contribution to the scarce literature in this area. In addition to these key theoretical contributions, the plan to use a neurolinguistics algorithm and the critical slowing down technique near tipping points along with qualitative interviews and machine learning algorithms for text classification, all of which have never been used together before or applied on big data, is a methodological contribution to the techniques available to online radicalisation researchers.

**Acknowledgments.** The author wishes to thank Prof Terry Bossomaier (Charles Sturt University) for his contribution and A/Prof Patrick Walsh (Charles Sturt University) and Rachel MacCulloch (Charles Sturt University) for their helpful comments and suggestions.

# References

1. Al-Saggaf, Y.: Understanding online radicalisation using data science. Int. J. Cyber Warf. Terror. (IJCWT) **6**(4), 12–27 (2016)
2. Bergin, A.: The internet as a platform for radicalisation. In: Proceedings of the Strategic Policy Forum, 5 May 2009, pp. 1–2. Australian Strategic Policy Institute, Perth (2009)
3. Bermingham, A., Conway, M., McInerney, L., O'Hare, N., Smeaton, A.F.: Combining social network analysis and sentiment analysis to explore the potential for online radicalisation. In: International Conference on Advances in Social Network Analysis and Mining, ASONAM 2009, pp. 231–236. IEEE, July 2009
4. Edwards, C., Gribbon, L.: Pathways to violent extremism in the digital era. RUSI J. **158**(5), 40–47 (2013)
5. Reynolds, T.: Ethical and legal issues surrounding academic research into online radicalisation: a UK experience. Crit. Stud. Terror. **5**(3), 499–513 (2012)
6. Scanlon, J.R., Gerber, M.S.: Forecasting violent extremist cyber recruitment. IEEE Trans. Inf. Forensics Secur. **10**(11), 2461–2470 (2015)
7. Spaaij, R., Hamm, M.S.: Key issues and research agendas in lone wolf terrorism. Stud. Confl. Terror. **38**(3), 167–178 (2015)
8. Torok, R.: Discourses of terrorism: the role of Internet technologies (social media and online propaganda) on Islamic radicalisation, extremism and recruitment post 9/11. Unpublished PhD Thesis. Edith Cowan University (2016)
9. Wadhwa, P., Bhatia, M.P.S.: Tracking on-line radicalization using investigative data mining. In: 2013 National Conference on Communication (NCC), pp. 1–5. IEEE, February 2013
10. Aly, A.: Online radicalisation and the Muslim Diaspora. In: Proceedings of the Strategic Policy Forum, pp. 7–8. Australian Strategic Policy Institute, Perth, Australia, 5 May 2009
11. McCauley, C., Moskalenko, S.: Mechanisms of political radicalization: pathways toward terrorism. Terror. Politi. Violence **20**(3), 415–433 (2008)
12. Borum, R.: Radicalization into violent extremism I: a review of social science theories. J. Strat. Secur. **4**(4), 7–36 (2011). https://doi.org/10.5038/1944-0472.4.4.1
13. Upal, M.A.: Confronting Islamic Jihadist movements. J. Terror. Res. **6**(2), 57–69 (2015)
14. Scanlon, J.R., Gerber, M.S.: Automatic detection of cyber-recruitment by violent extremists. Secur. Inf. **3**(1), 1–10 (2014)

15. Kernot, D., Bossomaier, T., Bradbury, R.: Novel text analysis for investigating properties of self: did Shakespeare and Thomas Kyd write Edward III? (2017)
16. Kernot, D., Bossomaier, T., Bradbury, R.: Stylometric techniques for multiple author clustering: Shakespeare's authorship in the Passionate Pilgrim. Int. J. Adv. Comput. Sci. Appl. **8**, 1–8 (2017)
17. Kernot, D., Bossomaier, T., Bradbury, R.: Novel text analysis for investigating personality: identifying the dark lady in Shakespeare's Sonnets. J. Quant. Linguist. **24**, 255–272 (2017)
18. Kernot, D., Bossomaier, T., Bradbury, R.: The impact of depression and apathy on sensory language. Open J. Modern Linguist. **7**, 8–32 (2017)
19. Scheffer, M., et al.: Anticipating critical transitions. Science **338**, 344–348 (2012)
20. Al-Saggaf, Y., Kharabsheh, R.: Political online communities in Saudi Arabia: the major players. In: Hongladarom, S. (ed.) Proceedings of the Third Asia Pacific Computing and Philosophy Conference, pp. 27–47. The Center for Ethics of Science and Technology, Chulalongkorn University, Bangkok (2009)
21. Al-Saggaf, Y., Weckert, J.: Political online communities (POCs) in Saudi Arabia. In: Marshall, S., Taylor, W., Yu, X. (eds.) Encyclopaedia of Developing Regional Communities with ICT, pp. 557–563. Idea Group Reference, Hershey (2006)
22. Al-Saggaf, Y.: Exploring political online forums in Saudi Arabia through thematic content analysis. In: Hongladarom, S. (ed.) Computing and Philosophy in Asia, pp. 13–30. Cambridge Scholars Publishing, Newcastle (2007)
23. Al-Saggaf, Y., Simmons, P.: Social media in Saudi Arabia: exploring its use during two natural disasters. Technol. Forecast. Soc. Chang. **95**, 3–15 (2015). https://doi.org/10.1016/j.techfore.2014.08.013
24. SproutSocial. https://sproutsocial.com/insights/facebook-stats-for-marketers/
25. Torok, R.: Developing an explanatory model for the process of online radicalisation and terrorism. Secur. Inf. **2**(1), 1–10 (2013)
26. Del Vicario, M., et al.: The spreading of misinformation online. PNAS Early Ed. **113**(3), 554–559 (2016)
27. Ramswell, P.Q.: The utilization and leveraging of grievance as a recruitment tool and justification for terrorist acts committed by Islamic extremists. Small Wars J. (2014). http://smallwarsjournal.com/jrnl/art/the-utilization-and-leveraging-of-grievance-as-a-recruitment-tool-and-justification-for-ter
28. Bradbury, R., Bossomaier, T., Kernot, D.: Predicting the emergence of self-radicalisation through social media: a complex systems approach. In: Conway, M., Jarvis, L., Lehane, O., Macdonald, S., Nouri, L. (eds.) Terrorists' use of the internet: assessment and response, pp. 379–389. IOS Press, Amsterdam (2017)
29. Kernot, D., Bossomaier, T., Bradbury, R.: The stylometric impacts of ageing and life events on identity. J. Quant. Linguist. (2017). https://doi.org/10.1080/09296174.2017.1405719
30. AFP: Fighting terrorism (2018). https://www.afp.gov.au/what-we-do/crime-types/fighting-terrorism
31. Wilson, R.E., Gosling, S.D., Graham, L.T.: A review of Facebook research in the social sciences. Perspect. Psychol. Sci. **7**(3), 203–220 (2012)
32. Bandura, A.: Selective moral disengagement in the exercise of moral agency. J. Moral Educ. **31**, 101–119 (2002)
33. Al-Saggaf, Y., Chutikulrungsee, T.T.: Twitter usage in Australia and Saudi Arabia and influence of culture: an exploratory cross-country comparison. In: Paterno, D., Bourk, M., Matheson, D. (eds.) Refereed proceedings of the Australian and New Zealand Communication Association Conference: Rethinking communication, space and identity (2015). http://www.anzca.net/conferences/past-conferences/
34. Al-Saggaf, Y., Himma, K., Kharabsheh, R.: Political online communities in Saudi Arabia: the major players. J. Inf. Commun. Eth. Soc. **6**(2), 127–140 (2008)

# A Multiple Linear Regression Based High-Performance Error Prediction Method for Reversible Data Hiding

Bin Ma[1(✉)], Xiaoyu Wang[1], Bing Li[2], and Yunqing Shi[2]

[1] School of Information Science, Qilu University of Technology
(Shandong Academic of Science), Jinan 250300, China
sddxmb@126.com

[2] New Jersey Institute of Technology, New Jersey 07102, USA

**Abstract.** In this paper, a high-performance error-prediction method based on multiple linear regression (MLR) algorithm is proposed to improve the performance of reversible data hiding (RDH). The MLR matrix function indicates the inner correlation between the pixels and its neighbors is established adaptively according to the consistency of pixels in local area of a natural image, and thus the object pixel is predicted accurately with the achieved MLR function that satisfies the consistency of the neighboring pixels. Compared with conventional methods that only predict the object pixel with simple arithmetic combination of its surroundings pixel, the experimental results show that the proposed method can provide a sparser prediction-error image for data embedding, and thus improves the performance of RDH more effectively than those state-of-the-art error prediction algorithms.

**Keywords:** Multiple linear regression · Reversible data hiding
Prediction error · Embedded capacity

## 1 Introduction

Reversible data hiding (RDH) enables the embedding of secret message into a host image without loss of any original information. It considers not only extracting the hidden message correctly, but also recovering the original image exactly after data extraction [1]. Data hiding capacity and image fidelity are the two main important indicators of RDH algorithm. To improving the data embedding capacity and maintaining the quality of the marked images simultaneously is a big challenge in this area. At present, RDH based on difference expansion and RDH based on histogram shifting are two kinds of most prevalent methods being widely employed. In a difference expansion based RDH scheme, the secret messages are embedded by multiplying the difference between the object pixel and its predicted value (prediction-error); while, the RDH scheme based on histogram shifting achieves data embedding by translating the largest number of prediction errors. If the prediction-errors are small and distribute around "0" closely, the prediction-error image employed for data hiding would minimize the distortion of the marked image largely after data embedding.

© ICST Institute for Computer Sciences, Social Informatics and Telecommunications Engineering 2018
R. Beyah et al. (Eds.): SecureComm 2018, LNICST 255, pp. 441–452, 2018.
https://doi.org/10.1007/978-3-030-01704-0_25

As the secret messages are hidden into the redundant information of the host image, accurate error prediction algorithm can obtain small prediction-errors and thus the histogram distributes steeper around "0", causing the data embedding capacity is enhanced at the same marked image quality. Therefore, the study of high performance error predictor to improve the prediction accuracy of object pixel attracts more and more attentions. Tian [2] presented the first difference expansion based RDH scheme, through which the secret data can be embedded and extracted exactly without damage the original image. Thodi and Rodríguez [3] firstly provided the prediction-error expansion based RDH scheme. This new technique exploited the inherent correlation between the object pixel and its neighbors better than Tian's difference-expansion scheme. Therefore, the prediction-error expansion method reduced the image distortion at low embedding capacity and mitigates the capacity control problem. Fallahpour *et al.* [4] illustrated a lossless data hiding method based on the technique of gradient-adjusted prediction (GAP), in which the prediction-errors are computed and slightly modified with histogram shifting method, so as to hided more secret message at high PSNR. Later on, Sachnev *et al.* [5] proposed the rhombus error prediction method to embed secret message into an image, and a sorting technique is employed to record the prediction-errors according to the magnitude of its local variance. The sorted prediction errors and a size reduced location map allowed more data can be embedded into the image with less distortion. Yang and Tsai [6] provided an interleaving error prediction method, in which the numbers of predictive values are as many as the pixels, and all prediction-errors are transformed into image histogram to create higher peak bins to improve the embedding capacity. Recently, Dragoi and Coltuc [7] presented a local error prediction method and evaluated it with difference expansion based RDH scheme. For each pixel, a least square predictor is established from a square block centered on the pixel, and thus the smaller corresponding prediction-errors are obtained. The method is employed regardless of the predictor order or the prediction context, which enable it achieved higher reversible data hiding performance.

Although the traditional error prediction methods have greatly improved the accuracy of prediction errors by exploring the similarity between the object pixel and their neighborhoods, the inner correlation among adjacent pixels in the image is still not having been fully exploited. So, it is still instructive to explore more effective error prediction methods to improve the performance of reversible data hiding.

In this paper, a new kind of error prediction method based on multiple linear regression (MLR) is proposed. Unlike the conventional methods just employ the simple arithmetical combinations of the objective pixel's neighbors to represent its value, the proposed method explores the inner correlation among the object pixel and its neighborhoods. The method adaptively studies the inner relation among the object pixel and its neighbors, and then predicts the object pixel with the MLR function achieved from its neighboring pixels. According to the local consistency of the natural image, the prediction accuracy is highly improved and the value of the prediction-errors are minimized, which enable the image prediction-errors distribute around "0" closely and the histogram distribute steep. And thus, the performance of RDH scheme based on the proposed prediction-error image outperforms those state-of-the-art schemes based on conventional counterparts clearly.

The outline of the paper is as follows. The principle of MLR algorithm is introduced in Sect. 2. The error prediction method based on MLR algorithm for RDH is presented in Sect. 3. The experimental results of error prediction based on MLR algorithm are shown in 4. In Sect. 5, the comparisons of RDH performance based on the proposed prediction-error image and images from other state-of-the-art algorithms are demonstrated. Finally, conclusions are drawn in Sect. 6.

## 2 Multiple Linear Regression Algorithm Based Error Prediction

Multiple linear regression is a linear approach for modeling the relationship between a scalar dependent variable $Y$ and independent variables denoted by $X$. The relationships are modeled with the linear predictor whose unknown model parameters are estimated from the data, and such models are called linear models. The basic purpose of MLR is utilizing the independent variables to estimate another dependent variable and its variability.

The general model of multiple linear regression is

$$y_i = \beta_0 + \beta_1 x_{i1} + \beta_2 x_{i2} + \cdots + \beta_k x_{ik} + \varepsilon \tag{1}$$

Where, $\beta_0, \beta_1, \beta_2, \ldots, \beta_k$ are $k+1$ unknown parameters, $\beta_0$ is regression constant, $\beta_1, \beta_2, \ldots, \beta_k$ are called regression coefficients, $x_1, x_2, \ldots, x_k$ is variables that can be accurately measured, and $\varepsilon$ is random error.

In a multiple variable estimated system, where the variables comply with the same mapping regular, the MLR function can be expressed in matrix format as

$$Y = \beta X + \varepsilon \tag{2}$$

Where, $Y, \beta, X$ are as follows

$$y = \begin{bmatrix} y_1 \\ y_2 \\ \vdots \\ y_n \end{bmatrix} \quad \beta = \begin{bmatrix} \beta_0 \\ \beta_1 \\ \vdots \\ \beta_n \end{bmatrix} \quad \varepsilon = \begin{bmatrix} \varepsilon_1 \\ \varepsilon_1 \\ \vdots \\ \varepsilon_n \end{bmatrix} \quad X = \begin{bmatrix} 1 & x_{11} & x_{12} & \cdots & x_{1k} \\ 1 & x_{21} & x_{22} & \cdots & x_{2k} \\ \vdots & \vdots & \vdots & \cdots & \vdots \\ 1 & x_{n1} & x_{n2} & \cdots & x_{nk} \end{bmatrix} \tag{3}$$

The above matrix equation can be solved with the Least-Square method, so that the MLR function is constructed with respect to the known and unknown variables, which enables the sum of the squared deviations between the estimated and observed values of the model is as small as possible, i.e. the sum of squared residuals is smallest. At last, the value of the regression coefficients $\beta$ is calculated as formula (4), and the prediction of the object variables is achieved effectively.

$$\beta = (X^T X)^{-1} X^T Y \tag{4}$$

## 3  Multiple Linear Regression Based Objective Pixel Error Prediction

According to the consistency of pixels in local area of natural image, the neighboring pixels generally have similar values, and the neighboring pixels and the object pixel from same local area usually have close relation. Thus, the object pixel can be predicted by exploiting the inner relation among its neighboring pixels.

Suppose the object pixel to be predicted is $x_{m,n}$, its neighboring pixels are chosen as the prediction samples, and the prediction result is $x'_{m,n}$. The multiple linear regression predictor of the object pixel is

$$x'_{m,n} = \beta_0 + \beta_1 x_{m,n-1} + \beta_2 x_{m-1,n-1} + \ldots + \beta_k x_{m-1,n+1} + \varepsilon \tag{5}$$

Where, $x_{m,n-1}, x_{m-1,n-1}, \ldots, x_{m-1,n+1}$ are the neighbors of object pixel.

Considering the closely correlation of pixels distribute in local area of natural image, the object pixel and its neighbors usually comply with the same pixel prediction function, thus, the object pixel can be predicted with the same function of its neighboring pixels precisely. In the light of this principle, the object pixel is not predicted through simple arithmetical combinations with its neighboring pixels in our proposed scheme, but through the MLR function established from the neighboring pixels, and thus, the prediction accuracy of the object pixel is improved.

Let $x_{m,n}$ be the pixel to be predicted, choose 4 pixels around the object pixel as the prediction samples, at the same time, choose 4 neighboring pixels of each prediction sample as training samples. Construct the MLR matrix function with the training samples as variables $X$ and the prediction samples as variable $Y$. The MLR coefficients that indicate the inner correlation of pixels in local area are obtained by least-square method. Then, the object pixel is predicted with the achieved MLR equation which indicates the consistency relations of neighboring pixels in local area.

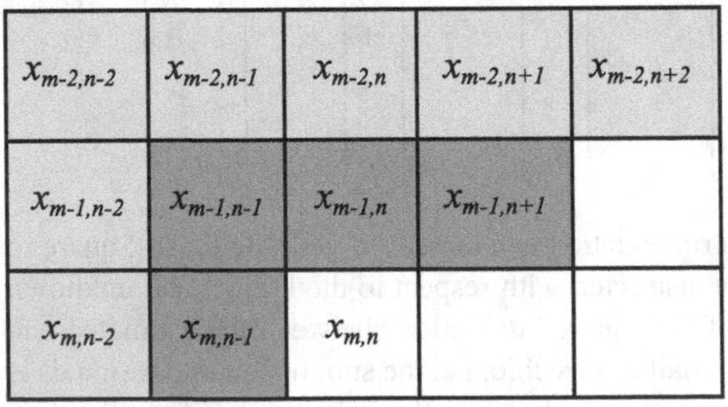

| $x_{m-2,n-2}$ | $x_{m-2,n-1}$ | $x_{m-2,n}$ | $x_{m-2,n+1}$ | $x_{m-2,n+2}$ |
|---|---|---|---|---|
| $x_{m-1,n-2}$ | $x_{m-1,n-1}$ | $x_{m-1,n}$ | $x_{m-1,n+1}$ | |
| $x_{m,n-2}$ | $x_{m,n-1}$ | $x_{m,n}$ | | |

**Fig. 1.** Pixel chosen method.

In the first stage, choose the four pixels at the top left of the object pixel $x_{m,n-1}, x_{m-1,n-1}, x_{m-1,n}, x_{m-1,n+1}$ (shown as Fig. 1, the Euclidean distance to object pixel is less than 2 pixels) as prediction samples, and every four pixels located at the upper left corner of each prediction pixel is chosen as the training sample. Then, the MLR matrix function is established according to the relationship between the training samples and the training pixels (shown as formula (6)).

$$
\begin{bmatrix} x_{m,n-1} \\ x_{m-1,n-1} \\ x_{m-1,n} \\ x_{m-1,n+1} \end{bmatrix} = \begin{bmatrix} x_{m,n-2} & x_{m-1,n-2} & x_{m-1,n-1} & x_{m-1,n} \\ x_{m-1,n-2} & x_{m-2,n-2} & x_{m-2,n-1} & x_{m-2,n} \\ x_{m-1,n-1} & x_{m-2,n-1} & x_{m-2,n} & x_{m-2,n+1} \\ x_{m-1,n} & x_{m-2,n} & x_{m-2,n+1} & x_{m-2,n+2} \end{bmatrix} \begin{bmatrix} \beta_1 \\ \beta_2 \\ \beta_3 \\ \beta_4 \end{bmatrix} + \begin{bmatrix} \varepsilon_1 \\ \varepsilon_2 \\ \varepsilon_3 \\ \varepsilon_4 \end{bmatrix} \quad (6)
$$

The MLR coefficients are obtained by Least-Squares method. As the optimal resolutions of MLR matrix function enable to minimize the sum of squared residuals (the residual is the difference between the estimated and original pixels), the optimal coefficients of a MLR function composed by the similar neighboring pixels are achieved.

In the following stage, the obtained MLR function and the four pixels locate at the upper left corner of the object pixel are employed to predict the object pixel value according to the formula (7).

$$
\hat{x}_{m,n} = \beta_1 x_{m,n-1} + \beta_2 x_{m-1,n-1} + \beta_3 x_{m-1,n} + \beta_4 x_{m-1,n+1} \quad (7)
$$

Finally, the prediction-error is obtained with the formula (8), where, the original pixel value is subtracted by its predicted value.

$$
e(i,j) = round(x(m,n) - \hat{x}(m,n)) \quad (8)
$$

To further exploit the inner correlations among adjacent pixels in the local area, the combination of training samples and the prediction samples can be altered to increase the number of training instances. Generally, the more pixel combinations are involved in MLR matrix function training stage, the more suitable MLR coefficients can be achieved, and the more accuracy object pixel prediction is obtained. More instances MLR function can be established according to formula (9). Where, the training instance is 8 (named $8 \times 4$), two times of the instance 4 in formula (6) (named $4 \times 4$).

$$
\begin{bmatrix} x_{m,n-1} \\ x_{m-1,n-1} \\ x_{m-1,n} \\ x_{m-1,n+1} \\ x_{m-1,n-1} \\ x_{m-1,n-1} \\ x_{m-1,n} \\ x_{m-1,n+1} \end{bmatrix} = \begin{bmatrix} x_{m,n-2} & x_{m-1,n-2} & x_{m-1,n-1} & x_{m-1,n} \\ x_{m-1,n-2} & x_{m-2,n-1} & x_{m-1,n} & x_{m,n-1} \\ x_{m-1,n-1} & x_{m-2,n-1} & x_{m-2,n} & x_{m-1,n+1} \\ x_{m-1,n} & x_{m-2,n} & x_{m-2,n+1} & x_{m-1,n+2} \\ x_{m-1,n-2} & x_{m-2,n-2} & x_{m-2,n-1} & x_{m-1,n} \\ x_{m-1,n-2} & x_{m-2,n-1} & x_{m-2,n} & x_{m-1,n} \\ x_{m-1,n-1} & x_{m-2,n} & x_{m-2,n+1} & x_{m-1,n+1} \\ x_{m-1,n} & x_{m-2,n+1} & x_{m-2,n+2} & x_{m-1,n+2} \end{bmatrix} \begin{bmatrix} \beta_1 \\ \beta_2 \\ \beta_3 \\ \beta_4 \end{bmatrix} + \begin{bmatrix} \varepsilon_1 \\ \varepsilon_2 \\ \varepsilon_3 \\ \varepsilon_4 \\ \varepsilon_5 \\ \varepsilon_6 \\ \varepsilon_7 \\ \varepsilon_8 \end{bmatrix} \quad (9)
$$

Apparently, the proposed method does not just rely on the simple arithmetical combination of pixels closely adjacent to the object pixel to predict the object pixel, but learns the inner correlations between the training samples and the prediction samples. According to the close relations of local pixels, the object pixel is predicted with the optimized MLR function established from its neighboring pixels. As the method adaptively learns the inner correlations of pixels distribute in local area, the accuracy of prediction is improved clearly compared with those coefficients fixed error prediction method.

## 4 Experimental Result and Discussion

To evaluate the performance of the proposed MLR based error prediction method, four well known standard $512 \times 512$ test images include *Lena*, *Baboon*, *Airplane* and *Tiffany* (see Fig. 2) from the image database of MISC are chosen to evaluate the performance of the proposed method. As image *Lena* and *Tiffany* have plenty of moderate frequency information, that is, it is moderate texture complexity; while image *Baboon* is high texture complexity, and image *Airplane* is with large uniform areas. Thus, experiments with these four images can evaluate the performance of the proposed error prediction method comprehensively.

In the experiment, the object pixel is predicted by four neighboring pixels locate on its upper left corner which are defined as prediction samples. It is supposed that the data embedding is from the lower right corner to the upper left corner, so that the value of the prediction samples are consistent before and after data embedding, and then the accurate pixel prediction is achieved. The training samples on the upper left corner of the prediction samples are employed to established the MLR function coefficients, and the objective pixel is predicted with the established MLR function and the four prediction samples.

Moreover, to enable the correct extraction of the embedded message and the lossless recovery of the original image, the left and right two columns as well as the top and bottom two rows of the image are not involved in the reversible data hiding process, while, they are generally reserved for additional information saving or other specific application. Therefore, the net amount of the pixels involved for RDH is $508 \times 508$ actually. Here, two kinds of MLR equations establish method (8 training instances and 4 training instances) are involved to evaluate the performance of the proposed method. Meanwhile, we compare the proposed error prediction method with other state-of-the-art error prediction methods such as Yang *et al.*'s method and Sachnev *et al.*'s method. Yang *et al.* proposed the interleaving prediction methods, in which the number of prediction-errors are as many as the pixels, Sachnev *et al.* presented the rhombus error prediction method for RDH. They all have achieved excellent experimental results in the process of object pixel error prediction. The experimental results are shown in Fig. 3.

**Fig. 2.** Test images of *Lena, Baboon, Airplane* and *Tiffany*

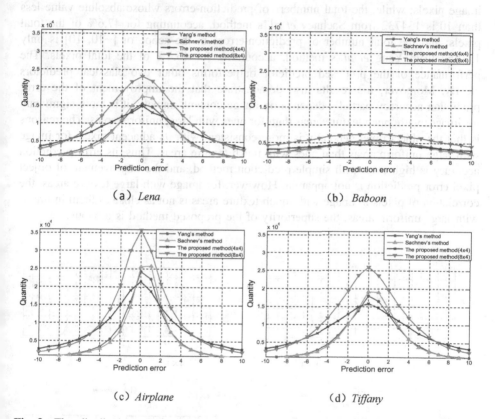

(a) *Lena*

(b) *Baboon*

(c) *Airplane*

(d) *Tiffany*

**Fig. 3.** The distribution of the prediction-errors from −10 to 10 of image *Lena, Baboon, Airplane* and *Tiffany*.

Figure 3 shows that the proposed scheme with 8 training instances achieves higher performance than other state-of-the-art schemes clearly. As for image *Lena*, the numbers of prediction-errors "0" obtained from the proposed method is 23190, while, it is 15518 for Yang *et al.*'s method, and 17668 for Sachnev *et al.*'s method. For image *Baboon*, the proposed scheme achieves better results than other two methods, the numbers of prediction-errors "0" are 7626, 5809, 5609 with the proposed method,

Yang *et al.*'s method and Sachnev *et al.*'s method separately. Even for image *Airplane*, the proposed scheme also achieves higher prediction accuracy than other two methods, it achieves 35808 prediction-error "0", well over 24265, 25643 prediction-error "0" with Yang *et al.*'s method and Sachnev *et al.*'s method. For image *Tiffany*, the numbers of prediction-error "0" is 25962 with the proposed method, but 18034 and 19207 with Yang *et al.*'s method and Sachnev *et al.*'s method. The experimental results also show that the number of prediction-errors in the scope of [−10, 10] obtained from the MLR algorithm is obviously better than from other algorithms. Take image *Lena* as an example, the total numbers of pixels with prediction-errors belongs to [−10, 10] is 226805 obtained from the proposed method (8 × 4), accounting for 86.5% of total image pixels; while, the total numbers of prediction-errors whose absolute value less than 10 is 134732 from Sachnev *et al.*'s method, accounting for 47.6% of the total pixels; and the total number of prediction-errors in the scope of [−10, 10] is only 121562 from Yang *et al.*'s method, accounting for 46.4% of the total pixels. The performance of the proposed predictor outperforms other two classical predictors clearly. Moreover, the results also demonstrate that the improvement of the error prediction accuracy partially depends on image content, namely, it is more significant for images with much texture areas than for ones with large uniform areas. The reasons is that the object pixel generally is more consistent with its adjacent pixels for image with large uniform areas than ones with much texture areas. Thus, its error prediction accuracy is high even with simple prediction method, and the improvement of object pixel error prediction is not apparent. However, for image with large texture areas, the correlation of pixels in image with much texture areas is not as close as them in image with large uniform areas, the superiority of the proposed method is obvious.

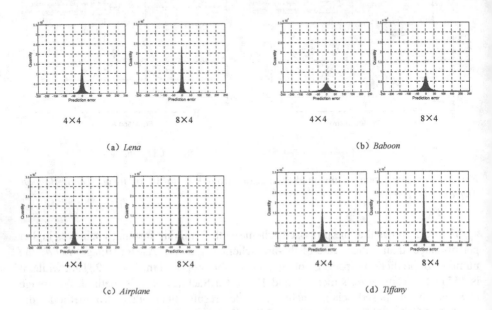

    4×4          8×4               4×4          8×4

(a) *Lena*                (b) *Baboon*

    4×4          8×4               4×4          8×4

(c) *Airplane*              (d) *Tiffany*

**Fig. 4.** The prediction-error histogram on four images with the proposed method.

Further, we compare the error prediction results of the proposed method with 4 and 8 training instances. As shown in Fig. 4, it is clear to see that the latter achieves higher prediction precision than the former. Take image *Lena* as an example, the numbers of prediction-errors "0" obtained with 4 training instances is 15015, while the numbers of prediction-errors "0" obtained with 8 training instances is 23190, which is increased by 54.4% compared with the former. More training instances can helps achieve higher error prediction accuracy. Figure 4 also demonstrates that the more accuracy the error prediction achieves, the steeper the curve is. It is obvious that image *Airplane* achieves the best prediction-error histogram and image *Baboon* is the worst one, while, image *Baboon* achieves the highest error prediction improvement. The reason is that for image with more uniform areas, the consistency of the adjacent pixels in a local area is strong, thus high accuracy error prediction is obtained, and the prediction-error histogram usually distribute steep around "0". However, our proposed method learns the inner relation between the object pixel and its neighbors and thus achieves more accurate pixel prediction than those schemes only predicted the object pixel with simple arithmetic combinations on its neighboring pixels. Thus, the propose scheme achieves better error prediction performance than conventional schemes, especially for image with much texture areas, where the object pixel has weak correlations.

Moreover, as it always be employed to evaluate the distortion of an image, we consider the mean square error (MSE) between the predicted and the original image. Figure 5 clearly appears that the proposed scheme outperforms other three classical predictors on four popular test image. Take image *Lena* as an example, it is clear to see that the MSE is 0.58 when the proposed method executed with 8 training instances, and 1.165 with 4 training instances, while the MSE are 1.10, 0.81 and 0.72 when the image predicted with Yang *et al.*'s, sachnev *et al.*'s and Dragoi *et al.*'s methods separately. The distortion of the predicted image formulated with the proposed method is small, especially when it executed with 8 training instances (Table 1).

**Table 1.** The MSE of predicted image for Yang *et al.*'s, Sachnev *et al.*'s, Dragoi *et al.*'s and the proposed method

| Test images | Yang's method | Sachnev's method | Dragoi's method | The proposed method | |
|---|---|---|---|---|---|
| | | | | $4 \times 4$ | $8 \times 4$ |
| Lena | 1.1 | 0.81 | 0.72 | 1.16 | 0.58 |
| Baboon | 6.84 | 7.96 | 5.87 | 8.89 | 3.11 |
| Airplane | 0.62 | 0.55 | 0.49 | 0.66 | 0.25 |
| Tiffany | 0.8 | 0.76 | 0.68 | 0.85 | 0.45 |

The reason of the experimental results is discussed as follows. Both the two methods of Yang *et al.*'s and Sachnev *et al.*'s employed fixed coefficient function to estimate the object pixel value. The Yang *et al.*'s method employed the two pixels at the left and right of the object pixel, and Sachnev *et al.*'s method employs the four pixels at the four directions of the object pixels (left, right, up and down) for object pixel error prediction. As the pixels distribute differently in a natural image, the object pixel prediction accuracy this different from one area to another. The more texture the host image has, the lower the prediction accuracy would be. Although Drogia *et al.*'s method predict the object pixel adaptively with pixels distribute in a local area, the marked and the original pixels are both involved for error prediction, its prediction accuracy is decreased apparently. On the other hand, our proposed scheme not just estimates the object pixel directly with simple arithmetical combination on its neighboring pixels, it establishes the MLR function and deciding its coefficients firstly from the neighboring pixels closely adjacent to the object pixel, and then predicts the object pixel with the achieved MLR function and its surrounding pixels. According to the consistency of pixels in local area of natural image, the error prediction accuracy is improved effectively.

## 5  Comparison of RDH on Different Prediction-Error Image

To further verify the superiority of the MLR based error prediction method, we compare the performance of difference expansion based RDH scheme on different prediction-error image formulated with Yang *et al.*'s method, Sachnev *et al.*'s method, Dragoi *et al.*'s method and the two proposed methods. Here, we choose difference expansion based RDH scheme, as it is a kind of simple but effective approach for data embedding. The comparison results on four classical images are shown in Fig. 6.

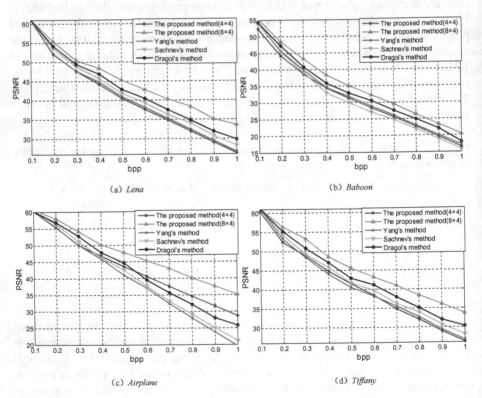

(a) *Lena*

(b) *Baboon*

(c) *Airplane*

(d) *Tiffany*

**Fig. 5.** RDH Performance based on the proposed method, Yang *et al.*'s method, Sachnev *et al.*'s method and Dragoi *et al.*'s method

It is clear to see that the performance of RDH based on the proposed method (8 training instances) outperforms other methods apparently, as the MLR algorithm can achieve more accuracy pixel value prediction, the prediction-error image has more "0" elements than others, and thus the marked image maintains high quality even after quite a lot data having been embedded.

When the data embedding rate reaches 0.5 Bit Per Pixel (BPP), for image *Lena*, we can find that the data embedding based on the proposed method are 40.52 dB (4 training instances) and 45.20 dB (8 training instances), which outperforms other three algorithm at 40.94 dB (Yang's method), 41.86 dB (Sachnev's method) and 42.80 dB (Dragoi's method) separately; for image *Airplane*, the PSNR are 43.48 dB (4 training instance), 47.85 dB (8 training instance),41.03 dB (Yang's method), 42.47 dB (Sachnev's method) and 44.65 dB (Dragoi's method) separately; and for image *Baboon*, the RDH based on the proposed prediction-error image also achieves excellent performance, the PSNR of the marked images are 31.31 dB (4 training instances), 35.10 dB (8 training instances), 31.80 dB (Yang's method), 29.99 dB (Sachnev's method) and 30.46 dB (Dragoi's method) seperately. Furtherly, for image *Tiffany*, the reversible data hiding based on the proposed prediction-error image achieves PSNR at 41.52 dB (4 training instances) and 45.56 dB (8 training instances),while the PSNR of the marked image with other three methods are 40.47 dB (Yang's method), 41.70 dB (Sachnev's method) and 42.88 dB (Dragoi's method) when the data embedding rate is 0.5 BPP.

As the MLR based error prediction method adaptively estimates the object pixel according to its neighboring pixels, for image with large uniform areas, the accuracy of prediction-error is similar for the proposed algorithm and other classical algorithms. However, if the image in rich in texture areas, it achieves higher error prediction performance than those fixed coefficients error prediction methods. Thus, the performance of the reversible data hiding based on the proposed prediction-error image is highly improved than those state-of-the-art schemes, especially for image with much texture areas. Figure 6 also shows that the proposed scheme achieves higher performance than others at moderate to high data embedding capacity, that is, when the data embedding capacity is low, all kinds of error prediction algorithms can provide sufficient prediction-errors "0" for data embedding, but with the embedding capacity increase, the error image with less prediction-errors "0" brings more image distortion than others. The better the error prediction algorithm is, the more accuracy the error prediction would be, and the higher the RDH performance is achieved.

# 6  Conclusion

In this paper, a new kind of error prediction method based on MLR algorithm is presented. The object pixel is predicted with MLR function and its neighboring pixels, where, the MLR is established from the neighboring pixels distribute closely to the object pixel. According to the consistency of the pixels in local area of natural image, the object pixel is predicted accurately. The experimental results compared with some state-of-the-art schemes show that the MLR based error prediction scheme achieves higher performance than others clearly. Moreover, the prediction-error image achieves with the proposed method also has been employed for RDH, and the results demonstrate that the RDH on the proposed prediction-error image outperforms the counterparts apparently, especially for image with much texture areas. The MLR based adaptive error prediction method can increase the object pixel prediction accuracy (minimize the prediction-error) largely and then improve image RDH performance in great extent.

## References

1. Shi, Y.Q., Li, X., Zhang, X., et al.: Reversible data hiding: advances in the past two decades. IEEE Access **4**, 3210–3237 (2016)
2. Tian, J.: Reversible data embedding using a difference expansion. IEEE Trans. Circ. Syst. Video Technol. **13**(8), 890–896 (2003)
3. Thodi, D.M., Rodriguez, J.J.: Prediction-error based reversible watermarking. In: 2004 International Conference on Image Processing, ICIP 2004, vol. 3, pp. 1549–1552. IEEE (2004)
4. Fallahpour, M.: Reversible image data hiding based on gradient adjusted prediction. IEICE Electron. Expr. **5**(20), 870–876 (2008)
5. Sachnev, V., Kim, H.J., Nam, J., et al.: Reversible watermarking algorithm using sorting and prediction. IEEE Trans. Circ. Syst. Video Technol. **19**(7), 989–999 (2009)
6. Yang, C.H., Yang, M.H.: Improving histogram-based reversible data hiding by interleaving predictions. IET Image Proc. **4**(4), 223–234 (2010)
7. Dragoi, I.C., Coltuc, D: Local-prediction-based difference expansion reversible watermarking. IEEE Trans. Image Process. **23**(4), 1779 (2014). (A Publication of the IEEE Signal Processing Society)

# A Secure AODV Protocol Improvement Scheme Based on Fuzzy Neural Network

Tongyi Xie[1], Jiawei Mo[2(✉)], and Baohua Huang[3]

[1] Research Department, Guangxi Institute of Education,
Nanning, Guangxi 530023, China
28922111@qq.com

[2] Department of Electrical and Computer Engineering,
Lushan College of Guangxi University of Science and Technology, Liuzhou,
Guangxi 545000, China
327998377@qq.com

[3] School of Computer and Electronic Information, Guangxi University,
Nanning, Guangxi 530004, China
bhhuang66@gxu.edu.cn

**Abstract.** Aiming at the possible attacks of malicious nodes in VANET (Vehicle ad hoc network). It is very important to select security nodes in the routing protocols for routing activities. A secure AODV (Ad hoc On-demand Distance Vector Routing) improvement scheme is proposed, namely SGF-AODV (Security AODV with GASA-FNN). This algorithm uses fuzzy neural network to compute node information about routing activities and obtains the trust value of nodes to evaluate the security of nodes. The algorithm considers node security and network environment equally, defends against malicious node attack and balances node utilization rate. In the routing maintenance phase, the parameters of the fuzzy neural network are optimized in real time using the genetic simulated annealing algorithm for the actual environment to ensure that the calculated node trust value is in line with the actual situation. Experiments show that, SGF-AODV relative to AODV, the average delay, packet loss rate, routing overhead are improved.

**Keywords:** Vehicular ad hoc networks · Node security · Fuzzy neural network AODV protocol

## 1 Introduction

AODV is a typical on-demand routing protocol, which is widely used in VANET and plays an important role in the development of VANET. In VANET, one of the most basic requirements is that the designed routing protocol is efficient, secure and capable of operating in unattended, harsh environments. Routing protocols not only to be able to stabilize link, to extend the network life cycle, but also to ensure the safety of the routing path, against malicious nodes. Therefore, it is very important to propose an improved AODV protocol based on security.

© ICST Institute for Computer Sciences, Social Informatics and Telecommunications Engineering 2018
R. Beyah et al. (Eds.): SecureComm 2018, LNICST 255, pp. 453–467, 2018.
https://doi.org/10.1007/978-3-030-01704-0_26

At present for this problem, many domestics and foreign literature on the AODV protocol has been studied and improved. The literature [2] proposes an improved TAODV routing protocol based on trust mechanism to determine whether the node is a malicious node by comparing the trust value of the node. The literature [3] put forward a way to prevent black hole attacks by hash chain, protect the volatile part of routing, and prevent malicious nodes from tampering with routing messages. The literature [4] constructs a new trust model, but there is no exact implementation in the routing process. The literature [5] uses a fixed time window to judge whether the node is selfish or not, and there is a delay in judging the behavior of the node. Although the protocol in the literature [6] can detect changes in node behavior, there is a problem of insufficient evidence in calculating the trust value. The literature [7] put forward that the TARF routing protocol uses a neighbor table to record the trust degree and energy consumption of each neighbor node, and is used to prevent attacks based on routing location. However, routing protocol increases routing load when broadcasting energy control packets. The literature [8] based on the AODV routing protocol, they use public key to encrypt and identify IP addresses. Encryption technology will increase many communication, computation and memory costs in the key distribution process.

In this paper, several factors that affect the security of nodes are dealt with, and then the fuzzy neural network based on genetic simulated annealing algorithm is used for fuzzy processing to get the quantified node trust values for routing activities. The node will save the latest calculated instance and the average trust value of all the current neighbors as the training data of the genetic simulated annealing algorithm. The protocol dynamically adjusts the parameters used in the fuzzy neural network and corresponds to the network conditions where the current node is located, which is more conducive to the protocols used in different network environments. Based on this, an improved AODV protocol with security is proposed based on the original AODV protocol. When the route is initiated, the trust value of the node is obtained by using the fuzzy neural network in conjunction with the packet repetition rate of the vehicle, the number of data packets and the correlation with the surrounding nodes. Eventually applied to the routing protocol activities, weakening the impact of malicious nodes, improve network security. The simulation results show that in combination with the AODV protocol, the protocol improves network performance under different sports environments.

## 2  A Trusted Secure Routing Protocol Based on Fuzzy Neural Network

### 2.1  Arithmetic Statement

In the process of protocol operation, the node will continue to distinguish the neighbor nodes' security and get the trust value. The node with lower trust value will also have lower weight in the process of routing. The structure is shown in Fig. 1.

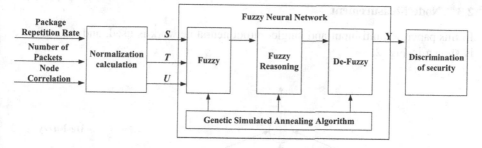

**Fig. 1.** The security of algorithm structure

## 2.2 Node Measurement

VANET internal nodes common several attacks are: random data packet loss in the process of forwarding; packet tampering and forgery; entice the surrounding nodes to send data packets to malicious nodes to launch black hole attacks. By analyzing these attacks, we can see that when the internal nodes are attacked, the repetition rate of data packets may be too large. When there are attacks such as black hole attacks and selective forwarding, there will be an abnormal number of packets sent. Neighboring The neighbor table corresponding to a node has a certain correlation, and the neighbor table between normal nodes should be repeated to some extent. Therefore, the packet content repetition rate, the number of packets [10], and the relevance of surrounding nodes can be used as detection factors for malicious nodes for the improved AODV algorithm. Based on the classical AODV protocol algorithm, the detection factors are extracted and normalized and integrated, and then the node trust value is obtained through the fuzzy processing.

The other node in the communication range of a node is called the neighbor node of the node. Set $N_i$ neighbor nodes $j$ of node $i$ to form $\Phi_i$ collection.

As shown in the formula 1, $S_{i,j}(t)$ represents the normalized packet repetition rate, $T_{i,j}(t)$ represents the packet transmission factor, and $U_{i,j}(t)$ represents the normalized node similarity. Among them, $p_{i,j}(t)$ is the number of packets at the t moment, $sp_{i,j}(t)$ is the number of repeated packets, and the delta $P(t)$ is the expected value of the number of packets. $U_{i,j}(t)$ is measured by Adamic-Adar [11] indexes. $N(i)$ is a neighbor set of nodes i, $c$ is the common neighbor of two nodes, $\log_k(c)$ is the logarithm of node degree.

$$\begin{cases} S_{i,j}(t) = \dfrac{p_{i,j}(t) - sp_{i,j}(t)}{P_{i,j}(t)} \\[2mm] T_{i,j}(t) = \dfrac{|p_{i,j}(t) - \Delta p(t)|}{p_{i,j}(t)} \\[2mm] U_{i,j}(t) = \dfrac{\sum\limits_{c \in N_{i,j}(t)} \frac{1}{\log_k(c)}}{\sum\limits_{c \in N_{i,j}(t)} 1} \end{cases} \qquad (1)$$

## 2.3    Node Measurement

In this paper, a multi-input and single-output neural network is used, and the structure is shown in Fig. 2.

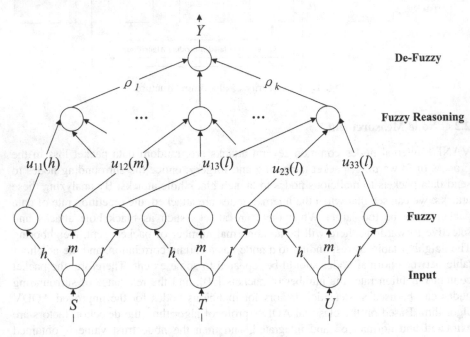

**Fig. 2.** Fuzzy neural network structure

The first layer is the input layer, which is responsible for passing the input variables to the second layer. The input value is the exact value and the number of nodes is the number of input variables. This layer has three neuron nodes, also known as three variables, $S$, $T$, and $U$.

The second layer is the fuzzy layer, which is mainly to blur the input values. The $S$, $T$, and $U$ are converted into three fuzzy subsets {high, middle and low}, which can be represented as {h, m, l}, and there are 9 nodes. $U_{ij}$ means $j$-th membership fuzzy subset of variables $i$. This article uses the gaussian function, expressed as a formula 2, $c_{ij}$, $\sigma_{ij}$ are all input parameters, including $c_{ij}$ ($i = 1, 2, 3$) determine the center of the gaussian function curve, and $\sigma_{ij}$ ($j = 1, 2, 3$) determine the width of the curve.

$$u_{ij}(X) = \exp\left(\frac{-(X - c_{ij})^2}{\sigma_{ij}^2}\right) \tag{2}$$

The third layer is the fuzzy rules reasoning layer. Each node of this layer corresponds to a fuzzy rule, which is connected to the fuzzy subset of every variable in the second layer, and there are 27 nodes, which correspond to 27 rules of inference. The fitness of each node is defined as formula 3.

$$\rho_k = \mu_{1j}\mu_{2j}\mu_{3j}; \ j = 1, 2, 3 \tag{3}$$

The fourth layer is the de-fuzzy layer. The fuzzy value of fuzzy inference is converted into an exact value, and the gravity method is used to blur it, and the output value of the neural network is obtained, and the expression is formula 4. The $\omega_k$ is the connection weight of the third and fourth layers, $Y$ is the deterministic solution of the problem and the node trust value.

$$Y = \frac{\sum\limits_{i=1}^{3}\sum\limits_{j=1}^{3} \omega_k \rho_k}{\sum\limits_{i=1}^{3}\sum\limits_{j=1}^{3} \rho_k} \tag{4}$$

In the fuzzy neural network, the parameters that need to be optimized are: $c_{ij}$ in the second layer gaussian function, the range of values [0, 1] and $\sigma_{ij}$, the range of values is [0, 0.25]. The connection weight value of the third and fourth layers is $\omega_k$, the range of values [0, 1]. In this paper, genetic simulated annealing algorithm is used for parameter optimization, and the default parameter is $c_{1j} = 0$, $c_{2j} = 0.5$, $c_{3j} = 1$, $\sigma_{ij} = 0.2$, and $\omega_k$ takes the random number in the domain.

## 2.4    The Genetic Simulation Algorithm Optimizes the Fuzzy Neural Network

In this paper, genetic algorithm as the main body, from a group of randomly generated initial population for the global optimal search process, first through the selection, crossover, mutation and other genetic operations to produce a new group of individuals, and then independent of the resulting each individual simulated annealing, and evaluation of new fitness groups, for individual selection, copying and other operations, the final result of its generation as individuals in the population. Run the process iteratively and iteratively until some termination condition is satisfied. In summary, there is a thought that the simulated annealing algorithm is dissolved in the running of the genetic algorithm, which not only has the advantages of the genetic algorithm and the simulated annealing algorithm but also overcomes the corresponding deficiencies [12].

The basic step of simulated genetic annealing algorithm:

- Step 1 Parameter initialization

The group scale $M$ takes 50, the maximum iteration number $N$ takes 200, the cross-probability $P_c$, the range of values [0.4, 0.99]; The variation probability $P_m$, the range of values [0.005, 0.01], the iteration count n initialized to zero.

- Step 2 Initializes the population

Chromosome coding method is: the first will be the second layer of the parameters of the Gaussian function $c$ domain is divided into three parts, such as the selection of equal interval defined each population size of random Numbers as the center value $c_{i1}$ respectively, $c_{i2}$, $c_{i3}$ initial value; And then, for the mean $\sigma_{ij}$ and the connection weight $\omega_k$, we take the random number in our domain as the initial value. Encode these real Numbers into chromosomes, and the length of the chromosome is the sum of the number of parameters (45 in this article). The specific coding method is as follows: $c_{11}c_{12} \dots c_{13}\sigma_{11} \dots \sigma_{33}\omega_1 \dots \omega_{27}$. The initial population of $M$ initial solutions is generated randomly, and the initial population should be larger than the specified size.

- Step 3 Output control

The fitness of each chromosome was calculated using the training data obtained during routine maintenance. The objective function is defined as formula 5. Where $y_k$ is the actual output of the neural network, $Y_k$ is the expected output of the neural network, and $E$ is the difference between the two outputs. The fitness function is desirable as formula 6, the closer the fitness is to 1, the better.

$$E = (Y_k - y_k)^2 \tag{5}$$

$$f(E) = \frac{1}{1+E} \tag{6}$$

When the iteration count reaches the maximum number of iterations, that is, when $n = N$, the algorithm ends and outputs the optimal individual.

When an individual reaches the progress requirement (the range of value [0.95, 0.99]), the individual is exported or entered the genetic operation.

- Step 4 Genetic manipulation

The number of iterations $n = n + 1$, the following selection, crossover, mutation operation to generate children, to determine whether to meet the output requirements, meet the output, does not meet the enter simulated annealing operation.

1. Selection, replication

Identify the highest fitness and minimum individuals in the current population and set up a global optimal individual. If an individual is found to be superior to the global optimal individual, the global optimal individual is substituted for the worst individual.

2. Crossover

Each individual generates a crossover probability $r$, in the range of [0, 1]. If $r > P_c$, then cross operation: suppose that individual $A = a_1a_2 \dots a_L$; Individual $B = b_1b_2 \dots b_L$. The $L$ is the individual length, and a parameter $i$ is randomly generated. The range of values is [$L, L - 1$]. After crossing operation, as showed by the formula 7. The algorithm always cross-operates the individual with the global optimal individual, which helps the individual inherit the excellent genetic factors.

$$A' = a_1a_2 \dots a_ib_{i+1} \dots b_l; B' = b_1b_2 \dots a_{i+1}a_{i+2} \dots a_l \tag{7}$$

3. Variation

Gene values at each individual locus randomly generate a sub-mutation probability $s$. If $s < Pm$, then this locus is mutated. This article uses the method of decimal gene mutation. That is, taking random numbers in the domain of definition.

- Step 5 Simulate annealing operation

Each individual in the new offspring produced by genetic manipulation is simulated annealing operation.

1. Initialization parameter

Initial temperature $t_0$, set to 1000; The number of iterations $i$, the initial value is $i = 0$; The initial solution $s = s_0$, each $t_i$ has an iteration number of the internal cycles of $N$, set to 200, and the temperature floor is set to $0.2\ t_0$.

2. Inner loop

Isothermal cycle. The current temperature $t = t_i$, the loop performs the following operations $N$ times:

The genetic value of $s'$ was randomly perturbed by 0.005, and the new solution $s$ were produced, and the fitness of the new solution was calculated using formula 8, and $f()$ was the fitness function.

$$\Delta f = f(s') - f(s) \tag{8}$$

Near to extend to a more optimal value is infinite, to use the Metropolis criterion to judge whether the new accepted: if $\Delta f < 0$, the new replaces the old solution; On the other hand, we randomly generate an acceptance probability $m$, and the range is $[0, 1]$. If the probability accepts a new solution, replace the old one. Under high temperature, it can accept the new state with a large energy difference between the current state and the current state. In the low temperature, only accept the new state with less energy than the current state.

3. Outer loop

To meet the termination conditions (to reach the upper limit of the outer cycle iteration or to the lower limit of the external circulation temperature), the current solution is output; The reverse cooling: $t_i + 1 = \beta t_i$, $i = i + 1$, $\beta$ is the cooling rate, take 0.95.

# 3  Improved Protocol Description

Security protocols are optimized for routing and routing maintenance protocol processes.

### 3.1  Routing Initiating

When a source node needs to communicate with a destination node, it first performs a route initiation process and broadcasts the RREQ (Route Request) packet to its neighboring neighbors.

The neighbor nodes that receive the RREQ package perform the following operations in turn:

1. Check for loop. If there is a loop, discard the RREP (Route Reply) package.
2. Check for duplicate RREQ packages. If repeated, discard the RREQ package.
3. Check whether the reverse routing has been established with the source node. Otherwise, the reverse path should be established with the source node to generate the previous hop route.
4. A delivery rate threshold of 0.5 for the neighbor node is set. Within a period, the neighbor node will update the delivery rate threshold based on the packet delivery of its own and its neighbors. When the delivery rate of the node is greater than 0.5 or greater than the threshold value of the delivery rate, the node trust value should be considered when forwarding the RREQ request. This can guarantee the delivery rate is greater than 0.5 when all nodes are always forward to participate in, and when the node environment are in a state of insecurity, by considering the trust value can choose the relative safety of the nodes involved in forwarding, raise the utilization ratio of nodes, and avoid the black hole nodes.
5. Considering neighbor node trust value, firstly calculates the average values of trust, all the neighbors trust in the trust value is less than 0.5 and less than the average value of node, marked as in a state of distrust of neighbor node, not participate in the current node routing process.
6. The process ends after the destination node is reached.

Through the statistics and analysis of the attacks and manifestations of the attacking nodes, the improved routing protocol comprehensively considers the main performance characteristics of the node security through the fuzzy neural network between adjacent nodes, which are respectively the packet repetition rate, the number of packets, and the relevance with surrounding nodes. In the mobile Ad Hoc network, the authentication of the node's output data not only depends on the historical data of the node itself, but also on the data of other nodes in the same area. The characteristics of node behavior often change with time, and the regularity has statistical characteristics. So, select the packet content of the repetition rate, the number of packets involved in measuring the trust value of the node. Analysis of the attacks on the attacking nodes reveals that for different neighboring nodes, the attacking nodes will be fake multiple fake identities to cheat the trust of the neighboring nodes, which has some weaknesses. For adjacent nodes in the same motion environment, their respective neighbor tables will have a greater probability of repetition. However, attack nodes have different identities among different neighboring nodes, which lead to their identities in the neighbor tables of all neighboring nodes of the attacked node are not uniform, that is, node relevance is low. Therefore, the improved Adamic-Adar algorithm can normalize the node relevancy, to measure the trust value of nodes in different situations.

The higher the node trust value, the better the node security and the lower the chance of attacking the node. Therefore, the node trust value needs to be considered according to the node environment when forwarding the RREQ request packet. The improved routing protocol participates in the route initiation process only when the node is in a safe state. It reduces the RREQ message forwarding volume, reduces the routing overhead, and ensures the link security to defend against black hole attacks.

## 3.2  Routing Maintenance

Through periodically sends the HELLO message to maintain connection between neighbor nodes, the improved routing protocol for stability calculation of encapsulation of the neighbor node in the HELLO message neighbor list, the node that receives the HELLO message performs a route maintenance procedure.

When a node first receives a HELLO message from a neighbor node, it first adds a neighbor to the neighbor table, and then uses the fuzzy neural network to calculate the node trust level of the corresponding node. The repetition rate, the number of groups, the correlation of surrounding nodes, and the average trust value of all current neighbors of the packet contents used in the current calculation are used as the training data of the simulated genetic annealing algorithm in the neighbor table. Each time a HELLO message is received from a neighbor node, the node first reads the node information encapsulated in the message, and then uses the fuzzy neural network to update the node trust value and then prolongs the lifetime of the corresponding neighbor node in the neighbor table. From time to time, the node will check whether the survival time of all the nodes is less than the current time. If the neighbor nodes are lost, the node will use the genetic simulated annealing algorithm to optimize the parameters of the fuzzy neural network.

When a node moves in a spatial scene, there are relatively few neighbor nodes around the node and the correlation with the surrounding nodes is relatively weak. However, as the number of nodes increases, the attack nodes will show a more obvious disadvantage in the node correlation. When the node is in an idle state, the traffic between the nodes is not large. The repetition rate of the contents of the node's packets and the number of the packets has little effect on the trust value of the nodes. When a node enters a busy state, the load of the node itself increases and other information exchanges frequently between nodes. The repetition rate of the packet content of the node and the size of the packet more reflects the level of node security.

Therefore, under different sport environment, the proportion of each trustworthy factor is different, and the fixed parameters cannot be used to calculate the fuzzy neural network. The improved routing protocols optimize the parameters of the fuzzy neural network using genetic simulated annealing based on the collected actual node data in different environments. The predicted trust value of the protocol of routing is close to the actual situation, which can adapt to different sport environments, increase the probability of the selected security nodes and further enhance the performance of routing protocols.

## 4 Performance Simulation and Analysis

In this paper, the network simulation software NS2 (Network Simulator Version 2) [13] is used to simulate the improved SGF-AODV protocol and the original AODV protocol. The attack method of malicious nodes is mainly based on black hole attacks. RREP messages are returned to any RREQ message, and none of the received data packets are forwarded. With Witch attacks, each malicious node will have two node sequence numbers and will randomly switch. The parameters of the simulation environment are shown in Table 1.

**Table 1.** Parameters of simulation environment

| Parameter | Substance | Parameter | Substance |
|---|---|---|---|
| Topology | 1000 m × 1000 m | Transmission range/m | 250 |
| Channel capacity | 2 M/s | Pause time/s | 0 |
| Routing protocols | SGF-AODV, AODV | Wireless transmission model | Two ray ground |
| Channel type | Wireless channel | The speed of nodes | 20–120 m/s |
| The number of nodes | 15–100 | Mac layer protocol | 802.11DCF |
| The number of links | 20 | Mobile model | Random way point |
| Traffic type | CBR | Queue type | PriQueue |
| Packet rate | 2 packets/s | Packet size/B | 512 |
| Channel capacity | 2 M/s | Pause time/s | 0 |
| Queue size | 64 | Simulation time | 300 s |

### 4.1 Experimental Results and Analysis

**When the number of vehicles is 100, the routing performance of the SGF-AODV protocol under the number of different black hole nodes is performed.**

Figure 3 shows the packet loss ratio of AODV protocol and SGF-AODV protocol as the number of black hole nodes increases. As the figure shows, as the number of black hole nodes increases, more RREQ packets are phagocytic, and the loss rate of the two protocols is on the rise. But because the SGF-AODV routing protocol using fuzzy neural network calculation of node trust value, select the high trust value of nodes participating in the routing initiated, reducing the probability of attack and attack; in the number of nodes in different situations by genetic simulated annealing algorithm to optimize the parameters of fuzzy neural network, change the node correlation in the node trust value weight calculation the increased probability of select safe node. so the packet loss SGF-AODV protocol packet loss rate is generally lower than the rate of AODV protocol.

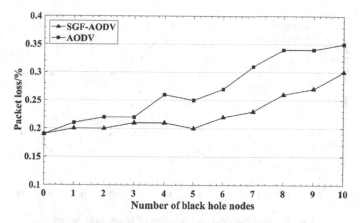

**Fig. 3.** Packet loss rate and the number of black hole nodes

Figure 4 shows the end-to-end average delay of AODV and SGF-AODV as the number of black hole nodes increases. In the environment with fewer black hole nodes, the SGF-AODV protocol preferentially selects the nodes with higher trust values to participate in the routing process, which causes certain network delay. However, routing protocol the parameters according to the specific conditions and avoids prolonged delay, so that the average delay does not show a large gap. With the increase of black hole nodes, the SGF-AODV protocol always selects the nodes with higher trust values to participate in the routing process and reduces the probability of routing requests being swallowed by the attacking nodes. Therefore, it can be seen from the figure that the average end-to-end delay of SGF-AODV is generally lower than that of the AODV protocol.

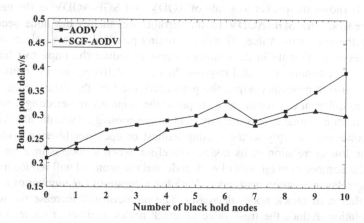

**Fig. 4.** Average delay and number of black hole nodes

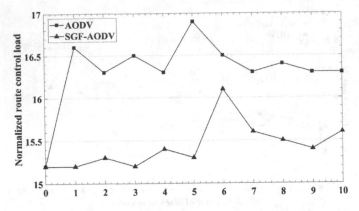

**Fig. 5.** Routing cost and number of black hole nodes

Figure 5 shows the normalized routing overhead of AODV and SGF-AODV as the number of black hole nodes increases. As the number of black hole nodes increases, the probability of losing RREQ increases and the number of control messages between nodes increases. Therefore, the routing overhead increases. However, since the SGF-AODV controls the forwarding of the RREQ through the node trust value in the routing initiation part, and uses the genetic simulated annealing algorithm to control the parameters, the weight of the node similarity in the fuzzy neural network is adjusted according to the condition of the black hole node. In different environments, SGF-AODV can select the security node to participate in the routing process to reduce the routing overhead required for initiating the route initiation due to the black hole node attack.

**When the ratio of the black hole nodes is ten percent, the routing performance of the SGF-AODV protocol under different number of vehicle nodes is performed.**

Figure 6 shows the packet loss rate of AODV and SGF-AODV as the number of nodes increases. The SGF-AODV routing protocol evaluates the node security by calculating the node trust value. Therefore, routing protocol always selects relatively secure nodes to participate in the routing process to reduce the impact of black-hole nodes of node communication and improve the packet delivery rate. In addition, SGF-AODV can also dynamically adjust the parameters used by the fuzzy neural network according to different environments to improve the accuracy of selecting a safe node. When the attacking node adopts the way of identity spoofing attack, the attacking node makes a confirmation reply to the routing request of each neighboring node, which leads to the low correlation of its nodes. Therefore, when a node is in a sparse environment, the number of neighbors of each node and the protocol will reduce the weight of the node relevance in the trust value. With the increase of the number of nodes, the node correlation of attack nodes decreases. The protocol will increase the weight of node correlation, reduce the trust value of attack nodes, and select security nodes to participate in routing activities to improve the packet delivery rate.

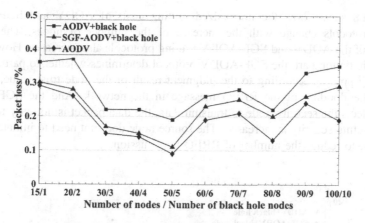

**Fig. 6.** Packet loss rate and number of nodes

Figure 7 shows the end-to-end average delay of two routing protocols, AODV and SGF-AODV, as the number of nodes increases. When selecting a node to participate in the routing process, the SGF-AODV protocol takes the amount of data packets sent and the repetition rate as influencing factors into the calculation of the trust value of the node. When the number of nodes is small, the SGF-AODV protocol mainly considers the packet repetition rate and improves the weight of the packet repetition rate in the node trust value, which helps the routing protocol to prevent the attack node from repeatedly sending attack messages and affecting the ad hoc network. When the number of nodes continues to increase, the communication between nodes is frequent, and the amount of data packets sent generally increases, affecting the judgment of node security. The protocol of SGF-AODV will reduce the weight of packet sending amount in the trust value of the fuzzy neural network node by simulating genetic annealing optimization algorithm parameters, and weaken the impact of attack denial of service attack on ad hoc network.

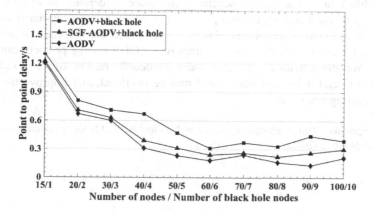

**Fig. 7.** Average delay and number of nodes

Figure 8 shows how the normalized routing costs of AODV and SGF-AODV routing protocols change with the increase of the number of nodes. The control overhead of the AODV and SGF-AODV routing protocols also increases. However, in the route initiation part, the SGF-AODV protocol determines whether to participate in the routing process according to the judgment result of the node trust value, thereby limiting the flooding of the RREQ message in the network. And the SGF-AODV always selects the security node to transmit data, the data packet is not easy to be lost and the routing security is increased. The source node does not need to initiate routing frequently, to reduce the number of RREQ transmission.

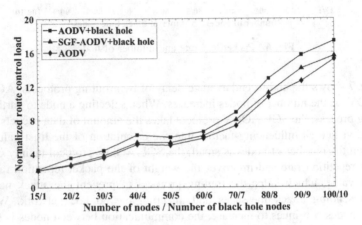

**Fig. 8.** Routing costs and number of nodes

## 5  Conclusion

Security is a hot issue in VANET research. Based on the fuzzy neural network, this paper proposes an improved AODV secure routing protocol suitable for VANET that can resist black hole attacks. The scheme takes into consideration of multiple attack modes in equilibrium and adjusts the parameters through genetic simulated annealing algorithm in different practical environments to improve the accuracy of node trust value. Experimental results show that the improved AODV routing protocol can choose to perform routine activities with safer nodes, reduce the packet loss rate, reduce the average end-to-end delay and normalized routing overhead, and improve the performance of routing protocols.

**Acknowledgments.** This work was supported by National Natural Science Foundation of China under Grant No. 61262072.

# References

1. Perkins, C., Belding-Royer, E., Das, S.: Request for comments: ad hoc on-demand distance vector (AODV) routing. Exp. Internet Soc. **6**(7), 90 (2003)
2. Jain, A., Prajapati, U., Chouhan, P.: Trust based mechanism with AODV protocol for prevention of black-hole attack in MANET scenario. In: Colossal Data Analysis and Networking, pp. 1–5. IEEE, CDAN (2016)
3. Shoja, M.K., Taheri, H., Vakilinia, S.: Preventing black hole attack in AODV through use of hash chain. In: Electrical Engineering, pp. 1–2. IEEE (2011)
4. Balakrishnan, V., Varadharajan, V., Lucs, P., et al.: Trust enhanced secure mobile ad-hoc network routing. In: International Conference on Advanced Information Networking and Applications Workshops, Salt Lake City, Utah, USA, pp. 21–33. IEEE Computer Society (2007)
5. Hiroki, U., Sonoko, T., Hiroshi, S.: An effective secure routing protocol considering trust in mobile ad hoc networks. IPSJ J. **55**, 649–658 (2014)
6. Umeda, S., Takeda, S., Shigeno, H.: Trust evaluation method adapted to node behavior for secure routing in mobile ad hoc networks. In: Eighth International Conference on Mobile Computing and Ubiquitous Networking, Melbourne, Australia, pp. 143–148. IEEE (2015)
7. Zhan, G., Shi, W., Deng, J.: Design and implementation of TARF: a trust-aware routing framework for WSNs. IEEE Trans. Dependable Secure Comput. **9**(2), 184–197 (2012)
8. Li, H., Singhal, M.: A secure routing protocol for wireless ad hoc networks. In: Hawaii International Conference on System Sciences, Hawaii, USA, p. 225a. IEEE (2006)
9. Singh, B., Srikanth, D., Kumar, C.R.S.: Mitigating effects of black hole attack in mobile ad-hoc NETworks: military perspective. In: IEEE International Conference on Engineering and Technology, Hammamet, Tunisia, pp. 21–22. IEEE (2016)
10. Zhu, Y.-S., Dou, G.-Q.: A dimensional trust based security data aggregation method in wireless sensor networks. J. Wuhan Univ. (Natural Science Edition). **59**(2), 193–197 (2013)
11. Adamic, L.A., Adar, E.: Friends and neighbors on the web. Soc. Netw. **25**(3), 211–230 (2003)
12. Xiao, W., Dong, H., Xin, Q.-L., et al.: Synthesis of large-scale multistream heat exchanger networks based on stream pseudo temperature. Chin. J. Chem. Eng. **14**(5), 574–583 (2006)
13. Rehmani, M.H., Saleem, Y.: Network simulator NS-2. J. Inst. Image Inf. Telev. Eng. **65**, 946–949 (2015)

# What's in a Downgrade? A Taxonomy of Downgrade Attacks in the TLS Protocol and Application Protocols Using TLS

Eman Salem Alashwali[1,2]([✉]) and Kasper Rasmussen[1]

[1] University of Oxford, Oxford, UK
{eman.alashwali,kasper.rasmussen}@cs.ox.ac.uk
[2] King Abdulaziz University (KAU), Jeddah, Saudi Arabia
ealashwali@kau.edu.sa

**Abstract.** A number of important real-world protocols including the Transport Layer Security (TLS) protocol have the ability to negotiate various security-related choices such as the protocol version and the cryptographic algorithms to be used in a particular session. Furthermore, some insecure application-layer protocols such as the Simple Mail Transfer Protocol (SMTP) negotiate the use of TLS itself on top of the application protocol to secure the communication channel. These protocols are often vulnerable to a class of attacks known as *downgrade attacks* which targets this negotiation mechanism. In this paper we create the first taxonomy of TLS downgrade attacks. Our taxonomy classifies possible attacks with respect to four different vectors: the protocol element that is targeted, the type of vulnerability that enables the attack, the attack method, and the level of damage that the attack causes. We base our taxonomy on a thorough analysis of fifteen notable published attacks. Our taxonomy highlights clear and concrete aspects that many downgrade attacks have in common, and allows for a common language, classification, and comparison of adowngrade attacks. We demonstrate the application of our taxonomy by classifying the surveyed attacks.

## 1 Introduction

A number of important real-world protocols, such as the Transport Layer Security protocol (TLS) [13,29], which is used by billions of people everyday to secure internet communications, support multiple protocol versions and algorithms, and allow the communicating parties to negotiate them during the handshake. Furthermore, some important legacy application-layer protocols that are *not* secure by design such as the Simple Mail Transfer Protocol (SMTP) [22] allow the communicating parties to negotiate upgrading the communication channel to a secure channel over a TLS layer. However, experience has shown that protocol developers tend to maintain support for weak protocol versions and algorithms, mainly to provide backward compatibility. In addition, empirical analysis of real-world deployment shows that a high percentage of SMTP servers that support

© ICST Institute for Computer Sciences, Social Informatics and Telecommunications Engineering 2018
R. Beyah et al. (Eds.): SecureComm 2018, LNICST 255, pp. 468–487, 2018.
https://doi.org/10.1007/978-3-030-01704-0_27

TLS and are capable of upgrading SMTP to SMTP-Secure (SMTPS) are configured in the "opportunistic security" mode [15], meaning that they "fail open",
and operate in an unauthenticated plaintext mode if the upgrade failed for any
reason, favoring functionality over security [9,17].

In a typical downgrade attack, an active network adversary[1] interferes with
the protocol messages, leading the communicating parties to operate in a mode
that is weaker than they prefer and support. In recent years, several studies
illustrated the practicality of downgrade attacks in widely used protocols such
as TLS. More dangerously, downgrade attacks can succeed even when only one
of the communicating parties supports weak choices as in [2,4].

There are plenty of reported downgrade attacks in the literature that pertain to TLS such as [2–6,16,17,24,27,33]. A close look at these attacks reveals
that they are not all identical: they target various elements of the protocol,
exploit various types of vulnerabilities, use various methods, and result in various levels of damage.

The existing literature lacks a taxonomy that shows the big picture outlook
of downgrade attacks that allows classifying and comparing them. To bridge
this gap, this paper presents a taxonomy of downgrade attacks with a focus on
the TLS protocol based on an analysis of fifteen notable published attacks. The
taxonomy helps in deriving answers to the following questions that arise in any
downgrade attack:

1. *What has been downgraded?*
2. *How is it downgraded?*
3. *What is the impact of the downgrade?*

Our downgrade attack taxonomy classifies downgrade attacks with respect
to four vectors: element (to answer: What has been downgraded?), vulnerability
and method (to answer: How is it downgraded?), and damage (to answer: What
is the impact of the downgrade?).

The aim of this paper is to provide a reference for researchers, protocol
designers, analysts, and developers that contributes to a better understanding
of downgrade attacks and its anatomy. Although our focus in this paper is on
the TLS protocol and the application protocols that use it, this does not limit
the paper's benefit to TLS. The paper can benefit the design, analysis, and
implementation of any protocol that has common aspects of TLS.

Our contribution is twofold: First, we provide the first taxonomy of TLS
downgrade attacks based on a thorough analysis of fifteen surveyed attacks.
Our taxonomy dissects complex downgrade attacks into clear categories and
provides a clean framework for reasoning about them. Second, although our
paper is not meant to provide a comprehensive survey, however, as a necessary
background, we provide a brief survey of all notable published TLS downgrade
attacks. Unlike the existing general surveys on TLS attacks, our survey is focused
on a particular family of attacks that are on the rise, and covers some important

---

[1] Throughout the paper we will use the terms: active network attacker, active network
adversary, and man-in-the-middle interchangeably.

recent downgrade attacks that none of the existing surveys [10, 26] (which date back to 2013) have covered.

The rest of the paper is organised as follows: in Sect. 2, we summarise related work. In Sect. 3, we provide an illustrative example of downgrade attacks. In Sect. 4, we describe the attacker model that we consider in our taxonomy. In Sect. 5, we describe the methodology we use to devise the taxonomy. In Sect. 6, we briefly survey fifteen cases of downgrade attacks in TLS. In Sect. 7, we present our taxonomy. In Sect. 8, we provide a discussion. In Sect. 9, we conclude. Finally, Appendix A provides a background in the TLS protocol.

## 2   Related Work

Bhargavan et al. [5] provide a formal treatment of downgrade resilience in cryptographic protocols and define downgrade security. In our work, we look at downgrade attacks from an informal and pragmatic point of view. We also consider downgrade attacks in a context beyond the key-exchange, e.g. in negotiating the use of TLS layer in multi-layers protocols such as SMTP.

The work of [10] and [26] provide surveys on TLS attacks in general. Their surveys cover some of the TLS downgrade attacks that we cover. However, our work is not meant to survey TLS downgrade attacks, but to analyse them to create a taxonomy of downgrade attacks and to provide a framework to reason about them. Furthermore, our work covers state-of-the-art TLS downgrade attacks that have not been covered in previous surveys such as downgrade attacks in draft-10 of the coming version of TLS (TLS 1.3) [5], the SLOTH attack [6], the DROWN attack [3], among others.

Howard and Longstaff [21] present a general taxonomy of computer and network attacks. Our approach is similar to the one taken in [21] in terms of presenting the taxonomy in logically connected steps. We have some common categories such as the vulnerability, but we also introduce our own novel categories such as the element and damage which classifies downgrade attacks at a lower level.

In [31] a taxonomy of man-in-the-middle attacks is provided. It is based on four tiers: "state", "target", "behaviour", and "vulnerability". Our taxonomy is particularly focused on downgrade attacks, thus provides further insights over the general man-in-the-middle taxonomy. We also have different perspectives. For example, although we share the vulnerability category, [31] present it in an exhaustive list of vulnerabilities such as "cipher block chaining", "compression", "export key", etc. while our approach is to focus on the source of the flaw that allows the attack. We end up with three vulnerability sub-categories: implementation, design, and trust-model, which are more likely to capture future attacks.

## 3   Downgrade Attacks, an Illustrative Example

Figure 1 shows an illustrative example of downgrade attacks in a simplified version of the TLS 1.2 protocol inspired by the Logjam attack [2]. Throughout the paper in the message sequence diagrams, we denote the communicating parties by client (initiator $I$) and server (responder $R$). We denote the man-in-the-middle by (MITM $M$). A background on the TLS protocol that is necessary to comprehend the example is provided in Appendix A.

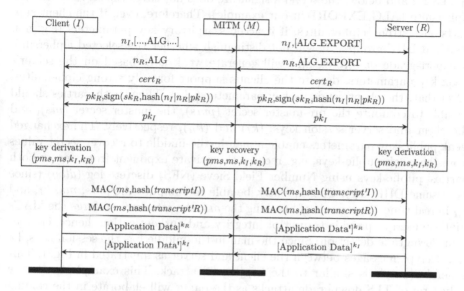

**Fig. 1.** Illustrative example of downgrade attack in a simplified version of TLS.

In this example, we assume certificate-based unilateral server-authentication mode using ephemeral Diffie-Hellman (DHE) key-exchange algorithm, and Message Authentication Code (MAC) to authenticate the exchanged handshake messages (the transcript). As depicted in Fig. 1 the client starts the handshake by sending its nonce ($n_I$) and a list of ciphersuites ([...,ALG,...]) to the server. The ciphersuite is a string (ALG) that defines the algorithms to be used in a particular session. In this example, we assume that the client's ciphersuites list contains only strong ciphersuites. The server must select one of the offered ciphersuites to be used in subsequent messages of the protocol. A man-in-the-middle modifies the client's proposed ciphersuites such that they offer only export-grade[2] ciphersuite ([ALG_EXPORT]), e.g. key-exchange with 512-bit DHE group. If the server supports export-grade ciphersuites, for example, to provide backward compatibility to legacy clients, it will select an export-grade one, misguided by the modified client message that offered only export-grade ciphersuites. Then, the server sends its nonce ($n_R$) and its selected ciphersuite ALG_EXPORT to the client. To avoid detection, the man-in-the-middle modifies the server's choice from ALG_EXPORT to ALG to make it acceptable for the client that may not support export-grade ciphersuites as is the case in most updated web browsers today. Then, the server sends its certificate ($cert_R$), followed by a message that

---

[2] Export-grade ciphers are weak ciphers with a maximum of 512-bit key for asymmetric encryption, and 40-bit key for symmetric encryption [34].

contains the server's public-key parameter $pk_R$, and a signed hash of the nonces ($n_I$ and $n_R$) and the server's public-key parameters $pk_R$. The signature is used to authenticate the nonces and the server's selected key parameters. However, in TLS 1.2 and below, the server's signature does not cover the server's selected ciphersuite (ALG_EXPORT in our example). Therefore, even if the client supports only strong ciphersuites, if it accepts arbitrary key parameters (e.g. non standard DHE groups), it will not distinguish whether the selected ciphersuite is export-grade or strong, and will generate weak keys based on the server's weak key parameters, despite the client's support for only strong ciphersuites. After that, the client sends its key parameter ($pk_I$). Then, both parties should be able to compute the pre-master secret ($pms$), the master secret ($ms$), and the client and server session keys, ($k_I$) and ($k_R$), respectively. The exchanged weak public-key parameters enable a man-in-the-middle to recover secret values from the weak public-keys, e.g. recover the private exponent from one or both parties' public-keys using Number Field Sieve (NFS) discrete log ($dlog$) (since we assume DHE key). Consequently, be able to compute the $pms$, $ms$, $k_I$, and $k_R$ in real-time. As a result of breaking the $ms$, the attacker can forge the MACs that are used to provide transcript integrity and authentication, hence, circumvent downgrade detection. Since the man-in-the-middle has the session keys, he can decrypt messages between the client and server as illustrated in Fig. 1. This general example is similar to the Logjam [2] attack. This example is not the only form of TLS downgrade attacks as the paper will elaborate in the coming sections.

## 4   Attacker Model

In our taxonomy, we assume an external man-in-the-middle attacker who can passively eavesdrop on, as well as actively inject, modify, or drop messages between the communicating parties. The attacker can also connect to multiple servers in parallel. Furthermore, the attacker has access to bounded computational resources that allow him to break weak cryptographic primitives.

## 5   Methodology

First, to devise the taxonomy, we analyse fifteen published cases of downgrade attacks that relate to TLS from: [2–6, 16, 17, 24, 27, 33] (some papers have more than one attack). These attacks represent all the notable published downgrade attacks that we are aware of, starting from the first version of TLS (SSL 2.0) until draft-10 of the upcoming version (TLS 1.3). We summarise them in Sect. 6. Second, we extract the features that characterise each attack (which we refer to as vectors), namely: the attacker targets an element that defines the mode of the protocol which can be the protocol algorithms, version, or the TLS layer, in order to modify or remove. The attacker also needs to exploit a vulnerability, which can be due to implementation, design, or trust-model. The downgrade is achieved by using a method which can be message modification, dropping, or injection.

Finally, the attack results in a damage which can be either broken security or weakened security. These four main vectors are intrinsic to any downgrade attack under the specified attacker model and can therefore be used to characterise each attack in that model. Third, after identifying the vectors, we devise the taxonomy. We define the notions of the taxonomy's categories and sub-categories in Sect. 7. Finally, we show the taxonomy's application in classifying known TLS downgrade attacks.

# 6   Downgrade Attacks in TLS, a Brief Survey

In this section, we briefly survey the TLS downgrade attacks that we have analysed in order to devise the taxonomy. We highlight the attack names in **Bold** and we use these names throughout the paper. We assume the reader's familiarity with the TLS technical details. The unfamiliar reader is advised to read Appendix A, which provides the required background to comprehend the rest of the paper.

Downgrade attacks have existed since the very early versions of TLS: SSL 2.0 [19] and SSL 3.0 [18]. SSL 2.0 suffers from the **"ciphersuite rollback"** attack, where the attacker limits SSL 2.0 strength to the "least common denominator", i.e. the weakest ciphersuite, by modifying the ciphersuites list in one or both of the Hello messages that both parties exchange so that they offer the weakest ciphersuite [32,33], e.g. export-grade or "NULL" encryption ciphersuites. To mitigate such attacks, SSL 3.0 mandated a MAC of the protocol's transcript in the Finished messages which needs to be verified by both parties to ensure identical views of the transcript (i.e. unmodified messages).

However, SSL 3.0 is vulnerable to the **"version rollback"** attack that works by modifying the client's proposed version from SSL 3.0 to SSL 2.0 [33]. This in turn leads SSL 3.0 servers that support SSL 2.0 to fall back to SSL 2.0. Hence, all SSL 2.0 weaknesses will be inherited in that handshake including the lack of integrity and authentication checks for the protocol's transcript as we described above, which render the downgrade undetected.

Another design flaw in SSL 3.0 allows a theoretical attack named the **"key-exchange rollback"** attack, which is a result of lack of authentication for the server's selected ciphersuite (which includes the name of the key-exchange algorithm) before the Finished MACs [33]. In this attack, the attacker modifies the client's proposed key-exchange algorithm from RSA to DHE, which makes the communicating parties have different views about the key-exchange algorithm. That is, the server sends DHE key parameters in the ServerKeyExchange message while the client treats them according to export-grade RSA algorithm. These mismatched views about the key-exchange result in generating breakable keys which are then used by the attacker to forge the Finished MACs to hide the attack, impersonate each party to the other, and to decrypt the application data.

In [24], an attack which we call the **"DHE key-exchange rollback"** is presented. It can be considered a variant of the **"key-exchange rollback"** in [33].

In this attack the attacker modifies the client's proposed key-exchange algorithm from DHE to ECDHE. As a result, the server sends a ServerKeyExchange that contains ECDHE parameters based on the client offer while the client treats them as DHE parameters. The client does not know the selected key-exchange algorithm by the server since the selected ciphersuite (which includes the key-exchange algorithm) is not authenticated in the ServerKeyExchange. Similar to the **"key-exchange rollback"** attack in [33], these mismatched views about the key-exchange algorithm result in breakable keys, which allow the attacker to recover the pre-master and master secretes. Consequently, be able to forge the Finished MACs to hide the modifications in the Hello messages, impersonate each party to the other, and decrypt the application data.

Version downgrade is not exclusive to SSL 3.0. The Padding Oracle On Downgraded Legacy Encryption **(POODLE)** attack [27] shows the possibility of version downgrade in recent versions of TLS (up to TLS 1.2) by exploiting the "downgrade dance", a client-side implementation technique that is used by some TLS clients (e.g. web browsers). It makes the client fall back to a lower version and retries the handshake if the initial handshake failed for any reason [27]. In the POODLE attack, a man-in-the-middle abuses this mechanism by dropping the ClientHello to lead the client to fall back to SSL 3.0. This in turn brings the specific flaw that is in the CBC padding in all block ciphers in SSL 3.0, which allows the attacker to decrypt some of the SSL session's data such as the cookies that may contain login passwords.

In [2], the **Logjam** attack is presented. It uses a method similar to the one we explained in the illustrative example in Sect. 3. The Logjam attack is applicable to DHE key-exchange. It works by modifying the Hello messages to misguide the server into selecting an export-grade DHE ciphersuite which result in weak DHE keys. As stated earlier, TLS up to version 1.2 does not authenticate the server's selected ciphersuite (which includes the key-exchange algorithm) until the Finished MACs. As a result, the client receives weak key parameters and generates weak keys based on the server's weak parameters. The lack of early authentication of the server's selected ciphersuite gives the attacker a window of time to recover the master secret from the weakly generated keys in real-time, before the Finished MACs. Consequently, the attacker can forge the Finished MACs to hide the modifications in the Hello messages, and decrypt the application data.

A similar attack called the Factoring RSA Export Keys **(FREAK)** attack [4] is performed using a method similar to the one used in the Logjam attack [2], which leads the server into selecting an export-grade ciphersuite. However, FREAK is applicable to RSA key-exchange and requires a client implementation vulnerability that makes a client that does not support export-grade ciphersuites accept a ServerKeyExchange message with weak ephemeral export-grade RSA key parameters, while the key-exchange algorithm is RSA (note that the ServerKeyExchange message must not be sent when the key-exchange algorithm is non-export-grade RSA [13]). However, the ServerKeyExchange is sent in export-grade RSA or in (EC)DHE key-exchange. This implementation vulnerability leads the client to use the export-grade RSA key parameters that are provided in the ServerKeyExchange to encrypt the pre-master secret instead of encrypting it with the long-term (presumably strong) RSA key that is provided in the server's Certificate. This results in breakable keys that can be used to forge the Finished MACs and decrypt the application data.

In [3], a variant of the Decrypting RSA using Obsolete and Weakened eNcryption (**DROWN**) attack (the "special DROWN") that exploits an OpenSSL server implementation bug [1] is presented. The attack enables a man-in-the-middle to force a client and server into choosing RSA key-exchange algorithm despite their preference for non-RSA (e.g. (EC)DHE) by modifying the Hello messages. The attacker then make use of a known flaw that can be exploited if the server's RSA key is shared with an SSLv2 server using an attack called Bleichenbacher attack [8] which enables the attacker to recover the plaintext of an RSA encryption (i.e. the pre-master secret) by using the SSLv2 server as a decryption oracle. If the attacker can break the pre-master secret, he can break the master secret and forge the Finished MACs to hide the attack, and be able to decrypt the application data.

Another case of downgrade attack is the **"Forward Secrecy rollback"** attack [4], in which the attacker exploits an implementation vulnerability to make the client fall back from Forward Secrecy (FS)[3] mode to non-FS mode by dropping the ServerKeyExchange message. However, non-FS mode does not result in immediate breakage of any security guarantee such as secrecy unless the long-term key that encrypts the session keys got broken after the session keys have been used to encrypt application data.

In [6], a downgrade attack in TLS 1.0 and TLS 1.1 is illustrated. The attack comes under a family of attacks named Security Losses from Obsolete and Truncated Transcript Hashes (**SLOTH**). This attack is possible due to the use of non collision resistant hash functions (MD5 and SHA-1) in the Finished MACs. The use of MD5 and SHA-1 is mandated by the TLS 1.0-1.1 specifications [11,12]. Non collision resistant hash functions allow the attacker to modify the Hello messages without being detected in the Finished MACs by creating a prefix-collision in the transcript hashes [6].

Downgrade attacks in multi-layered protocols that negotiate upgrading the connection to operate over TLS have been shown to be prevalent based on an empirical analysis of SMTP deployment in the IPv4 internet space [17]. In [17] they found evidence for corrupted STARTTLS commands which downgrade **SMTPS to SMTP** in more than 41,000 mail servers.

Similarly, downgraded TLS as a result of **proxied HTTPS** connections[4] has been shown to be prevalent. In [16], empirical data show that 10–40% of the proxied TLS connections advertise known broken cryptographic choices [16].

---

[3] Forward Secrecy (FS) is a property that guarantees that a compromised long-term key does not compromise past session keys [25]).

[4] A proxy refers to an entity that is located between the client and server that splits the TLS session into two separate sessions. As a result, the client encrypts the data using the proxy's public-key.

Downgrade attacks continued to appear until draft-10 of the coming version of TLS (TLS 1.3 [28]), where [5] report three possible downgrade attacks in TLS 1.3 draft-10. The first attack is similar in spirit to SSL 3.0 **"version rollback"** attack that we explained earlier in this section. In this attack, the attacker modifies the proposed version to TLS 1.2 and enjoys the vulnerabilities in TLS 1.2 that (in the presence of export-grade ciphersuites either on the server side or in both sides) enable him to break the master secret before the `Finished` MACs as in [2,4], hence circumventing downgrade detection.

The second attack in TLS 1.3 draft-10, which we call the **"downgrade dance version rollback"** attack, employs a method similar to the one employed in the POODLE attack [27], i.e. the attacker drops the initial handshake message one or more times to lead the clients that implement the "downgrade dance" mechanism to fall back to a lower version such as TLS 1.2, hence circumvent detection due to downgrade security weaknesses in TLS 1.2 and lower versions.

Finally, the third reported downgrade attack in TLS 1.3 draft-10, which we call the "`HelloRetry` **downgrade**" attack, occurs when an attacker injects a `HelloRetryRequest` message to downgrade the (EC)DHE group to a less preferred group despite the client and server preference to use another group. This attack can circumvent detection because the transcript hash restarts with every `HelloRetryRequest` [5]. However, consequent TLS 1.3 drafts mitigated this attack by continuing the hashes over retries [5].

## 7    Taxonomy of Downgrade Attacks

Based on the surveyed attacks in Sect. 6, we distill four vectors that characterise the surveyed downgrade attacks, namely: element, vulnerability, method, and damage. These vectors represent the taxonomy's main categories. We define the notions of the categories and sub-categories that we use in our taxonomy. Figure 2 summarises the taxonomy.

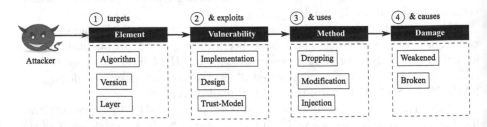

**Fig. 2.** A taxonomy of downgrade attacks in the TLS protocol and application protocols using TLS.

1. **Element:** The element refers to the protocol element that is being negotiated between the communicating parties. The element's value is intrinsic in

defining the protocol mode, i.e. the security level of the protocol run. The element is targeted by the attacker because either modifying or removing it will result in either a less secure, non secure, or less preferred mode of the protocol. We categorise the element into three sub-categories as follows:

(a) Algorithm: The algorithm refers to the cryptographic algorithms, e.g. key-exchange, encryption, hash, signature, etc. and their parameters such as block cipher modes of operation and key lengths, that are being negotiated to be used in subsequent messages of the protocol. Generally, in TLS, the main algorithms are represented by the ciphersuite, but they can also be represented by other parameters that are not part of the ciphersuite such as the extensions.

(b) Version: The version refers to the protocol version. A number of protocols including TLS allow their communicating parties to support multiple versions, negotiate the protocol version that both communicating parties will run, and allow them to fall back to a lower version to match the other party's version if the versions at both ends do not match.

(c) Layer: The layer refers to the whole TLS layer which is negotiated and optionally added in some legacy protocols. In such protocols like SMTP [22] for example, TLS encapsulation is negotiated through specific upgrade messages, e.g. STARTTLS [20], in order to upgrade the protocol from an insecure (plaintext and unauthenticated) to a secure (encrypted and/or authenticated) mode.

2. **Vulnerability:** Like any attack performed by an external man-in-the-middle, downgrade attacks require a vulnerability to be exploited. We categorise the vulnerability into three sub-categories as follows:

(a) Implementation: An implementation vulnerability refers to a faulty protocol implementation. The existence of implementation vulnerabilities can be due to various reasons, for example, a programmer's fault, a state-machine bug, or a malware that corrupted the code.

(b) Design: A design vulnerability refers to a flaw in the protocol design (i.e. the specifications). The protocol design is independent of the implementation. That is, even if the protocol was perfectly implemented, an attacker can exploit a design flaw to perform a downgrade attack.

(c) Trust-Model: A trust-model vulnerability refers to a flaw in the architectural aspect (the TLS ecosystem in our case) and the trusted parties involved in this architecture which is independent of the protocol design and implementation.

3. **Method:** The method refers to the method used by the attacker to perform the downgrade. We categorise the method into three sub-categories as follows:

(a) Modification: In the modification method, the attacker modifies the content of one or more protocol messages that negotiate the element (i.e. algorithm, version, layer). If the protocol does not employ any integrity nor authentication checks for the handshake transcript, the downgrade attack can be trivially performed. Otherwise, the attacker needs to find ways to circumvent the checks, for example, break the master secret or create colliding hashes for the transcript.

(b) Dropping: In the dropping method, the attacker drops one or more protocol messages (possibly more than once).

(c) Injection: In the injection method, the attacker sends a new message to one of the communicating parties by impersonating the party's peer, for example to request a different algorithm or version than what is initially offered by the communicating party. The injection method is trivial in the absence of transcript integrity and authentication checks. Otherwise, it requires circumventing the integrity and authentication checks.

4. **Damage:** The damage refers to the resulted damage after a successful downgrade attack. We categorise the damage into two sub-categories as follows:

(a) Broken Security: Broken security refers to downgrade attacks that result in allowing the attacker to break one or more main security goals that the protocol claims to guarantee. In TLS the guarantees are: secrecy, authentication, and integrity.

(b) Weakened Security: Unlike the broken security damage, weakened security does not result in immediate breakage of any of the main security guarantees. Instead, weakened security refers to attacks that result in making the communicating parties choose a non-recommended or less preferred mode, which is not broken yet.

## 8   Discussion

In Table 1, we show the taxonomy's application in classifying the surveyed TLS downgrade attacks. Then we discuss our reasoning in some of the noteworthy cases (we will refer to the attacks by their reference number according to the numbers in Table 1).

It should be noted that classifying attacks that have implementation is straightforward as is the case in the attacks: **04, 06, 07, 08, 09**, and **10** where their classifications in Table 1 are self-explanatory based on mapping the surveyed attacks description in Sect. 6 with the categories in Table 1. On the other hand, classifying either theoretical attacks such as **01, 02, 03, 05, 13, 14**, and **15**, or attacks that have been reported based on evidence from empirical data such as **11** and **12**, is less straightforward and requires making some assumptions.

Ideally the taxonomy helps in classifying concrete attacks that have implementation. However, for the sake of illustration, we make some assumptions (mostly worst case assumptions) to mimic a concrete attack case from the general attack that does not have an implementation. In the following, we elaborate more on these cases.

Attacks **01, 02**, and **03** are theoretical. We classify the damage on these attacks based on the worst case assumption as follows: In **01**, we assume that the attacker can select export-grade or "NULL" encryption ciphersuites, which breaks a main security guarantees of TLS. In **02**, once the attacker downgrades SSL 3.0 to SSL 2.0, he can perform attack **01** without being detected due to lack of downgrade security in SSL 2.0. In **03**, we assume that the attacker can break the master secret. Similar to the FREAK [4] and Logjam [2] attacks, this allows

**Table 1.** Classifying the surveyed downgrade attacks using our taxonomy. Attacks that are followed by "*" do not have an implementation and are either theoretical or based on evidence from measurement studies.

| No. | Attack | Element | | | Vuln. | | | Method | | | Damage | |
|---|---|---|---|---|---|---|---|---|---|---|---|---|
| | | Algorithm | Version | Layer | Implementation | Design | Trust-model | Dropping | Modification | Injection | Weakened | Broken |
| 01 | SSL 2.0 Ciphersuite rollback [33]* | ✓ | | | | ✓ | | | ✓ | | | ✓ |
| 02 | SSL 3.0 Version rollback [33]* | | ✓ | | | ✓ | | | ✓ | | | ✓ |
| 03 | SSL 3.0 key-exchange rollback [33]* | ✓ | | | | ✓ | | | ✓ | | | ✓ |
| 04 | DHE key-exchange rollback [24] | ✓ | | | | ✓ | | | ✓ | | | ✓ |
| 05 | TLS 1.0-1.1 SLOTH [6]* | | ✓ | | | ✓ | | | ✓ | | | ✓ |
| 06 | POODLE version downgrade [27] | | ✓ | ✓ | | | | | ✓ | | | ✓ |
| 07 | FREAK [4] | ✓ | | | ✓ | | | | ✓ | | | ✓ |
| 08 | DROWN [3] | ✓ | | | | | ✓ | | ✓ | | | ✓ |
| 09 | Forward Secrecy rollback [4] | ✓ | | | | ✓ | | ✓ | | | ✓ | |
| 10 | Logjam [2] | ✓ | | | | ✓ | | | ✓ | | | ✓ |
| 11 | SMTPS to SMTP [17]* | | | ✓ | | ✓ | | | ✓ | | | ✓ |
| 12 | Proxied HTTPS [16]* | | | ✓ | | | ✓ | | | ✓ | | ✓ |
| 13 | TLS 1.3 Version rollback [5]* | | ✓ | | | ✓ | | | ✓ | | | ✓ |
| 14 | TLS 1.3 Downgrade-dance version fallback [5]* | | ✓ | | ✓ | | | | ✓ | | | ✓ |
| 15 | TLS 1.3 HelloRetry downgrade [5]* | ✓ | | | ✓ | | | | | ✓ | ✓ | |

the attacker to forge the Finished MACs which enables him to impersonate the client and/or the server and decrypt the application data, and this breaks main security guarantees.

Attack **05** is a theoretical attack. Based on the worst case assumption, we classify the downgraded element under the version element. The attacker can modify the version as well as the algorithms and hide the attack by producing prefix collision in the transcript hashes which are computed using non collision resistant hashes (MD-5 and SHA1 based on the protocol design and specifications) that go into the Finished MACs. If the attacker succeeded in downgrading the version to a broken version such as SSL 3.0, he can break main security guarantees (e.g. the CBC flaw in the symmetric encryption in SSL 3.0), hence the damage in attack **05** is classified under broken category.

Although attack **08** has an implementation but it is quite complex attack and its vulnerability classification is noteworthy. We classified its vulnerability under the trust model. By contemplating the main cause that allows this downgrade attack to succeed we find the main reason lies in breaking the pre-master then the master secret that is then used to forge the Finished MACs, otherwise the attack will be detected. In this attack, the attacker can decrypt the pre-master secret if it is encrypted with an RSA key (even a strong 2048-bit RSA key), if the key is shared with an SSLv2 server (e.g. both servers uses the same certificate). Sharing RSA keys among servers is a trust-model vulnerability that allows the key sharing, rather than a protocol design nor implementation.

Attack 11 is based on evidence from real-world deployment. Based on the reported evidence described in [17], the method is classified under modification. However, dropping can also work as another method based on the STARTTLS specifications [20]. Since forcing TLS is not mandated by the SMTP protocol design and specifications, we do not consider the "fail open" local policy as an implementation vulnerability but a design one.

Attack 12 is widely known as HTTPS interception, where a man-in-the-middle (represented by a proxy) has full control over the TLS channel, which gives him the ability to downgrade TLS (algorithm, version, or layer). The empirical results in [16] shows an evidence of downgraded TLS version and algorithm due to proxied HTTPS. However, in fact, the man-in-the-middle can send the client's data to the server in cleartext. Therefore, based on the worst case assumption, the targeted element is classified under layer. The method is classified under injection since the man-in-the-middle injects a new message to the server by impersonating the client.

Attack 13 is similar in spirit to 02 that occurs in SSL 3.0 which is due to a design vulnerability. In TLS 1.3, the attack has been mitigated by redesigning the server's nonce to signal the received client's version [29].

Attack 14 is similar in spirit to 06 which targets the protocol version. If the attacker succeed in downgrading the version to a flawed version that has downgrade security weaknesses (as is the case in TLS 1.2 and below), the attacker can break main security guarantees based on the worst case assumption.

Attack 15 damage is classified under weakened security because as of this writing, no known broken (EC)DHE group elements are allowed in TLS 1.3 by design. Therefore, under the worst case assumption, the resulted damage leads both parties to agree on the least preferred DHE group.

Finally, as Table 1 shows, in most of the cases the resulted damage is broken security except in two cases.

## 9   Conclusion and Future Work

In conclusion, we introduce the first taxonomy of downgrade attacks in the TLS protocol and application protocols using TLS. Our taxonomy classifies downgrade attacks with respect to four vectors: element, vulnerability, method, and damage. It is based on a through analysis of fifteen TLS downgrade attack cases under the assumption of an external man-in-the-middle attacker model. In addition, we provided a brief survey of all notable published TLS downgrade attacks to date. Finally, we demonstrate our taxonomy's application in classifying known

TLS downgrade attacks. For future work, we plan to test the taxonomy on downgrade attacks in protocols other than TLS for potential generalisation of the taxonomy. Furthermore, we believe that the taxonomy has the potential of serving as a useful tool in devising downgrade attack severity assessment model, which can enable ranking the attack severity, which can help in identifying the attacks that require more research efforts to mitigate them.

**Acknowledgment.** The authors would like to thank Prof. Kenny Paterson, Prof. Andrew Martin, and Nicholas Moore for their feedback, and Mary Bispham, Ilias Giechaskiel, Jacqueline Eggenschwiler, and John Gallacher for proofreading earlier versions of this paper.

# Appendix A  The TLS Protocol

## A.1  TLS, a General Overview

The main goal of TLS is to provide a secure communication channel between two communicating parties [13], ideally client (initiator $I$) and server (responder $R$). TLS consists of two sub-protocols: the handshake protocol and the record protocol [13]. Briefly, the handshake protocol is responsible for version and ciphersuite negotiation, client and server authentication, and key exchange. On the other hand, the record protocol is responsible for carrying the protected application data, encrypted with the just negotiated keys in the handshake. As of this writing, TLS 1.2 [13] is the currently deployed standard. The coming version of TLS, TLS 1.3 [29], is still work in progress. Figure 3 shows the message sequence diagram for TLS 1.2 using Ephemeral Diffie-Hellman (EC)DHE[5] key-exchange [14], Fig. 4 shows TLS 1.2 using Rivest-Shamir-Adleman (RSA) key-exchange [30], and Fig. 5 illustrates the changes in the `Hello` messages in TLS 1.3 based on the latest draft (draft-25 as of this writing) [29]. Our scope in this paper is TLS in certificate-based unilateral server-authentication mode. In the diagrams, the messages are represented by their initials (e.g. CH refers to `ClientHello`). Throughout the paper, the protocol messages are distinguished by a `TypeWriter` font.

## A.2  TLS 1.2 Handshake Protocol

We briefly describe the TLS 1.2 handshake protocol in certificate-based unilateral server-authentication mode based on the Internet Engineering Task Force (IETF) standard's specifications [13]. A detailed description of the protocol can be found in [13]. As depicted in Fig. 3, the handshake protocol works as follows: First, the client sends a `ClientHello` (CH) message to initiate a connection with the server. This message contains: the maximum version of TLS that the client supports ($vmax_I$); the client's random value ($n_I$); optionally, a session identifier

---

[5] We use (EC)DHE as an abbreviation for: Elliptic-Curve Ephemeral Diffie-Hellman (ECDHE) or Ephemeral Diffie-Hellman (DHE).

if the session is resumed ($session_{ID}$); a list of ciphersuites that the client supports ordered by preference ($[a_1, \ldots, a_n]$); a list of compression methods that the client supports ordered by preference ($[c_1, \ldots, c_n]$); and finally, an optional list of extensions ($[e_1, \ldots, e_n]$).

Second, the server responds with a ServerHello (SH) message. This message contains: the server's selected TLS version ($v_R$); the server's nonce ($n_R$); optionally, a session identifier in case of session resumption ($session_{ID}$); the selected ciphersuite based on the client's proposed list ($a_R$); the selected compression method from the client's proposed list ($c_R$); and optionally, a list of the extensions that are requested by the client and supported by the server ($[e_1, \ldots, e_n]$). After that, the server sends a ServerCertificate (SC), which contains the server's certificate ($cert_R$) if server authentication is required. Then, if the key-exchange algorithm is (EC)DHE (see [14] for details about the DH algorithm), the server sends a ServerKeyExchange (SKE) message. This message must not be sent when the key-exchange algorithm is RSA (see [30] for details about the RSA algorithm). The ServerKeyExchange contains the server's (EC)DHE public-key parameters and a signature over a hash of the nonces ($n_I$ and $n_R$) and the (EC)DHE key parameters. In case of DHE (i.e. Finite Field DHE), the key parameters are: the prime ($p$), the generator ($g$), and the server's public value ($g^b$). We omit describing the ECDHE parameters and we refer the reader to [7] for details about ECDHE key parameters. Finally, the server sends a ServerHelloDone (SHD) to indicate to the client that it finished its part of the key-exchange.

Third, upon receiving the ServerHelloDone the client should verify the server's certificate and the compatibility of the server's selected parameters in the ServerHello. After that, the client sends a ClientKeyExchange (CKE) to set the pre-master secret. The content of the ClientKeyExchange depends on the key-exchange algorithm. If the key-exchange algorithm is RSA, the client sends the pre-master secret encrypted with the server's long-term RSA public-key ($[pms]^{pk_R}$) as illustrated in Fig. 4. If the key-exchange algorithm is DHE, the client sends its DHE public value ($g^a$) to allow the server to compute the shared DHE secret-key ($g^{ab}$) as illustrated in Fig. 3. After that, both parties compute the master secret ($ms$) and the session keys: ($k_I$) for the client, and ($k_R$) for the server, using Pseudo Random Functions PRFs as follows: ($kdf_{ms}$) takes the $pms$ and nonces as input and produces the $ms$, while ($kdf_k$) takes the $ms$ and nonces as input and produces the session keys $k_I$ and $k_R$. There are more than a pair for the session keys, i.e. separate key pairs for encryption and authentication, but we abstract away from these details and refer to the session keys in general by the key pair $k_I$ and $k_R$. Finally, the client sends ChangeCipherSpec (CCS) (this message is not considered part of the handshake and is not included in the transcript hash), followed by a ClientFinished (CF) which is encrypted by the just negotiated algorithms and keys. The ClientFinished verifies the integrity of the handshake transcript (i.e. the $log$ (We adopted the term $log$ from [5]). The ClientFinished content is computed using a PRF which serves as a Message Authentication Code (MAC) that we denote it by (mac) over a hash of the handshake transcript starting from the ClientHello up to, but not including, the ClientFinished (i.e. mac of $log_1$ as shown in Figs. 3 and 4), using the $ms$ as a key. This mac needs to be verified by the server.

Fourth, similar to the client, the server sends its ChangeCipherSpec (CCS) followed by a ServerFinished (SF) that consists of a mac over a hash of the server's transcript up to this point ($log_2$), which also needs to be verified by the client.

Once each communicating party has verified its peer's Finished message, they can now send and receive encrypted data using the established session keys $k_I$ and $k_R$. If "False Start" [23] is enabled, the client can send data just after its ClientFinished, and before it verifies the ServerFinished.

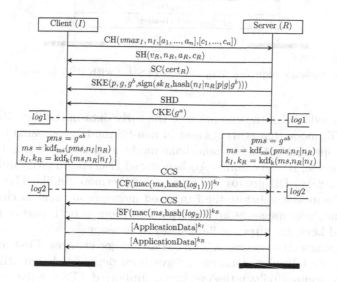

**Fig. 3.** Message sequence diagram for TLS 1.2 with (EC)DHE key-exchange.

## A.3  TLS 1.3 Handshake, Major Changes

This section is not meant to provide a comprehensive description of TLS 1.3, but to highlight some major changes in TLS 1.3 over its predecessor TLS 1.2. Similar to the previous section, we assume certificate-based unilateral server-authentication mode. A full description of the latest draft of TLS 1.3 (as of this writing) can be found in [29]. Figure 5 illustrates the Hello messages in TLS 1.3, where the TLS version and algorithms are negotiated.

One of the first changes in TLS 1.3 is prohibiting all known weak and unrecommended cryptographic algorithms such as RC4 for symmetric encryption, RSA and static DH for key-exchange, etc. In addition, TLS 1.3 enforces Forward Secrecy (FS) in both modes: the full handshake mode and the session

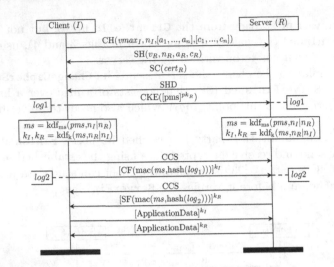

**Fig. 4.** Message sequence diagram for TLS 1.2 with RSA key-exchange.

resumption mode (with the exception of the early data in the Zero Round Trip Time (0-RTT) mode that is always sent in non-FS mode), compared to TLS 1.2, where FS is optional in the full handshake mode, and not possible in the session resumption mode. It also enforces Authenticated Encryption (AE) and standard (i.e. non arbitrary) DH groups and curves. Furthermore, unlike TLS 1.2 where all handshake messages before the Finished messages are sent in cleartext, all TLS 1.3 handshake messages are encrypted as soon as both parties have computed shared keys, i.e. after the ServerHello message.

The ClientHello message in TLS 1.3 has major changes. First, in terms of parameters, the following parameters have been deprecated (but still included for backward compatibility): the maximum supported TLS version ($vmax_I$) has been substituted by the "supported_versions" extension ($[v_1, \ldots, v_n]$); the session ID ($session_{ID}$) has been substituted by the "pre_shared_key" extension; the compression methods list $[c_1, \ldots, c_n]$ are not used any more and sent as a single byte set to zero ($c_I$). In addition, unlike TLS 1.2 where extensions are optional, in TLS 1.3, the ClientHello extensions are mandatory and must at least include the "supported_versions" extension. Second, in terms of behaviour, the server can optionally respond to a ClientHello with a HelloRetryRequest (HRR), a newly introduced message in TLS 1.3 that can be sent from server to client to request a new (EC)DHE group that has not been offered in the client's "key_share" extension ($[\ldots, (G_I, g^i), \ldots]$) which is a list of "key_share" entries ("KeyShareEntry") ordered by preference, but is supported in the client's "supported_groups" extension ($[\ldots, G_R, \ldots]$). The HelloRetryRequest can also be sent if the client has not sent any "key_share". After the HelloRetryRequest, the client sends a second ClientHello with the server's requested "key_share" ($[G_R, g^{i2}]$).

Upon receiving a ClientHello, if the client's offered parameters are supported by the server, the server responds with a ServerHello message. The

`ServerHello` has two major changes: First, unlike TLS 1.2 where the extensions field is optional, in TLS 1.3, the `ServerHello` must contain at least the "key_share" or "pre_shared_key" extensions (the latter is sent in case of session resumption which is beyond our paper's scope). Second, as a version downgrade attack defence mechanism (in addition to other mechanisms), the last eight bytes of the server's nonce $n_R$ are set to a fixed value that signals the TLS version that the server has received from the client. This allows the client to verify that the versions that were sent in the `ClientHello` have been received correctly by the server. This is because the nonces are signed in the TLS 1.3 `CertificateVerify` and in the TLS 1.2 `ServerKeyExchnage` as well.

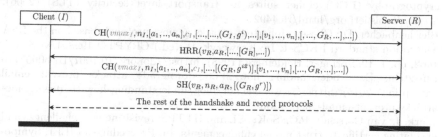

**Fig. 5.** Message sequence diagram for TLS 1.3 `Hello` messages with DHE key-exchange and `HelloRetryRequest`. Deprecated parameters that are included for backward compatibility are marked with gray color.

Finally, the TLS 1.2 `ServerKeyExchange` is not used in TLS 1.3. This is a result of shifting the key-exchange to the `Hello` messages, namely to the "key_share" and "pre_shared_key" extensions. The signature over the key parameters that is sent in the `ServerKeyExchange` in TLS 1.2 to authenticate the server's key parameters is now sent in a new message, namely the `ServerCertificateVerify` which is sent after the server's `Certificate` message. Most importantly, the signature in the `ServerCertificateVerify` is computed over a hash of the full transcript from the `Hello` messages up to the `Certificate`, and not only over the key parameters as in TLS 1.2 `ServerKeyExchange`. The signature over the full transcript provides protection against downgrade attacks that exploit the lack of ciphersuite authentication in the `ServerKeyExchange` as demonstrated in [2] and [4].

# References

1. CVE-2015-3197 (2015). https://cve.mitre.org/cgi-bin/cvename.cgi?name=CVE-2015-3197
2. Adrian, D., et al.: Imperfect forward secrecy: how Diffie-Hellman fails in practice. In: Proceedings of Conference on Computer and Communications Security (CCS), pp. 5–17 (2015)

3. Aviram, N., et al.: DROWN: breaking TLS using SSLv2. In: Proceedings of USENIX Security Symposium, pp. 689–706 (2016)
4. Beurdouche, B., et al.: A Messy state of the union: taming the composite state machines of TLS. In: Proceedings of IEEE Symposium on Security and Privacy (SP), pp. 535–552 (2015)
5. Bhargavan, K., Brzuska, C., Fournet, C., Green, M., Kohlweiss, M., Zanella-Béguelin, S.: Downgrade resilience in key-exchange protocols. In: Proceedings of IEEE Symposium on Security and Privacy (SP), pp. 506–525 (2016)
6. Bhargavan, K., Leurent, G.: Transcript collision attacks: breaking authentication in TLS, IKE, and SSH. In: Proceedings of Network and Distributed System Security Symposium (NDSS) (2016)
7. Blake-Wilson, S., Bolyard, N., Gupta, V., Hawk, C., Moeller, B.: Elliptic curve cryptography (ECC) cipher suites for transport layer security (TLS) (2006). https://tools.ietf.org/html/rfc4492
8. Bleichenbacher, D.: Chosen ciphertext attacks against protocols based on the RSA encryption standard PKCS-1. In: Krawczyk, H. (ed.) CRYPTO 1998. LNCS, vol. 1462, pp. 1–12. Springer, Heidelberg (1998). https://doi.org/10.1007/BFb0055716
9. Bursztein, E.: Understanding how TLS downgrade attacks prevent email encryption (2015). https://www.elie.net/blog/understanding-how-tls-downgrade-attacks-prevent-email-encryption
10. Clark, J., van Oorschot, P.C.: SoK: SSL and HTTPS: revisiting past challenges and evaluating certificate trust model enhancements. In: Proceedings of IEEE Symposium on Security and Privacy (SP), pp. 511-525 (2013)
11. Dierks, T., Allen, C.: The TLS protocol version 1.0 (1999). https://www.ietf.org/rfc/rfc2246.txt
12. Dierks, T., Rescorla, E.: The transport layer security (TLS) protocol version 1.1 (2006). https://tools.ietf.org/html/rfc4346
13. Dierks, T., Rescorla, E.: The transport layer security (TLS) protocol version 1.2 (2008). https://tools.ietf.org/html/rfc5246
14. Diffie, W., Hellman, M.: New directions in cryptography. IEEE Trans. Inf. Theory 22(6), 644–654 (1976)
15. Dukhovni, V.: Opportunistic security: some protection most of the time (2014). https://tools.ietf.org/html/rfc7435
16. Durumeric, Z., et al.: The security impact of HTTPS interception. In: Proceedings of Network and Distributed Systems Symposium (NDSS) (2017)
17. Durumeric, Z., et al.: Neither snow nor rain nor MITM...: an empirical analysis of email delivery security. In: Proceedings of Internet Measurement Conference (IMC), pp. 27–39 (2015)
18. Freier, A., Karlton, P., Kocher, P.: The secure sockets layer (SSL) protocol version 3.0 (2011). https://tools.ietf.org/html/rfc6101
19. Hickman, K.: SSL 0.2 protocol specification (2008). http://www-archive.mozilla.org/projects/security/pki/nss/ssl/draft02.html
20. Hoffman, P.: SMTP service extension for secure SMTP over transport layer security (2002). https://tools.ietf.org/html/rfc3207
21. Howard, J.D., Longstaff, T.A.: A common language for computer security incidents. Sandia National Laboratories (1998). https://prod.sandia.gov/techlib-noauth/access-control.cgi/1998/988667.pdf
22. Klensin, J.: Simple mail transfer protocol (2001). https://www.ietf.org/rfc/rfc2821.txt
23. Langley, A., Modadugu, N., Moeller, B.: Transport layer security (TLS) false start (2016). https://tools.ietf.org/html/rfc7918

24. Mavrogiannopoulos, N., Vercauteren, F., Velichkov, V., Preneel, B.: A cross-protocol attack on the TLS protocol. In: Proceedings of Conference on Computer and Communications Security (CCS), pp. 62–72 (2012)
25. Menezes, A.J., Van Oorschot, P.C., Vanstone, S.A.: Handbook of Applied Cryptography. CRC Press, Boca Raton (1996)
26. Meyer, C., Schwenk, J.: SoK: lessons learned from SSL/TLS attacks. In: Kim, Y., Lee, H., Perrig, A. (eds.) WISA 2013. LNCS, vol. 8267, pp. 189–209. Springer, Cham (2014). https://doi.org/10.1007/978-3-319-05149-9_12
27. Möller, B., Duong, T., Kotowicz, K.: This POODLE bites: exploiting the SSL 3.0 fallback (2014). https://www.openssl.org/~bodo/ssl-poodle.pdf
28. Rescorla, E.: The transport layer security (TLS) protocol version 1.3 draft-ietf-tls-tls13-10 (2015). https://tools.ietf.org/html/draft-ietf-tls-tls13-10
29. Rescorla, E.: The transport layer security (TLS) protocol version 1.3 draft-ietf-tls-tls13-25 (2018). https://tools.ietf.org/html/draft-ietf-tls-tls13-25
30. Rivest, R.L., Shamir, A., Adleman, L.: A method for obtaining digital signatures and public-key cryptosystems. Commun. ACM **21**(2), 120–126 (1978)
31. Stricot-Tarboton, S., Chaisiri, S., Ko, R.K.: Taxonomy of man-in-the-middle attacks on HTTPS. In: Proceedings of IEEE Trustcom/BigDataSE/ISPA, pp. 527–534 (2016)
32. Turner, S., Polk, T.: Prohibiting secure sockets layer (SSL) version 2.0 (2011). https://tools.ietf.org/html/rfc6176
33. Wagner, D., Schneier, B.: Analysis of the SSL 3.0 protocol. In: Proceedings of USENIX Workshop on Electronic Commerce (EC 96), pp. 29–40 (1996)
34. Wikipedia: Export of cryptography from the United States (2017). https://en.wikipedia.org/wiki/Export_of_cryptography_from_the_United_States

# An Approach to Enhance Understanding of Digital Forensics Technical Terms in the Presentation Phase of a Digital Investigation Using Multimedia Presentations

Niken Dwi Wahyu Cahyani[1,3], Ben Martini[1],
Kim-Kwang Raymond Choo[1,2(✉)], and Helen Ashman[1]

[1] School of Information Technology and Mathematical Sciences,
University of South Australia, Adelaide, SA 5095, Australia
niken.cahyani@mymail.unisa.edu.au, {ben.martini,
raymond.choo,helen.ashman}@unisa.edu.au
[2] Department of Information Systems and Cyber Security,
The University of Texas at San Antonio, San Antonio, TX 78249-0631, USA
raymond.choo@fulbrightmail.org
[3] Department of Informatics, Telkom University, Bandung, Indonesia
nikencahyani@telkomuniversity.ac.id

**Abstract.** This study examines the usage of multimedia presentations with a particular focus on the presentation phase within a trial context. The aim is to understand the extent to which multimedia presentations increase a lay person's understanding of technical terms and concepts in digital forensics. A questionnaire-based survey was conducted in Japan with 25 participants attending the United Nations Asia and Far East Institute for the Prevention of Crime and the Treatment of Offenders (UNAFEI) 160th international training course entitled "Contemporary Digital Forensic Investigations". Multimedia presentations in the form of videos were played with the aim of explaining three concepts: *cloud computing*, *botnet* and *forensic file recovery*. The findings of our survey showed that 84% of the participants had a better understanding after watching the videos. These results both support and extend findings from our previous research studies. The discussion on *material classification, background culture and language issues, video material*, and *other tools that would facilitate understanding and the needs of an expert* provide guidance for the practical implementation of multimedia presentations for their usage in a courtroom setting.

**Keywords:** Technical understanding · Digital forensics
Multimedia presentation · Evidence presentation · Judiciary training

## 1 Introduction

The presentation phase of a digital investigation is critical. Without a common understanding of terms used in the presentation of digital evidence, we cannot expect evidential information to be effectively conveyed from forensic practitioners to their audience. This understanding has the potential to influence the methods used as part of digital evidence examination, and in legal system a critical misunderstanding even has the potential to affect the court's verdict. An audience (e.g. judiciary members, legal teams) with a greater awareness of digital forensics and related techniques has the opportunity to delve deeper into an event and ask informed questions of the practitioners involved in the investigation.

The potential usage of multimedia presentation in a courtroom for the purpose of explaining an evidence has been highlighted in a study by Plowman [1]. The study describes the advantages of multimedia presentation as an efficient way to make persuasive presentations in a court, its positive impact on client and juror perceptions when used, and its effectiveness in terms of cost and time. The study also discusses the disadvantages of multimedia presentation, such as multimedia presentation's effect on the atmosphere of the courtroom, its admissibility and its cost for small organizations. Mayer [2] defines a multimedia instructional message as "a presentation consisting of words and pictures that is designed to foster meaningful learning" (p. 128). This definition is relevant to our topic of enhancing the understanding of technical terms used in digital forensics. His study underlines the potential of multimedia learning as it will be able to promote greater learner understanding.

In this paper, we discuss the findings from our examination of the usage of multimedia presentations to explain technical terms and concepts in digital forensics for legal communities and law enforcement officers, as we argue that multimedia presentations can be utilized to increase a layperson's understanding of technical terms and concepts in digital forensics. We conducted a face-to-face survey of professionals involved in legal system and law enforcement who attended training in Japan in 2015. In this survey, we utilized the same video dataset used in our previous research [3]. The results trend is similar to our previous studies [3–5], showing that the majority of participants increased their understanding after viewing relevant multimedia videos. This similarity in results strengthens the argument that multimedia presentations can be utilised in increasing a layperson's understanding of technical terms and concepts in digital forensics. These results highlight the potential for the use of multimedia presentations to improve understanding, within the context of the digital forensic presentation phase, during court proceedings.

## 2   The Need to Align Understanding in a Presentation Phase of a Digital Forensic Investigation

A contemporary description of forensic science is "[a]ny professional practice that provides scientific knowledge to the 'trier of fact'" [6] (p. 117). The process of providing the scientific knowledge derived from digital forensic investigations is commonly referred as a *presentation phase* [7]. In the context of presenting the findings to the court, the criticality of this phase in digital investigation is noted by Kessler and Fasulo [8]: "...regardless of what has been found, it is worthless if the information cannot be convincingly conveyed to a judge and jury." (p. 128).

Before going further into detail of criticality of same understanding in the presentation phase and what efforts that have been made to strengthen it, understanding its aims can give a clearer perspective. In general, the presentation phase is the last step of a digital investigation and is mainly concerned with presenting the investigation's findings and the methods used to reach those findings. Reith et al. [9] explain that the presentation phase is a key component in their abstract model of digital forensic procedures. This phase aims to deliver both a summary of findings and a detailed explanation in the form of a written report. Baryamureeba and Tushabe [10] term this phase "communication" which involves presenting final interpretations and a summary of an evidence. Meanwhile, Casey and Palmer [11] explicitly divide this phase into two steps as part of their investigative methodology: reporting (to report the conclusion's findings, the supporting evidence and the analysis process), and persuasion and testimony (to outline the detail of technical methods used in the form of an understandable explanation suitable for laypersons).

The importance of the presentation phase to reinforce understanding of its audience, particularly in digital investigations should not be understated. Without understanding the technology from where evidence was collected, the audience (e.g. judges, prosecutors, attorneys, and jury) may have difficulty in following the oral evidence presented by the expert witness, and therefore difficulty weighing the validity of the evidence and examining the investigation process (e.g. the soundness of the acquisition and analysis steps). This challenge increases the criticality of presentation phase. Moreover, digital evidence is known to be difficult to present in court because it naturally abstracts with no physical character [12]. For example, in reporting cloud computing related cases, a clear distinction is required between data generated by cloud service providers and data generated/owned by the suspect during the presentation phase. This is required as the evidence can be collected by a number of parties (e.g. cloud service providers, Internet Service Providers (ISPs) and Mobile Service Providers (MSPs) [13, 14]. In addition, a study has discussed challenges in forensic discovery within highly distributed and complex systems such as cloud environments which include presentation and visualization of evidence, and cross-jurisdictional aspects [15].

In considering the challenges inherent in communicating digital evidence and digital investigation processes, Reith et al. [9] mention that a report delivered in the presentation phase should consider its reader to be a layperson, and therefore suggest the use of short but precise terminology with a sufficient explanation of the detail. In the persuasion and testimony step of the investigative process proposed by Casey and Palmer [11], it is introduced that in this step, techniques and methods shall be considered to help the analyst and/or domain expert to deliver technical detail into understandable information for audiences. A similar argument by Yasinsac et al. [12] state that forensic science also requires appropriate training for its practitioners to be able to communicate the examination results clearly to a court.

The potential for multimedia presentations in enhancing the audience's understandings of complex terminologies has been highlighted in a number of studies, such as those of Carney and Feigenson [16] and Plowman [1]. In our recent studies, we also demonstrated the effectiveness of multimedia presentations (i.e. short videos) to improve participant's understanding of technical terminologies and concepts of digital forensics [3–5].

# 3 Multimedia Presentation Survey

## 3.1 Participants' Socio-Demographic Information

Our sample consists of 25 participants who attended the United Nations Asia and Far East Institute for the Prevention of Crime and the Treatment of Offenders (UNAFEI) 160th international training course entitled "Contemporary Digital Forensic Investigations" at Japan in 2015. Table 1 lists the demographics of the participants. There were no participants under 26 years old and almost half of our participants aged from 36 to 45. Participants' nationalities varied but 60% of participants originated from Asia, and more than 88% of participants do not use English as their first language.

**Table 1.** Demographic information

| Variable | Detail | n (%) |
|---|---|---|
| Age bracket | 26–35 | 6 (24) |
| | 36–45 | 12 (48) |
| | >45 | 7 (28) |
| Nationality | Africa | 3 (12) |
| | America | 3 (12) |
| | Asia | 15 (60) |
| | Europe | 2 (8) |
| | Oceania | 2 (8) |
| First language | English | 3 (12) |
| | Non-English | 22 (88) |
| Level of qualifications | Diploma or lower | 3 (12) |
| | Bachelor's degree | 8 (32) |
| | Master's degree | 13 (52) |
| | Blank | 1 (4) |
| Field of employment | Government agency | 23 (92) |
| | University | 2 (8) |
| Job title | Judge | 6 (24) |
| | Lawyer | 2 (8) |
| | Police Investigator | 6 (24) |
| | Prosecutor | 8 (32) |
| | Others | 3 (12) |
| Technical literacy | 1 (least) | 5 (20) |
| | 2 | 7 (28) |
| | 3 | 9 (36) |
| | 4 | 4 (16) |
| | 5 (most) | NA |

The highest qualification level held by the participants is a Master's degree and more than 50% of participants held this level of qualification. While most participants work in government agencies (more than 90%), a number of participants listed other professions such as judge, police investigator and prosecutor. "Other" job titles include chief executive officer, lecturer and court registrar. The remaining demographic information relates to a participant's own assessment of how they would score their technical literacy, meaning how familiar they are with technical terminologies and concepts. None of the participants selected the highest score (i.e. 5) with the majority selecting middle values (i.e. 2–3).

## 3.2  Materials

The multimedia presentation type used in this research is video with animation and narration. Three videos from our previous research [3] were reused to explain three concepts: Cloud computing, Botnet and Forensic file recovery. Cloud computing is selected because when investigating and/or presenting Internet artefacts, cloud services may also be involved as it is common now to store data on the cloud. Botnet is selected to provide an understanding of this form of attack technique and its exploitation using malware. The last term, forensic file recovery, is selected as it is a common process for acquiring digital evidence that has been deleted. The cloud computing and botnet videos have explicit term definition in their narration while an example of practical implementation is presented in both botnet and forensic file recovery videos. All participants viewed these three videos at the same time as a group.

Questions from our previous questionnaire [3] were also used in this study. There are three major parts to the questionnaire. The first part contains questions to gather demographic information of the participants and the information collected from this section is outlined in Table 1. In this first section, self-assessment questions, used to determine how the participants score their technical literacy, are asked. These questions are used to gauge participant's background knowledge in terms of their familiarity with general technical terminologies and concepts.

The second part is the main section of the questionnaire; where in total there are six questions to be asked to determine participants' understanding of the three tested terms. The first three questions are designed to be answered before the participants watch the videos. Below is the example of a question related to the first term; similar questions are asked of the botnet and forensic file recovery terms:

"Please outline your understanding of the term 'Cloud Computing'. – If you are completely unfamiliar with the term please write 'unfamiliar'."

The three remaining questions are to be answered after participants watched the videos, one by one, each after the related video is presented. Below, is one example of the questions that were asked to examine the participants' revised understanding of the related term:

"Having now viewed the Cloud Computing concept video, please outline your understanding of the term 'Cloud Computing'. – If you remain unfamiliar with the term please write 'unfamiliar'."

The last part of the questionnaire is intended to obtain participant's feedbacks. Feedback can be used to understand the gap between assessment procedure (i.e. our own, or institutional, evaluation of the assessment) and assessment practice (i.e. participant's satisfaction with the assessment) [17, 18]. In addition, for the purposes of our study, feedback is useful for examining the perceived usefulness of the multimedia presentation, and receiving the participants' input on other tools or methods that could be used to facilitate technical term understanding, and for collecting general comments on the questionnaire itself. To obtain that information, the following questions are asked:

- "On a scale of 1–5 (1 being the lowest score and 5 being the highest), how would you rate the usefulness of the multimedia presentation in enhancing your understanding of the three technical terminologies and concepts?"
- "Any comment on the multimedia presentations?"
- "What other tool(s) or method(s) do you think would facilitate the understanding of technical terminologies and concepts?"
- "Any further comments on matters raised in this questionnaire?"

## 3.3    Methods

An offline questionnaire and the three videos were used in a face-to-face survey of the 25 participants. The questionnaire papers were distributed manually and each video was played once before participants answered each related question. To ensure that each participant had the same opportunity to respond to the survey questions, the survey commenced and concluded concurrently for all participants.

To score participants' answers in terms of their understanding of the three selected terms, the holistic scoring method, which is discussed by Weigle [19], was applied. While this scoring method is mainly used in the composition literature to score writing assessment including open-ended questions [20, 21], in this study the method was adopted to score a participant's answer which is provided in a similar form to that of a short essay. A single score was assigned to a participant's answer based on the overall meaning of the answer, which includes information about the term or the concept and could be definition, explanation of its characteristics or its process, or its examples. This score is used as an indication of how familiar they were with the three terms, before and after they watched the videos.

Each answer was read and then scored against the scale outlined in Table 2. The minimum score is 0 and maximum score is 3 for each term. This scale is complemented by a set of sample answers for the "Cloud Computing" term, which can be referred to as a benchmark answer. The score is then categorised into four levels, namely: *None*, *Weak*, *Moderate* and *Strong*. If X is the participant's score, then the level of the participant's understanding is determined by following these rules:

If $X = 0$, then participants' understanding level is *None*;
else if $0 < X <= 1$, then participants' understanding level is *Weak*;
else if $1 < X <= 2$, then participants' understanding level is *Moderate*;
else if $2 < X <= 3$, then participants' understanding level is *Strong*.

In consideration of the subjectivity issues in marking essays [17], the following moderation strategy was conducted. Two markers were trained in the marking scheme

**Table 2.** Scoring scale

| Score | Level | Criteria |
|---|---|---|
| 2 < X <=3 | *Strong* | **An answer at this level**:<br>• effectively explains the meaning of the term<br>• accurately uses related keywords in its description<br>**Sample answer:**<br>Cloud computing is a pool of a virtualized computing resources that allows users to gain access to applications and data in a web-based environment on demand. It is categorised into three service models, namely: Infrastructure as a Service (IaaS), Platform as a Service (PaaS) and Software as a Service (SaaS). Cloud computing can be deployed into private, public, community-managed or hybrid settings |
| 1 < X <=2 | *Moderate* | **An answer at this level**:<br>• explains the term adequately but may be incomplete<br>• uses related keywords with occasional inaccuracy in its description<br>**Sample answer:**<br>Cloud computing is a virtualized computing resources that can be accessed by users on their demand. These resources are provided by an Internet provider to store data of a company or individual, outside their own system. It can be in private or public setting |
| 0 < X <=1 | *Weak* | **An answer at this level has the following weaknesses**:<br>• little or no detail, or irrelevant explanations<br>• no related keywords or uses them inappropriately<br>**Sample answer:**<br>Cloud computing is an Internet (public) resources |
| 0 | *None* | An answer is rated 0 if it contains no response, is "unfamiliar" or is off-topic |

before the scoring process. In the protocol, if the scores of the two markers differ by two levels, then a third marker is required. This situation did not arise during the scoring process for this study.

## 4   Key Results

Two key factors are analysed to determine benefits of utilising multimedia presentations to increase participants' understanding of technical concepts.

### 4.1   Participant's Technical Understanding

The grading results for participants' understanding of the terms cloud computing (term 1), botnet (term 2) and forensic file recovery (term 3) are listed in Table 3. By calculating their average understanding scores, the mean difference of the scores between before and after watching the videos is 0.91 with a standard deviation of 0.59. The

**Table 3.** Participant's understanding ratings

| | Term 1 | | | | Term 2 | | | | Term 3 | | | |
|---|---|---|---|---|---|---|---|---|---|---|---|---|
| | Before | | After | | Before | | After | | Before | | After | |
| | Score | Level | Score | Level | Score | Level | Score | Level | Score | Level | Score | Level |
| 1 | 0.000 | None | 0.000 | None | 0.000 | None | 0.000 | None | 0.000 | None | 0.000 | None |
| 2 | 0.000 | None | 0.000 | None | 0.000 | None | 0.000 | None | 0.000 | None | 0.000 | None |
| 3 | 0.000 | None | 0.000 | None | 0.000 | None | 0.000 | None | 0.500 | Weak | 1.000 | Weak |
| 4 | 0.000 | None | 1.250 | Moderate | 0.000 | None | 0.000 | None | 0.000 | None | 1.725 | Moderate |
| 5 | 0.875 | Weak | 1.000 | Weak | 0.000 | None | 2.100 | Strong | 0.125 | Weak | 1.975 | Moderate |
| 6 | 0.125 | Weak | 0.125 | Weak | 0.125 | Weak | 0.125 | Weak | 0.125 | Weak | 0.125 | Weak |
| 7 | 0.725 | Weak | 1.500 | Moderate | 0.750 | Weak | 1.500 | Moderate | 0.750 | Weak | 1.000 | Weak |
| 8 | 0.875 | Weak | 1.850 | Moderate | 0.000 | None | 1.975 | Moderate | 0.500 | Weak | 2.375 | Strong |
| 9 | 1.000 | Weak | 2.000 | Moderate | 0.875 | Weak | 2.250 | Strong | 1.500 | Moderate | 1.725 | Moderate |
| 10 | 1.725 | Moderate | 1.725 | Moderate | 1.500 | Moderate | 1.500 | Moderate | 0.250 | Weak | 0.250 | Weak |
| 11 | 1.125 | Moderate | 1.500 | Moderate | 1.125 | Moderate | 1.250 | Moderate | 0.000 | None | 1.725 | Moderate |
| 12 | 1.000 | Weak | 1.400 | Moderate | 1.250 | Moderate | 1.500 | Moderate | 0.250 | Weak | 2.750 | Strong |
| 13 | 0.000 | None | 1.975 | Moderate | 0.000 | None | 1.975 | Moderate | 0.000 | None | 1.850 | Moderate |
| 14 | 0.600 | Weak | 1.975 | Moderate | 0.725 | Weak | 1.500 | Moderate | 0.000 | None | 1.250 | Moderate |
| 15 | 0.500 | Weak | 1.375 | Moderate | 0.000 | None | 1.000 | Weak | 0.000 | None | 1.750 | Moderate |
| 16 | 0.000 | None | 0.500 | Weak | 0.000 | None | 0.500 | Weak | 1.000 | Weak | 1.500 | Moderate |
| 17 | 0.500 | Weak | 1.000 | Weak | 0.000 | None | 0.500 | Weak | 0.750 | Weak | 1.250 | Moderate |
| 18 | 0.000 | None | 1.875 | Moderate | 0.000 | None | 1.500 | Moderate | 0.000 | None | 1.750 | Moderate |
| 19 | 1.750 | Moderate | 2.500 | Strong | 0.000 | None | 2.625 | Strong | 0.000 | None | 1.500 | Moderate |
| 20 | 1.875 | Moderate | 2.875 | Strong | 1.875 | Moderate | 3.000 | Strong | 2.100 | Strong | 2.950 | Strong |
| 21 | 0.850 | Weak | 1.500 | Moderate | 0.000 | None | 1.500 | Moderate | 0.000 | None | 2.750 | Strong |
| 22 | 1.750 | Moderate | 2.750 | Strong | 1.375 | Moderate | 2.750 | Strong | 1.125 | Moderate | 2.625 | Strong |
| 23 | 1.250 | Moderate | 2.000 | Moderate | 1.000 | Weak | 1.375 | Moderate | 1.000 | Weak | 1.725 | Moderate |
| 24 | 0.375 | Weak | 1.250 | Moderate | 0.000 | None | 1.850 | Moderate | 0.375 | Weak | 2.000 | Moderate |
| 25 | 1.000 | Weak | 1.725 | Moderate | 1.250 | Moderate | 2.100 | Strong | 1.375 | Moderate | 1.975 | Moderate |

mean of the understanding scores before watching the videos is 0.56 with a standard deviation of 0.52 while the mean after watching the videos is 1.46 with a standard deviation of 0.77.

Participants' understanding is considered improved if their average score of the understanding after watching the three videos is better than before (i.e. the difference is greater than 0.00). Overall, 21 participants out of 25 (84%) demonstrated an increased understanding and they are categorised as improved.

Figure 1 represents the improvement in participants' understanding for the three terms. The five highest improvement scores are experienced by participants 13, 18, 21, 19, and 8, which are 1.933, 1.708, 1.633, 1.625, and 1.086, respectively. The majority of these participants identified as in the age range of 36–45 years old. English is not their native language and their job titles are varied; consisting of two judges, and one lawyer, police investigator and prosecutor. They are considered having low to moderate familiarity with technical terminologies and concepts as their technical literacy scores are notably 2, 1, 2, 3, and 2, respectively.

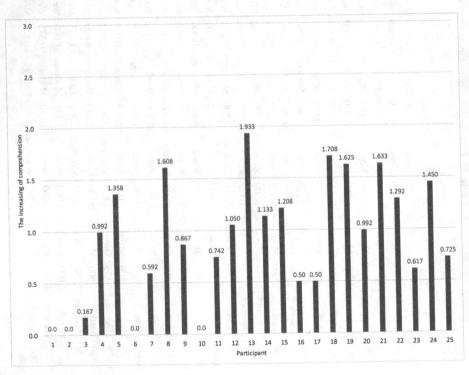

**Fig. 1.** Diagram representing the improvement in participants' understanding

## 4.2    Influence of Video Features on Participants' Level of Understanding

The key features of our videos are animation and narration. All three videos have these key features but feature different content (i.e. topic and purpose). These differentiations have the potential to influence participants' understanding. In this section, to examine this potential influence, we outline the shift in the understanding, using the category levels (None, Weak, Moderate and Strong) for each term.

Table 4 lists the number of participants who experienced increased understanding, grouped by the level of increase and then by video. In the remainder of this section, we focus on the groups that show an increase of two or more levels. The largest group of participants who increased by 2 levels did so after watching video 3 (9 participants), followed by video 2 (6 participants) and video 1 (3 participants). Videos 2 and 3 provide practical example in the delivery of their content. The greatest number of participants who improved their understanding by 3 levels (i.e. the highest increase, from *None* to *Strong*) did so after watching video 2 (2 participants), followed by video 3 (1 participants). It is noted that video 2 has the term's definition in addition to the practical example that is mentioned earlier.

**Table 4.** The increases in participants' level of understandings for each video

| Increase | Video | Number of participants |
|---|---|---|
| 1 level | Video 1 | 13 |
| | Video 2 | 9 |
| | Video 3 | 6 |
| 2 levels | Video 1 | 3 |
| | Video 2 | 6 |
| | Video 3 | 9 |
| 3 levels | Video 1 | 0 |
| | Video 2 | 2 |
| | Video 3 | 1 |

## 4.3    Participants' Feedback

In this section, participant feedback is presented in three parts. The first is participants' views of the usefulness of the multimedia presentations in enhancing their understanding. The second part is participant's opinions about other tools or methods that would facilitate their understanding, and lastly their feedback on the questionnaire itself.

### Feedback on the Multimedia Presentations

Figure 2 depicts the participants' subjective rating for the usefulness of multimedia presentations in enhancing their understanding of the three technical terminologies and concepts presented. The 25 participants were asked to rate the usefulness of the videos out of five, 8 of them give a rating of 4 for multimedia presentation usefulness and 7 of them a rating of 5. Only one participant gave a rating of 1.

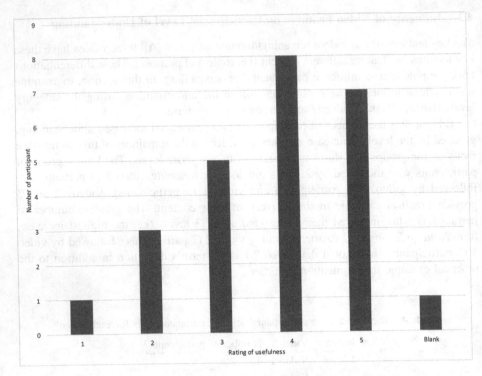

**Fig. 2.** Participant ratings of the usefulness of multimedia presentations

Nevertheless, there is no apparent relationship between a participant's subjective rating and their understanding improvements presented in Table 3. For example participant number 18 who only rates 2 for the usefulness rating, experienced a substantial enhancement of their understanding score (1.71 - from *None* to *Moderate*). Another example is the comparison between participant number 4 who provided a usefulness rating of 5 and other participants who rate 4 (e.g. participant number 13 and 19). While participant 4 rates higher of the usefulness of multimedia presentations than participants 13 and 19, in fact the two later participants experienced a greater increase in their understanding score.

Participants' written comments on the multimedia presentations are presented in Table 5. We grouped the comments based on participants' ratings in order to understand their connection. Here, we can see that those who provided low scores (i.e. 1 and 2) and blank, noted issues with sound or language, and indicated a difficultly in understanding the material.

**Opinions on Other Tools or Methods that Could Enhance Understanding**
Participants' opinions on tools or methods that would help to facilitate their understanding of technical terminologies and concepts is presented in Table 6. This table shows us that participants who give low scores would prefer the addition of practical examples and oral explanation by real person. Comparatively, in general, participants who give moderate and higher scores (i.e. 3–5) acknowledge the benefits of multimedia

**Table 5.** Feedback on the multimedia presentations

| Rating | Comments and suggestions |
|---|---|
| 1 | "Watching is better than listening, please let's speaker louder to hear easily" |
| 2 | "Video about cloud computing was useful, but the other two video was not, I feel"<br>"Professional presentation, but difficult for me to understand because of the level (high)" |
| 3 | "Language understandable to all participants" |
| 4 | "Understand clearly"<br>"Short and understandable interpretation of technical concepts"<br>"Multimedia presentation is very important in explaining technical terms because it helps the ordinary people to understand about ICT operates. It is a matter of converting technical terminologies into laymans term"<br>"Very helpful" |
| 5 | "The multimedia presentation was clear and understandable"<br>"Intelligible"<br>"Some so technical, other so interesting"<br>"Quite illuminating and constructive" |
| Blank | "Sometimes the language is a problem to understand a 100% of the material, and if we put music in the videos, it can be more difficult. So maybe I think that the music should be a little bit lower (special video #2)" |

**Table 6.** Opinions on other facilitating tools or methods

| Rating | Comments and suggestions |
|---|---|
| 1 | "It might be impossible but it is the best if practice rather than watching or listening" |
| 2 | "Oral explanation with some presentation sheets, by real person, not by videos"<br>"Theory + video + comments" |
| 3 | "More examples (for more understanding), use simple words and short PPT"<br>"Video presentation, power point explanation and references materials are essential"<br>"By inserting expert evidence such as video clips and other new technologies available and forensic evidence" |
| 4 | "Demonstrate using movie and video"<br>"I think it will be interesting to view/study during the lecture the concrete real cases about digital forensic investigation"<br>"Multimedia should be used to visualize. Examples should be used to explain each technical terminologies"<br>"Visual videos could be the most useful tool"<br>"If we have enough time, some small practical operating lesson"<br>"Site visits for greater appreciations of how ICT operates"<br>"I am not able to suggest any other method. But as for someone who comes from a country where cybercrime is yet to be seen I am happy as was presented"<br>"Multimedia presentations is OK! Maybe, the list of short explaining cases for me as prosecutor, would be useful for better understanding" |
| 5 | "Case studies and multimedia presentations will greatly assist understanding of technical terminologies"<br>"Animation"<br>"Just study more, and many others seminars, like workshops" |
| Blank | "Illustration. Interactive presentations" |

presentations and suggesting ways to improve the presentations (e.g. adding more examples and including case studies).

**Feedback on the Questionnaire**

The feedback relating to the questionnaire itself is outlined in Table 7. One participant highlights the difficulty in self-assessing technical literacy, and again the participants comment on the use of English as the delivery language in the videos and the need for material classification.

**Table 7.** Feedback on the questionnaire

| Comments and suggestions |
| --- |
| • "It is hard to rate my own technical literature because I always think that I lack knowledge. Knowledge is unlimited then although I know something else, it is not enough to rate me higher score" |
| • "Good for those whom use English as language" |
| • "Please use simple (easy) materials. Because your materials very difficult for lowers, especially for judges and prosecutors" |
| • "I only wish that more and more opportunities be given to … to attend similar workshops for attaining more knowledge pertaining to how cybercrime are committing" |

# 5 Discussion on the Practical Implementation of Multimedia Presentations When They Are Used in a Courtroom Context

It is important to note that in this study the videos were not displayed in a courtroom as part of the survey. Nevertheless, this study focuses to identify whether multimedia presentations can be utilised to increase a layperson's understanding of technical terms and concepts in a courtroom presentation context, rather than the effectiveness of multimedia presentations in widespread general learning situations.

The results from this study support and extend findings from our previous studies. We broaden our sample of participants from our previous studies in Indonesia, Taiwan and Singapore [3–5], by conducting the survey in a different country (i.e. Japan). The previous three studies indicate that the multimedia presentations (i.e. video with animation and narration) can assist in enhancing understanding of technical terminologies and concepts in digital forensics, and this current study supports those findings by extending their implications to judiciary and law enforcement communities from other countries.

The use of multimedia presentations in a court setting has been discussed by other authors, who have outlined the benefits and drawbacks [1, 16] and been utilised in the training for members of the judiciary [22, 23]. The research presented in this paper contributes by analysing empirical data to examine their effectiveness in increasing understanding of technical terms by court-related personnel. A brief comparison of the four studies we have conducted, is presented in Table 8. Based on the results of these papers, we conclude that any current or future implementation of multimedia presentation in a court setting are useful in increasing people's understanding, at least in the case of technical terminologies and concepts often used in the presentation of digital forensic findings.

The remainder of this section focuses on how to practically implement relevant feedback (presented in Table 9) in multimedia presentations to ensure an optimal outcome in terms of increasing participant understanding.

## 5.1 Material Classification

The need for material classification is evident in all of the four studies outlined in Table 9. This highlights not only the need to categorise the material into levels of expertise, but also to customise it for different professions. In our studies, the concept of participants' self-assessing their familiarity with technical terms can be used to measure a participant's background knowledge. This information can be utilised to assess each participant's current expertise and direct them to material suitable for their current level of understanding. However, difficulty in self-assessment was identified in our current study, for example where a participant strives to be objective and tends to give themselves a low score for technical literacy. This challenge is also recognised in a study by Hanrahan and Isaacs [24]. To examine participant's level of understanding prior to reviewing training materials, and it is suggested that self-assessment be combined with a simple assessment of understanding, such as the participant's score of understanding derived from their definition before watching the videos, as in this study.

While categorisation based on participants' level of expertise is relevant for training purposes, material differentiation based on the viewer's role may also help to increase the relevance of the materials in a court presentation context. For example, where explanations are mainly designed for judges or juries, material should be carefully prepared so that the audience can understand the main concepts of a technical term for without excessive or unnecessary detail. Conversely, that same detailed information might be of great value to police investigators. The suggested approach for members of the judiciary aligns with the findings of Armytage [25] who noted that, in the context of continuing judicial learning, the distinctive elements in the judicial profession (including their preferred learning styles) have implications on the design of their content and learning program.

## 5.2 Language Issues

The main results outlined in Table 8 suggest that despite the varying country of origin and language, our participants (i.e. judiciary members, law enforcement officers, and practitioners) commonly experience positive results in terms of increasing their understanding of digital forensic technical terms using multimedia presentations, which are presented in English. Nevertheless, participants often comment on the use of English as a delivery language in the videos. Even after we added subtitle, some of them still prefer the videos delivered in their native language [5]. The fact that most participants are likely not native English speakers and their level of proficiency in English remains unknown are issues identified in our studies. These issues potentially affect the effectiveness of the multimedia presentation to increase their understandings.

**Table 8.** Summary of multimedia presentation research

| Study | Cahyani et al. [4] | Cahyani et al. [3] | Cahyani et al. [5] | Current study |
|---|---|---|---|---|
| Materials | Three videos, presented in English: <br> - Cloud computing video <br> - Botnet video <br> - Forensic file recovery video | Three videos, presented in English: <br> - Cloud computing video <br> - Botnet video <br> - Forensic file recovery video | Three videos, presented in English with subtitle in Indonesia: <br> - Mobile forensics <br> - Time zone <br> - Hashing | Three videos, presented in English: <br> - Cloud computing video <br> - Botnet video <br> - Forensic file recovery video |
| Participants | They are participants of one international workshop in Singapore. They came from different nationalities. They are managers and directors from IT-related departments of financial institutions | *Linguistic group.* They came from different nationalities that attended an international seminar in Taiwan. They are linguistic academia (e.g. lecturer, teacher, and student) <br> *Judiciary group.* They are participants from a seminar in Indonesia. They are all Indonesian. Their professions are mixed of: <br> - Judge <br> - Legal administrator <br> - Police investigator <br> - Prosecutor | They are participants from three seminars in Indonesia. They are all Indonesian, comprising: <br> - Judge <br> - Police investigator <br> - Prosecutor <br> - Staff | Participants came from different nationalities, comprising: <br> - Judge <br> - Lawyer <br> - Police investigator <br> - Prosecutor |
| Main results | 8 of 9 participants experienced increasing understanding | 80.47% of 128 participants experienced increasing understanding | 100% of 121 participants experienced increasing understanding | 84% of 25 participants experienced increasing understanding |

Here, we acknowledge the influence of language and culture in learning process, such as those identified in clinical [26] and physics educations [27]. From those studies, strategies to decrease the influence of language can be learned and be considered. For example, this could be achieved by avoiding the use of culturally specific slang, idioms, and colloquialisms in the explanation and by getting reflection on the materials from audiences through their feedback. However, the use of audience's native language as a delivery language is strongly recommended to maximise their understanding.

**Table 9.** Summary of participants' comments and feedbacks

| Participants' comments and feedbacks | Cahyani et al. [4] | Cahyani et al. [3] | Cahyani et al. [5] | Current study |
|---|---|---|---|---|
| • Categorization of material difficulty or customization of material difficulty for the audience | √ | √ | √ | √ |
| • Presentation in the participant's native language | - | √ | √ | √ |
| • Adjustment of video speed/duration based on material | - | √ | √ | √ |
| • Utilisation of examples | - | √ | √ | √ |
| • Utilisation of case study | - | √ | √ | √ |
| • Utilisation of analogy | √ | - | √ | - |
| • Identification of the need for non-interactive methods (e.g. books, magazine, or texts) | - | √ | √ | √ |
| • Identification of the need for applied experiences (e.g. practical hands-on, role play, or site visit) | √ | - | - | √ |
| • Identification of the need for interactive methods, which includes the presence of instructor or expert | √ | √ | √ | √ |

## 5.3  Video Material

A number of findings from our studies relate to the video content. One content focused concern is balancing video duration with the scope of the topic being discussed. This might be related with the previous effort to classify material with the aim of maximising understanding of the topic being presented. Another key point is the importance of the use of examples, case studies, and analogy in the explanation of technical terminologies and concepts. The study presented in this paper also has feedback on this point, and its results highlighted the usefulness of definitions and examples as part of a video to enhance participants' understanding.

The use of multimedia presentations in a courtroom is highly dependent on the availability of supporting technologies. A study by Hout and de Bodo [28] on the topic of technologies, includes a discussion of animation and the tools needed for its courtroom presentation to judges and juries. Another study highlights more recent technologies to deliver multimedia presentations and considerations for using forensic animation for courtroom presentations [29, 30]. In practice, it is integral that both the display and audio devices are deployed sufficiently to be seen heard by all relevant audiences.

## 5.4  Other Tools that Would Facilitate Understanding and the Need of an Expert

Multimedia presentations (which are characterised by animation and narration) include a variety of other media such as text, images, and audio [31, 32]. The aim of the combination of these materials is to communicate a message in a more memorable way. It is not meant to replace other information sources such as books or slides. In other words, the use of multimedia presentations in a courtroom complements, rather than replaces, live presentation from a forensic practitioner or other expert witness. Direct presentation is still needed to provide the court with the opportunity to question the witness. For example, Hout and de Bodo [28] mention that "courtroom technology is a means to achieve persuasion, not an end in itself" (p. 76).

# 6  Conclusion

Robust presentation of evidence is a critical component of any digital investigation to ensure that the findings of digital forensics practitioners are clearly understood by the court. Many authors discuss the need for forensic soundness in their digital forensic approach, and generally this is linked with the requirement to ensure that evidence is admissible. However, we often focus principally on the forensic soundness of the technical processes and techniques used to obtain and analyse the electronic evidence. It can be argued that the soundness of the presentation of that evidence is of equal, or even greater, importance.

We posited that multimedia presentations have a role in helping to bridge this gap, and help the court to understand the evidence, and associated contextual information, as completely as the practitioner does. The need for a more complete understanding of an electronic evidence by those in the legal profession will only increase as with the growth in digital displacement of traditionally manual activities (e.g. the introduction of smartphone communications, Internet-of-Things (IoT) automated record keeping, and IP based CCTV) will come a corresponding increase in the importance of an electronic evidence to every case before the courts.

In this paper, we demonstrated that multimedia presentations (i.e. videos) that combine text, images, narration and animation improved 84% of our participants' understanding of digital forensic technical terms and concepts. Videos that provide case examples and are narrated in the participant's native language are preferred. Other methods that may help to increase understanding are also identified. They include practical experience and interactive presentations. The results of this study echoed the findings from our previous studies which highlight the potential effectiveness of utilising multimedia presentations as a learning tool to increase the understanding of digital forensics technical terms in the presentation phase of a digital investigation.

Future research will include exploring other types of multimedia presentation methods to more comprehensively evaluate the effectiveness of multimedia in enhancing teaching and learning, for example via developing e-learning package and collecting feedbacks at a centralized platform that can be accessible to a broader audience size from different countries.

# References

1. Plowman, J.K.: Multimedia in the courtroom: a valuable tool or smoke and mirrors. Rev. Litig. **15**, 415–430 (1995)
2. Mayer, R.E.: The promise of multimedia learning: using the same instructional design methods across different media. Learn. Instr. **13**(2), 125–139 (2003)
3. Cahyani, N.D.W., Martini, B., Choo, K.-K.R.: Effectiveness of multimedia presentations in improving understanding of technical terminologies and concepts: a pilot study. Aust. J. Forensic Sci. **49**, 1–17 (2016)
4. Cahyani, N.D.W., Martini, B., Choo, K.-K.R.: Using multimedia presentations to improve digital forensic understanding: a pilot study. In: 26th Australasian Conference on Information Systems, pp. 1–10. University of South Australia, South Australia (2015)
5. Cahyani, N.D.W., Martini, B., Choo, K.-K.R.: Using multimedia presentations to enhance the judiciary's technical understanding of digital forensic concepts: an Indonesian case study. In: 49th Annual Hawaii International Conference on System Sciences, pp. 5617–5626. IEEE Computer Society Press, Hawaii (2016)
6. Beckett, J., Slay, J.: Scientific underpinnings and background to standards and accreditation in digital forensics. Digit. Invest. **8**(2), 114–121 (2011)
7. McKemmish, R.: What is forensic computing? Trends Issues Crime Crim. Justice **118**, 1–6 (1999)
8. Kessler, G., Fasulo, M.: The case for teaching network protocols to computer forensics examiners. In: Conference on Digital Forensics, Security and Law, pp. 115–137. Association of Digital Forensics, Security and Law, United States (2007)
9. Reith, M., Carr, C., Gunsch, G.: An examination of digital forensic models. Int. J. Digit. Evid. **1**(3), 1–12 (2002)
10. Baryamureeba, V., Tushabe, F.: The enhanced digital investigation process model. In: Digital Forensic Research Conference, pp. 1–9. DFRWS, USA (2004)
11. Casey, E., Palmer, G.: The investigative process. In: Casey, E. (ed.) Digital Evidence and Computer Crime, 2nd edn, pp. 91–114. Academic Press, London (2004)
12. Yasinsac, A., Erbacher, R.F., Marks, D.G., Pollitt, M.M., Sommer, P.M.: Computer forensics education. IEEE Secur. Priv. Mag. **99**(4), 15–23 (2003)
13. Grispos, G., Storer, T., Glisson, W.: Calm before the storm: the challenges of cloud computing in digital forensics. Int. J. Digit. Crime Forensics **4**(2), 28–48 (2012)
14. Martini, B., Choo, K.-K.R.: An integrated conceptual digital forensic framework for cloud computing. Digit. Invest. **9**(2), 71–80 (2012)
15. Wolthusen, S.D.: Overcast: forensic discovery in cloud environments. In: 5th International Conference on IT Security Incident Management and IT Forensics, pp. 3–9. IEEE (2009)
16. Carney, B., Feigenson, N.: Visual persuasion in the Michael Skakel trial: enhancing advocacy through interactive media presentations. Crim. Justice **19**, 22–36 (2004)
17. Bloxham, S.: Marking and moderation in the UK: false assumptions and wasted resources. Assess. Eval. High Educ. **34**(2), 209–220 (2009)
18. Crook, C., Gross, H., Dymott, R.: Assessment relationships in higher education: the tension of process and practice. Brit. Educ. Res. J. **32**(1), 95–114 (2006)
19. Weigle, S.C.: Assessing Writing. Cambrigde University Press, Cambrigde (2002)
20. Barkaoui, K.: Variability in ESL essay rating processes: the role of the rating scale and rater experience. Lang. Assess. Q. **7**(1), 54–74 (2010)
21. Jongsma, E.A., Mellott, D.K.: Computerized system and method for teaching and assessing the holistic scoring of open-ended questions. IFI CLAIMS Patent Services (2004). http://www.google.com/patents/US6768894

22. Schmitt, G.R.: Online DNA training targets lawyers, judges. NIJ J. **256**, 16–18 (2007)
23. Varfi, T., Parmentier, S., Aertsen, I. (eds).: Developing judicial training for restorative justice: towards a European approach. European Forum for Restorative Justice, Leuven (2014)
24. Hanrahan, S.J., Isaacs, G.: Assessing self-and peer-assessment: the students' views. High Educ. Res. Dev. **20**(1), 53–70 (2001)
25. Armytage, L.: Educating Judges: Towards a New Model of Continuing Judicial Learning, 1st edn. Kluwer Law International, Alphen aan den Rijn (1996)
26. Ladyshewsky, R.: East meets west: the influence of language and culture in clinical education. Aust. J. Physiother. **42**(4), 287–294 (1996)
27. Morales, M.: Influence of culture and language sensitive physics on science attitude enhancement. Cult. Stud. Sci. Educ. **10**(4), 951–984 (2015)
28. Hout, K., de Bodo, R.: Technologies for courtroom presentation (with technical terms explained!). Pract. Litigator **7**(4), 61–76 (1996)
29. Sainato, V.: Evidentiary presentations and forensic technologies in the courtroom, the director's cut. J. Inst. Justice Int. Stud. **9**, 38–52 (2009)
30. Unger, P.J.: Technology for courtroom presentations. GP Solo **31**(5), 24–30 (2014)
31. Mayer, R.E., Moreno, R.: Aids to computer-based multimedia learning. Learn Instr. **12**(1), 107–119 (2002)
32. Prabhakaran, B.: Adaptive multimedia presentation strategies. Multimedia Tools Appl. **12**(2), 281–298 (2000)

# Event Reconstruction of Indonesian E-Banking Services on Windows Phone Devices

Niken Dwi Wahyu Cahyani[1,3], Ben Martini[1],
Kim-Kwang Raymond Choo[1,2(⊠)], and Helen Ashman[1]

[1] School of Information Technology and Mathematical Sciences,
University of South Australia, Adelaide, SA 5095, Australia
niken.cahyani@mymail.unisa.edu.au,
{ben.martini,raymond.choo,helen.ashman}@unisa.edu.au
[2] Department of Information Systems and Cyber Security,
The University of Texas at San Antonio, San Antonio, TX 78249-0631, USA
raymond.choo@fulbrightmail.org
[3] Department of Informatics, Telkom University, Bandung, Indonesia
nikencahyani@telkomuniversity.ac.id

**Abstract.** In this paper, a digital investigation of electronic (e)-banking services on the Windows Phone platform of nine Indonesian banks is undertaken. In the experiments, banking transactions (balance check, funds transfer and phone credit purchase) are performed using a Nokia Lumia 625. The digital evidence resulting from these transactions is acquired and analyzed using mobile forensic tools from Cellebrite and Micro Systemation AB. In order to reconstruct the transaction events, evidence objects are identified and related events are sequenced. Specifically, the findings relating to mobile banking activities identify eight digital evidence objects (SMS, email, call log, contact, media file, network packets, location and installed apps), and a physical object (account book - obtained from a physical investigation). Investigation questions of *who*, *what*, *when* and *how* are answered from the acquired evidence and the event sequence diagrams. The findings contribute to a better understanding of available mobile banking evidence on Windows Phone devices.

**Keywords:** Forensic science · Digital forensics · Investigative techniques
Event reconstruction · Windows phone forensics · Digital evidence
E-banking · Indonesian banks

## 1 Introduction

E-banking is a service provided by banks that delivers 24/7 banking transaction services. It includes SMS-banking, WAP-GPRS banking or Internet banking (I-banking), and mobile application-based banking or mobile banking. The substantial increases in telecommunications access may underlie banks' decision to deliver e-banking services, and broaden their support for a wide range of platforms. In Indonesia, e-banking services have been available in some form since the late 1990s. These services are becoming more widely-used in Indonesia with up to 80% of consumers surveyed having conducted mobile banking transactions in 2014, a leap of about a third from 58% in 2013 [1].

© ICST Institute for Computer Sciences, Social Informatics and Telecommunications Engineering 2018
R. Beyah et al. (Eds.): SecureComm 2018, LNICST 255, pp. 507–521, 2018.
https://doi.org/10.1007/978-3-030-01704-0_29

According to this report, by using mobile banking, Indonesian consumers are most enthusiastic in sending airtime (45%), checking their bank balance (30%) and transferring money (24%). The wide availability of e-banking services for mobile devices highlights the need for research in this area to inform forensic investigators, as these devices are likely to be the source of evidence in incidents, including WP8 devices.

This research aims to provide investigators with a better understanding of the types of digital evidence that can be acquired from Windows Phone devices (a relatively under-studied platform in comparison to Android and iOS devices) when investigating banking incidents and to what extent they can answer investigative questions: who, what, when, where and how. While the Windows Phone market share is only less than 0.22% in April 2018 [2], this research is necessary as it cannot be predicted which mobile platform will hold integral evidence.

In this paper, a case study was conducted to represent normal banking activities using the services of all Indonesian banks which support the Windows Phone platform in their e-banking services. Common financial transactions (i.e. funds transfer and purchases) and non-financial transactions (i.e. balance checks) were conducted during the experiments. Once the transactions were completed, the evidence was collected and the events were reconstructed and examined. The case study followed the event reconstruction phases proposed by Carrier and Spafford [3] and a delineating event sequence based on the Multilinear Events Sequencing (MES) approach [4].

This paper addresses the following two questions:

Q1: What banking activity evidence sources exist on Indonesian bank apps for Windows Phone devices?
Q2: How can detailed event reconstruction be undertaken based on evidence acquired from Indonesian bank apps for Windows Phone devices?

Following these two questions, we also examine how other evidence sources outside the phone may complete the event reconstruction.

## 2 Related Literature

To date, investigations on e-banking services have focused on the Android platform. One study based on Korean banks shows risk of financial loss by demonstrating an attack whereby seven Android banking apps are repackaged [5] in order to facilitate the transfer of money to an unintended recipient. A reverse engineering process to create forged apps was conducted by exploiting the apps' vulnerabilities (i.e. Android app distribution and repackaging vulnerability). After analyzing these vulnerabilities, the authors discussed possible technical actions as countermeasures, namely: restricting the self-signing of packages, code obfuscation and code attestation. A more recent study on forensic analysis and security assessment on Android banking apps was conducted by Chanajitt and Viriyasitavat [6]. The authors analyzed seven mobile banking apps in Thailand, and described forensic artefacts that could be recovered from the apps, including user information, the financial transactions and their timestamps. They also conducted a security assessment of the apps and revealed that it was also possible to modify these apps and install repackaged apps.

Compared to the Android platform, Windows Phone devices/apps forensics and banking apps forensics are understudied [7]. The relatively small number of Windows phone users might be one reason. However, it is not possible to predict what devices might be investigated in e-banking crime. Therefore, it is crucial to ensure that law enforcement and forensic investigators are operationally ready to investigate different mobile platforms, including Windows Phone devices. By considering that victims of cybercrime can be anywhere, this awareness is relevant not only for law enforcement in Indonesia, but also in other countries. Our previous studies on Windows Phone devices and apps gave an initial understanding of their digital artefacts and the support of mobile forensic tools in their data acquisitions [8, 9]. By using Nokia Lumia 625 and 735 (working in Windows Phone version 8.x), these studies show that physical acquisition can potentially extract prominent data such as phone book, call log, SMSs, and data files including apps data. Our studies only found that one of all the tested mobile forensic tools support physical acquisition on the devices. Also, the logical acquisition can only extract multimedia files. These results make investigations on Windows Phone more challenging.

Currently there is no study of mobile banking services on Windows Phone. This gap highlights the need for studying Windows Phone devices to examine the extent to which their digital evidence can contribute to an e-banking investigation.

## 3 Event Reconstruction Method

In conducting event reconstruction process, Carrier and Spafford [3] proposed an event reconstruction model that classifies an object's role based on a cause-and-effect approach. Evidence objects have a "cause" role if changing the object's state caused an event related to the incident. Conversely, evidence objects have an "effect" role if their state was changed by an event. The model consists of the following five phases:

1. Evidence examination;
2. Role classification;
3. Event Construction and testing;
4. Event sequencing; and
5. Hypothesis testing.

The first three phases focus on tasks in evidence object identification, assigning their role and reconstructing individual events related to the incident. Our study follows these steps to identify evidence sources from a phone, examine their linkages and to regenerate events that describe activities based on the available evidence. Within these phases, we aim to incorporate evidence sources collected from physical investigations to provide more complete information. This approach conforms with another study of Carrier and Spafford [10] about a model that integrates physical and digital crime scene investigations.

In the fourth phase (i.e. event sequencing phase), we identified that relational-based techniques can be used to sequence the events, as long as the objects and events have time information. In this phase to sequence our events, we used a method called Multilinear Events Sequencing (MES), which is based on the causal analysis technique [4].

It was used to emphasis the chronological order of our sequencing event based on the collected evidence. The MES methodology starts with the identification of the incident boundary, followed by sequencing constructed event blocks and their conditions in a flowchart. This step is followed by validation of the sequence, identification of causal relationships and identification of corrective actions. By using a MES diagram, delineating the beginning and the end of the incident sequence was described and finally incident hypotheses were tested.

## 4   Experiment

In this section, we discuss our case study environment in representing e-banking activities using a phone and acquisition procedure to extract data from the phone.

### 4.1   Environment and Requirements

We commenced our experiment by browsing and examining the available banking apps in the Windows Store. After verifying those apps with official information from the related banks' websites, nine Indonesian banks that deliver e-banking services on the Windows Phone platform were identified. At the time of the experiments, this covered all banks in Indonesia which provide e-banking services for their Windows Phone mobile devices' customers. These banks consisted of three central government banks (Bank1, Bank3 and Bank8), one local government bank (Bank7), two Syariah banks (Bank2 and Bank6) and three private banks (Bank4, Bank5 and Bank9). Based on the services they supported, there are five banks which provide SMS banking service, eight banks that provide I-banking service and four banks which deliver mobile banking service. A summary of the supported e-banking services is listed in Table 1.

**Table 1.**  Summary of the e-banking services and the conducted banking activities

| Bank | SMS banking | | | I-banking | | | Mobile banking | | |
|------|----|----|----|----|----|----|----|----|----|
|      | BC | FT | PR | BC | FT | PR | BC | FT | PR |
| 1 | √ | √ | √ | √ | √ | √* | NA | NA | NA |
| 2 | NA | NA | NA | √ | √ | √* | √ | √ | √ |
| 3 | √ | √ | √ | √ | √ | √* | NA | NA | NA |
| 4 | NA | NA | NA | √ | √ | √ | √ | √ | √* |
| 5 | √ | √ | √* | √ | √ | √* | NA | NA | NA |
| 6 | NA | NA | NA | NA | NA | NA | √ | √ | √ |
| 7 | √ | √ | √ | √ | √ | √ | NA | NA | NA |
| 8 | √ | √ | √ | √ | √ | √* | NA | NA | NA |
| 9 | NA | NA | NA | √ | √† | √* | √ | √ | √ |

*Transaction code from the bank is not received
†Transaction code from the bank is not displayed properly

For each service, three banking activities were conducted, namely: balance checks (BC), fund transfers (FT) and phone credit recharges (PR). These three activities are performed frequently by customers when they interact with electronic banking services.

For SMS banking services, we downloaded and installed four corresponding apps from Windows Store to our Nokia Lumia 625 while, one SMS banking service did not require an app to access its service; we could directly conduct banking transactions by sending an SMS to a specified number by the bank. Similarly, for mobile banking services, another four corresponding apps were downloaded and installed to the phone. Meanwhile, I-banking services were accessed by opening banks' I-banking URL using the Internet Explorer app from the phone.

In the experiments, balance check and fund transfer activities were performed successfully and we received success notifications as confirmation from the banks, with only one error occurred in the I-banking fund transfer of Bank 9. The transaction confirmation code from the bank was repeatedly displayed incompletely in its website. This incomplete code meant the related transaction could not proceed further. For phone credit recharge activities, obstacles were encountered with regard to the failure of verification step after we sent a PIN authorization code to the banks via the corresponding services. Nevertheless, as we aimed to simulate real activities of customers and examine how we can reconstruct their activities from phone data remnant, we accepted these problems as events that may occur in a real-world environment.

A Nokia Lumia 625 smartphone was chosen as the experiment device, as it uses the Windows Phone operating system (Windows Phone 8.1 update, v8.10.14234.375) and from our previous study [8], we identified that it is well supported by mobile forensic tools for data acquisition including physical acquisition. Two mobile forensic tools, UFED Touch ver. 5.0.1.508 with UFED Physical Analyser 5.0.1.12 from Cellebrite and XRY ver. 6.14 from Micro Systemation AB (MSAB), were used to acquire digital forensic data from the smartphone. The both tools support logical acquisition on the Nokia Lumia 625, while additionally, UFED supports physical and file system acquisitions as well on it.

## 4.2 Acquisition Procedure

Logical and file system acquisitions using the UFED tool were conducted first, and continued with logical acquisition using XRY. In order to maintain data integrity of the phone, the flight mode setting was turned on and the location services setting was turned off. After that, physical acquisition was applied to the phone with its SD card attached to anticipate identification of installed e-banking apps in this storage. The SIM card was removed in order to minimize the risk of status changes on stored SMS(s) or MMS(s) in this card (e.g. from unread to read).

Lastly, manual acquisition was performed by browsing data on the phone, aiming to complete and verify data acquisition results from previous acquisition methods. We are aware that manual acquisition may affect data integrity. Thus, in a real-world investigation, metadata including the hash value of the evidence (e.g. pictures and video recording) from the manual acquisition should be documented properly.

Besides acquiring digital data from the phone's memory, we also captured the network packets transmitted by the phone while we were conducting the banking transactions. A hotspot service by Connectify was set up to share the Internet connection and receive transmitted packets from the phone. Wireshark was then used to capture and analyze the packets. In general, capturing network packets from evidence devices is not practical as it requires access to the pre-incident environment and this is usually only possible with a court warrant. However, this scenario is considered as part of our experiments to gain a more complete understanding of the digital data that can be obtained from banking activities.

Based on the banking transactions in the experiments, we proposed three incident hypotheses. These hypotheses will be tested using the evidence located as part of the event reconstruction results in our findings:

1. Suspect conducts the banking transactions (to determine who the actor was and what transactions were performed)
2. The transactions were conducted using the seized Windows Phone smartphone (to determine how transactions are conducted, what apps and device that were used by the actor)
3. Transactions were conducted within the specified time, places and purposes (to determine when, where and why the transactions were performed).

## 5    Findings

In this section, data extraction results are presented first before we analyze them to form event reconstruction diagrams.

### 5.1    Extracted Data

Logical acquisitions were conducted using UFED and XRY tools, while file system and physical acquisitions were progressed using the UFED. All data has a timestamp and metadata. Table 2 lists types of data extracted from applied acquisition methods using the mobile forensic tools. The results presented in this table imply that physical acquisition provides a more complete dataset for the purpose of answering investigative questions (i.e. what, where, how and when) than the logical and file system methods.

Using the media files retrieved from the logical and file system extractions, we can determine information relating to the conducted e-banking transactions. These data are available when the customer takes a screenshot of the transaction or downloads its report (e.g. balance account), and saves them in the phone's storage. With the additional data extracted by the physical acquisition method, including SMS messages, email, and deleted media files, more investigative questions could be answered.

The utilization of the seized phone to conduct transactions via SMS banking was determined mainly from the extracted SMSs. From SIM card acquisition, it is noted that the mobile service provider stored both service-related contacts and SMSs on the SIM card, whereas user messages and contacts are stored in the phone's flash memory. While user messages and contacts may lead to examination of the user's banking transactions, the extracted data of mobile service provider are not directly related. Nevertheless, from an evidence perspective, they provide important information about

**Table 2.** Summary of data extracted from Nokia Lumia 625 using mobile forensic tools

| Extraction Method | Call log | Contact | SMS | Email | Media Files | Location | Installed apps |
|---|---|---|---|---|---|---|---|
| Logical | X | X | X | X | √ | √ | X |
| | What could be answered?<br>• (**What** and **When**) – The type and time of conducted e-banking transactions can be identified from extracted media files if customer make a screenshot of it and save it in phone's storage<br>• (**Where** and **When**) – Customer's position from physical investigation can be confronted with phone's location | | | | | | |
| File System | X | X | X | X | √ | √ | X |
| | What could be answered?<br>Similar with the benefits of logical acquisition (for answering **What, Where** and **When** questions), with the addition of extracted deleted media files. | | | | | | |
| Physical | √ | √ | √ | √ | √ | √ | √ |
| | What could be answered?<br>• Encompassing the benefits of logical and file system acquisitions (for answering the previous **What, Where** and **When** questions) with the addition on extracted deleted media files.<br>• (**What, How** and **When**) – The utilisation of the seized phone to conduct transactions on **SMS banking** was recognised mainly from the **extracted SMSs**, while **I-banking** primarily from the **extracted emails** when customer asked for emailing the copy of transactions. However, the question on the real person who conducted transactions/activities cannot be simply answered from these extracted data. | | | | | | |

what mobile service provider is used, activation date of the mobile service, and recharged credit activities for prepaid services. When necessary, such information may indicate to the investigator the need to request for additional supporting data from the mobile service provider or financial institution (e.g. pertaining to the conducted banking transactions). Meanwhile I-banking use was detected primarily from extracted emails (when the customer asked for an emailed copy of the transactions).

In the extracted SMSs and emails, Cellebrite Physical Analyzer did not decode the actor's identification (ID) from these artifacts; there was no record of the sender of the message or the receiver of a sent message. In the decoding process, this tool showed an error message while executing the NTFS plugin. This error might be the cause of the incomplete data and inconsistency of the messages. Likewise, the result of physical acquisition was not sufficient to recognize installed apps chiefly for mobile banking services, as its application data files cover only built-in apps on the phone, such as Alarms.exe, BootPrep.exe and Calc7.exe. Therefore, manual acquisition was needed to examine the following data: actor ID of messages, their status (e.g. read or sent) and apps' name, by manually browsing but not opening them. Additionally, evidence on the use of the mobile banking apps could be corroborated by network packet captures as this data might indicate accessed servers and time.

Meanwhile, discovering who was actually using the phone to access the banking services was challenging. In theory, anybody might have used the phone to access the services. Thus, we needed information about the registered customer. Information such as customer's name, address, and signature could be identified from deposit slips or account book.

## 5.2   Evidence Objects and Events Reconstruction

We classified extracted and collected data into evidence objects. There are eight digital evidence objects, namely: SMS, email, call log, contact, media file, network packets, location and installed apps, and one physical object which is an account book. SMS and email object classes are recognized from their type (i.e. SMS and email, respectively) while individual SMS messages and emails are identified by their initiating actor (i.e. sender and receiver), date and message content. Call logs and contacts are categorized by their type and individually recognized by their content and metadata. Media file objects and captured network packets are categorized by their types (e.g. document, audio, video and image) and individually categorized by their content and metadata. Installed apps are recognized from their type (e.g. .exe or .xap) and individually characterized from their name, the size of the installation file and their data. Lastly, the account book is also categorized by its type and individually identified by account number and name.

Table 3 lists information from extracted SMSs and emails as the main source of evidence to indicate the banking activities that were undertaken. Artifacts of the registration process (RP) include any data remnant found that can be used to identify the registration process of particular banking service. They contain instructions to guide customers to finish their banking service activation. These artifacts may contain confidential information such as activation codes and Personal Identification Numbers (PIN). Artifacts of registration notification (RN) contain confirmation of banking service activations or deactivations, including new PIN activations. They may contain customer IDs or part of the customer account number (e.g. the last three digits of a bank account number).

**Table 3.** The extracted SMSs and emails

| Bank | SMS Banking R* P‡ | N§ | T† P‡ | N§ | I-Banking R* P‡ | N§ | T† P‡ | N§ | Mobile Banking R* P‡ | N§ | T† P‡ | N§ |
|---|---|---|---|---|---|---|---|---|---|---|---|---|
| 1 | SMS | SMS | - | SMS | - | - | - | Email | | | | |
| 2 | | | | | - | - | SMS | - | SMS | - | - | - |
| 3 | - | - | SMS | SMS | SMS | - | SMS | Email | | | | |
| 4 | | | | | SMS | SMS | SMS | Email | SMS | SMS | SMS | SMS |
| 5 | - | - | SMS | SMS | - | SMS | SMS | Email | | | | |
| 6 | | | | | | | | | SMS | - | - | - |
| 7 | SMS | SMS | SMS | SMS | Email | Email | - | Email | | | | |
| 8 | - | - | SMS | SMS | - | - | - | - | | | | |
| 9 | | | | | - | - | - | - | SMS | - | SMS | - |

*Registration; †Transaction; ‡Process; §Notification

From transaction process (TP) artifacts, we are able to identify the step by step activities that form particular transactions. Especially for SMS banking services, we may be able to trace details of a customer's banking activities and related data for these actions. For example, the type of transaction (e.g. balance check or fund transfer), the recipient's account information (i.e. number and name of the account), and part of the customer's PIN. Transaction notification (TN) artifacts describe the bank's confirmations of banking activities. From these artifacts, we can determine the transaction types that have been undertaken, their status (whether successful or unsuccessful) and detailed transaction information. For example by undertaking a phone recharge transaction using a SMS banking service the following information was identified: name of the bank, date and time of transaction, recharged phone number, credit value, transaction fee, and reference number. For I-banking services, if the customer selected an option to send a transaction confirmation to an email address, then the email evidence object can provide notification artifacts for that transaction.

Call log and contact evidence objects are useful to examine communication between the customer and a bank call center. Whenever a customer needs assistance with banking services, calling the bank's customer service is a common option. In call log investigations, it is important to determine the called number, the call date and time, and its duration. For contact evidence objects, the UFED extracted the contact's name, their phone number and email address. We identified two contacts with a specific bank's name.

Media files were included as one of evidence objects in our examinations, which mainly consist of document, audio, image and video files. Although none of the bank apps directly create and store any of these files, the user may save media files relating to their banking activities (e.g. screenshots). Eight screenshot images were acquired from file system and logical acquisitions using UFED. Unexpectedly, compared to our previous work on Windows Phone (10), these files were not decoded by the physical acquisition method. Logical acquisition results from XRY confirm the Cellebrite logical and file system acquisition findings in terms of screenshots. However, with the XRY tool, there were issues extracting text files and decoding .xls and .ppt files.

We also used captured network packets as evidence objects. We note than in many situations this evidence will not always be available. However, when it is accessible and permissible, it is useful to provide a more complete understanding of potential incidents. Location data, based on Global Positioning System (GPS) data, is an important evidence object to determine where a phone was at a specific time.

The last evidence object considered was an account book. We utilized this physical evidence object to match the suspect's name and signature.

## 5.3   Events Sequencing and Test Hypotheses

Figures 1 and 2 present two examples of event sequences based on evidence objects and individual constructed events. As objects contain temporal information, and a timestamp for each event is known, we were able to sequence events based on their occurrences. In this sequence, we have four main actors: Suspect ($S$), Phone ($P$), Customer Service ($CS$) and Bank System ($BS$). For $BS$ actor, we added more information to describe the real actor that interacted with the user ($S$). As an example,

*BS*[BANKXXXXXXI] means that the sender of the SMS from the bank system is identified as BANKXXXXXXI.

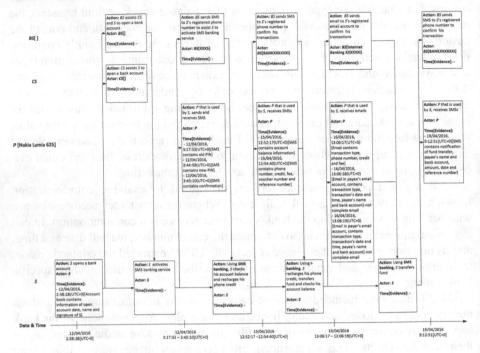

**Fig. 1.** Event sequencing of Bank1's banking transactions

We set only one condition for all events to occur: that the user has a working Internet connection. Evidence is selected only if it has a relationship with our hypothesis. For example, we found evidence that led to several failed-transaction attempts. While some failed transaction types could be useful evidence (e.g. failed PIN/code attempts), in these two examples we did not delineate the more detailed sequence of events that led to unsuccessful transactions. This is due to the fact that there was no unsuccessful transaction evidence extracted from Internet and mobile banking services, neither app data nor user data. However, in the case of SMS banking, failed transaction attempts can be identified from their confirmation SMS. For example, SMS confirmations of denied transactions were extracted for each failed transaction attempt by using the SMS banking service of Bank 7.

In the experiments, transactions were conducted with the phone's GPS service disabled to simulate a circumstance where users deliberately do not want their locations to be known. Under this condition, the phone's location could not be determined, because the information is not available. Naturally, when undertaking other activities with the GPS service enabled, the phone's location is identifiable. This location information contains timestamps (i.e. date and time), position (i.e. latitude and longitude),

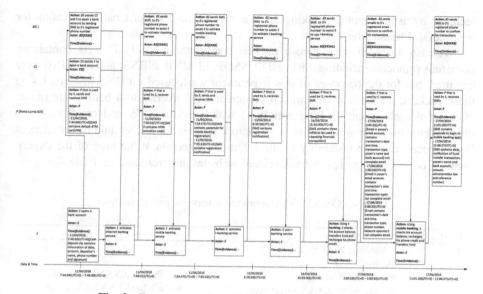

**Fig. 2.** Event sequencing of Bank4's banking transactions

place description, and source of information (e.g. application's name or media files). Experiments with the GPS service disabled complete our previous work on the same phone with GPS service enabled that successfully decoded phone's locations (10).

Figure 1 shows event sequencing for Bank1's transactions. It depicts that $S$ used their smartphone to conduct banking transactions from the 12th to the 19th of April 2016. Evidence of these transactions was retrieved from SMS, email and account book evidence objects. Digital evidence on $S$'s side (i.e. SMSs and emails) were extracted from $S$'s smartphone which is associated with a bank-registered phone number. For the SMS banking app, digital evidence such as their PIN, account balance, recharge phone number, and payee details are known. For the I-banking service, similar evidence artefacts are extracted from emails, except for PIN and account balance, which were not available.

However, as noted above, some emails were not completely decoded, and a manual acquisition was conducted to complete the extraction of this evidence. From the email message content, we obtained information about the purpose of the funds transfer transactions. Also, Fig. 1 shows that we did not identify timestamp (evidence) for some of $S$'s events. $S$'s action in these events can be verified by examining their effects on evidence outlined under actor $P$ (the phone). For example, $S$'s activation of the SMS banking service is verified by the three SMS messages located on the phone on the 12th of April 2016.

The event sequencing of Bank4 (Fig. 2) showed similar types of information to those found with Bank1. Extracted data such as the passcode for the mobile banking app, the mPIN for I-banking and transaction notifications, complete with their timestamps, provide important evidence to reconstruct related events. However, we cannot identify unsuccessful attempts of banking activities, see Table 1 (i.e. phone credit recharge by using a mobile banking app), as there is no SMS or email notification for unsuccessful transactions.

We also analyzed the network packets transmitted from $P$. Packets containing numerous protocols including ARP, UDP, SSDP, LLMNR, NBNS, and DHCPv6 were captured, but for the purposes of this experiment we focused on DNS packets. Using these packets, we were able to match particular DNS queries to a bank's site (as an effect of S's electronic banking activities) with previous SMS and email evidence objects. However, we were not able to capture packets for SMS banking activities at Bank1 because of the instability of the Internet connection at the time of the experiments. Coded DNS queries to bank-related websites are presented in Table 4.

**Table 4.** Coded DNS queries from network packet analysis

| Bank | Prominent Information |
|---|---|
| 1 | *SMS Banking*: Not applicable |
|   | *I-Banking*: |
|   | • XXXXXXi.co.id                • ib.bankXXXXXXi.co.id |
|   | • online.bankXXXXXXi.co.id     • olb.bankXXXXXXi.co.id |
|   | • business.bankXXXXXXi.co.id   • stat.bankXXXXXXi.co.id |
|   | • image.bankXXXXXXi.co.id |
| 2 | *Mobile Banking*: mbanking.bankXXXXXXat.co.id |
|   | *I-Banking*: ib.XXXXXXatbank.com |
| 3 | *SMS Banking*: - |
|   | *I-Banking*: ib.XXX.XX.Xd |
| 4 | *Mobile Banking*: mobile.XXXXXXXXXks.co.id |
|   | *I-Banking*: |
|   | • www.XXXXXXXXXks.co.id        • www2.XXXXXXXXXks.co.id |
|   | • cash.XXXXXXXXXks.co.id |
| 5 | *SMS Banking*: |
|   | • www.XXX.co.id                • www.XXXXXXk.co.id |
|   | *I-Banking*: |
|   | • www.XXXXXXk.co.id            • XXX.XXXbank.co.id |
| 6 | *Mobile Banking*: - |
| 7 | *SMS Banking*: - |
|   | *I-Banking*: XXXXson.bankXXXXm.co.id |
| 8 | *SMS Banking*: m.XXXXXXXX.com |
|   | *I-Banking*: |
|   | • www.XXX.XX.Xd                • ibXXX.XXX.co.id |
| 9 | *Mobile Banking*: |
|   | • mbanktrans.XXXXXXX.com        • m.XXXXXXa.com |
|   | *I-Banking*: m.XXXXXXa.com |

DNS query information can strengthen our hypothesis about the actual incident and complete our event reconstruction. The following two examples outline this process. By referring to Bank1's I-banking transactions (see Fig. 1), we know that emails containing transaction notifications were received between 13:06:17 (UTC+0) and 13:06:19 (UTC+0) on the 16th of April 2016. From the network packets captured, we were able to identify that $P$ accessed the XXXXXXi.co.id site at 12:34:55 (UTC+0), conducted several DNS queries for ib.bankXXXXXXi.co.id from 12:49:14 (UTC+0) to 12:49:30 (UTC+0) and accessed business.bankXXXXXXi.co.id between 12:47:17 (UTC+0) and 12:49:31 (UTC+0). All these DNS queries occurred just before the notification emails were received. These DNS queries strengthen our hypothesis that the transactions were conducted in this specific timeframe.

The second example is taken from transactions using Bank4's mobile banking. Notification SMSs were received on the 17th of April 2016, at 11:01:26 (UTC+0) and 11:06:27 (UTC+0). From the packet capture, we were able to determine that on the same day, mobile.XXXXXXXXXks.co.id was accessed at 10:56:53 (UTC+0), 10:57:37 (UTC+0) and 11:09:43 (UTC+0). These queries happened around the same time that $P$ received the notification SMSs. This example also increases the confidence in the event sequencing for Bank4's transactions.

Using these findings, we can test our incident hypothesis and seek to determine who conducted which activity and when it is happened. First, the account book was used to confirm the identity of $S$ as this physical evidence object has their name and signature. Secondly, we can verify that $S$ conducted the banking transactions, using their smartphone. We then determine the device that was used by $S$ by validating the phone's unique identifiers (e.g. MAC address). We compare these identifiers between device information from network packets and manual acquisition. We can also verify this using the device's recognized IMEI, which is identified from the physical and manual acquisition results. To confirm that the registered phone number is used on this device, we can trace the SIM number (MSISDN) of the attached SIM card from its cellular carrier by providing its ICCID and IMSI (extracted from SIM card individual acquisition) and compare it with the registered phone number at the bank.

Third, the congruence of the DNS query timestamps with the SMS and email timestamps could assist in validating the banking transaction type and its timeframe. Location of transactions may be able to be determined if a phone's location setting is turned on. Message content from notification emails can be analyzed further to attempt to determine the purpose for transactions.

## 6 Concluding Remarks

Accessing e-banking via mobile devices is a trend that is unlikely to fade away any time soon, and it is important for digital investigators to maintain an up-to-date and in-depth understanding of mobile devices. Most existing forensic studies focus on Android and iOS devices, and there are only a small number of papers that examined banking apps [5, 6]. In this paper, we analyzed e-banking services for Windows Phone platform that consist of five SMS banking, four mobile banking and eight I-banking services from all nine banks in Indonesia that support this platform.

We found that e-banking activities can be identified from combination of collected data from the phone, network packet captures and customer account book, particularly from Windows Phone device. Available evidence objects consisting of SMS, email, call log, contact, media files, location and installed apps are useful to define event reconstruction diagram and answer investigative questions. The presentation of this evidence in the event reconstruction diagram can facilitate a better understanding of the available evidence on their usefulness in an e-banking investigation.

Further work planned includes an investigation of other banking apps and their interactions with phone's operating system. While examination on.xap files would give more specific results on Windows Phone platform and deduce exclusive concerns in Indonesia, current acquisition results are insufficient to perform this examination. The physical acquisition result does not decode user applications' data, such as databases or executable files.

Here, this result confirms that the security model of Windows Phone 8 operating system (i.e. application security model, booting model and encryption model) might prevent the forensic tool from accessing the private app's data [8]. This limitation makes it difficult to collect digital artefacts based on the app's implementation and interaction with the operating system.

While examining digital artefacts and reconstructing banking activities are our main purposes, it could also be beneficial to identify the risk in the SMS banking's authentication method. This method asks customers to type a combination of their ATM pin numbers, for example the first and the fourth digits, in order to authenticate the customer to proceed with transactions. This method can be classified as a one-factor authentication method and it has been identified as the most convenient option for authenticating customer in e-banking [11, 12]. However, the risk is that it may make a complete ATM pin number recoverable from intact SMSs after a number of transactions. While the customers are reminded to delete those SMSs for security purposes they may not do so, thus the adoption of a one-time password system which is sent through SMS or token device is suggested to mitigate this risk.

To delineate the event reconstructions, this study combines artefacts from digital evidence objects (e.g. SMS, email, media file, network packets and location) and a physical one (i.e. account book). They are acquired from the combination of the four acquisition methods (logical, file system, physical and manual acquisitions) and network packet capture activity. This combination is conducted to complete the results of each method and in the same time to verify each other. The results show that five investigative questions (i.e. who, what, when, where and how) can be answered and event reconstruction diagrams can be presented.

Future research also includes extending the research to a wider range of financial apps such as mobile payment and mobile remittance apps that have the potential to be used in criminal activities (e.g. terrorism financing).

## References

1. Understanding Worldwide Attitudes, Behaviours and Trends in Mobile Content and Commerce. https://mobileecosystemforum.com/programmes/analytics/mef-country-report-indonesia/mef-country-report-indonesia-download/
2. Operating System Market Share. https://www.netmarketshare.com/operating-system-market-share.aspx
3. Carrier, B.D., Spafford, E.H.: Defining event reconstruction of digital crime scenes. J. Forensic Sci. **49**(6), 1291–1297 (2004)

4. Johnson, C.: Failure in Safety-Critical Systems: A Handbook of Incident and Accident Reporting. Glasgow University Press, Scotland (2003)
5. Jung, J.-H., Kim, J.Y., Lee, H.-C., Yi, J.H.: Repackaging attack on Android banking applications and its countermeasures. Wirel. Pers. Commun. **73**(4), 1421–1437 (2013)
6. Chanajitt, R., Viriyasitavat, W., Choo, K.-K.R.: Forensic analysis and security assessment of Android m-banking apps. Aust. J. Forensic Sci. 1–17 (2016)
7. Barmpatsalou, K., Damopoulos, D., Kambourakis, G., Katos, V.: A critical review of 7 years of mobile device forensics. Digit. Invest. **10**(4), 323–349 (2013)
8. Cahyani, N.D.W., Martini, B., Choo, K.-K.R., Al-Azhar, M.N.: Forensic data acquisition from cloud-of-things devices: Windows smartphones as a case study. Concurr. Comput. **29** (14), 1–16 (2017)
9. Cahyani, N.D.W., Ab Rahman, N.H., Glisson, W.B., Choo, K.-K.R.: The role of mobile forensics in terrorism investigations involving the use of cloud storage service and communication apps. Mobile Netw. Appl. **22**(2), 240–254 (2017)
10. Carrier, B., Spafford, E.H.: Getting physical with the digital investigation process. Int. J. Digit. Evid. **2**(2), 1–20 (2003)
11. Weir, C.S., Douglas, G., Richardson, T., Jack, M.: Usable security: user preferences for authentication methods in eBanking and the effects of experience. Interact. Comput. **22**(3), 153–164 (2010)
12. Gunson, N., Marshall, D., Morton, H., Jack, M.: User perceptions of security and usability of single-factor and two-factor authentication in automated telephone banking. Comput. Secur. **30**(4), 208–220 (2011)

# Author Index

Printed in the United States
By Bookmasters